# THE PROGRESSIVE YEARS

The Spirit and Achievement of American Reform

*By Otis Pease*

PARKMAN'S HISTORY:
The Historian as Literary Artist

# THE PROGRESSIVE YEARS

## YEARS

---

## The Spirit and Achievement of American Reform

---

SELECTED AND EDITED WITH INTRODUCTION
AND NOTES BY

*Otis Pease*

---

GEORGE BRAZILLER

NEW YORK 1962

## ACKNOWLEDGMENTS

Selections from Jane Addams' *Twenty Years at Hull-House* are reprinted with the permission of The Macmillan Company. Copyright 1910 by Phillips Publishing Company. Copyright 1910 by The Macmillan Company. Copyright 1938 by James Linn.

Selections from Woodrow Wilson are reprinted with the permission of the Yale University Press from *A Crossroads of Freedom* by John Wells Davidson. Copyright 1956 by the Yale University Press.

Selections from Theodore Roosevelt's autobiography are reprinted with the permission of Charles Scribner's Sons from *Theodore Roosevelt: an Autobiography*. Copyright 1913 by Charles Scribner's Sons. Renewal copyright 1941 by Edith K. Carow Roosevelt.

"The Hague Conference" is reprinted with the permission of Charles Scribner's Sons from *Mr. Dooley Says* by Finley Peter Dunne. Copyright 1910 by Charles Scribner's Sons. Renewal copyright 1938 by Margaret Dunne.

Selections from Walter Lippmann's *Drift and Mastery* are reprinted with the permission of the author.

"The Moral Equivalent of War" by William James is reprinted with the permission of Paul R. Reynolds & Son, Trustees for the Estate of Henry James.

# Preface

Anyone seeking to understand the complex domestic issues facing the United States in the 1960's might well turn first to an examination of the Progressive Era. Here was the seed bed out of which grew the New Deal and the Fair Deal and, in turn, the New Frontier. Here was a movement which irrevocably changed the role of the government in the economy, and which indelibly marked the thinking of several generations.

John F. Kennedy is the first American president from a post-Progressive generation, the first since Calvin Coolidge not to have entered manhood amidst Progressive excitement and debates. The New Frontier marks a considerable advance from the Progressive starting point, and many of the earlier leaders would have shrunk from accepting the dominant position the government has come to assume, yet the new generation is the logical heir of its Progressive forebears.

As Otis Pease points out in his illuminating Introduction and as the Progressives themselves fervently assert in the selections that follow, this was a young generation both thrilled and alarmed by the industrial civilization developing around them. These energetic young middle-class Americans of high purpose viewed with genuine pride the production miracles and the high living standards that the new industrialism already was achieving. But it was with troubled consciences that they viewed the continuing poverty, the spreading slums, and the all too prevalent corruption which industrialism in some instances had helped to create. Fundamentally optimistic, they did not wish to overthrow the existing order, but rather through a few minor adjustments to eliminate the malfunctioning. Mr. Dooley (the creation of Finley Peter Dunne) pointed out at the time, "Th' noise ye hear is not th' first gun iv a rivolution. It's on'y th' people iv th' United States batin' a carpet." And yet the changes the Progressives initiated in the first years of the century were in fact the opening guns of what by the 1960's had amounted to a quiet revolution.

The Progressives had discovered that private charity was not enough to remedy the nation's social and economic ills, and they turned increasingly to government for solutions. They hoped, through greater

v

democratization, to make government more responsive to the needs of the new era. One novelist wrote, "The way to have a Golden Age is to elect it by a . . . secret ballot." They hoped that through government at every level a balance could be brought into economic life: city ordinances to protect infants from unsafe milk; enforcement of Federal anti-trust laws to give protection against giant monopolies. As Pease points out, Progressives felt in the decades that followed that their solutions were too modest, but they were not prepared to accept formulas that seemed to them drastic. Nevertheless, their contribution to a broader participation by government was remarkable.

"Their achievement consisted in making it possible for a later generation to sanction what they could not. Meanwhile they had provided their society with something more: the conviction, which was never entirely to disappear, that it was the business of a democratic people to discover and to assert moral ideals worthy of man at his best, and that it was the business of the political process to honor them."

FRANK FREIDEL

To the memory of my father, 1888–1961

# Contents

# Editor's Note

I have constructed this book to reveal something of the first years of twentieth-century America through the writings of men and women who helped to shape those years. Rather than extract small selections from many sources, I have chosen from only a few writers unified selections substantial enough to convey the style of their thought and the depth of of their preoccupations. Only eleven men and one woman (besides the editor) have been entrusted with these years in this book, but they were for the most part extraordinary people. Theodore Roosevelt and Woodrow Wilson were American Presidents and accomplished historians; Roosevelt and Jane Addams each won a Nobel Prize for peace; Eugene Debs was a candidate for President and the embodiment of fundamental but responsible social dissent; Walter Lippmann was an advisor to a President; Frederic Howe, Lawrence Veiller, and Jane Addams were civic experts and reformers; Lincoln Steffens, Finley Peter Dunne, Howe, and Lippmann wrote influential journalism; and William James, writer, psychologist, philosopher, may have cast a deeper shadow than any of the rest. They were at once writers and doers. They embodied their age, they wrote to influence their age, and in consequence their writings can tell us much about their age.

Most of the selections presented here have been left substantially uncut. I have omitted footnotes whose functions were largely citation, and I have chosen to leave out occasional paragraphs of material I considered to be of little or no general interest to present readers. Omissions of this latter sort are indicated in the text. As a rule I have made use of coherent units of prose, such as articles, chapters, or groups of chapters. It is my hope that these selections will awaken interest in further reading, and I offer accordingly at the end of the book some recommendations for further reading: they represent personal enthusiasms as well as professional judgment.

I have believed it unnecessary to footnote the editorial and introductory material: it draws on the sources mentioned in the Suggestions for Further Reading and on the editor's general investigations made over several years of teaching and writing. The unfamiliar episode involving Brand Whitlock and Theodore Roosevelt (p. 386) is recorded in the Lincoln Steffens papers in the Columbia University Library. I am happy to pay my respects to the university libraries at Stanford, Washington (Seattle), Yale, and Columbia for efficient service and unfailing courtesies. To my wife Mary go special thanks for essential help and encouraging interest.

OTIS PEASE
Stanford University

March, 1962

# THE PROGRESSIVE YEARS

The Spirit and Achievement of American Reform

# Introduction

*Otis Pease*

Lincoln Steffens once told a story about America. In the 1890's, as so often before, a nation which had been running too fast had tripped and toppled on its face. Steelmakers banked their furnaces, corporate managers closed their doors, and ragged lines of the hungry and jobless roamed the disordered streets. But before even the initial panic—prelude to depression—had run its course, enterprising men could be found busily doctoring the old system, propping it to its feet, needling it into motion again. The *Evening Post* regularly sent Steffens to Wall Street to report the plans of the more "bullish" bankers and industrialists for the reorganization of business. The most bullish of all the bankers was J. Pierpont Morgan, and he was also the most powerful. He had been heard to declare that for the long pull "the bull side is the winning side in America. The United States is a bull country." Morgan's presence was fearsome. Not even his partners went near him unless sent for; and then, heart in mouth, they darted in like office boys. Steffens, a cub reporter, had never spoken to him. One day the Morgan firm issued a notice about some bonds, a statement so turgid and complicated that neither Steffens nor his editor could understand it. Picking up the notice and readying himself for an explosion, Steffens walked into Morgan's office and up to his desk.

"Mr. Morgan," he said, brave and afraid at once, "what does this statement mean?"

"Mean!" roared Morgan, his eyes glaring. "Mean! It means what it says. I wrote it myself, and it says what I mean."

"It doesn't say anything—straight," retorted the young journalist, so scared that he blazed right back at the great man.

Morgan clutched at his chair, and Steffens expected him to leap. "Oh come now, Mr. Morgan," said Steffens. "You may know a lot about figures and finance, but I'm a reporter, and I know as much as you do about English. And that statement isn't English."

For a moment Morgan continued to glare, then glanced at the piece of paper. "What's the matter with it?" he asked, suddenly mild.

Steffens suggested a few changes.

"Yes," said Morgan, "that is better. You fix it." Steffens did so and left. He later was told that Morgan sat watching him go, rapped for an associate to find out the reporter's name, and remarked, "Knows what he wants, and—and—gets it."

Times were changing in America. Restless young men who appeared to know what they wanted were beginning to confront their powerful elders with questions and proposals. They did not always do so in a spirit of dissent. Like Steffens they shared with Morgan the bullish confidence that a little reorganization here and there would permit the nation to push on, to grow. Steffens was no reformer—yet. He had come merely to inquire about progress from the man who embodied it. He was invited to help the man "fix" it a little, and he did. In another twenty years, the shoes would be reversed: the young inquirers into progress had become its custodians, they had infused it with revolutionary principles and fresh meaning, and they would now seek from the aged Morgans not advice on how to fix it but an accounting of what had previously been done to it that had required such a job of repair. In twenty years a new century had replaced the old. Here it was that the concept of growth or progress bestowed its name on an age. These years, for the reformers and the reformed alike, were the Progressive years.

The Progressive years present us at the outset with a puzzle. On the one hand, signs of progress filled the landscape. On the other hand, discontent with the results had set loose the unquiet energies of criticism and reform in every town and state.

To talk of progress was to cite tables of yearly gains—in population, bank clearings, tons of sugar consumed. Merely to watch a century of progress draw to a close generated extraordinary interest in the acceleration of progress itself as the distinctive feature of the bright century just begun. In the first new decade New York carved itself a subway system, Chicago a $40,000,000 drainage canal to divert sewage away from the lake, and San Francisco dug itself out from the rubble and ashes of an earthquake and rebuilt a white city on golden hills. While William Vanderbilt, Jr., drove his new French sports car from Newport to Boston and back at an unheard-of forty miles per hour, a quiet engineer named Ford had begun plans to put a cheap, serviceable automobile at the disposal of every crossroads farmer who could afford the incredibly low price of $600. In 1900 British scientists announced that a human voice had been conveyed electrically six miles across the air. Three years later two Americans lifted themselves off a North Carolina sand flat in a manmade machine; flying for fifty-nine seconds under their own power, they broke forever man's physical bond to the surface of the globe. Under the watchful eye of men like Morgan and Rockefeller industrial firms were regrouping their forces for a long stretch of prosperity; while the United States Steel Corporation was formed to take over Carnegie's efficient enterprise, the Standard Oil Company in one quarter paid 15 per cent on its stock. After the bitter years of uncertain employment and instability of wages the skilled workman and the more prosperous farmer found the first two decades of the new century a period of rising return on income and far steadier opportunities for work. Finally, the American people, fervent in the flag-waving of a short, glorious war, had appeared at one and the same time to be driving Spanish tyranny forever from democratic shores, acquiring a colonial empire, and striking chains from the wrists of hapless natives; in the wake of Dewey's cruise through Manila Bay the nation seemed to have become almost overnight not only prosperous but powerful, victorious, and selfless—in short, destined for greatness in a new century.

To talk of progress in America in 1900 was to talk of material improvements; but to call a man "progressive" was to label him a reformer, a man determined to improve his society, revise its laws, purify its politics, rearrange its economic awards, and invigorate its morals. The reform impulse had flowered in the nineties when the stark conditions of depression and industrial unrest made reform so compelling. Now that progress had returned, why were the critics still so insistent on change and the reformers so active? The answer lies partly in the fact that as the country became more of a single economic unit the reformers were compelled to shift their attention upward from city and state to the nation; one keynote of the Progressive years is the nationalizing of the reform efforts hitherto confined to local problems. More important is the possibility that with the return of good times (spurred on by the war with Spain) the gap between what is and what could be seemed all the less bearable. The triumph at Manila Bay was soon marred by the American army's systematic repression of the Filipino independence movement; the hopes of liberals, raised unnecessarily high by the apparent humanity of our war policy, turned to violent distaste at what semed at second glance to be merely the traditional instincts of colonialism. Meanwhile at home a rising tide of material expectations tugged at workaday minds and made them restless. Particularly was this true in the nation's cities, where rapid growth of wealth and poverty in close proximity accentuated the availability and promise of the new abundance. While urban life had improved for all classes, the disparity between the poor and the new rich was now the most visible feature of the urban landscape.

Americans who express concern today over a world-wide population

explosion are often surprised to discover that for over two centuries following the first colonial settlements the American people experienced the
highest birthrate in the Western world; we sustained this population explosion until we became industrialized; then, beginning with the 1880's,
our cities began to grow at an equally explosive rate. By 1910 the proportion of city dwellers in the nation had risen from 20 to 45 per cent while
the proportion of big city dwellers to small-town citizens rose even
faster; one-tenth of the entire nation lived in New York, Philadelphia,
and Chicago. They streamed in endlessly on a swelling tide—from upstate
farms and villages, and from the villages and towns of Germany, Austria,
Italy, Russia, the Balkans, and Canada. They were the beneficiaries of a
phenomenal decline in infant deaths throughout those regions of the
world touched by modern science. They came for the jobs no longer available on the mechanized farmlands but now to be found in expanding
industry in the large towns. There had always been cities; by 1900 the
national network of railroads—practically completed—could permit for
the first time the heavy concentration of large enterprises near centers
of labor rather than centers of raw material. Railroads could simultaneously provide the access to market which permitted Cleveland machine
shops to make enough steel lathes to sell all over the country, not merely
in northern Ohio, or New York garment makers to sell suits to Missouri
farmers as well as to New Jersey grocers. In short, while urban growth
was transforming America, an industrial revolution was transforming
urban life and through it the nation itself.

The rapidly exploding industrial city nurtured nearly every important
new advance in the social life of the nation. The need for power to
light the city street and push the street car bred the electrical utility
industry. The need for vertical space in the city produced the steel frame
and an architectural revolution. The necessities of a public health system
when masses of people crowded together drove the nation's people to
assure themselves pure water, clean milk, and sewage plants, and to
devise the complicated engineering they required. The demands of modern
urban technology led in turn to a pragmatic revolution in political thinking. The concepts of personal rights useful in a rural society proved mean-
ingless in a large city. Men were no longer free to use their property as
they pleased: if they owned a tenement, they were required to keep its
private hallways lit and accessible to the public; if they ran a private
trolley line, they were obliged to give dependable service; by city
ordinance they could not sell tubercular beef or spit on the sidewalk. Of
course the structure of city authority often lagged behind in archaic rural
attitudes, but in hundreds of growing localities forces were being generated which would soon eat away whatever grip laissez-faire was reputed
to have on the American people. In its turn would come a practical com-

mitment to piecemeal collectivism and to an impersonal and anonymous social environment. Yet curiously the collective anonymity of the city, together with its concentration of purchasing power and its unprecedented opportunities for wealth, was beginning to support a degree of independence and personal autonomy which no rural or frontier environment could match. To the thousands of hopeful city-bound Americans the city promised freedom from the repressive conformity of the small town.

If the growth of cities promised freedom, it also promised danger—and conflict.

In the first place close to one-third of the people crowded into the large cities had been brought up in European villages, and at least another third were their children. They came seeking work and a better life in a land free from the exactions of landlord and recruiting officer; but they also brought with them peasant village attitudes toward the social structure, where each person had a fixed role, where conflicts were resolved by authority and the cement of authority depended on systems of loyalty, favors, and personal relationships. It was inevitable that they held lightly those standards of reform democracy and town-meeting politics so traditional to the dominant middle classes; they gave their loyalty not to an impersonal system which they could not understand but to their ward boss, whom they could understand, who was often one of them and who understood them in turn, whose saloon was always open for a warm meal, for advice, for favors and support in the alien world around them. The boss controlled their grateful votes and rose to confront the middle classes with a power which seemed sometimes corrupt and always disturbing. Out of this political tension came further conflict and instability.

In the second place, despite the rising real wages and the increasing steadiness of work for the urban laborer, the wealthier classes were pulling still farther ahead of the rest in the new industrial cities. Between 1896 and 1910 the proportion of national income received by the richest 1 per cent of the people increased from 8 per cent to 15. While the total output of the nation's economy tripled in value, the total wages of all working people merely doubled, representing a relative loss in the wage earner's share of the gains in national productivity. During the severe depression of 1893-1896 the cost of living had declined sufficiently in the cities to permit workingmen lucky enough to keep their jobs a chance to scrape by. But in every large city could be seen the ragged lines of men without jobs, seeking a dole of bread from exhausted charity workers or from the helpful and unsentimental ward boss. Ten years later social investigators discovered to their shock that a decade of prosperity had not materially improved the lot of the poorer half of the urban working class. Though more of them had found steady work, their earnings averaged less than $600 a year at a time when even conservative social workers estimated that $800 was an absolute minimum income for a family of five if it were to get enough merely to eat and wear—and to burn for fuel in a precarious stove. That is what hurt—for half the working people, the same poverty in a time of visible affluence as had been their lot in the earlier years of obvious want.

Still more, the city embodied promise and despair in corrosive juxtaposition: the electric street car—and the slum at the end of the line; the incandescent street light—and the squalid alley, the unlit refuge of scrawny boys probing for food among the broken cans and the smashed gin bottles. The bright promise of immense technological progress threw into still darker shadow the failures of the social order to fulfill the promise for any below the favored half of the people. Poverty amid progress was what had driven Henry George to his pen and paper from sunny California and was to shatter the sensibilities of young women of means whose literary and moral education provided a standard against which the misery of the factory family's three-room tenement flat twelve blocks away beat as a shocking and galvanizing revelation.

It was often easy to assume that urban America of 1900 was divided into two classes: the wealthy, the educated, the politically adept, on the one hand; the unschooled, the wage-enslaved, the politically impotent, on the other. A rich class did exist, as did an urban poor, often within a block of each other, but mediating between them was a significant and lively middle class, possessed of enormous political power, economic skill, education, and moral ascendancy over both the tiny group of wealthy families at the top and the workingman who aspired to join it from below. One driving force behind urban reform was that the American urban economy in the 1900's had become so technically interdependent that the varying interests of economic classes had become more compellingly joined. The warehouse manager saw increasingly that his prosperity depended on coming to terms with the organized draymen, whose prosperity in turn hinged on the maintenance of a decent scale of wages throughout the laboring class. The stability of a clothing manufacturer's business required a stability of social relations in the city between managers and workers, and this implied in turn a government of dependable social service. The modern factory required a school system. The personnel manager came to discover that he had a stake in a minimum standard of living for the workmen who poured through his gates from the east side of town at the eight o'clock whistle. The factory towns in New England and along the Great Lakes were far removed from central Poland or provincial Italy, where classes and occupational groups remained separated by custom and by the fragmentization of economic interest. The industrial urban economy which transformed American society was beginning to stimulate among the middle classes an interest in assuring a minimum of well-being among all classes which shared a stake in the efficient functioning of the whole interlocking system.

But standing squarely in the way of such a system were long lines of the jobless, the quiet despair of the man with a job and barely the pay to keep himself fed, the indignity of those who returned home to window-less flats in wooden tenements, sharing three rooms with a wife, grand-father, and six children, sharing a bath with three other families. Standing in the way was the landlord, behind him the manager of the brothel, the seller of dope, the seller of "protection," the seller of funeral insurance, and behind them stood the precinct police captain. The web wound back through the littered streets and past the crowded public infirmary to the city hall, to the bank which financed the slum block, to the owner of the sweatshop clothing firm and to the cotton mill which supplied him his cloth. The frayed raggedness of urban life had always been present but somehow less visible. With the growing interdependence of all the na-tion's classes it had begun to appall and shock a substantial body of young men and women. From their response grew the first beginnings of the modern American state, our heritage from the Progressive years.

The reformers of that generation did not comprise more than a small segment of the young and middle-aged urban citizens, but they were educated far above the average, their professions placed them in a strategic position in society, and in consequence their influence grew all out of proportion to their numbers. Most were graduates of the small, rigorous Protestant colleges of New England and the Middle West, widely read in the classics and in the great tradition of social and philosophic speculation that formed the staple fare of the well-trained nineteenth-century mind. Most of them on graduation became lawyers, journalists, politicians, administrators, economists, or teachers; a striking number were women who became the pioneer social workers of the new century. Their distinguishing feature was a passion for writing. Their careers made them serious writers and kept them continually in touch with the currents of social thought sweeping the Western world. They studied the history of British labor and factory reform and the reports of municipal socialism emanating from New Zealand and from Bismarck's Germany. They were familiar with Charles Booth's study of the London slums and the massive statistics on poverty in northern England. Crossing the Atlantic to see for themselves how the East End settlement houses were run, they returned to confront the poverty of their own cities with a new confidence. Most of them confessed to having been profoundly affected by the moving social vision of Tolstoy, Ruskin, and Comte; no less influential were the acid insights of Shaw and Ibsen.

Fully as deep in their minds ran the reform idealism of the American past. Many of them had imbibed Emerson along with the moral activism of the Puritan tradition or the humanitarian principles of the Quakers. Some could recall parents and uncles who in their day had been jailed as abolitionists and ostracized for their support of women's rights. In scores of intellectual communities from Boston to Oberlin there dwelled elderly veterans scarred in earlier battles for reform, living tributes to a heritage of the fierce and rebellious creeds of equal rights, equal opportunities, and equal moral worth which had once left their searing mark on the minds of a rural Protestant republic. For some of the young progressives, a commitment to reform was almost a part of the air they breathed.

The two streams of influence, one from Europe and one from the American past, were soon swelled by a third major current, the belief that social values and behavior could be shaped in significant ways by man's purposive assault on his own environment. This assumption had grown in part from the revolution in biological science rooted in the writings of Charles Darwin and applied by other thinkers to the evolution of societies. Where Herbert Spencer had stressed the resistance of supposedly innate social traits to man-made changes, more sanguine writers modified the Darwinian stress on natural evolution by combining with it the assumptions of Comte and Marx, that the values and behavior of men generally depended not on inherited social predispositions or on the coercions of fixed patterns of thought innate in all men but rather on broad social and economic conditions which seemed plainly within the power of modern industrial societies to alter. In the hands of the urban reformers and when properly restricted in its application this view proved to be immensely liberating. Back of the ignorant, the lazy, the dissolute, there very seldom lay congenital defects or inherited traits of character but rather (it was said) lack of opportunity due to poverty and pervasive economic conditions. No longer did it seem unimportant or futile or immoral to attempt to restructure the social order. Men might still profoundly disagree over the formulas for changes; fewer and fewer continued to insist that valid changes could not be made.

More than any other American thinker it was William James who sharpened and reformulated the new currents of belief for his generation and enabled it to feel infinitely greater confidence in the value of what it was doing. Raised in New England, brilliantly educated abroad and at home, trained by his father, a poet and mystic, to respect and probe all categories of learning, James taught physiology at Harvard and moved rapidly into realms of psychology, philosophy, and ethics. In 1890 appeared his monumental and pioneering *Principles of Psychology*, which brought him world-wide acclaim and provided a base of influence for his immensely popular essays and lectures. By 1908 his views had coalesced into the doctrine of pragmatism. Rejecting the notion, popular with the scientific rebels of the nineteenth century, that truth can be objectively discovered, James developed the notion that truth is in fact created by man thinking, and from this came his central view that the value of an idea or the validity of a belief depends on its usefulness in affecting action, in creating the truths by which men live and with which they fashion their world.

The pragmatic position neatly bolstered the assumptions of the reform generation. It permitted the new liberals to feel less conscience-stricken, more moral, in employing social weapons such as the state which their fathers had by doctrine considered off limits. If the state can help man alter the environment and so create newer possibilities for his well-being, to that very extent the reformers need no longer see laissez-faire as a truth but as simply one of many possible strategies to be tested by experience. Pragmatism did not insist that reformers discard their goals of greater equality among classes, greater opportunity to make good, security of body and freedom of soul. It provided, rather, a formidable intellectual weapon for achieving these goals, an eternal skepticism of dogma, of yesterday's truths. Pragmatism did not propose that truths were infinitely malleable. "Mind engenders truth *upon* reality," insisted James in 1907. "The world resists some lines of attack on our part and opens herself to others, so that we must go with the grain of her willingness." Reformers were seeking not to enthrone an endless relativism but to remodel tested goals for a new age. Pragmatism bolstered their courage to do so.

What did the pragmatic vision imply for the nature of man and his social acts? First, it accepted the view that all people are of equal intrinsic worth. Societies will gain by protecting—not eliminating—the weak. Therefore, remake your criminals; care for your poor; treat your insane. School your young to use their minds, not their memories. Police your factories. Infuse the business ethos, the competitive tensions, with the spirit of respect for the equal rights of each. Second, the pragmatic vision implied that human nature is for the most part socially conditioned. Man's reason can solve most of his problems if given a chance. If you take steps to reduce the sting of poverty, you may succeed in curbing base passions. If you abolish economic privilege and favoritism, you may make it possible to end poverty altogether. It was at least worth-while to assume so, to believe that a society which supported the eight-hour day, decent housing and spacious parks, the secret ballot, public power, and the scientific administration of cities was creating merely the first essential conditions for a more noble and reasonable race of men. The abundance and prosperity of the nation made it possible to try.

The most widely known of the reformers were the journalists who exposed the conditions of the cities and states; yet curiously they did not begin as reformers. Men like Munsey and McClure, who owned magazines, and investigators like Steffens, Ray Stannard Baker, Samuel Hopkins Adams, and Ida Tarbell, who wrote for them, discovered that the restless middle-class readers had wearied of the memoirs of Civil War generals and traveling dilettantes in the pages of *Scribner's* and were ripe for articles about subjects which bore a direct relation to their own urban lives. The new editors sent their writers into the streets and into the corridors of the city halls and factories to find the material which would answer this new need. Perhaps it was inevitable that what began as an impulse to make money soon took on an unexpected life of its own. Readers who first sought only to be entertained became stimulated and disturbed over the implications of what they read, and the journalists themselves not infrequently turned crusaders, admired and took sides with the reformers, and sought to change what they had exposed. Often it was enough simply to present the facts, and the best of the journalists stuck so rigorously to the facts that they won virtually every libel suit brought against them. Merely in the choice of subject they possessed a weapon which they willingly used to help curb the power of ward politicians, require the pasteurization of milk and the inspection of butcher shops, regulate public transport, and support reform tickets which swept city, state, and even national elections. In time the business of exposure proved attractive to less able men, and the sensational and not especially accurate fulminations of Frank Lawson and David Graham Phillips led Theodore Roosevelt in a moment of irritation to describe the whole lot of them as muckrakers. Steffens, who continued to enjoy the President's favor, appropriated the title as a badge of distinction for himself and his colleagues, and long after the movement faded the muckrakers at their best still retained their deserved reputation as the principal catalyst for progressive reform.

Public indignation and the literature of exposure which fed it were, of course, nothing new in 1900. Behind the muckrakers stood the influence of Henry George's massive attack on poverty in the midst of progress, the trenchant essays of Henry Demarest Lloyd on the monopoly powers of Standard Oil, and the clinical but compassionate reporting of Jacob Riis on the urban slum. In 1885 the newly founded American Economic Association had stated that the positive intervention of the state in social affairs was "an indispensable condition to human progress," and a number of young economists such as Richard Ely, Simon Patten, E. R. A. Seligman, and Father John Ryan went on to advance the doctrine that labor in any Christian society should be guaranteed a "just wage" and consumers a "just price." In the 1890's earnest men and women, sometimes supported by liberal city churches, had run settlement houses and agencies of

social work; more often than not they had ranged themselves solidly behind the political crusaders in a battle to bring the power of the government to bear on the behavior of the private businessman.

What distinguished the reforms of the new century from those of the old
were the range and depth of its proposals for organized solutions—often
political and administrative solutions—to problems long recognized but
seldom systematically attacked. The writers of 1900 spoke no longer of
charity but of minimum wages and workmen's compensation, less of
social work and more of social security, slum clearance, employment
agencies, and tax reform. Many found a ready panacea in socialism, and by
1912 the Socialist Party was to reach the height of its influence with the
American voter, but except for a wide acceptance of municipally owned
utilities the core of the reform tradition did not embrace socialism. Not
Eugene Debs or Henry George but John Dewey would in later years
best represent its guiding spirit. That spirit stressed the view that the
modern social order, resting as it did on both science and democracy,
offered men their best hope of gaining a purposive mastery of the environment only if it provided at the same time an unlimited opportunity
for each individual to help shape his own goals and determine the goals
of his society. At the heart of Dewey's vision was the faith that intelligent
social action could and must generate among men the sort of sympathy
for one another that would insure both their collective well-being and
their individuality as creatures of dignity and moral worth.

Armed with such doctrines Americans by 1900 had begun to swarm
all over the capitalism they had inherited, probing, repairing, altering.
They believed that it was possible to build a limited welfare state for
universal, private ends. Their ideals were old, their weapons often new.
Here was an American substitute for the Marxist doctrines of class
violence. Here were men to insist that without a proletarian revolution a
middle class could construct a classless society. In the dawn of the
twentieth century the glow in the eastern sky may have seemed to the
worried disciples of Herbert Spencer only a dull pink, but to the progressive reformers the streaks of light promised an eternal morning.

The progressive reformer was at heart confident that American industrial
capitalism could be saved from its own weakness and injustices. He was
a constructive critic, but he was a critic nevertheless, and the ultimate
target of his discontent was the concentration of industrial and business
power which reached a climax in the first two years of the century. For
this subject he found a ready audience; fear of monopoly pervaded
nearly all ranks of the American community brought up to believe that
competition among numbers of small businessmen was indispensable to
a free society. Here the reformer tangled with an issue of almost insoluble

dimensions, for the system of free competition held within it the very force which was bound to destroy it: a race among winners who might win by such a margin as to destroy their competitors and end the game. Competition depended, then, on an effective legal and political framework, and despite the wide belief of nineteenth-century Americans in laissez-faire, regulations to preserve the game of competition had been slowly taking shape with the willing assent of most of the players.

Monopoly had always been an ugly word. Common law prohibited it. The Jacksonian Democrats had gained popularity by their crusade against Nicholas Biddle's Bank. Large and small business alike feared monopoly power among railroads and sought to restrict them by law. Yet as industrial America began to produce more goods than the market could absorb, price wars ensued, profits fell off, and the larger firms tried to save their position by making agreements on prices, marketing, and wages, and by eliminating or absorbing competitors. By this process large segments of the American economy in the 1890's had come under the sway of firms with substantial monopoly power. Most notorious and most consistently criticized was the Standard Oil trust. Other firms had cornered markets in sugar, whisky, agricultural machinery, and steel wire. Over a dozen states had passed antimonopoly laws, but they were badly drawn and confused in purpose, and monopolies were usually interstate in character. A national antitrust law, the Sherman Act, had been pushed through Congress on a wave of regional indignation by political strategists from the industrial states who had little use for such a law but who were promised in return support for a high tariff. So sweeping was the language of the Sherman Act, and so devoid of teeth, and so little enthusiasm did the Cleveland administration exhibit for disturbing the business community by enforcing it, that by 1895, when the Supreme Court virtually ruled it inoperative (in the famous E. C. Knight decision) few businessmen could have been terribly aware that it existed. In the next seven years over three hundred business mergers and combinations (directly affecting 5,300 separate firms) were chartered under the benign laws of a number of eastern states. Almost none were monopolies in a strict sense, but many of them exercised controlling power over their markets, and the largest—the United States Steel Corporation—brought under one management 170 separate firms and was capitalized at the unprecedented sum of almost $1,500,000,000. This gigantic holding company set the cap on J. P. Morgan's reputation. In the previous decade he had undertaken the partial reorganization of the nation's railroads, had gained virtual control of three of them, and had been called on to bail out the United States Treasury. The big businesses of America, declared the critics, not only resembled monopolies; they had become Morganized.

As antimonopoly sentiment grew, it tended to feed on a number of distinct and varied grievances, some fancied, some genuine. Trusts were popularly considered to have been formed to increase profits by raising prices, lowering wages, and ruining competitors with tactics which avoided an honest test of relative merit and often bordered on the criminal. There was little doubt concerning the existence of high profits: by 1900 Standard Oil's net earnings exceeded $80,000,000 and its annual return exceeded 40 per cent; by 1905 the net earnings of the American Tobacco Company exceeded its total capitalization; scores of other combinations reported impressive figures. Yet there was little public disposition to tax the profits or to challenge the integrity of the securities they were based on. As for prices, no very conclusive pattern existed to show that concentration of control either raised or lowered them to a significant degree, though combinations usually succeeded in reducing price fluctuations, often to the relief of firms doing business with them. Commodity prices in the relatively unorganized industries like farming rose twice as fast as the price of steel, sugar, and oil. Nor was there in fact any correlation between combination and low wages. Examples of oppressive labor policies and sweated wage scales could be found in some large industries such as steel, but they were even more prevalent among small businesses. The dubious competitive methods which had popularly been associated with the rise of Standard Oil—rebates, espionage, bribery, cutthroat pricing—were by no means unduplicated or unmatched among small and highly unstable firms. The ordinary consumer was more distressed at high profits than cutthroat prices, but his indignation over profits seldom stemmed from direct personal injury. Much of the original animus against trusts reflected the anguish of the small, beaten competitor, and behind the swelling agitation to curb the power of certain enterprises often stood other businesses equally powerful who consumed their products and services or who suffered some marked disadvantage of location. They objected less to the principles than to the practices of the trusts.

More serious and possibly more widespread than any other popular fear was that of the urban reformers and ordinary citizens who believed that such mammoth enterprises posed a first-class threat to the freedom and efficiency of representative government. Businessmen seeking monopoly franchises and special legislative privileges had warped and corrupted the political process in a score of cities and half a dozen states. Morgan's industrial and banking empire seemed to many worried liberals in both major parties influential enough to overshadow the national government itself. Washington had never been known to dictate to Wall Street; most Americans were ready to believe the reverse, and while they may have been wrong in their belief, they had known as an accepted fact of politics that the two centers of national power tended to negotiate with each other in a manner more befitting two sovereign governments than one democratic nation dealing with a segment of its people. It was little wonder that by 1900 reformers everywhere were beginning to assert that the central issue of their time was to restore the power and the operations of the government to the control of the ordinary citizen. They may have oversimplified the issue; but over the next dozen years most of their fellow citizens appeared quite effectively to agree with them.

State legislation provided the first cutting edge for progressivism. The capital cities of about fifteen states, most notably New York, New Jersey, Ohio, Michigan, Wisconsin, Iowa, Missouri, and California, in fact provided the major testing ground for what was distinctive and significant about reform as it moved into the new century. Here were passed laws prohibiting child labor, forbidding free railroad passes, unfair competitive practices, and corporate contributions to political campaigns, limiting the issuance of capital stock in chartered corporations, permitting direct primaries and home rule for city governments, setting maximum hours for railroad employees and for women in industry. Here were created effective public commissions to set railroad rates, inspect factories, regulate the operation of utilities, and reform the tax structure. By 1910 the political and economic climate of the industrial portions of America had undergone a partial but crucial change. True, laws were struck down by the courts, commissions fell into "safe" hands, legislators continued to receive and even seek corporate favors. The battle had continually to be refought, but perceptibly the battleline advanced, and within the first decade the climate in the nation's capital itself shifted the balance in favor of reform. New faces appeared on the Potomac—La Follette, Dolliver, Kent, Johnson, Borah, Norris, Beveridge, a score of other senators, congressmen, and cabinet members—fresh from local victories and possessed of a mandate to make the federal government once more effective in regulating interstate enterprise and in serving fundamental public needs more equitably and impartially than it had done for nearly two generations.

The hopes of the liberals quickly came to depend on the character and disposition of the new President, for the center of power within Congress and within both national parties, though shifting leftward, still lay with the conservatives. Never had the timing of tragedy proved so lucky for reform as when the shocking assassination of the "safe" and placid McKinley brought Vice President Theodore Roosevelt to the White House in September, 1901. Yet too much could be made of the role of chance: McKinley had shown himself more responsive to the demands for a liberal state than his predecessor Cleveland, who in turn had outdistanced both Harrison and Arthur; the drift of the nation was pulling the White

House with it, and the aggressive but moderate Roosevelt would have been a formidable contender for the Republican nomination in 1904 even had McKinley been permitted to finish his second term. In Roosevelt there seethed a potent blend of party professionalism, administrative talent, psychic energy, and reform morality. At each stage in his political career—as Police Commissioner for New York City in 1895, Governor of New York state in 1899, and now as effective boss of the Republican Party and President of the nation—his talents proved to be precisely right for the needs of the moment. At all periods progressives required the support of the party system, and Roosevelt was enough of an opportunist to make the system work. At the same time he possessed the instinct for power which led him unerringly in the direction that both the industrialists and the middle-class voters (for different reasons) wanted to go, which was perceptibly and steadily toward the positive state. While the liberals found in Roosevelt a politician uniquely fitted and more or less eager for the task of translating the reform impulse into politically acceptable terms, the conservatives could count on him only to moderate the impulse in the act of translating it. When Roosevelt, in short, seemed most like a drag on reform, he was often its most effective champion.

Roosevelt's first major task as President was to define for the federal government an acceptable position on the labor question. In the previous twenty years, depression and business instability had combined to produce explosive unrest among the laboring classes throughout the highly industrialized Northeast and in the western mining regions. Unions had grown in numbers and power, but what they had gained for the American laborer by 1900 they had gained almost singlehanded: at a time when the courts were hostile, the press abusive, the urban propertied classes fearful, and the farmers indifferent, the elaborate neutrality of the federal government in most major industrial disputes meant merely that troops would be used to restore order, terminate the strike, and usually permit management to gain its point. The American Federation of Labor and the Railroad Brotherhoods managed to survive the "unneutral neutrality" of the state, but their influence was felt mostly on behalf of the minority of skilled workmen, and in fact neither organization pressed for more than a change of rules whereby skilled labor and management might continue their bargaining under more equal terms but free from government interference. The less skilled workers plainly needed help from the state, and in 1902 a major crisis in labor relations gave the United Mine Workers, their only important spokesman, a chance to seek it. Rebuffed in their request for higher pay and for recognition of their union, the anthracite miners conducted an orderly and highly effective strike in the eastern Pennsylvania coal fields which lasted five months and produced a shortage of coal in eastern cities just as summer was giving

way to autumn. At first Roosevelt sought only to pressure the operators
into a private settlement and believed on legal advice that the federal
government was empowered to do nothing else. But the narrow stubborn-
ness of the coal operators and the incredible arrogance of their public
statements roused the nation's sympathy for the miners and infuriated
the President, who promptly threatened to use the army to seize and
run the mines. Important newspapers had already called for government
ownership, and a powerful group of businessmen, more liberal on the
subject of labor than were the coal barons, obtained the backing of J. P.
Morgan in a successful move to force the operators to agree to federal
arbitration.

The strike commission which Roosevelt appointed granted the miners
a pay raise but did not require management to extend recognition to the
union. The terms themselves were hardly a major victory for labor; yet
the President had shattered all precedent in his use of the power of his
office to force the operators to negotiate on terms more favorable than the
government had ever before supported. Roosevelt shared the dislike of
many of his class for radical positions; the man who had once thought
that social fomenters like Debs and Bryan should be taken out and
shot was not yet ready to let the more sanguine liberals in his party have
their way. But Roosevelt also correctly surmised that the public and the
business community were willing to give way enough to labor to preserve
industrial peace and prevent an intolerable buildup of working-class
tensions. Over the next dozen years the power of organized labor was
assured a more impartial political climate than it had ever known in the
nineteenth century, and by 1914 Gompers and the A.F.L. were able to
combine with the more militant progressives to persuade a reluctant
Woodrow Wilson to endorse the exemption of unions from the antitrust
laws and partial union protection from the use of court injunctions. Labor's
gains in the early twentieth-century reform movement were modest, but
the gains of no other class were more significant.

By far the most striking of Roosevelt's actions on behalf of reform
consisted of his drive to strengthen the national regulation of large
corporations and railroads. Early in his first term he had become convinced that while the growth of industrial combinations was not in itself
to be feared and was probably inevitable, it was certain to lead to a
dangerous centralization of economic power in private hands if it were
not subjected to rigorous federal supervision. Roosevelt had little use
for "trust-busting," and he pinned his first hopes on new legislation which
would replace the Sherman Act with a law requiring Federal incorporation of large enterprises and their careful policing by a powerful government commission. Finding this proposal to be politically impossible
(conservative Congressional leaders were aghast, and some liberals ex-

pressed doubts), Roosevelt proceeded to do what he could by executive action under the existing law. In 1902 his attorney-general announced a government suit under the Sherman Act to dissolve the Northern Securities Corporation, one of Morgan's holding companies whose formation had involved a spectacular fight for personal control of three transcontinental railroads. Wall Street was shocked and angered; it rightfully regarded the move as a major test of power between the business community and the government. In 1903 the Supreme Court ruled in favor of the government, and although Roosevelt still preferred regulation to dissolution of large corporations, he knew he had gained a strategic weapon of enormous value. The threat of a government suit was often sufficient to win cooperation from large business, and to show that he was not bluffing, Roosevelt in the next six years instigated suits against Standard Oil, American Tobacco, the New Haven Railroad, the Du Pont Company, the beef trust, and three dozen other combinations. He had already forged a similar weapon by setting up the Federal Bureau of Corporations, a fact-finding agency of the executive branch, which immensely strengthened his hand in negotiating with powerful businessmen who feared public exposure of their trade practices.

All this Roosevelt was able to achieve independently of Congress. The reformers, who were as yet no match for the conservatives who ran both houses, had reason to be grateful to the capable White House strategist who frequently appeared to be moving too slowly for their taste. When the inevitable showdown with Congress finally took place, Roosevelt's skill and willingness to compromise proved even more essential to the reform cause. It came in 1906 with the passage of the Hepburn Act, empowering the Interstate Commerce Commission to prescribe railroad rates (subject to review by the courts) and to examine the books of all railroads and utilities of an interstate character. Large shippers, most of the railroads, and the important banking houses which controlled them, arrayed themselves in a solid wall of political influence against the bill. Its proponents, numerous but divided, consisted largely of coal-mining states like West Virginia, small shippers from distant regions and cities who suffered from discriminatory rate-making, and the infant Chamber of Commerce. Convinced that his future effectiveness as a political leader rode on the outcome and that victory would provide the impetus for future reform, Roosevelt proceeded systematically to demoralize and undercut the opposition. His Bureau of Corporations furnished him with devastating information about Standard Oil's system of railroad rebates; and while friends of his among the reform journalists published a series of articles exposing the dishonesty of standard railroad policies, Roosevelt simultaneously made public his own evidence. The resulting outcry beat on the senatorial battleline and weakened it. Having openly spoken for a bill with sweeping powers of regulation, Roosevelt now suddenly agreed to compromise on its strongest clauses and supported a face-saving and largely superfluous provision for a broad judicial review. Such perfectly timed concessions, offered with a mixture of bargaining and pressure (1906 was a congressional election year), split the remainder of the opposing phalanx. The bill became law, and while Roosevelt had irritated a few progressives by failing to obtain all that he and they originally asked for, he was satisfied that he had gotten about all that he had really wanted and far more than had first seemed possible.

The Hepburn Act significantly advanced the entire concept of federal control of private industry. Within another year were to come effective inspection of the meat-packing industry and a Pure Food and Drug Law. Both were obtained by the familiar strategy of investigation, partial publicity accompanied by a threat of more, and strategically timed but largely irrelevant concessions. To cap his career as President, Roosevelt was then to arouse effective public support for the national practice of forestry, the regulation of timber supplies, the development of public waterways and irrigation, the continuous survey of public resources, and the voluntary conservation of those resources which remained in private control. Like the regulation of railroads and trusts and the policing of food, national resource policy was made possible partly by Roosevelt's flair for dramatizing the moral and public significance of issues which conservatives had generally regarded as purely economic and not subject to the political process. What assured the success of his policies was that they were built on a growing competence in the administration of public affairs in the states and in the nation, served by a body of reform-minded public officials increasingly capable of running an impartial regulatory state. Within a decade, during the crisis of national mobilization, the positive state first launched in 1906 was to become a reality.

The political momentum which Roosevelt so capably generated on behalf of reform proved in the meantime barely sufficient to carry through the presidential term of the far less dynamic Taft. An amiable man of ingrained conservatism, he displayed on occasion a devotion to legal niceties which served curiously to strengthen the government's hand in the regulation of business. Yet what reformers still required was an active friend at court, someone who could engender the sort of crusading enthusiasm necessary to refuel the progressive movement until such time as it could achieve larger victories and a firmer hold on the institutions of government. By 1911 the reformers had gained a balance of power within Congress, and it was now, ironically, the White House which had to be prodded, fought, and finally repudiated. Somewhat against his will Taft found himself in league with the dwindling ranks of standpatters in the Senate; yet in the face of such a formidable alliance the progressives still managed to strengthen the Hepburn Act, approve amendments to the Constitution to permit a federal income tax and the popular election of the Senate, and conduct an investigation of the banking system in preparation for major improvements in the structure of credit and currency. Their achievement was made easier by the Democratic sweep in the 1910 elections and plainly foreshadowed the twin nominations of Roosevelt and Wilson in 1912. Pitting two avowed reformers against each other (Taft was counted out of the race), this significant presidential battle constituted a massive endorsement for the continuation of progressivism. The momentum of the Roosevelt years had regained its vitality.

Woodrow Wilson's inauguration in 1913 launched the climactic years of the progressive era. It is true that the new President began with caution and like Roosevelt became bolder in reform leadership only as political necessities arose. This is perhaps to say that the liberal achievements building up for nearly a generation possessed by now a certain force of their own and that Wilson was astute enough to gauge their strength. Though reform had won a resounding vote in 1912, the Democratic segment of the electorate was still a minority in the nation, and it fell to Wilson to construct an effective major party out of what support he had and the approval he could win by his record. This he was never completely able to do: in 1916 the Democrats would hang onto the White House almost by their fingernails, and it is safe to say that their margin of victory depended on the promise of a continued search for neutrality in war; by 1918 they had lost partial control of Congress and in 1920 the progressive coalition was to disintegrate under the divisive questions of reform and peace. In the meantime progressivism under Wilson's imaginative leadership had managed to solidify and broaden its hold on American government. The President first demanded a lowering of the tariff, an issue Roosevelt had never dared touch and Taft had found to be dynamite. Calling Congress into early special session within a month of the inaugural, he delivered his tariff message in person, thereby breaking a century-long precedent and driving Roosevelt to exclaim, "Why didn't I think of that?" In six months Congress passed the first genuinely downward revision of the tariff in twenty years and provided in it the first collection of a federal income tax in its history. In breathtaking pace there followed within another year the Federal Reserve Act, the Clayton Antitrust Act (with clauses legalizing labor boycotts, picketing, and strikes), and the establishment of the Federal Trade Commission to carry out its provisions. Through the complex but not unfamiliar mutation of politics the Wilsonian formula for the federal policing of business managed to blend two antagonistic views: the flexible regulatory powers Roosevelt had sought, and the stricter emphasis on legal sanctions, even dissolution, as represented by the spirit of the Sherman Act and supported by most Democrats and Progressives from the West and the South. In forging such a record the Democrats found Wilson's leadership indispensable; no President had been more effective in exercising party discipline, in forcing compromise on friends and foes, or in arousing the public with the eloquence of his appeals.

Despite the liberalism of his rhetoric, Wilson, like Roosevelt, insisted on mediating, not choosing, between Wall Street and Main Street. Faced with a mild depression in 1913, he was anxious to gain the confidence of the business community. His appointments to the Federal Reserve Board and to the F.T.C. reflected cautious moderation, and for two years he managed to hold the progressives of both parties in tight rein. Yet he did so as much from choice as from instinct, and within another two years, building a record for 1916, he was hunting in full cry with the hounds. Under his firm prodding Congress extended federal loans and credits to farmers, authorized support for agricultural extension work, outlawed the sale of products from industries employing child labor, instituted an eight-hour day for railroad labor, and approved the appointment of Louis Brandeis, one of the most advanced liberals in American law, to that inner bastion of conservatism, the Supreme Court of the United States. Not since the Civil War had the national government achieved so much in so short a time, and not since its earliest years had it so completely fulfilled the expectations of those who were in advance of their time.

In retrospect Roosevelt and Wilson could be seen to have embodied both the virtues and the limitations of the reform vision. The limitations flowed in part from the virtues. In enlarging the opportunities for the middle-class capitalists, the men on the make, the reformers failed to perceive the equal need for a powerful labor movement; they tended, indeed, to view the interests of the middle class and the laboring class as partially in conflict. In fighting for a greater participation of individual citizens in the political process they sometimes ended in believing that the mere construction of a framework would generate wisdom in its use, that legislative reform would guarantee social change. Their achievement lay in taking first steps; their limitations appeared in their failure to envisage the shifts in strategy and in social thinking needed for the next steps. Nothing they did contributed more to the stability of modern society than their success in compelling the power of corporate enterprise to answer to public control and to appear responsive to public needs. Yet within the next decade their solutions proved too modest in the face of still greater business power and an increasingly unbalanced market. What was eventually to prevail was the conscious encouragement of organized power among rival interests and groups within the economic system, an encouragement backed by a strong administrative state and a flexible judiciary body. Such a solution the progressive generation was not completely prepared to sanction. Their achievement consisted in making it possible for a later generation to sanction what they could not. Meanwhile they had provided their society with something more: the conviction, which was never entirely to disappear, that it was the business of a democratic people to discover and to assert moral ideals worthy of man at his best, and that it was the business of the political process to honor them.

June, 1914, was a bright month for America. Henry Ford had announced a truly unprecedented wage of five dollars a day for the workers in his Highland Park plant. (The impact of this policy may be likened to an announcement in the 1960's that some motor company was offering a $7,500 minimum guaranteed annual salary to its entire work force.) In five thousand towns as the late spring sun slanted through the elms and the eucalyptus senior class orators spoke of the hopes and the promise of man. June, 1914, was the heyday of the Progressive years.

The United States seemed in that month a part of a larger victory. In the century since Waterloo there had taken place a more spectacular improvement in the material welfare of the average citizen of the western world than in any other period since the dawn of man. Everywhere in that world men had begun through science to command their environment. Men flew in the air, talked through wires, and watched flickers of light bring screens to life. The death rate had dropped. Fast trains roared under the Alps, through the Caucasus, and over the Sierras. Trade and travel had never been so free from papers, visas, passports. The middle classes controlled the destinies of four of the five greatest nation-states and a dozen of the lesser ones. The middle classes were dedicated to the development and protection of material progress. Their characteristic institutions embodied universal education, political democracy, economic liberalism, and the faith that these and the enlightened institution of international diplomacy would combine to abolish violence from the world. No one more perfectly represented a mood of reason and a pride in institutional achievement than the still vigorous William James, when in 1911 he posited his famous moral equivalent of war. Man's belligerence, he believed, could be successfully deflected into a struggle against nature to the end of controlling his own nature. No international organization, no police force, existed to keep peace, but it was everywhere thought that a kind of mutual national selfishness would keep social order. Modern war was simply too horrible and too costly. Great progressive nations had outgrown the regressive violence of barbarian tribes.

June, 1914, came and went. In a prosperous town in the Balkans an Austrian archduke clutched at his chest and slumped forward in his touring car. Blood from a bullet wound spread a slow stain over his crumpled uniform.

# PART I

# THE FIGHT AGAINST POVERTY AND PRIVILEGE

# The City

## *Frederic C. Howe*

*Most progressives fell in love with the city. For ambitious and well-educated citizens in small-town America (which was most of America before 1890) the fast-growing industrial metropolis promised to consummate their present dreams and stimulate new ones. The city touched with its wand budding administrators, social planners, hopeful lawyers, young men restless at the thought of remaining cautious merchants in rural market towns, young women shut off by barriers of custom from stimulating careers in the country counties where they were raised. Chicago beckoned Carl Sandburg, Clarence Darrow, Thorstein Veblen, Jane Addams, Theodore Dreiser (and Sister Carrie). To New York went Lincoln Steffens, Ida Tarbell, Charles Beard, and, by way of Cleveland, Frederic Howe.*

*Like all durable love affairs this flirtation with the city bogged down at times in disenchantment. Though progressives were often romantics, they were also realists, and when they wrote of urban life they did not fail to note its dislocations, its amorality and corruption, its nerve system of cash and calculation. To the progressives the city flaunted itself as a primary challenge for the construction of a social order built to modern humane specifications. When Lincoln Steffens exposed graft and corruption as the "shame" of the cities in 1903, his was a lover's quarrel, revealing only a little despair and a good deal of confidence in the political system; he noted that Chicago, at least, had half-freed itself from the "system" and was still "fighting on."*

*Steffens' breezy but clinical journalism was perfectly suited to arouse the interests of general readers everywhere in the anatomy of their city politics; equally influential were the writings of the active reform politicians, aimed less at the general reader than at their fellow specialists. Most prominent among them was Frederic C. Howe, lawyer, social worker, administrator, tax expert, politician, and writer in the front ranks of urban reform. By 1896, when not yet thirty, Howe had long*

25

*since shaken loose from the rigorous Scotch-Irish and Quaker piety of his parents' household in a small Pennsylvania town, had gained a Ph.D. from Johns Hopkins, a degree from the University of Halle in Germany, a degree in law, and a growing legal practice in Cleveland. Plunging into problems of urban social welfare, he was serving on the city council in 1902 when he shortly became a supporter of Tom Johnson, ex–utility baron, now hard headed reform mayor of Cleveland. Howe was subsequently to publish important books on taxation, on Wisconsin's state government, and on European municipal problems; he served a term in the Ohio Senate and on the Ohio Tax Commission, supported in quick succession the presidential candidacies of La Follette, Roosevelt, and Wilson in 1911 and 1912, and moved in and out of national politics as a writer and appointive official until his death in 1940.*

*The City: Hope of Democracy, published in 1905, was even then the work of no mere reform enthusiast but of an experienced public official and tax expert whose tempered vision of the city was to influence a generation of civic-minded Americans. The viewpoint and generalizations of The City closely paralleled those which Steffens had begun to advance, and it is apparent in the writings of both men that by 1905 each had profoundly influenced the other. As though to stress the modernness of his thought, Howe used the title page to label his book "an economic interpretation." The reader may determine for himself whether the phrase is appropriate, but in one major respect Howe's use of it to characterize his own outlook is significant. Was the political system corrupt? Did the economic order breed injustice and hardship? In the eyes of many middle-class citizens, evil flourished because the wrong crowd had seized power; reform involved merely the exposure of the crooks in office and their replacement with honest men. The question of good government seemed at bottom a question of good moral character. With this view the worldly-wise young experts of Howe's generation, men like Whitlock and Steffens, were notably impatient. Expecting honest men by their mere election to office to reform the political system made no more sense, as Mencken was later to observe, than to fill all the bawdy houses with virgins. Behind every city hall was a network of economic influence and a system of commercial interest and political privilege so pervasive as to involve most of the citizenry in ways that made the question of honest intentions and moral rectitude irrelevant. If you would reduce the corruption and abolish the privilege, apply your leverage to the economic arrangements which gave life to them. The basic proposition which made the early writings of Whitlock, Steffens, Beard, and Howe so significant was that by careful investigation intelligent men could uncover and gradually learn to control a few of the social forces which moved the political system.*

*Economic interpretations and formulas for action were, of course, ready at hand, notably the views of Karl Marx, but these writers owed little to Marx. Far more influential, especially on Howe, was the gigantic intellectual shadow which Henry George cast over many of the reform generations of the 1890's and the early twentieth century. George's writings provided the catalyst which had transformed Tom Johnson; his lieutenant Howe likewise fell convert to the elaborate social concepts of Progress and Poverty, and in a part of his writing presented here he championed a version of the Single Tax as the most effective sort of economic lever with which to alter the structure of the urban power. Howe's reputation and influence owed little to his view of the Single Tax and perhaps can be said to have grown in spite of it. It was his strength and that of his fellow progressives that they seldom hitched their hopes to single formulas. The problems of urban America were too complex for single formulas, and no one perceived this fact with greater clarity than the reformers who faced the problems day by day.*

The city has woven our lives into the lives of others. No longer is each household an independent one, producing for its own wants alone and supplied from within. The texture of the fabric has been altered. It is now closely woven. And this change is far more than an industrial one—a mere adjustment of mankind to his work. It is but part of man's desire for a larger life, for freer social intercourse, for amusement, as well as a response to the industrial revolution which has superseded domestic industry by the machine.

Within the city the game of life is played, and there are many capital prizes. Here, opportunity and fortune are to be found. Here business centres. Here life is full and human. The farm offers none of these things. It is barren of great possibilities, barren, even, of a living, the farmer says. The city is El Dorado, the promised land which fires the imagination. Failure may come, it is true, but there is the chance, and life, movement, and recreation even in failure. The saloon is something, while the streets, the parks, the theatre, the church, one's fellows, all make up the canvas of life even to the poorest.

And the city has given the world culture, enlightenment, and education along with industry and commercial opportunity. The advance in recent years in this regard has been tremendous. Compare our London, Paris, Berlin, or New York with these cities fifty years ago. Then, life in any large sense was limited to a few. To-day, to an ever-increasing mass of the population, opportunities are crowding one upon another. Not

Frederic C. Howe, *The City: Hope of Democracy* (New York: Scribner's, 1905), pp. 24-42, 61-90, 280-299.

only is education generously adapted to the needs of all, but night schools, art exhibitions, popular lectures and concerts, college settlements, the parks, playgrounds, a cheap press, labor organizations, the church, all these are bringing enlightenment at a pace never before dreamed of. Day by day opportunities gain in volume. A decade almost encompasses the history of such movements for democratic opportunity.

All this is enlarging life, modifying our civilization, deepening the significance of democracy. It is rendering possible a higher standard of living. A new conception of municipal purpose has come in. It is neither conscious nor defined as yet, but in the midst of the outward manifestations of municipal activity, an unrecognized broadening of the culture and life of the city is going on, of immense significance to the future.

Much of this is being expressed through private channels. But that the private activities of to-day will become the public ones of to-morrow is inevitable. The crèche, kindergarten, settlement, playgrounds, public baths, lodging houses, hospitals were inspired by private philanthropy. They are slowly passing under public control. Merely to enumerate what has been done during the past few years in the matter of school administration would form a chapter in itself. The same is true of the care of juvenile offenders. It is manifest in every department of city affairs. The possibility of life is increasing more rapidly than at any other period in the history of the world. It is less than a decade since Josiah Quincy, while Mayor of Boston, proposed the erection of public baths and gymnasiums and the opening of playgrounds in the poorer sections of the city. When made, the suggestion was assailed as socialistic. To-day, without protest, the City of Boston expends $500,000 annually for parks and playgrounds and over $100,000 annually for baths and gymnasiums. Over $3,000,000 has been expended for these purposes in a few year's time. There are now twenty-one playgrounds in the city; while summer camps, public concerts, bathing beaches, and public lavatories have still further added to the comfort of the poor. During this interval, appropriations for these purposes have crept into the budgets of nearly all of our large cities, while kindergartens, summer schools, manual training, free lectures, and public concerts are rapidly finding a place in city administration along with the expenditures for police, fire, and health protection.

But such a schedule of items is but a small part of the gain which civilization has made through the city. They are but evidences of the fact that life has become a social, not an isolated thing. The entire groundwork of society is being relaid under a system of closer political relationship. But a few generations ago, civilization was based on individualistic lines. The city has brought us whatever sense of social responsibility we now have. In a sense all this is socialism. We do not call it that. But neither does the German nor the Englishman call the undertakings of his city socialistic.

The humanizing forces of to-day are almost all proceeding from the city. They are creating a new moral sense, a new conception of the obligations of political life, obligations which, in earlier conditions of society, did not and could not exist. Step by step individual rights have been merged into larger social ones. And it is this very increase in public activities that renders the city as attractive to the rich as it is to the poor. In earlier days, even the most elementary public functions were performed by the individual. He paved, cleaned, and lighted the street before his door. He was his own constable. Such health protection as he enjoyed was the result of his own vigilance. Education was conducted at home or by the church. The library was a priestly possession, as was all learning. His house was his castle, even in the midst of the city, and society offered him little save the administration of justice and protection from foreign foes.

To-day the city protects his life and his property from injury. It safeguards his health in countless ways. It oversees his house-construction, and protects him from fire. It cleans and lights his streets, collects his garbage, supplies him with employees through free employment bureaus. It educates his children, supplies them with books, and in many instances with food. It offers him a library, and through the opening of branches almost brings it to his door. It offers nature in the parks; supplies him with opportunities for recreation and pleasure through concerts, lectures, and the like. It maintains a public market; administers justice; supplies nurses, physicians, and hospital service, as well as a cemetery for burial. It takes the refuse from his door and brings back water, gas, and frequently heat and power at the same time. It inspects his food, protects his life, and that of his children through public oversight of the conditions of factory labor. It safeguards him from contagious diseases, facilitates communication upon the streets, and in some instances offers opportunities for higher technical and professional education.

All these intrusions into the field of private business have involved no loss of freedom to the individual. Every increase of public activity has, in fact, added to personal freedom. Whatever the motive, the real liberty of the individual has been immeasurably enlarged through the assumption of these activities by the city.

And all this has been achieved at an insignificant cost. The expenditure of the average city of over a quarter of a million inhabitants ranges from $16 to $34 per capita, or from $60 to $136 per family, a sum which would scarcely pay for the education of a single child at a private institution. And while incompetence, extravagance, and frequently corruption have accompanied much of it, there are few who would contend that the private watchman is more efficient than the public fireman, that private education is better than public education, that the supply of gas from a private company is cheaper or better than the supply of water under public control.

Such are some of the palpable gains which the city has brought. But the real gain is far more than an enumeration of services or a schedule of activities. The real significance of it all is found in the fact that democracy has been forced into activities which have heretofore lain outside of the sphere of government. The relationships of society are changing. We are being drawn into an intimacy, a solidarity, which makes the welfare of one the welfare of all. A finer spirit is being born. The city is being socialized. It is coming to feel the cruelty of nature's laws and to alleviate their poignancy. The hospitals, parks, kindergartens, playgrounds, and reform schools were the first expression of this feeling. The movement has since changed in character. Its motives are justice, rather than philanthropy, and it is expressing itself in a demand for reform in our methods of taxation, the solution of the housing problem, in a desire for cheaper water, transportation, and light.

What the lines of future activity will be, we can only conjecture. Measured by what has been done in the past ten years, the change will be tremendous. For, once organized, modern democracy moves with increasing momentum. We may call it socialism if we will. This will scarce check its advance. And when these newer services come, their arrival will be welcomed by all classes just as were the public schools, libraries, parks, and water works, the police, fire, and health departments, whose control by the city has increased the happiness and safety of city life to all.

But along with the gain there is a loss account, a terrible loss account. The city has replaced simplicity, industrial freedom, and equality of fortune with complexity, dependence, poverty, and misery close beside a barbaric luxury like unto that of ancient Rome. Vice, crime, and disease have come in. The death rate has increased, while infectious diseases and infant mortality ravage the crowded quarters. The city has destroyed the home and substituted for it the hotel, flat, tenement, boarding house, and cheap lodging house. Our politics have suffered, and corruption has so allied itself with our institutions that many despair of democracy. The city exacts an awful price for the gain it has given us, a price that is being paid in human life, suffering, and the decay of virtue and the family. Just as in mediæval times, some of the burghers of a beleaguered town paid the forfeit of their lives that the others might live, so the modern city avenges itself upon humanity by vicariously taking of those who risk her favor.

According to the investigations of Charles Booth, a London-born family disappears in about three generations. Human life seems to require a ground wire to the sod, a connection with Mother Earth to maintain its virility. According to Mr. Galton, only about one-half as many children of artisans grow up in a typical manufacturing town, as in the case of the children of laboring people in a healthy country district. In the abyss of London, Paris, Berlin, New York, and Chicago, the family often ends with itself. It dies of town disease. The whirlpool of city life claims all in time. Those who fail, it claims at once. Were it not for the steady stream of rugged strength from the countryside, the city would ultimately lose its population.

And it is not alone those who win who have made the city. The police court docket produces such headlines for the daily press as: "Once a Millionaire," "Formerly a Leading Professional Man," "At One Time a Leader in Society, Now in the Workhouse." These failed. But they did not always fail. And the unnumbered thousands who have come to the city, the artisans, workmen, girls who gave their life to work so long as work was to be had, are part of the same sacrifice. They form the hecatomb of human life that the modern city, like an Oriental idol, exacts from society. And it is they who have built our homes, manned our industry, and amassed the wealth that they did not enjoy. Through them, wealth and culture have come. They are like the toilers of the hive, who by some hidden secret of nature fulfil their destiny in death for the well-being of the swarm.

Out of the three million five hundred thousand inhabitants in the great area of metropolitan New York, there are but twenty-five thousand persons who appear upon the tax-assessors' books as owners of personal property. But one person out of every one hundred and forty possesses sufficient property to warrant a return under the general property tax. And the number of persons owning real property is not much if any more. For in our cities the dweller has become a tenant. Mankind has been dispossessed of the soil. In Greater New York scarcely four per cent. of the families live in their own unencumbered homes, while on Manhattan Island the percentage falls to two percent. The city has given birth to a landless proletariat. The growth of population does this. Society creates a value and then is charged for the privilege of enjoying it. And neither thrift, economy, nor prudence can prevent it. For the average city dweller, even though he saved all of his earnings, could not possess himself of a freehold, or live upon it once secured.

And this loss, this sacrifice, is a vicarious one. The individual takes his chance, but his winnings or his losings alike go to the upbuilding of the city. The vagabond, the sick, the destitute, the prostitute, the flotsam and jetsam of the community who find their way to the cheap lodging house, the streets, the prisons, have lost their all, but they have contributed it to the city, to its industry and life. For the country does not breed this class, and few men are failures, outcasts, or criminals from choice. Any one who has taken the trouble to follow this human wreckage back through its terrible experience knows this. Men and women come to the city buoyant with hope, eager for work. At best, employment is precarious and irregular. This irregularity of city work is the most demoralizing thing of all. "When employment is precarious," says Professor Foxwell, "thrift and self-reliance are discouraged. The savings of years may be swallowed up in a few months. A fatalistic spirit is developed. Where all is uncertain, and there is not much to lose, reckless over-population is certain to be set at. These effects are not confined to the poorer classes. The business world is equally demoralized by industrial speculation. Careful prevision cannot reckon upon receiving its due return, and speculation of the purest gambling type is thereby encouraged. But the working class suffer most." Under these conditions, men live from hand to mouth. Once out of employment, the landlord closes the door upon them. Then comes the pawnshop to maintain life for a few weeks longer. Soon the cheap lodging house absorbs them with its filth and common helplessness. In time, the saloon is the only open door. And soon even it refuses to open to them. Loss of companionship, the most cruel loss of all, fills the cup to overflowing, and a sense of lost respect, helplessness, hopelessness, and utter alienation from society settles down. Then comes the charge of "vagrancy," "no visible means of support," "suspicion," which starts a new cycle of the police court and the workhouse with its brand of crime. Then freedom and vagrancy again, possibly some petty misdemeanor; then arrest, conviction, and ultimate extinction of self-respect, followed by the penitentiary and a life of regular crime. London, with less than one-fifth of the population of England and Wales, produces one-third of the crime. In Philadelphia, a city of high comfort, there is seven times as much crime to a given population as in the country districts; while in New York, nearly all of the offenders come from the cities. I have known men go through these experiences, men who were college-bred, men who were trained, women who had come to the city from necessity. I have known them pass from one social scale to another until they reached the marginal boarding house where the last stand was made. Every large city contains this class, not to speak of the infinitely larger number of artisans, unskilled workmen, common hands who cannot catch on. They do not know the ropes, even when opportunity, work, a livelihood is to be had.

This is part of the cost we pay for the city. It appears along with the mill, the factory, the sweatshop, and the counter. And this wreckage is incidental to the new civilization whose centre is the city, and which decays at the extremities among the very poor. In the rural districts it is not found. In the smaller towns only occasional traces of it appear.

We can calculate this cost of town disease with as much precision as an actuary can a mortuary table. Community by community, it is much the same. It rises in periods of depression and falls in periods of prosperity. It is diminished by work, education, recreation, and opportunity and is increased by ignorance, the tenement, and careless criminal administration. But the principal cause is industrial.

We find humanity making its last stand in the cheap lodging house, conscious of lost opportunity and departed respectability. It sits brooding at the shop counter, in the factory, and the sweatshop, where woman's virtue is battling for life on four or five dollars a week. One who follows the police patrol from the streets to the police stations, or spends an evening in the cheap lodging house, may see the beginning of the hardening round that ultimately ends in despair. Here the drag-net of hard times, irregular employment, loss of family gathers the flotsam and jetsam of the city; here are those who have been driven from the streets by cold, hunger, or the "move on" of the policeman. Companionship is gone, self-respect has vanished; for self-respect among the poor hinges upon work, and empty hands bring no welcome at home, in the saloon, or elsewhere. The beginning of the cycle is here, and we make little effort to stay its progress.

That this is not an overdrawn picture of modern city life the reports of public and private investigation confirm. Contemporary literature is filled with it. Here is the evidence of a man of science, Professor Thomas H. Huxley:

Any one who is acquainted with the state of the population of all great industrial centres, whether in this or other countries, is aware that amidst a large and increasing body of that population there reigns supreme . . . that condition which the French call *la misère*, a word for which I do not think there is an exact English equivalent. It is a condition in which the food, warmth, and clothing which are necessary for the mere maintenance of the functions of the body in their normal state cannot be obtained; in which men, women, and children are forced to crowd into dens wherein decency is abolished, and the most ordinary conditions of healthful existence are impossible of attainment; in which the pleasures within reach are reduced to brutality and drunkenness; in which the pains accumulate at compound interest in the shape of starvation, disease, stunted development, and moral degradation; in which the prospect of even steady and honest industry is a life of unsuccessful battling with hunger, rounded by a pauper's grave. . . . When the organization of society, instead of mitigating this tendency, tends to continue and intensify it; when a given social order plainly makes for evil and not for good, men naturally enough begin to think it high time to try a fresh experiment. I take it to be a plain truth that throughout industrial Europe there is not a single large manufacturing city which is free from a vast mass of people whose condition is exactly as described, and from a still greater mass who, living just on the edge of the social swamp, are liable to be precipitated into it.

Similar evidences are coming to light in America. And while we have no such exhaustive investigations as those of Mr. Charles Booth in London and Mr. B. S. Rountree in York, England, we have the testimony of those whose life has been identified with the poor and helpless of our great cities. In 1904 there were 700,000 persons in New York who were the recipients of relief from one agency or another. This is one-fifth of the population. In the previous year 60,463 families were evicted for the non-payment of rent in the Borough of Manhattan alone, or about fourteen per cent. of the total number of families. This means that 300,000 persons were unable to find the meagre means with which to pay for the squalid tenements that answer by the name of home; it was a number far in excess of the recorded evictions in all Ireland in ten years' time. It has been estimated by Mr. Robert Hunter that not less than fourteen per cent. of the people in good times and twenty per cent. in bad times are in distress. And still not more than one-half of the people actually in need ever apply for relief. According to the same authority the number of persons in poverty in the large industrial centres of America rarely falls below twenty-five per cent of the people. "I have not the slightest doubt," says Mr. Hunter, "that there are in the United States ten millions in precisely these conditions of poverty, but I am merely guessing, and there may be as many as fifteen or twenty millions."

Must the city, of necessity, exact such sacrifice? For the few inordinate wealth and luxury, for a numerous middle class a larger degree of comfort and convenience than society elsewhere offers, and for an ever-increasing residuum little save poverty, the tenement, and ultimate extinction? Or is the Rome of the days of the decaying Republic, the Rome of a few patrician families with hundreds of thousands of hopeless, landless, propertyless freemen clamoring for bread, the type to which even the modern democratic city is drifting?

Unquestionably such a tendency is already apparent in America. For no cities of the western world, saving London, Glasgow, and possibly two or three other British cities, offer a parallel to the conditions which exist in New York, Boston, Chicago, and elsewhere. There are certain economic tendencies in Anglo-Saxon institutions that seem to be inexorable. These tendencies are constantly increasing the masses of the poorer, whether or not they are constantly making the rich richer. Some of these tendencies have reached their logical conclusion in Great Britain, where they have produced a condition that is sapping the life of the nation. Similar forces are at work in America, which, if unchecked, will lead to an increasing proletariat.

For some years to come these tendencies may be ignored, but in the end they must be met if American civilization is to continue to higher development. For the life of the future is to be an urban life. And to an ever-increasing extent the city will continue to take its hostages in poverty, disease, and crime, from those who brave her favor.

It is difficult to believe that the advance in civilization which has made all nature tribute to man's energy should involve such a burden, or that the revolution in industry which has increased the productive power of the world a thousand-fold should of necessity leave an increasing proportion of mankind worse off than they were before. That the city should of necessity involve such a price seems a denial of human intelligence and the wisdom of God's plan. . . .

As we have seen, the American city is not all bad. Here and there a community has risen against the party, the boss, and the machine, and overthrown them. Such exhibits of municipal vitality tend to qualify the disheartening portrayals with which we are familiar. Moreover, whole departments of city life are administered on a relatively high plane of efficiency. In some cities the spoils system has been eliminated. Here and there sound business methods have come in, while reform movements have aroused the public to independent action in local elections. The schools, libraries, parks, and many other departments are responding to this change. Everywhere are many evidences of a higher civic sense, a more enlightened interest, a belief in the city and the possibilities of city life.

There yet remain many cities not touched by reform. Cincinnati, Philadelphia, St. Louis, and many others have failed to respond to the quickening uplift of other communities. At the same time, many departments of the city are in a state of arrested development. Councilmanic bodies are almost uniformly bad. The police, health, and street departments are backward or indifferently well administered. Corruption breaks out in city after city, and indictments, disclosures, and reform movements only serve to localize the disease.

From the mass of testimony now available, some explanation of the cause of the evils should be obtainable. We should be able to discover some influence that would account for the relative efficiency of some cities and the deplorable condition of others. We should be able to explain why some departments are honestly conducted while others are characterized by corruption.

The people are not dishonest. At most they are indifferent. The spoils system will not account for all the evil, for civil service reform has become an accomplished fact in New York, Boston, and Chicago. Nor can the blame be laid upon the ignorant foreign voter, for Philadelphia is the most American of our cities—and the worst. There is some influence back of all these, some influence that is universal, and at the same time powerful enough to engage the rich and the influential, the press and the party, the boss and the machine.

An examination of the conditions in city after city discloses one sleepless influence that is common to them all. Underneath the surface phenomena the activity of privilege appears, the privileges of the street railways, the gas, the water, the telephone, and electric-lighting companies. The connection of these industries with politics explains most of the corruption; it explains the power of the boss and the machine; it suggests the explanation of the indifference of the "best" citizen and his hostility to democratic reform. Moreover, it throws much light on the excellence of some departments of city life and the inefficiency of others, for the interest of the franchise corporations is centered in the council, in the executive departments, and in the tax-assessors. It does not extend to the schools, libraries, parks, and fire departments, departments which are free from the worst forms of corruption. But the city council awards franchises. It fixes the terms and the regulations under which the franchise corporations may use the streets. The executive enjoys the veto power. He controls permits, and exercises an influence upon the council and public opinion. The assessor determines the appraisal of property as well as the taxes to be paid. All these powers are of great importance, and their control of great value. The privilege of tax evasion may amount to hundreds of thousands of dollars a year. In the larger cities it is measured by millions. In 1903 the special franchises of the public service corporations in Greater New York were appraised at $235,184,325. This valuation is confessedly inadequate, and yet even it escaped taxation prior to the passage of the Ford Franchise Law, assessing the franchise as property.

The franchises themselves are even more valuable than the tax evasions. There is scarcely a city in America of over twenty-five thousand inhabitants in which their value does not exceed the amount of the municipal debt. Careful investigations have been made into this subject in a number of cities. The value in the market of the securities of the surface-railway, gas, and electric-lighting corporations in the Boroughs of Manhattan and the Bronx has been estimated at $400,000,000. The value of the physical property, exclusive of the franchise, is probably well within $125,000,000. Prior to the consolidation of the City of New York in 1898, the public debt, less the sinking fund, was but $141,916,520.

The cost of replacing the Third Avenue Metropolitan Railway system in New York has been estimated as within sixty million dollars, while the stocks and bonds issued on the property aggregate $165,000,000. In

1902 these securities possessed a market value of $221,000,000. The value of the franchise was therefore $161,000,000, or more than two and one-half times the amount of money actually in the system, and twenty million dollars more than the city's net debt in 1898.

The franchises enjoyed by a single corporation exceeded the total indebtedness of the most heavily bonded city in the world. This indebtedness represents parks, water works, aqueducts, fire and police departments, streets, sewers, docks, bridges, lands, hospitals, correctional institutions, colleges, schools, public buildings, armories, courthouses, museums, and all of the many investments which the city has made. But this was but one of the many franchise corporations of the city. It did not include other street-railway systems, the gas companies, the electric-light and telephone companies, the value of whose franchises is hundreds of millions of dollars more. The total value of the franchises in Greater New York has been estimated at $450,000,000. They are assessed for taxation at more than half this sum. At the present time, the total indebtedness of the city, exclusive of the sinking fund, is less than $400,000,000. The franchises of the metropolis, in excess of the physical value of the property, exceed the amount of the city's net debt. They amount to more than one hundred dollars for every man, woman, and child within the city, and their quotation in the market represents wealth in excess of the total appraisal for purposes of taxation of any city in America outside of New York, Philadelphia, Boston, and Chicago. For these grants, the city receives no return. They were obtained to some extent through the ignorance of public officials, but mainly through bribery, corruption and a political alliance with the Democratic Party in the city and the Republican Party in the state.

This is but part of the price that the city is paying to privilege. It is the price that all our cities are paying to those who have requited this gift by overturning our institutions. It is a price which many insist we should continue to pay, because of the alleged greater efficiency of private enterprise, and the fear that democracy is not equal to the additional burdens involved in the assumption of new obligations.

It was a franchise of imperial proportions to the United Gas Improvement Company that finally aroused the City of Philadelphia to resume the elemental means of government through petition, protest, and the vigilance committee. But while public indignation exhausted itself on the Board of Aldermen, the real offenders were higher up. For it was the big business men of the city that awakened the cupidity of city officials and inspired the theft of the city's most valuable asset from those who were its trustees.

In 1900, the Cleveland City Railroad was endeavoring to secure an extension of its franchises from the City Council, and the Chamber of

Commerce secured the appointment of an expert committee to examine into the value of its property. The committee estimated the cost of replacing the system at $3,869,327. This was less than half the value of the stock and bonds of the company then outstanding. And this did not include the franchises of another street railway, of two gas companies, one telephone company, and one electric-lighting company, the divergence between whose investment and capitalization was probably many times more than that of the railway system. In 1904 the total bonded debt of the City of Cleveland, exclusive of money in the sinking fund, but including the indebtedness of the water works, was but $18,877,000. The present market value of the franchises of the street railways of the city alone is probably about the same.

In the city of Toledo, Ohio, several railway systems have been consolidated through the issue of new stock. By this process $11,000,000 in bonds and $12,000,000 of stock have been placed upon the market. These issues have been marketed in the face of the fact that the franchises begin to expire in 1910, and that the plant could probably be duplicated for not to exceed $5,000,000.

Similar investigations have been made in the city of Chicago. The value of the physical property of the seven traction companies in that city has been appraised at $44,922,011; while the market value of the securities issued by the corporations amounts to $120,235,539. The public debt of the city in 1900 was $32,989,819, or $42,323,709 less than the value of the franchises of the traction interests alone.

The Cincinnati Street Railway Company and the Cincinnati Traction Company have issued securities on a fifty-year franchise in excess of $20,000,000, whereas the real investment made does not exceed one-half of this sum.

In Baltimore all the street railways and the electric-lighting company have been consolidated through the issue of over $65,000,000 in securities; whereas the public indebtedness of the city in 1900 was but $31,772,975. Such instances as these might be indefinitely extended, for these exhibits are by no means exceptional. In Philadelphia, Pittsburgh and other Eastern cities where franchises are perpetual, for 999 or 99 years, the amount of securities issued has been determined by the will of the promoters; but however excessive the capitalization may have been, in almost every instance the growth of the city, the increased demand for the services offered, and the diminished cost of production have brought the value of the stock up to par, and in many instances to far above par.

Here is a peculiar form of wealth. It scarcely existed fifty years ago. It is largely the results of the Dartmouth College Case, which decided that grants of this nature were contracts and could not be impaired by the state or the city. Reasonable legislation would have created a license, revocable at the will of the granting authority, but subject to compensation by the community for the actual investment made by the company. Such is the title enjoyed by other wealth; it is always subject to use by the public at its value in the market, which is its cost of replacement.

The value of these privileges or franchises runs into fabulous figures. Their existence is not dependent upon labor cost, but arises from a grant, a contract, a franchise from the community. In New York, Chicago, Philadelphia, and many other cities these anomalous values amount to tens of millions of dollars; while in hundreds of smaller cities their value amounts to hundreds of thousands. In every city of more than twenty-five thousand population they probably exceed in value the amount of the municipal debt.

It is these glittering prizes that lure men from the paths of ordinary industry, as do the gold fields of Alaska, South Africa, and the West. Here a lucky strike is like a bonanza mine. Year by year it increases in value by the growth in population. It is the most valuable possession in the hands of the people, a possession fairly regal in its proportions, and, as we shall see, endowed with power for the greatest evil or the greatest good, according to the policy adopted by the community. Its capitalized value would adorn the city with schoolhouses, parks, and playgrounds; it would pave streets, build sewers, and beautify the city with works of art. On the other hand, were the earnings retained by the city they would reduce the taxes, or if the price of the service were reduced to cost, it would relieve the most onerous of the burdens which urban life entails.

It is the contest for the possession of these privileges that breeds corruption and lures the unfit into politics. In this process, the boss has become the representative of the interests which have reduced our politics to a System of government. They have syndicated the party, and converted the blind submission of the people to party regularity into a marketable asset, which is bought and sold by campaign contributions for private ends.

All this is possible by reason of the fact that the privilege of supplying transportation, gas, water, lighting, and telephone service is a natural monopoly. Competition may be secured for a time, but combination inevitably follows. It has become an axiom of the business world that wherever combination is possible, competition is improbable. This has been demonstrated in hundreds of instances, and to-day there is scarcely a city in the United States where real competition in such service exists. Moreover, the charges of such companies are determined by the rule of monopoly, which is to collect what the traffic will bear. This rule must be qualified in so far as charges have been fixed by contract with the city. But most of these contracts were made many years ago, when these services were in their infancy and the cost of production was much higher than it is at present. Since the granting of these franchises watered securities have been added until it is impossible for the companies to lower rates, while the cities and states have been restrained in their efforts through the interference of the courts or the betrayal of the party to private influences. It is monopoly which gives these services their value. Competition cannot reach them, while their market is daily growing by the increase of population.

It is because these industries are monopolies, supplying a service of universal use, that securities may be issued, and sold, far in excess of the actual investment. This excess runs into the tens of millions of dollars, and it is this that represents the value of the franchise which is obtainable from the city. It is privileges such as these that invite corruption, and for their preservation perpetuate it. When millions may be made by the stroke of the pen, men will appear willing to adopt such measures as may be necessary to accomplish it, even though the means employed involve the crime of bribery, which Governor Folk of Missouri has termed "treason." In no other way can wealth be obtained so easily. In fact, it is only through privileges of some sort that wealth can be secured at all without human labor. And it is to secure and retain such privileges, to prevent their regulation, the reduction of charges, just taxation, and the like, that the boss, the machine, and the System have become the virtual government of city and state all over the Union.

In addition to all this, the difficulties of financing such properties have been reduced to a minimum. Money can be borrowed upon a franchise just as upon real estate. As a matter of fact, a grant of this kind is real estate. It is appurtenant to the land. Bankers will advance money upon a franchise when a manufacturing business would not command it, for in any growing city the earnings of such a property may be relied upon to increase at from five to ten per cent. a year. And the amount of securities which may be issued is determined not by the investment made, but by the earning capacity of the plant, as well as the speculative increase of the future.

In the confusion of causes, we have sought to avoid corruption by keeping our cities out of these businesses. In so doing we have invited the corruption we sought to escape, while business men have accepted the invitation, and remained to govern the city as well. Such a result is both natural and inevitable. We may safeguard our communities by reform associations, by the adoption of improved charters, by the abolition of the spoils system and the like; we may develop civic morality to a high level, we still have the "twentieth man," the man who is not bound by our organizations, the man who will not accept the new standards of conduct, but who will secure control of the party, dictate its nominations, bribe a city council, and, if necessary, the state legislature as well, in order to secure a franchise.

Does this seem an overdrawn picture—too narrow an explanation of the evil of city administration? Then read the tale of municipal corruption portrayed by J. Lincoln Steffens in *The Shame of the Cities*. It is true, Mr. Steffens does not limit the indictment to the privileged corporations. He lays the offense at the door of "business." But it is business, plus franchises and privileges, that has overturned our cities and brought shame to their citizens. For wealth without privilege does not organize to control parties, primaries, or conventions. The retail dealer, wholesale dealer, or manufacturer is not found in the council chamber. His offence is one of indifference. He probably cannot name the alderman from his ward. To him politics is a nuisance. He wants nothing from the city, for his business requires no favors. It depends upon his own energy, thrift, and enterprise. Chicago, "Half Free and Fighting On," as Mr. Steffens says, is not fighting business. Her Municipal Voters' League was not called into being as a vigilance committee to protect the city from ordinary wealth. During the past ten years, Chicago has been like a beleaguered camp, not for protection from without, but for protection from some of her own citizens. The contest within the city has been like that of the Guelphs and Ghibellines of Florence and the mediæval Italian cities. And to-day in Chicago, there is a powerful class who say: "Oh, damn reform; it hurts our business." It is the $75,000,000 of franchises that is hurt by reform. "Anarchy," privilege calls it, or "socialism." But again, it was not business that was hurt, it was graft. It was graft born of railway and gas franchises that turned Chicago over to the "gray wolves" of the Council. It was such graft that made the office of alderman worth fifty thousand dollars a year.

In 1896, the Council granted away six franchises of great value, despite the protests of the public. Some of these grants were made to a dummy who represented the Council combine. Some were used as "strikes" on the existing companies. The city got nothing from any of them. Ultimately, the Council was syndicated. The political machinery of the city was reduced to a System. But the System did not stop there. It could not, even if it would. It ran into the state. It organized both the Republican and the Democratic parties. It nominated and elected not only the members of the Council, the mayor, and the tax assessors, it entered state politics as well.

In 1886 and 1887 [says a report on the political condition of Chicago presented to the National Municipal League], Mr. Yerkes, for himself and his associates, chief of whom were Messrs. Elkins and Widener, of Philadelphia, secured control of a majority of the stock of the street-railway companies operating in the north and west divisions of the city. Then began the most remarkable era of financing and of political manipulation that Chicago has ever known. Securities have been piled on top of securities in the most confusing manner. Politically, Mr. Yerkes became the most powerful factor in the community.

He dominated conventions and made and unmade councils and mayors, all, of course, under cover as much as possible. During his later days he had nearly as much to say in naming Governors and in controlling the action of State Legislatures. But the very audacity of the man's plans finally proved his undoing, by furnishing to the people the shock necessary to stimulate them to effective action. Mr. Yerkes wanted more valuable grants than it was possible for the Council under law to vote him. He went to the Legislature of 1895 with bills, that were passed without much difficulty, but their final success was blocked by the veto of Governor Altgeld. Angered at this defeat of his project, Mr. Yerkes decided to name the next Governor of the state himself, and thus be sure of having there a man who would carry out his wishes, and in this he succeeded. But, in the meantime, the Legislature had become somewhat more sensitive to popular criticism, and in the face of public protest did not care to enact the bolder measures asked for by Mr. Yerkes, known as the Humphrey bills. The Legislature of 1897 did, however, pass, and the Governor approved, the Allen law, which made the position of the companies much stronger in many ways, and among other things authorized councils to make grants running for fifty-year periods.

It was such business as this that was hurt by reform in Chicago. It was not that of the merchant or the manufacturer. It was the business of dealing in a betrayal of the city's interests. It was the business of securing franchises from councils, legislatures, and governors, worth millions, that was in jeopardy. It was this that was injured, not business.

And any one familiar with city politics knows that the class so hurt by reform is not an insignificant one, limited to those seeking the franchises alone. It includes the thousands of stockholders; the bankers and brokers who advance money upon and handle the securities; the lawyers who represent, and the press that is controlled by them. Such business interests ramify into clubs and churches. They involve the best classes of the community; a class that is organized, that understands itself, and is perfectly alive to its own interests. It penetrates into social, business, and professional intercourse. And Chicago has been fighting—now down, now up again—not for some great public improvement, not for the upbuilding of the city and the rendering of it a more comfortable and beautiful place in which to live. Chicago has been like a nation engaged in civil war. All matters of domestic and local concern had to be abandoned in the face of a hostile enemy. Thus for the past ten years all the unfettered talent of that great metropolis of the West has been fighting for the city's protection. It has spent time, energy, and money sadly needed for positive good in the preservation of the city's interests. This contest has been not to prevent the honest barter of the city's streets, but to prevent these rights, whose value runs into the tens of millions of dollars, from being stolen from the community by modern business brigands.

Across the State of Illinois lies St. Louis. This city has been bound, gagged, and reduced to submission for so many years that the people hardly comprehend free government. They scarce remember the meaning of democracy. They are like castaways on a Pacific isle, who forget their mother tongue from disuse. So St. Louis had ceased to expect, ceased almost to believe in public honesty. And when Joseph W. Folk, as Circuit Attorney, began his indictments, the people stood dazed, unheeding, and without understanding the language which he used. The boodlers and the business men asked one another: "What does he want; what is his price?" They treated the city as a mastiff might his kennel. It was their domain, they had owned it for so long. So felt the English Stuarts towards Hampden. So the French Bourbons toward the Third Estate. Folk was an anachronism in Missouri. He is so still to a large portion of St. Louis. He excites the curiosity of the System as well as its anger and chagrin.

Here, as in Chicago, the fight has not been against business wealth, against property as such. The fight that has taken the lid off the city has shown that it was the franchises for street railways, contracts for electric lighting and the like that led to the syndicating of Boss Butler, the millionaire blacksmith. Through him the System controlled the election machinery, reduced the police to a Hessian brigade, and organized the entire city administration for private graft. It was to secure a street railway franchise that $125,000 was deposited in one of the trust companies of the city under an agreement that it was to be delivered to the Council combine when a franchise had been granted. It was another street-railway franchise, secured at a cost to the promoter of $250,000 in bribes, that was afterwards sold to a New York syndicate for $1,250,000. *In neither of these instances did the city receive anything.* It was franchise legislation that led the street railways to the state capital, where they organized the Legislature and paid $250,000 to the representatives of the people, for privileges that the railways did not possess, and could not secure from the city. It was for a lighting contract with the city of St. Louis that $47,500 was distributed by Boss Butler to the members of the Council combine, under the very eyes of indignant citizens, who sat in the Council gallery, ignorant of what was going on.

Who were the beneficiaries of these privileges; who have since defended Butler and the indicted public officials? It was the rich and influential citizens of St. Louis. It was they whom Butler represented. It was they who had organized the Democratic party, and through Butler dictated its nominations even for the Bench, and controlled the administration of justice for the protection of their friends and representatives. It was these men who opposed Folk. It was these men who trampled under foot the election laws, filled the booths with repeaters, and openly counted out the properly elected representatives of the people who were hostile to their designs.

In Cincinnati a former saloon keeper has become a millionaire banker. He gained this eminence, not through those traditional virtues that are inculcated in youth; not even through the gross levying of blackmail upon saloons, gambling houses, and dives. It came to him not through the barter and sale of public office. All these he used. To-day, Boss Cox rules the servile city of Cincinnati as a mediæval baron did his serfs. He rose to this eminence by binding together and to himself the rich and powerful members of the community, for whom he secured and protects the franchises of the street-railway, gas, and electric-lighting companies. They, in turn, became his friends and protectors, and through him, and for him, controlled the press and organized public opinion. Through his control of the local political machine, Boss Cox is able to dominate his party in the city as well as in the state; to nominate at will governors as well as members of the legislature, exactly as did Yerkes in Chicago and Butler in St. Louis. By means of this control, he is able to exempt millions of property from its proper burdens of taxation; he has aided in fastening upon the people of his city a fifty-year franchise; he has overthrown the school system of the commonwealth as well as the form of government of the cities; he has finally acquired rights of immense value in the canals of the state.

By means of this powerful combination, the city of Cincinnati has been terrorized into submission. Men speak in whispers of their disgrace, but none rise to overthrow it. Organized resistance has been destroyed, while the rich and privileged classes, the beneficiaries of the System, speak with approval of the government which Boss Cox "gives them."

At the other end of the state, in the city of Cleveland, the issues are the same, but the outcome different. Here for ten years the municipal contest has centred about street-railway, gas, and electric-lighting franchises. Recurring elections, both state and local, have turned on these issues. The Republican party has become as a pack of cards played by unseen hands in this great game. It has been used to secure and protect franchises of the local street-railway corporations, and relieve their property from taxation.

In former years these companies boldly entered politics the better to advance their interests. Their employees were the accredited bosses of the party machine. For years the City Council was dominated by these influences. Its personnel was made up prior to the primaries through a control of the party. After election, its committees were designated, its officers selected, and its policy controlled by the representatives of the corporations who made the Council Chamber the scene of their operations. Time and again the public has been organized like a *posse comitatus* for protection against the disposition of the city's streets without provision for the city's protection. Protests have been issued by the Chamber of Commerce and the Municipal Association. Immense campaign funds have been raised by the companies, and used without discrimination, now for the election of a Republican administration, now for the election of a Democratic one. For the business man in politics cares not at all for party. His allegiance is one of interest, not of principle.

Such were the conditions up to a short time ago. The present officials of the street-railway company have discountenanced such practices. In 1901 Tom L. Johnson was elected Mayor on the platform of lower fares, municipal ownership, and equitable taxation. Competing capital offered to construct and operate street-railway lines on a three-cent fare basis. A franchise was granted for the use of the streets and the work of construction commenced. Injunction after injunction suit was filed, preventing the city from using its open highways for this purpose. These resources failing, the charter of the city was overthrown by the courts for the purpose of tying the hands of a hostile administration.

Similar proceedings were begun in Toledo, where Samuel M. Jones had been elected Mayor on an Independent ticket, and had frustrated the railways in an attempted franchise. All of the municipal charters of the state were equally invalid; but their legality was only questioned in those cities where the public had awakened, and having overthrown the boss, declared themselves independent of his dictation. By the decision of the Supreme Court, the charter of the city of Cleveland was declared unconstitutional. With it, the charter of every other city in the state fell.

The city of Cleveland had a nearly model charter. It had been drafted by the Chamber of Commerce, and for ten years its constitutionality had been unquestioned. On the convening of a special session of the Legislature to enact a new municipal code for the cities of the state, the reform organizations presented what was known as the Cleveland plan of centralized responsibility. This plan bore the endorsement of the State Bar Association. It was approved by the National Municipal League. But this plan gave the Mayor too great powers and responsibilities. It enabled the people to concentrate their fight on one man. In the cities of Cleveland, Columbus, and Toledo, strong men, hostile to the designs of the privileged interests, had been chosen as Mayors. Instead of such a charter, the Legislature, at the command of Boss Cox, adopted a reactionary code, which distributed executive responsibility among the Mayor, and five or seven other officials, all elected by the people. Administrative power was divided, as was responsibility. Through this distribution, it was thought the ability of the people to protect themselves would be destroyed. By this measure, the well-being of nearly two million people, resident in the cities, was sacrificed to the private designs of privileged interests; municipal reform was set back a decade, and unnecessary pecuniary burdens were imposed upon the people. It is doubtful if organized greed has ever gone further than this in the promotion of its privileges.

For years, a similar contest has been carried on in Toledo. The street-railway franchises of the city are about to expire, and the companies are seeking their renewal. Local political contests have turned upon this issue and on more than one occasion the public turned out as a "Petition in Boots," and went to the Council Chamber determined to prevent by force, if necessary, the granting of a twenty-five-year franchise. Thus far they have been successful.

In Pennsylvania, the situation is even worse. In Pittsburgh the traction and public service corporations were owned or controlled by Magee and Flynn, the city's joint bosses. They formed an alliance with Senator Quay. Through the City Council, which they controlled, and the State Legislature, which was dominated by Senator Quay, they awarded to themselves "perpetual," "999," and "99" year franchises for the use of the city's streets. Magee and Flynn controlled both parties, and used the employees of their many corporations as part of the city machine. These great interests, with the railroads entering the city, formed the centre about which was grouped a general brokerage business in contracts, saloon and vice privilege, as well as all sorts of municipal jobbery, probably unsurpassed in the history of America. In Philadelphia, the story is the same. "Corrupt and contented," this city has been reduced to a state of subjection, through the System, which involves the railways, the traction and gas companies, and other privileges. From these as a base, corruption has gradually grown until it became perfected to all purposes.

Here, as in Ohio, the local and state machines have been merged into a System of government, which makes use of the overwhelming Republican majority, to trade in all kinds of franchises, grants, and immunities. And here the System has completely overthrown democratic government in state, city, county, and township. Legal forms and procedure still remain, but so overwhelming is the Republican majority, and so intimately is its control related to that of privileged wealth, that a return of the state to simple democratic ideals and purposes seems well-nigh impossible.

Everywhere the cause is the same. It is privilege, not wealth; franchises, not business; the few, not the many, that have overthrown our cities within the past few years. There is scarcely a large city of the country in which the public service corporations do not control or constantly seek to control the government. In many instances the Council is theirs, prior even to election. Through an alliance with the party, the corporations dictate aldermanic nominations. They supply candidates with funds, and place the machinery of the party at their disposal. Once elected, the alderman is controlled by friendship, favor, bribery, or the party caucus. The latter is used on the honest official, who would hotly resent direct bribery. In fact, as employed in city, state, and national affairs, the caucus is used quite as often to compel obedience to some corrupt proposition as for any other purpose. If this proves ineffectual, the official is ostracized from the party councils, is charged with a betrayal of party principles, and is treated as a pariah. In this way he is excluded from nomination on the party ticket.

Through such powerful influences the official comes to look upon the electors who place him in office as a sort of second constituency. The real constituency, the constituency to which he must account, is the boss who controls the caucus, disburses funds, and determines the party's policy. The disapproval of the boss is more feared than that of the community. For the average community is not yet sufficiently organized to be able to protect itself. An inspection of the treasurer's books of a campaign committee will show that almost all the money raised is supplied by these interests. The amount of their subscriptions, which in many instances are indiscriminately made to both parties, depends upon the exigencies of the occasion. Between elections, the party committee is made up. It is usually a Hessian brigade, interested only in party spoils.

On a larger scale, party machinery is used for similar purposes in the state. Party control is usually concentrated in one, or at most, in two hands. This control is gradually being centred in the United States Senate. It is no longer necessary to see the organization, but only the party boss. And through this "fence," men are nominated for the Bench and for the higher state offices with a knowledge approaching certainty as to what they will do under a given set of circumstances. Many, possibly most of them, are free from corruption through direct bribery or dishonesty, but through previous contact, pecuniary or political obligations, their attitude can be forecast with precision.

It is true, franchises and tax evasions do not explain all of the corruption of our cities. But it explains the organized, systematized corruption. The rest is unorganized, miscellaneous, occasional. Franchise interests form the keystone of the arch that supports the petty grafting. And were they removed, the System that has grown up about these interests would crumble before public opinion, because there is no other interest powerful enough to support it. The franchise interests are to the misgovernment of our cities what the regular army is to warfare. All other graft is guerilla-like in its methods, as well as its effectiveness. With a profit in sight of from $75,000,000 to $150,000,000 from a fifty-year grant in the Chicago streets, men will appear who are willing to spend such sums as may be necessary to control the machinery of the State of Illinois. In the City of New York, the opportunity to secure franchises, whose value runs into the hundreds of millions, and whose acquisition depends upon a control of the party, will warrant the expenditure of such time and money as the control of the party demands.

Further than this, there are no other interests in the community so dependent upon the public as are these. Other business enjoys no privileges. The vital principle of the franchise corporation is its grant. It exists through, its great value depends upon, its corrupting influences spring from this fact. And no other business is so readily organized to control the government. It possesses great wealth; it is schooled in political methods by daily contact with administrative agencies.

It is from these sources that the campaign contributions of state and city come. These contributions are neither solicited nor made with any pretence of patriotism. They are the price of protection from disturbance, or an earnest for some new privilege. And by common understanding the chairman of the city, state, or national committee is authorized to speak for the party in the barter for place or sale of legislation.

Such are the conditions prevailing in nearly every large city in the land. By insidiously undermining the party organization; by gradually gathering together an army of political hirelings maintained by their own campaign contributions; by the election of known men to positions of trust; by controlling platform declarations, party committees, and patronage; by all these means, backed by a class interest which involves a large portion of the community, a few great corporate interests have converted local government into a private agency responding to their will. Such a System as this is free from the noisome scandal that characterized earlier corruption. By virtue of this fact, its dangerous character is increased rather than diminished. There is less menace to the nation from miscellaneous corruption than there is from an organized System which wears the trappings of democracy, but which is in reality a well-organized and thoroughly false make-believe of popular government. For a despotism, monarchy, or republic, is not a matter of name. It is a matter of control. Liberty is not a thing of bills of rights, constitutions, or forms; it is a matter of practice. . . .

The city is not only the problem of our civilization, it is the hope of the future. In the city democracy is awakening, it is beginning to assert itself. Here life is free and eager and countless agencies coöperate to create a warmer sympathy, a broader sense of responsibility, and a more intelligent political sense. Already the city has attained a higher degree of political responsiveness than has the commonwealth which gave it being and which jealously resents its growing independence. In many instances it is better governed than is the state or the nation at large. It is freer from the more subtle forms of corruption. For the open bribe, the loan, or even the game of poker in which the ignorant councilman is permitted to win a handsome stake are not the only means employed. Self-interest, a class-conscious feeling, the fancied advantage of party may be as powerful a motive for evil as the more vulgar methods with which we are familiar. The sinister influences bent on maintaining the *status quo*, on the prevention of necessary legislation, the control of the party, the caucus, or the convention; methods which are in vogue in national and state affairs, may be even more dangerous to democracy than the acts which violate the criminal code and which are becoming intolerable to public opinion. Moreover, in national affairs, the public is less alert, much less able to act collectively or to concentrate attention upon a given issue. The same is true in state affairs, where the divergent interests of the country and the city render united action well-nigh impossible.

The city is also being aroused to social and economic issues as well as to political ones. It is constantly taking on new activities and assuming new burdens. Everything tends to encourage this, while many things render it imperative. By necessity we are forced to meet the burdens of a complex life. We cannot live in close association without common activities, without abandoning some of our liberties to regulation. Not only do health, comfort, and happiness demand this, self-protection necessitates it.

Some of the activities which the city has assumed, or will assume, have been suggested. Through them many of the losses which the city has created will be made good. By these means the city will become fuller of opportunity than the scattered rural life which it has displaced. A conscious housing policy will be adopted. The tenement will become habitable, comfortable, and safe. Cheap and rapid transit will lure the population from the crowded slum into smaller suburban centres. For the city of the future will cover a wide area.

The same motives that have opened up breathing spots in the form of parks, as well as public baths and gymnasiums, in the crowded quarters will, in time, lead to the establishment of city clubhouses, winter recreation centres, where such advantages as are now found in the social settlement will be offered. About these centres the life of the community will focus for study, play, recreation, and political activity. Here concerts, lectures, and human intercourse will be offered. A sense of the city as a home, as a common authority, a thing to be loved and cared for, will be developed. In the city club the saloon will find a rival. From such centres charity work will be carried on. Here neglected children will be cared for, here the boys and girls will find an opportunity of escape from the street, and the mother and father a common meeting ground which is now denied them. For city life not only destroys the home of the poor, it promotes divorce. The tenement drives its dwellers to the streets and to the saloon. Private philanthropy has done much to relieve this condition through the settlement, but the service it renders is as much a public one as are the parks, the hospitals, or the schools. For the settlement is the equivalent of the outdoor park. Even from a pecuniary point of view it is a good investment to the city. The settlement promotes order, it lessens crime, it reduces petty misdemeanors, and organizes the life and energy of the slum and turns it into good channels. The uniform testimony of police officials is to the effect that a settlement or a playground is as good as a half-dozen policemen.

When the city becomes its own factory inspector, the problem of school attendance will be simplified. Then the city will be able to coördinate its administration and enforce its own ordinances. With reduced cost of transportation, through the public ownership of the means of transit, with free books and possibly free luncheons to school children, compulsory education will become a possibility. For the problem of education is largely economic or industrial. Our cities are now in the illogical position of enforcing school attendance upon those who cannot afford even the insignificant cost of the same.

These reforms will be possible through home rule, through the city-republic. With the city free in these regards it will be able to raise the educational age, adopt manual-training and trades' schools, fit its instruction to local needs, and ultimately elevate the standard of life of all classes. With the city free, the administration of our correctional institutions may be fitted to the crime. Probation courts and city farm schools may then be established and provision made for those of tender years who, in many cities, are still imprisoned with criminals, branded with the mark of crime, a brand which they can never outlive, a memory which they can never forget, an influence that can never be eradicated. Then the city will be able to discriminate between the offences of ignorance and poverty and those of instinct. To-day they are all classed together. The poor who have unwittingly violated some local ordinance, such as blocking a sidewalk, driving a garbage cart without a license, failing to remove rubbish, or the like, when arrested, if unable to find bail, are cast into jail to await trial or to serve their time. An examination of the police-court blotter of the average city leads one to wonder if the offences of society against its own do not equal those of the individual against his fellows. Justice, as administered in these courts, probably hurts quite as much as it helps, and society, by its thoughtlessness, creates as much crime as it prevents. The solicitude of the common law for the occasional innocent has not been extended to the thousands of real innocents, to the children, the unfortunate, the ignorant, whom indifference punishes and, in punishing, destroys. Thousands of men and women are sent to the jails, workhouses, and penitentiary every year who should have been sent to the hospital, to an inebriate asylum, to the country, or, much better, given work. Their offence is of a negative sort. It is not wilful. It is industrial or economic; they could not catch on.

By natural processes inability to maintain life in store, factory, or sweat-shop produces the outcast woman, just as sickness, irregular employment, hard times yield their unvarying harvest of vagrants, with the sequence of the lodging house, the street, and ultimately a life of petty crime. Such a career is not often taken from choice, but by misfortune. And society often arrests, sentences, and punishes, when it should help and endeavor to reclaim by work, kindness, and assistance.

We have had our public schools for so long that we accept them as a commonplace. But we do not appreciate that the high schools are raising millions of citizens to an educated estate which was known to but a limited number a few years ago. The effect of this infusion of culture into our life is beginning to make itself felt. And in the years to come, when education has, in fact, become compulsory, and the school age has been raised to a higher standard, the effect will be tremendous. Along with the schools go the public libraries. Branches and distributing agencies are extending their influence into every part of the city. Through them opportunity is offered for a continuation of study, even after the door of the school has closed.

Provision for public concerts in summer as well as in winter has already found a place in many municipal budgets. With the development of the city club there will come public orchestras, art exhibitions, and the like that will brighten the life of the community. Something like this is already being done through the libraries which are being constructed with assembly halls and meeting rooms for this purpose. Here and there the idea is taking form of utilizing the public-school buildings as local clubs. The basement, gymnasiums, and assembly rooms are being opened in the evening and during the summer months. In time there will be a modification in their architecture, equipment, and facilities, so that they will be available for a multitude of purposes instead of the limited one of education. In New York City the school buildings are already being erected with roof-gardens, where music, recreation, and a common centre for the life of the locality are offered.

These are some of the things the new city will do. It will also care for the sick, as it now does in many cities, through district physicians or visiting nurses attached to the school departments. It will find work and maintain employment agencies. It will supervise factories, mills, and workshops. The latter function is now inadequately performed by the state at large, and the inefficiency of its performance is largely attributable to the fact that the state is attempting to supervise a matter of local concern. The regulation of the conditions of employment is as much a city function as is the preservation of the health and well-being of the community. It is also a necessary part of school administration.

All these functions are, in a sense, socialistic. But it is such activities as these, it is the care and protection of the people, that inspire love and affection for the city. For these new activities will enlarge our life, not limit it; will insure freedom, not destroy it; will give to the millions whose life goes to the city's upbuilding something more than ten hours of work, eight hours of sleep, a single room in a tenement for a home, and a few hours in the saloon as compensation for it all.

We have already taken the first steps toward such an end. Many of these activities are already performed in many cities without exciting comment. But nowhere have they been adopted as a conscious, working programme, unless it be in the county of London, the cities of Glasgow or Birmingham, or the parish of Battersea, where a coördinated idea of the city seems pretty highly developed. But amazing progress has been made in the United States within the past ten years. The most remarkable advance is in the cities of Boston, New York, Chicago, and Cleveland, which communities have been transformed in their tendencies if not in their achievements. We are probably in but the beginning of this movement which aims to relieve the cost of city life, to enlarge the opportunities for happiness, and save the oncoming generation from some of the losses which the industrial city has exacted.

How much farther the city will go in its activities is a matter of conjecture. That the educational development will continue is indicated by the impulse it has received in recent years, as well as the jealousy on the part of the public of anything which impairs its efficiency. The same is true of the public libraries, which are being supplemented in many cities by art galleries, public lectures, and concerts. The educational and recreative features of the twentieth-century city are assured, and these on a higher plane of efficiency as well as on a broader basis of culture than has anywhere yet been attempted. If our own cities are to follow the tendencies in England, Germany, France, and Belgium, it is likely that such functions will be greatly extended. Foreign cities are already going in for municipal milk bureaus, the supply of coal, for savings banks, not to speak of many enterprises of a purely competitive and commercial sort.

Many who assent to our advance in educational, recreative, and charitable activities hesitate at the extension of the community into the field of business. Yet the management of certain industries seems as necessary to the city's well-being as the functions already assumed. The discussion of municipal ownership has heretofore been confined to the natural monopolies, to the franchise corporations, the street railways, gas, water,

electric-lighting, telephone, power, and heating companies. These industries are inevitably monopolies. They occupy limited rights of way.
They exist by grant from the city. Their business is of a routine nature.
The services which they render are universally used. The public health,
our comfort and convenience demand that these services should be
supplied at a minimum cost. Urban life is so dependent upon them. Their
use cannot be avoided, and work, pleasure, education, and domestic
convenience are all intimately bound up with their cheap and proper
performance. Moreover, the value of such industries is a social one,
created by the very existence of the city, by its growth and development.
In this respect they differ widely from the purely competitive business.

It would seem to be a rule of general application that whatever is of
necessity a monopoly should be a public monopoly. Private monopoly
and political liberty seem to be irreconcilable. It is because of the conflict
between them that our politics have suffered, along with our convenience.
We have attempted to reconcile these two forces, with the result that
liberty has lost in the contest. There is abundant evidence that street-
railway fares under municipal ownership could be reduced to three,
possibly to two cents. In Germany they have been cut down to two and
one-half cents, while in England, where fares are adjusted by the zone
system, the average paid in many cities is much less. In Glasgow, the
average fare is one and three-fourths cents. In 1894 rates were reduced
thirty-three per cent. Since that time the lines have been electro-equipped
and greatly extended, while the number of passengers carried increased
in eight years from 86,500,000 to 177,000,000, or a growth of one hundred
per cent. Yet the net earnings of the Glasgow system, after all allowance
for working expenses and necessary maintenance, were $1,760,000 in 1903.
In the cities of New York and Cleveland, where an agitation has been on
for the public ownership of electric light and power, it has been shown by
reports of expert engineers that current could be produced and sold
the consumer at three cents a kilowatt hour. This is from one-half to one-
fifth what is usually charged by private companies.

Artificial gas is sold in the United States at from seventy-five cents
to two dollars a thousand cubic feet, the average charge being in the
neighborhood of a dollar and a quarter. In Great Britain the rate in the
municipal plants averages sixty-four cents a thousand, while in a number
of cities it is as low as fifty cents. The by-products of coal gas have
become so valuable that the gas itself is said to cost but little in the
mains. If this be true, public ownership would greatly reduce the cost
of light and fuel, while the problem of smoke abatement would be open
to solution through the use of gas as a fuel.

Moreover, many things are possible through public management that
cannot be achieved through private control. The streets and public ways

can be better lighted, while the use of gas can be greatly extended among the poor. For the city can adjust the rates, payments, and conditions of use so as to promote the convenience of the user. This is the policy adopted in Great Britain, where one person out of every five uses gas in the cities, the use being promoted by municipal coöperation in many ways.

In the discussion of municipal problems it is necessary to bear in mind that the issue of city life has become one of decent human existence. In England, it has become the most vital of imperial problems, for town disease has already affected her army, her industry, her life itself. Even in America the barest conveniences of life are denied to millions, conveniences that make life endurable to the majority of us. Every social adjustment involves some cost. Advancing society exacts some sacrifice. But under our present adjustment the sacrifice is borne by the many for the enjoyment of the few.

That democracy will seek to adjust these burdens so as to improve conditions of life is inevitable. The gain which has been made in the past ten years has been tremendous. Things that were denounced as socialistic but a few years ago are now accepted as commonplace. And greater and greater demands are being made in this direction each year. The time is not far distant when equality of chance, in so far as education is concerned, will be offered to all, while opportunities for recreation, which are now confined to a few and which a few years since were unknown to any, will become the common accessories of city life.

It is along these lines that the advance of society is to be made. It is to come about through the city. For here life is more active, while the government is close to the people. It is already manifest on every hand. Through the divorce of the city from state control this progress will be stimulated. The city will become a centre of pride and patriotism. Here art and culture will flourish. The citizen will be attached to his community just as were the burghers of the mediæval towns. Through direct legislation the city will be democratized. Public opinion will be free to act. Then the official will be holden to a real responsibility, while national politics will no longer dominate local affairs, for the test of the candidate for office will be his citizenship in the community which he serves.

At the same time the burden of existence will be materially relieved. The great cost of living within the city is largely attributable to ground rent on the one hand, and the cost of such services as transportation, gas, water, and fuel on the other. From one-fourth to one-half of the worker's income is absorbed by these charges. By the municipalization of the latter services and the reduction of charges to cost, a portion of this loss can be regained. Likewise, by a beautiful law of social adjustment, the burdens created by the growth of society, the ground rents of our cities, can be used to compensate the individual for the losses which he has incurred in making the city his home. Such a programme of tax reform is demanded by justice, not by charity. For if it be true that organized society creates this fund, then society should retake it for its own needs and the satisfaction of the wants which are created, and which are everywhere incidental to existence in the city.

Just as by a wonderful provision of nature the moisture is gathered up from the sea, to be later deposited upon the land, which it refreshes and renders productive, whence it is carried back again from mountain-side, hill, and prairie to the sea; so there is open to us a law of social life which performs the same refreshing and productive service. For the gathering together of mankind into close association, with its varied energies and activities, creates a social treasure; a treasure whose magnitude we are now able to measure, and which treasure, if retaken by society, will enable all of the burdens which close association involves, to be borne without cost to the dwellers therein.

This cycle of social production and social distribution, of rent and taxation, is like the circulation of the blood in the body. Surging from the heart, it is carried to the extremities, stimulating activities and enabling life to be carried on. From the extremities again, it is returned to the lungs, where it is purified and again returned to the heart.

Within the city there is a similar cycle. The crowding of mankind together has created a social fund. This fund is in excess of present needs, and the needs of government can never exceed it. In the creation of this fund mankind pays a price, a tribute for the privilege of city life; but a price that is now assumed by private collectors. Were society to retake this fund, it would repay the individual who has made the sacrifice what he has lost, it would offer him many of the common necessities of life and usher in an elevated standard of existence.

All this can be brought about through a reform in our methods of taxation. For the taxation of ground rents does not increase rents nor the cost of living. It merely shifts the burden on to him who enjoys the benefit. It cannot be shifted to any one else. It is like special assessments for paving, sewers, and the like. From this source all of the needs of the city can be satisfied. In many communities this principle has already been recognized. The city of Liverpool receives a half-million dollars annually from the lease of its common land. In certain cities in Germany, it has become the policy to buy up surrounding land in advance of the city's growth, and thus retain the benefits and the unearned increment of the city's expansion.

Through these means poverty would be relieved. For poverty is an eradicable thing. It is not a dispensation of Providence, as we interpret the scriptural expression with which we justify our inaction. Nor is it true that the poverty, which is everywhere increasing in our cities, is traceable to "Nature or the Devil, which has made some men weak and imbecile, and others lazy and worthless." Such men there are, and such there will probably always be. But poverty in city and country is largely the result of human laws. It is the natural, as it is the inevitable, product of legal institutions, which are open to correction. These institutions are most aggressively operative in Great Britain and America, where industrial progress is most advanced and wealth is most abundant. Especially in America is poverty traceable to the monopoly of the land and its withholding from use by those who would work it. In our cities it is the burden of rent, along with the franchise monopolies, that imposes the heaviest burden on the poor. Aside from this, within and about every large city, land is held out of use for speculative purposes, while the city is filled with men eager for an opportunity. It is this dog in the manger policy of acquiring and holding out of use land which other men would work that has changed the character of America within the past twenty years from a nation incredulous of poverty into a nation of rapidly increasing tenancy and landless men. It is this that closes opportunity and must of necessity reduce both nominal as well as real wages. Whatever may be the extent of poverty to-day (and we have recently had some alarming testimony, if not proof, of its widespread existence from the pen of Mr. Robert Hunter) the poverty of the next generation will be very great. For in no nation of western civilization has monopoly affixed its hold to industry as it has in the United States. With it has gone a marked increase in the cost of living, as well as a closing of opportunity. To this is to be added the injustice of our federal taxes, which are designed like an exaggerated poll-tax and fall almost exclusively on the poor. America is to-day struggling under a burden of monopoly charges in rent, franchise and railway privileges, and taxes on the necessities of life, unparalleled in the civilized world outside of Russia. The poor are held between the burden of unjust taxation on the one hand and monopoly on the other, and the result must inevitably be a decrease in wages, a reduction of the standard of living, and a great increase in poverty. In the cities it is within our power to lift the burden. The extension of the activities of the city and the reduction of the cost of service on municipal monopolies will do something. But the greatest gain will come through a change in our methods of taxation and the assumption of the unearned increment of the land for public uses.

But the fiscal advantages of the single tax upon land values are not the chief of the advantages which would follow. Through its introduction the bad tenement would disappear, while the vacant lands within and without the city would invite building. A stimulus to industry would result which would increase the demand for labor. This, in turn, would increase wages. But beyond all this a new freedom would arise, while the opportunity of access to the undeveloped resources of America would be like the discovery of a new continent. For while America is the richest country in the world in resources, its population per square mile is still less than one-tenth of that of many European countries.

Through such means as these the city will cease to be a necessary abyss of poverty. It is our institutions and our laws, not a divine ordinance or the inherent viciousness of humankind, that are at fault. Our evils are economic, not personal. Relief is possible through a change in our laws, in an increase in the positive agencies of the government, and the taxing for the common weal of those values which are now responsible for much of the common woe. It is not personal goodness that is demanded so much as public intelligence. For the worst of the evils under which America suffers are traceable to laws creating privileges. The evils can be largely corrected through their abolition. This is most easily obtainable in the city, for it is in the city that democracy is organizing and the power of privilege most rampant.

In the past, the extension of the functions of society has proceeded with an utter indifference to theoretical ideas as to the proper sphere of public activity. While political philosophers have debated the subject, society has ignored the proposals of individualism or socialism. While *a priori* philosophers have reduced the functions of the state to those of the constable, to the protection of life, liberty, and property from external and internal violence, public sentiment, unaided by the logic of any school, has contentedly accepted the formula of Locke that "the end of government was the welfare of mankind," which Thomas Huxley has said was "the noblest and at the same time briefest statement of the purpose of government known to man."

# Twenty Years at Hull-House

## *Jane Addams*

*Why would a woman comfortably raised in a mid-nineteenth-century small town deliberately seek a home in Chicago's industrial slums and devote her life to social reform? In her autobiography Jane Addams tells what she did and tells it with rare understanding and charm. She is less clear in telling us why she did it, but a careful reader can sight the answers by inference and indirection. Because so many reformers followed a similar path and because a significantly large number of them were women, to know why Jane Addams founded Hull-House and what she did there provides a central clue to the spirit of her era.*

*Jane Addams was the daughter of a miller who had settled in northern Illinois, on the hither edge of the largest basin of grain in North America. He had worked hard and prospered: railroads soon threaded west across the state and civil war was to push up the market for grain and land. By the year of Jane Addams' birth, 1860, he had become a state senator. In his industrious home the vaguely unsettling essays of Emerson blunted the stern rule of the Bible, and in a day when almost no women attended college this successful miller sent his restless daughter off to Rockford College, where she read voraciously in the classics, in philosophy and religion, and in the literature of modern English reform. By 1881, steeped in Tolstoy, Emerson, and Plato, she possessed a B.A. degree and resolved to make her education and her comfortable means count for something in the changing industrial (and predominantly man's) world. Eight years later she was ready to establish and run what soon became the most influential urban settlement house in the country; she was only thirty years of age.*

*Her experiment proved a landmark in American social reform. Through programs of individual activity and regeneration (which schools and community centers have since provided as a matter of course), and through the pressure of investigation and publicity undertaken by the politically adept welfare workers who resided there, Hull-House grew to*

*become a permanent experiment in education and community service. In
its heyday in the early years of the new century, its achievements embodied a major conviction of the progressive spirit: that by education and
service one may achieve the determined good will of each social class for
the others and reduce thereby the likelihood of human strife.*

*In that spirit, in 1910, she wrote the pages which follow. She was then
at the height of her career: her articles and reminiscences became hand-
books for early social reformers; she became the first woman on which
Yale University ever bestowed an honorary degree; she was shortly to join
the Bull Moose Progressives, whose international militancy she attempted
to soften with her crusading commitment to pacifism; and in 1931 she
would share the Nobel Prize for her efforts to establish world peace.*

*Twenty Years at Hull-House is one of the few great autobiographies
of a woman. On this occasion, at least, Jane Addams wrote with
poignancy, measured good humor, and, that rarest of qualities, a clear
eye for how she must have seemed to others. Her confrontation with
Tolstoy, included in this selection, is surely one of the most charming and
subtle commentaries in our literature on the strengths and limitations of
reformers.*

[After recounting the story of her early years and her college life, Jane
Addams notes that she had settled on a medical career. Her first year of
training was broken by a long illness, apparently the result of a spinal
ailment from childhood. Her physician advised her to postpone further
training and seek a rest in travel. She accordingly resolved to abandon
medicine and spend the next two years in Europe.]

### THE SNARE OF PREPARATION

The long illness left me in a state of nervous exhaustion with which I
struggled for years, traces of it remaining long after Hull-House was
opened in 1889. At the best it allowed me but a limited amount of energy,
so that doubtless there was much nervous depression at the foundation
of the spiritual struggles which this chapter is forced to record. However,
it could not have been all due to my health, for as my wise little notebook
sententiously remarked, "In his own way each man must struggle, lest the
moral law become a far-off abstraction utterly separated from his active
life."

It would, of course, be impossible to remember that some of these
struggles ever took place at all, were it not for these selfsame notebooks,
in which, however, I no longer wrote in moments of high resolve, but

Jane Addams, *Twenty Years at Hull-House* (New York: Macmillan, 1910), pp.
66-71, 85-112, 259-309, 342-358, 368-370.

judging from the internal evidence afforded by the books themselves, only in moments of deep depression when overwhelmed by a sense of failure.

One of the most poignant of these experiences, which occurred during the first few months after our landing upon the other side of the Atlantic, was on a Saturday night, when I received an ineradicable impression of the wretchedness of East London, and also saw for the first time the overcrowded quarters of a great city at midnight. A small party of tourists were taken to the East End by a city missionary to witness the Saturday night sale of decaying vegetables and fruit, which, owing to the Sunday laws in London, could not be sold until Monday, and, as they were beyond safe keeping, were disposed of at auction as late as possible on Saturday night. On Mile End Road, from the top of an omnibus which paused at the end of a dingy street lighted by only occasional flares of gas, we saw two huge masses of ill-clad people clamoring around two hucksters' carts. They were bidding their farthings and ha'pennies for a vegetable held up by the auctioneer, which he at last scornfully flung, with a gibe for its cheapness, to the successful bidder. In the momentary pause only one man detached himself from the groups. He had bidden in a cabbage, and when it struck his hand, he instantly sat down on the curb, tore it with his teeth, and hastily devoured it, unwashed and uncooked as it was. He and his fellows were types of the "submerged tenth," as our missionary guide told us, with some little satisfaction in the then new phrase, and he further added that so many of them could scarcely be seen in one spot save at this Saturday night auction, the desire for cheap food being apparently the one thing which could move them simultaneously. They were huddled into ill-fitting, cast-off clothing, the ragged finery which one sees only in East London. Their pale faces were dominated by that most unlovely of human expressions, the cunning and shrewdness of the bargain-hunter who starves if he cannot make a successful trade, and yet the final impression was not of ragged, tawdry clothing nor of pinched and sallow faces, but of myriads of hands, empty, pathetic, nerveless and workworn, showing white in the uncertain light of the street, and clutching forward for food which was already unfit to eat.

Perhaps nothing is so fraught with significance as the human hand, this oldest tool with which man has dug his way from savagery, and with which he is constantly groping forward. I have never since been able to see a number of hands held upward, even when they are moving rhythmically in a calisthenic exercise, or when they belong to a class of chubby children who wave them in eager response to a teacher's query, without a certain revival of this memory, a clutching at the heart reminiscent of the despair and resentment which seized me then.

For the following weeks I went about London almost furtively, afraid to look down narrow streets and alleys lest they disclose again this hideous human need and suffering. I carried with me for days at a time that curious surprise we experience when we first come back into the streets after days given over to sorrow and death; we are bewildered that the world should be going on as usual and unable to determine which is real, the inner pang or the outward seeming. In time all huge London came to seem unreal save the poverty in its East End. During the following two years on the continent, while I was irresistibly drawn to the poorer quarters of each city, nothing among the beggars of South Italy nor among the saltminers of Austria carried with it the same conviction of human wretchedness which was conveyed by this momentary glimpse of an East London street. It was, of course, a most fragmentary and lurid view of the poverty of East London, and quite unfair. I should have been shown either less or more, for I went away with no notion of the hundreds of men and women who had gallantly identified their fortunes with these empty-handed people, and who, in church and chapel, "relief works," and charities, were at least making an effort towards its mitigation.

Our visit was made in November, 1883, the very year when the *Pall Mall Gazette* exposure started "The Bitter Cry of Outcast London," and the conscience of England was stirred as never before over this joyless city in the East End of its capital. Even then, vigorous and drastic plans were being discussed, and a splendid program of municipal reforms was already dimly outlined. Of all these, however, I had heard nothing but the vaguest rumor.

No comfort came to me then from any source, and the painful impression was increased because at the very moment of looking down the East London street from the top of the omnibus, I had been sharply and painfully reminded of "The Vision of Sudden Death" which had confronted De Quincey one summer's night as he was being driven through rural England on a high mail coach. Two absorbed lovers suddenly appear between the narrow, blossoming hedgerows in the direct path of the huge vehicle which is sure to crush them to their death. De Quincey tries to send them a warning shout, but finds himself unable to make a sound because his mind is hopelessly entangled in an endeavor to recall the exact lines from the "Iliad" which describe the great cry with which Achilles alarmed all Asia militant. Only after his memory responds is his will released from its momentary paralysis, and he rides on through the fragrant night with the horror of the escaped calamity thick upon him, but he also bears with him the consciousness that he had given himself over so many years to classic learning—that when suddenly called upon for a quick decision in the world of life and death, he had been able to act only through a literary suggestion.

This is what we were all doing, lumbering our minds with literature that only served to cloud the really vital situation spread before our eyes. It seemed to me too preposterous that in my first view of the horror of East London I should have recalled De Quincey's literary description of the literary suggestion which had once paralyzed him. In my disgust it all appeared a hateful, vicious circle which even the apostles of culture themselves admitted, for had not one of the greatest among the moderns plainly said that "conduct, and not culture is three fourths of human life."

For two years in the midst of my distress over the poverty which, thus suddenly driven into my consciousness, had become to me the "Weltschmerz," there was mingled a sense of futility, of misdirected energy, the belief that the pursuit of cultivation would not in the end bring either solace or relief. I gradually reached a conviction that the first generation of college women had taken their learning too quickly, had departed too suddenly from the active, emotional life led by their grandmothers and great-grandmothers; that the contemporary education of young women had developed too exclusively the power of acquiring knowledge and of merely receiving impressions; that somewhere in the process of "being educated" they had lost that simple and almost automatic response to the human appeal, that old healthful reaction resulting in activity from the mere presence of suffering or of helplessness; that they are so sheltered and pampered they have no chance even to make "the great refusal." . . .

It is hard to tell just when the very simple plan which afterward developed into the Settlement began to form itself in my mind. It may have been even before I went to Europe for the second time, but I gradually became convinced that it would be a good thing to rent a house in a part of the city where many primitive and actual needs are found, in which young women who had been given over too exclusively to study, might restore a balance of activity along traditional lines and learn of life from life itself; where they might try out some of the things they had been taught and put truth to "the ultimate test of the conduct it dictates or inspires." I do not remember to have mentioned this plan to any one until we reached Madrid in April, 1888.

We had been to see a bull fight rendered in the most magnificent Spanish style, where greatly to my surprise and horror, I found that I had seen, with comparative indifference, five bulls and many more horses killed. The sense that this was the last survival of all the glories of the amphitheater, the illusion that the riders on the caparisoned horses might have been knights of a tournament, or the matadore a slightly armed gladiator facing his martyrdom, and all the rest of the obscure yet vivid associations of an historic survival, had carried me beyond the endurance of any of the rest of the party. I finally met them in the foyer stern and pale with disapproval of my brutal endurance, and but partially recovered from the faintness and disgust which the spectacle itself had produced upon them. I had no defense to offer to their reproaches save that I had not thought much about the bloodshed; but in the evening the natural and inevitable reaction came, and in deep chagrin I felt myself tried and condemned, not only by this disgusting experience but by the entire moral situation which it revealed. It was suddenly made quite clear to me that I was lulling my conscience by a dreamer's scheme, that a mere paper reform had become a defense for continued idleness, and that I was making it a *raison d'être* for going on indefinitely with study and travel. It is easy to become the dupe of a deferred purpose, of the promise the future can never keep, and I had fallen into the meanest type of self-deception in making myself believe that all this was in preparation for great things to come. Nothing less than the moral reaction following the experience at a bull-fight had been able to reveal to me that so far from following in the wake of a chariot of philanthropic fire, I had been tied to the tail of the veriest ox-cart of self-seeking.

I had made up my mind that next day, whatever happened, I would begin to carry out the plan, if only by talking about it. I can well recall the stumbling and uncertainty with which I finally set it forth to Miss Starr, my old-time school friend, who was one of our party. I even dared to hope that she might join in carrying out the plan, but nevertheless I told it in the fear of that disheartening experience which is so apt to afflict our most cherished plans when they are at last divulged, when we suddenly feel that there is nothing there to talk about, and as the golden dream slips through our fingers we are left to wonder at our own fatuous belief. But gradually the comfort of Miss Starr's companionship, the vigor and enthusiasm which she brought to bear upon it, told both in the growth of the plan and upon the sense of its validity, so that by the time we had reached the enchantment of the Alhambra, the scheme had become convincing and tangible although still most hazy in detail.

A month later we parted in Paris, Miss Starr to go back to Italy, and I to journey on to London to secure as many suggestions as possible from those wonderful places of which we had heard, Toynbee Hall and the People's Palace. So that it finally came about that in June, 1888, five years after my first visit in East London, I found myself at Toynbee Hall equipped not only with a letter of introduction from Canon Fremantle, but with high expectations and a certain belief that whatever perplexities and discouragement concerning the life of the poor were in store for me, I should at least know something at first hand and have the solace of daily activity. I had confidence that although life itself might contain many difficulties, the period of mere passive receptivity had come to an end, and I had at last finished with the everlasting "preparation for life," however ill-prepared I might be.

It was not until years afterward that I came upon Tolstoy's phrase "the snare of preparation," which he insists we spread before the feet of young people, hopelessly entangling them in a curious inactivity at the very period of life when they are longing to construct the world anew and to conform it to their own ideals.

### FIRST DAYS AT HULL-HOUSE

The next January found Miss Starr and myself in Chicago, searching for a neighborhood in which we might put our plans into execution. In our eagerness to win friends for the new undertaking, we utilized every opportunity to set forth the meaning of the settlement as it had been embodied in Toynbee Hall, although in those days we made no appeal for money, meaning to start with our own slender resources. From the very first the plan received courteous attention, and the discussion, while often skeptical, was always friendly. Professor Swing wrote a commendatory column in the *Evening Journal,* and our early speeches were reported quite out of proportion to their worth. I recall a spirited evening at the home of Mrs. Wilmarth, which was attended by that renowned scholar, Thomas Davidson, and by a young Englishman who was a member of the then new Fabian society and to whom a peculiar glamour was attached because he had scoured knives all summer in a camp of high-minded philosophers in the Adirondacks. Our new little plan met with criticism, not to say disapproval, from Mr. Davidson, who, as nearly as I can remember, called it, "one of those unnatural attempts to understand life through coöperative living."

It was in vain we asserted that the collective living was not an essential part of the plan, that we would always scrupulously pay our own expenses, and that at any moment we might decide to scatter through the neighborhood and to live in separate tenements; he still contended that the fascination for most of those volunteering residence would lie in the collective living aspect of the Settlement. His contention was, of course, essentially sound; there is a constant tendency for the residents to "lose themselves in the cave of their own companionship," as the Toynbee Hall phrase goes, but on the other hand, it is doubtless true that the very companionship, the give and take of colleagues, is what tends to keep the Settlement normal and in touch with "the world of things as they are." I am happy to say that we never resented this nor any other difference of opinion, and that fifteen years later Professor Davidson handsomely acknowledged that the advantages of a group far outweighed the weaknesses he had early pointed out. He was at that later moment sharing with a group of young men, on the East Side of New York, his ripest conclusions in philosophy and was much touched by their intelligent interest and absorbed devotion. I think that time has also justified our early contention that the mere foothold of a house, easily accessible, ample in space, hospitable and tolerant in spirit, situated in the midst of the large foreign colonies which so easily isolate themselves in American cities, would be in itself a serviceable thing for Chicago. I am not so sure that we succeeded in our endeavors "to make social intercourse express the growing sense of the economic unity of society and to add the social function to democracy." But Hull-House was soberly opened on the theory that the dependence of classes on each other is reciprocal; and that as the social relation is essentially a reciprocal relation, it gives a form of expression that has peculiar value. . . .

[Seeking the assistance of social workers and the public school authorities, Jane Addams set out to locate a house. In the tenement district of Halsted Street they found an old mansion well suited to their purposes.]

The house had passed through many changes since it had been built in 1856 for the homestead of one of Chicago's pioneer citizens, Mr. Charles J. Hull, and although battered by its vicissitudes, was essentially sound. Before it had been occupied by the factory, it had sheltered a second-hand furniture store, and at one time the Little Sisters of the Poor had used it for a home for the aged. It had a half-skeptical reputation for a haunted attic, so far respected by the tenants living on the second floor that they always kept a large pitcher full of water on the attic stairs. Their explanation of this custom was so incoherent that I was sure it was a survival of the belief that a ghost could not cross running water, but perhaps that interpretation was only my eagerness for finding folklore.

The fine old house responded kindly to repairs, its wide hall and open fireplaces always insuring it a gracious aspect. Its generous owner, Miss Helen Culver, in the following spring gave us a free leasehold of the entire house. Her kindness has continued through the years until the group of thirteen buildings, which at present comprises our equipment, is built largely upon land which Miss Culver has put at the service of the Settlement which bears Mr. Hull's name. In those days the house stood between an undertaking establishment and a saloon. "Knight, Death, and the Devil," the three were called by a Chicago wit, and yet any mock heroics which might be implied by comparing the Settlement to a knight quickly dropped away under the genuine kindness and hearty welcome extended to us by the families living up and down the street.

We furnished the house as we would have furnished it were it in another part of the city, with the photographs and other impedimenta we had collected in Europe, and with a few bits of family mahogany. While all the new furniture which was bought was enduring in quality, we were careful to keep it in character with the fine old residence. Probably no young matron ever placed her own things in her own house with more pleasure than that with which we first furnished Hull-House. We believed that the Settlement may logically bring to its aid all those adjuncts which the cutivated man regards as good and suggestive of the best life of the past.

On the 18th of September, 1889, Miss Starr and I moved into it. . . .

Halsted Street has grown so familiar during twenty years of residence, that it is difficult to recall its gradual changes—the withdrawal of the more prosperous Irish and Germans, and the slow substitution of Russian Jews, Italians, and Greeks. A description of the street such as I gave in those early addresses still stands in my mind as sympathetic and correct.

Halsted Street is thirty-two miles long, and one of the great thorough-fares of Chicago; Polk Street crosses it midway between the stockyards to the south and the ship-building yards on the north branch of the Chicago River. For the six miles between these two industries the street is lined with shops of butchers and grocers, with dingy and gorgeous saloons, and pretentious establishments for the sale of ready-made clothing. Polk Street, running west from Halstead Street, grows rapidly more prosperous; running a mile east to State Street, it grows steadily worse, and crosses a network of vice on the corners of Clark Street and Fifth Avenue. Hull-House once stood in the suburbs, but the city has steadily grown up around it and its site now has corners on three or four foreign colonies. Between Halsted Street and the river live about ten thousand Italians—Neopolitans, Sicilians, and Calabrians, with an occasional Lombard or Venetian. To the south on Twelfth Street are many Germans, and side streets are given over almost entirely to Polish and Russian Jews. Still farther south, these Jewish colonies merge into a huge Bohemian colony, so vast that Chicago ranks as the third Bohemian city in the world. To the northwest are many Canadian-French, clannish in spite of their long residence in America, and to the north are Irish and first-generation Americans. On the streets directly west and farther north are well-to-do English-speaking families, many of whom own their houses and have lived in the neighborhood for years; one man is still living in his old farmhouse.

The policy of the public authorities of never taking an initiative, and always waiting to be urged to do their duty, is obviously fatal in a neighborhood where there is little initiative among the citizens. The idea underlying our self-government breaks down in such a ward. The streets are inexpressibly dirty, the number of schools inadequate, sanitary legislation unenforced, the street lighting bad, the paving miserable and altogether lacking in the alleys and smaller streets, and the stables foul beyond description. Hundreds of houses are unconnected with the street sewer. The older and richer inhabitants seem anxious to move away as rapidly as they can afford it. They make room for newly arrived immigrants who are densely ignorant of civic duties. This substitution of the older inhabitants is accomplished industrially also, in the south and east quarters of the ward. The Jews and Italians do the finishing for the great clothing manufacturers, formerly done by Americans, Irish and Germans, who refused to submit to the extremely low prices to which the sweating system has reduced their successors. As the design of the sweating system is the elimination of rent from the manufacture of clothing, the "outside work" is begun after the clothing leaves the cutter. An unscrupulous contractor regards no basement as too dark, no stable loft too foul, no rear shanty too provisional, no tenement room too small for his workroom, as these conditions imply low rental. Hence these shops abound in the worst of the foreign districts where the sweater easily finds his cheap basement and his home finishers.

The houses of the ward, for the most part wooden, were originally built for one family and are now occupied by several. They are after the type of the inconvenient frame cottages found in the poorer suburbs twenty years ago. Many of them were built where they now stand; others were brought thither on rollers, because their previous sites had been taken for factories. The fewer brick tenement buildings which are three or four stories high are comparatively new, and there are few large tenements. The little wooden houses have a temporary aspect, and for this reason, perhaps, the tenement-house legislation in Chicago is totally inadequte. Rear tenements flourish; many houses have no water supply save the faucet in the back yard, there are no fire escapes, the garbage and ashes are placed in wooden boxes, which are fastened to the street pavements. One of the most discouraging features about the present system of tenement houses is that many are owned by sordid and ignorant immigrants. The theory that wealth brings responsibility, that possession entails at length education and refinement, in these cases fails utterly. The children of an Italian immigrant owner may "shine" shoes in the street, and his wife may pick rags from the street gutter, laboriously sorting them in a dingy court. Wealth may do something for her self-complacency and feeling of consequence; it certainly does nothing for her comfort or her children's improvement nor for the cleanliness of any one concerned. Another thing that prevents better houses in Chicago is the tentative attitude of the real estate men. Many unsavory conditions are allowed to continue which would be regarded with horror if they were considered permanent. Meanwhile, the wretched conditions persist until at least two generations of children have been born and reared in them.

In every neighborhood where poorer people live, because rents are supposed to be cheaper there, is an element which, although uncertain in the individual, in the aggregate can be counted upon. It is composed of people of former education and opportunity who have cherished ambitions and prospects, but who are caricatures of what they meant to be—"hollow ghosts which blame the living men." There are times in many lives when there is a cessation of energy and loss of power. Men and women of education and refinement come to live in a cheaper neighborhood because they lack the ability to make money, because of ill health, because of an unfortunate marriage, or for other reasons which do not imply criminality or stupidity. Among them are those who, in spite of untoward circumstances, keep up some sort of an intellectual life; those who are "great for books," as their neighbors say. To such the Settlement may be a genuine refuge.

In the very first weeks of our residence Miss Starr started a reading party in George Eliot's "Romola," which was attended by a group of young women who followed the wonderful tale with unflagging interest. The weekly reading was held in our little upstairs dining room, and two members of the club came to dinner each week, not only that they might be received as guests, but that they might help us wash the dishes afterwards and so make the table ready for the stacks of Florentine photographs.

Our "first resident," as she gayly designated herself, was a charming old lady who gave five consecutive readings from Hawthorne to a most appreciative audience, interspersing the magic tales most delightfully with recollections of the elusive and fascinating author. Years before she had lived at Brook Farm as a pupil of the Ripleys, and she came to us for ten days because she wished to live once more in an atmosphere where "idealism ran high." We thus early found the type of class which through all the years has remained most popular—a combination of a social atmosphere with serious study.

Volunteers to the new undertaking came quickly; a charming young girl conducted a kindergarten in the drawing room, coming regularly every morning from her home in a distant part of the North Side of the city. . . . [Another young girl] organized our first really successful club of boys, holding their fascinated interest by the old chivalric tales, set forth so dramatically and vividly that checkers and jackstraws were abandoned by all the other clubs on Boys' Day, that their members might form a listening fringe to "The Young Heroes."

I met a member of the latter club one day as he flung himself out of the house in the rage by which an emotional boy hopes to keep from shedding tears. "There is no use coming here any more, Prince Roland is dead," he gruffly explained as we passed. We encouraged the younger boys in tournaments and dramatics of all sorts, and we somewhat fatuously believed that boys who were early interested in adventurers or explorers might later want to know the lives of living statesmen and inventors. It is needless to add that the boys quickly responded to such a program, and that the only difficulty lay in finding leaders who were able to carry it out. This difficulty has been with us through all the years of growth and development in the Boys' Club until now, with its five-story building, its splendid equipment of shops, of recreation and study rooms, that group alone is successful which commands the services of a resourceful and devoted leader.

The dozens of younger children who from the first came to Hull-House were organized into groups which were not quite classes and not quite clubs. The value of these groups consisted almost entirely in arousing a higher imagination and in giving the children the opportunity which they could not have in the crowded schools, for initiative and for independent social relationships. The public schools then contained little hand work of any sort, so that naturally any instruction which we provided for the children took the direction of this supplementary work. But it required a constant effort that the pressure of poverty itself should not defeat the educational aim. The Italian girls in the sewing classes would count that day lost when they could not carry home a garment, and the insistence that it should be neatly made seemed a super-refinement to those in dire need of clothing. . . .

In those early days we were often asked why we had come to live on Halsted Street when we could afford to live somewhere else. I remember one man who used to shake his head and say it was "the strangest thing he had met in his experience," but who was finally convinced that it was "not strange but natural." In time it came to seem natural to all of us that the Settlement should be there. If it is natural to feed the hungry and care for the sick, it is certainly natural to give pleasure to the young, comfort to the aged, and to minister to the deep-seated craving for social intercourse that all men feel. Whoever does it is rewarded by something which, if not gratitude, is at least spontaneous and vital and lacks that irksome sense of obligation with which a substantial benefit is too often acknowledged.

In addition to the neighbors who responded to the receptions and classes, we found those who were too battered and oppressed to care for them. To these, however, was left that susceptibility to the bare offices of humanity which raises such offices into a bond of fellowship.

From the first it seemed understood that we were ready to perform the humblest neighborhood services. We were asked to wash the new-born babies, and to prepare the dead for burial, to nurse the sick, and to "mind the children."

Occasionally these neighborly offices unexpectedly uncovered ugly human traits. For six weeks after an operation we kept in one of our three bedrooms a forlorn little baby who, because he was born with a cleft palate, was most unwelcome even to his mother, and we were horrified when he died of neglect a week after he was returned to his home; a little Italian bride of fifteen sought shelter with us one November evening, to escape her husband who had beaten her every night for a week when he returned home from work, because she had lost her wedding ring; two of us officiated quite alone at the birth of an illegitimate child because the doctor was late in arriving, and none of the honest Irish matrons would "touch the likes of her"; we ministered at the deathbed of a young man, who during a long illness of tuberculosis had received so many bottles of whisky through the mistaken kindness of his friends, that the cumulative effect produced wild periods of exultation, in one of which he died.

We were also early impressed with the curious isolation of many of the immigrants; an Italian woman once expressed her pleasure in the red roses that she saw at one of our receptions in surprise that they had been "brought so fresh all the way from Italy." She would not believe for an instant that they had been grown in America. She said that she had lived in Chicago for six years and had never seen any roses, whereas in Italy she had seen them every summer in great profusion. During all that time, of course, the woman had lived within ten blocks of a florist's window; she had not been more than a five-cent car ride away from the public parks; but she had never dreamed of faring forth for herself, and no one had taken her. Her conception of America had been the untidy street in which she lived and had made her long struggle to adapt herself to American ways.

But in spite of some untoward experiences, we were constantly impressed with the uniform kindness and courtesy we received. Perhaps these first days laid the simple human foundations which are certainly essential for continuous living among the poor: first, genuine preference for residence in an industrial quarter to any other part of the city, because it is interesting and makes the human appeal; and second, the conviction, in the words of Canon Barnett, that the things which make men alike are finer and better than the things that keep them apart, and that these basic likenesses, if they are properly accentuated, easily transcend the less essential differences of race, language, creed and tradition.

Perhaps even in those first days we made a beginning toward that object which was afterwards stated in our charter: "To provide a center for a higher civic and social life; to institute and maintain educational and philanthropic enterprises, and to investigate and improve the conditions in the industrial districts of Chicago."

### TOLSTOYISM

The administration of charity in Chicago during the winter following the World's Fair had been of necessity most difficult for, although large sums had been given to the temporary relief organization which endeavored to care for the thousands of destitute strangers stranded in the city, we all worked under a sense of desperate need and a paralyzing consciousness that our best efforts were most inadequate to the situation.

During the many relief visits I paid that winter in tenement houses and miserable lodgings, I was constantly shadowed by a certain sense of shame that I should be comfortable in the midst of such distress. This resulted at times in a curious reaction against all the educational and philanthropic activities in which I had been engaged. In the face of the desperate hunger and need, these could not but seem futile and superficial. The hard winter in Chicago had turned the thoughts of many of us to these stern matters. A young friend of mine who came daily to Hull-House, consulted me in regard to going into the paper warehouse belonging to her father that she might there sort rags with the Polish girls; another young girl took a place in a sweatshop for a month, doing her work so simply and thoroughly that the proprietor had no notion that she had not been driven there by need; still two others worked in a shoe factory— and all this happened before such adventures were undertaken in order to procure literary material. It was in the following winter that the pioneer effort in this direction, Walter Wyckoff's account of his vain attempt to find work in Chicago, compelled even the sternest business man to drop his assertion that "any man can find work if he wants it."

The dealing directly with the simplest human wants may have been responsible for an impression which I carried about with me almost constantly for a period of two years and which culminated finally in a visit to Tolstoy—that the Settlement, or Hull-House at least, was a mere pretense and travesty of the simple impulse "to live with the poor," so long as the residents did not share the common lot of hard labor and scant fare.

Actual experience had left me in much the same state of mind I had been in after reading Tolstoy's "What to Do," which is a description of his futile efforts to relieve the unspeakable distress and want in the Moscow winter of 1881, and his inevitable conviction that only he who literally shares his own shelter and food with the needy, can claim to have served them.

Doubtless it is much easier to see "what to do" in rural Russia, where all the conditions tend to make the contrast as broad as possible between peasant labor and noble idleness, than it is to see "what to do" in the interdependencies of the modern industrial city. But for that very reason perhaps, Tolstoy's clear statement is valuable for that type of conscientious person in every land who finds it hard, not only to walk in the path of righteousness, but to discover where the path lies.

I had read the books of Tolstoy steadily all the years since "My Religion" had come into my hands immediately after I left college. The reading of that book had made clear that men's poor little efforts to do right are put forth for the most part in the chill of self-distrust; I became convinced that if the new social order ever came, it would come by gathering to itself all the pathetic human endeavor which had indicated the forward direction. But I was most eager to know whether Tolstoy's undertaking to do his daily share of the physical labor of the world, that labor which is "so disproportionate to the unnourished strength" of those by whom it is ordinarily performed, had brought him peace!

I had time to review carefully many things in my mind during the long days of convalescence following an illness of typhoid fever which I suffered in the autumn of 1895. The illness was so prolonged that my health was most unsatisfactory during the following winter, and the next May I went abroad with my friend, Miss Smith, to effect if possible a more complete recovery.

The prospect of seeing Tolstoy filled me with the hope of finding a clew to the tangled affairs of city poverty. I was but one of thousands of our contemporaries who were turning towards this Russian, not as to a seer—his message is much too confused and contradictory for that—but as to a man who has had the ability to lift his life to the level of his conscience, to translate his theories into action.

Our first few weeks in England were most stimulating. A dozen years ago London still showed traces of "that exciting moment in the life of the nation when its youth is casting about for new enthusiasms," but it evinced still more of that British capacity to perform the hard work of careful research and self-examination which must precede any successful experiments in social reform. Of the varied groups and individuals whose suggestions remained with me for years, I recall perhaps as foremost those members of the new London County Council whose far-reaching plans for the betterment of London could not but enkindle enthusiasm. It was a most striking expression of that effort which would place beside the refinement and pleasure of the rich, a new refinement and a new pleasure born of the commonwealth and the common joy of all the citizens, that at this moment they prized the municipal pleasure boats upon the Thames no less than the extensive schemes for the municipal housing of the poorest people. Ben Tillet, who was then an alderman, "the docker sitting beside the duke," took me in a rowboat down the Thames on a journey made exciting by the hundreds of dockers who cheering him as we passed one wharf after another on our way to his home at Greenwich; John Burns showed us his wonderful civic accomplishments at Battersea, the plant turning street sweepings into cement pavements, the technical school teaching boys brick laying and plumbing, and the public bath in which the children of the Board School were receiving a swimming lesson—these measures anticipating our achievements in Chicago by at least a decade and a half. The new Education Bill which was destined to drag on for twelve years before it developed into the children's charter, was then a storm center in the House of Commons. Miss Smith and I were much pelased to be taken to tea on the Parliament terrace by its author, Sir John Gorst, although we were quite bewildered by the arguments we heard there for church schools *versus* secular.

We heard Keir Hardie before a large audience of workingmen standing in the open square of Canning Town, outline the great things to be accomplished by the then new Labor Party, and we joined the vast body of men in the booming hymn

> When wilt Thou save the people,
> O God of Mercy, when!

finding it hard to realize that we were attending a political meeting. It seemed that moment as if the hopes of democracy were more likely to come to pass on English soil that upon our own. Robert Blatchford's stirring pamphlets were in every one's hands, and a reception given by Karl Marx's daughter, Mrs. Aveling, to Liebknecht before he returned to Germany to serve a prison term for his *lèse majesté* speech in the Reichstag, gave us a glimpse of the old-fashioned orthodox Socialist who had not yet begun to yield to the biting ridicule of Bernard Shaw although he flamed in their midst that evening.

Octavia Hill kindly demonstrated to us the principles upon which her well-founded business of rent collecting was established, and with pardonable pride showed us the Red Cross Square with its cottages marvelously picturesque and comfortable, on two sides, and on the third a public hall and common drawing-room for the use of all the tenants; the interior of the latter had been decorated by pupils of Walter Crane with mural frescoes portraying the heroism in the life of the modern workingman.

While all this was warmly human, we also had opportunities to see something of a group of men and women who were approaching the social problem from the study of economics; among others Mr. and Mrs. Sidney Webb who were at work on their Industrial Democracy; Mr. John Hobson who was lecturing on the evolution of modern capitalism.

We followed factory inspectors on a round of duties performed with a thoroughness and a trained intelligence which were a revelation of the possibilities of public service. When it came to visiting Settlements, we were at least reassured that they were not falling into identical lines of effort. Canon Ingram, who has since become Bishop of London, was then warden of Oxford House and in the midst of an experiment which pleased me greatly, the more because it was carried on by a churchman. Oxford House had hired all the concert halls—vaudeville shows we later called them in Chicago—which were found in Bethnal Green, for every Saturday night. The residents had censored the programs, which they were careful to keep popular, and any workingman who attended a show in Bethnal Green on a Saturday night, and thousands of them did, heard a program the better for this effort.

One evening in University Hall Mrs. Humphry Ward who had just returned from Italy, described the effect of the Italian salt tax in a talk which was evidently one in a series of lectures upon the economic wrongs which pressed heaviest upon the poor; at Browning House, at the moment, they were giving prizes to those of their costermonger neighbors who could present the best cared-for donkeys, and the warden, Herbert Stead, exhibited almost the enthusiasm of his well-known brother, for that crop of kindliness which can be garnered most easily from the acreage where human beings grow the thickest; at the Bermondsey Settlement they were rejoicing that their University Extension students had successfully passed the examinations for the University of London. The entire impression received in England of research, of scholarship, of organized public spirit, was in marked contrast to the impressions of my next visit in 1900, when the South African War had absorbed the enthusiasm of the nation and the wrongs at "the heart of the empire" were disregarded and neglected.

London, of course, presented sharp differences to Russia where social conditions were written in black and white with little shading, like a demonstration of the Chinese proverb, "Where one man lives in luxury, another is dying of hunger."

The fair of Nijni-Novgorod seemed to take us to the very edge of a civilization so remote and eastern, that the merchants brought their curious goods upon the backs of camels or on strange craft riding at anchor on the broad Volga. But even here our letter of introduction to Korolenko, the novelist, brought us to a realization of that strange mingling of a remote past and a self-conscious present which Russia presents on every hand. This same contrast was also shown by the pilgrims trudging on pious errands to monasteries, to tombs and to the Holy Land itself, with their bleeding feet bound in rags and thrust into bast sandals, and, on the other hand, by the revolutionists even then advocating a Republic which should obtain not only in political but also in industrial affairs.

We had letters of introduction to Mr. and Mrs. Aylmer Maude of Moscow, since well known as the translators of "Resurrection" and other of Tolstoy's later works, who, at that moment were on the eve of leaving Russia in order to form an agricultural colony in South England where they might support themselves by the labor of their hands. We gladly accepted Mr. Maude's offer to take us to Yasnaya Polyana and to introduce us to Count Tolstoy, and never did a disciple journey towards his master with more enthusiasm than did our guide. When, however, Mr. Maude actually presented Miss Smith and myself to Count Tolstoy, knowing well his master's attitude toward philanthropy, he endeavored to make

Hull-House appear much more noble and unique than I should have ventured to do.

Tolstoy standing by clad in his peasant garb, listened gravely but, glancing distrustfully at the sleeves of my traveling gown which unfortunately at that season were monstrous in size, he took hold of an edge and pulling out one sleeve to an interminable breadth, said quite simply that "there was enough stuff on one arm to make a frock for a little girl," and asked me directly if I did not find "such a dress" a "barrier to the people." I was too disconcerted to make a very clear explanation, although I tried to say that monstrous as my sleeves were they did not compare in size with those of the working girls in Chicago and that nothing would more effectively separate me from "the people" than a cotton blouse following the simple lines of the human form; even if I had wished to imitate him and "dress as a peasant," it would have been hard to choose which peasant among the thirty-six nationalities we had recently counted in our ward. Fortunately the countess came to my rescue with a recital of her former attempts to clothe hypothetical little girls in yards of material cut from a train and other superfluous parts of her best gown until she had been driven to a firm stand which she advised me to take at once. But neither Countess Tolstoy nor any other friend was on hand to help me out of my predicament later, when I was asked who "fed" me, and how did I obtain "shelter"? Upon my reply that a farm a hundred miles from Chicago supplied me with the necessities of life, I fairly anticipated the next scathing question: "So you are an absentee landlord? Do you think you will help the people more by adding yourself to the crowded city than you would by tilling your own soil?" This new sense of discomfort over a failure to till my own soil was increased when Tolstoy's second daughter appeared at the five-o'clock tea table set under the trees, coming straight from the harvest field where she had been working with a group of peasants since five o'clock in the morning, not pretending to work but really taking the place of a peasant woman who had hurt her foot. She was plainly much exhausted but neither expected nor received sympathy from the members of a family who were quite accustomed to see each other carry out their convictions in spite of discomfort and fatigue. The martyrdom of discomfort, however, was obviously much easier to bear than that to which, even to the eyes of the casual visitor, Count Tolstoy daily subjected himself, for his study in the basement of the conventional dwelling, with its short shelf of battered books and its scythe and spade leaning against the wall, had many times lent itself to that ridicule which is the most difficult form of martyrdom.

That summer evening as we sat in the garden with a group of visitors from Germany, from England and America, who had traveled to the remote Russian village that they might learn of this man, one could not forbear the constant inquiry to one's self, as to why he was so regarded as sage and saint that this party of people should be repeated each day of the year. It seemed to me then that we were all attracted by this sermon of the deed, because Tolstoy had made the one supreme personal effort, one might almost say the one frantic personal effort, to put himself into right relations with the humblest people, with the men who tilled his soil, blacked his boots and cleaned his stables. Doubtless the heaviest burden of our contemporaries is a consciousness of a divergence between our democratic theory on the one hand, that working people have a right to the intellectual resources of society, and the actual fact on the other, hand, that thousands of them are so overburdened with toil that there is no leisure nor energy left for the cultivation of the mind. We constantly suffer from the strain and indecision of believing this theory and acting as if we did not believe it, and this man who years before had tried "to get off the backs of the peasants," who had at least simplified his life and worked with his hands, had come to be a prototype to many of his generation.

Doubtless all of the visitors sitting in the Tolstoy garden that evening had excused themselves from laboring with their hands upon the theory that they were doing something more valuable for society in other ways. No one among our contemporaries has dissented from this point of view so violently as Tolstoy himself, and yet no man might so easily have excused himself from hard and rough work on the basis of his genius and of his intellectual contributions to the world. So far, however, from considering his time too valuable to be spent in labor in the field or in making shoes, our great host was too eager to know life to be willing to give up this companionship of mutual labor. One instinctively found reasons why it was easier for a Russian than for the rest of us, to reach this conclusion; the Russian peasants have a proverb which says: "Labor is the house that love lives in," by which they mean that no two people nor group of people, can come into affectionate relations with each other unless they carry on together a mutual task, and when the Russian peasant talks of labor he means labor on the soil, or, to use the phrase of the great peasant, Bondereff, "bread labor." Those monastic orders founded upon agricultural labor, those philosophical experiments like Brook Farm and many another, have attempted to reduce to action this same truth. Tolstoy himself has written many times his own convictions and attempts in this direction, perhaps never more tellingly than in the description of Lavin's morning spent in the harvest field, when he lost his sense of grievance and isolation and felt a strange new brotherhood for the peasants, in proportion as the rhythmic motion of his scythe became one with theirs.

At the long dinner table laid in the garden were the various traveling guests, the grown-up daughters, and the younger children with their governess. The countess presided over the usual European dinner served by men, but the count and the daughter who had worked all day in the fields, ate only porridge and black bread and drank only kvas, the fare of the hay-making peasants. Of course we are all accustomed to the fact that those who perform the heaviest labor, eat the coarsest and simplest fare at the end of the day, but it is not often that we sit at the same table with them while we ourselves eat the more elaborate food prepared by some one else's labor. Tolstoy ate his simple supper without remark or comment upon the food his family and guests preferred to eat, assuming that they, as well as he, had settled the matter with their own consciences.

The Tolstoy household that evening was much interested in the fate of a young Russian spy who had recently come to Tolstoy in the guise of a country schoolmaster, in order to obtain a copy of "Life," which had been interdicted by the censor of the press. After spending the night in talk with Tolstoy, the spy had gone away with a copy of the forbidden manuscript but, unfortunately for himself, having become converted to Tolstoy's views he had later made a full confession to the authorities and had been exiled to Siberia. Tolstoy holding that it was most unjust to exile the disciple while he, the author of the book, remained at large, had pointed out this inconsistency in an open letter to one of the Moscow newspapers. The discussion of this incident, of course, opened up the entire subject of non-resistance, and curiously enough I was disappointed in Tolstoy's position in the matter. It seemed to me that he made too great a distinction between the use of physical force and that moral energy which can override another's differences and scruples with equal ruthlessness.

With that inner sense of mortification with which one finds one's self at difference with the great authority, I recalled the conviction of the early Hull-House residents; that whatever of good the Settlement had to offer should be put into positive terms, that we might live with opposition to no man, with recognition of the good in every man, even the most wretched. We had often departed from this principle, but had it not in every case been a confession of weakness, and had we not always found antagonism a foolish and unwarrantable expenditure of energy?

The conversation at dinner and afterwards, although conducted with animation and sincerity, for the moment stirred vague misgivings within me. Was Tolstoy more logical than life warrants? Could the wrongs of life be reduced to the terms of unrequited labor and all be made right if each person performed the amount necessary to satisfy his own wants? Was it not always easy to put up a strong case if one took the naturalistic view of life? But what about the historic view, the inevitable shadings and modifications which life itself brings to its own interpretation? Miss Smith and I took a night train back to Moscow in that tumult of feeling which is always produced by contact with a conscience making one more of those determined efforts to probe to the very foundations of the mysterious world in which we find ourselves. A horde of perplexing questions, concerning those problems of existence of which in happier moments we catch but fleeting glimpses and at which we even then stand aghast, pursued us relentlessly on the long journey through the great wheat plains of South Russia, through the crowded Ghetto of Warsaw, and finally into the smiling fields of Germany where the peasant men and women were harvesting the grain. I remember that through the sight of those toiling peasants, I made a curious connection between the bread labor advocated by Tolstoy and the comfort the harvest fields are said to have once brought to Luther when, much perturbed by many theological difficulties, he suddenly forgot them all in a gush of gratitude for mere bread, exclaiming, "How it stands, that golden yellow corn, on its fine tapered stem; the meek earth, at God's kind bidding, has produced it once again!" At least the toiling poor had this comfort of bread labor, and perhaps it did not matter that they gained it unknowingly and painfully, if only they walked in the path of labor. In the exercise of that curious power possessed by the theorists to inhibit all experiences which do not enhance his doctrine, I did not permit myself to recall that which I knew so well—that exigent and unremitting labor grants the poor no leisure even in the supreme moments of human suffering and that "all griefs are lighter with bread."

I may have wished to secure this solace for myself at the cost of the least possible expenditure of time and energy, for during the next month in Germany, when I read everything of Tolstoy's that had been translated into English, German, or French, there grew up in my mind a conviction that what I ought to do upon my return to Hull-House, was to spend at least two hours every morning in the little bakery which we had recently added to the equipment of our coffee-house. Two hours' work would be but a wretched compromise, but it was hard to see how I could take more time out of each day. I had been taught to bake bread in my childhood not only as a household accomplishment, but because my father, true to his miller's tradition, had insisted that each one of his daughters on her twelfth birthday must present him with a satisfactory wheat loaf of her own baking, and he was most exigent as to the quality of this test loaf. What could be more in keeping with my training and tradition than baking bread? I did not quite see how my activity would fit in with that of the German union baker who presided over the Hull-House bakery but all such matters were secondary and certainly could be arranged. It may be that I had thus to pacify my aroused conscience before I could settle down to hear Wagner's "Ring" at Beyreuth; it may be that I had fallen a victim to the phrase, "bread labor"; but at any rate I held fast to the belief that I should do this, through the entire journey homeward, on land and sea, until I actually arrived in Chicago when suddenly the whole scheme seemed to me as utterly preposterous as it doubtless was. The half dozen people invariably waiting to see me after breakfast, the piles of letters to be opened and answered, the demand of actual and pressing human wants—were these all to be pushed aside and asked to wait while I saved my soul by two hours' work at baking bread?

Although my resolution was abandoned, this may be the best place to record the efforts of more doughty souls to carry out Tolstoy's conclusions. It was perhaps inevitable that Tolstoy colonies should be founded, although Tolstoy himself has always insisted that each man should live his life as nearly as possible in the place in which he was born. The visit Miss Smith and I made a year or two later to a colony in one of the southern States, portrayed for us most vividly both the weakness and the strange august dignity of the Tolstoy position. The colonists at Commonwealth held but a short creed. They claimed in fact that the difficulty is not to state truth but to make moral conviction operative upon actual life, and they announced it their intention "to obey the teachings of Jesus in all matters of labor and the use of property." They would thus transfer the vindication of creed from the church to the open field, from dogma to experience.

The day Miss Smith and I visited the Commonwealth colony of threescore souls, they were erecting a house for the family of a one-legged man, consisting of a wife and nine children who had come the week before in a forlorn prairie schooner from Arkansas. As this was the largest family the little colony contained, the new house was to be the largest yet erected. Upon our surprise at this literal giving "to him that asketh," we inquired if the policy of extending food and shelter to all who applied, without test of creed or ability, might not result in the migration of all the neighboring poorhouse population into the colony. We were told that this actually had happened during the winter until the colony fare of corn meal and cow peas had proved so unattractive that the paupers had gone back, for even the poorest of the southern poorhouses occasionally supplied bacon with the pone if only to prevent scurvy from which the colonists themselves had suffered. The difficulty of the poorhouse people had thus settled itself by the sheer poverty of the situation, a poverty so biting that the only ones willing to face it were those sustained by a conviction of its righteousness. The fields and gardens were being worked by an editor, a professor, a clergyman, as well as by artisans and laborers, the fruit thereof to be eaten by themselves and their families or by any other families who might arrive from Arkansas. The colonist were very conventional in matters of family relationship and had broken with society only in regard to the conventions pertaining to labor and property. We had a curious experience at the end of the day when we were driven into the nearest town. We had taken with us as a guest the wife of the president of the colony, wishing to give her a dinner at the hotel, because she had girlishly exclaimed during a conversation that at times during the winter she had become so eager to hear good music that it had seemed to her as if she were actually hungry for it, almost as hungry as she was for a beefsteak. Yet as we drove away we had the curious sensation that while the experiment was obviously coming to an end, in the midst of its privations it yet embodied the peace of mind which comes to him who insists upon the logic of life whether it is reasonable or not—the fanatic's joy in seeing his own formula translated into action. At any rate, as we reached the commonplace southern town of workaday men and women, for one moment its substantial buildings, its solid brick churches, its ordered streets, divided into those of the rich and those of the poor, seemed much more unreal to us than the little struggling colony we had left behind. We repeated to each other that in all the practical judgments and decisions of life, we must part company with logical demonstration; that if we stop for it in each case, we can never go on at all; and yet, in spite of this, when conscience does become the dictator of the daily life of a group of men, it forces our admiration as no other modern spectacle has power to do. It seemed but a mere incident that this group should have lost sight of the facts of life in their earnest endeavor to put to the test the things of the spirit.

I knew little about the colony started by Mr. Maude at Purleigh containing several of Tolstoy's followers who were not permitted to live in Russia, and we did not see Mr. Maude again until he came to Chicago on his way from Manitoba, whither he had transported the second group of Dukhobors, a religious sect who had interested all of Tolstoy's followers because of their literal acceptance of non-resistance and other Christian doctrines which are so strenuously advocated by Tolstoy. It was for their benefit that Tolstoy had finished and published "Resurrection," breaking through his long-kept resolution against novel writing. After the Dukhobors were settled in Canada, of the five hundred dollars left from the "Resurrection" funds, one half was given to Hull-House. It seemed possible to spend this fund only for the relief of the most primitive wants of food and shelter on the part of the most needy families.

PUBLIC ACTIVITIES AND INVESTIGATIONS

One of the striking features of our neighborhood twenty years ago, and one to which we never became reconciled, was the presence of huge wooden garbage boxes fastened to the street pavement in which the undisturbed refuse accumulated day by day. The system of garbage collecting was inadequate throughout the city but it became the greatest menace in a ward such as ours, where the normal amount of waste was much increased by the decayed fruit and vegetables discarded by the Italian and Greek fruit peddlers, and by the residuum left over from the piles of filthy rags which were fished out of the city dumps and brought to the homes of the rag pickers for further sorting and washing.

The children of our neighborhood twenty years ago played their games in and around these huge garbage boxes. They were the first objects that the toddling child learned to climb; their bulk afforded a barricade and their contents provided missiles in all the battles of the older boys; and finally they became the seats upon which absorbed lovers held enchanted converse. We are obliged to remember that all children eat everything which they find and that odors have a curious and intimate power of entwining themselves into our tenderest memories, before even the residents of Hull-House can understand their own early enthusiasm for the removal of these boxes and the establishment of a better system of refuse collection.

It is easy for even the most conscientious citizen of Chicago to forget the foul smells of the stockyards and the garbage dumps, when he is living so far from them that he is only occasionally made conscious of their existence but the residents of a Settlement are perforce constantly surrounded by them. During our first three years on Halsted Street, we had established a small incinerator at Hull-House and we had many times reported the untoward conditions of the ward to the city hall. We had also arranged many talks for the immigrants, pointing out that although a woman may sweep her own doorway in her native village and allow the refuse to innocently decay in the open air and sunshine, in a crowded city quarter, if the garbage is not properly collected and destroyed, a tenement-house mother may see her children sicken and die, and that the immigrants must therefore, not only keep their own houses clean, but must also help the authorities to keep the city clean.

Possibly our efforts slightly modified the worst conditions but they still remained intolerable, and the fourth summer the situation became for me absolutely desperate when I realized in a moment of panic that my delicate little nephew for whom I was guardian, could not be with me at Hull-House at all unless the sickening odors were reduced. I may well be ashamed that other delicate children who were torn from their families, not into boarding school but into eternity, had not long before driven me to effective action. Under the direction of the first man who came as a resident to Hull-House we began a systematic investigation of the city system of garbage collection, both as to its efficiency in other wards and its possible connection with the death rate in the various wards of the city.

The Hull-House Woman's Club had been organized the year before by the resident kindergartner who had first inaugurated a mothers' meeting. The members came together, however, in quite a new way that summer when we discussed with them the high death rate so persistent in our ward. After several club meetings devoted to the subject, despite the fact that the death rate rose highest in the congested foreign colonies and not in the streets in which most of the Irish American club women lived, twelve of their number undertook in connection with the residents, to carefully investigate the condition of the alleys. During August and September the substantiated reports of violations of the law sent in from Hull-House to the health department were one thousand and thirty-seven. For the club woman who had finished a long day's work of washing or ironing followed by the cooking of a hot supper, it would have been much easier to sit on her doorstep during a summer evening than to go up and down ill-kept alleys and get into trouble with her neighbors over the condition of their garbage boxes. It required both civic enterprise and moral conviction to be willing to do this three evenings a week during the hottest and most uncomfortable months of the year. Nevertheless, a certain number of women persisted, as did the residents and three city inspectors in succession were transferred from the ward because of unsatisfactory services. Still the death rate remained high and the condition seemed little improved throughout the next winter. In sheer desperation, the following spring when the city contracts were awarded for the removal of garbage, with the backing of two well-known business men, I put in a bid for the garbage removal of the nineteenth ward. My paper was thrown out on a technicality but the incident induced the mayor to appoint me the garbage inspector of the ward.

The salary was a thousand dollars a year, and the loss of that political "plum" made a great stir among the politicians. The position was no sinecure whether regarded from the point of view of getting up at six in the morning to see that the men were early at work; or of following the loaded wagons, uneasily dropping their contents at intervals, to their dreary destination at the dump; or of insisting that the contractor must increase the number of his wagons from nine to thirteen and from thirteen to seventeen, although he assured me that he lost money on every one and that the former inspector had let him off with seven; or of taking careless landlords into court because they would not provide the proper garbage receptacles; or of arresting the tenant who tried to make the garbage wagons carry away the contents of his stable.

With the two or three residents who nobly stood by, we set up six of those doleful incinerators which are supposed to burn garbage with the fuel collected in the alley itself. The one factory in town which could utilize old tin cans was a window weight factory, and we deluged that with ten times as many tin cans as it could use—much less would pay for. We made desperate attempts to have the dead animals removed by the contractor who was paid most liberally by the city for that purpose but who, we slowly discovered, always made the police ambulances do the work, delivering the carcasses upon freight cars for shipment to a soap factory in Indiana where they were sold for a good price although the contractor himself was the largest stockholder in the concern. Perhaps our greatest achievement was the discovery of a pavement eighteen inches under the surface in a narrow street, although after it was found we triumphantly discovered a record of its existence in the city archives. The Italians living on the street were much interested but displayed little astonishment, perhaps because they were accustomed to see buried cities exhumed. This pavement became the *casus belli* between myself and the street commissioner when I insisted that its restoration belonged to him, after I had removed the first eight inches of garbage. The matter was finally settled by the mayor himself, who permitted me to drive him to the entrance of the street in what the children called my "garbage phaëton" and who took my side of the controversy.

A graduate of the University of Wisconsin, who had done some excellent volunteer inspection in both Chicago and Pittsburgh, became my deputy and performed the work in a most thoroughgoing manner for three years. During the last two she was under the régime of civil service for in 1895, to the great joy of many citizens, the Illinois legislature made that possible.

Many of the foreign-born women of the ward were much shocked by this abrupt departure into the ways of men, and it took a great deal of explanation to convey the idea even remotely that if it were a womanly task to go about in tenement houses in order to nurse the sick, it might be quite as womanly to go through the same district in order to prevent the breeding of so-called "filth diseases." While some of the women enthusiastically approved the slowly changing conditions and saw that their housewifely duties logically extended to the adjacent alleys and streets, they yet were quite certain that "it was not a lady's job." A revelation of this attitude was made one day in a conversation which the inspector heard vigorously carried on in a laundry. One of the employees was leaving and was expressing her mind concerning the place in no measured terms, summing up her contempt for it as follows: "I would rather be the girl who goes about in the alleys than to stay here any longer!"

And yet the spectacle of eight hours' work for eight hours' pay, the even-handed justice to all citizens irrespective of "pull," the dividing of responsibility between landlord and tenant, and the readiness to enforce obedience to law from both, was, perhaps, one of the most valuable demonstrations which could have been made. Such daily living on the part of the office holder is of infinitely more value than many talks on civics for, after all, we credit most easily that which we see. The careful inspection combined with other causes, brought about a great improvement in the cleanliness and comfort of the neighborhood and one happy day, when the death rate of our ward was found to have dropped from third to seventh in the list of city wards and was so reported to our Woman's Club, the applause which followed recorded the genuine sense of participation in the result, and a public spirit which had "made good." But the cleanliness of the ward was becoming much too popular to suit our all-powerful alderman and, although we felt fatuously secure under the régime of civil service, he found a way to circumvent us by eliminating the position altogether. He introduced an ordinance into the city council which combined the collection of refuse with the cleaning and repairing of the streets, the whole to be placed under a ward superintendent. The office of course was to be filled under civil service regulations but only men were eligible to the examination. Although this latter regulation was afterwards modified in favor of one woman, it was retained long enough to put the ninteenth ward inspector out of office.

Of course our experience in inspecting only made us more conscious of the wretched housing conditions over which we had been distressed from the first. It was during the World's Fair summer that one of the Hull-House residents in a public address upon housing reform used as an example of indifferent landlordism a large block in the neighborhood occupied by small tenements and stables unconnected with a street sewer, as was much similar property in the vicinity. In the lecture the resident spared neither a description of the property nor the name of the owner. The young man who owned the property was justly indignant at this public method of attack and promptly came to investigate the condition of the property. Together we made a careful tour of the houses and stables and in the face of the conditions that we found there, I could not but agree with him that supplying South Italian peasants with sanitary appliances seemed a difficult undertaking. Nevertheless he was unwilling that the block should remain in its deplorable state, and he finally cut through the dilemma with the rash proposition that he would give a free lease of the entire tract to Hull-House, accompanying the offer, however, with the warning remark, that if we should choose to use the income from the rents in sanitary improvements we should be throwing our money away.

Even when we decided that the houses were so bad that we could not undertake the task of improving them, he was game and stuck to his proposition that we should have a free lease. We finally submitted a plan that the houses should be torn down and the entire tract turned into a playground, although cautious advisers intimated that it would be very inconsistent to ask for subscriptions for the support of Hull-House when we were known to have thrown away an income of two thousand dollars a year. We, however, felt that a spectacle of inconsistency was better than one of bad landlordism and so the worst of the houses were demolished, the best three were sold and moved across the street under careful provision that they might never be used for junk-shops or saloons, and a public playground was finally established. Hull-House became responsible for its management for ten years, at the end of which time it was turned over to the City Playground Commission although from the first the city detailed a policeman who was responsible for its general order and who became a valued adjunct of the House.

During fifteen years this public-spirited owner of the property paid all the taxes, and when the block was finally sold he made possible the playground equipment of a near-by school yard. On the other hand, the dispossessed tenants, a group of whom had to be evicted by legal process before their houses could be torn down, have never ceased to mourn their former estates. Only the other day I met upon the street an old Italian harness maker, who said that he had never succeeded so well anywhere else nor found a place that "seemed so much like Italy."

Festivities of various sorts were held on this early playground, always a May day celebration with its Maypole dance and its May queen. I remember that one year the honor of being queen was offered to the little girl who should pick up the largest number of scraps of paper which littered all the streets and alleys. The children that spring had been organized into a league and each member had been provided with a stiff piece of wire upon the sharpened point of which stray bits of paper were impaled and later soberly counted off into a large box in the Hull-House alley. The little Italian girl who thus won the scepter took it very gravely as the just reward of hard labor, and we were all so absorbed in the desire for clean and tidy streets that we were wholly oblivious to the incongruity of thus selecting "the queen of love and beauty."

It was at the end of the second year that we received a visit from the warden of Toynbee Hall and his wife, as they were returning to England from a journey around the world. They had lived in East London for many years, and had been identified with the public movements for its betterment. They were much shocked that, in a new country with conditions still plastic and hopeful, so little attention had been paid to experiments and methods of amelioration which had already been tried; and they looked in vain through our library for blue books and governmental reports which recorded painstaking study into the conditions of English cities.

They were the first of a long line of English visitors to express the conviction that many things in Chicago were untoward not through paucity of public spirit but through a lack of political machinery adapted to modern city life. This was not all of the situation but perhaps no casual visitor could be expected to see that these matters of detail seemed unimportant to a city in the first flush of youth, impatient of correction and convinced that all would be well with its future. The most obvious faults were those connected with the congested housing of the immigrant population, nine tenths of them from the country, who carried on all sorts of traditional activities in the crowded tenements. That a group of Greeks should be permitted to slaughter sheep in a basement, that Italian women should be allowed to sort over rags collected from the city dumps, not only within the city limits but in a court swarming with little children, that immigrant bakers should continue unmolested to bake bread for their neighbors in unspeakably filthy spaces under the pavement, appeared incredible to visitors accustomed to careful city regulations. I recall two visits made to the Italian quarter by John Burns— the second, thirteen years after the first. During the latter visit it seemed to him unbelievable that a certain house owned by a rich Italian should have been permitted to survive. He remembered with the greatest minuteness the positions of the houses on the court, with the exact space between the front and rear tenements, and he asked at once whether we had been able to cut a window into a dark hall as he had recommended thirteen years before. Although we were obliged to confess that the landlord would not permit the window to be cut, we were able to report that a City Homes Association had existed for ten years; that following a careful study of tenement conditions in Chicago, the text of which had been written by a Hull-House resident, the association had obtained the enactment of a model tenement-house code, and that their secretary had carefully watched the administration of the law for years so that its operation might not be minimized by the granting of too many exceptions in the city council. Our progress still seemed slow to Mr. Burns because in Chicago the actual houses were quite unchanged, embodying features long since declared illegal in London. Only this year could we have reported to him, had he again come to challenge us, that the provisions of the law had at last been extended to existing houses and that a conscientious corps of inspectors under an efficient chief, were fast remedying the most glaring evils, while a band of nurses and doctors were following hard upon the "trail of the white hearse."

The mere consistent enforcement of existing laws and efforts for their advance often placed Hull-House, at least temporarily, into strained relations with its neighbors. I recall a continuous warfare against local landlords who would move wrecks of old houses as a nucleus for new ones in order to evade the provisions of the building code, and a certain Italian neighbor who was filled with bitterness because his new rear tenement was discovered to be illegal. It seemed impossible to make him understand that the health of the tenants was in any wise as important as his undisturbed rents.

Nevertheless many evils constantly arise in Chicago from congested housing which wiser cities forestall and prevent; the inevitable boarders crowded into a dark tenement already too small for the use of the immigrant family occupying it; the surprisingly large number of delinquent girls who have become criminally involved with their own fathers and uncles; the school children who cannot find a quiet spot in which to read or study and who perforce go into the streets each evening; the tuberculosis superinduced and fostered by the inadequate rooms and breathing spaces. One of the Hull-House residents, under the direction of a Chicago physician who stands high as an authority on tuberculosis and who devotes a large proportion of his time to our vicinity, made an investigation into housing conditions as related to tuberculosis with a result as startling as that of the "lung block" in New York.

It is these subtle evils of wretched and inadequate housing which are often most disastrous. In the summer of 1902 during an epidemic of typhoid fever in which our ward, although containing but one thirty-sixth of the population of the city, registered one sixth of the total number of deaths, two of the Hull-House residents made an investigation of the methods of plumbing in the houses adjacent to conspicuous groups of fever cases. They discovered among the people who had been exposed to the infection, a widow who had lived in the ward for a number of years, in a comfortable little house of her own. Although the Italian immigrants were closing in all round her, she was not willing to sell her property and to move away until she had finished the education of her children. In the meantime she held herself quite aloof from her Italian neighbors and could never be drawn into any of the public efforts to secure a better code of tenement-house sanitation. Her two daughters were sent to an eastern college. One June when one of them had graduated and the other still had two years before she took her degree, they came to the spotless little house and to their self-sacrificing mother for the summer holiday. They both fell ill with typhoid fever and one daughter died because the mother's utmost efforts could not keep the infection out of her own house. The entire disaster affords, perhaps, a fair illustration of the futility of the individual conscience which would isolate a family from the rest of the community and its interests.

The careful information collected concerning the juxtaposition of the typhoid cases to the various systems of plumbing and nonplumbing, was made the basis of a bacteriological study by another resident, Dr. Alice Hamilton, as to the possibility of the infection having been carried by flies. Her researches were so convincing that they have been incorporated into the body of scientific data supporting that theory, but there were also practical results from the investigation. It was discovered that the wretched sanitary appliances through which alone the infection could have become so widely spread, would not have been permitted to remain, unless the city inspector had either been criminally careless or open to the arguments of favored landlords.

The agitation finally resulted in a long and stirring trial before the civil service board of half of the employees in the Sanitary Bureau, with the final discharge of eleven out of the entire force of twenty-four. The inspector in our neighborhood was a kindly old man, greatly distressed over the affair, and quite unable to understand why he should not have used his discretion as to the time when a landlord should be forced to put in modern appliances. If he was "very poor," or "just about to sell his place," or "sure that the house would be torn down to make room for a factory," why should one "inconvenience" him? The old man died soon after the trial, feeling persecuted to the very last and not in the least understanding what it was all about. We were amazed at the commercial ramifications which graft in the city hall involved and at the indignation which interference with it produced. Hull-House lost some large subscriptions as the result of this investigation, a loss which, if not easy to bear, was at least comprehensible. We also uncovered unexpected graft in connection with the plumbers' unions, and but for the fearless testimony of one of their members, could never have brought the trial to a successful issue.

Inevitable misunderstanding also developed in connection with the attempt on the part of Hull-House residents to prohibit the sale of cocaine to minors, which brought us into sharp conflict with many druggists. I recall an Italian druggist living on the edge of the neighborhood, who finally came with a committee of his fellow countrymen to see what Hull-House wanted of him, thoroughly convinced that no such effort could be disinterested. One dreary trial after another had been lost through the inadequacy of the existing legislation and after many attempts to secure better legal regulation of its sale, a new law with the coöperation of many agencies was finally secured in 1907. Through all this the Italian druggist, who had greatly profited by the sale of cocaine to boys, only felt outraged and abused. And yet the thought of this campaign brings before my mind with irresistible force, a young Italian boy who died—a victim to the drug at the age of seventeen. He had been in our kindergarten as a handsome merry child, in our clubs as a vivacious boy, and then gradually there was an eclipse of all that was animated and joyous and promising, and when I at last saw him in his coffin, it was impossible to connect that haggard shriveled body with what I had known before.

A midwife investigation, undertaken in connection with the Chicago Medical Society, while showing the great need of further state regulation in the interest of the most ignorant mothers and helpless children, brought us into conflict with one of the most venerable of all customs. Was all this a part of the unending struggle between the old and new, or were these oppositions so unexpected and so unlooked for merely a reminder of that old bit of wisdom that "there is no guarding against interpretations"? Perhaps more subtle still, they were due to that very super-refinement of disinterestedness which will not justify itself, that it may feel superior to public opinion. Some of our investigations of course had no such untoward results, such as "An Intensive Study of Truancy" undertaken by a resident of Hull-House in connection with the compulsory education department of the Board of Education and the Visiting Nurses Association. The resident, Mrs. Britton, who, having had charge of our children's clubs for many years, knew thousands of children in the neighborhood, made a detailed study of three hundred families tracing back the habitual truancy of the children to economic and social causes. This investigation preceded a most interesting conference on truancy held under a committee of which I was a member from the Chicago Board of Education. It left lasting results upon the administration of the truancy law as well as the coöperation of volunteer bodies.

We continually conduct small but careful investigations at Hull-House, which may guide us in our immediate doings such as two recently undertaken by Mrs. Britton, one upon the reading of school children before new books were bought for the children's club libraries, and another on the proportion of tuberculosis among school children, before we opened a little experimental outdoor school on one of our balconies. Some of the Hull-House investigations are purely negative in result; we once made an attempt to test the fatigue of factory girls in order to determine how far overwork superinduced the tuberculosis to which such a surprising number of them were victims. The one scientific instrument it seemed possible to use was an ergograph, a complicated and expensive instrument kindly lent to us from the physiological laboratory of the University of Chicago. I remember the imposing procession we made from Hull-House to the factory full of working women, in which the proprietor allowed us to make the tests; first there was the precious instrument on a hand truck guarded by an anxious student and the young physician who was going to take the tests every afternoon; then there was Dr. Hamilton the resident in charge of the investigation, walking with a scientist who was interested to see that the instrument was properly installed; I followed in the rear to talk once more to the proprietor of the factory to be quite sure that he would permit the experiment to go on. The result of all this preparation, however, was to have the instrument record less fatigue at the end of the day than at the beginning, not because the girls had not worked hard and were not "dog tired" as they confessed, but because the instrument was not fitted to find it out.

For many years we have administered a branch station of the federal

post office at Hull-House, which we applied for in the first instance because our neighbors lost such a large percentage of the money they sent
to Europe, through the commissions to middle men. The experience in the
post office constantly gave us data for urging the establishment of postal
savings as we saw one perplexed immigrant after another turning away
in bewilderment when he was told that the United States post office did
not receive savings.

We find increasingly, however, that the best results are to be obtained
in investigations as in other undertakings, by combining our researches
with those of other public bodies or with the State itself. When all the
Chicago Settlements found themselves distressed over the condition of
the newsboys who, because they are merchants and not employees, do not
come under the provisions of the Illinois child labor law, they united in
the investigation of a thousand young newsboys, who were all inter-
viewed on the streets during the same twenty-four hours. Their school
and domestic status was easily determined later, for many of the boys
lived in the immediate neighborhoods of the ten Settlements which had
undertaken the investigation. The report embodying the results of the
investigation recommended a city ordinance containing features from the
Boston and Buffalo regulations, and although an ordinance was drawn up
and a strenuous effort was made to bring it to the attention of the aldermen, none of them would introduce it into the city council without newspaper backing. We were able to agitate for it again at the annual meeting
of the National Child Labor Committee which was held in Chicago in
1908, and which was of course reported in papers throughout the entire
country. This meeting also demonstrated that local measures can sometimes be urged most effectively when joined to the efforts of a national
body. Undoubtedly the best discussions ever held upon the operation and
status of the Illinois law, were those which took place then. The needs
of the Illinois children were regarded in connection with the children of
the nation and advanced health measures for Illinois were compared with
those of other states.

The investigations of Hull-House thus tend to be merged with those of
larger organizations, from the investigation of the social value of saloons
made for the Committee of Fifty in 1896, to the one on infant mortality
in relation to nationality, made for the American Academy of Science in
1909. This is also true of Hull-House activities in regard to public movements, some of which are inaugurated by the residents of other Settlements, as the Chicago School of Civics and Philanthropy, founded by
the splendid efforts of Dr. Graham Taylor for many years head of Chicago
Commons. All of our recent investigations into housing have been under
the department of investigation of this school with which several of the
Hull-House residents are identified, quite as our active measures to
secure better housing conditions have been carried on with the City

Homes Association and through the coöperation of one of our residents who several years ago was appointed a sanitary inspector on the city staff.

Perhaps Dr. Taylor himself offers the best possible example of the value of Settlement experience to public undertakings, in his manifold public activities of which one might instance his work at the moment upon a commission recently appointed by the governor of Illinois to report upon the best method of Industrial Insurance or Employer's Liability Acts, and his influence in securing another to study into the subject of Industrial Diseases. The actual factory investigation under the latter is in charge of Dr. Hamilton, of Hull-House, whose long residence in an industrial neighborhood as well as her scientific attainment, give her peculiar qualifications for the undertaking.

And so a Settlement is led along from the concrete to the abstract, as may easily be illustrated. Many years ago a tailors' union meeting at Hull-House asked our coöperation in tagging the various parts of a man's coat in such wise as to show the money paid to the people who had made it; one tag for the cutting and another for the buttonholes, another for the finishing and so on, the resulting total to be compared with the selling price of the coat itself. It quickly became evident that we had no way of computing how much of this larger balance was spent for salesmen, commercial travelers, rent and management, and the poor tagged coat was finally left hanging limply in a closet as if discouraged with the attempt. But the desire of the manual worker to know the relation of his own labor to the whole is not only legitimate but must form the basis of any intelligent action for his improvement. It was therefore with the hope of reform in the sewing trades that the Hull-House residents testified before the Federal Industrial Commission in 1900, and much later with genuine enthusiasm joined with trades-unionists and other public-spirited citizens in an industrial exhibit which made a graphic presentation of the conditions and rewards of labor. The large casino building in which it was held was filled every day and evening for two weeks, showing how popular such information is, if it can be presented graphically. As an illustration of this same moving from the smaller to the larger, I might instance the efforts of Miss McDowell of the University of Chicago Settlement and others, in urging upon Congress the necessity for a special investigation into the condition of women and children in industry because we had discovered the insuperable difficulties of smaller investigations, notably one undertaken for the Illinois Bureau of Labor by Mrs. Van der Vaart of Neighborhood House and by Miss Breckinridge of the University of Chicago. This investigation made clear that it was as impossible to detach the girls working in the stockyards from their sisters in industry, as it was to urge special legislation on their behalf.

In the earlier years of the American Settlements, the residents were sometimes impatient with the accepted methods of charitable administration and hoped, through residence in an industrial neighborhood, to discover more coöperative and advanced methods of dealing with the problems of poverty which are so dependent upon industrial maladjustment. But during twenty years, the Settlements have seen the charitable people, through their very knowledge of the poor, constantly approach nearer to those methods formerly designated as radical. The residents, so far from holding aloof from organized charity, find testimony, certainly in the National Conferences, that out of the most persistent and intelligent efforts to alleviate poverty, will in all probability arise the most significant suggestions for eradicating poverty. In the hearing before a congressional committee for the establishment of a Children's Bureau, residents in American Settlements joined their fellow philanthropists in urging the need of this indispensable instrument for collecting and disseminating information which would make possible concerted intelligent action on behalf of children.

Mr. Howells has said that we are all so besotted with our novel reading that we have lost the power of seeing certain aspects of life with any sense of reality because we are continually looking for the possible romance. The description might apply to the earlier years of the American settlement, but certainly the later years are filled with discoveries in actual life as romantic as they are unexpected. If I may illustrate one of these romantic discoveries from my own experience, I would cite the indications of an internationalism as sturdy and virile as it is unprecedented which I have seen in our cosmopolitan neighborhood: when a South Italian Catholic is forced by the very exigencies of the situation to make friends with an Austrian Jew representing another nationality and another religion, both of which cut into all his most cherished prejudices, he finds it harder to utilize them a second time and gradually loses them. He thus modifies his provincialism for if an old enemy working by his side has turned into a friend, almost anything may happen. When, therefore, I became identified with the peace movement both in its International and National Conventions, I hoped that this internationalism engendered in the immigrant quarters of American cities might be recognized as an effective instrument in the cause of peace. I first set it forth with some misgiving before the Convention held in Boston in 1904 and it is always a pleasure to recall the hearty assent given to it by Professor William James.

I have always objected to the phrase "sociological laboratory" applied to us, because Settlements should be something much more human and spontaneous than such a phrase connotes, and yet it is inevitable that the residents should know their own neighborhoods more thoroughly than any other, and that their experiences there should affect their convictions.

Years ago I was much entertained by a story told at the Chicago Woman's Club by one of its ablest members in the discussion following a paper of mine on "The Outgrowths of Toynbee Hall." She said that when she was a little girl playing in her mother's garden, she one day discovered a small toad who seemed to her very forlorn and lonely, although as she did not in the least know how to comfort him, she reluctantly left him to his fate; later in the day, quite at the other end of the garden, she found a large toad, also apparently without family and friends. With a heart full of tender sympathy, she took a stick and by exercising infinite patience and some skill, she finally pushed the little toad through the entire length of the garden into the company of the big toad, when, to her inexpressible horror and surprise, the big toad opened his mouth and swallowed the little one. The moral of the tale was clear applied to people who lived "where they did not naturally belong," although I protested that was exactly what we wanted—to be swallowed and digested, to disappear into the bulk of the people.

Twenty years later I am willing to testify that something of the sort does take place after years of identification with an industrial community. . . .

## THE VALUE OF SOCIAL CLUBS

From the early days at Hull-House, social clubs composed of English speaking American born young people grew apace. So eager were they for social life that no mistakes in management could drive them away. I remember one enthusiastic leader who read aloud to a club a translation of "Antigone," which she had selected because she believed that the great themes of the Greek poets were best suited to young people. She came into the club room one evening in time to hear the president call the restive members to order with the statement, "You might just as well keep quiet for she is bound to finish it, and the quicker she gets to reading, the longer time we'll have for dancing." And yet the same club leader had the pleasure of lending four copies of the drama to four of the members, and one young man almost literally committed the entire play to memory.

On the whole we were much impressed by the great desire for self-improvement, for study and debate, exhibited by many of the young men. This very tendency, in fact, brought one of the most promising of our earlier clubs to an untimely end. The young men in the club, twenty in number, had grown much irritated by the frivolity of the girls during their long debates, and had finally proposed that three of the most "frivolous" be expelled. Pending a final vote, the three culprits appealed to certain of their friends who were members of the Hull-House Men's Club, between whom and the debating young men the incident became the cause of a quarrel so bitter that at length it led to a shooting. Fortunately the shot missed fire, or it may have been true that it was "only intended for a scare," but at any rate, we were all thoroughly frightened by this manifestation of the hot blood which the defense of woman has so often evoked. After many efforts to bring about a reconciliation, the debating club of twenty young men and the seventeen young women, who either were or pretended to be sober minded, rented a hall a mile west of Hull-House severing their connection with us because their ambitious and right-minded efforts had been unappreciated, basing this on the ground that we had not urged the expulsion of the so-called "tough" members of the Men's Club, who had been involved in the difficulty. The seceding club invited me to the first meeting in their new quarters that I might present to them my version of the situation and set forth the incident from the standpoint of Hull-House. The discussion I had with the young people that evening has always remained with me as one of the moments of illumination which life in a Settlement so often affords. In response to my position that a desire to avoid all that was "tough" meant to walk only in the paths of smug self-seeking and personal improvement leading straight into the pit of self-righteousness and petty achievement and was exactly what the Settlement did not stand for, they contended with much justice that ambitious young people were obliged for their own reputation, if not for their own morals, to avoid all connection with that which bordered on the tough, and that it was quite another matter for the Hull-House residents who could afford a more generous judgment. It was in vain I urged that life teaches us nothing more inevitably than that right and wrong are most confusingly confounded; that the blackest wrong may be within our own motives, and that at the best, right will not dazzle us by its radiant shining, and can only be found by exerting patience and discrimination. They still maintained their wholesome bourgeois position, which I am now quite ready to admit was most reasonable.

Of course there were many disappointments connected with these clubs when the rewards of political and commercial life easily drew the members away from the principles advocated in club meetings. One of the young men who had been a shining light in the advocacy of municipal reform, deserted in the middle of a reform campaign because he had been offered a lucrative office in the city hall; another even after a course of lectures on business morality, "worked" the club itself to secure orders for custom-made clothing from samples of cloth he displayed, although the orders were filled by ready-made suits slightly refitted and delivered at double their original price. But nevertheless, there was much to cheer us as we gradually became acquainted with the daily living of the vigorous young men and women who filled to overflowing all the social clubs.

We have been much impressed during our twenty years, by the ready adaptation of city young people to the prosperity arising from their own increased wages or from the commercial success of their families. This quick adaptability is the great gift of the city child, his one reward for the hurried changing life which he has always led. The working girl has a distinct advantage in the task of transforming her whole family into the ways and connections of the prosperous when she works down town and becomes conversant with the manners and conditions of a cosmopolitan community. Therefore having lived in a Settlement twenty years, I see scores of young people who have successfully established themselves in life, and in my travels in the city and outside, I am constantly cheered by greetings from the rising young lawyer, the scholarly rabbi, the successful teacher, the prosperous young matron buying clothes for her blooming children. "Don't you remember me? I used to belong to a Hull-House club." I once asked one of these young people, a man who held a good position on a Chicago daily, what special thing Hull-House had meant to him, and he promptly replied, "It was the first house I had ever been in where books and magazines just lay around as if there were plenty of them in the world. Don't you remember how much I used to read at that little round table at the back of the library? To have people regard reading as a reasonable occupation changed the whole aspect of life to me and I began to have confidence in what I could do."

Among the young men of the social clubs a large proportion of the Jewish ones at least obtain the advantages of a higher education. The parents make every sacrifice to help them through the high school after which the young men attend universities and professional schools, largely through their own efforts. From time to time they come back to us with their honors thick upon them; I remember one who returned with the prize in oratory from a contest between several western State universities, proudly testifying that he had obtained his confidence in our Henry Clay Club; another came back with a degree from Harvard University saying that he had made up his mind to go there the summer I read Royce's "Aspects of Modern Philosophy" with a group of young men who had challenged my scathing remark that Herbert Spencer was not the only man who had ventured a solution of the riddles of the universe. Occasionally one of these learned young folk does not like to be reminded that he once lived in our vicinity, but that happens rarely, and for the most part they are loyal to us in much the same spirit as they are to their own families and traditions. Sometimes they go further and tell us that the standards of tastes and code of manners which Hull-House has enabled them to form, have made a very great difference in their perceptions and estimates of the larger world as well as in their own reception there. Five out of one club of twenty-five young men who had held together for eleven years, entered the University of Chicago but although the rest of the Club called them the "intellectuals," the old friendships still held.

In addition to these rising young people given to debate and dramatics, and to the members of the public school alumni associations which meet in our rooms, there are hundreds of others who for years have come to Hull-House frankly in search of that pleasure and recreation which all young things crave and which those who have spent long hours in a factory or shop demand as a right. . . .

The social clubs form a basis of acquaintanceship for many people living in other parts of the city. Through friendly relations with individuals, which is perhaps the sanest method of approach, they are thus brought into contact, many of them for the first time, with the industrial and social problems challenging the moral resources of our contemporary life. During our twenty years hundreds of these non-residents have directed clubs and classes, and have increased the number of Chicago citizens who are conversant with adverse social conditions and conscious that only by the unceasing devotion of each, according to his strength, shall the compulsions and hardships, the stupidities and cruelties of life be overcome. The number of people thus informed is constantly increasing in all our American cities, and they may in time remove the reproach of social neglect and indifference which has so long rested upon the citizens of the new world. I recall the experience of an Englishman who, not only because he was a member of the Queen's Cabinet and bore a title, but also because he was an able statesman, was entertained with great enthusiasm by the leading citizens of Chicago. At a large dinner party he asked the lady sitting next to him what our tenement-house legislation was in regard to the cubic feet of air required for each occupant of a tenement bedroom; upon her disclaiming any knowledge of the subject, the inquiry was put to all the diners at the long table, all of whom showed surprise that they should be expected to possess this information. In telling me the incident afterward, the English guest said that such indifference could not have been found among the leading citizens of London, whose public spirit had been aroused to provide such housing conditions as should protect tenement dwellers at least from wanton loss of vitality and lowered industrial efficiency. When I met the same Englishman in London five years afterwards, he immediately asked me whether Chicago citizens were still so indifferent to the conditions of the poor that they took no interest in their proper housing. I was quick with that defense which an American is obliged to use so often in Europe, that our very democracy so long presupposed that each citizen could care for himself that we are slow to develop a sense of social obligation. He smiled at the familiar phrases and was still inclined to attribute our indifference to sheer ignorance of social conditions.

The entire social development of Hull-House is so unlike what I predicted twenty years ago, that I venture to quote from that ancient writing as an end to this chapter.

The social organism has broken down through large districts of our great cities. Many of the people living there are very poor, the majority of them without leisure or energy for anything but the gain of subsistence.

They live for the moment side by side, many of them without knowledge of each other, without fellowship, without local tradition or public spirit, without social organization of any kind. Practically nothing is done to remedy this. The people who might do it, who have the social tact and training, the large houses, and the traditions and customs of hospitality, live in other parts of the city. The club houses, libraries, galleries and semi-public conveniences for social life are also blocks away. We find workingmen organized into armies of producers because men of executive ability and business sagacity have found it to their interests thus to organize them. But these working men are not organized socially; although lodging in crowded tenement houses, they are living without a corresponding social contact. The chaos is as great as it would be were they working in huge factories without foreman or superintendent. Their ideas and resources are cramped, and the desire for higher social pleasure becomes extinct. They have no share in the traditions and social energy which make for progress. Too often their only place of meeting is a saloon, their only host a bartender; a local demagogue forms their public opinion. Men of ability and refinement, of social power and university cultivation, stay away from them. Personally, I believe the men who lose most are those who thus stay away. But the paradox is here: when cultivated people do stay away from a certain portion of the population, when all social advantages are persistently withheld, it may be for years, the result itself is pointed to as a reason and is used as an argument, for the continued withholding.

It is constantly said that because the masses have never had social advantages, they do not want them, that they are heavy and dull, and that it will take political or philanhropic machinery to change them. This divides a city into rich and poor; into the favored, who express their sense of the social obligation by gifts of money, and into the unfavored, who express it by clamoring for a "share"—both of them actuated by a vague sense of justice. This division of the city would be more justifiable, however, if the people who thus isolate themselves on certain streets and use their social ability for each other, gained enough thereby and added sufficient to the sum total of social progress to justify the withholding of the pleasures and results of that progress, from so many people who ought to have them. But they cannot accomplish this for the social spirit discharges itself in many forms, and no one form is adequate to its total expression.

# The Tenement House Problem

## *Robert De Forest* and *Lawrence Veiller*

*At the dead center of the urban reformer's consciousness stood the modern slum. No feature of American life in the new century more starkly silhouetted poverty against the hopeful backdrop of progress. In every city there festered the ramshackle houses with their motley mixture of tenants, the despairing and the indifferent, the foreigner and the country cousin. Chicago and the sociologist's Middletown alike were scarred with urban decay, but the multi-storied New York tenements exceeded every other slum in the sheer horror of their physical squalor, and none had been so continuously investigated or trenchantly described. In 1890 Jacob Riis, police reporter and writer, had published his widely influential* How the Other Half Lives. *Twelve years later he followed it with a sequel called* The Battle for the Slums *and he continued to pour out articles, reports, and lectures on the growing problem. Riding a crest of publicity and popular interest, a body of distinguished citizens and earnest social workers in 1895, headed by Richard Watson Gilder, the genteel editor of the* Century *magazine, had published a survey of slum conditions, and many of their recommendations became law.*

*No longer was it enough to probe and expose; urban social reform was becoming an elaborate network of commissions, legislative drafting, and the technical policing of a thousand stubborn details. The Gilder commission exerted only a minimal force on the New York tenements and the social conditions they embodied. In the work of translating the indignation of spare-time crusaders into a full-bodied statutory program, reformers came to believe with Abram Hewitt, liberal mayor of New York, that in social causes "everything takes ten years." It remained for Lawrence Veiller, a bearded, brisk young man with a brilliant mind and a sure instinct for political maneuver, to infuse the moral ardor of Gilder's generation with the hard-hitting professional competence necessary to make reform stick. When only eighteen he earned his B.A. from City College, where he discovered the writings of Ruskin and Carlyle, entered settlement work among the working poor, and studied building practices as an employee of the municipal government. In 1900 Veiller was only twenty-eight, but his prodigious career in the next ten years was to make him the father of modern housing reform in America. Outraged at the failure of a New York City Building Code Commission to disturb the dominant interests of the contractors and the landlords in the drafting of a new code, Veiller persuaded Robert De Forest, a philanthropist and chairman of a powerful charity organization, to sponsor a Tenement Housing Exhibition. It remained on view for several months and attracted ten thousand visitors. Among the shocked viewers of Veiller's cardboard model of the famous Canal Street slum (in which 2,781 residents shared 264 toilets and not a single bathtub) was Governor Theodore Roosevelt, who responded with characteristic force: "Tell me what you want and I will help you get it." With the Governor's help and some adroit political wire-pulling De Forest and his young colleague got what they wanted—a state-sponsored Tenement Housing Commission and the authority to investigate and recommend legislation safe from the obstructive tactics of Tammany Hall and the local housing interests. From the labors of De Forest and Veiller, who headed the Commission, there came a two-volume report, the principal section of which is presented here.*

*This remarkable document led in turn to the famous "New Law" of 1901 governing the erection and care of tenement houses in the state of New York, and a permanent Tenement Housing Department (De Forest and Veiller in charge) to carry out the provisions of the new law. In the subsequent abolition of the infamous "dumbbell" tenement houses and in the construction of model housing laws which governed the expansion of New York for the next generation and were later copied all over the United States, fewer crusaders of the progressive generation could show more conspicuous achievement in specific reforms than Robert De Forest and Lawrence Veiller. The technical proficiency of the report and the hard-boiled but compassionate realism of its authors, their awareness of the inescapable economic facts of the tenement coupled with their moral indignation against those who would exploit defenseless citizens, and above all the confidence that man's environment can yield to social control in the interests of human justice—all these attributes of the work which follows were characteristic of the reform spirit of the progressive era.*

Of all the great social problems of modern times incident to the growth of cities, none is claiming public attention in a greater degree than that of the housing of the working people. Mere housing, however, that is,

Robert W. De Forest and Lawrence Veiller, eds., *The Tenement House Problem* (New York: Macmillan, 1903), pp. 3-14, 18-21, 24-32, 38-40, 42-55, 412-417.

merely providing shelter, does not solve this problem. It only aggravates it by herding men and women together under conditions which inevitably tend to produce disease and crime. It is only by providing homes for the working people, that is, by providing for them not only shelter, but shelter of such a kind as to protect life and health and to make family life possible, free from surroundings which tend to immorality, that the evils of crowded city life can be mitigated and overcome. Nor does it concern only the working classes who are to be sheltered. It is of vital moment to all the inhabitants of every city, and particularly to those of every city governed by democratic rule. Homes are quite as much needed to make good citizens as to make good men. According as the working people are provided with better or poorer homes will the government, morals, and health of a city be better or worse.

In most cities the housing problem is the problem of the small house rather than of the large tenement. It is such in Philadelphia; it is such to a large extent in Buffalo. In New York, however, as in no other city in the country, it is the problem of the tenement house—the problem of the five, six, or even seven story building usually on a lot 25 feet in width and with as many as three or four families on each floor.

Nothing short of a personal inspection of the great tenement districts of New York can give any adequate realization of the importance of the questions involved—questions affecting, not only the health, morality, and welfare of the people living in those districts, but also having a most potent influence upon the political conditions of the whole city and of the entire State. A city which in the size of its population and number of its voters already includes about one-half of the inhabitants and voters of the State must necessarily exercise a powerful influence in State affairs. Of the 3,437,202 inhabitants of New York City, 2,372,079, or more than two-thirds, live in tenement houses, as these houses are defined by law. In Greater New York there are 82,652 of these buildings, of which 42,700 are located in Manhattan, 33,771 in the Borough of Brooklyn, 4365 in the Borough of the Bronx, 1398 in the Borough of Queens, and 418 in the Borough of Richmond.

The housing problem is not a new question. It began to claim attention in England and in this country in the early part of the nineteenth century, and as the growth of cities has developed has claimed attention more and more. So much effort has been expended in European cities to remedy the evils of bad housing that the Commission had hoped to find in such European cities useful suggestions and precedent. It has accordingly carefully investigated the housing conditions and tenement regulations of the large cities of Europe and of the leading cities of this country. This study has not been without valuable result in the direct line of inquiry; but it has demonstrated beyond question that it is in

New York that the most serious tenement house problem in the world is to be found, and the Commission finds that to the history of tenement house development and regulation in this city it must look for present conclusions and for the remedies for these evils.

Attention was first called to the subject here in 1834 by the City Inspector of the Board of Health at a time when the population of New York was about 270,000. The first Legislative Commission of inquiry was appointed in 1856. The Council of Hygiene of the Citizens' Association made its comprehensive report on this subject in 1865. The first tenement house law followed in 1867. The first practical illustration of improved methods of construction was made in Brooklyn in 1876 and did much to stimulate tenement house reform in 1877 and 1878. The second tenement house law was enacted in 1879. The second State Commission was appointed in 1884, and its recommendations led to important amendments of the law in 1887. The third State Commission was appointed in 1894, and as a result of its labors the tenement house law was amended and other desirable legislation was secured in the following year.

To the Commission of 1884 and to the Commission of 1894, as well as to the first Assembly Commission of 1856, and the many faithful workers who followed them, this Commission wishes to publicly state its obligations and to place itself only in the line of succession. The legislation which has followed the report of each Commission and the public sentiment which their action has aroused, has been in the main progressive; but too often the gain made at the time when public opinion has been centred on this subject has been lost when this interest has been diverted and the field left open for selfish interests to assert themselves. Some of the evils of fifty years ago, cellar dwellings and lack of sanitary arrangements, have been corrected in some degree; but the same evils which seemed most serious to the first Commission of 1856—lack of light and ventilation, insufficient protection against fire, surroundings so unclean and uncomfortable as to make home life almost impossible—are still the chief evils of the present day and have been intensified by the more recent types of tenements. Although additional legislation has been had upon these subjects at different intervals, it has not kept pace with the conditions sought to be remedied. In 1864 the tenement population of New York was 486,000 and the number of tenement houses 15,511. In 1900 the tenement population of the same city, now the Borough of Manhattan, was 1,585,000 and the number of tenement houses 42,700. With all the remedial legislation and regulation which has been put into operation since the enactment of the first tenement house law in 1867, the present type of tenement house—the six-story double-decker—occupying 75 per cent of a 25-foot lot, with four families on a floor, gives to its occupants less light and less ventilation, less fire protection and less comfortable surroundings, than the average tenement of fifty years ago, which was lower in height, occupied less lot space, and sheltered fewer people.

That there are great evils in our tenement house conditions, and that these evils should be remedied, is a general proposition universally accepted; but, like similar generalities, its acceptance leads nowhere unless particular evils are defined and particular remedies pointed out. The first question is, therefore, What are the particular evils to be remedied?

No one who is at all familiar personally with tenement house life in New York, no one who without personal familiarity reads the description of tenement house life from the point of view of the tenant and inspector contained in the special paper on this subject which forms part of this report, can fail to realize that the chief evil to be remedied is the tenement house itself.

Adequate light and air, perfect sanitation, even passable home environment, cannot be provided by the best tenement house which is commercially possible on Manhattan Island—that is, by the best tenement house which can be built with sufficient prospect of income to warrant its erection. Such a tenement house, even if only five stories high, occupying only 65 per cent of the lot and accommodating only three families on a floor, situated, as it either is at the outset or soon will be, among other buildings of the same or greater height, must necessarily lack, especially in its lower apartments, some of these desirable conditions. Ideal conditions in these particulars can only be attained when each family occupies its own separate house. The fewer families in each house and the larger air space around it, the nearer approach to this ideal.

Inquiry naturally directs itself, therefore, first to the question whether the inherent evils of the tenement house system can be remedied, and whether we can look forward at any near future to housing the working classes of New York in separate or smaller houses as the laboring men of many other cities are accommodated. The near realization of rapid transit and closer and quicker connection with the Boroughs of Brooklyn and Queens by bridge and tunnel would seem to make such a development possible.

Undoubtedly better transit facilities will enable some of the more ambitious and better paid tenement dwellers to provide themselves with separate homes in the outlying districts; but from the special inquiry made into this subject by the Commission, the results of which are summarized in its special report on small houses, it is evident that the bulk of the laboring classes will still continue to live in tenement houses.

A family which now pays from $12 to $18 a month for its apartment in a tenement house must be able to pay at least $20 a month for a separate house in the suburbs, a reason sufficient in itself to keep it in the tenement. Other influences—familiarity with tenement life, which, however distasteful to previous generations, has now perforce grown into a habit, the natural inclination of our large foreign population to group itself in neighborhoods on national lines, and other causes equally potent—all tend in the same direction.

Concluding, therefore, that the tenement house system must continue in New York, the question presents itself, What evils not inherent in the system admit of remedy? These are the practical questions before the Commission. The most serious evils may be grouped as follows:

(1) Insufficiency of light and air due to narrow courts or air shafts, undue height, and to the occupation by the building or by adjacent buildings of too great a proportion of lot area.

(2) Danger from fire.

(3) Lack of separate water-closet and washing facilities.

(4) Overcrowding.

(5) Foul cellars and courts, and other like evils, which may be classed as bad housekeeping.

Of the three first-named groups of evils, all are evils of construction which admit of remedy both in buildings hereafter constructed and those which already exist, if that remedy can wisely be applied.

In new buildings it would be possible to insure light and air by preventing the occupation of more than one-half the lot area, and by prescribing larger courts. It would be possible to make fireproof construction mandatory, and thus minimize all danger from fire. In old buildings it would be possible to cut in courts or air shafts so that every living or sleeping room should have a window opening to the outer air, and it would be possible to substitute fireproof stairs for the wooden stairs now used in these buildings. All these changes would be desirable. The immediate effect, however, of seeking to enforce them at the present time, in the case of new tenements, would probably be to prevent their erection by making them commercially too costly; and as respects the old tenements, to vacate many of them for living purposes, because the cost of such alterations would be more than would be justified by any probable revenue that could be expected from them after the changes had been made.

Tenement house reform would not be practical which went so far as to put a stop to building new tenement houses. Nor would it be practical if it compelled such extensive changes in old tenements that owners would turn them to other uses.

The result in both cases would be to decrease the supply of tenement accommodation, and to either force more people into this diminished space, which would mean more overcrowding, or to force some people out, in which case competition would raise rents.

Reform of such a kind would harm most the very persons it sought to aid.

The only difference of opinion between the members of the Commission has been, not as to what conditions were desirable, but as to how far these conditions could be attained without producing such consequences; that is, how far present evils could be prevented in new buildings without increasing their cost to such an extent as to practically prevent their erection, and how far they could be remedied in old buildings without such an expense as to be practically prohibitory, and to prevent their continuing to be occupied for living purposes.

For instance, there is not a member of the Commission who would not gladly limit the height of non-fireproof tenements to four stories, if it were practicable so to do, and, indeed, one leading architect has suggested that such limitation should be placed at three stories.

### THE TYPICAL NEW YORK TENEMENT

Some knowledge of the prevailing kind of New York tenement house must necessarily precede any consideration of its evils and their remedies. It is known as the "double-decker," "dumb-bell" tenement, a type which New York has the unenviable distinction of having invented. It is a type unknown to any other city in America or Europe.

Although the housing problem is one of the leading political questions of the day in England, the conditions which exist there are ideal compared to the conditions in New York. The tall tenement house, accommodating as many as 100 to 150 persons in one building, extending up six or seven stories into the air, with dark, unventilated rooms, is unknown in London or in any other city of Great Britain. It was first constructed in New York about the year 1879, and with slight modifications has been practically the sole type of building erected since, and is the type of the present day. It is a building usually five or six or even seven stories high, about 25 feet wide, and built upon a lot of land of the same width and about 100 feet deep. The building as a rule extends back 90 feet, leaving the small space of ten feet unoccupied at the rear, so that the back rooms may obtain some light and air. This space has continued to be left open only because the law has compelled it. Upon the entrance floor there are generally two stores, one on each side of the building, and these sometimes have two or three living rooms back of them. In the centre is the entrance hallway, a long corridor less than 3 feet wide and extending back 60 feet in length. This hallway is nearly always totally dark, receiving no light except that from the street door and a faint light that comes from the small windows opening upon the stairs, which are placed at one side of the hallway. Each floor above is generally divided into four sets of apartments, there being seven rooms on each side of the hall, extending back from the street to the rear of the building. The front apartments generally consist of four rooms each and the rear apartments of three rooms, making altogether fourteen upon each floor, or in a seven-story house eighty-four rooms exclusive of the stores and rooms back of them. Of these fourteen rooms on each floor, only four receive direct light and air from the street or from the small yard at the back of the building. Generally, along each side of the building is what is termed an "air shaft," being an indentation of the wall to a depth of about 28 inches, and extending in length for a space of from 50 to 60 feet. This shaft is entirely enclosed on four sides, and is, of course, the full height of the building, often from 60 to 72 feet high. The ostensible purpose of the shaft is to provide light and air to the five rooms on each side of the house which get no direct light and air from the street or yard; but as the shafts are narrow and high, being enclosed on all four sides, and without any intake of air at the bottom, these rooms obtain, instead of fresh air and sunshine, foul air and semi-darkness. Indeed it is questionable whether the rooms would not be more habitable and more sanitary with no shaft at all, depending for their light and air solely upon the front and back rooms into which they open; for each family, besides having the foul air from its own rooms to breathe, is compelled to breathe the emanations from the rooms of some eleven other families; nor is this all, these shafts act as conveyors of noise, odors, and disease, and when fire breaks out serve as inflammable flues, often rendering it impossible to save the buildings from destruction.

A family living in such a building pays for four rooms of this kind a rent of from $12 to $18 a month. Of these four rooms only two are large enough to be deserving of the name of rooms. The front one is generally about 10 feet 6 inches wide by 11 feet 3 inches long; this the family use as a parlor, and often at night, when the small bedrooms opening upon the air shaft are so close and ill-ventilated that sleep is impossible, mattresses are dragged upon the floor of the parlor, and there the family sleep, all together in one room. In summer the small bedrooms are so hot and stifling that a large part of the tenement house population sleep on the roofs, the sidewalks, and the fire-escapes. The other room, the kitchen, is generally the same size as the parlor upon which it opens, and receives all its light and air from the "air shaft," or such a supply as may come to it from the front room. Behind these two rooms are the bedrooms, so called, which are hardly more than closets, being each about 7 feet wide and 8 feet 6 inches long, hardly large enough to contain a bed. These rooms get no light and air whatsoever, except that which comes from the "air shaft," and except on the highest stories are generally almost totally dark. Upon the opposite side of the public hall is an apartment containing four exactly similar rooms, and at the rear of the building there are, instead of four rooms on each side of the hallway, but three, one of the bedrooms being dispensed with. For these three rooms in the rear the rent is generally throughout the city from $10 to $15 a month. In the public hallway, opposite the stairs, there are provided two water-closets, each water-closet being used in common by two families and being lighted and ventilated by the "air shaft," which also lights and ventilates all the bedrooms. In the newer buildings there is frequently provided, in the hallway between the two closets, a dumb-waiter for the use of the tenants.

It is not to be wondered at, therefore, that with such a kind of tenement house repeated all over the different parts of this city, and forming practically the only kind of habitation for the great mass of the people, the tenement house system has become fraught with so much danger to the welfare of the community. The effect upon the city population of the form of congregated living found in our tenement houses is to be seen, not only in its results upon the health of the people, but upon their moral and social condition as well. The public mind is just now especially aroused over the manifestation of one special form of vice in tenement districts. It is not to be wondered at that vice in various forms should manifest itself in the tenements; the wonder is that there is not more vice in such districts. The tenement districts of New York are places in which thousands of people are living in the smallest space in which it is possible for human beings to exist—crowded together in dark, ill-ventilated rooms, in many of which the sunlight never enters and in most of which fresh air is unknown. They are centres of disease, poverty, vice, and crime, where it is a marvel, not that some children grow up to be thieves, drunkards, and prostitutes, but that so many should ever grow up to be decent and self-respecting. All the conditions which surround childhood, youth, and womanhood in New York's crowded tenement quarters make for unrighteousness. They also make for disease. There is hardly a tenement house in which there has not been at least one case of pulmonary tuberculosis within the last five years, and in some houses there have been as great a number as twenty-two different cases of this terrible disease. From the tenements there comes a stream of sick, helpless people to our hospitals and dispensaries, few of whom are able to afford the luxury of a private physician, and some houses are in such bad sanitary condition that few people can be seriously ill in them and get well; from them also comes a host of paupers and charity seekers. The most terrible of all the features of tenement house life in New York, however, is the indiscriminate herding of all kinds of people in close contact, the fact, that, mingled with the drunken, the dissolute, the improvident, the diseased, dwell the great mass of the respectable working-men of the city with their families.

## THE LINE OF REMEDIAL ACTION

That many of the evils of such a tenement house system can be remedied by legislation there is no doubt. They have arisen largely because of the absence of wise, restrictive legislation. That it is the duty of the State to remedy these evils can also not be doubted, and the State has recognized this duty repeatedly for the past forty years. . . .

The tenement house problem in New York is a threefold one, and its solution lies along three definite lines of action:

FIRST. To provide proper types of new tenement houses for the future by means of adequate restrictive legislation, and to forbid the erection of any others.

SECOND. To remedy the errors of past years by altering and improving old tenement houses so as to make them fit for human habitation.

THIRD. To maintain present and future tenement houses in sanitary condition by adequate supervision.

The present tenement laws are a series of amendments to existing statutes, and since the passage of the first tenement house act have never been codified. The result has been that the laws contain many conflicting sections and many serious inconsistencies, and are in their requirements often illogical, with the still further defect that they are imperfectly arranged and often couched in language so involved that it is almost impossible for the ordinary builder or architect to understand them without calling in the services of a lawyer. The Commission, therefore, has prepared a complete code of tenement house laws, and has sought to so arrange and express their various provisions as to make the law plain to all persons. In so doing it has endeavored, so far as possible, to retain the substance of past legislation.

As has been stated, the greatest evil of the present day is the lack of light and air, and it is in the new type of building which is being erected at the present time that this evil is especially felt. As a result of this lack of light and air, we find that the dread disease of pulmonary tuberculosis has become practically epidemic in this city. The testimony taken before the Tenement House Commission at its public hearings, in which leading physicians and specialists upon this subject testified, shows that there are over eight thousand deaths a year in New York City due to this disease alone; that there are at least twenty thousand cases of well-developed and recognized pulmonary tuberculosis in the city, and in addition a large number of obscure or incipient cases. The connection between this disease and the character of the tenement houses in which the poor people live is of the very closest.

The work of the Committee of 1865 was due in large part to the epidemics of typhus fever, smallpox, and similar diseases existing at that time, caused largely by the unsanitary condition of the tenement houses. The chief problem then was to do away with filth and provide tenement houses with proper sanitary conveniences. To-day the problem is different. There are no longer epidemics of typhus and typhoid fever in this city, although recent developments have shown how easy it is for a disease like smallpox to find a foothold in the tenements, despite the watchful measures of the Board of Health. There exists at the present time, however, a much more serious epidemic caused by the peculiar evils of the tenement houses at the present time—pulmonary tuberculosis.

It was the testimony of all the physicians who testified before the Tenement House Commission that the conditions in the tenement houses were directly responsible for the tremendous extent and spread of this contagious disease, and that the first and most important step to be taken to check it was the improvement of the tenement house, especially with regard to light and air.

### THE AIR SHAFT

Bearing these facts in mind, it becomes evident that the present type of "air shaft" must be done away with in all future tenement houses. Practically all the witnesses who testified before the Commission united in the opinion that the "air shaft" was the most serious evil of the present tenement house. This testimony came from people who live in tenement houses, from settlement and charity workers living in tenement districts, from physicians, from tenement house owners, and from every one who has had any knowledge or experience of this subject. One of the witnesses said that the "air shaft" should not be called an air shaft, but should be called "a foul air shaft," and we find that it has even been designated as "a culture tube on a gigantic scale." The objections to the "air shaft" are that, owing to its narrowness and height, it cannot possibly afford light to the rooms, but only semi-darkness; that, owing to the same narrowness and height, and also to the fact that it is generally enclosed on four sides, it is impossible for it to furnish fresh air to the rooms, but instead it simply becomes a stagnant well of foul air emptied from each one of the rooms opening upon it, which sometimes are as many as sixty. Many persons testified that the air from these shafts was so foul and the odors so vile that they had to close the windows opening into them, and in some cases the windows were permanently nailed up for this reason. Moreover, the tenants often use the air shaft as a receptacle for garbage and all sorts of refuse and indescribable filth thrown out of the windows, and this mass of filth is often allowed to remain, rotting at the bottom of the shaft for weeks without being cleaned out.

From other points of view than that of light and air the air shaft stands condemned. It serves as a conveyor of smells and noise and is one of the greatest elements in destroying privacy in the tenement house. Through it one hears the sounds that occur in the rooms of every other family in the building, and often in these narrow shafts the windows of one apartment look directly into the windows of another apartment not more than 5 feet away. Privacy under such conditions is not only difficult, but impossible. The attention of the Commission has been called to the fact that these conditions have led in numerous cases to grave immorality.

From the point of view of danger from fire the "air shaft" is equally objectionable. The fire department for years has protested against it as one of the most serious evils with which it has to contend in fighting tenement house fires. From the investigation of the way in which fire spreads through tenement houses made by this Commission, embracing all tenement house fires occurring during the past two years and a half in this city, we find that 26 per cent, or over one-fourth, of all the fires spread by means of the "air shaft." It is not at all surprising that this should be the case, because such a shaft in case of fire must necessarily become nothing more than a tremendous flue.

The Commission therefore recommends that such narrow "air shafts" be absolutely prohibited in all future tenement houses, and that proper courts sufficiently large to secure adequate light and ventilation to all rooms be required. . . .

## DARK HALLWAYS

The evils of the dark, unventilated hallways have been recognized ever since the first effort was made to remedy tenement house conditions; and the first law in regard to tenement houses sought to remedy these evils by providing that the halls on each floor should open directly to the external air with suitable windows, and should have no room or other obstruction at the end. A proviso was added, however, giving discretionary power to the Board of Health to permit other means of lighting and ventilating these halls. This provision of the law has been reënacted in every amendment of the law since 1867. It has practically never been enforced. The effect of the dark, unventilated hallway upon health is serious. Any one who has had much experience in tenement houses knows that the majority of the hallways are pitch-black; that a person enters from the street, gropes his way along the wall, and stumbles up the stairs as best he can; that, being unventilated, the halls retain the odors that have come from the different apartments, odors of cooking as well as accumulated odors of every kind. Moreover, being dark, the tenants do not care whether the halls are clean or not, as no one can see the dirt, and they at a very early date become very filthy. More serious, even, than the evils due to dirt and the lack of ventilation are the moral evils of these places.

The following part of a letter from the vicar of St. Augustine's Chapel, which has been signed by twelve other clergymen who at different times have worked at this chapel, expresses better than can be done in any other way the dangers of the dark hallway:

For nearly thirty years I have been vicar of this church, which is situated in almost the centre of the East Side tenement district of New York City.

From confidential communications that have been made to me by the young women themselves, I know that numbers of respectable girls have been seduced at the very thresholds of their homes. A party, or the theatre, or a ball, and a late supper with wine, leading to improper liberties in the lonely streets on the way home, then the dark and at that time lifeless halls and stairways of the tenement, and the sin is done, the apartment door alone hiding the erring daughter from the sleeping mother. Whatever the girl's wishes may be, she can do nothing—shame prevents her from crying out then and there, and arousing the whole house.

The fact is, dark halls and staircases are destructive to morality, since they give constant opportunities and furnish most plausible excuses for personal familiarities of the worst kind between the sexes.

The reports of previous Commissions point conclusively to the same facts, yet, notwithstanding this, practically nothing has been done to remedy these evils. The Tenement House Commission of 1894, thoroughly aware of this evil, sought to remedy it, and provided, in the law which was enacted as a result of their recommendations, that in every hallway that was not light the owner should keep a light burning upon each floor from sunrise to ten o'clock at night. This law, however, has become a dead letter, and the Board of Health makes practically no attempt to enforce this provision. This Commission has sought, therefore, to devise some way by which such halls can be kept lighted. It is obvious that a law requiring the light to be kept burning is very difficult of enforcement, because when the inspector's back is turned the light will be turned out. The Commission has sought, therefore, to substitute for this provision of the law a provision which when once enforced will stay enforced. It recommends, therefore, that wherever a tenement house hallway is now dark the wooden panels in the doors shall be removed and glass panels substituted, or if this be not done that a proper window be placed at the end of the hall leading to the outer air. Either one of these things will greatly remedy the existing conditions.

These requirements will apply to the tenement houses that are already constructed. In regard to the new buildings to be erected in the future, the Commission has provided that every public hallway shall have a window opening to the outer air so that such hallways shall be light, and the evils that have existed in former tenement houses may not be repeated in the new.

The Commission has also recommended that a light shall be kept burning in the public hallways of all tenement houses upon the entrance floor, and also upon the second floor above, every night from sunset to sunrise throughout the year, and that upon all other floors such a light shall be kept burning from sunset until ten o'clock at night. This requirement has been urged upon the Commission with practical unanimity, not only from the point of view of morality, but also for the purpose of preventing fires. The Fire Department has been especially desirous that such a law should be enacted.

FIRE PROTECTION

The Commission has given most serious attention to the subject of danger from fires in tenement houses. There has been a very strong feeling on the part of a certain element in the community demanding that all future tenement houses shall be constructed fireproof throughout. The Commission, however, after very carefully weighing this subject and after having estimates made as to the additional cost of such fireproof construction, finds that to make it compulsory at the present time will place too heavy a burden upon the owners of tenement houses and also upon tenement house dwellers. That if such a method of construction were made compulsory, rents in tenement houses—already high—would be raised to such a point that tenement house dwellers would seriously suffer. The Commission has therefore sought to secure every safeguard possible in respect to fire without going to the extreme measure of making fireproof tenements compulsory. It has limited the height of future non-fireproof tenement houses to five stories, except in the case of a building having a width of 40 feet or more, in such cases permitting the buildings to be erected to a height of six stories or 67 feet. The laws of this State in 1896 limited the height of all non-fireproof buildings to 70 feet, which does not vary much from this requirement. The Commission has come to these conclusions in regard to the height of non-fireproof tenement houses only after the most serious consideration and discussion of all the questions involved. It is the one point about which there has been an earnest difference of opinion between the members of the Commission, a considerable part of the Commission wishing to go farther in restricting the height of non-fireproof tenement houses to five stories under all circumstances, and permitting no non-fireproof tenement house to exceed this height. The majority of the Commission, however, having in mind the practical and commercial considerations involved, did not see their way clear to making such recommendations at the present time. They find that while the greater part of the tenement houses in this city are

five stories high, and that only 3 per cent of all these buildings are six
stories high, yet the tenement houses being erected at the present time
are permitted under certain conditions to be even as high as seven stories
and basement without the building being made fireproof, and also that
about one-half the new tenement houses erected during the past year
have been over five stories in height. . . .

[The report continues with a discussion of tenement courtyards, fire
escapes, cellars, and the proportion of tenement space to the lot
occupied.]

### SEPARATE WATER-CLOSET ACCOMMODATIONS

In regard to the subject of water-closet accommodations, the Commission recommends that in every tenement house erected in future a
separate water-closet shall be provided for each family within the apartments. This, the Commission believes, is required by common decency
and morals, and no one who has made any recommendation to them
has not agreed with this view. As a matter of fact, the Commission finds
that it is becoming the practice for builders to provide separate water-
closet accommodations in new tenement houses from motives of self-
interest, although the present law only requires one water-closet for
every two families. In 61 per cent of the new tenement houses examined,
it was found that a private water-closet was provided for each family.

### GENERAL SANITARY PROVISIONS

In regard to the subject of plumbing, the Commission finds that on
the whole the present plumbing law as embodied in the Building Code
is adequate if properly enforced. It would add, however, one or two
additional recommendations: That the water-closet compartments shall
be provided with proper means of lighting the same at night, and that
all plumbing pipes, wherever possible, be exposed, or that, if such pipes
are covered, they shall be arranged in such a way that access can be
had to them without cutting open the floors or partitions; also that where
they pass through floors or through the partitions the space shall be made
air-tight with some non-combustible material, so as to prevent the spread
of fire from floor to floor, and also to prevent the passage of air from
one room to another. This will also be beneficial in checking the spread
of contagious disease.

The Commission also recommends that in existing tenement houses
the following requirements of the present law be continued in force:
That such houses be provided with a proper and adequate water supply;
that they shall be kept at all times in a clean condition; that proper
receptacles shall be provided at all times for ashes, garbage, refuse, etc.;

that there shall be a janitor or housekeeper for every tenement house where there are eight families or more.

The Commission also recommends that at the bottom of every shaft or court there shall be a door so as to permit these shafts to be cleaned out, it having developed that such shafts are often covered at the bottom with rubbish which it is almost impossible to remove, owing to the fact that there is no means of access to the shaft.

The Commission has carefully considered the provisions of the present law in regard to the use of wall paper in tenement houses, and has recommended that no change be made in that portion of the law which requires that where any wall paper is placed upon a wall or ceiling the existing wall paper shall be removed and the wall or ceiling shall be thoroughly cleansed. The other provision, however, of the present law upon this subject, that the walls and ceilings of every tenement house shall be whitewashed once a year, the Commission has not found itself able to recommend. While it appreciates the sanitary advantages of such a requirement in some cases, it is manifestly unfair to apply this law to the better grade of apartment houses and flats. Such an application of it would cause not only hardship, but great discomfort, and would be deemed by the tenants an unwarrantable interference with their natural rights and liberties. The Commission has, therefore, recommended that this portion of the law be repealed. It has, however, required that the walls and ceilings of the cellars shall be whitewashed once a year; this the Commission considers essential. It has also recommended further that the walls of all air shafts shall either be whitewashed at least once in three years or shall be painted a light color at least once every five years.

The above statement summarizes the more important recommendations of the Commission in regard to tenement houses to be erected in the future.

NON-ENFORCEMENT OF THE LAWS IN EXISTING TENEMENT HOUSES

In regard to the existing tenement houses, the Commission is of opinion that the most serious evils are due to the lack of proper, adequate sanitary supervision. When it is borne in mind that there are in Greater New York 82,652 tenement houses, containing a population of 2,372,079 persons, and that the entire corps of sanitary inspectors of the Department of Health devoting their time to this work is sixty-one inspectors for the entire city, including the Bronx, Brooklyn, and the other boroughs, as well as Manhattan, it is not to be wondered at that grave evils exist, or that the sanitary condition of the tenements is one which calls for the most effective remedies. It is obviously a physical impossibility for so small a corps of men to make the slightest pretence of adequately inspecting such buildings. The law calls for a semiannual inspection of all tenement houses. This has developed practically into a tenement house census twice a year, and the entire time of the Sanitary Squad of policemen detailed by the Police Department to secure the enforcement of the tenement house laws is taken up with this work. The officials of the Department of Health stated in their testimony before the Commission, that, with the exception of the census referred to, it had become the practice in the Health Department to inspect tenement houses only upon complaint, and that the entire time of the inspectors was taken up in investigating such complaints and seeing that they were remedied, and that it was absolutely impossible for the department to make a thorough inspection of the tenement houses on its own initiative. Until there is an adequate corps of sanitary inspectors to inspect the lower grade of tenement houses thoroughly at least once a month, there is little hope that the evils of the existing tenement houses will be remedied. The value of such an inspection cannot be overestimated. The report of the inspector employed by the Commission shows that his mere presence in buildings, without giving any orders or without any legal proceedings being brought, was of the most beneficial effect, and that it had a salutary moral influence in remedying bad conditions. If this is so in the case of one man attempting to use no authority, it is not difficult to conceive what results could be accomplished if a systematic, thorough, and frequent inspection of the tenements were made.

The Commission finds, however, that the Department of Health is charged with many other duties besides the duty of tenement house inspection. It has, for instance, the management of four hospitals; the recording of death, birth, and marriage statistics for the entire city; the prevention of the spread of contagious and infectious diseases; the disinfecting of all buildings; the inspection of mercantile establishments, and the granting of permits to school children to work; milk inspection, meat, fish, fruit, and food inspection; the regulation of offensive trades; the prohibition of smoke nuisances; the management of bacteriological laboratories; the production of antitoxin; the medical inspection of schools and school children; the analysis of the water supply; the removal of dead animals from the streets; the inspection of the elevated railroad, etc., etc. It is apparent that, with all these other duties to perform, the work of the supervision and sanitary maintenance of 82,000 tenement houses is apt to be somewhat neglected.

The report of every previous Tenement House Commission has called attention to the fact that the Department of Health has not had a sufficient number of inspectors to properly perform its duties, and as a consequence, the number of such inspectors has been from time to time slightly increased. This, however, has failed to meet the situation.

It is to be noted also that there is no special bureau of the Health Department for the supervision of the tenement houses, nor is there any official or employee of this department devoting his entire time to such work, but that the inspectors are given districts throughout the city and are required to inspect all buildings within these districts. The fact that the department no longer makes inspections on its own initiative, but does most of its work on complaint of citizens, shows that a radical change is imperative. It should not be necessary for any considerable number of such complaints to be filed. There should be systematic, regular, thorough, and adequate inspection of all the tenement houses in this city at all times. If such inspection were carried on, the greater part of the tenement house evils would be remedied without the necessity for the filing of complaints, or for taking legal proceedings, or for the issuance of the numerous "orders" that are now issued by the Department of Health. To any one of experience in sanitary affairs, it is obvious that if such inspection is properly carried out the sanitary evils will very greatly diminish. It has been the history of Glasgow and all other well-administered municipalities. In Glasgow there are 150 sanitary inspectors and in London about 230. While the Commission appreciates that so large a force means additional outlay by the city, it believes that any sum of money likely to be spent for this work would be a paying investment both to the city and the State. . . .

### FINANCIAL SIDE OF THE TENEMENT HOUSE PROBLEM

Probably no subject has been more carefully reviewed by the Commission than the practicability of the legislation proposed, and its effect on property interests. In the many discussions had by the Commission, it is safe to say that the point of view of the tenement house owner has been considered quite as much as the point of view of the tenant, and properly so, for though the interests of landlord and tenant, superficially considered, may seem to be divergent, in the ultimate analysis they are identical. The Commission presents with this report two special papers upon this subject, one dealing with the question of rentals and returns upon tenement house property, both of the ordinary kind and also of improved tenements; the other treating the phases of the problem involved in the ordinary methods of building tenement houses upon building loans as a speculation.

The report of the first Tenement House Commission of 1856 and other early reports on this subject are replete with accusations against the greed of landlords, and the profits on tenement house property are stated in these reports at figures which now seem almost fabulous. Undoubtedly, at those times the demand for tenement house accommodation was in excess of the supply, partly incidental to the extraordinary increase of immigration. At the present time the amount of accommodation is fairly in advance of the demand, and indeed the investigations of the Commission show that over 9 per cent of the room accommodation in tenement houses is vacant. So many varying circumstances affect the rental of the new tenement house that it is very difficult to determine the average net returns now received from such investments. The new house, which either needs or has but small expenditure for repairs, and is under efficient management, may produce a large net income, while the same house built a few years ago in which many repairs have already become necessary and which has inefficient management, may produce but little. The figures in every case would be misleading from the point of view of permanent investment.

Dr. Elgin R. L. Gould, in the special report on this subject, which follows this general report, concludes that the average net return on the ordinary class of tenements now being erected, without any mortgage placed upon the property, is 5.81 per cent, and that when a mortgage is placed upon the property, for about 60 per cent of its entire cost, that the average net profit on such property is 7.03 per cent.

The Commission finds that substantial profits are realized in speculative operations, not only by the building loan operator, but also by the speculative builder, before the tenement house has been purchased by the ultimate investor, and that this system of middlemen tends, as in other industries, to increase the cost to the consumer, who is in this case the tenant. The Commission has not thought it practicable to recommend any specific legislation upon this subject, but is of the opinion that the plan of granting certificates to the owners of new tenement houses will tend to remedy some abuses in construction which now exist. The Commission would also call attention to the evils resulting from the inferior grade of workmanship employed in many tenement houses. In the ordinary tenement house the Commission finds that the work is generally of a low grade, and that such property is apt to deteriorate in a very short time. The result is not only a loss to the investor, but a loss to the tenement dweller. It means discomfort, and also means that he must pay higher rents to meet the increasing bills for repairs which each year grow greater.

This report has so far been devoted to the main evils of tenement houses due to faulty construction and lack of proper supervision. There are, however, other phases of the tenement house problem which are of vital moment to the welfare of the community and which deserve serious consideration. For some of these we have deemed it our duty to recommend legislation. In regard to others, while we appreciate the necessity for a change in the existing conditions, and mention them in this report, we have not deemed it within our duties to make specific recommendations.

There are also many suggestions which have been carefully considered by the Commission, among which are several which call for special mention. . . .

## TENEMENT HOUSE LIMITS

Among the suggestions which have been made to the Commission was one that a law should be passed establishing tenement house limits, similar to the present fire limits of the city, so that after a certain date no tenement house should be allowed to be built outside of such limits. This recommendation was made with the purpose of safeguarding the outlying sections of the city from the evils that exist in the lower portions.

The enactment of such a law, however, involves many varied questions, to which the Commission has not been able to give sufficient consideration to warrant it at this time in making any recommendations.

## MUNICIPAL TENEMENTS

Still another suggestion was that New York, following in this respect the example of some cities in Great Britain, should build model tenements for its people at public expense. The Commission is not prepared to recommend such an enlargement of municipal functions. No good purpose could be thereby served. At most such public buildings would better the living conditions of a favored few, who had sufficient influence to secure apartments in them, and even these would better their living conditions at the sacrifice of self-dependence. If such model tenements are intended to set an example and to demonstrate what can be done to provide better housing conditions, they will furnish no better demonstration than private benevolence has furnished in the past and can be relied upon to furnish in the future. If they are intended to house the working people, they can at most house only a very small proportion, and by so housing this small proportion they will prevent the greater number from being effectively housed by other means, for private enterprise will not compete with municipal bounty, and when cities begin to build tenements other tenement building will cease. No large city can provide homes for all its working people. So vast a project could not be seriously contemplated. If by providing for a few it prevented provision for the many, the average condition of the working classes would be worse than before the city began to build. Nor would there be any limit to the scope of municipal building operations if once they were begun. If cities, however, are to become landlords at all, where should the wage line be drawn between those for whom they should and those for whom they should not provide? Where, in practice, would the line be drawn in American cities where democracy reigns supreme, and the limit of public bounty would be ulti-mately fixed by popular vote? Even if municipal building did not stop private enterprise, and the municipal buildings were managed without favoritism or those evils which too often attend government ownership, other objections would still exist. Tenement house management is largely a question of good housekeeping and prompt business method, involving wide discretion and full power. The average city official would not be likely to be a good housekeeper; nor, even if he were able to forget that he owed his place in some degree at least to those whom he was aiding his city to house, could he use prompt business methods and exercise individual discretion under the necessarily cumbrous and mechanical methods of government system. The municipal tenement would inevitably be forced to the wall in competition with similar buildings under private ownership. Its rooms would be frequently vacant or its rents would be lowered to hold tenants, and it would become, more than before, an in-creasing burden to the taxpayer, without any corresponding good to the working classes. Moreover, such buildings would introduce a new ele-ment into public service, already sufficiently complex, and add so many more to the already large number of government servants. If tenanted with a view to votes, they might be so located and utilized by the political party in power as to perpetuate its control.

## TAX EXEMPTION FOR MODEL TENEMENTS

Another suggestion was that the building of model tenments which conformed to certain specified requirements of plan should be encour-aged by making them, wholly or partly, exempt from taxation, either per-petually or for a term of years. If municipal aid is to be extended at all to tenement house building, this would be more effective and open to less objection than any other method. It would be more effective because it would probably insure the building of more tenements than could be erected under municipal ownership. It would be less objectionable because this increased accommodation for the working classes could be thus ob-tained at less expense to the city. However large a decrease in the tax revenue of the city would be thereby effected, it would undoubtedly be less than the increased tax burden which would follow municipal building and municipal management of such buildings. The Commission, however, is not ready to recommend any such change in the present system of taxation. It would be a distant departure from our present public policy, which taxes alike all real estate used for business or private purposes. It would diminish tax revenue. It would change property values by arti-ficially decreasing the value of the improved tenement completed this year, and artificially increasing the value of the same tenement built next year. It would immediately increase the income of the property owners whose new tenements were exempted from tax burdens, and would only remotely decrease the rents of the wage-earners, in whose interests it was adopted, for until the increase in tenement accommodation became very marked it is not likely that rent rates would be diminished. It would involve drawing some line between tenements for the poorer classes which were to be encouraged by exemption, and other tenements not intended to be so exempt. Drawing such a line would be extremely difficult, however it were to be drawn, whether on the number of rooms to the apartment, or the size of the rooms, or otherwise. The exemption would be likely to be abused, and be claimed by those who were not intended to share in these benefits.

It seems to us proper, however, to point out that the construction of improved dwellings for the laboring classes on any large scale is far more likely to depend on the efforts of corporations than of individuals, and that the present statutes regarding taxation restrain the efforts of corporations in this direction. Individual investors may erect tenement houses and pay simply the tax on real estate, but corporations making precisely the same investment must pay the annual tax on their capital stock in addition to the same tax on the real estate. The experience of London and many other large cities besides New York proves that the construction of improved dwellings for working people on any such scale as may respond in fair degree to the needs of a great city is certain to depend mostly on the efforts of corporations, because individuals shrink from undertakings which involve a large expenditure of money, a large responsibility for administration, and the necessity of a close supervision with the prospect of only a modest return on the investment.

The State would lose nothing by relieving the capital stock of companies whose sole object is to erect improved dwellings from annual taxation on their stock, because all such corporations can, and we believe do now, avoid the extra taxation by incurring mortgage indebtedness; but this proceeding repels many conservative philanthropic investors. Thus, while the State gains nothing, the movement for the construction of improved dwellings for working people is retarded under the present laws. Such legislation as would place corporations whose sole investment is in real estate on the same basis as individual property owners by relieving them from annual taxation on their stock, would be equitable and would stimulate the construction of improved dwellings for the laboring classes.

This question, however, relates rather to the general policy of the State respecting taxation than to the special sphere of this Commission.

HOW THE CITY CAN AND SHOULD AID TENEMENT HOUSE DWELLERS

There are expenditures clearly within the sphere of municipal action which the city can and should make for the benefit of its tenement house population.

The streets in tenement districts should be paved with asphalt or other smooth pavement so that they can be more readily kept clean. This is especially desirable in the crowded tenement parts of the city, where the street is constantly used by so large a part of the population, and particularly by the children. It is far more important there than in other residential districts. Gratifying progress in this direction has been made in the tenement house quarters of New York. These streets should be kept clean, and garbage and ashes should be promptly removed. Prompt and complete performance of these municipal duties is nowhere more important than among the tenements. The standard of street cleaning has been notably raised within recent years.

The streets should be well lighted. In this direction, too, there has been improvement. There should be more public conveniences and lavatories. There should be more small parks and playgrounds. There should be public bathing facilities.

Within these spheres there is ample scope for municipal activity and expenditure, and it is within these spheres that such activity and expenditure can accomplish the greatest good for the greatest number . . .

### PROSTITUTION IN THE TENEMENT HOUSES

In the course of its investigations the Commission has become painfully aware of one evil from which it believes tenement house dwellers should be protected, and protected as they are not under existing conditions and existing laws. That evil is the introduction of the practice of prostitution into reputable tenement houses. The forcible and earnest protest of one of our best known moral and religious leaders has properly awakened all classes of society to the horrors of this situation. But the determination of the Commission to investigate the evil dated back to the very beginning of the Commission's work, many months prior to the publication of that protest and to the recent anti-vice crusade.

The steady growth of vice in the tenement houses has come under the personal observation of members of the Commission. Its special investigations, reënforced by the unanimous testimony of many witnesses, including the tenement house dwellers, labor representatives, and philanthropic workers, lead it to most earnestly protest against such conditions.

It appears that prostitution has spread greatly among the tenement houses. This condition has recently grown worse, nor does it appear that there has been sufficient effort on the part of the public authorities to suppress it. Evidence has been submitted that the protests of the dwellers in the tenement houses immediately affected, as well as those of their neighbors, have been alike unheeded, and in spite of the best efforts of careful parents, the very house in which a family has dwelt, selected because it was thought to be free from this curse, has furnished the temptation against which parental care and anxiety have been in vain. The dangers of this situation to those of tender age in the tenement houses is alarming. We have ascertained that when dissolute women enter a tenement house their first effort is to make friends with the children. Children have been lured into their rooms, where they have beheld sights from which they should be protected. Frequently these women engage one family in the tenement to do their laundry work, another to do their cooking, and still further financial arrangements are made with the housekeeper. The patronage which they can distribute is thus utilized to make friends and to purchase the silence of those who might otherwise object to their presence. The children of respectable families are often sent to the prostitutes on various errands, and because of the gifts made to the children these women become important personages in the house and their affairs the subject of frequent conversation. The familiarity with vice, often in its most flagrant forms, possessed by very young children because of the condition just described has profoundly impressed the Commission. Several physicians have informed us that though they as children had lived in quarters of the city where prostitution existed, they had not possessed a tenth of the knowledge of it which they find almost universal among tenement house children of the present day. The anxiety of reputable parents living in houses upon which these harlots have descended is most pitiful. One of our charity workers stated that she had heard women living in tenement houses thus infected bemoan the birth of a daughter because of their fear of the dangers to which she would be exposed. And the same worker declared that scarcely a day passed that some woman did not confide to her a mother's anxiety and despair regarding this situation.

But it is not the children alone who are contaminated! Boys and young men living in the tenement houses are tempted, and become addicted to habits of immorality, because of the constant temptation placed before them almost at the door of their home. Still more distressing is the condition of young girls. Such girls are often working in difficult situations with long hours, small pay, and hard work. When they return to their homes tired and perhaps discouraged at the end of the day's toil, they see their neighbors living lives of apparent ease, dressing far better than they can afford to dress on their limited wages, and showing by their manner that they feel themselves superior to those who are foolish enough to toil when they might be at leisure. The very sight of this contrast with their own condition raises despairing questions, disappointments, and bitterness. After the shock occasioned by the knowledge of the character of the prostitutes has subsided, as it inevitably will, if the evil is encountered daily, the girls are led to consider seriously the words of the tempters. The fall of many girls, daughters of honest and reputable parents, has, undoubtedly, been due to this contamination. From the statement of many in a position to know facts, we have been led to believe that more girls have been started, in recent years, upon a life of immorality, because of their associations in the tenement houses, than by all other means combined that supply this traffic.

Voicing the protests of tenement house dwellers, clergymen, teachers, and many others interested in the welfare of tenement house people, the Commission recommends legislation of a stringent character for the suppression of prostitution in tenement houses. While there may be serious difference of opinion regarding the subject as a whole, there can be no difference of opinion regarding the enforced mingling in the same house of old and young with prostitutes and their procurers. Wherever this evil may exist, and however it may be dealt with, it should be absolutely eradicated from the dwellings of the poor.

For these reasons the Commission recommends the enactment of more severe penalties against prostitution in tenement houses. Its proposed code subjects a tenement house, any part of which is used as a house of prostitution, to a penalty of $1000 which is to be made a lien upon the premises. The fact that a tenement house is used for such purposes is made presumptive evidence that it is so occupied with the knowledge of the owner or lessee, with a proviso that such presumption may be rebutted by appropriate evidence. An innocent owner is protected by providing that the lease may be void at his option in case the tenement house be so used. The general reputation of the premises in the neighborhood is made competent evidence of such use of a house, with the proviso that such evidence shall not be sufficient to warrant a judgment without corroborative evidence, and women who reside in or commit prostitution in a tenement house are made punishable by imprisonment instead of by fine as has been customary.

### POLICY

Prostitution, however, is not by any means the only form of vice to be found in tenement districts. The very serious evils of certain forms of gambling and their effects upon the general morale of the community, as well as their effect upon its industrial well-being, has been set forth in one of the special reports presented by the Commission. The temptations of the game of policy, it appears, are especially open to the tenement house dweller, and the Commission urges upon the Legislature that every means be taken to stamp out and eradicate this serious menace to the welfare of the community.

### TENEMENT HOUSE LABOR

The Commission has made an investigation of the conditions of labor in the tenement houses, especially with reference to the making of garments, artificial flowers, and feathers. The evils of cigar making in such buildings, regarding which a forceful presentation was made to the Legislature ten years ago, have to a large extent disappeared. Through the invention of a machine called the suction table, the manufacture of cigars is being gradually removed into factories; and it is the opinion of those best acquainted with the trade, that it will soon disappear from the tenement houses. But the opinions of workers in this trade regarding the general conditions of tenement house labor are in accord with the statements of workers in other trades and our own investigations.

The law requiring the licensing of work carried on in tenement houses has undoubtedly led to certain improvements, but the very attempt to enforce the law has furnished additional proof of the undesirability of the conditions. Where workers apply for a license they may be investigated, but if a license is refused, it is not always possible to be sure that work will be discontinued; and if the license is not applied for, it will only be by chance that the tenement house workshop will be discovered.

Tenement house labor is generally carried on in the dwelling room of the family, where old and young are crowded in with the workers. The danger of contagion when any member of the family is ill, therefore, is very great. A member of the Commission has seen garments piled on the floor in the midst of dirt and rubbish, garments stacked on the bed and some of them used as pillows for sick children, and in one instance garments were found stored in the same room with a sick man apparently in an advanced stage of tuberculosis. Such conditions the Commission regards as a serious menace to public health. It believes that manufacturing cannot be continued in the tenement houses with safety to the general public except at great expense in the way of investigation and supervision, in view of the immense amount of labor at present carried on in tenement houses. The Commission does not, however, feel warranted in recommending the absolute abolition of tenement house labor. It recommends the amendment of Chapter 191 of the Laws of 1899 by the insertion of a proviso that no license shall be issued for any room in a tenement house containing less than 1250 cubic feet of air, or used for the purpose of cooking, eating, or sleeping, or for children, or otherwise than as a workshop. This recommendation regarding the size of the room in which labor should be allowed is based upon knowledge of the constant use by all the members of the family of any room connected with a living apartment. It is also based upon the universally accepted fact that the average tenement house family consists of five members, though undoubtedly in frequent instances the boarders taken by such families make the average size higher. Among the Italian garment workers it has been frequently found that two and even three families, making a total of from ten to fifteen individuals, occupy a single apartment. But taking the conservative estimate and applying the provision of the law that a workshop must have at least 250 cubic feet of space for each worker, the Commission believes that 1250 feet should be required as the minimum size of any workroom in a tenement house, because experience has shown that an average of not less than five persons will use the room for a greater or less part of the day.

This requirement of space seems especially important in view of the disposition of builders to make the living room of the family constantly smaller and smaller.

The Commission also recommends an increase in the force of the Factory Inspector's Department, to enable him to adequately enforce the law in tenement houses.

### SANITARY CONDITIONS

The results of examinations of a number of typical tenement houses which form the subject of a special report included with the Commission's report, show on the whole that the present plumbing laws, with one or two slight exceptions, are, if properly enforced, entirely adequate to meet the present needs. They also point out serious evils in old tenement houses, which imperatively call for remedy.

### DEATH-RATES

The subject of death-rates in tenement house districts is one which the Commission carefully considered at the beginning of its work, especially as to whether it was desirable to make a study of death-rates in such districts as compared with other districts of the city. After consultation, however, with leading experts upon this subject, Dr. John S. Billings, Dr. Roger S. Tracy, and Professor Franklin H. Giddings, it was found that no data upon this subject could be obtained that would point to any definite conclusion, without more extended study than could possibly be given within the time at the disposal of the Commission, because of the fact that so many elements enter into the question that it is difficult to draw reliable conclusions. The Commission finds from such study of this subject as it has made that the death-rate cannot be deemed a criterion of bad sanitary conditions. In certain blocks of the Italian quarter of the city there is a very high death-rate, while in certain other blocks, half a mile away, in the Jewish quarter, the death-rate is only one-half as great as the average death-rate of the city; yet in the latter district there was a greater population, the tenement houses were taller, and the general sanitary conditions were worse. Similar instances may be observed in other parts of the city. The explanation of this lies in the fact that race characteristics, the character of occupation, the nature of the soil on which the building is located, and numerous other elements must also be taken into consideration.

## IMMIGRATION

The subject of immigration is intimately connected with the tenement house problem in this city. Its varying volume and the proportion which different nationalities bear to each other are set forth in the special report on this subject. While the Commission appreciates that no State legislation is practicable upon this subject, yet it would call attention to the fact that the tenement house system is exerting quite as detrimental an effect upon the newly arrived immigrant as the newly arrived immigrant is exerting on the tenement house.

## TENEMENT EVILS AS SEEN BY THE TENANTS

The Commission has at all times sought from tenement dwellers their views upon this subject, believing that they, better than any one else, know the evils that need to be remedied. It has, therefore, submitted with this report a special paper containing the views of a number of such persons. It has been stated so often in the past that tenement dwellers will not appreciate improvements in tenement houses, that it seemed to the Commision especially important that the tenement house dweller should speak for himself on the subject, in his own way. . . .

## TESTIMONY OF A TENANT

(Testimony given at a hearing of the Tenement House Commission held on November 26, 1900.)

Mr. Henry Moscowitz then took the witness chair and was interrogated by the secretary:

*The Secretary.*—Where do you reside?

*Mr. Moscowitz.* 05 Forsyth Street.

*The Secretary.*—Is that a tenement house?

*Mr. Moscowitz.*—Yes, sir.

*The Secretary.*—How long have you lived in tenement houses?

*Mr. Moscowitz.*—Seventeen years.

*The Secretary.*—Practically most of your life?

*Mr. Moscowitz.*—Yes, sir.

*The Secretary.*—In that time do you remember about how many tenement houses you have lived in?

*Mr. Moscowitz.*—Fourteen.

*The Secretary.*—Fourteen different buildings?

*Mr. Moscowitz.*—Yes, sir.

*The Secretary.*—So that you feel you are competent to speak on the condition of tenement houses from your own experience?

*Mr. Moscowitz.*—Yes, sir.

*The Secretary*—Have you resided generally in one part of the city?

*Mr. Moscowitz.*—Yes; in the lower East Side.

*The Secretary.*—What have you got to say about the air shaft; do you think it is a good thing?

*Mr. Moscowitz.*—I think it is decidedly a bad thing. I must confirm the statements by other witnesses that the air shaft is a breeder of disease, and especially that there can be no fresh air in any building with an air shaft, from my experience, because of the refuse thrown down in the air shaft, the stench is so vile and the air is so foul that the occupants do not employ the windows as a means of getting air.

*The Secretary.*—Do these shafts furnish light to the rooms, in your experience?

*Mr. Moscowitz.*—They do not. They do not furnish light because the windows are very often dirty. That is one thing; they are not cleaned by the tenants very often and I will explain it that it is a hopeless task; the windows cannot be made clean during the day.

*The Secretary.*—Why is that?

*Mr. Moscowitz.*—Well, there is dirt and dust comes down the walls and strikes the windows.

*The Secretary.*—Do you mean from the apartments above?

*Mr. Moscowitz.*—Apartments above.

*The Secretary.*—People shake things out of the windows?

*Mr. Moscowitz.*—Yes, and throw things.

*The Secretary.*—That is not the fault of the air shaft, but of the tenants?

*Mr. Moscowitz.*—Yes, sir.

*The Secretary.*—Are there any other objections to the air shaft?

*Mr. Moscowitz.*—It destroys privacy.

*The Secretary.*—How does it do that?

*Mr. Moscowitz.*—I know where I lived in a house where there was a family opposite, the windows which are usually diagonal, I heard everything, especially loud noises, and when the windows are not covered one sees into the house.

*The Secretary.*—You have observed that in numbers of cases?

*Mr. Moscowitz.*—I have observed that in every case.

*The Secretary.*—Do you think that the tenement houses should be restricted in height?

*Mr. Moscowitz.*—Decidedly. I think that no tenement house ought to be built over five stories high. It is injurious to the health of the women.

*The Secretary.*—In what way?

*Mr. Moscowitz.*—The women complain, and I know this to be a fact, there is a Jewish word "Stiegen," the stairs. Families who live on the third floor complain that they have to go up and down, and I know that many a woman has complained of the side ache to me because of the "stiegen."

*The Secretary.*—Is it true that because of the stairs many of the women in the tenement houses seldom go down into the street and outdoors?

*Mr. Moscowitz.*—Decidedly true. I know this for a fact; that they do not visit their neighbors often. Complaints, serious complaints are made, "Why don't you come to visit me?" and they say "We live so high up we seldom come."

*The Secretary.*—Do you know of many families where the mother does not go out oftener than twice a week?

*Mr. Moscowitz.*—I do.

*The Secretary.*—Would you say that was a very general practice?

*Mr. Moscowitz.*—Very general, yes.

*The Secretary.*—You think that has a bad effect on the health of the people?

*Mr. Moscowitz.*—Very bad effect.

*The Secretary.*—Are there any other reasons why you object to tall buildings?

*Mr. Moscowitz.*—I think the children are kept in the street a good deal; the parents, especially the mother, very often loses sight of the children, and she has to open the windows and shout down for the little one at play when she wants it in the room, and the parents cannot trace the children; cannot keep track of them.

*The Secretary.*—Are the hallways in most tenement houses you have observed light or dark?

*Mr. Moscowitz.*—Dark.

*The Secretary.*—How dark?

*Mr. Moscowitz.*—Well, they are dark in most houses that I have lived in. One tumbles over human obstacles and other obstacles, especially little children.

*The Secretary.*—Are the rooms dark or light in most of the tenement houses you have lived in?

*Mr. Moscowitz.*—The bedrooms are dark. The kitchen and the front room called the parlor is light.

*The Secretary.*—Have you any recommendation to make with reference to baths on the East Side in tenement houses?

*Mr. Moscowitz.*—Yes, sir; I think that baths are very essential. Because there are no baths in the tenement houses many of the tenants do not bathe as often as they otherwise would. I can say from experience that many tenants do not bathe more than six times a year, and often less, and not because they would not take advantage of the opportunity, but there are no opportunities.

*The Secretary.*—Cannot they take a bath in the rooms?

*Mr. Moscowitz.*—No, they cannot. There are no baths there.

*The Secretary.*—Cannot they take a tub and bathe in that way?

*Mr. Moscowitz.*—Well, they may take a tub, but they do not do that very often.

*The Secretary.*—Why, is it difficult?

*Mr. Moscowitz.*—I believe it is difficult. The tubs are narrow in the tenements.

*The Secretary.*—You mean the wash-tubs?

*Mr. Moscowitz.*—The wash-tubs, yes.

*The Secretary.*—Have you ever seen a bath-tub in a tenement house?

*Mr. Moscowitz.*—Never.

*The Secretary.*—Never in seventeen years?

*Mr. Moscowitz.*—Never in seventeen years.

*The Secretary.*—It has been stated that bath-tubs, when put in tenement houses, have been used for the storage of coal. Have you ever heard of such a thing?

*Mr. Moscowitz.*—It is the same story I have heard time and time again.

*The Secretary.*—From your knowledge of the people do you think it is true?

*Mr. Moscowitz.*—It is decidedly not true.

*The Secretary.*—Is it not the fact that the people buy their coal mostly by the pail, so that they could not store it in bath-tubs?

*Mr. Moscowitz.*—That is true.

*The Secretary.*—Have you known of cases where the water supply in tenements has been deficient?

*Mr. Moscowitz.*—Yes, sir; in the summer-time very often the water supply is deficient, and people are deprived of water for half a day. I have known that to be the case in two instances of my own knowledge, and the particular water supply is deficient in tenements which have closets in the hallways. This is a fact which is general. From my own observations in the tenements where the closets are situated in the hall, the stench is very noticeable, and the reason, I believe, is because there is not a sufficient flush in the closet. I do not know whether it is compulsory for the landlord to supply a certain thickness of pipe, but I surely think it ought to be because I have noticed that the water supply is not sufficient in the closets situated in the hallways.

*The Secretary.*—Have you noticed the practice of people sleeping on the roofs and in the street in the summer-time?

*Mr. Moscowitz.*—Yes, sir, I have, because I myself have done so.

*The Secretary.*—Why?

*Mr. Moscowitz.*—Because it was too hot to sleep in the room in the summer-time.

*The Secretary.*—Is this practice general?

*Mr. Moscowitz.*—It is general.

*The Secretary.*—What proportion would you say of the people in the summer-time sleep on the roofs and in the street?

*Mr. Moscowitz.*—I think about one-third of the people sleep on the roofs in my observation.

*The Secretary.*—And you attribute that entirely to the heat of the rooms?

*Mr. Moscowitz.*—Decidedly so, and to the air in the summertime.

*The Secretary.*—How often in seventeen years have you seen a sanitary inspector?

*Mr. Moscowitz.*—Never.

*The Secretary.*—How often have you seen a light burning in a dark hallway in the daytime?

*Mr. Moscowitz.*—I have a dim recollection of having seen one about twelve years ago in a tenement on Essex Street.

*The Secretary.*—Do you think the tenement house system is a good thing for the community?

*Mr. Moscowitz.*—A very bad thing for the community.

*The Secretary.*—Why?

*Mr. Moscowitz.*—Because, first, it destroys the privacy of the home. Then I believe the most serious thing is that it disintegrates the home.

*The Secretary.*—In what way?

*Mr. Moscowitz.*—The home is very unattractive for the children and they are glad to get out to meet their friends. They want to supply a social need, and they go out and meet other friends and the home has no tie upon them. The father—there is not the authority of the parent that existed in the old country, and I believe because the child is not at home as often as he should be. The tenement house is a decidedly disintegrating influence in the family, and that is seen especially on the East Side to-day.

*The Secretary.*—I have always understood that among the Jewish people the patriarchal form of government was very strong and the authority of the father very strong?

*Mr. Moscowitz.*—Yes.

*The Secretary.*—Do you mean to say that this is being weakened by the tenement houses?

*Mr. Moscowitz.*—The tenement house is not the only thing, but a very strong influence. I believe the entire economic conditions in this country are another influence, and I will state decidedly that I think the tenement house life is a strong influence in that direction.

*The Secretary.*—Would you have us infer from your statement that the young men and young women have to meet each other on the street because the home is unattractive?

*Mr. Moscowitz.*—Well, they meet each other on the streets, and in club-rooms, and in settlements, but very few I think meet each other there. In dancing academies, in social clubs, in balls and receptions.

*The Secretary.*—And you think this is a bad thing?

*Mr. Moscowitz.*—Decidedly a bad thing, because of another point, the tenement house life destroys a certain delicacy of feeling, which is noticeable in one brought up in a good home. That is a decided characteristic of the young men and women living in the tenement houses, that they are too socially dependent.

# The Struggle for Self-Government

## *Lincoln Steffens*

*"My special business," declared Lincoln Steffens in 1907, "is to write about graft, grafters, and American political injustice generally." An imaginative, intelligent university graduate from California's exuberant gilded age, Steffens drew on his father's prosperity for two years of restless study in Europe before determining to report and write in the urban world of Tammany Hall, Jacob Riis, Police Commissioner Theodore Roosevelt, and Wall Street's J. P. Morgan. By 1903 it had become everyone's business to read about graft, grafters, and injustice. In undertaking to investigate the political corruption of America's largest cities Steffens was only following his readers' interests and his employer's nose for salable news. He soon became preeminent in digging for the hidden and buried facts of machine government and boss rule, and he even won the unlikely respect of some of the bosses he exposed—and immortalized.*

*His courage in probing for facts was conspicuous, as was the skill with which he made them come alive in colloquial and personal vignettes, but it was his sophistication in interpreting the facts that made him the ablest and most persistently read of the reform journalists. For one thing, his long experience as a reporter and the flexibility of a mind trained in philosophy discouraged him from dividing people into the good and the bad. Though not the first, he was the most effective writer to suggest with appropriate irony that honesty in government can be corrupting, that the form of government is often the shadow cast by the exercise of real power elsewhere, that representative government was better than good government, and that honest bosses were less to be feared than inefficient reformers. In the second place, Steffens was eventually to surpass his fellow muckrakers in his ability to formulate generalizations about the nature of corruption in urban government under modern capitalism. Did corruption spring from the ineradicable greed in man's nature? Could it more plausibly be traced to the social arrangements whereby all citizens held a crucial stake in a profit-seeking business system? Steffens' interest*

131

*in questions like these was not immediately apparent in his reporting, and the book reviewers regretted that this journalist did not possess the insights of Bryce or Tocqueville. Insights worthy of Bryce were present but obscure and imperfectly worked out; they would not become persuasively clear until the remarkable* Autobiography, *twenty-five years later. In his original journalism the tentativeness of his interpretations belied the breezy assurance of his manner and imparted to his articles what Louis Filler has described as an "air of tense expectancy." We are not certain of the conclusion, for neither was he; nor, in analyzing the political process, was it possible for anyone to be.*

*In* The Shame of the Cities *Steffens demonstrated repeatedly how the fortunes of reformers in the city rose and fell with their success in the state. Particularly was this true in St. Louis, Chicago, New York, and the cities of Ohio. (In this connection the experiences of Frederic Howe and Lawrence Veiller in achieving reform are especially significant.) Steffens was soon impelled to follow up his investigation of cities with a series on the politics of a number of states. Published as a book in 1906 and hopefully entitled* The Struggle for Self-Government, *it featured as a central episode in progressive reform the career of Robert La Follette and the politics of Wisconsin. It is this chapter we are reprinting below.*

*Elected governor of Wisconsin in 1900, La Follette was twice returned to office and resigned in 1905 to become United States Senator. His success was a tribute to the skill with which he welded a coalition of Populists, Grangers, Laborites, silver men, University professors, and immigrant Norwegian farmers into an astonishingly tight-disciplined party which ruled the state for fourteen years and by its example continued to influence the nation for the next thirty. By the time La Follette left the state for Washington he had gained a national reputation as the one truly successful but uncorrupted political reformer.*

*How was he able to do this? La Follette readily fit Steffens' formula for an effective democratic leader. Years of party politics as a district attorney had taught him the wisdom of constructing not just a platform of popular ideals but a ruthless machine to carry them out. Rather than set out to destroy "the system," a mistake reformers often made, he successfully converted it into what Steffens insisted was an efficient engine for democratic government. In this instructive piece concerning political reform in Wisconsin (subtitled "Representative Government Restored"), Steffens defines clearly what the progressive generation meant by the "system," suggests why it seemed of central concern to them, and allows the reader to conclude that possibly the truly remarkable achievement of twentieth-century America has been a generally successful fusion of the "boss system" and its party machines with the ancient but revolutionary ideal of representative government.*

## WISCONSIN: REPRESENTATIVE GOVERNMENT RESTORED

The story of the State of Wisconsin is the story of Governor La Follette. He is the head of the State. Not many Governors are that. In all the time I spent studying the government of Missouri I never once had to see or name the Governor of Missouri, and I doubt if many of my readers know who he was. They need not. He was only the head of the paper government described in the Constitution, and most Governors are simply "safe men" set up as figureheads by the System, which is the actual government that is growing up in the United States in place of the "government of the people, by the people, and for the people, which shall not perish from the earth." The System, as we have found it, is a reorganization of the political and financial powers of the State by which, for boodle of one sort or another, the leading politicians of both parties conduct the government in the interest of those leading businesses which seek special privileges and pay for them with bribes and the "moral" support of graft. And a "safe man" is a man who takes his ease, honors, and orders, lets the boss reign, and makes no trouble for the System.

There is trouble in Wisconsin. Bounded on the east by Lake Michigan, on the north by Lake Superior, on the west by the Mississippi River, Wisconsin is a convenient, rich, and beautiful State. New England lumbermen stripped fortunes of forest off it, and, uncovering a fat soil watered by a thousand lakes and streams, settlers poured in from Northwestern Europe and made this new Northwest ripen into dairy farms and counties of golden wheat. From the beginning Wisconsin has paid, nor is there now any material depression or financial distress in the State. Yet there is trouble in Wisconsin. What is the matter? I asked a few hundred people out there to explain it, and though some of them smiled and others frowned, all gave substantially one answer: "La Folletteism." They blame one man.

Robert Marion La Follette was born on a farm in Dane County, Wisconsin, June 14, 1855. His father was a Kentucky-bred French Huguenot; his mother was Scotch-Irish. When the boy was eight months old the father died, leaving the mother and four children, and, at the age of fourteen, "Little Bob," as his followers still call him, became the head of the family. He worked the farm till he was nineteen years old, then sold it and moved the family to Madison, the county-seat and capital of the State. If, with this humble start, La Follette had gone into business, his talents might have made him a captain of industry; and then, no matter

Lincoln Steffens, *The Struggle for Self-Government* (New York: McClure, Phillips, 1906), pp. 79-119. This chapter was originally written in October, 1904, and bears as a subheading, "The Story of La Follette's War on the Railroads that Ruled His State."

how he won it, his success would have made him an inspiration for youth. But he made a mistake. He entered the State University with the class of '79. Even so, he might have got over his college education, but his father's French blood (perhaps) stirred to sentiment and the boy thrilled for glory. He had a bent for oratory. In those days debates ranked in the Western colleges where football does now, and "Bob" La Follette won, in his senior year, all the oratorical contests, home, State, and interstate. His interstate oration was on *Iago*, and his round actor's head was turned to the stage, till John McCullough advised him that his short stature was against that career. Also, he says, his debts chained him to the earth. He had to go to work, and he went to work in a law office. In five months he was admitted to the bar, and in February, 1880, he opened an office and began to practice. A year or so later the young lawyer was running for an office.

"They" say in Wisconsin that La Follette is ambitious; that he cannot be happy in private life; that, an actor born, he has to be on a stage. I should say that a man who can move men, as La Follette can, would seek a career where he could enjoy the visible effect of his eloquence. But suppose "they" are right and the man is vain—I don't care. Do you? I have noticed that a public official who steals, or, like Lieutenant-Governor Lee, of Missouri, betrays his constituents, may propose to be Governor, without being accused of ambition. "They" seem to think a boodler's aspirations are natural. He may have a hundred notorious vices; they do not matter. But a "reformer," a man who wants to serve his people, he must be a white-robed, spotless angel, or "they" will whisper that he is— what? A thief? Oh, no; that is nothing; but that he is ambitious. This is the System at work. It was the System in Missouri that, after spending in vain thousands of dollars to "get something on Folk," passed about the damning rumor that he was ambitious. And so in Wisconsin, "they" will take you into a back room and warn you that La Follette is ambitious. I asked if he was dishonest. Oh dear, no. Not that. Not a man in the State, not the bitterest foe of his that I saw, questioned La Follette's personal integrity. So I answered that we wanted men of ambition; that if we could get men to serve us in public life, not for graft, not for money, but for ambition's sake, we should make a great step forward.

Mr. La Follette has ambition. He confessed as much to me, but he is after a job, not an office; Governor La Follette's ambition is higher and harder to achieve than any office in the land.

The first office he sought was that of District Attorney of Dane County, and, although his enemies declare that the man is a radical and was from the start a radical, I gathered from the same source that his only idea at this time was to "pose" before juries "and win cases." Mr. La Follette married in this year (a classmate), and he says he thought of the small but regular salary of the District Attorney. However this may be, he won the office and he won his cases, so he earned his salary. District Attorney La Follette made an excellent record. That is freely admitted, but my attention was called to the manner of his entrance into politics, as proof of another charge that is made against him in Wisconsin. "They" say La Follette is a politician.

"They" say in Missouri that Folk is a politician. "They" say in Illinois that Deneen is a politician. "They" say in the United States that President Roosevelt is a politician. "They" are right. These men are politicians. But what of it? We have blamed our politicians so long for the corruption of our politics that they themselves seem to have been convinced that a politician is necessarily and inherently bad. He isn't, of course. Only a bad politician is bad, and we have been discovering in our studies of graft that a bad business man is worse. To succeed in reform, a man has to understand politics and play the game, or the bad business man will catch him, and then—what will he be? He will be an "impracticable reformer," and that, we all know, is awful.

"Bob" La Follette is a politician. Irish, as well as French, he was born a master of the game, and he did indeed prove his genius in that first campaign. Singlehanded he beat the System. Not that he realized then that there was such a thing. All the young candidate knew when he began was that E. W. Keyes, the postmaster at Madison, was the Republican State boss, and, of course, absolute master of Dane County, where he lived. La Follette was a Republican, but he had no claim of machine service to the office he wanted, and he felt that Boss Keyes and Philip L. Spooner, the local leader, would be against him, so he went to work quietly. He made an issue; La Follette always has an issue; but his first one wasn't very radical. It had been the practice of District Attorneys to have assistants at the county's expense, and La Follette promised, if elected, to do all his own work. With this promise he and his friends canvassed the county, house by house, farm by farm, and, partly because they were busy by day, partly because they had to proceed secretly, much of this politics was done at night. The scandal of such "underhand methods" is an offense to this day to the men who were beaten by them. Mr. "Phil" Spooner (the Senator's brother) speaks with contempt of La Follette's "night riders." He says the La Follette workers went about on horseback after dark and that he used to hear them gallop up to their leader's house late at night. Of course he knows now that they were coming to report and plot, but he didn't know it then. And Boss Keyes, who is still postmaster at Madison, told me he had no inkling of the conspiracy till the convention turned up with the delegates nearly all instructed for La Follette for District Attorney. Then it was too late to do anything.

Boss Keyes thought this showed another defect in the character of La Follette. "They" say in Wisconsin that the Governor is "selfish, dictatorial, and will not consult." "They" said that about Folk in Missouri, when he refused to appoint assistants dictated by Boss Butler. Wall Street said it about Roosevelt when he refused to counsel with Morgan upon the advisability of bringing the Northern Securities case, but the West liked that in Roosevelt. The West said it about Parker when he sent his gold telegram to the Democratic National Convention, but the East liked that in Parker. There must be something back of this charge, and a boss should be able to explain it. Boss Keyes cleared it up for me. He said that at the time "Bob" was running for District Attorney, "a few of us here were—well, we were managing the party and we were usually consulted about—about things generally. But La Follette, he went ahead on his own hook, and never said a word to—well, to me or any of us." So it's not a matter of dictation, but of who dictates, and what. In the case of La Follette, his dictatorial selfishness consisted in this, that he "saw" the people of the county and the delegates, not "us," not the System. No wonder he was elected. What is more, he was reëlected; he kept his promises, and, the second time he ran, La Follette was the only Republican elected on the county ticket.

During the two terms of District Attorney La Follette, important changes were occurring in the Wisconsin State system beyond his ken. Boss Keyes was deposed and Philetus Sawyer became the head of the State. This does not mean that Sawyer was elected Governor; we have nothing to do with Governors yet. Sawyer was a United States Senator. While Keyes was boss, the head of the State was in the post-office at Madison, and it represented, not the people, but the big business interests of the State, principally lumber and the railways, which worked well together and with Keyes. There were several scandals during this "good fellow's" long reign, but big business had no complaint to make against him. The big graft in this Northwestern State, however, was lumber, and the typical way of getting hold of it wholesale, was for the United States to make to the State grants which the State passed on to railway companies to help "develop the resources of the State." Railroad men were in lumber companies, just as lumbermen were in the railway companies, so railway companies sold cheap to the lumber companies, which cleared the land—for the settlers. This was business, and while it was necessary to "take care" of the Legislature, the original source of business was the Congress, and that was the place for the head of the System. Keyes had wished to go to the Senate, but Sawyer thought he might as well go himself. He had gone, and now, when Keyes was willing to take the second seat, the business men decided that, since it was all a matter of business, they might as well take it out of politics. Thus Senator

Sawyer became boss, and, since he was a lumberman, it was no more than fair that the other seat should go to the railroads. So the big business men got together and they bought the junior United States Senatorship for the Honorable John C. Spooner.

At Marinette, Wisconsin, lives to-day a rich old lumberman, Isaac Stephenson. He was associated for years with Senator Sawyer and the other enemies of the Republic in Wisconsin, and he left them because they balked an ambition of his. Having gone over, however, he began to see things as they are, and not many men to-day are more concerned over the dangers to business of the commercial corruption of government than this veteran who confesses that he spent a quarter of a million in politics.

Once he and Senator Sawyer were comparing notes on the cost to them of United States Senatorships.

"Isaac," said Sawyer, "how much did you put in to get the Legislature for Spooner that time?"

"It cost me about twenty-two thousand, Philetus. How much did you put in?"

"Why," said Sawyer, surprised, "it cost me thirty thousand. I thought it cost you thirty."

"No, it cost me thirty to get it for you when you ran."

Friends of mine, who are friends of Senator Spooner in Washington, besought me, when they heard I was going to Wisconsin, to "remember that Spooner is a most useful man in the Senate," and I know and shall not forget that. Able, deliberate, resourceful, wise, I believe Senator Spooner comes about as near as any man we have in that august chamber to-day to statesmanship, and I understand he loathes many of the practices of politics. But the question to ask about a representative is, what does he represent?

Senator Spooner, at home, represented the railroads of his State. He served a term in the Wisconsin assembly, and he served the railroads there. After that he served them as a lobbyist. I do not mean that he went to Madison now and then to make arguments for his client. Mr. Spooner spent the session there. Nor do I mean to say that he paid bribes to legislators; there are honest lobbyists. But I do say that Mr. Spooner peddled passes, and any railroad man or any grafter will tell you that this is a cheap but most effective form of legislative corruption. United States Senator Spooner, then, is a product, a flower, perhaps, but none the less he is a growth out of the System, the System which is fighting Governor La Follette.

The System was fighting La Follette 'way back in those days, but the young orator did not know it. He was running for Congress. So far as I can make out, he was seeking only more glory for his French blood and a wider field to shine in, but he went after his French satisfaction in a Scotch-Irish fashion. Boss Keyes told me about it. Keyes had been reduced to the control only of his Congressional district, and, as he said, "We had it arranged to nominate another man. The place did not belong to Dane County. It was another county's turn, but Bob didn't consult us." Bob was consulting his constituents again, and his night riders were out. The System heard of it earlier than in the District Attorney campaign, and Keyes and Phil Spooner and the other leaders were angry. Keyes did want to rule that Congressional district; it was all he had, and Phil Spooner (who now is the head of the street railway system of Madison) sensed the danger in this self-reliant young candidate.

"What's this I hear about you being a candidate for Congress?" he said to La Follette one day. "Don't you know nobody can go to Congress without our approval? You're a fool."

But La Follette's men were working, and they carried all except three caucuses (primaries that are something like town meetings) against the ring. The ring bolted, but the people elected him; the people sent La Follette to Congress at the same time they elected the legislators that sent John C. Spooner to the United States Senate.

When La Follette had been in Washington a few weeks, Senator Sawyer found him out and became "like a father" to him. "Our boy" he called him, for La Follette was the "youngest member." The genial old lumberman took him about and introduced him to the heads of departments and finally, one day, asked him what committee he would like to go on. La Follette said he would prefer some committee where his practice in the law might make him useful, and Sawyer thought "Public Lands" would about do. He would "fix it." Thus the System was coming after him, but it held back; there must have been a second thought. For the Speaker put La Follette not on "Public Lands," but on "Indian Affairs."

The Governor to-day will tell you with a relish that he was so green then that he began to "read up on Indians"; he read especially Boston literature on that subject, and he thought of the speeches he could make on Indian wrongs and rights. But there was no chance for an orator. The committee worked and "our boy" read bills. Most of these bills were hard reading and didn't mean much when read. But by and by one came along that was "so full of holes that," as the Governor says, "even I could see through it." It provided for a sale of pine on the Menominee reservation in Wisconsin. Mr. La Follette took it to the (Cleveland's) Commissioner of Indian Affairs, and this official said he thought it "a little the worst bill of the kind that I have ever seen. Where did it come from?" They looked and they saw that it had been introduced by the member from Oshkosh (Sawyer's home district). None the less, Mr. La Follette wanted a report, and the Commissioner said he could have one if he would sit down and write for it. The report so riddled the bill that it lay dead in the committee. One day the Congressman who introduced it asked about it.

"Bob, why don't you report my bill?" he said.

"Bill," said Bob, "did you write that bill?"

"Why?"

"It's a steal."

"Let it die then. Don't report it. I introduced it because Sawyer asked me to. He introduced it in the Senate and it is through their committee."

Sawyer never mentioned the bill, and the incident was dropped with the bill. Some time after, however, a similar incident occurred, and this time Sawyer did mention it. The Indian Affairs Committee was having read, at the rate of two hours a day, a long bill to open the big Sioux Indian reservation in Dakota, by selling some eleven million acres right through the center. It was said to be a measure most important to South Dakota, and no one objected to anything till the clerk droned out a provision to ratify an agreement between the Indians and certain railroads about a right of way and some most liberal grants of land for terminal town sites. La Follette interrupted, and he began to talk about United States statutes which provided not so generously, yet amply, for land grants to railways, when a Congressman from a neighboring State leaned over and said:

"Bob, don't you see that those are your home corporations?"

Bob said he saw, and he was willing to grant all the land needed for railway purposes, but none for town site schemes. When the committee rose, and La Follette returned to his seat in the house, a page told him Senator Sawyer wanted to see him. He went out and the Senator talked to him for an hour in a most fatherly way, with not a word concerning the Sioux bill till they were about to separate. Then, quite by the way, he said:

"Oh, say, when that Sioux Injun bill comes up there's a little provision in it for our folks which I wish you to look after."

La Follette said the bill was up then, that they had just reached the "little provision for our folks," and that he was opposing it.

"Why, is that so?" said Sawyer. "Let's sit down and——" they had another hour, on town sites. It was no use, however. La Follette "wouldn't consult." Sawyer gave up reasoning with him, but he didn't give up "the little provision." Political force was applied, but not by the senior Senator. The System had other agents for such work.

Henry C. Payne arrived on the scene. Payne was chairman of the Republican State Central Committee of Wisconsin, and we have seen in other States what the legislative functions of that office are. Payne reached Washington forty-eight hours after La Follette's balk, and he went at him hard. All sorts of influence was brought to bear, and when La Follette held out, Payne became so angry that he expressed himself—and the spirit of the System—in public. To a group in the Ebbitt House he said:

"La Follette is a damned fool. If he thinks he can buck a railroad with five thousand miles of continuous line, he'll find he's mistaken. We'll take care of him when the time comes."

The State machine fought the Congressman in his own district, and so did Keyes and the "old regency" at Madison, but La Follette, the politician, had insisted upon a Congressman's patronage, all of it, and he had used it to strengthen himself at home. La Follette served three terms in Congress, and when he was defeated in 1890, for the fourth, he went down with the whole party in Wisconsin. This complete overthrow of the Republicans was due to two causes, the McKinley tariff (which La Follette on the Ways and Means Committee helped to frame) and a piece of State school legislation which angered the foreign and Catholic voters. We need not go into this, and the Democratic administration which resulted bears only indirectly on our story.

One of the great grafts of Wisconsin (and of many another State) was the public funds in the keeping of the State Treasurer. The Republicans, for years, had deposited these moneys in banks that stood in with the System, and the treasurer shared with these institutions the interest and profits. He, in turn, "divided up" with the campaign fund and the party leaders. The Democrats were pledged to break up this practice and sue the extreasurers. Now these treasurers were not all "good" for the money, and when the suits were brought, as they were in earnest, the treasurers' bondsmen were the real defendants. Chief among these was Senator Sawyer, the boss who had chosen the treasurers and backed them and the practice for years. Sawyer was alarmed. It was estimated that there had been $30,000 a year in the graft; the Attorney-General was going back twenty years, and his suits were for the recovery of all the back interest. Several hundred thousand dollars was at stake. And the judge before whom the cases were to be tried was Robert J. Siebecker, brother-in-law and former law partner of Robert M. La Follette.

One day in September, 1891, La Follette received from Sawyer a letter asking for a meeting in the Plankington Hotel, Milwaukee. The letter had been folded first with the letter head on, then this was cut off and the sheet refolded; and, as if secrecy was important, the answer suggested by Sawyer was to be the one word "Yes" by wire. La Follette wired "Yes," and the two men met. There are two accounts of what occurred. La Follette said Sawyer began the interview with the remark that "nobody knows that I'm to meet you to-day"; he spoke of the treasury cases and pulled out and held before the young lawyer a thick roll of bills. Sawyer's subsequent explanation was that he proposed only to retain La Follette, who, however, insists that Sawyer offered him a cash bribe for his influence with Judge Siebecker.

Since Sawyer is dead now, we would better not try to decide between the two men on this particular case, but there is no doubt of one general truth: that Philetus Sawyer was the typical captain of industry in politics; he debauched the politics of his State with money. Old Boss Keyes was bad enough, but his methods were political—patronage, deals, etc., and he made the government represent special interests. But when the millionaire lumberman took charge, he came with money; with money he beat Keyes; and money, his and his friends', was the power in the politics of his régime.

His known methods caused no great scandal so long as they were confined to conventions and the Legislature, but the courts of Wisconsin had the confidence of the State, and the approach of money to them made people angry. And the story was out. La Follette, after consultation with his friends, told Judge Siebecker what had happened, and the Judge declined to hear the case. His withdrawal aroused curiosity and rather sensational conjectures. Sawyer denied one of these, and his account seeming to call for a statement from La Follette, the young lawyer told his story. Sawyer denied it and everybody took sides. The cases were tried, the State won, but the Republican Legislature, pledged though it was to recover in full, compromised. So the System saved its boss.

But the System had raised up an enemy worthy of all its power. La Follette was against it. "They" say in Wisconsin that he is against the railroads, that he "hates" corporate wealth. It is true the bitterest fights he has led have been for so-called anti-railroad laws, but "they" forget that his original quarrel was with Sawyer, and that, if hatred was his impulse, it probably grew out of the treasury case "insult." My understanding of the state of his mind is that before that incident, La Follette thought only of continuing his Congressional career. After it, he was for anything to break up the old Sawyer machine. Anyhow, he told me that, after the Sawyer meeting, he made up his mind to stay home and break up the System in Wisconsin. And, La Follette did not originate all that legislation. Wisconsin was one of the four original Granger States. There seems to have been always some discontent with the abuse of the power of the railways, their corrupting influence, and their escape from just taxation. So far as I can make out, however, some of the modern measures labeled La Folletteism, sprang from the head of a certain lean, clean Vermont farmer, who came to the Legislature from Knapp, Wisconsin. I went to Knapp. It was a long way around for me, but it paid, for now I can say that I knew A. R. Hall. He is a man. I have seen in my day some seventeen men, real

men, and none of them is simpler, truer, braver than this ex-leader of the
Wisconsin Assembly; none thinks he is more of a failure and none is more
of a success.

Hall knows that there is a System in control of the land. Sometimes
I doubt my own eyes, but Hall knows it in his heart, which is sore and
tired from the struggle. He went to the Legislature in 1891. He had lived
in Minnesota and had served as an Assemblyman there. When he went
to the Legislature in Wisconsin, one of the first demands upon him was
from a constituent who wanted not a pass, but several passes for himself
and others. Hall laughed at the extravagance of the request, but when he
showed it to a colleague, the older Assemblyman took it as a matter of
course and told him he could get all the passes he cared to ask for from
the railroad lobbyist. "I had taken passes myself in Minnesota," Hall
told me, "but I was a legislator; it was the custom, and I thought nothing
of it." A little inquiry showed him that the custom in Wisconsin was an
abuse of tremendous dimensions. Legislators took "mileage" for themselves, their families, and for their constituents till it appeared that no
man in the State was compelled to pay his fare. Hall had not come there
as a reformer; like the best reformers I have known, experience of the facts
started him going, and his reforms developed as if by accident along
empirical lines. Hall says he realized that the legislators had to deliver
votes—legislation—for these pass privileges, and he drew an anti-pass
resolution which was offered as an amendment to the Constitution. It was
beaten. Not only the politicians, the railroads also fought it, and together
they won in that session. But Hall, mild-spoken and gentle, was a fighter,
so the anti-pass measure became an issue.

One day Assemblyman Hall happened to see the statement of earnings
of a railroad to its stockholders. Railroads in Wisconsin paid by way of
taxes a percentage on their gross receipts, and, as Hall looked idly over
the report, he wondered how the gross receipts item would compare with
that in the statement to the State Treasurer. He went quietly about his
investigation, and he came to the conclusion that, counting illegal rebates,
the State reports were from two to five millions short. So he asked for a
committee to investigate, and he introduced also a bill for a State railroad
commission to regulate railroad rates. This was beaten, and a committee
which was sent to Chicago to look up earnings reported for the railways.
But this was not enough. Hall was "unsafe" and he must be kept out of
the Legislature. So, in 1894, "they" sent down into Dunn County men and
money to beat Hall for the renomination. They got the shippers out
against him (the very men who were at the mercy of the roads), and one
of these business men handled the "barrel" which, as he said himself, he
"opened at both ends." Hall had no money and no organization, but he
knew a way to fight. The caucuses were held in different places at different times, and Hall went about posting bills asking the voters to as-

semble one hour before time and listen to him. At these preliminary meetings he explained just what was being done and why; he said that he might not be right, but he had some facts, which he gave, and then he declared he was not against the railroads, that he only wished to make sure that they were fulfilling their obligations and not abusing their power. "I had only been trying to serve honorably the people I represented, and it was hard to be made to fight for your political life, just for doing that. But we won out. Those voters went into those caucuses and Dunn County beat the bribery. They then tried to buy my delegates."

Mr. Hall was leaning against the railroad station as he said this. We had gone over the night before, his twelve years' fight, up to his retirement the year before, and we were repeating now. He was looking back over it all, and a hint of moisture in his eyes and the deep lines in his good face made me ask:

"Does it pay, Mr. Hall?"

"Sometimes I think it does, sometimes I think it doesn't. Yes, it does. Dunn County——" He stopped. "Yes, it does," he added. "They used to cartoon me. They lampooned and they ridiculed, they abused and they vilified. They called me a demagogue; said I was ambitious; asked what I was after, just as they do La Follette. But he is a fighter. He will never stop fighting. And if I had served them, I could have had anything, just as he could now. It is hard and it hurts, when you're only trying to do your duty and be fair. But it does pay. They don't question my motives now, any more."

No, they don't question Hall's motives any more. When "they" became most heated in their denunciations of the Governor and all his followers, I would ask them, the worst haters, "What about A. R. Hall?" and the change was instantaneous.

"Now, there's a man," they would say; not one, but everybody to whom I mentioned A. R. Hall.

When La Follette began his open fight against the System in 1894, he took up the issues of inequalities in taxation, machine politics, and primary elections. Hall and La Follette were friends and they had talked over these issues together in La Follette's law office in Madison, during the sessions. "They" say in Wisconsin that La Follette is an opportunist. They say true. But so is Folk an opportunist, and so are the Chicago reformers —as to specific issues. So are the regular politicians who, in Wisconsin, for example, adopted later these same issues in the platform. The difference is this: the regulars wanted only to keep in power so as to continue the profitable business of representing the railroads and other special interests; Hall and La Follette really wanted certain abuses corrected, and La Follette was, and is, for any sound issue that will arouse the people of Wisconsin to restore representative government.

In 1894 La Follette carried his issues to the State convention with a candidate for Governor, Nils P. Haugen, a Norse-American who had served in Congress and as a State railroad commissioner. La Follette and his followers turned up with one-third of the delegates. The regulars, or "Stalwarts," as they afterward were called, were divided, but Sawyer, declaring it was anybody to beat La Follette, managed a combination on W. H. Upham, a lumberman, and Haugen was beaten. Hall was there, by the way, with an anti-pass plank, and Hall also was beaten.

The contest served only to draw a line between the La Follette "Half-breeds" and the "Stalwarts," and both factions went to work on their organizations. Upham was elected, and the Stalwarts, who had been living on federal patronage, now had the State. They rebuilt their State machine. La Follette, with no patronage, continued to organize, and his method was that which he had applied so successfully in his early independent fights for District Attorney and Congressman. He went straight to the voters.

"They" say in Wisconsin that La Follette is a demagogue, and if it is demagogy to go thus straight to the voters, then "they" are right. But then Folk also is a demagogue, and so are all thorough-going reformers. La Follette from the beginning has asked, not the bosses, but the people for what he wanted, and after 1894 he simply broadened his field and re-doubled his efforts. He circularized the State, he made speeches every chance he got, and if the test of demagogy is the tone and style of a man's speeches, La Follette is the opposite of a demagogue. Capable of fierce invective, his oratory is impersonal; passionate and emotional himself, his speeches are temperate. Some of them are so loaded with facts and such closely knit arguments, that they demand careful reading, and their effect is traced to his delivery, which is forceful, emphatic, and fascinating. His earnestness carries the conviction of sincerity, and the conviction of his honesty of purpose he has planted all over the State by his Halfbreed methods.

What were the methods of the Sawyer-Payne-Spooner Republicans? In 1896 the next Governor of Wisconsin had to be chosen. The Stalwarts could not run Governor Upham again. As often happens to "safe men," the System had used him up; his appointments had built up the machine, his approval had sealed the compromise of the treasury cases. Someone else must run. To pick out his successor, the Stalwart leaders held a meeting at St. Louis, where they were attending a national convention, and they chose for Governor Edward W. Scofield. There was no demagogy about that.

La Follette wished to run himself; he hoped to run and win while Sawyer lived, and he was holding meetings, too. But his meetings were all over the State, with voters and delegates, and he was making headway. Lest he might fall short, however, La Follette made a political bargain.

He confesses it, and calls it a political sin, but he thinks the retribution which came swift and hard was expiation. He made a deal with Emil Baensch, by which both should canvass the State for delegates, with the understanding that whichever of the two should develop the greater strength was to have both delegations. La Follette says he came into convention with enough delegates of his own to nominate him, and Boensch had seventy-five or so besides. The convention adjourned over night without nominating and the next morning La Follette was beaten. He had lost some of his own delegates, and Baensch's went to Scofield.

La Follette's lost delegates were bought. How the Baensch delegates were secured, I don't know, but Baensch was not a man to sell for money. It was reported to La Follette during the night that Baensch was going over, and La Follette wrestled with and thought he had won him back, till the morning balloting showed. As for the rest, the facts are ample to make plain the methods of the old ring. Sawyer was there; and there was a "barrel." I saw men who saw money on a table in the room in the Pfister Hotel, where delegates went in and out, and newspaper men present at the time told me the story in great detail. But there is better evidence than this. Men to whom bribes were offered reported to their leader that night. The first warning came from Captain John T. Rice, of Racine, who (as Governor La Follette recalls) said: "I have been with the old crowd all my life and I thought I knew the worst, but they have no right to ask me to do what they did to-night. I won't tell you who, but the head of the whole business asked me to name my price for turning over the Union Grove delegation from you to Scofield." There are many such personal statements, some of them giving prices—cash, and federal and State offices—and some giving the names of the bribery agents. The Halfbreed leaders tried to catch the bribers with witnesses, but failed, and at midnight Charles F. Pfister, a Milwaukee Stalwart leader, called on La Follette, who repeated to me what he said:

"La Follette, we've got you beaten. We've got your delegates. It won't do you any good to squeal, and if you'll behave yourself we'll take care of you."

So La Follette had to go on with his fight. He would not "behave." His followers wanted him to lead an independent movement for Governor; he wouldn't do that, but he made up his mind to lead a movement for reform within the party, and his experience with corrupt delegates set him to thinking about methods of nomination. The System loomed large with the growth of corporate wealth, the power of huge consolidations over the individual, and the unscrupulous use of both money and power. Democracy was passing, and yet the people were sound. Their delegates at home were representatives, but shipped on passes to Milwaukee, treated, "entertained," and bribed, they ceased to represent. The most important reform was to get the nomination back among the voters themselves. Thus La Follette, out of his own experience, took up this issue—direct primary nominations by the Australian ballot.

During the next two years La Follette made a propaganda with this issue and railroad taxation, the taxation of other corporations—express and sleeping car companies which paid nothing—and the evils of a corrupt machine that stood for corrupting capital. He sent out circulars and litera- ture, some of it the careful writings of scientific authors, but, most effective of all, were the speeches he made at the county fairs. When the time for the next Republican State convention came around in 1898, he held a conference with some thirty of his leaders in Milwaukee, and he urged a campaign for their platform alone, with no candidate. The others insisted that La Follette run, and they were right in principle. As the event proved, the Stalwarts were not afraid of a platform, if they could be in office to make and carry out the laws. La Follette ran for the nomination and was beaten—by the same methods that were employed against him in '96; cost (insider's estimate), $8,000. Scofield was re- nominated.

But the La Follette-Hall platform was adopted—anti-pass, corporation taxation, primary election reform, and all. "They" say now in Wisconsin that La Follette is too practical; that he has adopted machine methods, etc. During 1896, 1897, and 1898 they were saying he was an impracticable reformer, and yet here they were adopting his impracticable theories. And they enacted some of these reforms. The agitation (for La Follette is indeed an "agitator") made necessary some compliance with public demand and platform promises, so Hall got his anti-pass law at last; a commission to investigate taxation was appointed, and there was some other good legislation. Yet, as Mr. Hall said, "In effect, that platform was repudiated." The railway commission reported that the larger companies, the Chicago, Milwaukee & St. Paul and the Northwestern, respectively, did not pay their proportionate share of the taxes, and a bill was introduced by Hall to raise their assessments. It passed the House, but the Senate had and has a "combine" like the Senates of Missouri and Illinois, and the combine beat the bill.

The failures of the Legislature left all questions open, and La Follette and his followers continued their agitation. Meanwhile Senator Sawyer died, and when the next gubernatorial election (1900) approached, all hope of beating La Follette was gone. The Stalwarts began to come to him with offers of support. One of the first to surrender was J. W. Babcock, Congressman and national politician. Others followed, but not John C. Spooner, Payne, and Pfister, not yet. They brought out for the nomination John M. Whitehead, a State Senator with a clean reputation and a good record. But in May (1900) La Follette announced his candidacy on a ringing platform, and he went campaigning down into the strongest Stalwart counties. He carried enough of them to take the heart out of the old ring. All other candidates withdrew, and Senator Spooner, who is a timid man, wrote a letter which, in view of his subsequent stand for reëlection, is a remarkable document; it declared that he was unalterably determined not to run again for the Senate. La Follette was nominated unanimously, and his own platform was adopted. The victory was complete. Though the implacable Stalwarts supported the Democratic candidate, La Follette was elected by 102,000 plurality.

Victory for reform is often defeat, and this triumph of La Follette, apparently so complete, was but the beginning of the greatest fight of all in Wisconsin, the fight that is being waged out there now. Governor La Follette was inaugurated January 7, 1901. The legislature was overwhelmingly Republican and apparently there was perfect harmony in the party. The Governor believed there was. The Stalwart-Halfbreed lines were not sharply drawn. The Halfbreeds counted a majority, especially in the House, and A. R. Hall was the "logical" candidate for Speaker. It was understood that he coveted the honor, but he proposed and it was decided that, in the interest of peace and fair play, a Stalwart should take the chair. The Governor says that the first sign he had of trouble was in the newspapers which, the day after the organization of the legislature, reported that the Stalwarts controlled and that there would be no primary election or tax legislation. The Governor, undaunted, sent in a firm message calling for the performance of all platform promises, and bills to carry out these pledges were introduced under the direction of the La Follette leaders, Hall and Judge E. Ray Stevens, the authority of the primary election bill. These developed the opposition. There were two (alternative) railway tax bills; others to tax other corporations; and, later, a primary election bill—nothing that was not promised by a harmonious party, yet the outcry was startling and the fight that followed was furious. Why?

I have seen enough of the System to believe that that is the way it works. Just such opposition, with just such cries of "boss," "dictator," etc., arise against any Governors who try to govern in the interest of the people. And I believe they will find their Legislatures organized and corrupted against them. But in the case of La Follette there was a "misunderstanding." In the year (1900) when everything was La Follette, Congressman Babcock, Postmaster-General Payne, and others sought to bring together the great ruling special interests and the inevitable Governor. Governor La Follette said, like President Roosevelt, that he would represent the corporations of his State, just as he would represent all other interests and persons; but no more. He would be "fair." Well, that was "all we want," they said, and they way seemed smooth. It was like the incident in St. Louis when Folk told the boodlers he would "do his duty," and the boodlers answered, "Of course, old man."

But some railroad men said La Follette promised in writing to consult with them before bringing in railroad bills; there was a certain famous letter written in the spring of 1900 to Thomas H. Gill, an old friend of the Governor, who is counsel to the Wisconsin Central Railroad; this letter put the Governor on record. Everywhere I went I heard of this document, and though the noise of it had resounded through the State for four years, it had never been produced. Here it is:

MADISON, WIS., MAY 12th, 1900.

DEAR TOM:

You have been my personal and political friend for twenty years. Should I become a candidate for the nomination for Governor, I want your continued support, if you can consistently accord it to me. But you are the attorney for the Wisconsin Central R. R. Co., and I am not willing that you should be placed in any position where you could be subjected to any criticism or embarrassment with your employers upon my account. For this reason, I desire to state to you in so far as I am able my position in relation to the question of railway taxation, which has now become one of public interest, and is likely to so continue until rightly settled. This I can do in a very few words.

Railroad corporations should pay neither more nor less than a justly proportionate share of taxes with the other taxable property of the State. If I were in a position to pass officially upon a bill to change existing law, it would be my first care to know whether the rate therein proposed was just in proportion to the property of other corporations and individuals as then taxed, or as therein proposed to be taxed. The determination of that question would be controlling. If such rate was less than the justly proportionate share which should be borne by the railroads, then I should favor increasing it to make it justly proportionate. If the proposed rate was more than the justly proportionate share, in comparison with the property of other corporations, and of individuals taxed under the law, then I should favor decreasing to make it justly proportionate.

In other words, I would favor equal and exact justice to each individual and to every interest, yielding neither to clamor on the one hand, nor being swerved from the straight course by any interest upon the other. This position, I am sure, is the only one which could commend itself to you, and cannot be criticised by any legitimate business honestly managed.

The Mr. Gill to whom this letter was addressed is one of the most enlightened and fair-minded corporation lawyers that I ever met, even in the West, where corporation men also are enlightened. He convinced me that he and the other railroad men really did expect more consideration than the Governor gave them, and so there may have been a genuine misunderstanding. But after what I have seen in Chicago, St. Louis, and Pittsburgh, and in Missouri and Illinois and the United States, I almost am persuaded that no honest official in power can meet the expectations of great corporations; they have been spoiled, like bad American children, and are ever ready to resort to corruption and force. That was their recourse now.

Governor La Follette says he learned afterward that during the campaign, the old, corrupt ring went about in the legislative districts, picking and "fixing" legislators, and that the plan was to discredit him with defeat by organizing the Legislature against him. However this may be, it is certain that when his bills were under way, there was a rush to the lobby at Madison. The regular lobbyists were reinforced with special agents; local Stalwart leaders were sent for, and federal office-holders; United States Senators hurried home, and Congressmen; and boodle, federal patronage, force, and vice were employed to defeat bills promised in the platform. Here is a statement by Irvine L. Lenroot, now the Speaker of the Assembly. He says:

From the first day of the session the railroad lobbyists were on the ground in force, offering courtesies and entertainments of various kinds to the members. Bribery is a hard word, a charge, which never should be made unless it can be substantiated. The writer has no personal knowledge of money being actually offered or received for votes against the bill. It was, however, generally understood in the Assembly that any member favoring the bill could better his financial condition if he was willing to vote against it. Members were approached by representatives of the companies and offered lucrative positions. This may not have been done with any idea of influencing votes.

The reader will draw his own conclusions. It was a matter of common knowledge that railroad mileage could be procured if a member was "right." Railroad lands could be purchased very cheaply by members of the Legislature. It was said if a member would get into a poker game with a lobbyist, the member was sure to win. Members opposed to Governor La Follette were urged to vote against the bill, because he wanted it to pass. A prominent member stated that he did not dare to vote for the bill, because he was at the mercy of the railroad companies, and he was afraid they would ruin his business by advancing his rates, if he voted for it.

I went to Superior and saw Mr. Lenroot, and he told me that one of the "members approached by representatives of the companies and offered positions" was himself. He gave his bribery stories in detail, and enabled me to run down and verify others; but the sentence that interested me most in his statement was the last. The member who did not dare vote for the railway tax bill, lest the railways raise the freight on his goods and ruin his business, confessed to Governor La Follette and others. Another member stated that in return for his treason to his constituents, a railroad quoted him a rate that would give him an advantage over his competitors.

Well, these methods succeeded. The policy of the administration was not carried out. Some good bills passed, but the session was a failure. Not content with this triumph, however, the System went to work to beat La Follette, and to accomplish this end, La Follette's methods were adopted, or, rather, adapted. A systematic appeal was to be made to public opinion. A meeting of the leading Stalwarts was held in the eleventh story of an office building in Milwaukee, and a Permanent Republican League of the State of Wisconsin was organized. This became known as the "Eleventh Story League." A manifesto was put out "viewing with alarm the encroachments of the executive upon the legislative branch of the government," etc., etc. (The encroachments of boodle business upon all branches of the government is all right.) An army of canvassers was dispatched over the State to interview personally every voter in the State and leave with him books and pamphlets. Now this was democratic and fair, but that League did one thing which is enough alone to condemn the whole movement. It corrupted part of the country press. This is not hearsay. The charge was made at the time these papers swung round suddenly, and the League said it did not bribe the editors; it "paid for space for League editorial matter, and for copies of the paper to be circulated." This is bribery, as any newspaper man knows. But there was also what even the League business man would call bribery; newspaper men all over the State told me about direct purchase—and cheap, too. It is sickening, but, for final evidence, I saw affidavits, published in Wisconsin, by newspaper men, who were approached with offers which they refused, and by others who sold out, then threw up their contracts and returned the bribes, for shame or other reasons.

These "democratic" methods failed. When the time arrived for the next Republican State convention, the Stalwarts found that the people had sent up delegates instructed for La Follette, and he was nominated for a second term. What could the Stalwarts do? They weren't even "regular" now. La Follette had the party, they had only the federal patronage and the Big Business System. But the System had resources. Wherever a municipal reform movement has hewed to the line, the leaders of it, like Folk and the Chicago reformers, have seen the forces of corruption retire from one party to the other and from the city to the State. This Wisconsin movement for State reform now had a similar experience. The Wisconsin System, driven out of the Republican, went over to the Democratic party; that had not been reformed; beaten out of power in the State, it retreated to the towns; they had not been reformed.

The System in many of the Wisconsin municipalities was intact. There had been no serious municipal reform movements anywhere, and the citizens of Milwaukee, Oshkosh, Green Bay, etc., were pretty well satisfied, and they are still, apparently. "We're nothing like Minneapolis, St. Louis, and the rest," they told me with American complacency. Green Bay was exactly like Minneapolis; we know it because the wretched little place has been exposed since. And Marinette and Oshkosh, unexposed, are said by insiders to be "just like Green Bay." As for Milwaukee, that is St. Louis all over again.

District Attorney Bennett has had grand juries at work in Milwaukee since 1901, and he has some forty-two persons indicted—twelve aldermen, ten supervisors, nine other officials, one State Senator, and ten citizens; four convictions and three pleas of guilty. The grafting so far exposed is petty, but the evidence in hand indicates a highly perfected boodle system. The Republicans had the county, the Democrats the city, and both the council and the board of supervisors had combines which grafted on contracts, public institutions, franchises, and other business privileges. The corrupt connection of business and politics was shown; the informants were merchants and contractors, mostly small men, who confessed to bribery. The biggest caught so far is Colonel Pabst, the brewer, who paid a check of $1,500 for leave to break a building law. But all signs point higher than beer, to more "legitimate" political business. As in Chicago, a bank is the center of this graft (The First National Bank, the president of which is now in the penitentiary), and public utility companies are back of it. The politicians in the boards of management, now or formerly, show that. It is a bipartisan system all through. Henry C. Payne, while chairman of the Republican State Central Committee, and E. C. Wall (the man the Wisconsin Democracy offered to the National Democratic Convention for President of the United States), while chairman of the Democratic State Central Committee, engineered a consolidation of Milwaukee street railway and electric lighting companies, and, when the job was done, Payne became manager of the street railway, Wall of the light company. But this was "business." There was no scandal about it. The great scandal of Milwaukee was the extension of street railway franchises, and the men who put that through were Charles F. Pfister, the Stalwart Republican boss, and David S. Rose, the Stalwart Democratic Mayor. Money was paid; the extension was boodled through. The Milwaukee *Sentinel* reprinted a paragraph saying Pfister, among others, did the bribing, and thus it happened that the Stalwarts got that paper. Pfister sued for libel, but when the editors (now on the Milwaukee *Free Press*) made answer that their defense would be proof of the charge, the millionaire traction man bought the paper and its evidence, too. It is no more than fair to add—as Milwaukee newspaper men always do (with delight)—that the paper had very little evidence, not nearly so much as Pfister seemed to think it had. As for Mayor Rose, his friends declare that he has told them, personally and convincingly, that he got not one cent for his service. But that is not the point. Mayor Rose fought to secure for special interests a concession which sacrificed the common interests of his city. I am aware that he defends the terms of the grants as fair, and they would seem so in the East, but the West is intelligent on special privileges, and Mayor Rose lost to Milwaukee the chance Chicago seized to tackle the public utility problem. Moreover, Rose knew that his council was corrupt before it was proven so; he told two business men that they couldn't get a privilege they sought honestly from him without bribing aldermen. Yet he ridiculed as "hot air" an investigation which produced evidence enough to defeat at the polls, in a self-respecting city, the head of an administration so besmirched. Nevertheless, Milwaukee reëlected Rose; good citizens say that they gave the man the benefit of the doubt— the man, not the city.

But this is not the only explanation. The System was on trial with Mayor Rose in that election, and the System saved its own. The Republicans, with the Rose administration exposed, had a chance to win, and they nominated a good man, Mr. Guy D. Goff. Pfister, the Stalwart Republican boss, seemed to support Goff; certainly the young candidate had no suspicion to the contrary. He has now, however. When the returns came in showing that he was beaten, Mr. Goff hunted up Mr. Pfister, and he found him. Mr. Goff, the Republican candidate for Mayor, found Charles F. Pfister, the Stalwart Republican boss, rejoicing over the drinks with the elected Democratic Mayor, David S. Rose!

I guess Mr. Goff knows that a bipartisan System rules Milwaukee, and, by the same token, Governor La Follette knows that there is a bipartisan System in Wisconsin. For when Governor La Follette beat the Stalwarts in the Republican State convention of 1902, those same Stalwarts combined with the Democrats. Democrats told me that the Republican Stalwarts dictated the "Democratic" anti-La Follette platform, and that Pfister, the "Republican" boss, named the "safe man" chosen for the "Democratic" candidate for Governor to run again La Follette—said David S. Rose.

"They" say in Wisconsin that La Follette is a Democrat; that "he appeals to Democratic voters." He does. He admits it, but he adds that it is indeed to the Democratic voters that he appeals—not to the Democratic machine. And he gets Democratic votes. "They" complain that he has split the Republican party; he has, and he has split the Democratic party, too. When "they" united the two party rings of the bipartisan System against La Follette in 1902, he went out after the voters of both parties, and those voters combined; they beat Rose, the two rings, and the System. The people of Wisconsin reëlected La Follette, the "unsafe," and that is why the trouble is so great in Wisconsin. The System there is down.

There is a machine, but it is La Follette's. When he was reëlected, the Governor organized his party, and I think no other of his offenses is quite so heinous in Stalwart eyes. They wanted me to expose him as a boss who had used State patronage to build up an organization. I reminded "them" that their federal patronage is greater than La Follette's State patronage, and I explained that my prejudice was not against organization; their kind everywhere had been urging me so long to believe that organization was necessary in politics that I was disposed to denounce only those machines that sold out the party and the people. And as for the "boss"— it is not the boss in an elective office where he is responsible that is so bad, but the irresponsible boss back of a safe figurehead; this is the man that is really dangerous. They declared, however, that Governor La Follette had sacrificed good service to the upbuilding of his machine. This is a serious charge. I did not go thoroughly into it. Cases which I investigated at Stalwart behest, held, with one exception, very little water, and I put no faith in the rest. But, for the sake of argument, let us admit that the departments are not all that they should be. What then? As in Chicago, the fight in Wisconsin is for self-government, not "good" government; it is a fight to reëstablish a government representative of all the people. Given that; remove from control the Big Business and the Bad Politics that corrupt all branches of the government, and "good" government will come easily enough. But Big Business and Bad Politics are hard to beat.

The defeat of Rose did not beat them. The Stalwarts still had the Senate, and they manned the lobby to beat the railroad tax and the primary election bills. But Governor La Follette outplayed them at the great game. He long had been studying the scheme for a State commission to regulate railway freight rates. It was logical. If their taxes were increased the roads could take the difference out of the people by raising freight rates. Other States had such commissions, and in some of them, notably Iowa and Illinois, the rates were lower than in Wisconsin. Moreover, we all know railroads give secret rebates and otherwise discriminate in favor of individuals and localities.

When then, the battle lines were drawn on the old bills in the Legislature of 1903, the Governor threw into the fight a bristling message calling for a commission to regulate railway rates. The effect was startling. "Populism!" "Socialism!" "they" cried, and they turned to rend this new bill. They let the tax bill go through to fight this fresh menace to "business." They held out against the primary election bill also, for if that passed they feared the people might keep La Follette in power forever. Even that, however, they let pass finally, with an amendment for a referendum. Concentrating upon the rate commission bill, Big Business organized business men's mass metings throughout the State, and with the help of favored or timid shippers, sent committees to Madison to protest to the Legislature. Thus this bill in the interests of fair business was beaten by business, and, with the primary election referendum, is an issue in this year's campaign (1904).

As I have tried to show, however, the fundamental issue lies deeper. The people of Wisconsin understand this. The Stalwarts dread the test at the polls. But what other appeal was there? They knew one. When the Republican State convention met this year, the Stalwarts bolted; whatever the result might have been of a fight in the convention, they avoided it and held a separate convention in another hall, which, by the way, they had hired in advance. The Halfbreeds renominated La Follette; the Stalwarts put up another ticket. To the Stalwart convention came Postmaster-General Payne, United States Senators Spooner and Quarles, Stalwart Congressmen and federal officeholders—the Federal System. The broken State System was appealing to the United States System, and the Republican National Convention at Chicago was to decide the case. And it did decide—for the System. I attended that convention, and heard what was said privately and honestly. The Republicans who decided for Payne-Spooner-Pfister-Babcock, et al., said "La Follette isn't really a Republican anyhow."

Isn't he? That is a most important question. True, he is very democratic essentially. He helped to draw the McKinley tariff law and he is standing now on the national Republican platform; his democracy consists only in the belief that the citizens elected to represent the people should represent the people, not the corrupt special interests. Both parties should be democratic in that sense. But they aren't. Too often we have found both parties representing graft—big business graft. The people, especially in the West, are waking to a realization of this state of things, and (taking a hint from the Big Grafters) they are following leaders who see that the way to restore government representative of the common interests of the city or State, is to restore to public opinion the control of the dominant party. The Democrats of Missouri have made their party democratic; the Republicans of Illinois have made their party democratic. The next to answer should be the people of Wisconsin. The Stalwarts hope the courts will decide. They hope their courts will uphold the decision of the National Republican Party, that they, who represent all that is big and bad in business and politics, are the regular "Republicans." This isn't right. The people of Wisconsin are not radicals; they are law-abiding, conservative, and fair. They will lay great store by what their courts shall rule, but this is a question that should be left wholly to the people themselves. And they are to be trusted, for no matter how men may differ about Governor La Follette otherwise, his long, hard fight has developed citizenship in Wisconsin—honest, reasonable, intelligent citizenship. And that is better than "business"; that is what business and government are for—men.

# PART II

# LABOR IN A MIDDLE-CLASS SOCIETY

# Report of the Industrial Relations Commission

## *Basil M. Manly*

*The social issue which most continually distracted the minds of citizens in the progressive era was the fact of class conflict. Americans viewed the problem in mixed ways. A small but important number were professed Socialists who believed that capital and labor would clash in an inevitable (though not necessarily a violent) showdown, from which would emerge a classless nation. A greater number rejected Socialism as irrelevant or undesirable and deplored the class warfare they associated with it. Most citizens longed for a social order free from strife, a single middle class nourished on a respect for the rights of property and persons under a rule of law.*

*To the perceptive citizen, however, evidence was abundantly clear that this order had not yet arrived. In the single generation between 1885 and 1915 no less than three federally sponsored fact-finding commissions were empowered to investigate the impact of industrialism on the economic and social order and to prescribe remedies to Congress for what they uncovered. In 1903 the second (and most thorough) of the three commissions published nineteen fat volumes of testimony which documented what many people believed on hunch, that while the productive achievements of American industrialism were awesome they had been gained at the price of a substantial growth in monopoly power and an apparent aggravation of social injustice. National progressivism brought little relief. Between 1903 and 1913 conflicts between management and labor were to smolder and flare with increasing heat. After the bombing of the Los Angeles* Times *and with the violence in western mining camps still fresh in public memory, the outgoing Congress of 1912 authorized the appointment of a third federal commission to probe specifically into the causes of the current labor unrest.*

*In the following year the new President, Woodrow Wilson, announced*

157

*the appointment of a nonpartisan Commission on Industrial Relations, a nine-member body intended to represent management, labor, and the public in equal numbers. For its chairman Wilson originally sought the services of John R. Commons, professor of economics at the University of Wisconsin, specialist in the labor movement and a friend of Robert La Follette; but Commons declined the chairmanship under pressure of other work, though he agreed to serve on the Commission and to head its staff of investigators, and Wilson turned to Frank P. Walsh, a successful criminal lawyer and aggressive liberal from Kansas. Walsh quickly dominated the work of the Commission. Calling on over seven hundred witnesses to testify, he organized a dramatic series of hearings deliberately designed to highlight the problems of conflict between capital and labor; he hired a number of carefully picked investigators to report independently to him on a number of leading industrial disputes and social problems; and he put into the charge of Basil Manly, a capable analyst from the Bureau of Labor Statistics and a strong liberal like himself, the crucial task of writing the final report and casting the Commission's recommendations into persuasive form.*

*The findings ran to eleven volumes and took a large staff of workers two years to complete. The members of the Commission were in basic agreement in their support of the factual evidence but split sharply over the conclusions and recommendations which Basil Manly drew from the evidence. Walsh and the three "labor" representatives supported Manly on most major issues, while the three "business" representatives supported a vigorous and lengthy dissent submitted by John Commons and Mrs. Borden Harriman. The major disagreement was over whether the future of the labor movement lay in collective bargaining or in more direct political action; but though the issue was crucial to the ultimate fate of the reform movement, it did not involve the validity of the report in what it revealed of the deterioration of industrial relations over the previous twenty years. This was the central point in Manly's narrative summary, which is reproduced below.*

*Manly's report struck hard. In its bald assertion that beneath the middle class of Americans there existed 25,000,000 wage earners whose condition of life and whose political rights placed them only slightly above the status of the traditional European proletariat, it exposed the one most vulnerable feature of the era which had been largely concealed from view. Stressing a central theme of progressive reformers the author hammered most sharply at the courts as having perverted justice and perpetuated the inequality of the social classes before the law. But as a reward for its frankness, the Commission suffered a not uncommon fate. Submitting its report (and dissent), it disbanded, and then was forced to watch the cautious legislators skirt around the controversial recommendations and finally shelve them. Imperceptibly, under the impact of war, depression, and the growth of a direct federal interest in labor-management stability, bits and pieces of the Commission's work took root in public policy. Less important for its influence than for what it revealed and represented, it had already entered into the disturbing image which sensitive citizens beheld in the mirror of their own times.*

INTRODUCTION

The question of industrial relations assigned by Congress to the Commission for investigation is more fundamental and of greater importance to the welfare of the Nation than any other question except the form of our Government. The only hope for the solution of the tremendous problems created by industrial relationship lies in the effective use of our democratic institutions and in the rapid extension of the principles of democracy to industry.

The *immediate* effects of the form and character of industrial organization are, however, greater and closer to the lives and happiness of all classes of citizens than even the form and character of our political institutions. The ordinary man, whether employer or worker, has relatively little contact with the Government. If he and his family are well-fed, well-housed, and well-clothed, and if he can pay for the education of his children, he can exist even under an autocratic monarchy with little concern, until some critical situation develops in which his own liberty is interfered with or until he is deprived of life or property by the overwhelming power of his tyrannical ruler. But his industrial relations determine every day what he and his family shall eat, what they shall wear, how many hours of his life he shall labor and in what surroundings. Under certain conditions where his individual or corporate employer owns or controls the community in which he lives, the education of his children, the character and prices of his food, clothing and house, his own actions, speech and opinions, and in some cases even his religion, are controlled and determined, in so far as the interests of the employer make it desirable for him to exercise such control. Such conditions are established and maintained not only through the dictation of all working conditions by the employer, but by his usurpation or control of the functions and machinery of political government in such communities.

In the available time it has been impossible to ascertain how general such conditions are, but it is clearly indicated by the investigations that in isolated industrial, mining, or agricultural communites, whch are owned or controlled by single individuals or corporations, and in which the employees are unorganized, industrial feudalism is the rule rather than the exception.

Commission on Industrial Relations, *Final Report of Basil M. Manly, Director of Research and Investigation,* United States Senate, 64th Congress, 1st Session, Document 415 (Washington D.C.: Government Printing Office, 1915), I, pp. 1-65.

In such communities democratic government does not, as a rule, exist, except in name or form, and as a consequence there now exist within the body of our Republic industrial communities which are virtually principalities, oppressive to those dependent upon them for a livelihood and a dreadful menace to the peace and welfare of the Nation.

Such conditions as these are the direct and inevitable consequence of the industrial relations which exist in such communities. Political freedom can exist only where there is industrial freedom; political democracy only where there is industrial democracy.

Such industrial democracy has been established in a greater or less degree in certain American industries or for certain classes of employees. But between conditions of industrial democracy and industrial feudalism there are almost infinite gradations marking the stages of evolution which have been reached. In every case, however, investigation has shown that the degree of political freedom and democracy which exists is conditioned by the industrial status of the citizens who form the majority of the community.

The problems of industrial relations, therefore, demand the attention of Congress not only because they determine the life, security and happiness of the twenty-five million citizens of the United States who occupy the position of wage earners, but because they affect for good or evil the Government of localities and States, and to a smaller degree that of the Nation itself. What each of these wage earners shall eat, what he shall wear, where he shall live, and how long and under what conditions he shall labor, are determined by his industrial status and by his relation individually or collectively to the person or corporation employing him. Similarly and almost as directly this relationship determines whether the machinery of government shall be used for or against his welfare, whether his vote shall count for or against his own interest, whether he shall be tried by a jury of his peers or a jury selected in collusion with the employing company, or, under conditions of so-called martial law, by no jury whatever; whether in fact he shall be a free man or be deprived of every right guaranteed by Federal and State constitutions, imprisoned without warrant for the commission of crimes of which he may be innocent, or forcibly deported from the community or State in which he has made his home. For these reasons it seems desirable at the outset to suggest a recommendation to Congress that these problems of industrial relationship should occupy their due prominence in the deliberations of that Honorable Body, and that the entire machinery of the Federal Government should be utilized to the greatest possible degree for the correction of such deplorable conditions as have been found to exist.

The lack of a proper industrial relationship and the existence of bad labor conditions is a matter of the most serious moment during times of peace, but the events of the past year have demonstrated how enormously their menace to the welfare of a nation is increased during a period of war. The present European war is being fought on the farms and in the factories as much as in the trenches. The effective mobilization of our industrial resources is as important, simply from the standpoint of war, as is the mobilization of our military and naval forces.

It is equally important that action should be taken now, and not after war is a reality.

An attempt has been made in the succeeding pages of this report to suggest some of the measures which should be adopted, with a full realization, however, that no action will be effective which does not come through an understanding by the American people of the essential facts regarding industrial conditions. Practically, there are only two alternatives for effective action: First, the creation of a huge system of bureaucratic paternalism such as has been developed in Germany; second, action which removes the many existing obstacles which prevent effective organization and co-operation, reserving for performance by the Gevornment only those services which can not be effectively conducted by voluntary organizations, and those which are of such vital importance to the entire Nation that they should not be left to the hazard of private enterprise.

In closing this introductory statement, it is proper to append a quotation from Carlyle, the great Scotch historian, which contains in a few eloquent sentences the very heart of the situation in American industry:

With the working people, again, it is not so well. Unlucky! For there are from twenty to twenty-five millions of them. Whom, however, we lump together into a kind of dim compendious unity . . . as "the masses." Masses indeed: and yet, singular to say, the masses consist all of units . . . every unit of whom has his own heart and sorrows; stands covered there with his own skin, and if you prick him he will bleed. Every unit of these masses is a miraculous man, even as thou thyself art; struggling with vision or with blindness for *his* infinite kingdom (this life which he has got, once only, in the middle of eternities); with a spark of the divinity, what thou callest an immortal soul, in him!

Clearly a difficult "point" for government, that of dealing with these masses; if indeed it be not rather the sole point and problem of government, and all other points mere accidental crotchets, superficialities, and beatings of the wind! For let charter-chests, use and wont, law common and special, say what they will, the masses count to so many millions of units; made, to all appearance, by God, whose earth this is declared to be. . . .

LABOR CONDITIONS IN THE PRINCIPAL INDUSTRIES, INCLUDING AGRICULTURE

In considering the conditions of labor in American industries, it has seemed that they could be judged or appraised only by comparing conditions as they actually exist with what knowledge and experience shows that they might easily be made during the immediate future if proper action were taken to utilize the resources of our Nation efficiently and distribute the products equitably.

As against this view there has been an attempt by some persons to urge the judgment of all things by comparison with the past. Much stress has been laid by certain witnesses upon the alleged improvement of the condition of the workers during the past quarter century.

This point, however, is regarded as generally immaterial. The crux of the question rather is, Have the workers received a fair share of the enormous increase in wealth which has taken place in this country, during the period, as a result largely of their labors? The answer is emphatically —No!

The wealth of the country between 1890 and 1912 increased from 65 to 187 billions, or 188 per cent, whereas the aggregate income of wage earners in manufacturing, mining, and transportation has risen between 1889 and 1909 only 95 per cent, from 2516 millions in 1889 to 4916 millions in 1909. Furthermore, the wage earners' share of the net product of industry in the case of manufactures was only 40.2 per cent in 1909 as compared with 44.9 per cent in 1889.

Similarly, the attempt to dismiss deplorable labor conditions in the United States by arguments that they are better than in European countries is repugnant. To say that conditions are better than in Great Britain, for example, is simply to say that somewhat less than one-third of the population is in a state of absolute poverty, for that was the condition reported by the latest British Commission. It should be a matter of shame also to boast that the condition of American laborers is better than that of laborers in the "black bread belt" of Germany.

That conditions are, as a matter of fact, but little better is proved conclusively by the almost complete cessation of immigration from Germany, England, and France. No better proof of the miserable condition of the mass of American workers need be sought than the fact that in recent years laborers in large numbers have come to this country only from Russia, Italy, Austria-Hungary and the backward and impoverished nations of southern and eastern Europe.

With the inexhaustible natural resources of the United States, her tremendous mechanical achievements, and the genius of her people for organization and industry, there can be no natural reason to prevent every able-bodied man of our present population from being well fed, well housed, comfortably clothed, and from rearing a family of moderate size in comfort, health and security. How far this idea is actually achieved is discussed in some detail in the following pages.

It is evident both from the investigations of this Commission and from the reports of all recent Governmental bodies that a large part of our industrial population are, as a result of the combination of low wages and unemployment, living in a condition of actual poverty. How large this proportion is can not be exactly determined, but it is certain that at least one-third and possibly one-half of the families of wage earners employed in manufacturing and mining earn in the course of the year less than enough to support them in anything like a comfortable and decent condition. The detailed evidence is presented in a separate report which is submitted for transmittal to Congress. At this point it is sufficient to call attention to the results of the most exhaustive and sweeping official investigation of recent years, that of the Immigration Commission, which reported to Congress in 1909. This investigation secured detailed information regarding the daily or weekly earnings of 619,595 employees of all classes in our basic manufacturing industries and in coal mining, and information regarding income and living conditions for 15,726 families.

It was found that the incomes of almost two-thirds of these families (64 per cent) were less than $750 per year and of almost one-third (31 per cent) were less than $500, the average for all being $721. The average size of these families was 5.6 members. Elaborate studies of the cost of living made in all parts of the country at the same time have shown that the very least that a family of five persons can live upon in anything approaching decency is $700. It is probable that, owing to the fact that the families investigated by the Immigration Commission were, to a large extent, foreign born, the incomes reported are lower than the average for the entire working population; nevertheless, even when every allowance is made for that fact, the figures show conclusively that between one-half and two-thirds of these families were living below the standards of decent subsistence, while about one-third were living in a state which can be described only as abject poverty.

American society was founded and for a long period existed upon the theory that the family should derive its support from the earnings of the father. How far we have departed from this condition is shown by the fact that 79 per cent of the fathers of these families earned less than $700 per year. In brief, only one-fourth of these fathers could have supported their families on the barest subsistence level without the earnings of other members of the family or income from outside sources.

Other facts collected in this investigation show conclusively that a very large proportion of these families did not live in decency and comfort. Thirty per cent kept boarders and lodgers, a condition repugnant to every ideal of American family life, especially in the crowded tenements or tiny cottages in which the wage earners of America characteristically live. Furthermore, in 77 per cent of the families two or more persons occupied each sleeping room, in 37 per cent three or more persons, and in 15 per cent four or more persons.

The most striking evidence of poverty is the proportion of pauper burials. The repugnance of all classes of wage earners of all races to pauper burial is such that everything will be sacrificed and heavy debts incurred rather than permit any member of the family to lie in the "potters' field"; nevertheless in New York City one out of every twelve corpses is buried at the expense of the city or turned over to physicians for dissection.

The terrible effects of such poverty may be outlined in a few paragraphs, but their far-reaching consequences could not be adequately shown in a volume.

Children are the basis of the State; as they live or die, as they thrive or are ill-nourished, as they are intelligent or ignorant, so fares the State. How do the children of American workers fare?

It has been proved by studies here and abroad that there is a direct relation between poverty and the death rate of babies; but the frightful rate at which poverty kills was not known, at least for this country, until very recently, when through a study made in Johnstown, Pa., by the Federal Children's Bureau, it was shown that the babies whose fathers earned less than $10 per week died during the first year at the appalling rate of 256 per 1000. On the other hand, those whose fathers earned $25 per week or more died at the rate of only 84 per 1000. The babies of the poor died at three times the rate of those who were in fairly well-to-do families. The tremendous significance of these figures will be appreciated when it is known that one-third of all the adult workmen reported by the Immigration Commission earned less than $10 per week, even exclusive of time lost. On the showing of Johnstown these workmen may expect one out of four of their babies to die during the first year of life.

The last of the family to go hungry are the children, yet statistics show that in six of our largest cities from 12 to 20 per cent of the children are noticeably underfed and ill-nourished.

The minimum amount of education which any child should receive is certainly the grammar school course, yet statistics show that only one-third of the children in our public schools complete the grammar school course, and less than 10 per cent finish high school. Those who leave are almost entirely the children of the workers, who, as soon as they reach working age, are thrown, immature, ill-trained, and with no practical knowledge, into the complexities of industrial life. In each of four industrial towns studied by the Bureau of Labor Statistics, more than 75 per cent of the children quit school before reaching the seventh grade.

The great seriousness of this condition is even more acutely realized when it is known that in the families of the workers 37 per cent of the mothers are at work and consequently unable to give the children more than scant attention. Of these mothers 30 per cent keep boarders and lodgers and 7 per cent work outside the home.

As a final statement of the far-reaching effects of the economic condition of American wage earners, it seems proper to quote the following statement of the Chicago Commission on Crime, which after thorough investigation has reported during the past year:

The pressure of economic conditions has an enormous influence in producing certain types of crime. Unsanitary housing and working conditions, unemployment, wages inadequate to maintain a human standard of living, inevitably produce the crushed or distorted bodies and minds from which the army of crime is recruited. The crime problem is not merely a question of police and courts, it leads to the broader problems of public sanitation, education, home care, a living wage, and industrial democracy.

The other factors in the conditions under which labor is employed in American industry, such as working hours, regularity of employment, safety and sanitation, are left for later discussion. Suffice it to say in this connection that while in certain fields great improvements have been made, the general situation is such that they accentuate rather than relieve the deplorable effects of inadequate income which have been pointed out.

As a picture of American industry, this presentation is undeniably gloomy and depressing, but as a diagnosis of what is wrong with American labor conditions, it is true and exact. There are of course many bright spots in American industry, where workmen are well paid and regularly employed under good working conditions in the determination of which they have some share. But, even as the physician pays little attention to the good eyes and sound teeth of a patient whose vital organs are diseased, so impressive is the urgent need for attention to the diseased spots in industry, it is felt to be unnecessary to waste time in word pictures of conditions which are all right or which may be depended upon to right themselves.

In agriculture there is no array of exact figures which can be quoted to show the condition of labor. But, speaking generally, the available evidence indicates clearly that while in some sections agricultural laborers are well paid and fairly treated, the condition of the mass is very much like that of the industrial workers.

Moreover, there is a peculiar condition in agriculture, which merits a brief but strong statement at this point as a preface to a more detailed discussion later. The most alarming fact in American agriculture is the rapid growth of tenacy. In 1910 there were 37 tenant-operated farms in each 100 farms in the United States, as compared with 28 in 1890, an increase of 32 per cent during 20 years. No nation-wide investigation of the condition of tenant farmers has ever been made, but in Texas, where the investigations of this Commission were thorough and conclusive, it was found not only that the economic condition of the tenant was extremely bad, but that he was far from being free, while his future was regarded as hopeless. Badly housed, ill-nourished, uneducated and hopeless, these tenants continue year after year to eke out a bare living, moving frequently from one farm to another in the hope that something will turn up. Without a large family the tenant cannot hope to succeed or break even, so in each tenant family numerous children are being reared to a future which under present conditions will be no better than that of their parents, if as good. The wife of a typical tenant farmer, the mother of eleven children, stated in her testimony before the Commission that in addition to the rearing of children, making their clothes and doing the work of the house, she always helped with the crops, working up to within three or four months before children were born, and that during all the years of her married life she had had no ready-made dresses and only three hats. The investigations of this Commission in that rich and generally prosperous section of the country only confirm and accentuate the statements of the Federal Industrial Commission which reported in 1902:

The result of this system [share tenancy] is that the renters rarely ever succeed in laying by a surplus. On the contrary, their experiences are so discouraging that they seldom remain on the same farm for more than a year. They are not only unable to lay by any money, but their children remain uneducated and half clothed. The system is apparently one of the most undesirable, so far as its effect on the community is concerned.

Similarly, the Public Lands Commission reported in 1905:

There exists and is spreading in the West a tenant or hired labor system which not only represents a relatively low industrial development, but whose further development carries with it a most serious threat. Politically, socially and economically this system is indefensible.

The condition of agricultural laborers can not, however, be dismissed without referring to the development of huge estates which are operated by managers with hired labor on what may properly be called a "factory system." The conditions upon such estates are deplorable not only because of the extremely low wages paid (80 cents per day in the case of one which was carefully investigated), but even more because these estates, embracing within their boundaries entire counties and towns, are a law unto themselves and the absolute dictators of the lives, liberties and happiness of their employees. It is industrial feudalism in an extreme form. Such estates are, as a rule, the property of absentee landlords, who are for the most part millionaires, resident in the eastern States or in Europe.

EXISTING RELATIONS BETWEEN EMPLOYERS AND EMPLOYEES

Considering the whole field of American industry, there are almost infinite variations of relationship between employers and employees, ranging from the individual worker, hired by a single employer, as in domestic service and agriculture, to the huge corporation with a hundred thousand stockholders and a quarter of a million employees. Relationship varies from that of direct contact to a situation where the employee, together with thousands of his fellow-workers, is separated by hundreds of miles from the individuals who finally control his employment and of whose existence he is usually entirely ignorant.

A thorough discussion of the relationships which exist under these various forms of industrial organization would be not only tedious but useless for all practical purposes. The typical form of industrial organization is the corporation: In transportation approximately 100 per cent of the wage earners are employed by corporations; in mining, 90 per cent, and in manufacturing, 75 per cent. Moreover, it is under this form that the great problems of industrial relations have developed.

The actual relationship which exists between employers and employees under the artificial conditions which characterize the corporate form of organization can not be understood without an analysis of the different elements which go to make up the typical corporation. The actual ownership of a corporation is vested in the stockholders and bondholders, whose only interest in the industry is represented by certificates upon the basis of which they expect the payment of interest or dividends at stated intervals.

The control of the property, as far as operation is concerned, rests finally with the stockholders, or with some particular class of stockholders whose shares entitle them to vote. The stockholders, however, act through the Board of Directors, who are usually elected in such a way that they represent only the dominant interest. As far as the organization of the corporation is concerned, the principal function of the Board of Directors is to select the executive officials. These executive officials, either directly or indirectly, select the numerous superintendents, foremen and petty bosses by whom the direct operation of the enterprise is managed and through whom all the workers are hired, discharged and disciplined.

This is a skeleton of corporate organization. To understand its operations it is necessary to examine the functions and responsibilities of the different parts of the organization.

Theoretically and legally, the final control and responsibility rests with the stockholders, but in actual practice a very different situation is found. The relationship of stockholders to a corporation is anything but permanent; in a busy week on Wall street, the number of shares bought and sold in one of the great corporations will greatly exceed the total number of shares that are in existence. The stockholders as a class, therefore, have no guiding interest in the permanent efficiency of the corporation as regards either the preservation of its physical property or the maintenance of an efficient productive organization. Stocks are bought either as a speculation or as an investment, and in case either the physical property deteriorates or the productive organization tends to become inefficient, the well-informed stockholder generally takes no steps to correct the condition, but merely throws his stock upon the market. This marks a very real and definite distinction from the actual ownership of a property or business which must be kept in good condition by its owner as regards both plant and organization. If all industries were owned and operated by individuals, there might be some reason to hope that generally satisfactory wages and physical conditions might be attained through the education of the owner to a realization that permanent success depended absolutely upon the maintenance of the plant in the best condition and the permanent satisfaction of the legitimate demands of the workers, but with the impersonal, remote and irresponsible status of control by stock ownership, such a hope must be purely illusory. The ordinary stockholder in a large corporation actually occupies a less direct relationship to the corporation in which he is interested, has less knowledge of its actual operations, and less control over its management, than the ordinary citizen has over local, state and national governments.

Boards of Directors in theory are responsible for and would naturally be expected to maintain supervision over every phase of the corporation's management, but, as a matter of fact, we know that such supervision is maintained only over the financial phase of the business, controlling the acquisition of money to operate the business and distributing the profits. Actual direction generally exists only through the removal of executive officials who fail to deliver the expected profits, and through the appointment of their successors.

Upon the testimony of financiers representing, as directors, hundreds of corporations, the typical director of large corporations is not only totally ignorant of the actual operations of such corporations, whose properties he seldom, if ever, visits, but feels and exercises no responsibility for anything beyond the financial condition and the selection of executive officials. Upon their own statements, these directors know nothing and care nothing about the quality of the product, the condition and treatment of the workers from whose labor they derive their income, nor the general management of the business.

As far as operation and actual management are concerned, the executive officials are practically supreme. Upon their orders production is increased or decreased, plants are operated or shut down and upon their recommendations wages are raised or lowered. But even they have little direct contact with the actual establishment of working conditions, and no relation at all with the rank and file of the workers. They act upon the recommendations of superintendents, whose information comes from their assistants and foremen and from the elaborate statistics of modern business, which account for every piece of material and product, show the disposition of every penny that comes and goes, but ignore, as though they did not exist, the men and women whose labor drives the whole mechanism of business.

Here, then, is the field of industrial relations: Masses of workers on the one side dealing in some manner with foremen and superintendents on the other, behind whom is an organization of executive officials, representing in turn the Board of Directors, who are the chosen representatives of the stockholders.

The crux of the whole question of industrial relations is: Shall the workers for the protection of their interests be organized and represented collectively by their chosen delegates, even as the stockholders are represented by their Directors and by the various grades of executive officials and bosses?

In considering this issue the first question that presents itself is: Why should such representation be demanded as a necessity? Not only are the executive officials, superintendents and bosses, some witnesses have urged before the Commission, for the most part humane and well-intentioned men, but they know that the interests of the business depend upon the welfare of the workers and, if unhindered, will pay the best wages and create the best working conditions that the business can afford. Organization and representation are therefore argued to be unnecessary and tending only to promote friction and interfere with the management of the business.

Let us grant the high character and good intentions of officials, and consider the statement of the workers in reply.

They say that in modern corporate business the actions of officials are governed not by their personal intentions, but by the inexorable demands for interest and dividends, and are driven not by their desire to create a permamently successful business with a contented labor force, but by the never-relaxed spur of the comparative cost-sheet. The constant demand is for high production at low cost, not through improvements and good conditions which might give them next year, but this very month. In the high pressure of business, every superintendent knows that if his plant is at the bottom of the comparative scale for two months his position topples, and if for three months it is virtually gone. He can not afford to experiment with changes that will not give immediate results. If he were his own master he might take a chance, knowing that the loss of this year would be compensated by gains under better conditions next year, but the monthly cost-sheet does not wait for next year; it demands results now.

But it may be said that, if he can not improve conditions himself, he can at least recommend them to his superiors to be transmitted to the Board of Directors for approval. This might indeed be done, and with the extension of an understanding among managers that low production costs may be secured with high wages, probably would be to an increasing extent, except that Boards of Directors scorn such abstractions as the high-wage-low-cost theory, and habitually insist that managers shall buy labor, as they buy material, in the cheapest market. Moreover, raising wages is traditionally unpopular among stockholders and directors, and recommendations for better conditions, particularly if they involve new capital, are frowned upon. Neither the stockholders nor the directors have to live on wages or work in the existing surroundings, and profits deferred are considered profits lost.

The workers, therefore, deny the potency of even good intentions on the part of managers, and point to labor history which they allege shows that at best only isolated cases can be pointed out where marked improvements have taken place except in response to repeated demands from the workers or to forestall the growth of threatened organization. They point also to such facts as that children of 12 years or younger were not only employed in the factories (as they still are in some States where there has been little aggressive agitation), but almost without exception were insisted upon by the employers as a necessity.

The evidence of this character, which is summarized elsewhere, seems to be conclusive of the necessity for organization and representation under modern business conditions. But even if it were not necessary, it is difficult to see any reason why what is demanded and required by stockholders should be denied to workers. It would be as illogical for stockholders individually to attempt to deal with the representatives of the unions, as it is for the individual worker to attempt to deal with executive officials, representing the organized stockholders.

### CAUSES OF INDUSTRIAL UNREST

It is presumed that Congress had in mind, in directing the Commission to inquire into the "causes of dissatisfaction in the industrial situation," something far different from that "dissatisfaction with the present which is the hope of the future," that desire for better things which drives men forever forward. Such dissatisfaction is the mainspring of all progress, and is to be desired in every nation, in all walks of life.

It is believed that Congress intended the inquiry to be directed to that unrest and dissatisfaction which grows out of the existence of intolerable industrial conditions, and which, if unrelieved, will in the natural course of events rise into active revolt or, if forcibly suppressed, sink into sullen hatred.

Of the existence of such unrest ample evidence has been found. It is the basis of the establishment and growth of the I. W. W., whose card-carrying members number only a few thousands but which, as "a spirit and a vocabulary," permeates to a large extent enormous masses of workers, particularly among the unskilled and migratory laborers. But entirely apart from those who accept its philosophy and creed, there are numberless thousands of workers, skilled and unskilled, organized and unorganized, who feel bitterly that they and their fellows are being denied justice, economically, politically, and legally. Just how widespread this feeling is, or whether there is imminent danger of a quickening into active, nation-wide revolt, none can say. But no one who reads the papers from which the workers get their ideas and inspiration; no one who has studied with care the history of such strikes as those at Lawrence and Paterson, in West Virginia and Colorado, and has understood the temper of the strikers; no one who has associated with large numbers of workers in any part of the country, can fail to be impressed by the gravity of the situation.

This sense of tension and impending danger has been expressed by numerous witnesses before the Commission, but by none more forcibly than by Mr. Daniel Guggenheim, a capitalist whose interests in mines and industrial plants extend to every part of the country.

*Chairman Walsh.* What do you think has been accomplished by the philanthropic activities of the country in reducing suffering and want among the people?

*Mr. Guggenheim.* There has a great deal been done. If it were not for what has been done and what is being done we would have revolution in this country.

The sources from which this unrest springs are, when stated in full detail, almost numberless. But upon careful analysis of their real character they will be found to group themselves almost without exception under four main sources which include all the others. These four are:

1. Unjust distribution of wealth and income.

2. Unemployment and denial of an opportunity to earn a living.

3. Denial of justice in the creation, in the adjudication, and in the administration of law.

4. Denial of the right and opportunity to form effective organizations.

## 1. Unjust Distribution of Wealth and Income

The conviction that the wealth of the country and the income which is produced through the toil of the workers is distributed without regard to any standard of justice, is as widespread as it is deep-seated. It is found among all classes of workers and takes every form from the dumb resentment of the day laborer, who, at the end of a week's back-breaking toil, finds that he has less than enough to feed his family while others who have done nothing live in ease, to the elaborate philosophy of the "soap-box orator," who can quote statistics unendingly to demonstrate his contentions. At bottom, though, there is the one fundamental, controlling idea that income should be received for service and for service only, whereas, in fact, it bears no such relation, and he who serves least, or not at all, may receive most.

This idea has never been expressed more clearly than in the testimony of Mr. John H. Walker, President of the Illinois State Federation of Labor:

A working man is not supposed to ask anything more than a fair day's wage for a fair day's work; he is supposed to work until he is pretty fairly tuckered out, say eight hours, and when he does a fair day's work he is not supposed to ask for any more wages than enough to support his family, while with the business man the amount of labor furnishes no criterion for the amount they receive. People accept it as all right if they do not do any work at all, and accept it as all right that they get as much money as they can; in fact, they are given credit for getting the greatest amount of money with the least amount of work; and those things that are being accepted by the other side as the things that govern in everyday life, and as being right, have brought about this condition, this being in my judgment absolutely unfair; that is, on the merits of the proposition in dealing with the workers.

The workers feel this, some unconsciously and some consciously, but all of them feel it, and it makes for unrest, in my judgment, and there can be no peace while that condition obtains.

In the highest paid occupations among wage earners, such as railroad engineers and conductors, glass-blowers, certain steel-mill employees, and a few of the building trades, the incomes will range from $1,500 to $2,000 at best, ignoring a few exceptional men who are paid for personal qualities. Such an income means, under present-day conditions, a fair living for a family of moderate size, education of the children through high school, a small insurance policy, a bit put by for a rainy day—and nothing more. With unusual responsibilities or misfortunes, it is too little, and the pinch of necessity is keenly felt. To attain such wages, more-over, means that the worker must be far above the average, either in skill, physical strength, or reliability. He must also have served an apprenticeship equal in length to a professional course. Finally, and most important, he or his predecessors in the trade must have waged a long, aggressive fight for better wages, for there are other occupations whose demand for skill, strength and reliability are almost as great as those mentioned, where the wages are very much less.

These occupations, however, include but a handful compared to the mass of the workers. What do the millions get for their toil, for their skill, for the risk of life and limb? That is the question to be faced in an industrial nation, for these millions are the backbone and sinew of the State, in peace or in war.

First, with regard to the adult workmen, the fathers and potential fathers, from whose earnings, according to the "American standard," the support of the family is supposed to be derived.

Between one-fourth and one-third of the male workers 18 years of age and over, in factories and mines, earn less than $10 per week; from two-thirds to three-fourths earn less than $15, and only about one-tenth earn more than $20 a week. This does not take into consideration lost working time for any cause.

Next are the women, the most portentously growing factor in the labor force, whose wages are important, not only for their own support or as the supplement of the meager earnings of their fathers and husbands, but because, through the force of competition in a rapidly extending field, they threaten the whole basis of the wage scale. From two-thirds to three-fourths of the women workers in factories, stores and laundries, and in industrial occupations generally, work at wages of less than $8 a week. Approximately one-fifth earn less than $4 and nearly one-half earn less than $6 a week.

Six dollars a week—what does it mean to many? Three theater tickets, gasoline for the week, or the price of a dinner for two; a pair of shoes, three pairs of gloves, or the cost of an evening at bridge. To the girl it means that every penny must be counted, every normal desire stifled, and each basic necessity of life barely satisfied by the sacrifice of some other necessity. If more food must be had than is given with 15 cent dinners, it must be bought with what should go for clothes; if there is need for a new waist to replace the old one at which the forewoman has glanced reproachfully or at which the girls have giggled, there can be no lunches for a week and dinners must cost five cents less each day. Always too the room must be paid for, and back of it lies the certainty that with slack seasons will come lay-offs and discharges. If the breaking point has come and she must have some amusement, where can it come from? Surely not out of $6 a week.

Last of all are the children, for whose petty addition to the stream of production the Nation is paying a heavy toll in ignorance, deformity of body or mind, and premature old age. After all, does it matter much what they are paid? for all experience has shown that in the end the father's wages are reduced by about the amount that the children earn. This is the so-called "family wage," and examination of the wages in different industries corroborates the theory that in those industries, such as textiles, where women and children can be largely utilized, the wages of men are extremely low.

The competitive effect of the employment of women and children upon the wages of men, can scarcely be overestimated. Surely it is hard enough to be forced to put children to work, without having to see the wages of men held down by their employment.

This is the condition at one end of the social scale. What is at the other?

Massed in millions, at the other end of the social scale, are fortunes of a size never before dreamed of, whose very owners do not know the extent nor, without the aid of an intelligent clerk, even the sources, of their incomes. Incapable of being spent in any legitimate manner, these fortunes are burdens, which can only be squandered, hoarded, put into so-called "benefactions" which for the most part constitute a menace to the State, or put back into the industrial machine to pile up ever-increasing mountains of gold.

In many cases, no doubt, these huge fortunes have come in whole or in part as the rich reward of exceptional service. None would deny or envy him who has performed such service the richest of rewards, although one may question the ideals of a nation which rewards exceptional service only by burdensome fortunes. But such reward can be claimed as a right only by those who have performed service, not by those who through relationship or mere parasitism chance to be designated as heirs. Legal right, of course, they have by virtue of the law of inheritance, which, however, runs counter to the whole theory of American society and which was adopted, with important variations, from the English law, without any conception of its ultimate results and apparently with the idea that it would prevent exactly the condition which has arisen. In effect the American law of inheritance is as efficient for the establishment and maintenance of families as is the English law, which has bulwarked the British aristocracy through the centuries. Every year, indeed, sees this tendency increase, as the creation of "estates in trust" secures the ends which might be more simply reached if there were no prohibition of "entail." According to the income tax returns for ten months of 1914, there are in the United States 1598 fortunes yielding an income of $100,000 or more per year. Practically all of these fortunes are so invested and hedged about with restrictions upon expenditure that they are, to all intents and purposes, perpetuities.

An analysis of 50 of the largest American fortunes shows that nearly one-half have already passed to the control of heirs or to trustees (their vice regents) and that the remainder will pass to the control of heirs within twenty years, upon the deaths of the "founders." Already, indeed, these founders have almost without exception retired from active service, leaving the management ostensibly to their heirs but actually to executive officials upon salary.

We have, according to the income tax returns, forty-four families with incomes of $1,000,000 or more, whose members perform little or no useful service, but whose aggregate incomes, totalling at the very least fifty millions per year, are equivalent to the earnings of 100,000 wage earners at the average rate of $500.

The ownership of wealth in the United States has become concentrated to a degree which is difficult to grasp. The recently published researches of a statistician of conservative views [Professor Willard I. King] have shown that as nearly as can be estimated tho distribution of wealth in the United States is as follows:

The "Rich," 2 per cent of the people, own 60 per cent of the wealth.

The "Middle Class," 33 per cent of the people, own 35 per cent of the wealth.

The "Poor," 65 per cent of the people, own 5 per cent of the wealth.

This means in brief that a little less than two million people, who would make up a city smaller than Chicago, own 20 per cent more of the Nation's wealth than all the other ninety millions.

The figures also show that with a reasonably equitable division of wealth, the entire population should occupy the position of comfort and security which we characterize as Middle Class.

The actual concentration has, however, been carried very much further than these figures indicate. The largest private fortune in the United States, estimated at one billion dollars, is equivalent to the aggregate wealth of 2,500,000 of those who are classed as "poor," who are shown in the studies cited to own on the average about $400 each.

Between the two extremes of superfluity and poverty is the large middle class—farmers, manufacturers, merchants, professional men, skilled artisans, and salaried officials—whose incomes are more or less adequate for their legitimate needs and desires, and who are rewarded more or less exactly in proportion to service. They have problems to meet in adjusting expenses to income, but the pinch of want and hunger is not felt, nor is there the deadening, devitalizing effect of superfluous, unearned wealth.

From top to bottom of society, however, in all grades of incomes, are an innumerable number of parasites of every conceivable type. They perform no useful service, but drain off from the income of the producers a sum whose total can not be estimated.

This whole situation has never been more accurately described than by Hon. David Lloyd-George in an address on "Social Waste":

I have recently had to pay some attention to the affairs of the Sudan, in connection with some projects that have been mooted for irrigation and development in that wonderful country. I will tell you what the problem is— you may know it already. Here you have a great, broad, rich river upon which both the Sudan and Egypt depend for their fertility. There is enough water in it to fertilize every part of both countries; but if, for some reason or other, the water is wasted in the upper regions, the whole land suffers sterility and famine. There is a large region in the Upper Sudan, where the water has been absorbed by one tract of country, which, by this process, has been converted into a morass, breeding nothing but pestilence. Properly and fairly husbanded, distributed, and used, there is enough to fertilize the most barren valley and make the whole wilderness blossom like the rose.

That represents the problem of civilization, not merely in this country but in all lands. Some men get their fair share of wealth in a land and no more —sometimes even the streams of wealth overflow to waste over some favored regions, often producing a morass, which poisons the social atmosphere. Many have to depend on a little trickling runlet, which quickly evaporates with every commercial or industrial drought; sometimes you have masses of men and women whom the flood at its height barely reaches, and then you witness parched specimens of humanity, withered, hardened in misery, living in a desert where even the well of tears has long ago run dry.

Besides the economic significance of these great inequalities of wealth and income, there is a social aspect which equally merits the attention of Congress. It has been shown that the great fortunes of those who have profited by the enormous expansion of American industry have already passed, or will pass in a few years, by right of inheritance to the control of heirs or to trustees who act as their "vice regents." They are frequently styled by our newspapers "monarchs of industry," and indeed occupy within our Republic a position almost exactly analogous to that of feudal lords.

These heirs, owners only by virtue of the accident of birth, control the livelihood and have the power to dictate the happiness of more human beings than populated England in the Middle Ages. Their principalities, it is true, are scattered and, through the medium of stock-ownership, shared in part with others; but they are none the less real. In fact, such scattered, invisible industrial principalities are a greater menace to the welfare of the Nation than would be equal power consolidated into numerous petty kingdoms in different parts of the country. They might then be visualized and guarded against; now their influence invisibly permeates and controls every phase of life and industry.

"The king can do no wrong" not only because he is above the law, but because every function is performed or responsibility assumed by his ministers and agents. Similarly our Rockefellers, Morgans, Fricks, Vanderbilts and Astors can do no industrial wrong, because all effective action and direct responsibility is shifted from them to the executive officials who manage American industry. As a basis for this conclusion we have the testimony of many, among which, however, the following statements stand out most clearly:

*Mr. John D. Rockefeller, Jr.*
. . . those of us who are in charge there elect the ablest and most upright

and competent men whom we can find, in so far as our interests give us the opportunity to select, to have the responsibility for the conduct of the business in which we are interested as investors. We can not pretend to follow the business ourselves.

*Mr. J. Pierpont Morgan.*
*Chairman Walsh.* In your opinion, to what extent are the directors of corporations responsible for the labor conditions existing in the industries in which they are the directing power?
*Mr. Morgan.* Not at all I should say.

The similitude, indeed, runs even to mental attitude and phrase. Compare these two statements:

*Mr. John D. Rockefeller, Jr.*
My appreciation of the conditions surrounding wage-earners and my sympathy with every endeavor to better these conditions are as strong as those of any man.

*Louis XVI.*
There is none but you and me that has the people's interest at heart. ("*Il n'y a que vous et moi qui aimions le peuple.*")

The families of these industrial princes are already well established and are knit together not only by commercial alliances but by a network of intermarriages which assures harmonious action whenever their common interest is threatened.

Effective action by Congress is required, therefore, not only to readjust on a basis of compensation approximating the service actually performed, the existing inequalities in the distribution of wealth and income, but to check the growth of an hereditary aristocracy, which is foreign to every conception of American Government and menacing to the welfare of the people and the existence of the Nation as a democracy.

The objects to be attained in making this readjustment are: To reduce the swollen, unearned fortunes of those who have a superfluity; to raise the underpaid masses to a level of decent and comfortable living; and at the same time to accomplish this on a basis which will, in some measure, approximate the just standard of income proportional to service.

The discussion of how this can best be accomplished forms the greater part of the remainder of this report, but at this point it seems proper to indicate one of the most immediate steps which need to be taken.

It is suggested that the Commission recommend to Congress the enactment of an inheritance tax, so graded that, while making generous provision for the support of dependents and the education of minor children, it shall leave no large accumulation of wealth to pass into hands which had no share in its production. The revenue from this tax, which we are informed would be very great, should be reserved by the Federal Government for three principal purposes:

1. The extension of education.

2. The development of other important social services which should properly be performed by the Nation, which are discussed in detail elsewhere.

3. The development, in cooperation with States and municipalities, of great constructive works, such as road building, irrigation and reforestation, which would materially increase the efficiency and welfare of the entire Nation.

We are informed by counsel not only that such a tax is clearly within the power of Congress, but that upon two occasions, namely, during the Civil War and in 1898, such graded inheritance taxes were enacted with scarcely any opposition and were sustained by the Supreme Court, which held that the inheritance tax was not a direct tax within the meaning of the Constitution. We are aware that similar taxes are levied in the various States, but the conflict with such State taxes seems to have presented little difficulty during the period in which the tax of 1898 was in effect. Under any circumstances this need cause no great complication, as the matter could be readily adjusted by having the Federal Government collect the entire tax and refund a part to the States on an equitable basis.

There is no legislation which could be passed by Congress the immediate and ultimate efforts of which would be more salutary or would more greatly assist in tempering the existing spirit of unrest.

## 2. Unemployment and Denial of Opportunity to Earn a Living

As a prime cause of a burning resentment and a rising feeling of unrest among the workers, unemployment and the denial of an opportunity to earn a living is on a parity with the unjust distribution of wealth. They may on final analysis prove to be simply the two sides of the same shield, but that is a matter which need not be discussed at this point. They differ in this, however, that while unjust distribution of wealth is a matter of degree, unemployment is an absolute actuality, from which there is no relief but soul-killing crime and soul-killing charity.

To be forced to accept employment on conditions which are insufficient to maintain a decent livelihood is indeed a hardship, but to be unable to get work on any terms whatever is a position of black despair.

A careful analysis of all available statistics shows that in our great basic industries the workers are unemployed for an average of at least one-fifth of the year, and that at all times during any normal year there is an army of men, who can be numbered only by hundreds of thousands, who are unable to find work or who have so far degenerated that they can not or will not work. Can any nation boast of industrial efficiency when the workers, the source of her productive wealth, are employed to so small a fraction of their total capacity?

Fundamentally this unemployment seems to rise from two great causes, although many others are contributory. First, the inequality of the distribution of income, which leaves the great masses of the population (the true ultimate consumers) unable to purchase the products of industry which they create, while a few have such a superfluity that it can not be normally consumed but must be invested in new machinery for production or in the further monopolization of land and natural resources. The result is that in mining and other basic industries we have an equipment in plant and developed property far in excess of the demands of any normal year, the excess being, in all probability, at least 25 per cent. Each of these mines and industrial plants keeps around it a labor force which, on the average, can get work for only four-fifths of the year, while at the same time the people have never had enough of the products of those very industries—have never been adequately fed, clothed, housed, nor warmed—for the very simple reason that they have never been paid enough to permit their purchase.

The second principal cause lies in the denial of access to land and natural resources even when they are unused and unproductive, except at a price and under conditions which are practically prohibitive. This situation, while bound up with the land and taxation policies of our States and Nation, also rests fundamentally upon the unjust distribution of wealth. Land or mineral resources in the hands of persons of average income must and will be used either by their original owners or by some more enterprising person. By the overwhelming forces of economic pressure, taxation, and competition they can not be permitted to lie idle if they will produce anything which the people need. Only in the hands of large owners—free from economic pressure, able to evade or minimize the effects of taxation and to await the ripening of the fruits of unearned increment—can land be held out of use if its products are needed.

There can be no more complete evidence of the truth of this statement than the condition of the farms of 1000 acres and over, which, valued at two and one-third billion dollars, comprise 19 per cent of all the farm land of the country and are held by less than one per cent of the farm owners. The United States Census returns show that in these 1000-acre farms only 18.7 per cent of the land is cultivated as compared with 60 to 70 per cent in farms of from 50 to 499 acres. Furthermore, it is well known that the greater part of these smaller farms which are left uncultivated are held by real estate men, bankers and others who have independent sources of income. More than four-fifths of the area of the large holdings is being held out of active use by their 50,000 owners, while 2,250,000 farmers are struggling for a bare existence on farms of less than 50 acres, and an untold number who would willingly work these lands are swelling the armies of the unemployed in the cities and towns.

A basic theory of our Government, which found expression in the Homestead Acts, was that every man should have opportunity to secure land enough to support a family. If this theory had been carried out and homesteads had either gone to those who would use them productively or remained in the hands of the Government, we should not yet have a problem of such a character. But these acts were evaded; land was stolen outright by wholesale, and fraudulent entries were consolidated into enormous tracts which are now held by wealthy individuals and corporations.

The Public Lands Commission, after an exhaustive inquiry, reported in 1905:

Detailed study of the practical operation of the present land laws shows that their tendency far too often is to bring about land monopoly rather than to multiply small holdings by actual settlers.

. . . Not infrequently their effect is to put a premium on perjury and dishonest methods in the acquisition of land. It is apparent, in consequence, that in very many localities, and perhaps in general, a larger proportion of the public land is passing into the hands of speculators than into those of actual settlers making homes. . . . Nearly everywhere the large landowner has succeeded in monopolizing the best tracts, whether of timber or agricultural land.

To one who has not read the preceding statements carefully, there may seem to be a contradiction in proposing to prevent great capitalists from creating an excess of productive machinery and overdeveloping mineral resources, while pointing out the necessity of forcing land and other natural resources into full and effective use by the people. The two propositions are, as a matter of fact, as fundamentally distinct as monopoly and freedom. The capitalist increases his holdings in productive machinery and resources only because through monopolization and maintenance of prices he hopes to reap rewards for himself or increase his power, while the aim in desiring the full development of land and other resources by the people is that they, producing for themselves, may enjoy a sufficiency of good things and exchange them for the products of others, and thus reduce to a minimum the condition of unemployment.

There are, of course, many other causes of unemployment than the inequality of wealth and the monopolization of land which there is no desire to minimize. Chief among these are immigration, the inadequate organization of the labor market, the seasonal character of many industries, and the personal deficiencies of a very large number of the unemployed. It can not be denied that a considerable proportion of the men who fill the city lodging houses in winter are virtually unemployables, as a result of weakness of character, lack of training, the debasing effects of lodging house living and city dissipation, and, last but not least, the conditions under which they are forced to work in the harvest fields and lumber, railroad and construction camps. The seasonal fluctuations of our industries are enormous, employing hundreds of thousands during the busy season and throwing them out on the community during the dull season, and almost nothing has been done to remedy this condition. It would be difficult to imagine anything more chaotic and demoralizing than the existing methods of bringing workmen and jobs together. Certain measures for dealing with these conditions, which are discussed elsewhere in the report, need to be pushed forward with all possible vigor. But it may be confidently predicted that the unemployment situation will not be appreciably relieved until great advances have been made in the removal of the two prime causes—unjust distribution of wealth and monopolization of land and natural resources.

The most direct methods of dealing with the inequality of wealth have already been briefly discussed and will be considered elsewhere in the report. With respect to the land question, however, the following basic suggestions are submitted:

1. Vigorous and unrelenting prosecution to regain all land, water power and mineral rights secured from the Government by fraud.

2. A general revision of our land laws, so as to apply to all future land grants the doctrine of "superior use," as in the case of water rights in California, and provision for forfeiture in case of actual nonuse. In its simplest form the doctrine of "superior use" implies merely that at the time of making the lease the purpose for which the land will be used must be taken into consideration, and the use which is of greatest social value shall be given preference.

3. The forcing of all unused land into use by making the tax on nonproductive land the same as on productive land of the same kind, and exempting all improvements. . . .

The unemployed have aptly been called "the shifting sands beneath the State." Surely there is no condition which more immediately demands the attention of Congress than that of unemployment, which is annually driving hundreds of thousands of otherwise productive citizens into poverty and bitter despair, sapping the very basis of our national efficiency and germinating the seeds of revolution.

## 3. Denial of Justice

No testimony presented to the Commission has left a deeper impression than the evidence that there exists among the workers an almost universal conviction that they, both as individuals and as a class, are denied justice in the enactment, adjudication, and administration of law, that the very instruments of democracy are often used to oppress them and to place obstacles in the way of their movement towards economic, industrial, and political freedom and justice. Many witnesses, speaking for millions of workers as well as for themselves, have asserted with the greatest earnestness that the mass of the workers are convinced that laws necessary for their protection against the most grievous wrongs can not be passed except after long and exhausting struggles; that such beneficient measures as become laws are largely nullified by the unwarranted decisions of the courts; that the laws which stand upon the statute books are not equally enforced, and that the whole machinery of government has frequently been placed at the disposal of the employers for the oppression of the workers; that the Constitution itself has been ignored in the interests of the employers; and that constitutional guaranties erected primarily for the protection of the workers have been denied to them and used as a cloak for the misdeeds of corporations.

If it be true that these statements represent the opinions of the mass of American workers, there is reason for grave concern, for there are twenty-five millions of them, of whom three millions are welded together into compact organizations.

But if it be true that these charges are justified; if, in fact, our legislators, our judges and executives, do not afford equal consideration to the workers and are concerned with protecting the rights of property rather than the rights of men, and at times even become the instruments for the oppression of the poor and humble, then the situation demands and must receive the prompt and decisive action of every right thinking man in order that these evils may be eradicated and justice and liberty established in the place of injustice and oppression.

Before examining the evidence, it should be understood that it is not charged that such acts of injustice are universal but that they occur so frequently and in such diverse parts of the country that any man may reasonably fear that he himself or those with whom he is associated may at any time be the victim of injustice or discrimination. It has been urged, and perhaps properly, that the charges would be sustained if it were found that such acts of injustice had been committed only upon rare occasions, if it should also be established that such injustices were allowed to stand without redress, and if those who were guilty of their commission were left unimpeached and unpunished.

An enormous mass of evidence bearing upon these charges has been presented to the Commission by witnesses or collected by its staff. This material is presented in some detail in another part of the report, but the summary which follows may be regarded as reasonably full and exact.

*First, with regard to the enactment of laws, it is charged that the workers have been unable to secure legislation to protect them against grievous wrongs, except after exhausting struggles against overwhelming odds and against insidious influences.*

The evidence bearing upon this question has dealt with the history of three principal lines of legislation in which the evils sought to be remedied are now universally admitted to have been very great, involving wanton destruction of life, the exploitation of women and children, and the practical enslavement of American seamen. A careful examination has been made of the history of attempts to secure adequate legislation to prevent child labor, to protect women against extreme hours of labor and night work, to secure the safety of factories, railroads and mines, and to provide for the safety, comfort and liberty of seamen.

The history of child labor legislation shows that although agitation for the protection and education of children began during the early part of the nineteenth century in Massachusetts, Rhode Island, Connecticut, New York and Pennsylvania, no adequate legislation was obtained until nearly the end of the century. Time after time in each of these industrial States the sentiment of the public was aroused, organization was effected, and well-drafted bills were introduced only to be killed in committee, emasculated or killed on the floor of the legislature, or passed with exceptions which rendered them entirely ineffective. Even the attempt to reduce the hours of children below 12 per day was bitterly contested and met by every known trick of legislative chicanery. The whole history of the contest for adequate child labor legislation is even now being repeated in some of the Southern states, where laws prohibiting the employment of children are bitterly contested and beaten session after session by legislators, unsympathetic or controlled by the cotton-mill interests.

Similarly, although the movement to restrict the working hours of women and to prohibit night work began in Massachusetts and Pennsylvania as early as 1840, the first legislation limiting the hours was the 10-hour bill passed in Massachusetts, in 1874, and night work went unregulated until the passage of the act of 1899 in Nebraska.

The movement for safety of life and limb in the factories and workshops, although pushed with great vigor in almost every session of the State legislatures after 1880, secured only a few acts providing for such obvious matters as the guarding of set screws and gears, but made practically no provision for their enforcement. No really effective action to promote safety took place until, after many years of hard fighting, the first workmen's compensation acts were passed between 1900 and 1910, which for the first time made the unsafe condition of factories directly expensive.

Even upon the railroads, where the safety of the public as well as of the workers was involved, at least ten years of constant agitation on the part of the railroad brotherhoods and various interested citizens was necessary before the first Federal act providing for safety appliances was passed in 1893.

In the case of the movement to secure the safety, comfort, and liberty of seamen, it is a matter of record that Andrew Furuseth, President of the Seamen's Union, backed not only by all the members of his own organization but by the entire American labor movement, attended each session of Congress and devoted his whole energies to securing legislation upon this subject for the entire period of 22 years from 1893 to 1915, when the Seamen's Bill finally became a law.

Other evidence has been presented covering the long fights to secure legislation to remove the evils of company stores, payment in scrip, prison labor, arbitrary deductions from wages, "sweating," tenement houses, and a number of other matters upon which adequate legislation has not yet been secured, except perhaps in a few States, although there has been unremitting agitation upon these questions for more than half a century. This evidence shows clearly that the workers have just grounds for the charge that the legislatures have been criminally slow in acting for the relief of grievous wrongs and have used every subterfuge to escape adequate and aggressive action, even while thousands of men, women, and children were being killed, maimed, or deformed as a result of their negligence.

Evidence has further been presented to show that such a condition has not been the result entirely of the complacency or slothfulness of legislators, but that powerful influences have been at work to prevent such remedial legislation. The most convincing evidence presented upon this phase of the question is the record of the National Association of Manufacturers and its allied organizations, as contained in the testimony and findings before Congressional committees, in the printed reports of that Association, and in the testimony before the Commission of the representatives of various state employers' associations. The substance of this evidence is so well known to Congress and to the public that it is necessary here to call attention only to the fact that the efforts of such associations in preventing the enactment of practically all legislation intended to improve the condition or advance the interests of workers were not confined to Congress, but were even more effective in the State legislatures.

The persistent and bitter manner in which the railroads fought the laws providing for safety appliances, although the measures were moderate and necessary not only for the safety of the traveling public but for the efficient operation of the roads, is well known to Congress.

Perhaps the most significant statement regarding the insidious influences of this character is contained in a letter from Mr. L. M. Bowers, Chairman of the Board of Directors of the Colorado Fuel & Iron Co., to the Secretary of Mr. John D. Rockefeller, Jr., under date of May 13, 1913.

The Colorado Fuel and Iron Company for many years were accused of being the political dictator of southern Colorado, and in fact were a mighty power in the entire state. When I came here it was said that the C. F. & I. Co. voted every man and woman in their employ without any regard to their being naturalized or not; and even their mules, it used to be remarked, were registered if they were fortunate enough to possess names. Anyhow, a political department was maintained at a heavy expense. I had before me the contributions of the C. F. & I. Co. for the campaign of 1904, amounting to $80,605.00, paid out personally by President Hearne. All the vouchers and checks I have examined personally, all of which were payable to Albert A. Miller, upon which he drew the currency and, it is said, handed the money over to Mr. Hearne, who paid it out. So far as I can discover, not one particle of good was accomplished for the company; but Mr. Hearne was an aspirant for the position of United States senator and devoted a vast amount of time and money with this end in view, I have no doubt.

The company became notorious in many sections for their support of the liquor interests. They established saloons everywhere they possibly could. This department was managed by one John Kebler, a brother of the one-time president of the company, who died, about the time I came here, a victim of his own intemperate habits. A sheriff, elected by the votes of the C. F. & I. Co. employees, and who has been kept in office a great many years, established himself or became a partner in sixteen liquor stores in our coal mines. To clean up the saloons and with them the gambling hells and houses of prostitution, has been one of the things that Mr. Welborn and I have devoted an enormous amount of time to during the past five years. The decent newspapers everlastingly lampooned the C. F. & I. Co. at every election; and I am forced to say the company merited, from a moral standpoint, every shot that was fired into their camp.

Since I came here not a nickel has been paid to any politician or political party. We have fought the saloons with all the power we possess. We have forbidden any politician from going into our camps, and every subordinate official connected with the Company has been forbidden to influence our men to vote for any particular candidate. We have not lobbied in the Legislature, but have gone directly to the Governor and other able men and have demanded fair treatment.

*Second, it is charged by the workers that after wholesome and necessary laws are passed they are in large part nullified by the courts* either upon technicalities of a character which would not be held to invalidate legislation favorable to the interests of manufacturers, merchants, bankers, and other property owners, or thrown out on the broad ground of unconstitutionality, through strained or illogical construction of constitutional provisions. It is argued that such action is doubly evil because the power to declare legislative acts unconstitutional has been assumed by the courts in the face of a complete absence of legal sanction, in complete disregard of early decisions denying the possession of such power, and in complete contrast to the practices of the courts in every other country of the civilized world. It is not within our province to decide whether or not this assumption of power by the courts was justified. It is sufficient here merely to examine the evidence bearing upon the allegations that laws necessary for the correction of grave industrial abuses are nullified by strained interpretations or for reasons which would be insufficient in other cases, and that they are held unconstitutional upon pretexts which in reality are the outgrowth of economic bias on the part of the judges. . . .

Probably there are no other cases which have created so much bitterness as those of personal injury in which the plaintiffs have been denied recovery of damages on the principles of "fellow servant," "assumption of risk" and "contributory negligence," and the obstacles which have been created by the courts to prevent the removal of these defenses for the employer have served only to intensify the feeling. The contrast in attitude of the judges can not better be shown than by considering that while they have held each employee of a corporation responsible under these three principles not only for his own involuntary acts but for the physical condition of the entire property and the conduct of each of his fellow workers, they have repeatedly absolved officials, directors and stockholders from responsibility for accidents, even when the unsafe condition of the property had been published, or when orders had been issued which were directly responsible for the accidents. It would hardly be an exaggeration to say that if the courts had held officials and directors to as great a degree of responsibility as employees for the condition of the property and the actions of their agents, there is hardly one who would have escaped punishment for criminal negligence. According to the best estimates, approximately 35,000 persons were killed last year in American industry, and at least one-half of these deaths were preventable. What would be the situation if the courts, following the clear logic of their own decisions, should hold the stockholders, directors, and officials criminally responsible for each of the 17,500 preventable deaths to which attention has time after time been directed?

That the courts, including even the highest tribunal of the Nation, do allow their economic bias to influence them in holding laws unconstitutional is nowhere more clearly expressed than in the dissenting opinion of Mr. Justice Holmes in the case of *Lochner* v. *N. Y.*, wherein the right of the Legislature of New York to limit the hours of work in bakeries was involved. He said:

This case is decided upon an economic theory which a large part of the country does not entertain. If it were a question whether I agree with that theory [limiting the consecutive hours of labor in bakeries which may be required of an employee], I should desire to study it further and long before making up my mind. But I do not conceive that to be my duty, because I strongly believe that my agreement or disagreement has nothing to do with the right of a majority to embody their opinions in law.

. . . Some of these laws [referring to several which he has discussed] embody convictions or prejudices which judges are likely to share. Some may not, but a Constitution is not intended to embody a particular economic theory, whether of paternalism and the organic relation of the citizen to the State, or of *laissez faire*. It is made for people of fundamentally differing views, and the accident of our finding certain opinions natural and familiar or novel, and even shocking, ought not to conclude our judgment upon the question whether statutes embodying them conflict with the Constitution of the United States.

This statute of the State of New York, which had been sustained by the courts of New York, was thus held unconstitutional, we are assured by the highest possible authority, on the economic theories of five judges, whose bias is clearly reflected in the majority opinion. By that action not only were the bakers of New York deprived of all legal relief from the hardships of working long hours in underground bakeries, but the entire movement for relieving the condition of other workmen in similarly unhealthful occupations throughout the country was effectually checked for a decade. Can these judges, the workers ask, absolve themselves from responsibility for the thousands of lives which have been shortened as a result of their decisions, the ill-health and suffering of other thousands who contracted disease as a result of unduly long exposure to bad conditions and a lack of sufficient fresh air and leisure? The provision of the Constitution which was held to be violated by this act was the fourteenth amendment, designed solely to protect the emancipated negroes.

The wide range of the labor laws declared unconstitutional may be seen from the following list, which includes only those cases which may be clearly understood from their titles:

Requiring statement of cause of discharge.

Prohibiting blacklisting.

Protecting workmen as members of labor unions.

Restricting power of courts to grant injunctions, etc.

Protecting employees as voters (Federal).

Forbidding public employment office to furnish names of applicants to employers whose workmen were on strike.

Fixing rates of wages on public works.

Regulating weighing of coal at mines (four States).

Providing for small attorneys' fees in successful actions to recover wage claims.

Fixing the time of payment of wages.

Prohibiting use of "scrip."

Prohibiting or regulating company stores.

Fixing hours of labor in private employment.

Defining liability of employers for injuries. . . .

Finally, reference should be made to the history of the fight for the enactment of eight-hour legislation in Colorado, which illustrates the grounds upon which the workers not only of that State but throughout the Nation distrust legislatures, courts, and executive officials.

Although the eight-hour day was established in Colorado gold mines by agreement among the operators after the Cripple Creek strike of 1894, in the coal-mining industry a twenty-years struggle followed the miners' first attempt at legislation.

The eight-hour bill presented to the General Assembly in 1895, though supported by the Western Federation of Miners, the United Mine Workers of America, and labor organizations in general, was, upon reference to the Supreme Court for an advance opinion, reported as unconstitutional, and failed of enactment.

A bill brought successfully to enactment in 1899, and which was substantially a copy of the Utah law upheld by State and Federal Supreme Courts, was declared by the Colorado Supreme Court to be unconstitutional.

In 1901 the people adopted by an overwhelming vote an amendment to the Constitution which provided for eight-hour legislation. This was followed by the introduction in the next General Assembly (1903) of several bills, and by the inauguration of active opposition thereto on the part of corporations. No fewer than eleven anonymous bulletins were attributed to one officer of a smelting company.

On account of disagreements in conference, none of the several bills passed; and so great was the public outcry that at the extra session in July, 1903, each House passed resolutions blaming the other for the failure.

In the session of 1904-5 a bill substantially the same as the present law, and favored by all political parties, was so amended by Mr. Guggenheim as to be "absolutely worthless." It remained on the statute books, a dead letter, until 1911.

In 1911, House Bill 46 was passed. The operators succeeded in having it submitted to a referendum vote, and at the last moment they initiated a smelterman's eight-hour bill, the two came up on the same ballot, and in the succeeding confusion both were adopted by the people, because of their genuine interest in the passage of an eight-hour law.

The legislature of 1913 repealed both the laws so enacted in 1911, and reenacted House Bill 46, the present law. By a decision of the Supreme Court, allowing a "safety clutch," this law may not be referred.

The essential injustice and stupidity of this long fight of the employers against eight-hour legislation is strikingly shown by a letter from Mr. L. M. Bowers, Chairman of the Board of Directors of the Colorado Fuel & Iron Co., to Mr. J. D. Rockefeller, Jr., stating that after they saw that such legislation was inevitable, they tried out the eight-hour day in their mines and found that it was economically profitable. The Colorado Fuel & Iron Co. thereby is shown to have stubbornly resisted by every conceivable device, for a period of twenty years, a just law which was not only necessary for the health and welfare of its 12,000 miners but was actually profitable for the company itself.

The reason for the effectiveness of the opposition of the Colorado Fuel & Iron Co. is also shown in the letter quoted [on page 185] from Mr. Bowers to the secretary of Mr. Rockefeller, describing the complete and corrupt control which the Company exercised over the State Government during this period.

*Third, it is alleged by the workers that in the administration of law, both common and statute, there is discrimination by the courts against the poor and in favor of the wealthy and powerful.* It is further stated that this discrimination arises not only from the economic disabilities of the poor, which render them unable to employ equally skillful lawyers, to endure the law's delay, and to stand the expense of repeated appeals, but out of an actual bias on the part of the judges in favor of the wealthy and influential. It should arouse great concern if it be true that the courts do not resolve their doubts in favor of the poor and humble; how much graver then is the injustice if the judges do in fact lean toward the rich and mighty?

To establish this claim by the presentation of a sufficient number of cases would be a tedious task. Many such have been presented to the Commission, but can not be considered fully here. Instead, it would seem that in such cases we may safely rely upon the uncontradicted opinion of weighty authorities whose position removes from them any suspicion of bias.

Ex-President William H. Taft has said:

We must make it so that the poor man will have as nearly as possible an equal opportunity in litigating as the rich man; and under present conditions, ashamed as we may be of it, this is not the fact.

Prof. Henry R. Seager, of Columbia University, testified before the Commission:

I don't see how any fair-minded person can question but what our judges have shown a decided bias in favor of the employers. I would not be inclined to ascribe this so much to a class bias, although I think this is a factor, as to the antecedent training of judges. Under our legal system the principal task of the lawyer is to protect property rights, and the property rights have come to be concentrated more and more into the hands of corporations, so that the successful lawyer of today, in a great majority of cases, is the corporation lawyer. His business is to protect the rights of employers and corporations. It is from the ranks of successful lawyers, for the most part, that our judges are selected, and from that results inevitably a certain angle on the part of a majority of our judges.

The bias of the courts is nowhere more clearly shown than in cases involving persons and organizations with whose economic and social views the court does not agree. An interesting example may be cited in the case of *Warren* v. *U. S.,* 183 Fed. 718, where the editor of *Appeal to Reason,* Fred D. Warren, was sentenced by the Federal District Court to six months' imprisonment and a fine of $1500 for the circulation through the mails of matter offering a reward to anyone who would kidnap a certain governor for whom extradition had been refused.

The sentence was commuted by President Taft, against the protest of Warren, to a fine of $100 to be collected in a civil suit. In commenting on the sentence, President Taft is reported to have said:

The District Court evidently looked beyond the record of the evidence in this case and found that Warren was the editor and publisher of a newspaper engaged in a crusade against society and government.

Moreover, this is not a prosecution for criminal libel; it is a prosecution for what at best is the violation of a regulation as to the use of the mails. To visit such an offense with a severe punishment is likely to appear to the public to be an effort to punish the defendant for something that could not be charged in the indictment.

This obviously was not intended as a reflection upon the court, but the attitude of a large part of the workers is that if President Taft was justified in making such an assertion it was a case demanding impeachment of the judges involved rather than a commutation of sentence for Warren.

*Fourth, it is charged by the representatives of labor not only that courts have neglected or refused to protect workers in the rights guaranteed by the Constitution of the United States and of the several States, but that sections of the Constitution framed primarily to protect human rights have been perverted to protect property rights only and to deprive workers of the protection of rights secured to them by statutes.*

First, with regard to the Federal courts, it is startling and alarming to citizens generally, and particularly to workers, to learn that the consensus of Federal decisions is to the effect that the sections of the Constitution defining the rights of citizens to trial by jury, security from unwarranted arrest and search, free speech, free assembly, writ of habeas corpus, bearing of arms, and protection from excessive bail and cruel and unusual punishments, apply only to Federal jurisdiction and in reality protect the citizen only against the action of the Federal Government. The only sections protecting the personal rights of citizens under ordinary circumstances are the thirteenth amendment, prohibiting involuntary servitude, the fifteenth, protecting the right to vote, and the fourteenth, providing that "No State shall make or enforce any law which shall abridge the privileges or immunities of citizens of the United States; nor shall any State deprive any person of life, liberty, or property, without due process of law, nor deny any person within its jurisdiction the equal protection of the laws."

We are, however, informed by counsel who has examined the cases involved, that the fourteenth amendment has had no appreciable effect in protecting personal rights. According to the existing decisions, the due-process clause does not guarantee the right of trial by jury, nor does it necessitate indictment by grand juries, nor has it restrained arbitrary arrests and imprisonment on the part of State Governments when men are kidnaped in one State and carried to another.

Up to 1911 the United States Supreme Court intervened in 55 cases in which the fourteenth amendment was invoked. In 39 of these cases private corporations were the principal parties. Thirty-two statutes were affected by these decisions, and in only three, concerning the civil rights of negroes, were the personal rights of individual citizens involved. With the exceptions involving the rights of negroes in jury cases ( *e. g.*, *Strauder v. W. Va.*, 100 U. S. 303), the fourteenth amendment has not acted to secure or protect personal rights from State encroachment, but only to prevent encroachment on property rights. In all the other numerous cases in which the fourteenth amendment was invoked to protect personal rights, the attempt failed.

On the other hand there is abundant evidence of the great protection which it affords corporations and other forms of organized capital. On that point we may quote the statements of Mr. C. W. Collins, of the Alabama Bar, who analyzed the decisions of the United States Supreme Court through the October, 1910, term:

Private corporations are using it as a means to prevent the enforcement of State laws. Since 1891 a majority of cases under the Amendment have involved a corporation as the principal party . . . The increase of this kind of litigation runs parallel to the rise of the trust movement in America. At the 1909-10 term of the Court, out of a total of twenty-six opinions rendered under the Amendment, twenty involved a corporation as the principal party. . . . The Fourteenth Amendment is the easiest of all constitutional measures to invoke. In a country where economic activity is so intense and time so vital an element, it has been grasped as a sure measure of delay, with always the possibility of obtaining affirmative relief. The Amendment, though intended primarily as a protection to the negro race, has in these latter days become a constitutional guarantee to the corporations that no State action toward them can become effective until after years of litigation through the State and Federal courts to the Supreme Court of the United States. The course of the Amendment is running away from its originally intended channel.

The Fourteenth Amendment, although a humanitarian measure in origin and purpose, has been within recent years practically appropriated by the corporations. It was aimed at restraining and checking the powers of wealth and privilege. It was to be a charter of liberty for human rights against property rights. The transformation has been rapid and complete. It operates today to protect the rights of property to the detriment of the rights of man. It has become the Magna Charta of accumulated and organized capital.

It is thus quite clear that the fourteenth amendment not only has failed to operate to protect personal rights but has operated almost wholly for the protection of the property rights of corporations. These facts taken in conjunction with the many decisions, such as the Lochner case, in which the fourteenth amendment has been invoked to annul statutes designed to better conditions of life and work, must constitute just ground for grave concern not only to the workers but to every citizen who values his liberty.

With the "bills of rights" contained in the Constitutions of the several States, the situation, as far as the workers are concerned, is somewhat different, since in many jurisdictions these have been used upon numerous occasions to afford substantial protection to them in their personal rights. The workers call attention particularly, however, to the long list of statutes, city ordinances and military orders abridging freedom of speech and press, which not only have not been interfered with by the courts but whenever tested have almost uniformly been upheld by the State and Federal courts. They point also to the grave injuries done to workers individually and collectively by the thousands of arrests which have been made without just cause in labor disputes, without relief from either the courts or the executive; to the denial of the right to the writ of habeas corpus upon numerous occasions; to the fact that where, as for example in Los Angeles, San Diego and Fresno (Cal.), Spokane (Wash.), Minot (N. D.), Paterson (N. J.), Little Falls (N. Y.), Lawrence (Mass.), Idaho, Colorado, and West Virginia, workers have been grievously injured, brutally treated, or interfered with in the pursuit of their guaranteed rights by other classes of citizens or by officials, the courts have not interfered and the perpetrators have gone unpunished.

On the general question of martial law and habeas corpus a member of the staff has made an elaborate comparison of the cases arising from nonlabor disturbances with the cases arising from labor disturbances.

It is not necessary, and would require too much space, to recite these cases in full, but among the former may be mentioned the Milligan case, and other cases arising in the State courts of Indiana, Illinois, Kentucky, North Carolina, and Wisconsin (all during or immediately following the Civil War), and three cases in the courts of Kentucky, Ohio, and Oklahoma since that time; among the latter, *i. e.*, those arising from labor disturbances, are included the cases from Colorado, Idaho, Montana, Pennsylvania, and West Virginia. The results of such comparison are summarized in part as follows:

Although uniformly held that the writ of habeas corpus can only be suspended by the legislature, in these labor disturbances the executive has in fact suspended or disregarded the writ. In the labor cases the judiciary either disregards the fact that the writ has been suspended by the executive or evades the issue. In nonlabor cases the courts have protested emphatically when the executive attempted to interfere with the writ of habeas corpus.

In many instances in which the military has been in active operation because of nonlabor disturbances, the judiciary has almost without exception protested against the exercise of any arbitrary power and has almost uniformly attempted to limit that power.

In cases arising from labor agitations, the judiciary has uniformly upheld the power exercised by the military and in no case has there been any protest against the use of such power or any attempt to curtail it, except in Montana, where the conviction of a civilian by military commission was annulled.

Finally, it is impossible to imagine a more complete mockery of justice and travesty upon every conception of fair dealing than the innumerable decisions holding unconstitutional wise and salutary laws for the protection of workers, upon the ground that they violate the right of contract, even while the workers, whose rights are supposed to be affected, clamor for the maintenance of the statute. The appeal for the protection of the workers' rights in such cases comes invariably from the employers, and is urged against the protest of the workers, yet in almost unbroken succession the judges solemnly nullify the wisest acts of legislatures on just such specious, self-serving pleas. There are notable cases in which the judges have unmasked the mummery, as, for example, in *Holden* v. *Hardy*, where it was said:

Although the prosecution in this case was against the employer of labor, who, apparently, under the statute, is the only one liable, his defense is not so much that his right to contract has been infringed upon, but that the act works a peculiar hardship to his employees, whose right to labor as long as they please is alleged to be thereby violated. The argument would certainly come with better grace and greater cogency from the latter class.

There appear to be no reported cases in which the workers have urged that their rights are violated by such restrictive legislation, which in fact invariably originates with them; but the courts continue to hand down decisions "protecting the sacred right of contract of the worker," when the only person benefited is the employer, who is thus able to "turn the very Constitution itself into an instrument of inequality."

This entire situation is fraught with such grave dangers not only to the workers but to all citizens who value their individual liberty, that the Nation can not be entirely secure until those fundamental rights are affirmatively guaranteed to every citizen of the United States by the Federal Government. It is therefore earnestly recommended that Congress forthwith initiate an amendment to the Constitution securing these rights against encroachment by Federal, State or local governments or by private persons and corporations.

*Fifth, it is charged that the ordinary legal machinery provides no adequate means whereby laborers and other poor men can secure redress for wrongs inflicted upon them through the nonpayment of wages, through overcharges at company stores, through exorbitant hospital and other fees, fines and deductions, through fraud on the part of private employment offices, loan offices and installment houses, and through the "grafting" of foremen and superintendents.* The losses to wage earners from these sources are stated to amount each year to millions of dollars and to work untold hardship on a class of men who can ill afford to lose even a penny of their hard-won earnings.

These charges were thoroughly investigated in all parts of the country by an experienced member of the Commission's staff.

He cites, for example, that in California, where the situation has been more completely uncovered than elsewhere and where remedies are beginning to be applied, during the year ending June, 1914, 9621 claims were presented to the Commissioner of Labor alone. Of these, 7330 were for nonpayment of wages, of which 4904 were successfully settled and $110,912 of unpaid wages was collected. This is believed to have been only a small proportion of the total claims of laborers throughout the State, inasmuch as the number of claims was growing rapidly as the work of the Bureau became better known, and because, during a period of only ten months, over 2200 claims were presented to the State Commission on Immigration and Housing. The work of handling these claims and making its existence known to laborers throughout the State was just getting well under way, although with a small appropriation and inadequate force, when the collection of wage claims was suddenly checked by a decision of the State Court of Appeals that the Payment-of-Wages Law was unconstitutional on the ground that since it provided for fine or imprisonment where the wages of laborers were illegally retained, it was in effect a provision for imprisonment for debt.

The investigation in other States revealed equally bad or worse conditions, while in all except a few no efficient means existed by which these claims could be prosecuted. In conclusion our investigator reported:

*a.* The existing labor and life conditions of common laborers in this country produce immense numbers of justified labor complaints and claims, involving not only great sums of money in the aggregate but untold personal hardship and suffering.

*b.* The existing public and private legal institutions are utterly inadequate to secure justice to the laborers in the matter of these complaints and claims.

*c.* This situation has already created in the laborers distrust of the Government, of employers, and of the well-to-do classes generally, and is one of the contributory causes of the existing industrial unrest. . . .

[It is suggested that] the Commission recommend to Congress that, inasmuch as the immigrant laborers, who suffer most largely from these injustices, are ethically and legally wards of the Nation until they became citizens, the Bureau of Immigration of the Federal Department of Labor should be given the authority and necessary appropriations to establish, wherever it may seem necessary, in connection with its existing offices in all parts of the country, legal aid divisions which would freely and aggressively prosecute these claims and complaints on behalf of the immigrant laborers, and, if there are no constitutional or statutory barriers, on behalf also of American citizens.

*Sixth, it is charged by the workers that the courts, by the unwarranted extension of their powers in the issuance of injunctions, have not only grievously injured the workers individually and collectively upon innumerable occasions, but have, by the contempt procedure consequent upon disobedience to such injunctions, deprived the workers of the right, fundamental to anglo-Saxon institutions, to be tried by jury.*

This charge is not limited to members of trade unions, nor to workers, but is voiced also by many who have no reason for partisanship. For example, Mr. S. S. Gregory, former president of the American Bar Association, testified before the Commission:

These injunctions are based upon the theory that the man carrying on a business has a certain sort of property right in the good will or the successful conduct of that business; and that when several hundred or several thousand excited men gather around his premises where he carries his business on, and threaten everybody that comes in there to work, and possibly use violence, that that is such an unlawful interference with property right as may be the subject of protection in equity. And that view of the law has been sustained by the courts of practically all the States.

But the great difficulty about this was this, that having enjoined defendants, namely, striking workmen, perhaps from unlawful interference with the business of the employer, where that unlawful interference consisted in an attack or an assault and battery upon another man, to wit, perhaps a strikebreaker so-called, or one who was hired to take the place of one of the striking workmen, that thereafter the judge who had ordered the injunction and whose authority had been thus defied, was permitted to put the person charged with the breach of that injunction upon trial upon a charge of contempt, really for having committed an unlawful and criminal act.

Now the Constitution has thrown around the prosecution of criminals (the Constitutions State and Federal) a number of securities. They are entitled to trial by jury; they are entitled to be confronted by the witnesses who are to testify against them; they are entitled to be heard by counsel.

But none of those guaranties except perhaps the right to be heard by counsel is secured in contempt proceedings; and the obvious wisdom of permitting twelve men drawn from the body of the people to pass on questions of fact—men who are supposed to be prejudiced neither for nor against the parties, who know nothing about the case until they are sworn in the jury box, has so far commended itself to the wisdom of legislators and jurists to such a degree that it has become a permanent feature of our jurisprudence; and to provide that the court may proceed against parties for contempt, where the conduct charged against them is criminal, is really an evasion of the constitutional guaranties and a plain attempt to commit to equity jurisdiction over matters which it has been decided over and over again by all the courts that it has no jurisdiction with respect to, namely, the administration of the criminal law.

For instance, I might receive, as I leave the room of this tribunal today, a threatening letter from somebody saying they were going to kill me for something I had said, or had not said, before the Commission. Now, that involves personal loss possibly to my wife or those dependent upon me; but no court of equity would listen for a moment to a bill I should file saying "A B" or some other blackhand gentleman had threatened to kill me, or if filed by anybody dependent upon me, and therefore there should be an injunction to prevent him from killing me. That would be an absurdity—a legal absurdity; and none the less is it so where a man is enjoined from committing acts of violence in a strike to try him for contempt, without a trial by jury. And that has been an injustice that has rankled in the minds of everybody that has been a victim of it, and justly so.

Sir Charles Napier says, "People talk about agitators, but the only real agitator is injustice; and the only way is to correct the injustice and allay the agitation."

Judge Walter Clark, Chief Justice of the Supreme Court of North Carolina, also testified before the Commission as follows:

*Chairman Walsh.* Have you studied the effect of the use of injunctions in labor disputes generally in the United States, as a student of economics and the law?

*Judge Clark.* I do not think they can be justified, sir. . . . [Their effect] has been, of course, to irritate the men, because they feel that in an anglo-Saxon community every man has a right to a trial by jury and that to take him up and compel him to be tried by a judge, is not in accordance with the principles of equality, liberty, and justice.

*Chairman Walsh.* Do you think that has been one of the causes of social unrest in the United States?

*Judge Clark.* Yes, sir, and undoubtedly will be more so, unless it is remedied.

It is not within the province of the Commission to attempt to decide the question of whether or not the issuance of such injunctions is an unwarranted extension upon the part of the courts; but the weighty opinions cited above are very impressive and are convincing that the workers have great reason for their attitude. It is known, however, from the evidence of witnesses and from the information collected by the staff, that such injunctions have in many cases inflicted grievous injury upon workmen engaged in disputes with their employers, and that their interests have been seriously prejudiced by the denial of jury trial, which every criminal is afforded, and by trial before the judge against whom the contempt was alleged.

It is felt to be a duty, therefore, to register a solemn protest against this condition, being convinced of its injustice not only by reason of the evil effects which have resulted from this procedure, but by virtue of a conviction that no person's liberty can safely be decided by any one man, particularly when that man is the object of the alleged contempt.

The Clayton Act undoubtedly contains many features which will relieve this situation as far as the Federal courts are concerned, but it seems clear that it does not contain anything like a complete solution of the existing injustices, even for the limited field of Federal jurisdiction.

*Seventh, it is charged by the representatives of labor that laws designed for the protection of labor in workshops and mines and on railroads, are not effectively enforced, except in a few States.* This is a matter of considerable moment to labor, but it is, after all, regarded by the workers, since it concerns chiefly only their safety and comfort, as ranking far below the other matters discussed, which involve primarily their liberty and rights as freemen and, secondarily, their only means of bettering their condition. Moreover, it is almost entirely a matter of administration, which is discussed in detail elsewhere in the report. With the great attention which the method of administration is now receiving, not only from labor organizations but from civic organizations, and lately even from employers' associations, it is likely to reach a satisfactory stage before very long.

*Eighth, it is charged that in cases involving industrial questions, the workers are liable to great injustice by reason of the fact that in many localities they are excluded from juries either by the qualifications pre-*

*scribed (usually payment of property tax) or by the method of selection.*

In California, for example, it was testified that grave injustice had been done in many cases because the juries (composed only of property owners, for the most part employers) were greatly prejudiced against the defendants, whose program, if successful, would directly or indirectly affect the interests of the jurors.

Similarly, in Cook County, Illinois, which includes Chicago, it was found by a committee of the Lawyers' Association of Illinois that, although the system of selection by commissioners was intended to produce an impartial selection from all classes of the community, out of probably 1000 different occupations in Cook County the commissioners confine the selection of the great bulk of the jurors to the following ten occupations: Managers, superintendents, foremen, presidents and owners of companies, secretaries of companies, merchants, agents, salesmen, clerks and book-keepers.

To quote from the report:

There are 76,000 mechanics affiliated with the Building Trades Council in Chicago, yet in the 3,440 jurors investigated by your committee there are only 200 mechanics drawn from the 76,000 in the Building Trades Council.

There are about 200,000 mechanics belonging to the different labor organizations in Chicago, yet there are only about 350 mechanics drawn as jurors by the commissions in the 3,440 investigated, or about 10 per cent, when the percentage ought to be about 70 per cent.

The report of the committee adds:

Another comparison will show that out of these 3,440 jurors the commission took only 314 jurors from 130 different occupations, or an average of less than three jurors from each occupation, while from the ten favored occupations mentioned above, 1,723 jurors were picked, or the grossly excessive average of 172 from each of said ten occupations.

A similar situation was disclosed by the investigations of members of the staff in Paterson, N. J.

Finally, there is the very grave situation where, by putting aside the legal and customary methods, the jury is chosen by the sheriff or other officers, who may be unduly influenced by either party to the case. Such a situation, inimical in the extreme to the interests of the workers, has been conclusively proved to have existed in Colorado and in other mining districts.

In the belief that the right to trial by an impartial jury is necessary for the maintenance of justice, and that such impartiality can be secured only by including all classes of citizens, it is suggested that the Commission recommend that Federal and State statutes should be passed providing for the creation of juries by drawing the names from a wheel or other like device, which shall contain the name of *every qualified voter* in the district from which the jury is to be selected. The adoption of this method in Missouri and other States has resulted uniformly in securing impartial juries of much higher grade, and has also eliminated almost entirely the sources of corruption attending the selection of juries.

*Ninth, it is charged by the workers that, during strikes, innocent men are in many cases arrested without just cause, charged with fictitious crimes, held under excessive bail, and treated frequently with unexampled brutality for the purpose of injuring the strikers and breaking the strike.*

In support of this charge, the Commission has been furnished with evidence showing that in a number of recent strikes large numbers of strikers were arrested, but that only a small number were brought to trial, and relatively few were convicted of any serious offense; that those arrested were, as a rule, required to give heavy bail, far beyond their means, or were detained without trial until their effectiveness as strikers was destroyed; and that in many cases strikers were brutally treated by the police or by special deputies in the pay of the companies. A number of these strikes have been investigated by public hearings of the Commission, by members of its staff, or by other departments of the Federal Government. In each of the strikes investigated, the charges as made were in essentials substantiated.

In Paterson, N. J., which was investigated with unusual thoroughness and which, because of its size and its location in the most densely populated section, might be considered likely to be free from such abuses, it was found that during the strike of the silk workers, 2238 arrests charging unlawful assembly or disorderly conduct were made, and that in all there were 300 convictions in the lower courts. Men arrested for unlawful assembly were held in bail of $500 to $5000. The right of trial by jury was generally denied. Men were arrested for ridiculous reasons, as, for example, for standing on the opposite side of the street and beckoning to men in the mills to come out. This was the allegation on which the charge of unlawful assembly was placed against four men, and for which they were sent to jail in default of $500 bail, and, although never indicted, the charges still stand against them as a bar to their rights as citizens and voters. Men were fined arbitrarily, as in the case of one who was fined $10 for permitting strikers to sit on a bench in front of his house. Not more than $25 worth of damage was done during the entire strike, involving 25,000 workers, and there was no actual violence or attempt at violence on the part of the strikers during the entire strike. Under such conditions the editor of a local paper was arrested, charged with criminal libel, for comparing the conditions in Paterson with the rule of Cossacks; and four men who sold the paper on the streets also were arrested. The editor was tried and convicted in the lower court, but the verdict was set aside by the Supreme Court, while the four men, after being held several days in default of bail, were released without trial.

It is impossible to summarize the activities of the police and authorities during this strike better than by referring to the testimony of two of the leading citizens of Paterson, who said that they had resolved to get rid of the "agitators" and were ready to go beyond the law to accomplish their purpose. A full appreciation of the injustice committed during this strike can be secured only by reading the testimony taken at Paterson, and the reports of the Commission's investigators based upon the records of the police and the courts.

In Los Angeles and Indianapolis essentially the same conditions were found by the Commission, while in McKees Rocks, Bethlehem, and Westmoreland County, Pa., Lawrence, Mass., and Calumet, Mich., investigated by the Federal Department of Labor, essentially the same conditions of injustice were found to prevail. The conditions in West Virginia and Colorado, which were almost beyond belief and had the additional feature of military rule, will be discussed elsewhere.

An examination of the entire mass of evidence is convincing that such conditions are in fact typical of strikes which are serious enough to arouse the authorities, especially where the workers are unorganized before the strike and therefore lacking in influence in the community.

*Tenth, it is asserted by the workers that in many localities during strikes not only is one of the greatest functions of the State, that of policing, virtually turned over to employers or arrogantly assumed by them, but criminals employed by detective agencies and strikebreaking agencies are clothed, by the process of deputization, with arbitrary power and relieved of criminal liability for their acts.*

Only three such cases are cited here, though the Commission has in its records evidence regarding a considerable number. At Roosevelt, N. J., it was found by the Commission's investigators and later confirmed in court, that the office of sheriff was virtually turned over to one Jerry O'Brien, the proprietor of a so-called detective agency, that he imported a number of men of bad reputation and clothed them with the authority of deputies, and that on January 19, 1915, these criminals, without provocation, wantonly shot and killed two men, and wounded 17 others, who were on strike against the American Agricultural Chemical Company, which paid and armed the deputies.

Similarly, during the Calumet, Mich., strike, about 230 men were imported from detective agencies in eastern cities, 52 under pay from the county board of supervisors, which was made up almost entirely of copper company officials. The actions of these men were so wantonly brutal that they were censured by the local judge, but they went unchecked in their career of arrogant brutality, which culminated in their shooting, without provocation, into a house in which women and children were, killing two persons and wounding two others.

The recent strike in Bayonne, N. J., threw more light on these armed guards. During this strike one of the New York detective agencies furnished, for the protection of the Tidewater Oil Company's plant, men who were so vicious and unreliable that the officials of the company themselves say that their presence was sufficient to incite a riot. These men shot without provocation at anyone or everyone who came within sight, and the killing of at least three strikers in Bayonne, and the wounding of many more, is directly chargeable to these guards.

The character of the men who make a specialty of this kind of employment has never been more frankly described than in the testimony of Mr. L. M. Bowers, Chairman of the Board of Directors of the Colorado Fuel & Iron Company, who repeatedly referred to those in the employ of that company as "cut-throats," against whose character, he stated, he had frequently protested.

According to the statement of Berghoff Brothers & Waddell, who style themselves "labor adjusters" and who do a business of strike breaking and strike policing, there are countless men who follow this business at all times. They say they can put 10,000 armed men into the field inside of seventy-two hours. The fact that these men may have a criminal record is no deterrent to their being employed; and no check can be made on the men sent out by these companies on hurry calls.

When the question of providing the bail for these men arose, as a result of the killing of the strikers at Bayonne, the company attorney actually declined to furnish bail to them, on the ground that they were thugs of whom the company knew nothing and that it would not be responsible for their appearance.

In view of the endless crimes committed by the employees of the so-called detective agencies, who have been permitted to usurp a function that should belong only to the State, it is suggested that the Commission recommend to Congress either that such of these agencies as may operate in more than one State, or may be employed by corporations engaged in interstate commerce, or may use the mails, should be compelled to take out a Federal license, with regulations to insure the character of their employees and the limitation of their activities to the bona fide business of detecting crime, or that such agencies shall be utterly abolished through the operation of the taxing power or through denying them the use of the mails.

*Eleventh, it is charged that in many localities the entire system of civil Government is suspended during strikes and there is set up in its place a military despotism under so-called martial law.*

In West Virginia, for example, during the strike of coal miners in 1912, martial law was declared and the writ of habeas corpus denied, in the face of a direct prohibition by the Constitution of the State, in spite of the fact that the courts were open and unobstructed, and without reference to the protests of the strikers. Persons outside the military zone were arrested, dragged before military courts, tried and sentenced under so-called martial law. Upon appeal to the civil courts of the State, the actions of the military authorities were upheld in spite of the oath of the judges to support the Constitution, which in terms provided "that no citizen, unless engaged in the military service of the State, shall be tried or punished by any military court for any offense that is cognizable by the civil courts of the State," and further, "The privilege of the writ of habeas corpus shall not be suspended."

The decisions of the court stirred Hon. Edgar M. Cullen, a former Chief Judge of the Court of Appeals of New York (a witness before this Commission and recognized as unusually conservative and careful in his utterances), to make the following statements:

Under these decisions the life and liberty of every man within the State would seem to be at the mercy of the Governor. He may declare a state of war whether the facts justify such a declaration or not, and that declaration is conclusive upon the courts.

If he declares only a portion of the State to be in a state of war, under the decision in the second case a person in any other part of the State, however distant, may be arrested and delivered to the military authorities in the martial zone, and his fate, whether liberty or life, depends on the action of a military commission, for I know of no principle which authorizes a military commission to impose the punishment of imprisonment that would not equally authorize the imposition of the punishment of death. Under that doctrine, should armed resistance to the Federal authority justifying a suspension of the writ of habeas corpus occur in Arizona a citizen could, on a charge of aiding the insurrection, be dragged from his home in Maine and delivered to the military authorities in Arizona for trial and punishment.

The remedy suggested by the learned court, of impeachment by the legislature, would hardly seem of much efficacy. By impeachment the Governor could only be removed from office. He could not be further punished, however flagrant his opposition may have been, except by a perversion of the criminal law; for if the doctrine of the courts is correct he would not have exceeded his legal power.

The Governor might imprison or execute the members of the legislature, or even the learned judges of the Supreme Court themselves.

The attention of the Commission has also been directed by witnesses to the repeated occurrence of similar or, if possible, more extreme conditions in Colorado and Idaho, which testimony has been confirmed either by the investigations and hearings of the Commission or by the reports of responsible officials of the Federal Government. In Colorado, martial law has been in effect ten times since 1894. Similarly in Idaho, martial law has been in effect on several occasions. In both of these States not only have strikers been imprisoned by military courts, but thousands have been held for long periods in "bull pens," hundreds have been forcibly deported from the State, and so arrogant have the troops become upon occasions that they have refused to obey the mandates of the civil courts, although the constitutions of both States provide that the military shall always be in strict subordination to the civil power. In fact, on one occasion at least, when orders of the court for the production of prisoners had been ignored and the military officers were summoned before the court, they surrounded the courthouse with infantry and cavalry, came into court accompanied by soldiers with fixed bayonets, and stationed a gatling gun in a position commanding the courthouse. During the recent strike in Colorado the military was supreme and wielded its arbitrary power despotically and at times brutally.

*Twelfth, it is charged by the workers that in some localities the control by the employers of the entire machinery of government is so great that lawless acts on the part of agents of the employers go unheeded and unpunished, while vindictive action against the leaders of the strike is accomplished by methods unparalleled in civilized countries.* It is seldom that evidence sufficient to substantiate such sweeping charges can be secured even if the charges are true, but in the testimony and documents which have been gathered by the Commission there seems to be conclusive proof that in one State at least, Colorado, such a condition of complete domination of the State Government has prevailed and, it would seem, does still prevail.

First, Hon. Frederick Farrar, Attorney General of Colorado, testified in substance as follows:

As a result of a personal investigation into conditions in Las Animas and Huerfano Counties, Colo., in the summer of 1913, a very perfect political machine was found to exist. The head of this political machine is the sheriff, and it is conducted along lines very similar to those maintained by corrupt political organizations. It has a system of relief in case of need, and a system of giving rewards to its people. It was difficult to determine which was cause and which effect, but there was undoubtedly some relationship between the political machine and the coal companies. Witness believes the machine existed through its power as a machine over the coal companies, but has no knowledge of any money being used. His investigation did not lead into question of whether the machine controlled coroners' juries in cases of death from accidents in mines, etc., or of whether mining laws were obeyed.

Second, Hon. Thomas M. Patterson, formerly United States Senator, testified:

The men employed by the large mining companies have been used to gain political power. There is no doubt that it is the deliberate purpose of these companies to control the officials of the counties in which they are operating, and to have a great influence in the selection of judges and in the constitution of the courts. In this purpose they have been successful. Election returns from the two or three counties in which the large companies operate show that in the precincts in which the mining camps are located the returns are nearly unanimous in favor of the men or measures approved by the companies, regardless of party. The companies know whom they want elected, and do not hesitate, judging from the results, to make it known.

Third, State Senator Helen Ring Robinson testified in substance as follows:

As a member of the Committee of Privileges and Elections, which investigated conditions in Las Animas County, she listened for three weeks to the story of political conditions there. Long before the strike was ordered, she realized that the industrial situation was hopeless because the political situation appeared hopeless.

"I found that while the Counties of Las Animas and Huerfano are geographically a part of Colorado, yet industrially and politically they are a barony or a principality of the Colorado Fuel & Iron Company. Such situations of course must mean a knitting together of the industrial and political situation, and I don't wish to say that the Colorado Fuel & Iron Company have limited their efforts to Las Animas and Huerfano Counties. If that were so, the situation in the State itself would not be so seriously affected by them; but they have in time past reached out beyond the boundaries of their principality and made and unmade Governors; men who desire positions of high place in Colorado would be very loath to antagonize them whether they lived in Las Animas or Routt County or in Denver, and it would not matter in that case to which political party they belonged."

Attention should be called to another aspect of the control of the machinery of government by one class for the oppression of another. The scales of justice have in the past swung far in one direction—legislatures, courts and administrative officers under the domination of corporations have grievously wronged the workers. There is grave danger that, if the workers assert their collective power and secure the control of government by the massing of their numbers, the scales may swing equally far in the other direction and every act of injustice, every drop of blood, every moment of anguish, be repaid in full, not upon some obscure and humble worker, but upon those who now glory in the sense of boundless power and security.

In the few cases in which the workers have momentarily secured control of local situations, they have followed the examples that have been set and have in many instances used their power unjustly and oppressively. In Colorado, for example, during the strikes in the metal mines, where the

Western Federation of Miners controlled a camp, they followed the example of the operators and deported persons whom they deemed to be obnoxious. Similarly, during the fight between two factions of the Western Federation of Miners in Butte, Mont., the dominant faction forced several persons to leave the city and set aside the ordinary processes of law. It is inevitable that this should be the case, and it is remarkable only that the masses of workers, even when acting as mobs, show greater self-restraint than do organizations made up of business men ordinarily regarded as upright, respectable and admirable citizens.

For the security and honor of the Nation the scales of justice must be brought to a stable equilibrium. This can be accomplished only by a realization by every citizen that every act of injustice, whether done in far-off states or at one's very door, whether affecting a friend or an enemy, is in its consequences an invasion of one's own security and a menace to one's liberty.

There is reason, however, to expect that no sober and well considered action for the removal of these abuses will be taken, and one may, without being an alarmist, share the fears expressed by Judge Seymour D. Thompson:

The dangerous tendencies and extravagant pretensions of the courts which I have pointed out ought not to be minimized, but ought to be resisted. Their resistance ought not to take place as advised by Jefferson, by "meeting the invaders foot to foot," but it ought to take place under the wise and moderate guidance of the legal profession, but the danger is that the people do not always so act. In popular governments, evils are often borne with stolid patience until a culminating point is reached, when the people burst into sudden frenzy and redress their grievances by violent and extreme measures, and even tear down the fabric of government itself. There is danger, real danger, that the people will see at one sweeping glance that all the powers of their Government, Federal and State, lie at the feet of us lawyers, that is to say, at the feet of a judicial oligarchy; that those powers are being steadily exercised in behalf of the wealthy and powerful classes, and to the prejudice of the scattered and segregated people; that the power thus seized includes the power of amending the Constitution; the power of superintending the action, not merely of Congress, but also of the State Legislatures; the power of degrading the powers of the two houses of Congress, in making those investigations which they may deem accessory to wise legislation, to the powers which an English court has ascribed to British Colonial legislatures . . . holding that a venal legislature, temporarily vested with power, may corruptly bargain away those essential attributes of sovereignty and for all time; that corporate franchises bought from corrupt legislatures are sanctified and placed forever beyond recall by the people; that great trusts and combinations may place their yokes upon the necks of the people of the United States, who must groan forever under the weight, without remedy and without hope; that trial by jury and the ordinary criminal justice of the States, which ought to be kept near the people, are to be set aside, and Federal court injunctions substituted therefor; that those injunctions extend to preventing laboring men quitting their employment, although they are liable to be discharged by their employers at any time, thus creating and perpetuating a state of slavery. There is danger that the people will see these things all at once; see their enrobed judges doing their thinking on the side of the rich and powerful; see them look with solemn cynicism upon the sufferings of the masses, nor heed the earthquake when it begins to rock beneath their feet; see them present a spectacle not unlike that of Nero fiddling while Rome burns. There is danger that the people will see all this at one sudden glance, and that the furies will then break loose and that all hell will ride on their wings.

It is true that Judge Thompson spoke 19 years ago, but the real danger lies in the fact that during that period we have done little to remove the evils cited by him, and that there is even reason to fear that we have simply moved nearer to the danger line instead of away from it.

In considering the action which needs to be taken it has been urged by some that the end to be achieved is to place personal rights on a parity with property rights. It is necessary to render a firm protest and warning against the acceptance of such an ideal. The establishment of property rights and personal rights on the same level can leave only a constant and ever growing menace to our popular institutions. With the acceptance of such an ideal our democracy is doomed to ultimate destruction. Personal rights must be recognized as supreme and of unalterable ascendency over property rights.

Relief from these grave evils can not be secured by petty reforms. The action must be drastic and directed at the roots from which these evils spring.

With full recognition of the gravity of the suggestions, it seems necessary to urge the Commission to make the following recommendations:

1. That Congress forthwith initiate an amendment to the Constitution providing in specific terms for the protection of the personal rights of every person in the United States from encroachment by the Federal and State Governments and by private individuals, associations and corporations. The principal rights which should be thus specifically protected by the power of the Federal Government are the privilege of the writ of habeas corpus, the right to jury trial, to free speech, to peaceful assemblage, to keep and bear arms, to be free from unreasonable searches and seizures, to speedy public trial, and to freedom from excessive bail and from cruel and unusual punishments.

2. That Congress immediately enact a statute or, if deemed necessary, initiate a constitutional amendment, specifically prohibiting the courts from declaring legislative acts unconstitutional.

3. That Congress enact that in all Federal cases where the trial is by jury, all qualified voters in the district shall be included in the list from which jurors are selected and that they shall be drawn by the use of a wheel or other device designed to promote absolute impartiality.

4. That Congress drastically regulate or prohibit private detective agencies doing business in more than one State, employed by a company doing an interstate business, or using the mails in connection with their business. Such regulation, if it is feasible, should include particularly the limitation of their activities to the *bona fida* functions of detecting crime, and adequate provision should be made for the rigid supervision of their organization and personnel.

### 4. Denial of the Right of Organization

The previous discussion of the causes of industrial unrest has dealt with the denial of certain fundamentals to which the workers believe they have natural and inalienable rights, namely, a fair distribution of the products of industry, the opportunity to earn a living, free access to unused land and natural resources, and just treatment by legislators, courts and executive officials. A more serious and fundamental charge is, however, contained in the allegation by the workers that, in spite of the nominal legal right which has been established by a century-long struggle, almost insurmountable obstacles are placed in the way of their using the only means by which economic and political justice can be secured, namely, combined action through voluntary organization. The workers insist that this right of organization is fundamental and necessary for their freedom, and that it is inherent in the general rights guaranteed every citizen of a democracy. They insist that "people can free themselves from oppression only by organized force. No people could gain or maintain their rights or liberties acting singly, and any class of citizens in the State subject to unjust burdens or oppression can gain relief only by combined action."

The demand for organization and collective action has been misunderstood, it is claimed, because of the belief among a large number of citizens that its purpose was simply to secure better wages and better physical conditions. It has been urged, however, by a large number of witnesses before the Commission that this is a complete misconception of the purposes for which workers desire to form organizations. It has been pointed out with great force and logic that the struggle of labor for organization is not merely an attempt to secure an increased measure of the material comforts of life, but is a part of the age-long struggle for liberty; that this struggle is sharpened by the pinch of hunger and the exhaustion of body and mind by long hours and improper working conditions; but that even if men were well fed they would still struggle to be free. It is not denied that the exceptional individual can secure an economic sufficiency either by the sale of his unusual ability or talent, or by sycophantic subservience to some person in authority, but it is insisted that no individual can achieve freedom by his own efforts. Similarly, while it is admitted that in some cases exceptional employers treat their employees with the greatest justice and liberality, it is held to be a social axiom that no group of workers can become free except by combined action, nor can the mass hope to achieve any material advance in their condition except by collective effort.

Furthermore, it is urged by the representatives of labor that the efforts of individuals who are bent upon bettering their own condition without reference to their health or to the interests of others, directly injure each of their fellow workers and indirectly weaken the whole fabric of society.

It is also pointed out that the evolution of modern industry has greatly increased the necessity for organization on the part of wage earners. While it is not admitted that the employer who has only one employee is on an economic equality with the person who is employed by him, because of the fact that the employer controls the means of livelihood, which gives him an almost incalculable advantage in any bargain, nevertheless this condition of inequality is held to have been enormously increased by the development of corporations controlling the livelihood of hundreds of thousands of employees, and by the growth of employers' associations whose members act as a unit in questions affecting their relations with employees.

There have been many able and convincing expositions of this belief by witnesses before the Commission, but there is no other which seems to have so completely covered the entire field as the testimony of Mr. Louis D. Brandeis, who, as he stated, has studied this problem from the standpoint both of employers and of employees:

My observation leads me to believe that while there are many single things —single causes—contributing causes to unrest, that there is one cause which is fundamental, and it is the necessary conflict between—the contrast between —our political liberty and the industrial absolutism.

We are as free politically perhaps as it is possible for us to be. Every man has his voice and vote and the law has endeavored to enable, and has succeeded practically in enabling, him to exercise his political franchise without fear. He, therefore, has his part, and certainly can secure an adequate part of the government of the country in all of its political relations—in all relations which are determined by legislation or governmental administration. On the other hand, in dealing with industrial problems the position of the ordinary worker is exactly the reverse. And the main objection, as I see it, to the large corporation is, that it makes possible—and in many cases makes inevitable— the exercise of industrial absolutism. It is not merely the case of the individual worker against employer, which, even if he is a reasonably sized employer, presents a serious situation calling for the interposition of a union to protect the individual. But we have the situation of an employer so potent, so well organized, with such concentrated forces and with such extraordinary powers of reserve and the ability to endure against strikes and other efforts of a union, that the relatively loosely organized masses of even strong unions are unable to cope with the situation.

We are dealing here with a question not of motive, but of condition. Now the large corporation and the managers of the large corporation—of the powerful corporation—are probably in large part actuated by motives just the same as an employer of a tenth of their size. Neither of them, as a rule, wishes to have his liberty abridged; but the smaller concern usually comes to the conclusion that it is necessary that it should be, where there is an important union found. But when you have created a great power, when there exist these powerful organizations who can afford—not only can successfully summon forces from all parts of the country—but can afford to use tremendous amounts of money in any conflict to carry out what they deem to be their business principles, you have necessarily a condition of inequality between the two contending forces. The result is that contests undertaken doubtless with the best motives and with strong conviction of what is for the best interests not only of the company but of the community, lead to absolutism. In all cases of these large corporations the result has been to develop a benevolent absolutism—an absolutism all the same; and it is that which makes the great corporation so dangerous. It is because you have created within the State a state so powerful that the ordinary forces existing are insufficient to meet it.

Now, to my mind the situation of the worker that is involved—and I noted, Mr. Chairman, that when you put the question you put the question of physical condition—unrest, in my mind, never can be removed, and fortunately never can be removed, by mere improvement of the physical and material condition of the working man. If it were, we should run great risk of improving their material condition and reducing their manhood. We must bear in mind all the time that however much we may desire material improvement and must desire it for the comfort of the individual, that we are a democracy; and that we must have, above all things, men; and it is the development of manhood to which any industrial and social system must be directed. We are committed not only to social justice in the sense of avoiding things which bring suffering and harm and unequal distribution of wealth; but we are committed primarily to democracy, and the social justice to which we are headed is an incident of our democracy, not an end itself. It is the result of democracy, but democracy we must have. And therefore the end to which we must move is a recognition of industrial democracy as the end to which we are to work, and that means this: It means that the problems are not any longer, or to be any longer, the problems of the employer. The problems of his business—it is not the employer's business. The union can not shift upon the employer the responsibility for the conditions, nor can the employer insist upon solving, according to his will, the conditions which shall exist; but the problems which exist are the problems of the trade; they are the problems of employer and employee. No possible degree of profit-sharing, however liberal, can meet the situation. That would be again merely dividing the proceeds of business. That might do harm or it might do good, dependent on how it is applied.

No mere liberality in the division of the proceeds of industry can meet this situation. There must be a division not only of the profits, but a division of the responsibilities; and the men must have the opportunity of deciding, in part, what shall be their condition and how the business shall be run. They also, as a part of that responsibility, must learn that they must bear the results, the fatal results, of grave mistakes, just as the employer. But the right to assist in producing the results, the right, if need be, the privilege of making mistakes, is a privilege which can not be denied to labor, just as we must insist on their sharing the responsibilities for the result of the business.

Now to a certain extent we get that result—are gradually getting it—in smaller businesses. The grave objection to the large business is that almost inevitably, from its organization, through its absentee stockholdership, through its remote directorship, through the creation practically of stewards to take charge of the details of the operation of the business and coming into direct relation with labor, we lose that necessary cooperation which our own aspirations—American aspirations—of democracy demand. And it is in that, in my opinion, that we will find the very foundation of the unrest; and no matter what is done with the superstructure, no matter how it may be improved one way or the other, unless we reach that fundamental difficulty, the unrest will not only continue, but, in my opinion, will grow worse.

It is very significant that out of 230 representatives of the interests of employers, chosen largely on the recommendations of their own organizations, less than half a dozen have denied the propriety of collective action on the part of employees. A considerable number of these witnesses have, however, testified that they denied in practice what they admitted to be right in theory. A majority of such witnesses were employers who in the operation of their business maintained what they, in accordance with common terminology, called the "open shop." The theory of the "open shop," according to these witnesses, is that workers are employed without any reference to their membership or nonmembership in trade unions; while, as a matter of fact, it was found upon investigation that these employers did not, as a rule, willingly or knowingly employ union men. Nevertheless, this is deemed by the Commission to be a minor point. The "open shop," even if union men are not discriminated against, is as much a denial of the right of collective action as is the "antiunion shop." In neither is the collective action of employees permitted for the purpose of negotiating with reference to labor conditions. Both in theory and in practice, in the absence of legislative regulation, the working conditions are fixed by the employer.

It is evident, therefore, that there can be at best only a benevolent despotism where collective action on the part of employees does not exist.

A great deal of testimony has been introduced to show that employers who refuse to deal collectively with their workmen do in fact grant audiences at which the grievances of their workmen may be presented. One is repelled rather than impressed by the insistence with which this idea has been presented. Every tyrant in history has on stated days granted audiences to which his faithful subjects might bring their complaints against his officers and agents. At these audiences, in theory at least, even the poorest widow might be heard by her sovereign in her search for justice. That justice was never secured under such conditions, except at the whim of the tyrant, is sure. It is equally sure that in industry justice can never be attained by such a method.

The last point which needs to be considered in this connection is the attitude frequently assumed by employers that they are perfectly willing to deal with their own employees collectively, but will resist to the end dealing with any national organization, and resent the intrusion of any persons acting for their employees who are not members of their own labor force. In practice these statements have been generally found to be specious. Such employers as a rule oppose any effective form of organization among their own employees as bitterly as they fight the national unions. The underlying motive of such statements seems to be that as long as organizations are unsupported from outside they are ineffective and capable of being crushed with ease and impunity by discharging the ringleaders. Similarly, the opposition to the representation of their employees by persons outside their labor force, seems to arise wholly from the knowledge that as long as the workers' representatives are on the payroll they can be controlled, or, if they prove intractable, they can be effectually disposed of by summary dismissal.

To suggest that labor unions can be effective if organized on less than a national scale, seems to ignore entirely the facts and trend of present-day American business. There is no line of organized industry in which individual establishments can act independently. Ignoring for the time the centralization of control and ownership, and also the almost universal existence of employers' associations, the mere fact of competition would render totally ineffective any organization of employees which was limited to a single establishment. Advance in labor conditions must proceed with a fair degree of uniformity throughout any line of industry. This does not indeed require that *all* employees in an industry must belong to a national organization, for experience has shown that wherever even a considerable part are union members, the advances which they secure are almost invariably granted by competitors, even if they do not employ union men, in order to prevent their own employees from organizing.

The conclusions upon this question, however, are not based upon theory, but upon a thorough investigation of typical situations in which the contrast between organization and the denial of the right of organization could best be studied. The Commission has held public hearings and has made thorough investigations in such industrial communities as Paterson, N. J., Los Angeles, Cal., Lead, S. D., and Colorado, where the right of collective action on the part of employees is denied. These investigations have shown that under the best possible conditions, and granting the most excellent motives on the part of employers, freedom does not exist either politically, industrially, or socially, and that the fiber of manhood will inevitably be destroyed by the continuance of the existing situation. Investigations have proved that although the physical and material conditions may be unusually good, as, for example, in Lead (S. D.), they are the price paid for the absolute submission of the employees to the will of the employing corporation. Such conditions are, moreover, shown by the hearings of the Commission and by the investigations of its staff to be unusual. Los Angeles, for example, although exceptionally endowed in location, climate and natural resources, was sharply criticised for the labor conditions which had developed during its "open shop" regime even by Mr. Walter Drew, representing several of the largest associations which contend for the "open shop." It is significant that the only claim ordinarily made for the conditions in such establishments or localities is that "they are as good as are secured by the union." As a matter of fact, there are few establishments which make this boast, and in the majority the conditions were found to be far below any acceptable standards.

The Commission has also, through public hearings and the investigations of its staff, made a thorough and searching investigation of the conditions in those industries and establishments where collective action, through the medium of trade unions and joint agreements exists. It has not been found that the conditions in such industries are ideal, nor that friction between employers and the unions is unknown; nor has it been found that the employees in such industries have entirely achieved economic, political and industrial freedom, for these ideals can not be gained until the fundamental changes in our political and economic structure, which have already been referred to, have in some way been accomplished. It has been found, however, that the material conditions of the workers in such industries and establishments are on a generally higher plane than where workers are unorganized; that important improvements in such conditions have been achieved as the direct result of organization; that the friction which exists in such industries and establishments has been reduced rather than increased by organization; and that the workers at least have secured a basis upon which their political and economic freedom may ultimately be established.

The evils of graft, "machine politics," factional fights and false leadership, which have been found sometimes to exist in such organized industries, are those which are inevitable in any democratic form of organization. They are the same evils which have accompanied the development of the American Nation, and of its States and municipalities. Such evils as we have found to exist are indeed to be condemned, but a study of the history of these organizations seems to show clearly that there is a tendency to eradicate them as the organizations become stronger and as the membership becomes more familiar with the responsibilities and methods of democratic action. Furthermore, there is a fundamental principle which applies in this field as in all other lines of human activity. This principle is contained in the following contrast: In democratic organizations such evils and excesses as may arise tend to disrupt and destroy the organization and are therefore self-eradicating; while in an autocracy, evils and excesses tend inevitably to strengthen the existing autocrat and can be eradicated only in the event of a revolt on the part of those who suffer from such evils. This is the history not only of every form of artificial association, but of nations.

The fundamental question for the Nation to decide, for in the end public opinion will control here as elsewhere, is whether the workers shall have an effective means of adjusting their grievances, improving their condition, and securing their liberty, through negotiation with their employers, or whether they shall be driven by necessity and oppression to the extreme of revolt. Where men are well organized, and the power of employers and employees is fairly well balanced, agreements are nearly always reached by negotiation; but, even if this fails, the strikes or lockouts which follow are as a rule merely cessations of work until economic necessity forces the parties together again to adopt some form of compromise. With the unorganized, there is no hope of achieving anything except by spontaneous revolt. Too often has it been found that during the delay of attempted negotiations, the leaders are discharged, and new men are found ready to take the place of those who protest against conditions. Without strike funds or other financial support, the unorganized must achieve results at once; they can not afford to wait for reason and compromise to come into play. Lacking strong leaders and definite organization, such revolts can only be expected to change to mob action on the slightest provocation.

Looking back over the industrial history of the last quarter-century, the industrial disputes which have attracted the attention of the country and which have been accompanied by bloodshed and violence have been revolutions against industrial oppression, and not mere strikes for the improvement of working conditions. Such revolutions in fact were the railway strikes of the late eighties, the Homestead strike, the bituminous coal strike of 1897, the anthracite strikes of 1900 and 1903, the strike at McKees Rocks in 1909, the Bethlehem strike of 1910, the strikes in the textile mills at Lawrence, Paterson and Little Falls, many of the strikes in the mining camps of Idaho and Colorado, the garment workers' strikes in New York and other cities, and the recent strikes in the mining districts of West Virginia, Westmoreland Co., Pa., and Calumet, Mich.

As a result, therefore, not only of fundamental considerations but of practical investigations, the results of which are described in detail hereinafter, it would appear that every means should be used to extend and strengthen organizations throughout the entire industrial field. Much attention has been devoted to the means by which this can best be accomplished, and a large number of suggestions have been received. As a result of careful consideration, it is suggested that the Commission recommend the following action:

1. Incorporation among the rights guaranteed by the Constitution of the unlimited right of individuals to form associations, not for the sake of profit but for the advancement of their individual and collective interests.

2. Enactment of statutes specifically protecting this right and prohibiting the discharge of any person because of his membership in a labor organization.

3. Enactment of a statute providing that action on the part of an association of individuals not organized for profit, shall not be held to be unlawful where such action would not be unlawful in the case of an individual.

4. That the Federal Trade Commission be specifically empowered and directed by Congress, in determining unfair methods of competition to take into account and specially investigate the unfair treatment of labor in all respects, with particular reference to the following points:

a. Refusal to permit employees to become members of labor organizations.

b. Refusal to meet or confer with the authorized representatives of employees.

5. That the Department of Labor, through the Secretary of Labor or any other authorized official, be empowered and directed to present to the Federal Trade Commission, and to prosecute before that body, all cases of unfair competition arising out of the treatment of labor which may come to its attention.

6. That such cases, affecting as they do the lives of citizens in the humblest circumstances, as well as the profits of competitors and the peace of the community, be directed by Congress to have precedence over all other cases before the Federal Trade Commission.

# Unionism and Socialism

## Eugene V. Debs

*In the early twentieth century organized labor faced two ways. The growth and the victories of trade unions as an answer to the power of industrialists had come mixed with such failures and frustrations that there were bound to arise from within the ranks disillusioned and impatient leaders determined to redirect the strategy of the labor movement. Such a man was Eugene Debs, and the American Socialism he forged, while ultimately powerless of itself, left its mark on all the political movements which it touched and provided a focus and a release for some profound and dynamic social currents in the progressive era.*

*The son of Alsatian immigrants, Debs grew up near the railroad shops in Terre Haute, Indiana, went to work in 1869 when a boy of fourteen, and for the next twenty-five years made the labor movement his life. He soon became a union organizer, tramping frozen streets in dreary company towns at constant risk of harassment from unfriendly police. Later he helped run the Brotherhood of Local Firemen and edited their magazine. By 1890 he had already moved out on the advanced fringe of labor, for he came to believe that its future lay in industrial unionism—the solid organization of all workers in a given plant regardless of their craft so as to confront as a unit the businessmen with whom they had to deal. Debs soon constructed one of the first successful industrial unions, the American Railway Union, and when in April, 1894, it had won a major strike against the Great Northern Railroad, Debs' career in the labor movement was established.*

*But hard on success came failure. 1894 was a year of paralyzing depression and industrial unrest. To support the workers at the Pullman factories in South Chicago in their strike against a paternalistic and arbitrary management, Debs' union called for a boycott against the railroads in Chicago and sought the support of all labor in a general strike. Sensing defeat, Gompers and the A.F.L. backed away, and the Railway Union succeeded merely in arousing against itself the massed forces of federal troops and the federal courts. The boycott and strike were crushed, and Debs was jailed for six months on a conviction of the charge of civil contempt. He soon came to believe that labor's struggle for better terms within the existing social system was hopelessly unequal, that if the class of employers could call to their rescue the power of the public—its armies and its judges—then the struggle required more than a labor movement: it demanded a class war. Debs had entered prison a pragmatic but fervent trade unionist; he left prison more than half convinced of Socialism, and by 1900 the American Railway Union had become the Socialist Party of the United States and Debs its most effective orator, evangelist, and prophet.*

*The selection which follows appeared in 1904 as a pamphlet setting forth Debs' views as a presidential candidate on the crucial relationship between trade unions and the Socialist movement. It is one of the most powerfully reasoned pieces Debs ever wrote. The reader will note here a characteristic and familiar animus against the "petty capitalism" of the moderate trade unionists. (Gompers won Debs' special scorn for having lent his support to Mark Hanna's Civic Federation, an organization of businessmen designed to win labor's cooperation by making moderate concessions to unionism.) Another familiar but compelling note is Debs' confident certainty that the Socialist state was only a few years off. Debs perhaps could be forgiven for believing in the imminent success of his movement. By 1912 his presidential vote was to top 900,000, and the Socialist Party could boast among its supporters five daily papers, 250 weeklies, fifty mayors, and one congressman. What is more significant is his assertion that all unions—even industrial unions—are at best only an economic tool and that by 1904 this tool had failed to win social justice or even economic security for the wage earner. Rather, Debs asserted repeatedly that labor needed a political tool—a militant party, organized to wage and win a class war (with ballots) and subsequently to run the government and destroy the corrosive relation between private property and the state. The focal concern for Debs, as for the authors of the Industrial Relations Report, was the corrupton and debasement of the nation's legal system.*

*In this and in the uncompromising rhetoric in defense of the struggle against property, Debs shows himself and his party as fundamentally Marxist in conception and philosophy. Yet Debs rejected violence and preferred to take a curiously progressive view toward the class struggle: he defined it as a contest which would pit "all who contribute" to society against those few capitalists who were merely owners, parasites on the economic system. No wonder Debs shared the liberal reformer's faith in peaceable majority rule: the lopsided struggle was foreordained from the start! Does not Debs lead us to infer that for most Socialists of 1904,*

*as well as for workingmen, trade unionists and progressives, the distinc-*
*tion between those who produce and those who merely profit was the*
*most appealing and useful moral boundary to be drawn in the land of*
*industrial promise?*

The labor question, as it is called, has come to be recognized as the foremost of our time. In some form it thrusts itself into every human relation, and directly or indirectly has a part in every controversy.

A thousand "solutions" of the labor question find their way into print, but the question not only remains unsolved, but steadily assumes greater and graver proportions. The nostrums have no effect other than to prove their own inefficacy.

There has always been a labor question since man first exploited man in the struggle for existence, but not until its true meaning was revealed in the development of modern industry did it command serious thought or intelligent consideration, and only then came any adequate conception of its importance to the race.

Man has always sought the mastery of his fellow-man. To enslave his fellow in some form and to live out of his labor has been the mainspring of human action.

To escape submission, not in freedom, but in mastery over others, has been the controlling desire, and this has filled the world with slavery and crime.

In all the ages of the past, human society has been organized and maintained upon the basis of the exploitation and degradation of those who toil. And so it is today.

The chief end of government has been and is to keep the victims of oppression and injustice in subjection.

The men and women who toil and produce have been and are at the mercy of those who wax fat and scornful upon the fruit of their labor.

The labor question was born of the first pang of protest that died unvoiced in the breast of unrequited toil.

The labor movement of modern times is the product of past ages. It has come down to us for the impetus of our day, in pursuit of its worldwide mission of emancipation.

Unionism, as applied to labor in the modern sense, is the fruit and flower of the last century.

In the United States, as in other countries, the trade union dates from the beginning of industrial society.

During the colonial period of our history, when agriculture was the

Eugene V. Debs, *Unionism and Socialism* (Terra Haute, Ind.: printed as a pamphlet, 1904).

principal pursuit, when the shop was small and work was done by hand with simple tools, and the worker could virtually employ himself, there was no unionism among the workers.

When machinery was applied to industry, and mill and factory took the place of the country blacksmith shop; when the workers were divorced from their tools and recruited in the mills; when they were obliged to compete against each other for employment; when they found themselves in the labor market with but a low bid or none at all upon their labor power; when they began to realize that as toolless workingmen they were at the mercy of the tool-owning masters, the necessity for union among them took root, and as industry developed, the trade union movement followed in its wake and became a factor in the struggle of the workers against the aggressions of their employers.

In his search for the beginnings of trade unionism in our country, Prof. Richard T. Ely, in his "Labor Movement in America," says: "I find no traces of anything like a modern trades union in the colonial period of American history, and it is evident, on reflection, that there was little need, if any, of organization on the part of labor at that time.

"Such manufacturing as was found consisted largely in the production of values-in-use. Clothing, for example, was spun and woven, and then converted into garments in the household for its various members. The artisans comprised chiefly the carpenter, the blacksmith and the shoe maker; many of whom worked in their own little shops with no employes, while the number of subordinates in any one shop was almost invariably small, and it would probably have been difficult to find a journeyman who did not expect, in a few years, to become an independent producer."

This was the general condition from the labor standpoint at the close of the eighteenth century. But with the dawn of the new century and the application of machinery and the spread of industry that followed came the beginning of the change. The workers gradually organized into unions and began to take active measures to increase their wages and otherwise improve their condition. Referring to this early period in the rise of unionism, the same author records the incident of one of the first strikes as follows: "Something very like a modern strike occurred in the year 1802. The sailors in New York received $10 a month, but wished an increase of $4 a month, and endeavored to enforce their demands by quitting work. It is said that they marched about the city, accompanied by a band, and compelled seamen, employed at the old wages, to leave their ships and join them. But the iniquitous combination and conspiracy laws, which viewed concerted action of laborers as a crime, were then in force in all modern lands, and 'the constables were soon in pursuit, arrested the leader, lodged him in jail, and so ended the earliest of labor strikes.'"

This sounds as if it had been the occurrence of yesterday, instead of more than a hundred years ago. The combination and conspiracy laws have been repealed, but the labor leader fares no better now than when these laws were still on the statute books. The writ of injunction is now made to serve the purpose of the master class, and there is no possible situation in which it cannot be made to apply and as swiftly and surely strike the vital point and paralyze the opposition to the master's rule.

We need not at this time trace the growth of the trade union from its small and local beginnings to its present national and international proportions; from the little group of hand-workers in the service of an individual employer to the armies of organized and federated workers in allied industries controlled by vast corporations, syndicates and trusts. The fact stands forth in bold relief that the union was born of necessity and that it has grown strong with the development of industry and the increasing economic dependence of the workers.

A century ago a boy served his apprenticeship and became the master of his trade. The few simple tools with which work was then done were generally owned by the man who used them; he could provide himself with the small quantity of raw material he required, and freely follow his chosen pursuit and enjoy the fruit of his labor. But as everything had to be produced by the work of his hands, production was a slow process, meagre of results, and the worker found it necessary to devote from twelve to fifteen hours to his daily task to earn a sufficient amount to support himself and family.

It required most of the time and energy of the average worker to produce enough to satisfy the physical wants of himself and those dependent upon his labor.

There was little leisure for mental improvement, for recreation or social intercourse. The best that can be said for the workingman of this period is that he enjoyed political freedom, controlled in large measure his own employment, by virtue of his owning the tools of his trade, appropriated to his own use the product of his labor and lived his quiet, uneventful round to the end of his days.

This was a new country, with boundless stretches of virgin soil. There was ample room and opportunity, air and sunlight for all.

There was no millionaire in the United States; nor was there a tramp. These types are the products of the same system. The former is produced at the expense of the latter, and both at the expense of the working class. They appeared at the same time in the industrial development and they will disappear together with the abolition of the system that brought them in existence.

The application of machinery to productive industry was followed by tremendous and far-reaching changes in the whole structure of society.

First among these was the change in the status of the worker, who, from an independent mechanic or small producer, was reduced to the level of a dependent wage-worker. The machine had leaped, as it were, into the arena of industrial activity, and had left little or no room for the application of the worker's skill or the use of his individual tools.

The economic dependence of the working class became more and more rigidly fixed—and at the same time a new era dawned for the human race.

The more or less isolated individual artisans were converted into groups of associated workers and marshalled for the impending social revolution.

It was at this time that the trades-union movement began to take definite form. Unorganized, the workers were not only in open competition with each other for the sale of their labor power in the labor market, but their wages could be reduced, and their hours of labor lengthened at will, and they were left practically at the mercy of their employers.

It is interesting to note the spirit evinced by the pioneers of unionism, the causes that impelled them and the reasons they assigned for banding themselves together in defense of their common interests. In this connection we again quote from Professor Ely's "Labor Movement in America," as follows:

The next event to attract our attention in New York is an address delivered before "The General Trades Unions of the City of New York," at Chatham street chapel, on December 2, 1833, by Eli Moore, president of the union. This General Trades Union, as its name indicates, was a combination of subordinate unions "of the various trades and arts in New York City and its vicinity," and is the earliest example in the United States, so far as I know, of those Central Labor Unions which attempt to unite all the workingmen in one locality in one body, and which have now become so common among us. The address of Mr. Moore is characterized by a more modern tone than is found in most productions of the labor leaders of that period. The object of these unions is stated to be "to guard against the encroachments of aristocracy, to preserve our natural and political rights, to elevate our moral and intellectual condition, to promote our pecuniary interests, to narrow the line of distinction between the journeyman and employer, to establish the honor and safety of our respective vocations upon a more secure and permanent basis, and to alleviate the distress of those suffering from want of employment."

This is a remarkably clear statement of the objects of unionism in that early period, and indicates to what extent workingmen had even then been compelled to recognize their craft interests and unite and act together in defense thereof.

So far, and for many years later, the effects of trades-unions were confined to defensive tactics, and to the amelioration of objectionable conditions. The wage-system had yet to develop its most offensive features and awaken the workers to the necessity of putting an end to it as the only means of achieving their freedom; and it was this that finally forced the extension of organized activity from the economic to the political field of labor unionism.

As the use of machinery became more general and competition became more intense; as capital was centralized and industry organized to obtain better results, the workers realized their dependence more and more, and unionism grew apace. One trade after another fell into line and raised the banner of economic solidarity. Then followed strikes and lockouts and other devices incident to that form of warfare. Sometimes the unionists gained an advantage, but more often they suffered defeat, lost courage and abandoned the union, only to return to the scene of disaster with renewed determination to fight the battle over again and again until victory should at last perch upon the union banner.

Oh, how many there were, whose names are forgotten, who suffered untold agonies to lay the foundation of the labor movement, of whose real mission they had but the vaguest conception!

These pioneers of progress paved the way for us, and deserve far more at our hands than we have in our power to do for them. We may at best rescue their nameless memory from the darkness of oblivion, and this we undertake to do with the liveliest sense of obligation for the service they rendered, and the sacrifices they made in the early and trying stages of the struggle to improve the condition and advance the welfare of their fellow-toilers.

The writer has met and known some of these untitled agitators of the earlier day, whose hearts were set on organizing their class, or at least, their branch of it, and who had the courage to undertake the task and accept all the bitter consequences it imposed.

The union men of today have little or no conception of what the pioneer unionists had to contend with when they first started forth on their mission of organization. The organizer of the present time has to face difficulties enough, it is true, but as a rule the road has at least been broken for his approaching footsteps; the union has already been organized and a committee meets him at the station and escorts him to the hotel.

Far different was it with the pioneer who left home without "scrip in his purse," whose chief stock consisted in his ability to "screw his courage to the sticking point" and whom privation and hardship only consecrated more completely to his self-appointed martyrdom.

Starting out, more than likely, after having been discharged for organizing a local union of his craft, or for serving on a committee, or interceding for a fellow, or "talking back" to the boss, or any other of the numerous acts which mark the conduct of the manly worker, distinguishing him from his weak and fawning brother, and bringing upon him the reprobation of his master—starting out to organize his fellow-workers, that they might fare better than fell to his lot, he faced the world without a friend to bid him welcome, or cheer him onward. Having no money for railroad fare he must beat his way, but such a slight inconvenience does not deter him an instant. Reaching his destination he brushes up as well as his scanty toilet will allow and then proceeds with due caution to look up "the boys," careful to elude the vigilance of the boss, who has no earthly use for a worthless labor agitator.

We shall not attempt to follow our pioneer through all his tortuous windings, nor have we space to more than hint at the story of his cruel persecution and pathetic end.

Our pioneer, leaving home, in many an instance, never saw wife and child again. Repulsed by the very men he was hungering to serve, penniless, deserted, neglected and alone, he became "the poor wanderer of a stormy day," and ended his career a nameless outcast. Whatever his frailties and faults, they were virtues all, for they marked the generous heart, the sympathetic soul who loves his brother and accepts for himself the bitter portion of suffering and shame that he may serve his fellowman.

The labor agitator of the early day held no office, had no title, drew no salary, saw no footlights, heard no applause, never saw his name in print, and fills an unknown grave.

The labor movement is his monument, and though his name is not inscribed upon it, his soul is in it, and with it marches on forever.

From the small beginnings of a century ago the trades-union movement, keeping pace with the industrial development, has become a tremendous power in the land.

The close of the Civil War was followed by a new era of industrial and commercial activity, and trades-unions sprang up on every hand. Local organizations of the same craft multiplied and were united in national bodies, and these were in time bound together in national and international federation.

The swift and vast concentration of capital and the unprecedented industrial activity which marked the close of the nineteenth century were followed by the most extraordinary growth in the number and variety of trades-unions in the history of the movement; yet this expansion, remarkable as it was, has not only been equalled, but excelled, in the first years of the new century, the tide of unionism sweeping over the whole country, and rising steadily higher, notwithstanding the efforts put forth from a hundred sources controlled by the ruling class to restrain its march, impair its utility or stamp it out of existence.

The history of the last thirty years of trades-unionism is filled with stirring incident and supplies abundant material for a good-sized volume. Organizations have risen and fallen, battles have been fought with varying results, every device known to the ingenuity of the ruling class has been employed to check the movement, but through it all the trend has been steadily toward a more perfect organization and a more comprehensive grasp of its mighty mission. The strikes and boycotts and lockouts which occurred with startling frequency during this period, some of them accompanied by riots and other forms of violence, tell their own tragic story of the class struggle which is shaking the foundations of society, and will end only with the complete overthrow of the wage-system and the freedom of the working class from every form of slavery.

No strike has ever been lost, and there can be no defeat for the labor movement.

However disastrous the day of battle has been, it has been worth its price, and only the scars remain to bear testimony that the movement is invincible and that no mortal wound can be inflicted upon it.

What has the union done for the worker? Far more than these brief pages will allow us to place on record.

The union has from its inception taught, however imperfectly, the fundamental need of solidarity; it has inspired hope in the breast of the defeated and despairing worker, joining his hand with the hand of his fellow-worker and bidding them lift their bowed bodies from the earth and look above and beyond the tribulations of the hour to the shining heights of future achievement.

The union has fought the battles of the worker upon a thousand fields, and though defeated often, rallied and charged again and again to wrest from the enemy the laurels of victory.

The union was first to trace in outline the lesson above all others the workingman needs to learn, and that is the collective interest and welfare of his class, in which his own is indissolubly bound, and that no vital or permanent change of conditions is possible that does not embrace his class as a whole.

The union has been a moral stimulus as well as a material aid to the worker; it has appealed to him to develop his faculties and to think for himself; to cultivate self-reliance and learn to depend upon himself; to have pride of character and make some effort to improve himself; to sympathize with and support his fellow-workers and make their cause his own.

Although these things have as yet been only vaguely and imperfectly accomplished, yet they started in and have grown with the union, and to this extent the union has promoted the class-conscious solidarity of the working-class.

It is true that the trades-union movement has in some essential respects proved a disappointment, but it may not on this account be repudiated as a failure. The worst that can in truth be said of it is that it has not kept up with the procession of events, that it lacks the progressive spirit so necessary to its higher development and larger usefulness, but there are reasons for this and they suggest themselves to the most casual student of the movement.

When workingmen first began to organize unions every effort was made by the employing class to stamp out the incipient "rebellion." This was kept up for years, but in spite of all that could be done to extinguish the fires of revolt, the smouldering embers broke forth again and again, each time with increased intensity and vigor; and when at last it became apparent to the shrewder and more far-seeing members of the capitalist family that the union movement had come to stay, they forthwith changed their tactics, discarding their frowns and masking their features with the most artful smiles as they extended their greeting and pronounced their blessing upon this latest and greatest benefaction to the human race.

In fewer words, seeing that they could not head it off, they decided to take it by the hand and guide it into harmless channels.

This is precisely the policy pursued, first and last, by the late Marcus A. Hanna, and it will not be denied that he had the entire confidence of the capitalist class and that they clearly recognized his keen perception, astute diplomacy and sagacious leadership in dealing with the union movement.

Mr. Hanna denominated the national leaders of the trades-unions as his "lieutenants"; had the "Civic Federation" organized and himself elected president, that he and his lieutenants might meet upon equal ground and as often as necessary; he slapped them familiarly on the back, had his picture taken with them and cracked jokes with them; and all the time he was doing this he was the *beau idéal* of Wall Street, the ruling voice in the capitalist councils, and all the trusts, syndicates and combines, all the magnates, barons, lords and plutocrats in one voice proclaimed him the ruler of rulers, the political prophet of their class, the corner stone and central pillar in the capitalist temple.

Mr. Hanna did not live to see his plan of "benevolent feudalism" consummated, nor to be elected President of the United States, as his Wall Street admirers and trades-union friends intended, but he did live long enough to see the gathering clouds of the social revolution on the political horizon; and to prevent the trades-union movement from becoming a factor in it, he taxed the resources of his fertile brain and bended all the energies of his indomitable will. Clearer sighted than all others of his class, he was promptly crowned their leader. He saw what was coming and prepared to meet and defeat it, or at least put off the crisis to a later day.

The trades-union movement must remain a "pure and simple" organization. It must not be subject to the laws of evolution; it must be securely anchored to its conservative, time-honored policy, hold fast to its good name and preserve inviolate all the traditions of the past. Finally, it must eschew politics as utterly destructive of trades-union ends, and above all, beware of and guard against the contamination of Socialism, whose breath is disruption and whose touch is death.

That was the position of Senator Hanna; it is that of the smaller lights who are serving as his successors. It is this position that is taken by the press, the pulpit and the politician; it is this position that is reflected in the trades-union movement itself, and voiced by its officials, who are at once the leaders of labor and the lieutenants of capital, and who, in their dual role, find it more and more difficult to harmonize the conflicting interests of the class of whom they are the leaders and the class of whom they are the lieutenants.

It is not claimed for a moment that these leaders are corrupt in the sense that they would betray their trust for a consideration. Such charges and intimations are frequently made, but so far as we know they are baseless and unjust in almost every instance; and it is our opinion that an accusation of such gravity is never justified, whatever the circumstances, unless the proof can be furnished to support the charge and convict the offender.

But the criticism to which these leaders are properly subject is that they fear to offend the capitalist class, well knowing that the influence of this class is potential in the labor union, and that if the labor lieutenant fails of obedience and respect to his superior capitalist officers, he can soon be made to feel their displeasure, and unless he relents, his popularity wanes and he finds himself a leader without an office.

The late Peter M. Arthur, of the Brotherhood of Locomotive Engineers, was a conspicuous example of this kind of leadership. There was frequently the most violent opposition to him, but his standing with the railway corporations secured him in his position, and it was simply impossible to dislodge him. Had he been radical instead of conservative, had he stood wholly on the side of the engineers instead of cultivating the good offices of the managers and placating the corporations, he would have been deposed years ago and pronounced a miserable failure as a labor leader.

The capitalist press has much to do with shaping the course of a labor leader; he shrinks from its cruel attacks and he yields, sometimes unconsciously, to its blandishments and honeyed phrases, and in spite of himself becomes a servile trimmer and cowardly time-server.

The trades-union movement of the present day has enemies within and without, and upon all sides, some attacking it openly and others insidiously, but all bent either upon destroying it or reducing it to unresisting impotency.

The enemies of unionism, while differing in method, are united solidly upon one point, and that is in the effort to misrepresent and discredit the men who, scorning and defying the capitalist exploiters and their minions, point steadily the straight and uncompromising course the movement must take if it is to accomplish its allotted task and safely reach its destined port.

These men, though frequently regarded as the enemies, are the true friends of trades-unionism and in good time are certain to be vindicated.

The more or less open enemies have inaugurated some interesting innovations during the past few years. The private armies the corporations used some years ago, such as Pinkerton mercenaries, coal and iron police, deputy marshals, etc., have been relegated to second place as out of date, or they are wholly out of commission. It has been found after repeated experiments that the courts are far more deadly to trades-unions, and that they operate noiselessly and with unerring precision.

The rapid fire injunction is a great improvement on the gatling gun. Nothing can get beyond its range and it never misses fire.

The capitalists are in entire control of the injunction artillery, and all the judicial gunner has to do is to touch it off at their command.

Step by step the writ of injunction has invaded the domain of trades-unionism, limiting its jurisdiction, curtailing its powers, sapping its strength and undermining its foundations, and this has been done by the courts in the name of the institutions they were designed to safeguard, but have shamelessly betrayed at the behest of the barons of capitalism.

Injunctions have been issued restraining the trades-unions and their members from striking, from boycotting, from voting funds to strikes, from levying assessments to support their members, from walking on the public highway, from asking non-union men not to take their places, from meeting to oppose wage reductions, from expelling a spy from membership, from holding conversation with those who had taken or were about to take their jobs, from congregating in public places, from holding meetings, from doing anything and everything, directly, indirectly, or any other way, to interfere with the employing class in their unalienable right to operate their plants as their own interests may dictate, and to run things generally to suit themselves.

The courts have found it in line with judicial procedure to strike every weapon from labor's economic hand and leave it defenseless at the mercy of its exploiter; and now that the courts have gone to the last extremity in this nefarious plot of subjugation, labor, at last, is waking up to the fact that it has not been using its political arm in the struggle at all; that the ballot which it can wield is strong enough not only to disarm the enemy, but to drive that enemy entirely from the field.

The courts, so notoriously in control of capital, and so shamelessly perverted to its base and sordid purposes are, therefore, exercising a wholesome effect upon trades-unionism by compelling the members to note the class character of our capitalist government and driving them to the inevitable conclusion that the labor question is also a political question and that the working class must organize their political power that they may wrest the government from capitalist control and put an end to class rule forever.

Trades-unionists for the most part learn slowly, but they learn surely, and fresh object lessons are prepared for them every day.

They have seen a Democratic President of the United States send the federal troops into a sovereign state of the Union in violation of the constitution, and in defiance of the protest of the governor and the people, to crush a body of peaceable workingmen at the behest of a combination of railroads bent on destroying their union and reducing them to vassalage.

They have seen a Republican President refuse to interpose his executive authority when militarism, in the name of the capitalist class, seized another sovereign state by the throat and strangled its civil administration to death while it committed the most dastardly crimes upon defenseless workingmen in the annals of capitalist brutality and military despotism.

They have seen a composite Republican-Democratic Congress, the legislative tool of the exploiting class, pass a military bill which makes every citizen a soldier and the President a military dictator.

They have seen this same Congress, session after session, making false promises to deluded labor committees; pretending to be the friends of workingmen and anxious to be of service to them, while at the same time in league with the capitalist lobby and pledged to defeat every measure that would afford even the slightest promise of relief to the working class. The anti-injunction bill and the eight hour measure, pigeon-holed and rejected again and again in the face of repeated promises that they should pass, tell their own story of duplicity and treachery to labor of the highest legislative body in the land.

They have seen Republican governors and Democratic governors order out the militia repeatedly to shoot down workingmen at the command of their capitalist masters.

They have seen these same governors construct military prisons and "bull pens," seize unoffending workingmen without warrant of law and thrust them into these vile quarters for no other reason than to break up their unions and leave them helpless at the feet of corporate rapacity.

They have seen the Supreme Court of the nation turn labor out without a hearing, while the corporation lawyers, who compose this august body, and who hold their commissions in virtue of the "well done" of their capitalist retainers, solemnly descant upon the immaculate purity of our judicial institutions.

They have seen state legislatures, both Republican and Democratic, with never an exception, controlled bodily by the capitalist class and turn the committees of labor unions empty-handed from their doors.

They have seen state supreme courts declare as unconstitutional the last vestige of law upon the statute books that could by any possibility be construed as affording any shelter or relief to the labor union or its members.

They have seen these and many other things and will doubtless see many more before their eyes are opened as a class; but we are thankful for them all, painful though they be to us in having to bear witness to the suffering of our benighted brethren.

In this way only can they be made to see, to think, to act, and every wrong they suffer brings them nearer to their liberation.

The "pure and simple" trade-union of the past does not answer the requirements of today, and they who insist that it does are blind to the changes going on about them, and out of harmony with the progressive forces of the age.

The attempt to preserve the "autonomy" of each trade and segregate it within its own independent jurisdiction, while the lines which once separated them are being obliterated, and the trades are being interwoven and interlocked in the process of industrial evolution, is as futile as to declare and attempt to enforce the independence of the waves of the sea.

A modern industrial plant has a hundred trades and parts of trades represented in its working force. To have these workers parcelled out to a hundred unions is to divide and not to organize them, to give them over to factions and petty leadership and leave them an easy prey to the machinations of the enemy. The dominant craft should control the plant or, rather, the union, and it should embrace the entire working force. This is the industrial plan, the modern method applied to modern conditions, and it will in time prevail.

The trade autonomy can be expressed within the general union, so far as that is necessary or desirable, and there need be no conflict on account of it.

The attempt of each trade to maintain its own independence separately and apart from others results in increasing jurisdictional entanglements, fruitful of dissension, strife and ultimate disruption.

The work of organizing has little, if any, permanent value unless the work of education, the right kind of education, goes hand in hand with it.

There is no cohesiveness in ignorance.

The members of a trade-union should be taught the true import, the whole object of the labor movement and understand its entire program.

They should know that the labor movement means more, infinitely more, than a paltry increase in wages and the strike necessary to secure it; that while it engages to do all that possibly can be done to better the working conditions of its members, its higher object is to overthrow the capitalist system of private ownership of the tools of labor, abolish wage-slavery and achieve the freedom of the whole working class and, in fact, of all mankind.

Karl Marx recognized the necessity of the trade union when he said, ". . . The general tendency of capitalist production is not to raise, but to sink the average standard of wages or to push the value of labor more or less to its minimum limit. Such being the tendency of things in this system, is this saying that the working class ought to renounce their resistance against the encroachments of capital, and abandon their attempts at making the best of the occasional chances for their temporary improvement? If they did, they would be degraded to one level mass of broken wretches past salvation. . . . By cowardly giving way in their every-day conflict with capital, they would certainly disqualify themselves for the initiating of any larger movement."

Marx also set forth the limitations of the trade-union and indicated the true course it should pursue as follows:

At the same time, and quite apart from the general servitude involved in the wage system, the working class ought not to exaggerate to themselves the ultimate working of these every-day struggles. They ought not to forget that they are fighting with effects, but not with the causes of those effects; that they are retarding the downward movement, but not changing its direction; that they are applying palliatives, not curing the malady. They ought, therefore, not to be exclusively absorbed in these unavoidable guerrilla fights incessantly springing up from the never-ceasing encroachments of capital or changes of the market. They ought to understand that, with all the miseries it imposes upon them, the present system simultaneously engenders the material conditions and the social forms necessary for an economic reconstruction of society. Instead of the conservative motto, "A fair day's wages for a fair day's work!" they ought to inscribe on their banner the revolutionary watchword, "Abolition of the wage system." . . .

Trades unions work well as centers of resistance against the encroachments of capital. They fail partially from an injudicious use of their power. They fail generally from limiting themselves to a guerrilla war against the effects of the existing system, instead of simultaneously trying to change it, instead of using their organized forces as a lever for the final emancipation of the working class, that is to say, the ultimate abolition of the wage system.

In an address to the Knights of St. Crispin, in April, 1872, Wendell Phillips, the eloquent orator and passionate hater of slavery in every form, said:

"I hail the Labor movement for the reason that it is my only hope for democracy."

Wendell Phillips was right; he spoke with prophetic insight. He knew that the labor movement alone could democratize society and give freedom to the race.

In the same address he uttered these words, which every trade-unionist should know by heart:

"Unless there is a power in your movement, industrially and politically, the last knell of democratic liberty in this Union is struck."

The orator then proceeded to emphasize the urgent need of developing the political power of the movement; and it is just this that the trade-unionist should be made to clearly understand.

The cry, "no politics in the union," "dragging the union into politics," or "making the union the tail of some political kite," is born of ignorance or dishonesty, or a combination of both. It is echoed by every ward-heeling politician in the country. The plain purpose is to deceive and mislead the workers.

It is not the welfare of the union that these capitalist henchmen are so much concerned about, but the fear that the working class, as a class, organized into a party of their own, will go into politics, for well they know that when that day dawns their occupation will be gone.

And this is why they employ their time in setting the union against the political party of the working class, the only union labor party there ever was or ever will be, and warning the members against the evil designs of the Socialists.

The important thing to impress upon the mind of the trade-unionist is that it is his duty to cultivate the habit of doing his own thinking.

The moment he realizes this he is beyond the power of the scheming politician, the emissary of the exploiter, in or out of the labor movement.

The trades-union is not and can not become a political machine, nor can it be used for political purposes. They who insist upon working class political action not only have no intention to convert the trades-union into a political party, but they would oppose any such attempt on the part of others.

The trades-union is an economic organization with distinct economic functions and as such is a part, a necessary part, but a part only of the Labor Movement; it has its own sphere of activity, its own program and is its own master within its economic limitations.

But the labor movement has also its political side and the trades-unionist must be educated to realize its importance and to understand that the political side of the movement must be *unionized* as well as the economic side; and that he is not in fact a union man at all who, although a member of the union on the economic side, is a non-unionist on the political side; and while striking for, votes against the working class.

The trades-union expresses the economic power and the Socialist Party expresses the political power of the Labor movement.

The fully developed labor-unionist uses both his economic and political power in the interest of his class. He understands that the struggle between labor and capital is a *class* struggle; that the working class are in a great majority, but divided, some in trades-unions and some out of them, some in one political party and some in another; that because they are divided they are helpless and must submit to being robbed of what their labor produces, and treated with contempt; that they must unite their class in the trades-union on the one hand and in the Socialist Party on the other hand; that industrially and politically they must act together as a class against the capitalist class and that this struggle is a class struggle, and that any workingman who deserts his union in a strike and goes to the other side is a scab, and any workingman who deserts his party on election day and goes over to the enemy is a betrayer of his class and an enemy of his fellow-man.

Both sides are organized in this class struggle, the capitalists, however, far more thoroughly than the workers. In the first place the capitalists are, comparatively, few in number, while the workers number many millions. Next, the capitalists are men of financial means and resources, and can buy the best brains and command the highest order of ability the market affords. Then again, they own the earth, and the mills and mines and locomotives and ships and stores and the jobs that are attached to them, and this not only gives them tremendous advantage in the struggle, but makes them for the time the absolute masters of the situation.

The workers, on the other hand, are poor as a rule, and ignorant as a class, *but they are in an overwhelming majority.* In a word, they have the power, but are not conscious of it. This then is the supreme demand: to make them conscious of the power of their class, or class-conscious workingmen.

The working class alone does the world's work, has created its capital, produced its wealth, constructed its mills and factories, dug its canals, made its roadbeds, laid its rails and operates its trains, spanned the rivers with bridges and tunnelled the mountains, delved for the precious stones that glitter upon the bosom of vulgar idleness and reared the majestic palaces that shelter insolent parasites.

The working class alone—and by the working class I mean all useful workers, all who by the labor of their hands or the effort of their brains, or both in alliance, as they ought universally to be, increase the knowledge and add to the wealth of society—the working class alone is essential to society and therefore the only class that can survive in the world-wide struggle for freedom.

We have said that both classes, the capitalist class and the working class are organized for the class struggle, but the organizations, especially that of the workers, is far from complete; indeed, it would be nearer exact to say that it has but just fairly begun.

On the economic field of the class struggle the capitalists have their Manufacturers' Association, Citizens' Alliance, Corporations' Auxiliary, and—we must add—Civic Federation, while on the political field they have the Republican Party and the Democratic Party, the former for large capitalists and the latter for small capitalists, but both of them for capitalists and both against the workers.

Standing face to face with the above named economic and political forces of the capitalists the workingmen have on the economic field their trades-unions, and on the political field their working class Socialist Party.

In the class struggle the workers must unite and fight together as one on both economic and political fields.

The Socialist Party is to the workingman politically what the trades-union is to him industrially; the former is the party of his class, while the latter is the union of his trade.

The difference between them is that while the trades-union is confined to the trade, the Socialist Party embraces the entire working class, and while the union is limited to bettering conditions under the wage system, the party is organized to conquer the political power of the nation, wipe out the wage system and make the workers themselves the masters of the earth.

In this program, the trades-union and the Socialist Party, the economic and political wings of the labor movement, should not only not be in conflict, but act together in perfect harmony in every struggle whether it be on the one field or the other, in the strike or at the ballot box. The main thing is that in every such struggle the workers shall be united, shall in fact be unionists and no more be guilty of scabbing on their party than on their union, no more think of voting a capitalist ticket on election day and turning the working class over to capitalist robbery and misrule than they would think of voting in the union to turn it over to the capitalists and have it run in the interest of the capitalist class.

To do its part in the class struggle the trades-union need no more go into politics than the Socialist Party need go into the trades. Each has its place and its functions.

The union deals with trade problems and the party deals with politics.

The union is educating the workers in the management of industrial activities and fitting them for co-operative control and democratic regulation of their trades—the party recruiting and training and drilling the political army that is to conquer the capitalist forces on the political battlefield; and having control of the machinery of government, use it to transfer the industries from the capitalists to the workers, from the parasites to the people.

In his excellent paper on "The Social Opportunity," published in a recent issue of the *International Socialist Review,* Dr. George D. Herron, discussing trades-unions and their relation to the Socialist Party, and the labor movement in general, clearly sees the trend of the development and arrives at conclusions that are sound and commend themselves to the thoughtful consideration of all trades-unionists and Socialists. Says Dr. Herron:

On the one side, it is the trade-unionist who is on the firing line of the class struggle. He it is who blocked the wheels of the capitalist machine; he it is who has prevented the unchecked development of capitalist increase; he it is who has prevented the whole labor body of the world from being kept forever at the point of mere hunger wages; he it is who has taught the workers of the world the lesson of solidarity, and delivered them from that wretched and unthinking competition with each other which kept them at the mercy of capitalism; he it is who has prepared the way for the co-operative common-wealth. On the other hand, trade unionism is by no means the solution of the workers' problem, nor is it the goal of the labor struggle. It is merely a capitalist line of defense within the capitalist system. Its existence and its struggles are necessitated only by the existence and predatory nature of capitalism.

. . . Organized labor has an instinct that far outreaches its intelligence, and that far outreaches the intelligence of the preaching and teaching class—the instinct that the workers of the world are bound up together in one common destiny; that their battle for the future is one; and that there is no possible safety or extrication for any worker unless all the workers of the world are extricated and saved from capitalism together.

. . . Until the workers shall become a clearly defined socialist movement, standing for and moving toward the unqualified co-operative commonwealth, while at the same time understanding and proclaiming their immediate interests, they will only play into the hands of their exploiters, and be led by their betrayers.

It is the Socialist who must point this out in the right way. He is not to do this by seeking to commit trade-union bodies to the principles of Socialism. Resolution or commitments of this sort accomplish little good. Nor is he to do it by taking a servile attitude toward organized labor, nor by meddling with the details or the machinery of the trade-unions. Not by trying to commit Socialism to trade-unionism, nor trade-unionism to Socialism, will the Socialist end be accomplished. It is better to leave the trade-unions do their distinctive work, as the workers' defense against the encroachments of capital-ism, as the economic development of the worker against the economic develop-ment of the capitalist, giving unqualified support and sympathy to the struggles of the organized worker to sustain himself in his economic sphere. But let the Socialist also build up the character and harmony and strength of the socialist movement as a political force, that it shall command the respect and confidence of the worker, irrespective of his trade or his union obligations. It is urgent that we so keep in mind the difference between the two developments that neither shall cripple the other. The Socialist movement, as a political development of the workers for their economic emancipation, is one thing; the trade-union development, as an economic defense of the workers within the capitalist system, is another thing. Let us not interfere with the internal affairs of the trade-unions, or seek to have them become distinctively political bodies in themselves, any more than we would seek to make a distinctive political body in itself of a church, or a public school, or a lawyer's office. But let us attend to the harmonious and commanding development of the Socialist political movement as the channel and power by which labor is to come to its emancipation and its commonwealth.

We have quoted thus at length to make clear the position of the writer who has given close study to the question and in the paper above quoted has done much to light the way to sound tactics and sane procedure.

It is of vital importance to the trades-union that its members be class-conscious, that they understand the class struggle and their duty as union men on the political field, so that in every move that is made they will have the goal in view, and while taking advantage of every opportunity to secure concessions and enlarge their economic advantage, they will at the same time unite at the ballot box, not only to back up the economic struggle of the trades-union, but to finally wrest the government from capitalist control and establish the working class republic.

### SOCIALISM

There are those who sneeringly class Socialism among the "isms" that appear and disappear as passing fads, and pretend to dismiss it with an impatient wave of the hand. There is just enough in this great world movement to them to excite their ridicule and provoke their contempt. At least they would have us think so and if we take them at their word their ignorance does not rise to the level of our contempt, but entitles them to our pity.

To the workingman in particular it is important to know what Socialism is and what it means.

Let us endeavor to make it so clear to him that he will readily grasp it and the moment he does he becomes a Socialist.

It is our conviction that no workingman can clearly understand what Socialism means without becoming and remaining a Socialist. It is simply impossible for him to be anything else and the only reason that all workingmen are not Socialists is that they do not know what it means.

They have heard of Socialism—and they have heard of anarchy and of other things all mixed together—and without going to any trouble about it they conclude that it is all the same thing and a good thing to let alone.

Why? Because the capaitalist editor has said so; the politician has sworn to it and the preacher has said amen to it, and surely that ought to settle it.

But it doesn't. It settles but one thing and that is that the capitalist is opposed to Socialism and that the editor and politician and preacher are but the voices of the capitalist. There are some exceptions, but not enough to affect the rule.

Socialism is first of all a political movement of the working class, clearly defined and uncompromising, which aims at the overthrow of the prevailing capitalist system by securing control of the national government and by the exercise of the public powers, supplanting the existing capitalist class government with Socialist administration—that is to say, changing a republic in name into a republic in fact.

Socialism also means a coming phase of civilization, next in order to the present one, in which the collective people will own and operate the sources and means of wealth production, in which all will have equal right to work and all will co-operate together in producing wealth and all will enjoy all the fruit of their collective labor.

In the present system of society, called the capitalist system, since it is controlled by and supported in the interest of the capitalist class, we have two general classes of people; first, capitalists, and second, workers. The capitalists are few, the workers are many; the capitalists are called capitalists because they own the productive capital of the country, the lands, mines, quarries, oil and gas wells, mills, factories, shops, stores, warehouses, refineries, tanneries, elevators, docks, wharves, railroads, street cars, steamships, smelters, blast furnaces, brick and stone yards, stock pens, packing houses, telegraph wires and poles, pipe lines, and all other sources, means and tools of production, distribution and exchange. The capitalist class who own and control these things also own and control, of course, the millions of jobs that are attached to and inseparable from them.

It goes without saying that the owner of the job is the master of the fellow who depends upon the job.

Now why does the workingman depend upon the capitalist for a job? Simply because the capitalist owns the tools with which work is done, and without these the workingman is almost as helpless as if he had no arms.

Before the tool became a machine, the worker who used it also owned it; if one was lost or destroyed he got another. The tool was small; it was for individual use and what the workingman produced with it was his own. He did not have to beg some one else to allow him to use his tools —he had his own.

But a century has passed since then, and in the order of progress that simple tool has become a mammoth machine.

The old hand tool was used by a single worker—and owned by him who used it.

The machine requires a thousand or ten thousand workers to operate it, but they do not own it, and what they produce with it does not go to them, but to the capitalist who does own it.

The workers who use the machine are the slaves of the capitalist who owns it.

They can only work by his permission.

The capitalist is a capitalist solely for profit—without profit he would not be in business an instant. That is his first and only consideration.

In the capitalist system profit is prior to and more important than the life or liberty of the workingman.

The capitalist's profit first, last and always. He owns the tools and only allows the worker to use them on condition that he can extract a satisfactory profit from his labor. If he cannot to do this the tools are not allowed to be used—he locks them up and waits.

The capitalist does no work himself; that is, no useful or necessary work. He spends his time watching other parasites in the capitalist game of "dog eat dog," or in idleness or dissipation. The workers who use his tools give him all the wealth they produce and he allows them a sufficient wage to keep them in working order.

The wage is to the worker what oil is to the machine.

The machine cannot run without lubricant and the worker cannot work and reproduce himself without being fed, clothed and housed; this is his lubricant and the amount he requires to keep him in running order regulates his wage.

Karl Marx, in his "Wage, Labor and Capital," makes these points clear in his own terse and masterly style. We quote as follows:

The free laborer sells himself, and that by fractions. From day to day he sells by auction, eight, ten, twelve, fifteen hours of his life to the highest bidder—to the owner of the raw material, the instruments of work and the means of life; that is, to the employer. The laborer himself belongs neither to an owner nor to the soil; but eight, ten, twelve, fifteen hours of his daily life belong to the man who buys them. The laborer leaves the employer to whom he has hired himself whenever he pleases; and the employer discharges him whenever he thinks fit; either as soon as he ceases to make a profit out of him or fails to get as high a profit as he requires. But the laborer whose only source of earning is the sale of his labor power cannot leave *the whole class of its purchasers,* that is the capitalist class, without renouncing his own existence. He does not belong to this or that particular employer, but he does belong to the *capitalist class;* and more than that: it is his business to find an employer; that is, among this capitalist class it is his business to discover *his own particular purchaser*.

Coming to the matter of wages and how they are determined, Marx continues:

Wages are the price of a certain commodity, labor-power. Wages are thus determined by the same law which regulates the price of any other commodity.

Thereupon the question arises, how is the price of a commodity determined?

By means of competition between buyers and sellers and the relations between supply and demand—offer and desire.

. . . Now the same general laws which universally regulate the price of commodities, regulate, of course, *wages, the price of labor*.

Wages will rise and fall in accordance with the proportion between demand and supply; that is, in accordance with the conditions of the competition between capitalists as buyers and laborers as sellers of labor. The fluctuations of wages correspond in general with the fluctuation in the price of commodities. *Within these fluctuations the price of labor is regulated by its cost of production; that is, by the duration of labor which is required in order to produce this commodity, labor power.*

*Now what is the cost of production of labor power?*

*It is the cost required for the production of a laborer and for his maintenance as a laborer.*

. . . *The price of his labor is therefore determined by the price of the bare necessaries of his existence.*

This is the capitalist system in its effect upon the working class. They have no tools, but must work to live. They throng the labor market, especially when times are hard and work is scarce, and eagerly, anxiously look for some one willing to use their labor power and bid them in at the market price.

To speak of liberty in such a system is a mockery; to surrender is a crime.

The workers of the nation and the world must be aroused.

In the capitalist system "night has drawn her sable curtain down and pinned it with a star," and the great majority grope in darkness. The pin must be removed from the curtain, even though it be a star.

But the darkness, after all, is but imaginary. The sun is marching to meridian glory and the world is flooded with light.

Charlotte Perkins Stetson, the inspired evangel of the coming civilization, says:

> We close our eyes and call it night,
> And grope and fall in seas of light,
> Would we but understand!

Not for a moment do we despair of the future. The greatest educational propaganda ever known is spreading over the earth.

The working class will both see and understand. They have the inherent power of self-development. They are but just beginning to come into consciousness of their power, and with the first glimmerings of this consciousness the capitalist system is doomed. It may hold on for a time, for even a long time, but its doom is sealed.

Even now the coming consciousness of this world-wide working class power is shaking the foundations of all governments and all civilizations.

The capitalist system has had its day and, like other systems that have gone before, it must pass away when it has fulfilled its mission and made room for another system more in harmony with the forces of progress and with the onward march of civilization.

The centralization of capital, the concentration of industry and the co-operation of workingmen mark the beginning of the end. Competition is no longer "the life of trade." Only they are clamoring for "competition" who have been worsted in the struggle and would like to have another deal.

The small class who won out in the game of competition and own the trusts want no more of it. They know what it is, and have had enough. Mr. John D. Rockefeller needs no competition to give life to his trade, and his pious son does not expatiate upon the beauties of competition in his class at Sunday school.

No successful capitalist wants competition—for himself—he only wants it for the working class, so that he can buy his labor power at the lowest competitive price in the labor market.

The simple truth is, that competition in industrial life belongs to the past, and is practically outgrown. The time is approaching when it will be no longer possible.

The improvement and enlargement of machinery, and the ever increasing scale of production compel the concentration of capital and this makes inevitable the concentration and co-operation of the workers.

The capitalists—the successful ones, of course—co-operate on the one side; the workers—who are lucky enough to get the jobs—on the other side.

One side gets the profit, grow rich, live in palaces, ride in yachts, gamble at Monte Carlo, drink champagne, choose judges, buy editors, hire preachers, corrupt politics, build universities, endow libraries, patronize churches, get the gout, preach morals and bequeath the earth to their lineal descendants.

The other side do the work, early and late, in heat and cold; they sweat and groan and bleed and die—the steel billets they make are their corpses. They build the mills and all the machinery; they man the plant and the thing of stone and steel begins to throb. They live far away in the out-skirts, in cottages, just this side of the hovels, where gaunt famine walks with despair and *Les Misérables* leer and mock at civilization. When the mills shut down, they are out of work and out of food and out of home; and when old age begins to steal away their vigor and the step is no longer agile, nor the sinew strong, nor the hand cunning; when the frame begins to bend and quiver and the eye to grow dim, and they are no longer fit as labor power to make profit for their masters, they are pushed aside into the human drift that empties into the gulf of despair and death.

The system, once adapted to human needs, has outlived its usefulness and is now an unmitigated curse. It stands in the way of progress and checks the advance of civilization.

If by its fruit we know the tree, so by the same token do we know our social system. Its corrupt fruit betrays its foul and unclean nature and condemns it to death.

The swarms of vagrants, tramps, outcasts, paupers, thieves, gamblers, pickpockets, suicides, confidence men, fallen women, consumptives, idiots, dwarfed children; the disease, poverty, insanity and crime rampant in every land under the sway of capitalism rise up and cry out against it, and hush to silence all the pleas of its *mercenaries* and strike the knell of its doom.

The ancient and middle-age civilizations had their rise, they ruled and fell, and that of our own day must follow them.

Evolution is the order of nature, and society, like the units that compose it, is subject to its inexorable law.

The day of individual effort, of small tools, free competition, hand labor, long hours and meagre results is gone never to return. The civilization reared upon this old foundation is crumbling.

The economic basis of society is being transformed.

The working class are being knit together in the bonds of co-operation, they are becoming conscious of their interests as a class, and marshalling the workers for the class struggle and collective ownership.

With the triumph of the workers the mode of production and distribution will be completely revolutionized.

Private ownership and production for profit will be supplanted by social ownership and production for use.

The economic interests of the workers will be mutual. They will work together in harmony instead of being arrayed against each other in competitive warfare.

The collective workers will own the machinery of production, and there will be work for all and all will receive their socially due share of the product of their co-operative labor.

It is for this great work that the workers and their sympathizers must organize and educate and agitate.

The Socialist movement is of the working class itself; it is from the injustice perpetrated upon, and the misery suffered by this class that the movement sprang, and it is to this class it makes its appeal. It is the voice of awakened labor arousing itself to action.

As we look abroad and see things as they are, the capitalists intrenched and fortified and the workers impoverished, ignorant and in bondage, we are apt to be overawed by the magnitude of the task that lies before the Socialist movement, but as we become grounded in the Socialist philosophy, as we understand the process of economic determinism and grasp the principles of industrial and social evolution the magnitude of the undertaking, far from daunting the Socialist spirit, appeals to each comrade to enlist in the struggle because of the very greatness of the conflict and the immeasurable good that lies beyond it, and as he girds himself and touches elbows with his comrades his own latent resources are developed and his blood thrills with new life as he feels himself rising to the majesty of a man.

Now he has found his true place, and though he be reviled against and ostracized, traduced and denounced, though he be reduced to rags, and tormented with hunger pangs, he will bear it all and more, for he is battling for a principle, he has been consecrated to a cause and he cannot turn back.

To reach the workers that are still in darkness and to open their eyes, that is the task, and to this we must give ourselves with all the strength we have, with patience that never fails and an abiding faith in the ultimate victory.

The moment a worker sees himself in his true light he severs his relations with the capitalist parties, for he realizes at once that he no more belongs there than Rockefeller belongs in the Socialist Party.

What is the actual status of the workingman in the capitalist society of today?

Is he in any true sense a citizen?

Has he any basis for the claim that he is a free man?

First of all, he cannot work unless some capitalist finds it to his interest to employ him.

Why not? Because he has no tools and man cannot work without them.

Why has he no tools? Because tools in these days are, as a rule, great machines and very costly, and in the capitalist system are the private property of the capitalists.

This being true, the workingman, before he can do a tap of work, before he can earn a dime to feed himself, his wife or his child, must first consult the tool-owning capitalist; or, rather, his labor-buying superintendent. Very meekly, therefore, and not without fear in his heart and trembling in his knees, he enters the office and offers his labor power in exchange for a wage that represents but a part, usually a small part, of what his labor produces.

His offer may be accepted or rejected.

Not infrequently the "boss" has been annoyed by so many job-hunters that he has become irritable, and gruffly turns the applicant away.

But admitting that he finds employment, during working hours he is virtually the property of his master.

The bell or the whistle claims him on the stroke of the hour. He is subject to the master's shop regulations and these, of course, are established solely to conserve his master's interests. He works, first of all, for his master, who extracts the surplus value from his labor, but for which he would not be allowed to work at all. He has little or no voice in determining any of the conditions of his employment.

Suddenly, without warning, the shop closes down, or he is discharged and his wage, small at best, is cut off. He has to live, the rent must be paid, the wife and children must have clothing and food, fuel must be provided, and yet he has no job, no wages and no prospect of getting any.

Is a worker in that position free?

Is he a citizen?

A man?

No! He is simply a wage-slave, a job-holder, while it lasts, here today and gone tomorrow.

For the great body of wage-workers there is no escape; they cannot rise above the level of their class. The few who do are the exceptions that prove the rule.

And yet there are those who have the effrontery to warn these wage-slaves that if they turn to Socialism they will lose all incentive to work, and their individuality will fade away.

Incentive and individuality forsooth! Where are they now?

Translated into plain terms, this warning means that a slave who is robbed of all he produces, except enough to keep him in producing condition, as in the present system, has great incentive to work and is highly individualized, but if he breaks his fetters and frees himself and becomes his own master and gets all his labor produces, as he will in Socialism, then all incentive to work vanishes, and his individuality, so used to chains and dungeons, unable to stand the air of freedom, withers away and is lost forever.

The capitalists and their emissaries who resort to such crude attempts at deception and imposture betray the low estimate they place on the intelligence of their wage-workers and also show that they fully understand to what depths of ignorance and credulity these slaves have sunk in the wage-system.

In the light of existing conditions there can be no reform that will be of any great or permanent benefit to the working class.

The present system of private ownership must be abolished and the workers themselves made the owners of the tools with which they work, and to accomplish this they must organize their class for political action and this work is already well under way in the Socialist Party, which is composed of the working class and stands for the working class on a revolutionary platform, which declares in favor of the collective ownership of the means of production and the democratic management of industry in the interest of the whole people.

What intelligent workingman can hold out against the irresistible claim the Socialist movement has upon him? What reason has he to give? What excuse can he offer?

None! Not one!

The only worker who has an excuse to keep out of the Socialist movement is the unfortunate fellow who is ignorant and does not know better. He does not know what Socialism is. That is his misfortune. But that is not all, nor the worst of all. He thinks he knows what it is.

In his ignorance he has taken the word of another for it, whose interest it is to keep him in darkness. So he continues to march with the Republican Party or shout with the Democratic Party, and he no more knows why he is a Republican or Democrat than he knows why he is not a Socialist.

It is impossible for a workingman to contemplate the situation and the outlook and have any intelligent conception of the trend and meaning of things without becoming a Socialist.

Consider for a moment the beastly debasement to which womanhood is subjected in capitalist society. She is simply the property of man to be governed by him as may suit his convenience. She does not vote, she has no voice and must bear silent witness to her legally ordained inferiority.

She has to compete with man in the factories and workshops and stores, and her inferiority is taken advantage of to make her work at still lower wages than the male slave gets who works at her side.

As an economic dependent, she is compelled to sacrifice the innate refinement, the inherent purity and nobility of her sex, and for a pallet of straw she marries the man she does not love.

The debauching effect of the capitalist system upon womanhood is accurately registered in the divorce court and the house of shame.

In Socialism, woman would stand forth the equal of man—all the avenues would be open to her and she would naturally find her fitting place and rise from the low plane of menial servility to the dignity of ideal womanhood.

Breathing the air of economic freedom, amply able to provide for herself in Socialist society, we may be certain that the cruel injustice that is now perpetrated upon her sex and the degradation that results from it will disappear forever.

Consider again the barren prospect of the average boy who faces the world today. If he is the son of a workingman his father is able to do but little in the way of giving him a start.

He does not get to college, nor even to the high school, but has to be satisfied with what he can get in the lower grades, for as soon as he has physical growth enough to work he must find something to do, so that he may help support the family.

His father has no influence and he can get no preferred employment for him at the expense of some other boy, so he thankfully accepts any kind of service that he may be allowed to perform.

How hard it is to find a place for that boy of yours!

What shall we do with Johnnie? and Nellie? is the question of the anxious mother long before they are ripe for the labor market.

"The child is weak, you know," continues the nervous, loving little mother, "and can't do hard work; and I feel dreadfully worried about him."

What a picture! Yet so common that the multitude do not see it. This mother, numbered by thousands many times over, instinctively understands the capitalist system, feels its cruelty and dreads its approaching horrors which cast their shadows upon her tender, loving heart.

Nothing can be sadder than to see a mother take the boy she bore by the hand and start to town with him to peddle him off as merchandise to some one who has use for a child-slave.

To know just how that feels one must have had precisely that experience.

The mother looks down so fondly and caressingly upon her boy; and he looks up into her eyes so timidly and appealingly as she explains his good points to the business man or factory boss, who in turn inspects the lad and interrogates him to verify his mother's claims, and finally informs them that they may call again the following week, but that he does not think he can use the boy.

Well, what finally becomes of the boy? He is now grown, his mother's worry is long since ended, as the grass grows green where she sleeps— and he, the boy? Why, he's a factory hand—a *hand*, mind you, and he gets a dollar and a quarter a day when the factory is running.

That is all he will ever get.

He is an industrial life prisoner—no pardoning power for him in the capitalist system.

No sweet home, no beautiful wife, no happy children, no books, no flowers, no pictures, no comrades, no love, no joy for him.

Just a hand! A human factory hand!

Think of a hand with a soul in it!

In the capitalist system the soul has no business. It cannot produce profit by any process of capitalist calculation.

The working hand is what is needed for the capitalist's tool and so the human must be reduced to a hand.

No head, no heart, no soul—simply a hand.

A thousand hands to one brain—the hands of workingmen, the brain of a capitalist.

A thousand dumb animals, in human form—a thousand slaves in the fetters of ignorance, their heads having run to hands—all these owned and worked and fleeced by one stock-dealing, profit-mongering capitalist.

This is capitalism!

And this system is supported alternately by the Republican Party and the Democratic Party.

These two capitalist parties relieve each other in support of the capitalist system, while the capitalist system relieves the working class of what they produce.

A thousand hands to one head is the abnormal development of the capitalist system.

A thousand workingmen turned into hands to develop and gorge and decorate one capitalist paunch!

This brutal order of things must be overthrown. The human race was not born to degeneracy.

A thousand heads have grown for every thousand pairs of hands; a thousand hearts throb in testimony of the unity of heads and hands; and a thousand souls, though crushed and mangled, burn in protest and are pledged to redeem a thousand men.

Heads and hands, hearts and souls, are the heritage of all.

Full opportunity for full development is the unalienable right of all.

He who denies it is a tyrant; he who does not demand it is a coward; he who is indifferent to it is a slave; he who does not desire it is dead.

The earth for all the people! That is the demand.

The machinery of production and distribution for all the people! That is the demand.

The collective ownership and control of industry and its democratic management in the interest of all the people! That is the demand.

The elimination of rent, interest and profit and the production of wealth to satisfy the wants of all the people! That is the demand.

Co-operative industry in which all shall work together in harmony as the basis of a new social order, a higher civilization, a real republic! That is the demand.

The end of class struggles and class rule, of master and slave, of ignorance and vice, of poverty and shame, of cruelty and crime—the birth of freedom, the dawn of brotherhood, the beginning of MAN! That is the demand.

This is Socialism!

# Mr. Dooley on the Labor Troubles and on Immigration

## Finley Peter Dunne

*Squarely in the midst of the American people of 1900 stood Mr. Martin Dooley, saloon keeper and sage, formerly of Ireland but mostly a citizen of Archey Road, Sixth Ward, Chicago. Broad of brogue, pugnacious but kind in middle age, wise to the ways of precinct politics, Mr. Dooley read his newspaper and observed the world around him with a penetrating mixture of skepticism and sentimentality, indignation and detachment. He ridiculed sham, punctured pomposity, and with merciless irony dissected popular prejudices—including his own, which were abundant. "Ye have a r-right to ye'er opinyon," Mr. Dooley once admonished his friend Hennessy, "an' ye'll hold it annyhow, whether ye have a r-right to it or not. Like most iv ye'er fellow-citizens, ye start impartial. Ye don't know annything about th' case. If ye knew annything, ye'd not have an opinyon wan way or th'other."*

*Mr. Dooley shared the reformer's view of the privileged plutocrat ("Niver steal a dure-mat. If ye do, ye'll be invistigated, hanged, an' maybe rayformed. Steal a bank, me boy, steal a bank") and the cynic's view of the reformer ("A rayformer thinks he was ilicted because he was a rayformer, whin th' thruth iv th' matther is he was ilicted because no wan knew him"). Imperialists, military heroes, and Englishmen did not enchant him; but neither did the Boer or the Filipino patriot. As will be evident from the following selections, his sharp eye pierced through the professional American and the professional Irishman alike, and as did many self-made men who were committed to survive in the jungle of small urban enterprise, he confronted the prospect of a protracted conflict between labor and capital with a sympathy for the former that only slightly concealed his irritation with both. The common denominator of his thought was a keen moral perspective which is the essence of humor, and what imparted to Mr. Dooley's humor its enduring quality was the kind of detachment from the events of the larger world which was distinctly and peculiarly the detachment of the working man, the immigrant, or simply the average uncom-*

245

*mitted wage-earning citizen who constituted the great mass of urban America. Little wonder that he became the most popular and certainly one of the most incisively funny commentators in the progressive era.*

*Mr. Dooley was, of course, a fiction, the happy conception of Finley Peter Dunne, a Chicago journalist and editorial writer, and so successfully did Dunne create Mr. Dooley that the character soon overshadowed the author. Born in 1867 of Irish parents of comfortable means, Dunne reported and wrote for three newspapers, covered the sporting world and the police court, managed a city desk, ran the Chicago Journal, and later worked in New York for Collier's and for Steffens' American magazine. A contemporary of Stephen Crane, Frank Norris, Theodore Dreiser, a friend of Whitlock, Steffens, Mark Twain, and Theodore Roosevelt, he belonged to the notable race of brash, iconoclastic literary realists who were overturning the orthodoxies of American writing at the turn of the century, and his career as commentator and essayist spanned forty years of political and social ferment; but nothing else he wrote measured up to the trenchant humor and incomparably successful dialect of Mr. Dooley's observations. Modeled originally in 1893 on a philosophical bartender whose saloon on Archer Avenue was usually crowded with journalists and lawyers, Mr. Dooley was content to expound his opinions with increasing acclaim in local newspapers when he suddenly rose to national view with his inspired comments "On His Cousin George" (Admiral Dewey) and with related essays on the Spanish-American War, the sort of national enterprise which provided a man of Mr. Dooley's temperament with an unrivaled opportunity for ironic comment on public affairs. Soon after Cousin George there followed Dooley's popular but devastating "book review" of Theodore Roosevelt's Rough Riders, which produced for Dunne an invitation from the delighted and unabashed governor to visit him at Oyster Bay. In the next ten years Mr. Dooley's comments on the world became as familiar to the American public as those of Theodore Roosevelt himself.*

*The two essays offered here are rendered exactly as written: to reduce them to straight English would destroy most of the bite and the savor of the first and possibly the last truly inspired Irish saloonkeeper in American letters. The dialect in fact grows on one after a page or two, and the insights tend never to be forgotten.*

THE LABOR TROUBLES

"I see th' sthrike has been called off," said Mr. Hennessy.

"Which wan?" asked Mr. Dooley. "I can't keep thrack iv thim. Some-

Finley Peter Dunne, *Dissertations by Mr. Dooley* (New York: Scribner's, 1906), pp. 59-64; *Observations by Mr. Dooley* (New York: Scribner's, 1902), pp. 49-54.

body is sthrikin' all th' time. Wan day th' horseshoers are out, an' another day th' teamsters. Th' Brotherhood iv Molasses Candy Pullers sthrikes, an' th' Amalgymated Union iv Pickle Sorters quits in sympathy. Th' carpinter that has been puttin' up a chicken coop f'r Hogan knocked off wurruk whin he found that Hogan was shavin' himsilf without a card fr'm th' Barbers' Union. Hogan fixed it with th' walkin' dillygate iv th' barbers, an' th' carpinter quit wurruk because he found that Hogan was wearin' a pair iv non-union pants. Hogan wint down-town an' had his pants unionized an' come home to find that th' carpinter had sthruck because Hogan's hens was layin' eggs without th' union label. Hogan injooced th' hens to jine th' union. But wan iv thim laid an egg two days in succission an' th' others sthruck, th' rule iv th' union bein' that no hen shall lay more eggs thin th' most reluctant hen in th' bunch.

"It's th' same ivrywhere. I haven't had a sandwich f'r a year because ivry time I've asked f'r wan ayether th' butchers or th' bakers has been out on sthrike. If I go down in a car in th' mornin' it's eight to wan I walk back at night. A man I knew had his uncle in th' house much longer than ayether iv thim had intinded on account iv a sthrike iv th' Friendly Brotherhood iv Morchuary Helpers. Afther they'd got a permit fr'm th' walkin' dillygate an' th' remains was carrid away undher a profusyon iv floral imblims with a union label on each iv thim, th' coortege was stopped at ivry corner be a picket, who first punched th' mourners an' thin examined their credintials. Me frind says to me: 'Uncle Bill wud've been proud. He was very fond iv long fun'rals, an' this was th' longest I iver attinded. It took eight hours, an' was much more riochous goin' out thin comin' back,' he says.

"It was diff'rent whin I was a young man, Hinnissy. In thim days Capital an' Labor were frindly, or Labor was. Capital was like a father to Labor, givin' it its boord an' lodgin's. Nayether intherfered with th' other. Capital wint on capitalizin', an' Labor wint on laborin'. In thim goolden days a wurrukin' man was an honest artisan. That's what he was proud to be called. Th' week befure iliction he had his pitcher in th' funny pa-apers. He wore a square paper cap an' a leather apron, an' he had his ar-rm ar-round Capital, a rosy binivolint old guy with a plug-hat an' eye-glasses. They were goin' to th' polls together to vote f'r simple old Capital.

"Capital an' Labor walked ar-rm in ar-rm instead iv havin' both hands free as at prisint. Capital was contint to be Capital, an' Labor was used to bein' Labor. Capital come ar-round an' felt th' ar-rm iv Labor wanst in a while, an' ivry year Mrs. Capital called on Mrs. Labor an' congratylated her on her score. Th' pride iv ivry artisan was to wurruk as long at his task as th' boss cud afford to pay th' gas bill. In return f'r his fidelity he got a turkey ivry year. At Chris'mas time Capital gathered his happy fam'ly around him, an' in th' prisince iv th' ladies iv th' neighborhood give thim a short oration. 'Me brave la'ads,' says he, 'we've had a good year. (Cheers.) I have made a millyon dollars. (Sinsation.) I atthribute this to me supeeryor skill, aided be ye'er arnest efforts at th' bench an' at th' forge. (Sobs.) Ye have done so well that we won't need so manny iv us as we did. (Long an' continyous cheerin'.) Those iv us who can do two men's wurruk will remain, an', if possible, do four. Our other faithful sarvants,' he says, 'can come back in th' spring,' he says, 'if alive,' he says. An' th' bold artysans tossed their paper caps in th' air an' give three cheers f'r Capital. They wurruked till ol' age crept on thim, and thin retired to live on th' wish-bones an' kind wurruds they had accumylated.

"Nowadays 'tis far diff'rent. Th' unions has desthroyed all individjool effort. Year be year th' hours iv th' misguided wurrukin' man has been cut down, till now it takes a split-second watch to time him as he goes through th' day's wurruk. I have a gintleman plasthrer frind who tells me he hasn't put in a full day in a year. He goes to his desk ivry mornin' at tin an' sthrikes punchooly at iliven. 'Th' wrongs iv th' wurrukin' men mus' be redhressed,' says he. 'Ar-re ye inthrested in thim?' says I. 'Ye niver looked betther in ye'er life,' says I. 'I niver felt betther,' he says. 'It's th' out-iv-dure life,' he says. 'I haven't missed a baseball game this summer,' he says. 'But,' he says, 'I need exercise. I wish Labor Day wud come around. Th' boys has choose me to carry a life-size model iv th' Masonic Temple in th' parade,' he says.

"If I was a wurrukin' man I'd sigh f'r th' good ol' days, whin Labor an' Capital were frinds. Those who lived through thim did. In thim times th' arrystocracy iv labor was th' la-ads who r-run th' railroad injines. They were a proud race. It was a boast to have wan iv thim in a fam'ly. They niver sthruck. 'Twas again' their rules. They conferred with Capital. Capital used to weep over thim. Ivry wanst in a while a railroad prisidint wud grow red in th' face an' burst into song about thim. They were a body that th' nation might well be proud iv. If he had a son who asked f'r no betther fate, he wud ask f'r no betther fate f'r him thin to be a Brotherhood iv Locmotive Ingineers. Ivrybody looked up to thim, an' they looked down on ivrybody, but mostly on th' bricklayers. Th' bricklayers were niver bulwarks iv th' constichoochion. They niver conferred with Capital. Th' polis always arrived just as th' conference was beginnin'. Their motto was a long life an' a merry wan; a brick in th' hand is worth two on th' wall. They sthruck ivry time they thought iv it. They sthruck on th' slightest provocation, an' whin they weren't provoked at all. If a band wint by they climbed down th' laddhers an' followed it, carryin' banners with th' wurruds: 'Give us bread or we starve,' an' walked till they were almost hungry. Ivry Saturdah night they held a dance to protest again' their wrongs. In th' summer-time th' wails iv th' oppressed bricklayers wint up fr'm countless picnics. They sthruck in sympathy with annybody.

Th' union wint out as wan man because they was a rumor that th' super-intintendent iv th' rollin'-mills was not nice to his wife. Wanst they sthruck because Poland was not free.

"What was th' raysult? Their unraisoning demands fin'lly enraged Capital. To-day ye can go into a bricklayer's house an' niver see a capital-ist but th' bricklayer himsilf. Forty years ago a bricklayer was certain iv twelve hours wurruk a day, or two hours more thin a convicted burglar. To-day he has practically nawthin' to do, an' won't do that. They ar-re out iv wurruk nearly all th' time an' at th' seashore. Jus' as often as ye read 'Newport colony fillin' up,' ye read, 'Bricklayers sthrike again.' Ye very sil-dom see a bricklayer nowadays in th' city. They live mostly in th' counthry, an' on'y come into town to be bribed to go to wurruk. It wud pay anny man who is buildin' a house to sind thim what money he has be mail an' go live in a tent.

"An' all this time, how about th' arrystocracy iv labor, th' knights iv th' throttle? Have thcy been deprived iv anny hours iv labor? On th' conthry, they have steadily increased, ontil to-day there is not a knight iv th' throttle who hasn't more hours iv wurruk in a day thin he can use in a week. In th' arly mornin', whin he takes his ir'n horse out iv th' stall, he meets th' onforchnit, misguided bricklayer comin' home in a cab fr'm a sthrike meetin'. Hardly a year passes that he can't say to his wife: 'Mother, I've had an increase.' 'In wages?' 'No, in hours.' It's th' old story iv th' ant an' th' grasshopper—th' ant that ye can step on an' th' grasshopper ye can't catch.

"Well, it's too bad that th' goolden days has passed, Hinnissy. Capital still pats Labor on th' back, but on'y with an axe. Labor rayfuses to be threated as a frind. It wants to be threated as an inimy. It thinks it gets more that way. They ar-re still a happy fam'ly, but it's more like an English fam'ly. They don't speak. What do I think iv it all? Ah, sure, I don't know. I belong to th' onforchnit middle class. I wurruk hard, an' I have no money. They come in here undher me hospital roof, an' I furnish thim with cards, checks, an' refrishmints. 'Let's play without a limit,' says Labor. 'It's Dooley's money.' 'Go as far as ye like with Dooley's money,' says Capital. 'What have ye got?' 'I've got a straight to Roosevelt,' says Labor. 'I've got ye beat,' says Capital. 'I've got a Supreme Court full of injunctions.' Manetime I've pawned me watch to pay fr th' game, an' I have to go to th' joolry-store on th' corner to buy a pound iv beef or a scuttle iv coal. No wan iver sthrikes in sympathy with me."

"They ought to get together," said Mr. Hennessy.

"How cud they get anny closer together thin their prisint clinch?" asked Mr. Dooley. "They're so close together now that those that ar-re between thim ar-re crushed to death."

IMMIGRATION

"Well, I see Congress has got to wurruk again," said Mr. Dooley.

"The Lord save us fr'm harm," said Mr. Hennessy.

"Yes, sir," said Mr. Dooley, "Congress has got to wurruk again, an' manny things that seems important to a Congressman 'll be brought up befure thim. 'Tis sthrange that what's a big thing to a man in Wash'nton, Hinnissy, don't seem much account to me. Divvle a bit do I care whether they dig th' Nicaragoon Canal or cross th' Isthmus in a balloon; or whether th' Monroe docthrine is enfoorced or whether it ain't; or whether th' thrusts is abolished as Teddy Rosenfelt wud like to have thim or encour- aged to go on with their neefaryous but magnificent entherprises as th' Prisidint wud like; or whether th' water is poured into th' ditches to re- claim th' arid lands iv th' West or th' money f'r thim to fertilize th' arid pocket-books iv th' conthractors; or whether th' Injun is threated like a depindant an' miserable thribesman or like a free an' indepindant dog; or whether we restore th' merchant marine to th' ocean or whether we lave it to restore itsilf. None iv these here questions inthrests me, an' be me I mane you an' be you I mane ivrybody. What we want to know is, ar-re we goin' to have coal enough in th' hod whin th' cold snap comes; will th' plumbin' hold out, an' will th' job last.

"But they'se wan question that Congress is goin' to take up that you an' me are inthrested in. As a pilgrim father that missed th' first boats, I must raise me claryon voice again' th' invasion iv this fair land be th' paupers an' arnychists iv effete Europe. Ye bet I must—because I'm here first. 'Twas diff'rent whin I was dashed high on th' stern an' rockbound coast. In thim days America was th' refuge iv th' oppressed iv all th' wurruld. They cud come over here an' do a good job iv oppressin' thim- silves. As I told ye I come a little late. Th' Rosenfelts an' th' Lodges bate me be at laste a boat lenth, an' be th' time I got here they was stern an' rockbound thimsilves. So I got a gloryous rayciption as soon as I was towed off th' rocks. Th' stars an' sthripes whispered a welcome in th' breeze an' a shovel was thrust into me hand an' I was pushed into a sthreet excyvatin' as though I'd been born here. Th' pilgrim father who bossed th' job was a fine ol' puritan be th' name iv Doherty, who come over in th' Mayflower about th' time iv th' potato rot in Wexford, an' he made me think they was a hole in th' breakwather iv th' haven iv refuge an' some iv th' wash iv th' seas iv opprission had got through. He was a stern an' rock- bound la-ad himsilf, but I was a good hand at loose stones an' wan day— but I'll tell ye about that another time.

"Annyhow, I was rayceived with open arms that sometimes ended in a clinch. I was afraid I wasn't goin' to assimilate with th' airlyer pilgrim fathers an' th' instichoochions iv th' counthry, but I soon found that a long swing iv th' pick made me as good as another man an' it didn't require a gr-reat intellect, or sometimes anny at all, to vote th' dimmycrat ticket, an' befure I was here a month, I felt enough like a native born American to burn a witch. Wanst in a while a mob iv intilligint collajeens, whose grandfathers had bate me to th' dock, wud take a shy at me Pathrick's Day procission or burn down wan iv me churches, but they got tired iv that befure long; 'twas too much like wurruk.

"But as I tell ye, Hinnissy, 'tis diff'rent now. I don't know why 'tis diff'rent but 'tis diff'rent. 'Tis time we put our back again' th' open dure an' keep out th' savage horde. If that cousin iv ye'ers expects to cross, he'd betther tear f'r th' ship. In a few minyits th' gates 'll be down an' whin th' oppressed wurruld comes hikin' acrost to th' haven iv refuge, they'll do well to put a couplin' pin undher their hats, f'r th' Goddess iv Liberty 'll meet thim at th' dock with an axe in her hand. Congress is goin' to fix it. Me frind Shaughnessy says so. He was in yisterdah an' says he: ' 'Tis time we done something to make th' immigration laws sthronger,' says he. 'Thrue f'r ye, Miles Standish,' says I; 'but what wud ye do?' 'I'd keep out th' offscourin's iv Europe,' says he. 'Wud ye go back?' says I. 'Have ye'er joke,' says he. ' 'Tis not so seeryus as it was befure ye come,' says I. 'But what ar-re th' immygrants doin' that's roonous to us?' I says. 'Well,' says he, 'they're arnychists,' he says; 'they don't assymilate with th' counthry,' he says. 'Maybe th' counthry's digestion has gone wrong fr'm too much rich food,' says I; 'perhaps now if we'd lave off thryin' to digest Rockyfellar an' thry a simple diet like Schwartzmeister, we wudden't feel th' effects iv our vittels,' I says. 'Maybe if we'd season th' immygrants a little or cook thim thurly, they'd go down betther,' I says.

" 'They're arnychists, like Parsons,' he says. 'He wud've been an immygrant if Texas hadn't been admittcd to th' Union,' I says. 'Or Snolgosh,' he says. 'Has Mitchigan seceded?' I says. 'Or Gittoo,' he says. 'Who come fr'm th' effete monarchies iv Chicago, west iv Ashland Av'noo,' I says. 'Or what's-his-name, Wilkes Booth,' he says. 'I don't know what he was— maybe a Boolgharyen,' says I. 'Well, annyhow,' says he, 'they're th' scum iv th' earth.' 'They may be that,' says I; 'but we used to think they was th' cream iv civilization,' I says. 'They're off th' top annyhow. I wanst believed 'twas th' best men iv Europe come here, th' la-ads that was too sthrong and indepindant to be kicked around be a boorgomaster at home an' wanted to dig out f'r a place where they cud get a chanst to make their way to th' money. I see their sons fightin' into politics an' their daughters tachin' young American idee how to shoot too high in th' public school, an' I thought they was all right. But I see I was wrong. Thim boys out there towin' wan heavy foot afther th' other to th' rowlin' mills is all arnychists. There's warrants out f'r all names endin' in 'inski, an' I think I'll board up me windows, f'r,' I says, 'if immygrants is as dangerous to this counthry as ye an' I an' other pilgrim fathers believe they are, they'se enough iv thim sneaked in already to make us aborigines about as infloointial as the prohibition vote in th' Twinty-ninth Ward. They'll dash again' our stern an' rock-bound coast till they bust it,' says I.

"'But I ain't so much afraid as ye ar-re. I'm not afraid iv me father an' I'm not afraid iv mesilf. An' I'm not afraid iv Schwartzmeister's father or Hinnery Cabin Lodge's grandfather. We all come over th' same way, an' if me ancestors were not what Hogan calls rigicides, 'twas not because they were not ready an' willin', on'y a king niver come their way. I don't believe in killin' kings, mesilf. I niver wud've sawed th' block off that curly-headed potintate that I see in th' pitchers down town, but, be hivins, Presarved Codfish Shaughnessy, if we'd begun a few years ago shuttin' out folks that wudden't mind handin' a bomb to a king, they wudden't be enough people in Mattsachoosetts to make a quorum f'r th' Anti-Impeeryal S'ciety,' says I. 'But what wud ye do with th' offscourin' iv Europe?' says he. 'I'd scour thim some more,' say I.

"An' so th' meetin' iv th' Plymouth Rock Assocyation come to an end. But if ye wud like to get it together, Deacon Hinnissy, to discuss th' immygration question, I'll sind out a hurry call f'r Schwartzmeister an' Mulcahey an' Ignacio Sbarbaro an' Nels Larsen an' Petrus Gooldvink, an' we'll gather to-night at Fanneilnoviski Hall at th' corner iv Sheridan an' Sigel sthreets. All th' pilgrim fathers is rayquested f'r to bring interpreters."

"Well," said Mr. Hennessy, "divvle th' bit I care, on'y I'm here first, an' I ought to have th' right to keep th' bus fr'm bein' overcrowded."

"Well," said Mr. Dooley, "as a pilgrim father on me gran' nephew's side, I don't know but ye're right. An' they'se wan sure way to keep thim out."

"What's that?" asked Mr. Hennessy.

"Teach thim all about our instichoochions befure they come," said Mr. Dooley.

# PART III

# THE NATIONAL PROGRESSIVE VISION

# Report of the Country Life
# Commission

*With the one-sided election of Theodore Roosevelt to the presidency in
1904 the mood of reform so central to the progressive era now began to
influence the course of national and state politics. Progressivism showed
itself in a number of distinctive ways. It aimed to establish a balance of
economic power where economic forces had gotten out of balance and
where, in consequence, specific classes of people felt their economic
security threatened. Thus the Roosevelt administration sought to persuade
employers to bargain in good faith with organized workers, to prevent
railroads from setting rates which penalized shippers on the basis of their
regional isolation, and to ride herd on large corporations as a protection
for smaller businesses. National progressives aimed to enlarge the role of
the government in the necessary policing of a modern industrial state: to
bolster regulations governing conditions of work, to control the interstate
sale of products closely affecting the health of citizens, to investigate and
publicize conditions which cried out for relief. High on their list of hopes
to be fulfilled was a centralized national effort to increase the supply and
availability of the natural resources of the country and to control their
consumption.*

*Progressives in nation and state not only possessed a distinctive pro-
gram; they pursued their program with a distinctive attitude and spirit.
They believed that a truly worth-while civilization rested primarily on a
continuously expanding stock of material goods and a wide body of
scientific knowledge and technological skills spread widely through the
population. Yet their gauge for national well-being did not end with a
count of motor cars, cattle sales, and bank clearings. They attached as
great an importance to growth in public health, slum clearance, and average yearly wages, while central to their expectations for national progress
was a faith in mass education as the ultimate guarantee of equal and
universal opportunity. National progressives approached their problems
with an enthusiasm for experts, for the comprehensive plan left in the*

*charge of intelligent men of good education, strong ideals of service, even
a trace of* noblesse oblige. *Yet the most successful reformers also championed the central mechanisms of democracy—the referendum, the political party, and "home rule." Overlapping their vision of what ought to be
was a cold-eyed awareness of things as they were.*

*The program and spirit of national progressivism is revealed with re-
markable clarity in the report which Theodore Roosevelt's specially appointed Country Life Commission submitted to him in early 1909 upon
his request for a study of the state of rural American society and for
remedies for its deficiencies. Readers familiar with Roosevelt's professional
career will recall that though he spent virtually all of it in as urban an
environment as one could find in the entire world, he regularly escaped
to the country, the ranch, or the wilderness; that no cause he fought for
became so charged with his own moral convictions as did the conservation
of natural resources; and that having thrown his political weight with
bruising effectiveness into the battle for better urban government and
conditions of life, he not unnaturally came to believe that rural society
might yield to a similar assault. In 1900 well over half the nation's
people still lived in the "country" as the census defined it. To anyone
sharing Roosevelt's nationalistic enthusiasm for the moral and physical
strengthening of the American people at a time when, as it seemed to him,
destiny was about to tap the nation for the role of a world power, what
more imperative task remained in the final year of his presidential career
than to extend the progressive dream to the outer countryside?*

*The* Country Life Report *(offered here virtually entire) deserves close
attention as a document of progressivism. It finds most of rural America
in the early 1900's deficient in civilization and impervious to progress.
For this it blames the economic power of large urban (and generally
eastern) corporations, the setting of discriminatory railroad rates, the
profits of the middleman, and the private monopolizing of natural resources. The Commission is concerned not with the productivity of the
top half of the nation's farmers (1897 to 1919 were years of remarkable
prosperity and technological growth in agriculture), but with the improvement of the way of life on the average farm; here one can glimpse the
traditional preoccupation of American political theorists with the small
family farm as one pole of democracy. Yet it is plain that the Commissioners' perspective on the country is rooted in a commitment to a very
different standard of life. Their enthusiasm for the inherent virtues of
country life seems a little perfunctory: their values are thoroughly urban,
and their moral vision consists of the hope that intelligent social engineering (in America this has been more urban than rural) will reinvigorate a
retarded rural hinterland. The Commission sets forth in particularly robust
terms a progressive faith in the power of the school and the church in*

*transforming social life. Revealing the experimental cast of mind which
John Dewey so brilliantly exemplified in precisely the same era, the report
makes clear that country schools, "burdened with tradition," were a disgrace to the nation in their failure to relate education to the daily life of
rural people. Let it also be noted how clearly the Commission implies
that the nation's farmers ought to create for themselves the political power
which alone can assure them the fruits of reform: they must learn to lobby,
to bargain, to school themselves in the techniques of political action.*

*The* Country Life Report, *then, succinctly embodied the reform spirit.
And therein lies irony. For the fate of this document suggests another,
less-understood fact of progressivism: reform went as often spotted with
failure as graced with success. With almost monumental frigidity Congress
spurned the Commission's findings, refused to appropriate funds for
further publication and circulation, and even considered forbidding the
President to appoint similar commissions without specific congressional
approval. The reasons are unclear, but some may be surmised. Trailing at
the end of Roosevelt's regime, this hand-picked body of intellectuals, including Walter Hines Page and Gifford Pinchot, two devoted personal
supporters of the controversial President, may unwittingly have provided
Congress with simply too much of a temptation to express a safe defiance
of the man who had ridden roughshod over it for so long. Nor, having
transmitted the report to Congress, did Roosevelt push it with more than
earnest verbal support. Perhaps he was wise not to commit too many of
his heavy battalions to a doubtful fight: there was little here in the way of
specific recommendations for Congress to work on, and what there was
seemed desirable but hardly crucial in a period of general economic well-
being.*

*But though Congress shelved the report, the issues it raised continued
to plague the nation until the most urgent of them were solved. The
federal government soon committed itself to the support of rural highways
and a parcel post service. Eventually, urban salesmanship talked its way
into every crossroads store; automobiles, radio, and city-educated school
teachers broke down the boundaries betwen town and country; and the
Great Depression impelled the New Deal to infuse the numerous rural
enclaves of poverty—especially in the South—with that national energy
which the Country Life Commission had so forcefully urged on the progressive generation thirty years before.*

Broadly speaking, agriculture in the United States is prosperous and
the conditions in many of the great farming regions are improving. The

*Report of the Country Life Commission,* United States Senate, 60th Congress, 2d
Session, Document 705 (Washington, D.C.: Government Printing Office, 1909), pp.
20-65.

success of the owners and cultivators of good land, in the prosperous regions, has been due partly to improved methods, largely to good prices for products, and also to the general advance in the price of farm lands in these regions. Notwithstanding the general advance in rentals and the higher prices of labor, tenants also have enjoyed a good degree of prosperity, due to fair crops, and an advance in the price of farm products approximately corresponding to the advance in the price of land. Farm labor has been fully employed and at increased wages, and many farm hands have become tenants and many tenants have become landowners.

There is marked improvement, in many of the agricultural regions, in the character of the farm home and its surroundings. There is increasing appreciation on the part of great numbers of country people of the advantage of sanitary water supplies and plumbing, of better construction in barns and all farm buildings, of good reading matter, of tasteful gardens and lawns, and the necessity of good education.

Many institutions are also serving the agricultural needs of the open country with great effectiveness, as the United States Department of Agriculture, the land-grant colleges and experiment stations, and the many kinds of extension work that directly or indirectly emanate from them. The help that these institutions render to the country-life interests is everywhere recognized. State departments of agriculture, national, state, and local organizations, many schools of secondary grade, churches, libraries, and many other agencies are also contributing actively to the betterment of agricultural conditions.

There has never been a time when the American farmer was as well off as he is to-day, when we consider not only his earning power, but the comforts and advantages he may secure. Yet the real efficiency in farm life, and in country life as a whole, is not to be measured by historical standards, but in terms of its possibilities. Considered from this point of view, there are very marked deficiencies. There has been a complete and fundamental change in our whole economic system within the past century. This has resulted in profound social changes and the redirection of our point of view on life. In some occupations the readjustment to the new conditions has been rapid and complete; in others it has come with difficulty. In all the great series of farm occupations the readjustment has been the most tardy, because the whole structure of a traditional and fundamental system has been involved. It is not strange, therefore, that development is still arrested in certain respects; that marked inequalities have arisen; or that positive injustice may prevail even to a very marked and widespread extent. All these difficulties are the results of the unequal development of our contemporary civilization. All this may come about without any intention on the part of anyone that it should be so. The problems are nevertheless just as real, and they must be studied and remedies must be found.

These deficiencies are recognized by the people. We have found, from the testimony not only of the farmers themselves but of all persons in touch with farm life, more or less serious agricultural unrest in every part of the United States, even in the most prosperous regions. There is a widespread tendency for farmers to move to town. It is not advisable, of course, that all country persons remain in the country; but this general desire to move is evidence that the open country is not satisfying as a permanent abode. This tendency is not peculiar to any region. In difficult farming regions, and where the competition with other farming sections is most severe, the young people may go to town to better their condition. In the best regions the older people retire to town, because it is socially more attractive and they see a prospect of living in comparative ease and comfort on the rental of their lands. Nearly everywhere there is a townward movement for the purpose of securing school advantages for the children. All this tends to sterilize the open country and to lower its social status. Often the farm is let to tenants. The farmer is likely to lose active interest in life when he retires to town, and he becomes a stationary citizen, adding a social problem to the town. He is likely to find his expenses increasing and is obliged to raise rents to his tenant, thereby making it more difficult for the man who works on the land. On his death his property enriches the town rather than the country. The withdrawal of the children from the farms detracts from the interest and efficiency of the country school and adds to the interest of the town school. Thus the country is drained of the energy of youth on the one hand and the experience and accumulation of age on the other, and three problems more or less grave are created—a problem for the town, a problem for the public school, and also a problem of tenancy in the open country.

The farming interest is not, as a whole, receiving the full rewards to which it is entitled, nor has country life attained to anywhere near its possibilities of attractiveness and comfort. The farmer is necessarily handicapped in the development of social life and in the conduct of his business because of his separateness, the small volume of his output, and the lack of capital. He often begins with practically no capital, and expects to develop his capital and relationships out of the annual business itself; and even when he has capital with which to set up a business and operate it the amount is small when compared with that required in other enterprises. He is not only handicapped in his farming but is disadvantaged when he deals with other business interests and with other social groups. It is peculiarly necessary, therefore, that Government should give him adequate consideration and protection. There are difficulties of the separate man, living quietly on his land, that government should understand.

I. PURPOSE AND METHODS OF THE COMMISSION

The commission is requested to report on the means that are "now available for supplying the deficiencies which exist" in the country life of the United States and "upon the best methods of organized permanent effort in investigation and actual work" along the lines of betterment of rural conditions.

The President's letter appointing the commission is as follows:

OYSTER BAY, N. Y., *August 10, 1908.*

MY DEAR PROFESSOR BAILEY: No nation has ever achieved permanent greatness unless this greatness was based on the wellbeing of the great farmer class, the men who live on the soil; for it is upon their welfare, material and moral, that the welfare of the rest of the nation ultimately rests. In the United States, disregarding certain sections and taking the nation as a whole, I believe it to be true that the farmers in general are better off to-day than they ever were before. We Americans are making great progress in the development of our agricultural resources. But it is equally true that the social and economic institutions of the open country are not keeping pace with the development of the nation as a whole. The farmer is, as a rule, better off than his forbears; but his increase in well-being has not kept pace with that of the country as a whole. While the condition of the farmers in some of our best farming regions leaves little to be desired, we are far from having reached so high a level in all parts of the country. In portions of the South, for example, where the Department of Agriculture, through the farmers' cooperative demonstration work of Doctor Knapp, is directly instructing more than 30,000 farmers in better methods of farming, there is nevertheless much unnecessary suffering and needless loss of efficiency on the farm. A physician, who is also a careful student of farm life in the South, writing to me recently about the enormous percentage of preventable deaths of children, due to insanitary condition of southern farms, said:

"Personally, from the health point of view, I would prefer to see my own daughter, 9 years old, at work in a cotton mill than have her live as tenant on the average southern tenant one-horse farm. This apparently extreme statement is based upon actual life among both classes of people."

I doubt if any other nation can bear comparison with our own in the amount of attention given by the Government, both Federal and State, to agricultural matters. But practically the whole of this effort has hitherto been directed toward increasing the production of crops. Our attention has been concentrated almost exclusively on getting better farming. In the beginning this was unquestionably the right thing to do. The farmer must first of all grow good crops in order to support himself and his family. But when this has been secured the effort for better farming should cease to stand alone, and should be accompanied by the effort for better business and better living on the farm.

It is at least as important that the farmer should get the largest possible return in money, comfort, and social advantages from the crops he grows as that he should get the largest possible return in crops from the land he farms. Agriculture is not the whole of country life. The great rural interests are human interests, and good crops are of little value to the farmer unless they open the door to a good kind of life on the farm.

This problem of country life is in the truest sense a national problem. In an address delivered at the semicentennial of the founding of agricultural colleges in the United States a year ago last May, I said:

"There is but one person whose welfare is as vital to the welfare of the whole country as is that of the wage-worker who does manual labor, and that is the tiller of the soil—the farmer. If there is one lesson taught by history, it is that the permanent greatness of any State must ultimately depend more upon the character of its country population than upon anything else. No growth of cities, no growth of wealth can make up for loss in either the number or the character of the farming population. . . .

"The farm grows the raw material for the food and clothing of all our citizens; it supports directly almost half of them; and nearly half the children of the United States are born and brought up on the farms. How can the life of the farm family be made less solitary, fuller of opportunity, freer from drudgery, more comfortable, happier, and more attractive? Such a result is most earnestly to be desired. How can life on the farm be kept on the highest level, and, where it is not already on that level, be so improved, dignified, and brightened as to awaken and keep alive the pride and loyalty of the farmer's boys and girls, of the farmer's wife, and of the farmer himself? How can a compelling desire to live on the farm be aroused in the children that are born on the farm? All these questions are of vital importance not only to the farmer but to the whole nation. . . .

"We hope ultimately to double the average yield of wheat and corn per acre; it will be a great achievement; but it is even more important to double the desirability, comfort, and standing of the farmer's life."

It is especially important that whatever will serve to prepare country children for life on the farm and whatever will brighten home life in the country and make it richer and more attractive for the mothers, wives, and daughters of farmers should be done promptly, thoroughly, and gladly. There is no more important person, measured in influence upon the life of the nation, than the farmer's wife, no more important home than the country home, and it is of national importance to do the best we can for both.

The farmers have hitherto had less than their full share of public attention along the lines of business and social life. There is too much belief among all our people that the prizes of life lie away from the farm. I am therefore anxious to bring before the people of the United States the question of securing better business and better living on the farm, whether by cooperation between farmers for buying, selling, and borrowing; by promoting social advantages and opportunities in the country; or by any other legitimate means that will help to make country life more gainful, more attractive, and fuller of opportunities, pleasures, and rewards for the men, women, and children of the farms.

I shall be very glad indeed if you will consent to serve upon a commission on country life, upon which I am asking the following gentlemen to act: Prof. L. H. Bailey, New York State College of Agriculture, Ithaca, N. Y., chairman; Mr. Henry Wallace, Wallace's Farmer, Des Moines, Iowa; President Kenyon L. Butterfield, Massachusetts Agricultural College, Amherst, Mass.; Mr. Gifford Pinchot, United States Forest Service; Mr. Walter H. Page, editor of The World's Work, New York.

My immediate purpose in appointing this commission is to secure from it such information and advice as will enable me to make recommendations to Congress upon this extremely important matter. I shall be glad if the commission will report to me upon the present condition of country life, upon what means are now available for supplying the deficiencies which exist, and upon the best methods of organized permanent effort in investigation and actual work along the lines I have indicated. You will doubtless also find it necessary to suggest means for bringing about the redirection or better adaptation of rural schools to the training of children for life on the farm. The national and state agricultural departments must ultimately join with the various farmers' and agricultural organizations in the effort to secure greater efficiency and attractiveness in country life.

In view of the pressing importance of this subject I should be glad to have you report before the end of next December. For that reason the commission will doubtless find it impracticable to undertake extensive investigations, but will rather confine itself to a summary of what is already known, a statement of the problem, and the recommendation of measures tending toward its solution. With the single exception of the conservation of our natural resources, which underlies the problem of rural life, there is no other material question of greater importance now before the American people. I shall look forward with the keenest interest to your report.

Sincerely, yours,                                                    THEODORE ROOSEVELT.

Prof. L. H. BAILEY,
    *New York State College of Agriculture, Ithaca, N. Y.*

Subsequently Charles S. Barrett, of Georgia, and William A. Beard, of California, were added to the commission.

The means that may be suggested for amelioration of country life fall under one or more of three general classes: (*a*) Definite recommendations for executive or legislative action by the Federal Government; (*b*) suggestions for legislative enactment on the part of States; (*c*) suggestions or recommendations to the public at large as to what the commission thinks would be the most fruitful lines of action and policy on the part of individuals, communities, or States.

The problem before the commission is to state, with some fullness of detail, the present conditions of country life, to point out the causes that may have led to its present lack of organization, to suggest methods by which it may be redirected, the drift to the city arrested, the natural rights of the farmer maintained, and an organized rural life developed that will promote the prosperity of the whole nation.

We are convinced that the forces that make for rural betterment must themselves be rural. We must arouse the country folk to the necessity for action, and suggest agencies which, when properly employed, will set them to work to develop a distinctly rural civilization.

In making its inquiries, the commission has had constantly in mind the relation of the farmer to his community and to society in general. It has made no inquiry into problems of technical farming except as they may have bearing on general welfare and public questions.

The commission has not assumed that country-life conditions are either good or bad, nor is it within its province to compare country conditions with city conditions; but it has assumed that we have not yet arrived at that state of society in which conditions may not be bettered.

It is our place, therefore, to point out the deficiencies rather than the advantages and the progress. In doing this we must be distinctly understood as speaking only in general terms. The conditions that we describe do not, of course, apply equally in all parts of the country, and we have not been able to make studies of the problems of particular localities.

Before discussing the shortcomings more fully, we may explain how the commission undertook its work.

The field of inquiry has been the general social, economic, sanitary, educational, and labor conditions of the open country. Within the time at its disposal, the commission has not been able to make scientific investigations into any of these questions, but, following the suggestion of the President, has endeavored to give "a summary of what is already known, a statement of the problem, and the recommendation of measures looking toward its solution." We have been able to make a rather extensive exploration or reconnoissance of the field, to arrive at a judgment as to the main deficiencies of country life in the United States to-day, and to suggest some of the means of supplying these deficiencies.

The commission and its work have met with the fullest cooperation and confidence on the part of the farmers and others, and the interest in the subject has been widespread. The people have been frank in giving information and expressing opinions, and in stating their problems and discouragements. There is every evidence that the people in rural districts have welcomed the commission as an agency that is much needed in the interest of country life, and in many of the hearings they have asked that the commission be continued in order that it may make thorough investigations of the subjects that it has considered. The press has taken great interest in the work, and in many cases has been of special service to the commission in securing direct information from country people.

The activities of the commission have been directed mainly along four lines: The issuing of questions designed to bring out a statement of conditions in all parts of the United States; correspondence and inquiries by different members of the commission, so far as time would permit, each in a particular field; the holding of hearings in many widely separated places; discussions in local meetings held in response to a special suggestion by the President.

As a means of securing the opinions of the people themselves on some of the main aspects of country life, a set of questions was distributed, as follows:

   I. Are the farm homes in your neighborhood as good as they should be under existing conditions?

  II. Are the schools in your neighborhood training boys and girls satisfactorily for life on the farm?

 III. Do the farmers in your neighborhood get the returns they reasonably should from the sale of their products?

  IV. Do the farmers in your neighborhood receive from the railroads, highroads, trolley lines, etc., the services they reasonably should have?

   V. Do the farmers in your neighborhood receive from the United States postal service, rural telephones, etc., the service they reasonably should expect?

  VI. Are the farmers and their wives in your neighborhood satisfactorily organized to promote their mutual buying and selling interest?

 VII. Are the renters of farms in your neighborhood making a satisfactory living?

VIII. Is the supply of farm labor in your neighborhood satisfactory?

  IX. Are the conditions surrounding hired labor on the farms in your neighborhood satisfactory to the hired man?

   X. Have the farmers in your neighborhood satisfactory facilities for doing their business in banking, credit, insurance, etc.?

  XI. Are the sanitary conditions of farms in your neighborhood satisfactory?

 XII. Do the farmers and their wives and families in your neighborhood get together for mutual improvement, entertainment, and social intercourse as much as they should?

What, in your judgment, is the most important single thing to be done for the general betterment of country life?

(NOTE. Following each question are the subquestions: (a) Why? (b) What suggestions have you to make?)

About 550,000 copies of the circular questions were sent to names supplied by the United States Department of Agriculture, state experiment stations, farmers' societies, women's clubs, to rural free deliverymen, country physicians and ministers, and others. To these inquiries about 115,000 persons have now replied, mostly with much care and with every evidence of good faith. Nearly 100,000 of these circulars have been arranged and some of the information tabulated in a preliminary way by the Census Bureau. In addition to the replies to the circulars, great numbers of letters and carefully written statements have been received, making altogether an invaluable body of information, opinion, and suggestion.

Hearings were held in 24 states through all parts of the nation by the whole commission, or part of it, between November 9 and December 22, 1908; and frequently two or more long sessions were held. Very full notes were taken of the proceedings. They were attended by good audiences, in some instances overflowing the hall. At several, especially in the Northwest, delegates were in attendance representing associations and communities in the vicinity, who were anxious to present their views and needs. Speeches were numerous and usually short and pithy, and represented every sort of person concerned with rural life, including many women, who contributed much to the domestic and educational aspects of the subject. The governors and principal officials of the States were often present; and also the presidents and professors of institutions of learning, clergymen, physicians, librarians, and others, but the bulk of the speakers and audiences was country people. No attempt was made to follow a definite programme of questioning, but general discussions proceeded, with an occasional show of hands or outburst of applause to signify general assent to the speaker's words. . . .

## II. THE MAIN SPECIAL DEFICIENCIES IN COUNTRY LIFE

The numbers of problems and suggestions that have been presented to the commission in the hearings and through the correspondence are very great. We have chosen for special discussion those that are most significant and that seem most to call for immediate action. The main single deficiency is, of course, lack of the proper kind of education, but inasmuch as the redirection of educational methods is also the main remedy for the shortcomings of country life, as also of any other life, the discussion of it may be reserved for Part III.

### 1. *Disregard of the Inherent Rights of Land Workers*

Notwithstanding an almost universal recognition of the importance of agriculture to the maintenance of our people there is nevertheless a widespread disregard of the rights of the men who own and work the land. This results directly in social depression, as well as in economic disadvantage.

The organized and corporate interests represented in mining, manufacturing, merchandising, transportation, and the like, seem often to hold the idea that their business may be developed and exploited without regard to the farmers, who should, however, have an equal opportunity for enjoyment of the land, forests, and streams and of the right to buy and sell in the open markets without prejudice.

The question of the moral intention of the consolidated interests is not involved in these statements. The present condition has grown up, and without going into the reasons it is imperative that we recognize these disadvantages to country-life interests and seek to correct them. The way in which discriminating conditions may arise is well illustrated in the inequalities of taxation of farm property. It is natural that visible and stationary property should be taxed freely under our present system; it is equally natural that invisible and changeable property should tend to evade taxation. The inevitable result is that the farmer's property bears an unjust part in taxation schemes.

Nor is this disregard of the inherent rights of the land worker confined to corporations and companies or to the recognized inequalities of taxation. It is often shared by cities. Instead of taking care of their own undesirables, they often turn them off on the country districts. The "fringe" of a city thereby becomes a low-class or even vicious community, and its influence often extends far into the country districts. The commission hears complaints that hoboes are driven from the cities and towns into the country districts, where there is no machinery for controlling them.

The subjects to which we are here inviting attention are, of course, not confined to country life alone. They express an attitude toward public questions in general. We look for the development of a sentiment that will protect and promote the welfare of all the people whenever there is a conflict with the interests of a small or particular class.

The handicaps that we now have specially in mind may be stated under four heads: Speculative holding of lands; monopolistic control of streams; wastage and monopolistic control of forests; restraint of trade.

*(a) Speculative holding of lands.* Certain landowners procure large areas of agricultural land in the most available location, sometimes by questionable methods, and hold it for speculative purposes. This not only withdraws the land itself from settlement, but in many cases prevents the development of an agricultural community. The smaller landowners are isolated and unable to establish their necessary institutions or to attract the attention of the market. The holding of large areas by one party tends to develop a system of tenantry and absentee farming. The whole development may be in the direction of social and economic ineffectiveness. In parts of the West and South this evil is so pronounced that persons have requested the commission to recommend measures of relief by restricting, under law, the size of speculative holdings of agricultural lands.

A similar problem arises in respect to the utilization of the swamp lands of the United States. According to the reports of the United States Geological Survey, there are more than 75,000,000 acres of swamp land in this country, the greater part of which are capable of reclamation at probably a nominal cost as compared to their value. It is important to the development of the best type of country life that the reclamation of the lands in rural regions proceed under conditions insuring their subdivision into small farm units and their settlement by men who would both own them and till them. Some of these lands are near the centers of population. They become a menace to health, and they often prevent the development of good social conditions in very large areas of country. As a rule, they are extremely fertile. They are capable of sustaining an agricultural population numbering many millions, and the conditions under which these millions must live are properly a matter of national concern. In view of these facts, the Federal Government should act to the fullest extent of its constitutional powers in securing the reclamation of these lands under proper safeguards against speculative holding and landlordism. It may be that in the case of those lands ceded to the States for the purpose of reclamation, the greater part of which are unreclaimed, there exists a special authority on the part of the Federal Government by reason of failure to comply with the terms of the grant; and there should be a vigorous legal inquiry into the present rights of the Government with respect to them, followed, if the status warrants it, by legal steps to rescind the grants and to begin the practical work of reclamation.

*(b) Monopolistic control of streams.* The legitimate farming interests of the whole country would be vastly benefited by a systematic conservation and utilization, under the auspices of the State and Federal Governments, of our waterways, both great and small. Important advantages of these waterways are likely to be appropriated in perpetuity and without adequate return to the people by monopolistic interests that deprive the permanent agricultural inhabitants of the use of them.

The rivers are valuable to the farmers as drainage lines, as sources of irrigation supply, as carriers and equalizers of transportation rates, as a readily available power resource, and for the raising of food fish. The wise development of these and other uses is important to both agricultural and other interests; their protection from monopoly is one of the first responsibilities of government. The streams belong to the people; under a proper system of development their resources would remain an estate of all the people, and become available as needed. A broad constructive programme involving coordinate development of the many uses of streams, under conditions insuring their permanent control in the interest of the people themselves, is urgently needed, and none should be more concerned in this than the farmers.

River navigation affords the best and cheapest transportation of farm products of a nonperishable nature. The rivers afford the best means of competition with railroads, because river carriage is cheap, and because the rivers once opened by the Government for navigation are open to all, and monopoly of their use should be an impossibility. Interest in river improvement for the purpose of navigation is very keen among the farmers who actually use river transportation, and to some extent among farmers who enjoy advantages in railway rates due to parallel water lines; but the great mass of farmers, while complaining of what they affirm to be unjust and exorbitant railway rates, have given too little thought to the means of relief with which nature has favored them. This is probably due to lack of knowledge of the actual economies of river transportation. For example, one community located 200 miles from a former head of navigation ships wheat by rail to a market that is 1,033 miles distant, at a cost of 21 cents per bushel, yet it showed no interest in the reopening of the channel that would reduce the train haul to less than one-fifth the distance.

This failure to consider the waterways is probably due very largely to the high rates per ton-mile charged by railroads for short hauls. Under the present methods of fixing the railway tariffs, local rates are often almost or quite as great as between points far distant, and there is small inducement to use cheap river freights because of the cost of reaching the river banks. The remedy for this lies in two directions: It must come either from a rearrangement of freight schedules, which may involve a complete change in the present policy of the railway companies with reference thereto, or by means of competition by independent or local companies.

It must be remembered, also, that no interests inimical to the public welfare should be allowed to acquire permanent control of the stream banks. Facilities for ready and economical approach are practically as important as the channels themselves.

River transportation is not usually antagonistic to railway interests. Population and production are increasing rapidly, with corresponding increase in the demands made on transportation facilities. It may be reasonably expected that in the evolution of the transportation business, the rivers will eventually carry a large part of the freight that does not require prompt delivery, while the railways will carry that requiring expeditious handling. This is already foreseen by leading railway men; and its importance to the farmer is such that he should encourage and aid, by every means in his power, the movement for large use of the rivers. The country will produce enough business to tax both streams and railroads to their utmost.

In many regions the streams afford facilities for the development of power, which, since the successful inauguration of electrical transmission, is available for local rail lines and offers the best solution of local transportation problems. In many parts of the country local and interurban lines are providing transportation to farm areas, thereby increasing the facilities for moving crops and adding to the profit and convenience of farm life. Notwithstanding this development, however, there seems to be a very general lack of appreciation on the part of farmers of the possibilities of this water-power resource as a factor in governing transportation costs.

The streams may also be used as a source of small water power on thousands of farms. This is particularly true of the small streams. Much of the manual labor about the house and barn can be performed from transmission of power from small water wheels running on the farms themselves or in the neighborhood. This power could be used for electric lighting and for small manufacture. It is more important that small power be developed on the farms of the United States than that we harness Niagara.

Unfortunately, the tendency of the present laws is to encourage the acquisition of these resources on easy terms, or on their own terms, by the first applicants, and the power of the streams is rapidly being acquired under conditions that lead to the concentration of ownership in the hands of monopolies. This state of things constitutes a real and immediate danger, not to the country-life interests alone, but to the entire nation, and it is time that the whole people become aroused to it.

The laws under which water is appropriated or flowage rights secured for power were enacted prior to the introduction of electrical transmission, and, consequently, before there was any possibility of water power becoming of more than local importance or value. Monopoly of water power was practically impossible while the sources and uses were alike isolated, but the present ability to concentrate the power of streams and to develop transportation, manufacturing, heating, and lighting on a vast scale invites monopolization.

It appears as a result of governmental investigation that practically in the last five years there has been a very significant concentration of water powers; that this concentration has now placed about 33 per cent of the total developed water powers of the country under the control of a group of 13 companies or interests; that there are very strong economic and technical reasons forcing such concentration. The rapid concentration already accomplished, together with the obvious technical reasons for further control and the financial advantages to be gained by a substantial monopoly, justifies the fear that the concentration already accomplished is but the forerunner of a far greater degree of monopoly of water power. Unless the people become aroused to the danger to their interests, there will probably be developed a monopoly greater than any the world has yet seen.

The development of power plants and of industries using this power ought to be encouraged by every legitimate and proper means. It should not be necessary, however, to grant perpetual rights in order to encourage this development. There should be no perpetual grant of water-power privileges. On the contrary, the ownership of the people should be perpetually maintained, and grants should be in the nature of terminable franchises.

The irrigation water should be protected. Farm life in the irrigated regions is usually of an advanced type, due principally to the small size of farms and the resulting social and educational advantages and to intensive agriculture. Because of these facts the development of the arid regions by irrigation may be a distinct contribution to the improvement of the country life of the nation. In the use of streams for irrigation, as in other uses, monopoly should be discouraged. The ownership of water for irrigation is no less important than the ownership of land; "water-lordism" is as much to be feared as landlordism. In the irrigated regions the water is more valuable than the land to which it is applied; the availability of the water supply often gives to the land all the value that it has, and when this is true it must follow that the farmer must own both the water and the land if he is to be master of his own fortunes. One of the very best elements of any population is the independent home-owning farmer, and the tendency of government, so far as may be practicable, should be toward securing the ownership of the land by the man who lives on it and tills it. It should seek to vest in the farmer of the irrigated region the title to his water supply and to protect his tenure of it. The national reclamation act, under which large areas of arid land are now being placed under irrigation, is commended as a contribution to the development of a good country life in the West, not alone because it renders available for settlement large areas of previously worthless land, but still more because it insures to settlers the ownership of both the land and the water.

The need to utilize the streams is to be considered in the East as well as in the West.

The commission suggests that a special inquiry be made of the control and stream resources of the United States, with the object of protecting the people in their ownership and of reserving to agricultural uses such benefits as should be reserved for these purposes.

*(c) Wastage and control of forests.* The forests have been exploited for private gain until not only has the timber been seriously reduced, but until streams have been ruined for navigation, power, irrigation, and common water supplies and whole regions have been exposed to floods and disastrous soil erosion. Probably there has never occurred a more reckless destruction of property that of right should belong to all the people. These devastations are checked on the government lands, but similar devastation in other parts of the country is equally in need of attention. The commission has heard strong demands from farmers for the establishment of forest reservations in the White Mountains and the Southern Appalachian region to save the timber and to control the sources of streams, and no statements in opposition to the proposal. Measures should be enacted creating such reservations. The forests as well as the streams should be saved from monopolistic control.

The conservation of forests and brush on watershed areas is important to the farmer along the full length of streams, regardless of the distance between the farm and these areas. The loss of soil in denuded areas increases the menace of flood, not alone because of the more rapid run-off, but by the filling of channels and the greater erosion of stream banks when soil matter is carried in suspension.

Loss of soil by washing is a serious menace to the fertility of the American farm. A high authority on this subject recently made the statement that soil wash is "the heaviest impost borne by the American farmer."

The wood-lot property of the country needs to be saved and increased. Wood-lot yield is one of the most important crops of the farm, and is of great value to the public in controlling streams, saving the run-off, checking winds, and in adding to the attractiveness of the region. In many regions, where poor and hilly lands prevail, the town or county could well afford to purchase forest land, expecting thereby to add to the value of the property and eventually to make the forests a source of revenue. Such communal forests in Europe yield revenue to the cities and towns by which they are owned and managed.

*(d) Restraint of trade.*   The commission has heard much complaint, in all parts of the country and by all classes of farmers, of injustice, inequalities, and discrimination on the part of transportation companies and middlemen. These are the most universal direct complaints that have been presented to the commission. If the statements can be trusted, the business of farming as a whole is greatly repressed by lack of mutual understanding and good faith in the transportation and marketing of agricultural produce.

Without expressing an opinion on these questions, we feel that there should be a free understanding between transportation companies and farmers in respect to their mutual business. We find that farmers who have well-informed opinions on tariff, education, and other public questions are yet wholly uninformed in respect to the transportation man's point of view on freight rates and express rates that may be in dispute. A disposition on the part of all parties to discuss the misunderstandings fairly would probably accomplish much.

The whole matter of railway freight rates should be made more understandable. There should be a simplifying or codifying of rates that will enable the farmer or a group of farmers or of other citizens who use the railways to ascertain readily from the published tariffs the actual rate on any given commodity between two points. Railway rate making is fundamentally a matter of public importance. The rates are a large factor in the development of population; in many instances the railway rates determine both the character of the population and the development of industry. The railway companies, by their rates, may decide where the centers of distribution shall be, what areas shall develop manufactures, and other special industries. To the extent that they do this they exercise a purely public function, and for this reason alone, if for no other, the Government should exercise a wise supervision over the making and publication of rates. Favoritism to large shippers has been one of the principal abuses of the transportation business and has contributed to the growth of monopolies of trade. While rebating is largely discontinued, it is very generally believed that this favoritism is still practiced, in various forms, to an extent that works a hardship on the small shipper and the unorganized interests. Complaint is not confined to steam roads alone, but is directed toward the trolley lines as well. There is a feeling that trolley systems should be feeders to the steam roads, and that these systems, which are rapidly being extended through rural districts, should afford to farmers a freight service that is ready, rapid, and cheap. It is charged that this is not done; that steam lines discourage the use of the trolleys for freight, or absorb them and eliminate competition, to the detriment of the farm population which they should most benefit.

The Interstate Commerce Commission exercises a most valuable governmental function. It is a body to which complaint may be made of any rate considered to be unreasonable. It has been of great benefit to the farmers of the country. What is needed now is a careful study of the railway situation with a view to reaching and correcting abuses and practices still in existence that operate against the unorganized and the rural interests.

In this connection attention is invited to the fact that many States have railway commissions charged with the duty of protecting the public from paying exorbitant freight rates, and farmers who feel that they are charged more than is fair should see to it, first, that their state railway commissions are composed of men who will do their duty; and second, that these men are sustained in honest efforts to do their duty with fairness to all concerned. The charge is frequently made that these commissions are not effective; but as they are a part of the machinery of the State, it would seem that the farmers have here an excellent opportunity to serve their interests by active devotion to a plain political duty.

Dissatisfaction with the prevailing systems of marketing is very general. There is a widespread belief that certain middlemen consume a share of agricultural sales out of all proportion to the services they render, either to the consumer or the producer, making a larger profit—often without risk—in the selling of the product than the farmer makes in producing it. We have no desire to condemn middlemen as a class. We have no doubt that there are many businesses of this kind that are conducted on a square-deal basis, but we are led to believe that grave abuses are practiced by unscrupulous persons and firms, and we recommend a searching inquiry into the methods employed in the sale of produce on commission.

*(e) Remedies for the disregard of the inherent rights of the farmer.* We need, in the first place, as a people, to recognize the necessary rights of the individual farmer to the use of the native resources and agencies that go with the utilization of agricultural lands and to protect him from hindrance and encroachment in the normal development of his business. If the farmer suffers because his business is small, isolated, and unsyndicated, then it is the part of government to see that he has a natural opportunity among his fellows and a square deal.

In the second place, we need such an attitude of government, both state and national, as will safeguard the separate and individual rights of the farmer, in the interest of the public good. As a contribution toward this attitude, we commend the general policy of the present administration to safeguard the streams, forests, coal lands, and phosphate lands, and in endeavoring to develop a home-owning settlement in the irrigated regions.

At the moment, one of the most available and effective single means of giving the farmer the benefit of his natural opportunities is the enlargement of government service to the country people through the post-office. We hold that a parcels post and a postal savings bank system are necessities; and as rapidly as possible the rural free delivery of mails should be extended. Everywhere we have found the farmers demanding the parcels post. It is opposed by many merchants, transportation organizations, and established interests. We do not think that the parcels post will injure the merchant in the small town or elsewhere. Whatever will permanently benefit the farmer will benefit the country as a whole. Both town and country would readjust themselves to the new conditions. We recognize the great value of the small town to the country districts and would not see it displaced or crippled; but the character of the open country largely makes or unmakes the country town.

In order that fundamental correctives may be applied, we recommend that a thoroughgoing study or investigation be made of the relation of business practices and of taxation to the welfare of the farmer, with a view to ascertaining what discriminations and deficiencies may exist, whether legislation is needed, and to give publicity to the entire subject. This investigation should include the entire middleman system, farmers' cooperative organizations, transportation rates and practices, taxation of agricultural property, methods of securing funds on reasonable conditions for agricultural uses, and the entire range of economic questions involved in the relation of the farmer to the accustomed methods of doing business.

We find that there is need of a new general attitude toward legislation, in the way of safeguarding the farmer's natural rights and interests. It is natural that the organized and consolidated interests should be strongly in mind in the making of legislation. We recommend that the welfare of the farmer and countryman be also kept in mind in the construction of laws. We specially recommend that his interests be considered and safeguarded in any new legislation on the tariff, on regulation of railroads, control or regulating of corporations and of speculation, river, swamp, and forest legislation, and public-health regulation. At the present moment it is especially important that the farmer's interests be well considered in the revision of the tariff. One of the particular needs is such an application of the reciprocity principle as to open European markets for our flour, meats, and live cattle. One of the great economic problems of our agriculture is how to feed the corn crop and other grains profitably, for it must be fed if the fertility of the land is to be maintained; to dispose of the crop profitably requires the best markets that can be secured.

## 2. Highways

The demand for good highways is general among the farmers of the entire United States. Education and good roads are the two needs most frequently mentioned in the hearings. Highways that are usable at all times of the year are now imperative not only for the marketing of produce, but for the elevation of the social and intellectual status of the open country and the improvement of health by insuring better medical and surgical attendance.

The advantages are so well understood that arguments for better roads are not necessary here. Our respondents are now concerned largely with the methods of organizing and financing the work. With only unimportant exceptions, the farmers who have expressed themselves to us on this question consider that the Federal Government is fairly under obligation to aid in the work.

We hold that the development of a fully serviceable highways system is a matter of national concern, coordinate with the development of waterways and the conservation of our native resources. It is absolutely essential to our internal development. The first thing necessary is to provide expert supervision and direction and to develop a national plan. All the work should be cooperative between the Federal Government and the States. The question of federal appropriation for highway work in the States may well be held in abeyance until a national service is provided and tested. We suggest that the United States Government establish a highway engineering service, or equivalent organization, to be at the call of the States in working out effective and economical highway systems.

### 3. Soil Depletion and Its Effects

A condition calling for serious comment is the lessening productiveness of the land. Our farming has been largely exploitational, consisting of mining the virgin fertility. On the better lands this primitive system of land exploitation may last for two generations without results pernicious to society, but on the poorer lands the limit of satisfactory living conditions may be reached in less than one generation.

The social condition of any agricultural community is closely related to the available fertility of the soil. "Poor land, poor people," and "rough land, rough people" have long since passed into proverbs. Rich land well farmed does not necessarily mean high ideals or good society. It may mean land greed and dollar worship; but, on the other hand, high ideals can not be realized without at least a fair degree of prosperity, and this can not be secured without the maintenance of fertility.

When the land begins to yield with difficulty the farmer may move to new land, develop a system of self-sustaining agriculture (becoming thereby a real farmer), or be driven into poverty and degradation. The first of these results has been marked for many years, but it is now greatly checked because most of the available lands have been occupied. The second result—the evolution of a really scientific and self-perpetuating agriculture—is beginning to appear here and there, mostly in the long-settled regions. The drift to poverty and degradation is pronounced in many parts of the country. In every region a certain class of the population is forced to the poor lands, becoming a handicap to the community and constituting a very difficult social problem.

There are two great classes of farmers—those who make farming a real and active constructive business, as much as the successful manufacturer or merchant makes his effort a business; and those who merely passively live on the land, often because they can not do anything else, and by dint of hard work and the strictest economy manage to subsist. Each class has its difficulties. The problems of the former class are largely those arising from the man's relation to the whole at large. The farmer of the latter class is not only powerless as against trade in general, but is also more or less helpless in his own farming problems. In applying corrective measures, we must recognize these two classes of persons.

When no change of system has followed the depletion of the virgin fertility, the saddest results have followed. The former owners have often lost the land, and a system of tenantry farming has gradually developed. This is marked in all regions that are dominated by a one-crop system of agriculture. In parts of the Southern States this loss of available fertility is specially noticeable, particularly where cotton is the main if not the only crop. In some parts of the country this condition and the social results are pathetic, and particularly where the farmers, whether white or black, by reason of poverty and lack of credit and want of experience in other kinds of farming, are compelled to continue to grow cotton. Large numbers of southern farmers are still obliged to mortgage their unplanted crop to secure the means of living while it is growing; and, as a matter of course, they pay exorbitant prices for the barest necessities of life. The only security that the man can give, either to the banker or the merchant, is cotton, and this forces the continued cultivation of a crop that decreases the soil fertility in a country of open winters where the waste by erosion is necessarily at the maximum. The tenants have little interest in the land, and move from year to year in the vain hope of better luck. The average income of the tenant-farmer family growing cotton is about $150 a year; and the family usually does not raise its poultry, meat, fruit, vegetables, or breadstuffs. The landlords in large sections are little better off than the tenants. The price of the product is manipulated by speculators. The tenant farmer, and even the landlord, is preyed upon by other interests, and is practically powerless. The effect of the social stratification into landlord, tenant, and money-lending merchant still further complicates a situation that in some regions is desperate and that demands vigorous treatment.

The recent years of good prices for cotton have enabled many farmers to get out of debt and to be able to handle their own business. These farmers are then free to begin a new system of husbandry. The problems still remain, however, of how to help the man who is still in bondage.

While these conditions are specially marked in the cotton-growing States, they are arising in all regions of a single-crop system, except, perhaps, in the case of fruit regions and vegetable regions. They are beginning to appear in the exclusive wheat regions, where the yields are constantly growing less and where the social life is usually monotonous and barren. The hay-selling system of many parts of the Northeastern States presents similar results, as does also the exclusive corn growing for the general market when stock raising is not a part of the business.

The loss of fertility in the Northern States is less rapid because of the climatic conditions that arrest the winter waste; fewer landlords, and these for the most part retired farmers who live near their farms and largely control the methods of cultivating the land; and a different kind of agriculture and a different social structure. It is, however, serious enough even in the Northern States, and especially in the Mississippi Valley, particularly when lands are held as an investment by capitalists who know nothing about farming and care only for annual returns, and also when held by speculators in the hope of harvesting the unearned increment, which has been large of late years, due probably to some world-wide cause which it is beyond our province to discuss. In any case, whether North or South, it has become a matter of very serious concern, whether farmers are to continue to dominate and direct the policy of the people as they do now in large part in the more prosperous agricultural sections, or whether because of soil deterioration they shall become a dependent class or shall be tenants in name but laborers in fact and working for an uncertain wage.

Fortunately, there is abundant evidence on every hand, both North and South, that the fertility of the soil can be maintained, or where it has been greatly decreased can be restored at least approximately to its virgin fertility. The hope of the future lies in the work of the public institutions that are devoted to the new agriculture. The United States Department of Agriculture, experiment stations, colleges of agriculture, and other agencies are making great progress in correcting these and other deficiencies, and these institutions deserve the sympathetic support of all the people. The demonstration work of the Department of Agriculture in the Southern States is a marked example of the good that can be done by teaching the people how to diversify their farming and to redeem themselves from the bondage of an hereditary system. Similar work is needed in many parts of the United States, and it is already under way, in various forms, under the leadership of the land-grant institutions.

The great agricultural need of the open country is a system of diversified and rotation farming, carefully adapted in every case to the particular region. Such systems conserve the resources of the land and develop diversified and active institutions. Nor is this wastage of soil resources peculiar to one-crop systems, although it is more marked in such cases. It is a general feature of our agriculture, due to a lack of appreciation of our responsibility to society to protect and save the land. Although we have reason to be proud of our agricultural achievements, we must not close our eyes to the fact that our soil resources are still being lost through poor farming.

This lessening of soil fertility is marked in every part of the United States, even in the richest lands of the prairies. It marks the pioneer stage of land usage. It has now become an acute national danger, and the economic, social, and political problems arising out of it must at once receive the best attention of statesmen. The attention that has been given to these questions is wholly inadequate to the urgency of the dangers involved.

## 4. Agricultural Labor

There is a general, but not a universal, complaint of scarcity of farm labor. This scarcity is not an agricultural difficulty alone, but one phase for expression of the general labor-supply problem.

So long as the United States continues to be a true democracy it will have a serious labor problem. As a democracy, we honor labor, and the higher the efficiency of the labor the greater the honor. The laborer, if he has the ambition to be an efficient agent in the development of the country, will be anxious to advance from the lower to the higher forms of effort, and from being a laborer himself he becomes a director of labor. If he has nothing but his hands and brains, he aims to accumulate sufficient capital to become a tenant, and eventually to become the owner, of a farm home. A large number of our immigrants share with the native-born citizen this laudable ambition. Therefore there is a constant decrease of efficient farm labor by these upward movements.

At the same time, there is a receding column of farm owners who, through bad management, have become farm tenants, and who from farm tenants may become farm laborers. While the percentage of this class is small, there are, nevertheless, some who fail to make good, and if they are tenants farm for a living rather than as a business, and if laborers become watchers of the sun rather than efficient workers.

The farm labor problem, however, is complicated by several special conditions, such as the fact that the need for labor is not continuous, the lack of conveniences of living for the laborer, long hours, the want of companionship, and in some places the apparently low wages. Because of these conditions the necessary drift of workmen is from the open country to the town. On the part of the employer the problem is complicated by the difficulty of securing labor, even at the relatively high prices now prevailing, that is competent to handle modern farm machinery and to care for live stock and to handle the special work of the improved dairy. It is further complicated in all parts of the country by the competition of railroads, mines, and factories, which, by reason of shorter hours, apparently higher pay, and the opportunities for social diversion and often of dissipation, attract the native farm hand to the towns and cities.

The difficulty of securing good labor is so great in many parts of the country that farmers are driven to dispose of their farms, leaving their land to be worked on shares by more or less irresponsible tenants, or selling them outright, often to foreigners. All absentee and proxy farming (which seems to be increasing) creates serious social problems in the regions thus affected. There is not sufficient good labor available in the country to enable us to farm our lands under present systems of agriculture and to develop our institutions effectively. Our native labor supply could be much increased by such hygienic measures as would lessen the unnecessary death rate among country children and insure better health to workmen.

So long as the labor supply is not equal to the demand the country can not compete with the town in securing labor. The country must meet the essential conditions offered by the town or change the kind of farming.

The most marked reaction to the labor difficulty is the change in modes of farm management, whereby farming is slowly adapting itself to the situation. In some cases this change is in the nature of more intensive and businesslike methods whereby the farmer becomes able to secure a better class of labor and to employ it more continuously. More frequently, however, the change is in the nature of a simplification of the business and a less full and active farm life. In the sod regions of the Northeast the tendency is toward a simple or even a primitive nature farming, with the maximum of grazing and meadow and the minimum of hand labor. In many States the more difficult lands are being given up and machinery farming is extending. This results in an unequal development of the country as a whole, with a marked shift in the social equilibrium. The only real solution of the present labor problem must lie in improved methods of farming. These improvements will be forced by the inevitable depletion of soil fertility under any and all one-crop systems in every part of the country, and realized by the adoption on the part of intelligent, progressive farmers of a rotation of crops and a system of husbandry that will enable them to employ their labor by the year and thereby secure a higher type of workman by providing him a home with all its appurtenances. The development of local industries will also contribute to the solution of the problem.

The excessive hours of labor on farms must be shortened. This will come through the working out of the better farm scheme just mentioned and substituting planning for some of the muscular work. Already in certain regions of well-systematized diversified farming the average hours of labor are less than ten.

There is a growing tendency to rely on foreigners for the farm labor supply, although the sentiment is very strong in some regions against immigration. It is the general testimony that the native American labor is less efficient and less reliable than much of the foreign labor. This is due to the fact that the American is less pressed by the dire necessity to labor and to save, and because the better class of laborers is constantly passing on to land ownership on their own account. Because of their great industry and thrift certain foreigners are gradually taking possession of the land in some regions, and it seems to be only a question of time until they will drive out the native stock in those regions.

The most difficult rural labor problem is that of securing household help on the average farm. The larger the farm the more serious the problem becomes. The necessity of giving a suitable education to her children deprives the farm woman largely of home help; while the lure of the city, with its social diversions, more regular hours of labor, and its supposed higher respectability, deprives her of help bred and born in the country. Under these circumstances she is compelled to provide the food that requires the least labor. This simple fact explains much of the lack of variety, in the midst of the greatest possible abundance, so often complained of on the farmer's table. The development of the creamery system over large sections of the country has relieved the farmer's wife of a heavy burden. This gives the hint for further improvement. The community laundering and other work could be done in an establishment connected with the creamery. Labor-saving appliances in the future will greatly lighten the burdens of those who are willing to use them. With the teaching of home subjects in the schools, household labor will again become respectable as well as easier and more interesting.

There is widespread conviction that the farmer must give greater attention to providing good quarters to laborers and to protect them from discouragement and from the saloon. The shortage of labor seems to be the least marked where the laborer is best cared for. It is certain that farming itself must be so modified and organized as to meet the labor problem at least halfway. While all farmers feel the shortage of help, the commission has found that the best farmers usually complain least about the labor difficulty.

The liquor question has been emphasized to the commission in all parts of the country as complicating the labor question. It seems to be regarded as a burning country life problem. Intemperance is largely the result of the barrenness of farm life, particularly of the lot of the hired man. The commission has made no inquiry into intemperance as such, but it is impressed, from the testimony that has accumulated, that drunkenness is often a very serious menace to country life, and that the saloon is an institution that must be banished from at least all country districts and rural towns if our agricultural interests are to develop to the extent to which they are capable. The evil is specially damning in the South, because it seriously complicates the race problem. Certain States have recently adopted prohibitory regulations, but liquor is shipped into dry territory from adjoining regions, and the evil is thereby often increased. Dry territories must rouse themselves to self-preservation in the face of this grave danger, and legislation must be enacted that will protect them. When a State goes dry, it should be allowed to keep dry.

There is most urgent need for a quickened public sentiment on this whole question of intoxication in rural communities in order to relieve country life of one of its most threatening handicaps. At the same time it is incumbent on every person to exert his best effort to provide the open country with such intellectual and social interests as will lessen the appeal and attractiveness of the saloon.

The best labor, other things being equal, is resident labor. Such reorganization of agriculture must take place as will tend more and more to employ the man the year round and to tie him to the land. The employer bears a distinct responsibility to the laborer, and also to society, to house him well and to help him to contribute his part to the community welfare.

Eventually some kind of school or training facilities must be provided for the farm laborer to cause him to develop skill and to interest him intellectually in his work.

Some kind of simple saving institution should also be developed in order to encourage thrift on the part of the laborer. It would be well, also, to study systems of life insurance in reference to farm workmen. The establishment of postal savings banks should contribute toward greater stability of farm labor.

The development of various kinds of cooperative buying and selling associations might be expected to train workmen in habits of thrift, if the men were encouraged to join them.

## 5. Health in the Open Country

Theoretically the farm should be the most healthful place in which to live, and there are numberless farmhouses, especially of the farm-owner class, that possess most excellent modern sanitary conveniences. Still it is a fact that there are also numberless other farmhouses, especially of the tenant class, and even numerous rural schoolhouses, that do not have the rudiments of sanitary arrangement. Health conditions in many parts of the open country, therefore, are in urgent need of betterment. There are many questions of nation-wide importance, such as soil, milk, and water pollution; too much visiting in case of contagious diseases; patent medicines, advertising quacks, and intemperance; feeding of offal to animals at local slaughterhouses and general insanitary conditions of those houses not under federal or other rigid sanitary control; in some regions unwholesome and poorly prepared and monotonous diet; lack of recreation; too long hours of work.

Added to these and other conditions, are important regional questions, such as the extensive spread of the hook-worm disease in the large Gulf-Atlantic States, the prevalence of typhoid fever and malaria, and other difficulties due to neglect in the localities.

In general, the rural population is less safeguarded by boards of health than is the urban population. The physicians are farther apart and are called in later in case of sickness, and in some districts medical attendance is relatively more expensive. The necessity for disease prevention is therefore self-evident, and it becomes even more emphatic when we recall that infection may be spread from farms to cities in the streams and also in the milk, meat, and other farm products. Quite aside from the humanitarian point of view, the aggregate annual loss to the nation from insanitary conditions on the farms must, when expressed in money values, reach an enormous sum, and a betterment of these conditions is a nation-wide obligation.

There is great need for the teaching of the simplest and commonest laws of hygiene and sanitation in all the schools. The people need knowledge, and no traditions should prevent them from having it. How and what to eat, the nature of disease, the importance of fresh air, the necessity of physical training even on the farm, the ineffectiveness or even the danger of nostrums, the physical evils of intemperance, all should be known in some useful degree to every boy and girl on leaving school.

Some of the most helpful work in improving rural sanitary conditions and in relieving suffering is now proceeding from women's organizations. This work should be encouraged in every way. We especially commend the suggestion that such organizations, and other interests, provide visiting nurses for rural communities when they are needed.

We find urgent need for better supervision of public health in rural communities on the part of States and localities. The control is now likely to be exercised only when some alarming condition prevails. We think that the Federal Government should be given the right to send its health officers into the various States on request of these States, at any time, for the purpose of investigating and controlling public health; it does not now have this right except at quarantine stations, although it may attend to diseases of domestic animals. It should also engage in publicity work on this subject.

### 6. Woman's Work on the Farm

Realizing that the success of country life depends in very large degree on the woman's part, the commission has made special effort to ascertain the condition of women on the farm. Often this condition is all that can be desired, with home duties so organized that the labor is not excessive, with kindly cooperation on the part of husbands and sons, and with household machines and conveniences well provided. Very many farm homes in all parts of the country are provided with books and periodicals, musical instruments, and all the necessary amenities. There are good gardens and attractive premises and a sympathetic love of nature and of farm life on the part of the entire family.

On the other hand, the reverse of these conditions often obtains, sometimes because of pioneer conditions and more frequently because of lack of prosperity and of ideals. Conveniences for outdoor work are likely to have precedence over those for household work.

The routine work of woman on the farm is to prepare three meals a day. This regularity of duty recurs regardless of season, weather, planting, harvesting, social demands, or any other factor. The only differences in different seasons are those of degree rather than of kind. It follows, therefore, that whatever general hardships, such as poverty, isolation, lack of labor-saving devices, may exist on any given farm, the burden of these hardships falls more heavily on the farmer's wife than on the farmer himself. In general, her life is more monotonous and the more isolated, no matter what the wealth or the poverty of the family may be.

The relief to farm women must come through a general elevation of country living. The women must have more help. In particular these matters may be mentioned: Development of a cooperative spirit in the home, simplification of the diet in many cases, the building of convenient and sanitary houses, providing running water in the house and also more mechanical help, good and convenient gardens, a less exclusive ideal of money getting on the part of the farmer, providing better means of communication, as telephones, roads, and reading circles, and developing of women's organizations. These and other agencies should relieve the woman of many of her manual burdens on the one hand and interest her in outside activities on the other. The farm woman should have sufficient free time and strength so that she may serve the community by participating in its vital affairs.

We have found good women's organizations in some country districts, but as a rule such organizations are few or even none, or where they exist they merely radiate from towns. Some of the stronger central organizations are now pushing the country phase of their work with vigor. Mothers' clubs, reading clubs, church societies, home economics organizations, farmers' institutes, and other associations can accomplish much for farm women. Some of the regular farmers' organizations are now giving much attention to domestic subjects, and women participate freely in the meetings. There is much need among country women themselves of a stronger organizing sense for real cooperative betterment. It is important also that all rural organizations that are attended chiefly by men should discuss the home-making subjects, for the whole difficulty often lies with the attitude of the men.

There is the most imperative need that domestic, household, and health questions be taught in all schools. The home may well be made the center of rural school teaching. The school is capable of changing the whole attitude of the home life and the part that women should play in the development of the best country living.

## III. THE GENERAL CORRECTIVE FORCES THAT SHOULD BE SET IN MOTION

The ultimate need of the open country is the development of community effort and of social resources. Here and there the commission has found a rural neighborhood in which the farmers and their wives come together frequently and effectively for social intercourse, but these instances seem to be infrequent exceptions. There is a general lack of wholesome societies that are organized on a social basis. In the region in which the Grange is strong this need is best supplied.

There is need of the greatest diversity in country-life affairs, but there is equal need of a social cohesion operating among all these affairs and tying them all together. This life must be developed, as we have said, directly from native or resident forces. It is neither necessary nor desirable that an exclusive hamlet system be brought about in order to secure these ends. The problem before the commission is to suggest means whereby this development may be directed and hastened directly from the land.

The social disorder is usually unrecognized. If only the farms are financially profitable, the rural condition is commonly pronounced good. Country life must be made thoroughly attractive and satisfying, as well as remunerative and able to hold the center of interest throughout one's lifetime. With most persons this can come only with the development of a strong community sense of feeling. The first condition of a good country life, of course, is good and profitable farming. The farmer must be enabled to live comfortably. Much attention has been given to better farming, and the progress of a generation has been marked. Small manufacture and better handicrafts need now to receive attention, for the open country needs new industries and new interests. The schools must help to bring these things about.

The economic and industrial questions are, of course, of prime importance, and we have dealt with them; but they must all be studied in their relations to the kind of life that should ultimately be established in rural communities. The commission will fail of its purpose if it confines itself merely to providing remedies or correctives for the present and apparent troubles of the farmer, however urgent and important these troubles may be. All these matters must be conceived of as incidents or parts in a large constructive programme. We must begin a campaign for rural progress.

To this end local government must be developed to its highest point of efficiency, and all agencies that are capable of furthering a better country life must be federated. It will be necessary to set the resident forces in motion by means of outside agencies, or at least to direct them, if we are to secure the best results. It is specially necessary to develop the cooperative spirit, whereby all people participate and all become partakers.

The cohesion that is so marked among the different classes of farm folk in older countries can not be reasonably expected at this period in American development, nor is it desirable that a stratified society should be developed in this country. We have here no remnants of a feudal system, fortunately no system of entail, and no clearly drawn distinction between agricultural and other classes. We are as yet a new country with undeveloped resources, many faraway pastures which, as is well known, are always green and inviting. Our farmers have been moving, and numbers of them have not yet become so well settled as to speak habitually of their farm as "home." We have farmers from every European nation and with every phase of religious belief often grouped in large communities, naturally drawn together by a common language and a common faith, and yielding but slowly to the dominating and controlling forces of American farm life. Even where there was once social organization, as in the New England town (or township), the competition of the newly settled West and the wonderful development of urban civilization have disintegrated it. The middle-aged farmer of the Central States sells the old homestead without much hesitation or regret and moves westward to find a greater acreage for his sons and daughters. The farmer of the Middle West sells the old home and moves to the Mountain States, to the Pacific coast, to the South, to Mexico, or to Canada.

Even when permanently settled, the farmer does not easily combine with others for financial or social betterment. The training of generations has made him a strong individualist, and he has been obliged to rely mainly on himself. Self-reliance being the essence of his nature, he does not at once feel the need of cooperation for business purposes or of close association for social objects. In the main, he has been prosperous, and has not felt the need of cooperation. If he is a strong man, he prefers to depend on his own ability. If he is ambitious for social recognition, he usually prefers the society of the town to that of the country. If he wishes to educate his children, he avails himself of the schools of the city. He does not as a rule dream of a rural organization that can supply as completely as the city the four great requirements of man—health, education, occupation, society. While his brother in the city is striving by moving out of the business section into the suburbs to get as much as possible of the country in the city, he does not dream that it is possible to have most that is best of the city in the country.

The time has come when we must give as much attention to the constructive development of the open country as we have given to other affairs. This is necessary not only in the interest of the open country itself, but for the safety and progress of the nation.

It is impossible, of course, to suggest remedies for all the shortcomings of country life. The mere statement of the conditions, as we find them, ought of itself to challenge attention to the needs. We hope that this report of the commission will accelerate all the movements that are now in operation for the betterment of country life. Many of these movements are beyond the reach of legislation. The most important thing for the commission to do is to apprehend the problem and to state the conditions.

The philosophy of the situation requires that the disadvantages and handicaps that are not a natural part of the farmer's business shall be removed, and that such forces shall be encouraged and set in motion as will stimulate and direct local initiative and leadership.

The situation calls for concerted action. It must be aroused and energized. The remedies are of many kinds, and they must come slowly. We need a redirection of thought to bring about a new atmosphere, and a new social and intellectual contact with life. This means that the habits of the people must change. The change will come gradually, of course, as a result of new leadership; and the situation must develop its own leaders.

Care must be taken in all the reconstructive work to see that local initiative is relied on to the fullest extent, and that federal and even state agencies do not perform what might be done by the people in the communities. The centralized agencies should be stimulative and directive, rather than mandatory and formal. Every effort must be made to develop native resources, not only of material things, but also of people.

It is necessary to be careful, also, not to copy too closely the reconstructive methods that have been so successful in Europe. Our conditions and problems differ widely from theirs. We have no historical, social peasantry, a much less centralized form of government, unlike systems of land occupancy, wholly different farming schemes, and different economic and social systems. Our country necessities are peculiarly American.

The correctives for the social sterility of the open country are already in existence or under way, but these agencies all need to be strengthened and especially to be coordinated and federated; and the problem needs to be recognized by all the people. The regular agricultural departments and institutions are aiding in making farming profitable and attractive, and they are also giving attention to the social and community questions. There is a widespread awakening, as a result of this work. This awakening is greatly aided by the rural free delivery of mails, telephones, the gradual improvement of highways, farmers' institutes, cooperative creameries and similar organizations, and other agencies.

The good institutions of cities may often be applied or extended to the open country. It appears that the social evils are in many cases no greater in cities in proportion to the number of people than in country districts; and the very concentration of numbers draws attention to the evils in cities and leads to earlier application of remedies. Recently much attention has been directed, for example, to the subject of juvenile crime, and the probation system in place of jail sentences for young offenders is being put into operation in many places. Petty crime and immorality are certainly not lacking in rural districts, and it would seem that there is a place for the extension of the probation system to towns and villages.

Aside from the regular churches, schools, and agricultural societies, there are special organizations that are now extending their work to the open country, and others that could readily be adapted to country work. One of the most promising of these newer agencies is the rural library that is interested in its community. The libraries are increasing, and they are developing a greater sense of responsibility to the community, not only stimulating the reading habit and directing it, but becoming social centers for the neighborhood. A library, if provided with suitable rooms, can afford a convenient meeting place for many kinds of activities and thereby serve as a coordinating influence. Study clubs and traveling libraries may become parts of it. This may mean that the library will need itself to be redirected so that it will become an active rather than a passive agency; it must be much more than a collection of books.

Another new agency is the county work of the Young Men's Christian Association, which, by placing in each county a field secretary, is seeking to promote the solidarity and effectiveness of rural social life, and to extend the larger influence of the country church. The commission has met the representatives of this county work at the hearings, and is impressed with the purpose of the movement to act as a coordinating agency in rural life.

The organizations in cities and towns that are now beginning to agitate the development of better play, recreation, and entertainment offer a suggestion for country districts. It is important that recreation be made a feature of country life, but we consider it to be important that this recreation, games and entertainment, be developed as far as possible from native sources rather than to be transplanted as a kind of theatricals from exotic sources.

Other organizations that are helping the country social life, or that might be made to help it, are women's clubs, musical clubs, reading clubs, athletic and playground associations, historical and literary societies, local business men's organizations and chambers of commerce, all genuinely cooperative business societies, civic and village improvement societies, local political organizations, granges and other fraternal organizations, and all groups that associate with the church and school.

There is every indication, therefore, that the social life of the open country is in process of improvement, although the progress at the present moment has not been great. The leaders need to be encouraged by an awakened public sentiment, and all the forces should be so related to each other as to increase their total effectiveness while not interfering with the autonomy of any of them.

The proper correctives of the underlying structural deficiencies of the open country are knowledge, education, cooperative organizations, and personal leadership. These we may now discuss in more detail.

## 7. Need of Agricultural or Country Life Surveys

The time has now come when we should know in detail what our agricultural resources are. We have long been engaged in making geological surveys, largely with a view to locating our mineral wealth. The country has been explored and mapped. The main native resources have been located in a general way. We must now know what are the capabilities of every agricultural locality, for agriculture is the basis of our prosperity and farming is always a local business. We can not make the best and most permanent progress in the developing of a good country life until we have completed a very careful inventory of the entire country.

This inventory or census should take into account the detailed topography and soil conditions of the localities, the local climate, the whole character of streams and forests, the agricultural products, the cropping systems now in practice, the conditions of highways, markets, facilities in the way of transportaion and communication, the institutions and organizations, the adaptability of the neighborhood to the establishment of handicrafts and local industries, the general economic and social status of the people and the character of the people themselves, natural attractions and disadvantages, historical data, and a collation of community experience. This would result in the collection of local fact, on which we could proceed to build a scientifically and economically sound country life.

Beginnings have been made in several States in the collection of these geographical facts, mostly in connection with the land-grant colleges. The United States Department of Agriculture is beginning by means of soil surveys, study of farm management, and other investigations, and its demonstration work in the Southern States is in part of this character. These agencies are beginning the study of conditions in the localities themselves. It is a kind of extension work. All these agencies are doing good work; but we have not yet, as a people, come to an appreciation of the fact that we must take account of stock in detail as well as in the large. We are working mostly around the edges of the problem and feeling of it. The larger part of the responsibility of this work must lie with the different States, for they should develop their internal resources. The whole work should be coordinated, however, by federal agencies acting with the States, and some of the larger relations will need to be studied directly by the Federal Government itself. We must come to a thoroughly nationalized movement to understand what property we have and what uses may best be made of it. This in time will call for large appropriations by State and nation.

In estimating our natural resources we must not forget the value of scenery. This is a distinct asset, and it will be more recognized as time goes on. It will be impossible to develop a satisfactory country life without conserving all the beauty of landscape and developing the people to the point of appreciating it. In parts of the East a regular system of parking the open country of the entire State is already begun, constructing the roads, preserving the natural features, and developing the latent beauty in such a way that the whole country becomes part of one continuing landscape treatment. This in no way interferes with the agricultural utilization of the land, but rather increases it. The scenery is, in fact, capitalized, so that it adds to the property values and contributes to local patriotism and to the thrift of the commonwealth.

## 8. *Need of a Redirected Education*

The subject of paramount importance in our correspondence and in the hearings is education. In every part of the United States there seems to be one mind, on the part of those capable of judging, on the necessity of redirecting the rural schools. There is no such unanimity on any other subject. It is remarkable with what similarity of phrase the subject has been discussed in all parts of the country before the commission. Everywhere there is a demand that education have relation to living, that the schools should express the daily life, and that in the rural districts they should educate by means of agriculture and country life subjects. It is recognized that all difficulties resolve themselves in the end into a question of education.

The schools are held to be largely responsible for ineffective farming, lack of ideals, and the drift to town. This is not because the rural schools, as a whole, are declining, but because they are in a state of arrested development and have not yet put themselves in consonance with all the recently changed conditions of life. The very forces that have built up the city and town school have caused the neglect of the country school. It is probable that the farming population will willingly support better schools as soon as it becomes convinced that the schools will really be changed in such a way as to teach persons how to live.

The country communities are in need of social centers—places where persons may naturally meet, and where a real neighborhood interest exists. There is difference of opinion as to where this center should be, some persons thinking it should be in the town or village, others the library, others the church or school or grange hall. It is probable that more than one social center should develop in large and prosperous communities. Inasmuch as the school is supported by public funds, and is therefore an institution connected with the government of the community, it should form a natural organic center. If the school develops such a center, it must concern itself directly with the interests of the people. It is difficult to make people understand what this really means, for school-teaching is burdened with tradition. The school must express the best cooperation of all social and economic forces that make for the welfare of the community. Merely to add new studies will not meet the need, although it may break the ground for new ideas. The school must be fundamentally redirected, until it becomes a new kind of institution. This will require that the teacher himself be a part of the community and not a migratory factor.

The feeling that agriculture must color the work of rural public schools is beginning to express itself in the interest in nature study, in the introduction of classes in agriculture in high schools and elsewhere, and in the establishment of separate or special schools to teach farm and home subjects. These agencies will help to bring about the complete reconstruction of which we have been speaking. It is specially important that we make the most of the existing public-school system, for it is this very system that should serve the real needs of the people. The real needs of the people are not alone the arts by which they make a living, but the whole range of their customary activities. As the home is the center of our civilization, so the home subjects should be the center of every school.

The most necessary thing now to be done for public-school education in terms of country life is to arouse all the people to the necessity of such education, to coordinate the forces that are beginning to operate, and to project the work beyond the schools for youth into continuation schools for adults. The schools must represent and express the community in which they stand, although, of course, they should not be confined to the community. They should teach health and sanitation, even if it is necessary to modify the customary teaching of physiology. The teaching should be visual, direct, and applicable. Of course the whole tendency of the schools will be ethical if they teach the vital subjects truthfully; but particular care should be taken that they stand for the morals of the pupils and of the communities.

We find a general demand for federal encouragement in educational propaganda, to be in some way cooperative with the States. The people realize that the incubus of ignorance and inertia is so heavy and so widespread as to constitute a national danger, and that it should be removed as rapidly as possible. It will be increasingly necessary for the national and state governments to cooperate to bring about the results that are needed in agricultural and other industrial education.

The consideration of the educational problem raises the greatest single question that has come before the commission, and which the commission has to place before the American people. Education has now come to have vastly more significance than the mere establishing and maintaining of schools. The education motive has been taken into all kinds of work with the people, directly in their homes and on their farms, and it reaches mature persons as well as youths. Beyond and behind all educational work there must be an aroused intelligent public sentiment; to make this sentiment is the most important work immediately before us. The whole country is alive with educational activity. While this activity may all be good, it nevertheless needs to be directed and correlated, and all the agencies should be more or less federated.

The arousing of the people must be accomplished in terms of their daily lives or of their welfare. For the country people this means that it must be largely in terms of agriculture. Some of the colleges of agriculture are now doing this kind of work effectively although on a pitiably small scale as compared with the needs. This is extension work, by which is meant all kinds of educational effort directly with the people, both old and young, at their homes and on their farms; it comprises all educational work that is conducted away from the institution and for those who can not go to schools and colleges. The best extension work now proceeding in this country—if measured by the effort to reach the people in their homes and on their own ground—is that coming from some of the colleges of agriculture and the United States Department of Agriculture. Within the last five or ten years the colleges of agriculture have been able to attack the problem of rural life in a new way. This extension work includes such efforts as local agricultural surveys, demonstrations on farms, nature study, and other work in schools, boys' and girls' clubs of many kinds, crop organizations, redirection or rural societies, reading clubs, library extension lectures, traveling schools, farmers' institutes, inspections of herds, barns, crops, orchards, and farms, publications of many kinds, and similar educational effort directly in the field.

To accomplish these ends, we suggest the establishment of a nation-wide extension work. The first, or original, work of the agricultural branches of the land-grant colleges was academic in the old sense; later there was added the great field of experiment and research; there now should be added the third coordinate branch, comprising extension work, without which no college of agriculture can adequately serve its State. It is to the extension department of these colleges, if properly conducted, that we must now look for the most effective rousing of the people on the land.

In order that all public educational work in the United States may be adequately studied and guided, we also recommend that the United States Bureau of Education be enlarged and supported in such a way that it will really represent the educational activities of the nation, becoming a clearing house, and a collecting, distributing, and investigating organization. It is now wholly inadequate to accomplish these ends. In a country in which education is said to be the national religion, this condition of our one expressly federal educational agency is pathetic. The good use already made of the small appropriations provided for the bureau shows clearly that it can render a most important service if sufficient funds are made available for its use.

## 9. Necessity of Working Together

It is of the greatest consequence that the people of the open country should learn to work together, not only for the purpose of forwarding

their economic interests and of competing with other men who are organized, but also to develop themselves and to establish an effective
community spirit. This effort should be a genuinely cooperative or common effort in which all the associated persons have a voice in the management of the organization and share proportionately in its benefits.
Many of the so-called "cooperative" organizations are really not such,
for they are likely to be controlled in the interest of a few persons rather
than for all and with no thought of the good of the community at large.
Some of the societies that are cooperative in name are really strong
centralized corporations or stock companies that have no greater interest
in the welfare of the patrons than other corporations have.

At present the cooperative spirit works itself out chiefly in business
organizations devoted to selling and buying. So far as possible, these
business organizations should have more or less social uses; but even if
the organizations can not be so used, the growth of the cooperative spirit
should of itself have great social value, and it should give the hint for
other cooperating groups. There is great need of associations in which
persons cooperate directly for social results. The primary cooperation is
social and should arise in the home, between all members of the family.

The associations that have an educational purpose are very numerous,
such as the common agricultural societies and clubs devoted to stock
raising, fruit growing, grain growing, poultry keeping, floriculture, bee
culture, and the like, mostly following the lines of occupation. These
are scarcely truly cooperative, since they usually do not effect a real
organization to accomplish a definite end, and they may meet only once
or twice a year; they hold conventions, but usually do not maintain a
continuous activity. These societies are of the greatest benefit, however,
and they have distinct social value. No doubt a great many of them
could be so reorganized or developed as to operate continuously throughout the year and become truly cooperative in effort, thereby greatly
increasing their influence and importance.

A few great farmers' organizations have included in their declarations
of purposes the whole field of social, educational, and economic work.
Of such, of national scope, are Patrons of Husbandry and the Farmers'
Union. These and similar large societies are effective in proportion as
they maintain local branches that work toward specific ends in their
communities.

While there are very many excellent agricultural cooperative organizations of many kinds, the farmers nearly everywhere complain that there
is still a great dearth of association that really helps them in buying and
selling and developing their communities. Naturally the effective cooperative groups are in the most highly developed communities; the general
farmer is yet insufficiently helped by the societies. The need is not so

much for a greater number of societies as for a more complete organization within them and for a more continuous active work.

Farmers seem to be increasingly feeling the pressure of the organized interests that sell to them and buy from them. They complain of business understandings or agreements between all dealers, from the wholesaler and jobber to the remote country merchants, that prevent farmers and their organizations from doing an independent business.

The greatest pressure on the farmer is felt in regions of undiversified one-crop farming. Under such conditions he is subject to great risk of crop failure; his land is soon reduced in productiveness; he usually does not raise his home supplies, and is therefore dependent on the store for his living, and his crop, being a staple and produced in enormous quantities, is subject to world prices and to speculation, so that he has no personal market. In the exclusive cotton and wheat regions the hardships of the farmer and the monotony of rural life are usually very marked. Similar conditions are likely to obtain in large-area stock ranging, hay raising, tobacco growing, and the like. In such regions great discontent is likely to prevail and economic heresies to breed. The remedy is diversification in farming on one hand and organization on the other.

The commission has found many organizations that seem to be satisfactorily handling the transporting, distributing, and marketing of farm products. They are often incorporated stock companies, in which the cooperators have the spur of money investment to hold them to their mutual obligations. In nearly all cases the most successful organizations are in regions that are strongly dominated by similar products, as fruit, dairy, grain, or live stock.

Two principles may be applied in these business societies: In one class the organization is in the nature of a combination, and attempts to establish prices and perhaps to control the production; in the other class the organization seeks its results by studying and understanding the natural laws of trade and taking advantage of conditions and regulating such evils as may arise, in the same spirit as a merchant studies them, or as a good farmer understands the natural laws of fertility.

With some crops, notably cotton and the grains, it is advantageous to provide cooperative warehouses in which the grower may hold his products till prices rise, and also in which scientific systems of grading of the products may be introduced. In certain fruit regions community packing houses have proved to be of the greatest benefit. In the meantime the cotton or grain in the warehouse becomes, for business purposes, practically as good as cash (subject to charge for insurance) in the form of negotiable warehouse receipts. This form of handling products is now coming to be well understood, and, combined with good systems of farming, it is capable of producing most satisfactory results.

Organized effort must come as the voluntary expression of the people; but it is essential that every State should enact laws that will stimulate and facilitate the organization of such cooperative associations, care being taken that the working of the laws be not cumbersome. These laws should provide the associations with every legal facility for the transaction of the business in which they are to engage. They are as important to the State as other organizations of capital and should be fostered with as much care, and their members and patrons be adequately safeguarded. It is especially important that these organizations be granted all the powers and advantages given to corporations or other aggregations of capital, to the end that they may meet these corporations on equal legal ground when it is necessary to compete with them. Such laws should not only protect the cooperative societies but should provide means that will allow the societies to regulate themselves, so that they may be safeguarded from becoming merely commercial organizations through the purchase or control of the stock by dealers in the products that they handle. It is not unlikely that federal laws may also be needed to encourage cooperation.

Organized associative effort may take on special forms. It is probable, for example, that cooperation to secure and to employ farm labor would be helpful. It may have for its object the securing of telephone service (which is already contributing much to country life, and is capable of contributing much more), the extension of electric lines, the improvement of highways, and other forms of betterment. Particular temporary needs of the neighborhood may be met by combined effort, and this may be made the beginning of a broader permanent organization.

A method of cooperative credit would undoubtedly prove of great service. In other countries credit associations loan money to their members on easy terms and for long enough time to cover the making of a crop, demanding security not on the property of the borrower but on the moral warranty of his character and industry. The American farmer has needed money less, perhaps, than land workers in some other countries, but he could be greatly benefited by a different system of credit, particularly where the lien system is still in operation. It would be the purpose of such systems, aside from providing loans on the best terms and with the utmost freedom consistent with safety, to keep as much as possible of the money in circulation in the open country where the values originate. The present banking systems tend to take the money out of the open country and to loan it in town or to town-centered interests. We suggest that the national-bank examiners be instructed to determine, for a series of years, what proportion of the loanable funds of rural banks is loaned to the farmers in their localities, in order that data may be secured on this question. All unnecessary drain from the open country should be checked, in order that the country may be allowed and encouraged to develop itself.

It is essential that all rural organizations, both social and economic, should develop into something like a system, or at least that all the efforts be known and studied by central authorities. There should be, in other words, a voluntary union of associative effort, from the localities to the counties, States, and the nation. Manifestly, government in the United States can not manage the work of voluntary rural organization. Personal initiative and a cultivated cooperative spirit are the very core of this kind of work; yet both State and National Government, as suggested, might exert a powerful influence toward the complete organization of rural affairs.

Steps should be taken whereby the United States Department of Agriculture, the State departments of agriculture, the land-grant colleges and experiment stations, the United States Bureau of Education, the normal and other schools, shall cooperate in a broad programme for aiding country life in such a way that each institution may do its appropriate work at the same time that it aids all the others and contributes to the general effort to develop a new rural social life.

## 10. The Country Church

This commission has no desire to give advice to the institutions of religion nor to attempt to dictate their policies. Yet any consideration of the problem of rural life that leaves out of account the function and the possibilities of the church, and of related institutions, would be grossly inadequate. This is not only because in the last analysis the country life problem is a moral problem, or that in the best development of the individual the great motives and results are religious and spiritual, but because from the pure sociological point of view the church is fundamentally a necessary institution in country life. In a peculiar way the church is intimately related to the agricultural industry. The work and the life of the farm are closely bound together, and the institutions of the country react on that life and on one another more intimately than they do in the city. This gives the rural church a position of peculiar difficulty and one of unequaled opportunity. The time has arrived when the church must take a larger leadership, both as an institution and through its pastors, in the social reorganization of rural life.

The great spiritual needs of the country community just at present are higher personal and community ideals. Rural people need to have an aspiration for the highest possible development of the community. There must be an ambition on the part of the people themselves constantly to progress in all of those things that make the community life wholesome, satisfying, educative, and complete. There must be a desire to develop a permanent environment for the country boy and girl, of which they will become passionately fond. As a pure matter of education, the countryman must learn to love the country and to have an intellectual appreciation of it. More than this, the spiritual nature of the individual must be kept thoroughly alive. His personal ideals of conduct and ambition must be cultivated.

Of course the church has an indispensable function as a conservator of morals. But from the social point of view, it is to hold aloft the torch of personal and community idealism. It must be a leader in the attempt to idealize country life.

The country church doubtless faces special difficulties. As a rule, it is a small field. The country people are conservative. Ordinarily the financial support is inadequate. Often there are too many churches in a given community. Sectarian ideas divide unduly and unfortunately. While there are many rural churches that are effective agents in the social evolution of their communities, it is true that as a whole the country church needs new direction and to assume new responsibilities. Few of the churches in the open country are provided with resident pastors. They are supplied mostly from the neighboring towns and by a representative of some single denomination. Sometimes the pulpit is supplied by pastors of different denominations in turn. Without a resident minister the church work is likely to be confined chiefly to services once a week. In many regions there is little personal visitation except in cases of sickness, death, marriage, christening, or other special circumstance. The Sunday school is sometimes continued only during the months of settled weather. There are young people's organizations to some extent, but they are often inactive or irregular. The social activity of the real country church is likely to be limited to the short informal meetings before and after services and to suppers that are held for the purpose of raising funds. Most of the gatherings are designed for the church people themselves rather than for the community. The range of social influence is therefore generally restricted to the families particularly related to the special church organization, and there is likely to be no sense of social responsibility for the entire community.

In the rural villages there are generally several or a number of churches of different denominations, one or more of which are likely to be weak. The salaries range from $400 to $1,000. Among Protestants there is considerable denominational competition and consequent jealousy or even conflict. United effort for cooperative activity is likely to be perfunctory rather than sympathetic and vital. The pastor is often overloaded with station work in neighboring communities.

It is not the purpose of the commission to discuss the difficulties of the rural church at this time nor to present a solution for them, but in the interests of rural betterment it seems proper to indicate a few considerations that seem to be fundamental.

1. In New England and in some other parts of the North the tremendous drawback of denominational rivalry is fairly well recognized and active measures for church federation are well under way. This does not mean organic union. It means cooperation for the purpose of trying to reach and influence every individual in the community. It means that "some church is to be responsible for every square mile." When a community is overchurched, it means giving up the superfluous church or churches. When a church is needed, it means a friendly agreement on the particular church to be placed there. This movement for federation is one of the most promising in the whole religious field, because it does not attempt to break down denominational influence or standards of thought. It puts emphasis, not on the church itself, but on the work to be done by the church for all men—churched and unchurched. It is possible that all parts of the country are not quite ready for federation, although a national church federation movement is under way. But it hardly seems necessary to urge that the spirit of cooperation among churches, the diminution of sectarian strife, the attempt to reach the entire community, must become the guiding principles everywhere if the rural church is long to retain its hold.

The rural church must be more completely than now a social center. This means not so much a place for holding social gatherings, although this is legitimate and desirable, but a place whence constantly emanates influences that go to build up the moral and spiritual tone of the whole community. The country church of the future is to be held responsible for the great ideals of community life as well as of personal character.

2. There should be a large extension of the work of the Young Men's Christian Association into the rural communities. There is apparently no other way to grip the hearts and lives of the boys and young men of the average country neighborhood. This association must regard itself as an ally of the church, with a special function and a special field.

3. We must have a complete conception of the country pastorate. The country pastor must be a community leader. He must know the rural problems. He must have sympathy with rural ideals and aspirations. He must love the country. He must know country life, the difficulties that the farmer has to face in his business, some of the great scientific revelations made in behalf of agriculture, the great industrial forces at work for the making or the unmaking of the farmer, the fundamental social problems of the life of the open country.

Consequently, the rural pastor must have special training for his work. Ministerial colleges and theological seminaries should unite with agricultural colleges in this preparation of the country clergyman. There should be better financial support for the clergyman. In many country districts it is pitiably small. There is little incentive for a man to stay in a country parish, and yet this residence is just what must come about. Perhaps it will require an appeal to the heroic young men, but we must have more men going into the country pastorates, not as a means of getting a foothold, but as a permanent work. The clergyman has an excellent chance for leadership in the country. In some sections he is still the dominating personality. But everywhere he may become one of the great community leaders. He is the key to the country church problem.

### 11. Personal Ideals and Local Leadership

Everything resolves itself at the end into a question of personality. Society or government can not do much for country life unless there is voluntary response in the personal ideals of those who live in the country. Inquiries by the commission, for example, find that one reason for the shift from the country to town is the lack of ideals in many country homes and even the desire of the countryman and his wife that the children do not remain on the farm. The obligation to keep as many youths on the farms as are needed there rests on the home more than on the school or on society.

It is often said that better rural institutions and more attractive homes and yards will necessarily follow an increase in profitableness of farming; but, as a matter of fact, high ideals may be quite independent of income, although they can not be realized without sufficient income to provide good support. Many of the most thrifty farmers are the least concerned about the character of the home and school and church. One often finds the most attractive and useful farm homes in the difficult farming regions. On the other hand, some of the most prosperous agricultural regions possess most unattractive farm premises and school buildings. Many persons who complain most loudly about their incomes are the last to improve their home conditions when their incomes are increased; they are more likely to purchase additional land and thereby further emphasize the barrenness of home life. Land hunger is naturally strongest in the most prosperous regions.

When an entire region or industry is not financially prosperous, it is impossible, of course, to develop the best personal and community ideals. In the cotton-growing States, for example, the greatest social and mental development has been apparent in the years of high prices for cotton; and the same is true in exclusive wheat regions, hay regions, and other large areas devoted mainly to one industry.

While it is of course necessary that the farmer receive good remuneration for his efforts, it is nevertheless true that the money consideration is frequently too exclusively emphasized in farm homes. This consideration often obscures every other interest, allowing little opportunity for the development of the intellectual, social, and moral qualities. The open country abounds in men and women of the finest ideals; yet it is necessary to say that other ends in life than the making of more money and the getting of more goods are much needed in country districts; and that this, more than anything else, will correct the unsatisfying nature of rural life.

Teachers of agriculture have placed too much relative emphasis on the remuneration and production sides of country life. Money hunger is as strong in the open country as elsewhere, and as there are fewer opportunities and demands for the expenditure of this money for others and for society, there often develops a hoarding and a lack of public spirit that is disastrous to the general good. So completely does the money purpose often control the motive that other purposes in farming often remain dormant. The complacent contentment in many rural neighborhoods is itself the very evidence of social incapacity or decay.

It must not be assumed that these deficiencies are to be charged as a fault against the farmer as a group. They are rather to be looked on as evidence of an uncorrelated and unadjusted society. Society is itself largely to blame. The social structure has been unequally developed. The townsman is likely to assume superiority and to develop the town in disregard of the real interests of the open country or even in opposition to them. The city exploits the country; the country does not exploit the city. The press still delights in archaic cartoons of the farmer. There is as much need of a new attitude on the part of the townsman as on the part of the farmer.

This leads us to say that the country ideals, while derived largely from the country itself, should not be exclusive; and the same applies to city and village ideals. There should be more frequent social intercourse on equal terms between the people of the country and those of the city or village. This community of interests is being accomplished to a degree at present, but there is hardly yet the knowledge and sympathy and actual social life that there should be between those who live on the land and those who do not. The business men's organizations of cities could well take the lead in some of this work. The country town in particular has similar interests with the open country about it; but beyond this, all people are bettered and broadened by association with those of far different environment.

We have now discussed some of the forces and agencies that will aid in bringing about a new rural society. The development of the best country life in the United States is seen, therefore, to be largely a question of guidance. The exercise of a wise advice, stimulus, and direction from some central national agency, extending over a series of years, could accomplish untold good, not only for the open country, but for all the people and for our institutions.

In the communities themselves, the same kind of guidance is needed, operating in good farming, in schools, churches, societies, and all useful public work. The great need everywhere is new and young leadership, and the commission desires to make an appeal to all young men and women who love the open country to consider this field when determining their careers. We need young people of quality, energy, capacity, aspiration, and conviction, who will live in the open country as permanent residents on farms, or as teachers, or in other useful fields, and who, while developing their own business or affairs to the greatest perfection, will still have unselfish interest in the welfare of their communities. The farming country is by no means devoid of leaders, and is not lost or incapable of helping itself, but it has been relatively overlooked by persons who are seeking great fields of usefulness. It will be well for us as a people if we recognize the opportunity for usefulness in the open country and consider that there is a call for service.

L. H. Bailey
Henry Wallace
Kenyon L. Butterfield
Walter H. Page
Gifford Pinchot
C. S. Barrett
W. A. Beard

# Mr. Dooley on National Housecleaning

## *Finley Peter Dunne*

"*Th' noise ye hear is not th' first gun iv a rivolution. It's on'y th' people iv th' United States batin' a carpet.*" *Finley Peter Dunne's comment on the fever of national reform was written at the height of his muckraking exposures of business and politics. Here, as always, Mr. Dooley's perspective made it difficult for his readers ever again to view the issues with total sobriety and earnestness.*

"*Idarem*" *Tarbell had published a two-volume study of Rockefeller's Standard Oil empire. Norman Hapgood wrote for* Collier's. *William Travis Jerome and Joseph Folk were leading reformers in city and state. Folk in particular had been made the hero of Steffens' first articles on the "shame" of the cities.*

"It looks to me," said Mr. Hennessy, "as though this counthry was goin' to th' divvle."

"Put down that magazine," said Mr. Dooley. "Now d'ye feel betther? I thought so. But I can sympathize with ye. I've been readin' thim mesilf. Time was whin I sildom throubled thim. I wanted me fiction th' day it didn't happen, an' I cud buy that fr a penny fr'm th' newsboy on th' corner. But wanst in a while some homefarin' wandhrer wud jettison wan in me place, an' I'd frequently glance through it an' find it in me lap whin I woke up. Th' magazines in thim days was very ca'ming to th' mind. Angabel an' Alfonso dashin' fr a marredge license. Prom'nent lady authoressesses makin' pomes at th' moon. Now an' thin a scrap over whether Shakespeare was enthered in his own name or was a ringer, with th' long-shot players always again Shakespeare. But no wan hurt.

Finley Peter Dunne, *Dissertations by Mr. Dooley* (New York: Scribner's, 1906), pp. 257-262.

Th' idee ye got fr'm these here publications was that life was wan glad, sweet song. If annything, ivrybody was too good to ivrybody else. Ye don't need to lock th' dure at night. Hang ye'er watch on th' knob. Why do polismen carry clubs? Answer, to knock th' roses off th' throlley-poles. They were good readin'. I liked thim th' way I like a bottle iv white pop now an' thin.

"But now whin I pick me fav'rite magazine off th' flure, what do I find? Ivrything has gone wrong. Th' wurruld is little betther thin a convict's camp. Angabel an' Alfonso ar-re about to get marrid whin it is discovered that she has a husband in Ioway an' he has a wife in Wis-consin. All th' pomes be th' lady authoressesses that used to begin: 'Oh, moon, how fair!' now begin: 'Oh, Ogden Armour, how awful!' Shake-speare's on'y mintioned as a crook. Here ye ar-re. Last edition. Just out. Full account iv th' Crimes iv Incalculated. Did ye read Larsen last month on 'Th' use iv Burglars as Burglar Alarums'? Good, was it? Thin read th' horrible disclosures about th' way Jawn C. Higgins got th' right to build a bay-window on his barber-shop at iliven forty-two Kosciusko Avnoo, South Bennington, Arkansaw. Read Wash'n'ton Bliffens's dhread-ful assault on th' board iv education iv Baraboo. Read Idarem on Jawn D.; she's a lady, but she's got th' punch. Graft ivrywhere. 'Graft in th' Insurance Comp'nies,' 'Graft in Congress,' 'Graft in th' Supreem Coort,' 'Graft be an Old Grafter,' 'Graft in Lithrachoor,' be Hinnery James; 'Graft in Its Relations to th' Higher Life,' be Dock Eliot; 'Th' Homeeric Legend an' Graft; Its Cause an' Effect; Are They th' Same? Yes and No,' be Norman Slapgood.

"An' so it goes, Hinnissy, till I'm that blue, discouraged, an' broken-hearted I cud go to th' edge iv th' wurruld an' jump off. It's a wicked, wicked, horrible, place, an' this here counthry is about th' thoughest spot in it. Is there an honest man among us? If there is throw him out. He's a spy. Is there an institution that isn't corrupt to its very foundations? Don't ye believe it. It on'y looks that way because our graft iditor hasn't got there on his rounds yet. Why, if Canada iver wants to increase her popylation all she has to do is to sind a man in a balloon over th' United States to yell: 'Stop thief!' At th' sound iv th' wurruds sivinty millyon men, women, an' little scoundhrelly childher wud skedaddle f'r th' fron-tier, an' lave Jerome, Folk, an' Bob La Follette to pull down th' blinds, close th' dure, an' hang out a sign: 'United States to rent.' I don't thrust anny man anny more. I niver did much, but now if I hear th' stealthy step iv me dearest frind at th' dure I lock th' cash dhrawer. I used to be nervous about burglars, but now I'm afraid iv a night call fr'm th' Chief Justice iv th' Supreem Coort or th' prisidint iv th' First National Bank.

"It's slowly killin' me, Hinnissy, or it wud if I thought about it. I'm

sorry George Wash'n'ton iver lived. Thomas Jefferson I hate. An' as f'r
Adam, well, if that joker iver come into this place I'd—but I mustn't
go on.

"Do I think it's all as bad as that? Well, Hinnissy, now that ye ask
me, an' seein' that Chris'mas is comin' on, I've got to tell ye that this
counthry, while wan iv th' worst in th' wurruld, is about as good as th'
next if it ain't a shade betther. But we're wan iv th' gr-reatest people in
th' wurruld to clean house, an' th' way we like best to clean th' house is
to burn it down. We come home at night an' find that th' dure has been
left open an' a few mosquitoes or life-insurance prisidints have got in,
an' we say: 'This is turr'ble. We must get rid iv these here pests.' An'
we take an axe to thim. We desthroy a lot iv furniture an' kill th' canary
bird, th' cat, th' cuckoo clock, an' a lot iv other harmless insects, but
we'll fin'lly land th' mosquitoes. If an Englishman found mosquitoes in
his house he'd first thry to kill thim, an' whin he didn't succeed he'd
say: 'What pleasant little humming-bur-rds they ar-re. Life wud be very
lonesome without thim,' and he'd domesticate thim, larn thim to sing
'Gawd Save th' King,' an' call his house Mosquito Lodge. If these here
inthrestin' life-insurance scandals had come up in Merry ol' England
we'd niver hear iv thim, because all th' boys wud be in th' House iv
Lords be this time, an' Lord Tontine wud sit hard on anny scheme to
have him searched be a lawyer fr'm Brooklyn. But with this here nation
iv ours somebody scents something wrong with th' scales at th' grocery-
store an' whips out his gun, another man turns in a fire alarm, a third
fellow sets fire to th' Presbyterian Church, a vigilance comity is formed
an' hangs ivry foorth man; an' havin' started with Rockyfellar, who's
tough an' don't mind bein' lynched, they fin'lly wind up with desthroyin'
me because th' steam laundhry has sint me home somebody else's collars.

"It reminds me, Hinnissy, iv th' time I lived at a boardin'-house kept
be a lady be th' name iv Doherty. She was a good woman, but her idee
iv life was a combination iv pneumony an' love. She was niver still. Th'
sight iv a spot on th' wall where a gintleman boorder had laid his head
afther dinner would give her nervous prostration. She was always
polishin', scrubbin', sweepin', airin'. She had a plumber in to look at th'
dhrains twice a week. Fifty-two times a year there was a rivolution in
th' house that wud've made th' Czar iv Rooshya want to go home to rest.
An' yet th' house was niver really clean. It looked as if it was to us. It
was so clean that I always was ashamed to go into it onless I'd shaved.
But Mrs. Doherty said no; it was like a pig-pen. 'I don't know what to
do,' says she. 'I'm worn out, an' it seems impossible to keep this house
clean.' 'What is th' throuble with it?' says she. 'Madam,' says me frind
Gallagher, 'wud ye have me tell ye?' he says. 'I wud,' says she. 'Well,'
says he, 'th' throuble with this house is that it is occupied entirely be

human bein's,' he says. 'If 'twas a vacant house,' he says, 'it cud aisily be kept clean,' he says.

"An' there ye ar-re, Hinnissy. Th' noise ye hear is not th' first gun iv a rivolution. It's on'y th' people iv th' United States batin' a carpet. Ye object to th' smell? That's nawthin'. We use sthrong disinfectants here. A Frinchman or an Englishman cleans house be sprinklin' th' walls with cologne; we chop a hole in th' flure an' pour in a kag iv chloride iv lime. Both are good ways. It depinds on how long ye intind to live in th' house. What were those shots? That's th' housekeeper killin' a couple iv cock-roaches with a Hotchkiss gun. Who is that yellin'? That's our ol' frind High Fi-nance bein' compelled to take his annual bath. Th' housecleanin' season is in full swing, an' there's a good deal iv dust in th' air; but I want to say to thim neighbors iv ours, who're peekin' in an' makin' remarks about th' amount iv rubbish, that over in our part iv th' wurruld we don't sweep things undher th' sofa. Let thim put that in their pipes an' smoke it."

"I think th' counthry is goin' to th' divvle," said Mr. Hinnissy, sadly.

"Hinnissy," said Mr. Dooley, "if that's so I congratylate th' wurruld."

"How's that?" asked Mr. Hennessy.

"Well," said Mr. Dooley, "f'r nearly forty years I've seen this counthry goin' to th' divvle, an' I got aboord late. An' if it's been goin' that long an' at that rate, an' has got no nearer thin it is this pleasant Chris'mas, thin th' divvle is a divvle iv a ways further off thin I feared."

# A Confession of Faith

## *Theodore Roosevelt*

*It came like a warm wind on a turning tide, clearing the sluggish fogs of Washington. In hope or in dread everyone felt the unmistakable vigor, the exuberant eagerness to govern, the boyish impulse to set in motion every engine of energy within his reach. Theodore Roosevelt, at forty-three the nation's youngest President, displayed the untiring drive of a man ten years younger. What a contrast to the preceding generation of chief executives! Only a little older than he, they had moved in their day like men in their seventies. Limited in their political vision, narrow in their cultural range, they had exemplified the meager administrative needs of a half-developed commercial economy, businessmen had assumed in the 1880's that almost anyone could run the government, and consequently almost anyone did. Roosevelt's spirit and style was a light-year removed from such mediocrity. The most versatile President since Thomas Jefferson, raised in the comfortable circumstances of the Roosevelt clan, schooled at Harvard, by choice an earnest professional in politics, he had ranched and hunted in the Dakotas, had administered a civil service, a police force, and a navy, had trained and led into battle a regiment of volunteers, had governed the most populous state in the union, and through it all wrote a dozen volumes of history and biography and corresponded actively with the literary and cultural arbiters of his generation. One of his distinguished contemporaries described him as "a combination of St. Vitus and St. Paul."*

*The contrast with the passing generation of political leaders went beyond personality. Roosevelt's predecessors hesitated to exercise their power even when Congress shared it with them; but Roosevelt was so in love with power that he could not resist wielding it even before others had quite let go. From Johnson through McKinley the party in office tended to ride off with the President; but Roosevelt, confronted with two quarreling factions which threatened to split at every fork in the road, kept them by goad and promise pulling in the direction he wished*

305

*them to go. When at last the western insurgents and the eastern stalwarts flew apart on divergent paths in defiance of the man who was no longer President, this supremely confident political warrior simply refused to choose between two horses he could not control and switched over, as it were, to a more docile bull moose, even though he did not seriously expect that it would take him very far.*

*For one of Roosevelt's most pressing and delicate tasks was to keep the Republican Party from breaking up. In the early years of the party's growth, in war, reconstruction, and reunion, its strength lay in its uneasy alliance of small freehold western farmer with the northeastern manu-facturer. Gradually the businessmen gained in influence, and the western farmers grew restive. While the political contrast between East and Mid-west was never as clear as some historians have implied, forces building up in the West with the insistence of thunderclouds threatened to swamp the prevailing Republican standpatters. The agrarian and small-town wing of the party called for the regulation of railroads and monopolies and an end to the alliance between finance capitalists and the federal treasury, favored a tariff balanced more equitably between the needs of producers and consumers everywhere, and insisted on the opportunity for local governments to heed the popular will in the building of a regulatory state free from judicial restraint. So long as Roosevelt ran the administration and bossed the party, the western bloc remained reason-ably satisfied, if not ecstatic, with occasional legislative victories and frequent promises of more. By 1909 Roosevelt had instituted a wave of spectactular antitrust prosecutions against oil, tobacco, and agricultural machinery manufacturers, and had adroitly pressed Congress into passing laws to abolish rebates, empower the government to set aside railroad rates, create new national forest reserves, and crack down on the sale of adulterated food and drugs in interstate commerce. By inclination a moderate reformer, Roosevelt was also a political realist, and he con-tinued to nudge the party leftward to accommodate the growing popular support for the midwesterners. At the same time Roosevelt made certain that Aldrich and the eastern Old Guard were kept secure in their con-trol of the party hierarchy. When he left the White House in 1909 he was outwardly confident that Taft, whose candidacy he had forced on both the doubting party leaders and the suspicious progressives, would fill the roles of political middleman and party whip as skillfully as he had filled them.*

*Roosevelt had misjudged his man. Taft possessed neither the experi-ence, the psychic energy, nor the conviction necessary to keep the right wing of the party within talking distance of the left. Passive by tempera-ment, he made a fetish of constituted authority and soon found himself siding with the Old Guard on nearly every issue that involved party regularity. The consequences were disastrous: the midterm elections of*

*1910 swept out of office substantial numbers of Republican stalwarts and a not inconsiderable number of moderates. Deprived of their essential access to the executive branch and spurred on by the victories of Democratic reformers, the swelling band of reform Republicans defied their congressional leaders and party bosses, called themselves insurgents, and formed bold plans to overthrow Taft and seize control of the party in time for a 1912 triumph. Many turned to La Follette, who announced his candidacy in 1911, swiftly constructed a platform of insurgent principles, and attracted an organization of powerful supporters who called themselves the National Progressive Republican League. Conspicuously missing from the roster was the name of Roosevelt, but La Follette believed the chances of gaining his endorsement were good. In recent months the Colonel had openly staked out an astonishingly radical position on major economic and social problems. Dubbed the New Nationalism, it plainly implied support for at least the principles of the insurgents. Liberal hopes soared. At last it appeared that Republicanism could be made over—from within.*

*But La Follette in turn had misjudged Roosevelt. For ten months the ex-President evaded all invitations to join the Progressive League. Distrusting La Follette's leadership and apparently convinced that 1912 was to be a Democratic year, Roosevelt was entirely willing to let Taft be renominated and bear the burden of defeat, leaving himself thereafter free to reorganize the party. Then in October, 1911, Roosevelt's already cooling friendship with Taft broke sharply over Taft's determination to prosecute the United States Steel Corporation for violations of the Sherman Antitrust Act, violations which were implied as having occurred in 1907 with the connivance of the White House. In white heat Roosevelt denied the implication and then proceeded to defend the wisdom of regulating large corporations by executive agreement rather than by cumbersome legal action. By nature as restless out of office as a cowpuncher without a horse, and now furious at Taft for having so slurred the man who had put him in the White House, the ex-President was not hard to convince that he himself ought to run again. "My hat is in the ring," he declared dramatically in early 1912. This was what many of La Follette's nominal supporters were waiting to hear. Scores of progressives soon deserted the League to rally behind their old friend; from the Taft forces a sizable number of regulars, sensing a winner, also joined up, while a small but crucial body of well-heeled industrialists, captained by George Perkins (of United States Steel) shortly announced that Roosevelt was now a more acceptable candidate than Taft. As the nomination neared, La Follette's candidacy disintegrated, while Roosevelt and Taft assailed each other in language which became at times almost hysterical with abuse.*

*Roosevelt quickly discovered that while he could count on the support of the mass of Republican voters, the Taft forces had gained complete command of the convention proceedings. The cries of "Thief!" were probably justified but largely irrelevant: Taft gained the nomination by methods long sanctified in political usage if not in democratic theory; and rather than surrender the party to an uncertain winner whose political views and very presence were now so irksome, the stalwarts preferred to nominate a certain loser who would not challenge their own continuous control of the party. When it became clear that Roosevelt's challenge had failed, his outraged supporters walked out. Six weeks later, in August, 1912, they returned to the same convention hall to hail Roosevelt as the candidate of the Progressive Party of America, and in response to their tumultuous welcome he addressed them in what he described as "A Confession of Faith." With two small omissions it is reprinted here as it was given.*

*If this "confession" was not radical enough, he later said, "then I do not know what radicalism is." It was more. It was a statement of long-developing personal conviction; and it was smart politics. Since Roosevelt was now not likely under any circumstances to regain the support of the Old Guard, his one chance to win the presidency lay in attracting the votes of some ultra-progressive Democrats dissatisfied with the more cautious doctrines of Woodrow Wilson. Privately Roosevelt admitted that his cause was lost, but he had destroyed his home base, and it was out of the question at this point to forsake the jubilant throng which had gathered with his prior encouragement to nominate him. His political future now seemed to hinge on how good a showing he could make against both Taft and Wilson. Were he to press closely on the winner's heels, he would possess formidable bargaining power in the negotiations he fully expected to undertake with the Republican bosses once Taft had been driven from the field. Meanwhile he must not waste his unique opportunity to construct the truly advanced bastion of progressivism which he had now come so firmly to believe in. If he could not gain victory for a truncated party, he could at least gain votes for his own future and for the future of his creed.*

*"I feel fit as a bull moose," Roosevelt had cried to the delighted reporters at the start of the campaign, and this characteristic outburst quickly provided his ebullient followers with a sorely needed party emblem. Enthusiasm, convictions, and money were abundantly in evidence at the Progressive convention that August. Politically speaking, there was little else. An almost palpable air of uplift obscured the usual political hurrah, the calculated bedlam, the cuspidors, the bourbon, and the cigars; nor did the delegates need the boost of artificial claques. In the spirit of religious enthusiasts they opened and closed the proceedings with the lilt of popular hymns bearing new verses:*

The moose has left the wooded hill; his call rings through the land.
It's a summons to the young and strong to join with willing hand:
To fight for right and country; to strike down a robber band,
And we'll go marching on.

*A similar earnestness pervaded the party platform. Solidly buttressing Roosevelt's "radicalism," it flung in the face of the dwindling conservatives in both major parties a panoply of advanced doctrines: support for sweeping electoral reforms popular among all progressives, the promises of minimum wages for women, workman's compensation and social insurance, prohibition of child labor, restrictions on labor injunctions, a tariff of moderate protection, currency reform, a graduated inheritance tax, and the popular recall of judicial decisions. Here was idealism rampant. "There was room on that platform," remarked Donald Richberg later, "for anyone who had seen Peter Pan and believed in fairies."*

*Be that as it may, the Bull Moose campaign had also found room in its command post for George Perkins and Frank Munsey, two millionaires whose financial support Roosevelt had insisted on gaining before he would even consent to run. Outraged foes of big business were numerous among the delegates, and when they discovered that Roosevelt had forced the platform committee to strike out all mention of trust-busting, some were quick to denounce Perkins and demand he take his money and go home. But in fact Roosevelt's convictions about trust regulation long antedated his friendship with Perkins; he did not need Perkins to help him keep a tight rein on the antitrust forces. Nor was Perkins likely to quit the cause, despite his threat to do so when an antitrust plank temporarily appeared in the platform. Without his money there would have been no Bull Moose ticket—and hence no popular spokesman in 1912 for the kind of trust policy Perkins so ardently desired.*

*The dangers plainly lay elsewhere. The Bull Moose Party was all head and heart, and not even two millionaires could provide it with a body. In almost no state except California were Roosevelt's supporters able to build machines and run successful candidates. Professional politicians preferred to stick with their organizations, and many reformers had no other choice if they wished to continue in politics. The remarkable vote Roosevelt gained in November revealed no revolution in the party system but an endorsement of a man of immense personal appeal, a progressive at home and a nationalist abroad, temporarily hitched to a third party whose fate probably did not concern many voters one way or another. In four more years Roosevelt was to return to the Republican Party, and most of his followers would either return with him or become Democrats. The third party was doomed. There were, its leader later remarked, "no loaves, no fishes."*

*Even in defeat Roosevelt's campaign, so well built on his "Confession of*

*Faith," seriously affected the future of progressivism. Its political vision set in motion a galaxy of younger stars: in its ranks for 1912 were enlisted Harold Ickes, George Norris, Norman Thomas, Alfred Landon, Walter Lippmann, and Dean Acheson. It pushed Wilson somewhat farther left in 1912 than he had at first seemed willing to go; by 1914 the Democrat doctrines resembled more and more the vigorous views of the Bull Moose, and two years later Wilson moved still farther in a bold reach for a slice of Roosevelt's old following, without whose support he could not have won reelection. Roosevelt's 1912 decision may also be considered in part responsible for the Republican Party's failure in the next fifteen years to accommodate itself to reform doctrines. Those who deserted the party to "stand at Armageddon" left the stalwarts in complete control of the fort. Though progressivism soon seized a few outlying states, the Old Guard were not forced to surrender the keys to the higher party bastion until the later era of Hoover, Landon, Willkie, and Dewey. And yet no single man in public life had done more than Theodore Roosevelt to pry loose the operative ideals of American politics from their rural and small-town roots. In the unchecked growth of twentieth-century industrialism these ideals required new roots, else they might have been choked off. Roosevelt was the first American of enormous ability and popularity to insist that the modern industrial system be held responsive to the ideals of a political democracy. It was because of what he fought for that his successor, Woodrow Wilson, was enabled to bring national progressivism to full flower.*

To you, men and women who have come here to this great city of this great State formally to launch a new party, a party of the people of the whole Union, the National Progressive party, I extend my hearty greeting. You are taking a bold and a greatly needed step for the service of our beloved country. The old parties are husks, with no real soul within either, divided on artificial lines, boss-ridden and privilege-controlled, each a jumble of incongruous elements, and neither daring to speak out wisely and fearlessly what should be said on the vital issues of the day. This new movement is a movement of truth, sincerity, and wisdom, a movement which proposes to put at the service of all our people the collective power of the people, through their governmental agencies, alike in the nation and in the several States. We propose boldly to face the real and great questions of the day, and not skilfully to evade them as do the old parties. We propose to raise aloft a standard to which

Theodore Roosevelt, "A Confession of Faith," address before the national convention of the Progressive Party, Chicago, August 6, 1912, reproduced in *Works*, (New York: Scribner's, 1926), xix, 358-411.

all honest men can repair, and under which all can fight, no matter what their past political differences, if they are content to face the future and no longer to dwell among the dead issues of the past. We propose to put forth a platform which shall not be a platform of the ordinary and insincere kind, but shall be a contract with the people; and, if the people accept this contract by putting us in power, we shall hold ourselves under honorable obligation to fulfil every promise it contains as loyally as if it were actually enforceable under the penalties of the law.

The prime need to-day is to face the fact that we are now in the midst of a great economic evolution. There is urgent necessity of applying both common sense and the highest ethical standard to this movement for better economic conditions among the mass of our people if we are to make it one of healthy evolution and not one of revolution. It is, from the standpoint of our country, wicked as well as foolish longer to refuse to face the real issues of the day. Only by so facing them can we go forward; and to do this we must break up the old party organizations and obliterate the old cleavage lines on the dead issues inherited from fifty years ago.

Our fight is a fundamental fight against both of the old corrupt party machines, for both are under the dominion of the plunder league of the professional politicians who are controlled and sustained by the great beneficiaries of privilege and reaction. How close is the alliance between the two machines is shown by the attitude of that portion of those northeastern newspapers, including the majority of the great dailies in all the northeastern cities—Boston, Buffalo, Springfield, Hartford, Philadelphia, and, above all, New York—which are controlled by or representative of the interests which, in popular phrase, are conveniently grouped together as the Wall Street interests. The large majority of these papers supported Judge Parker for the presidency in 1904; almost unanimously they supported Mr. Taft for the Republican nomination this year; the large majority are now supporting Professor Wilson for the election. Some of them still prefer Mr. Taft to Mr. Wilson, but all make either Mr. Taft or Mr. Wilson their first choice; and one of the ludicrous features of the campaign is that those papers supporting Professor Wilson show the most jealous partisanship for Mr. Taft whenever they think his interests are jeopardized by the Progressive movement—that, for instance, any electors will obey the will of the majority of the Republican voters at the primaries, and vote for me instead of obeying the will of the Messrs. Barnes-Penrose-Guggenheim combination by voting for Mr. Taft. No better proof can be given than this of the fact that the fundamental concern of the privileged interests is to beat the new party. Some of them would rather beat it with Mr. Wilson; others would rather beat it with Mr. Taft; but the difference between Mr. Wilson and Mr. Taft they con-

sider as trivial, as a mere matter of personal preference. Their real fight
is for either, as against the Progressives. They represent the allied re-
actionaries of the country, and they are against the new party because
to their unerring vision it is evident that the real danger to privilege comes
from the new party, and from the new party alone. The men who presided
over the Baltimore and the Chicago Conventions, and the great bosses
who controlled the two conventions, Mr. Root and Mr. Parker, Mr.
Barnes and Mr. Murphy, Mr. Penrose and Mr. Taggart, Mr. Guggenheim
and Mr. Sullivan, differ from one another of course on certain points. But
these are the differences which one corporation lawyer has with another
corporation lawyer when acting for different corporations. They come
together at once as against a common enemy when the dominion of both
is threatened by the supremacy of the people of the United States, now
aroused to the need of a national alignment on the vital economic issues
of this generation.

Neither the Republican nor the Democratic platform contains the
slightest promise of approaching the great problems of to-day either
with understanding or good faith; and yet never was there greater need
in this nation than now of understanding and of action taken in good faith,
on the part of the men and the organizations shaping our governmental
policy. Moreover, our needs are such that there should be coherent action
among those responsible for the conduct of national affairs and those
responsible for the conduct of State affairs; because our aim should be
the same in both State and nation; that is, to use the government as an
efficient agency for the practical betterment of social and economic conditions throughout this land. There are other important things to be done,
but this is the most important thing. It is preposterous to leave such a
movement in the hands of men who have broken their promises as have
the present heads of the Republician organization (not of the Republican
voters, for they in no shape represent the rank and file of the Republican
voters). These men by their deeds give the lie to their words. There is no
health in them, and they cannot be trusted. But the Democratic party is
just as little to be trusted. The Underwood-Fitzgerald combination in
the House of Representatives has shown that it cannot safely be trusted
to maintain the interests of this country abroad or to represent the interests
of the plain people at home. The control of the various State bosses in the
State organizations has been strengthened by the action at Baltimore; and
scant indeed would be the use of exchanging the whips of Messrs. Barnes,
Penrose, and Guggenheim for the scorpions of Messrs. Murphy, Taggart,
and Sullivan. Finally, the Democratic platform not only shows an utter
failure to understand either present conditions or the means of making
these conditions better but also a reckless willingness to try to attract
various sections of the electorate by making mutually incompatible

promises which there is not the slightest intention of redeeming, and which, if redeemed, would result in sheer ruin. Far-seeing patriots should turn scornfully from men who seek power on a platform which with exquisite nicety combines silly inability to understand the national needs and dishonest insincerity in promising conflicting and impossible remedies.

If this country is really to go forward along the path of social and economic justice, there must be a new party of nation-wide and non-sectional principles, a party where the titular national chiefs and the real State leaders shall be in genuine accord, a party in whose counsels the people shall be supreme, a party that shall represent in the nation and the several States alike the same cause, the cause of human rights and of governmental efficiency. At present both the old parties are controlled by professional politicians in the interests of the privileged classes, and apparently each has set up as its ideal of business and political development a government by financial despotism tempered by make-believe political assassination. Democrat and Republican alike, they represent government of the needy many by professional politicians in the interests of the rich few. This is class government, and class government of a peculiarly unwholesome kind.

It seems to me, therefore, that the time is ripe, and overripe, for a genuine Progressive movement, nation-wide and justice-loving, sprung from and responsible to the people themselves, and sundered by a great gulf from both of the old party organizations, while representing all that is best in the hopes, beliefs, and aspirations of the plain people who make up the immense majority of the rank and file of both the old parties.

The first essential in the Progressive programme is the right of the people to rule. But a few months ago our opponents were assuring us with insincere clamor that it was absurd for us to talk about desiring that the people should rule, because, as a matter of fact, the people actually do rule. Since that time the actions of the Chicago Convention, and to an only less degree of the Baltimore Convention, have shown in striking fashion how little the people do rule under our present conditions.

We should provide by national law for presidential primaries. We should provide for the election of United States senators by popular vote. We should provide for a short ballot; nothing makes it harder for the people to control their public servants than to force them to vote for so many officials that they cannot really keep track of any one of them, so that each becomes indistinguishable in the crowd around him. There must be stringent and efficient corrupt-practices acts, applying to the primaries as well as the elections; and there should be publicity of campaign contributions during the campaign.

We should provide throughout this Union for giving the people in every State the real right to rule themselves, and really and not nominally to control their public servants and their agencies for doing the public business; an incident of this being giving the people the right themselves to do this public business if they find it impossible to get what they desire through the existing agencies. I do not attempt to dogmatize as to the machinery by which this end should be achieved. In each community it must be shaped so as to correspond not merely with the needs but with the customs and ways of thought of that community, and no community has a right to dictate to any other in this matter. But wherever representative government has in actual fact become non-representative there the people should secure to themselves the initiative, the referendum, and the recall, doing it in such fashion as to make it evident that they do not intend to use these instrumentalities wantonly or frequently, but to hold them ready for use in order to correct the misdeeds or failures of the public servants when it has become evident that these misdeeds and failures cannot be corrected in ordinary and normal fashion. The administrative officer should be given full power, for otherwise he cannot do well the people's work; and the people should be given full power over him.

I do not mean that we shall abandon representative government; on the contrary, I mean that we shall devise methods by which our government shall become really representative. To use such measures as the initiative, referendum, and recall indiscriminately and promiscuously on all kinds of occasions would undoubtedly cause disaster; but events have shown that at present our institutions are not representative—at any rate in many States, and sometimes in the nation—and that we cannot wisely afford to let this condition of things remain longer uncorrected. We have permitted the growing up of a breed of politicians who, sometimes for improper political purposes, sometimes as a means of serving the great special interests of privilege which stand behind them, twist so-called representative institutions into a means of thwarting instead of expressing the deliberate and well-thought-out judgment of the people as a whole. This cannot be permitted. We choose our representatives for two purposes. In the first place, we choose them with the desire that, as experts, they shall study certain matters with which we, the people as a whole, cannot be intimately acquainted, and that as regards these matters they shall formulate a policy for our betterment. Even as regards such a policy, and the actions taken thereunder, we ourselves should have the right ultimately to vote our disapproval of it, if we feel such disapproval. But, in the next place, our representatives are chosen to carry out certain policies as to which we have definitely made up our minds, and here we expect them to represent us by doing what we have decided ought to be done. All I desire to do by securing more direct control of the governmental agents and agencies of the people is to give the people the chance to make their representatives really represent them whenever the government becomes misrepresentative instead of representative.

I have not come to this way of thinking from closet study, or as a mere matter of theory; I have been forced to it by a long experience with the actual conditions of our political life. A few years ago, for instance, there was very little demand in this country for presidential primaries. There would have been no demand now if the politicians had really endeavored to carry out the will of the people as regards nominations for President. But, largely under the influence of special privilege in the business world, there have arisen castes of politicians who not only do not represent the people, but who make their bread and butter by thwarting the wishes of the people. This is true of the bosses of both political parties in my own State of New York, and it is just as true of the bosses of one or the other political party in a great many States of the Union. The power of the people must be made supreme within the several party organizations.

In the contest which culminated six weeks ago in this city I speedily found that my chance was at a minimum in any State where I could not get an expression of the people themselves in the primaries. I found that if I could appeal to the rank and file of the Republican voters, I could generally win, whereas, if I had to appeal to the political caste—which includes the most noisy defenders of the old system—I generally lost. Moreover, I found, as a matter of fact, not as a matter of theory, that these politicians habitually and unhesitatingly resort to every species of mean swindling and cheating in order to carry their point. It is because of the general recognition of this fact that the words politics and politicians have grown to have a sinister meaning throughout this country. The bosses and their agents in the National Republican Convention at Chicago treated political theft as a legitimate political weapon. It is instructive to compare the votes of States where there were open primaries and the votes of States where there were not. In Illinois, Pennsylvania, and Ohio we had direct primaries, and the Taft machine was beaten two to one. Between and bordering on these States were Michigan, Indiana, and Kentucky. In these States we could not get direct primaries, and the politicians elected two delegates to our one. In the first three States the contests were absolutely open, absolutely honest. The rank and file expressed their wishes, and there was no taint of fraud about what they did. In the other three States the contest was marked by every species of fraud and violence on the part of our opponents, and half the Taft delegates in the Chicago Convention from these States had tainted titles. The entire Wall Street press at this moment is vigorously engaged in denouncing the direct primary system and upholding the old convention system, or, as they call it, the "old representative system." They are so doing because they know that the bosses and the powers of special privilege have tenfold the chance under the convention system that they have when the rank and file of the people can express themselves at the primaries. The nomination of Mr. Taft at Chicago was a fraud upon the rank and file of the Republican party; it was obtained only by defrauding the rank and file of the party of their right to express their choice; and such fraudulent action does not bind a single honest member of the party.

Well, what the national committee and the fraudulent majority of the national convention did at Chicago in misrepresenting the people has been done again and again in Congress, perhaps especially in the Senate, and in the State legislatures. Again and again laws demanded by the people have been refused to the people because the representatives of the people misrepresented them.

Now, my proposal is merely that we shall give to the people the power, to be used not wantonly but only in exceptional cases, themselves to see to it that the governmental action taken in their name is really the action that they desire.

The American people, and not the courts, are to determine their own fundamental policies. The people should have power to deal with the effect of the acts of all their governmental agencies. This must be extended to include the effects of judicial acts as well as the acts of the executive and legislative representatives of the people. Where the judge merely does justice as between man and man, not dealing with constitutional questions, then the interest of the public is only to see that he is a wise and upright judge. Means should be devised for making it easier than at present to get rid of an incompetent judge; means should be devised by the bar and the bench acting in conjunction with the various legislative bodies to make justice far more expeditious and more certain than at present. The stick-in-the-bark legalism, the legalism that subordinates equity to technicalities, should be recognized as a potent enemy of justice. But this is not the matter of most concern at the moment. Our prime concern is that in dealing with the fundamental law of the land, in assuming finally to interpret it, and therefore finally to make it, the acts of the courts should be subject to and not above the final control of the people as a whole. I deny that the American people have surrendered to any set of men, no matter what their position or their character, the final right to determine those fundamental questions upon which free self-government ultimately depends. The people themselves must be the ultimate makers of their own Constitution, and where their agents differ in their interpretations of the Constitution the people themselves should be given the chance, after full and deliberate judgment, authoritatively to settle what interpretation it is that their representatives shall thereafter adopt as binding.

Whenever in our constitutional system of government there exist general prohibitions that, as interpreted by the courts, nullify, or may be used to nullify, specific laws passed, and admittedly passed, in the interest of social justice, we are for such immediate law, or amendment to the Constitution, if that be necessary, as will thereafter permit a reference to the people of the public effect of such decision under forms securing full deliberation, to the end that the specific act of the legislative branch of the government thus judicially nullified, and such amendments thereof as come within its scope and purpose, may constitutionally be excepted by vote of the people from the general prohibitions, the same as if that particular act had been expressly excepted when the prohibition was adopted. This will necessitate the establishment of machinery for making much easier of amendment both the National and the several State Constitutions, especially with the view of prompt action on certain judicial decisions—action as specific and limited as that taken by the passage of the Eleventh Amendment to the National Constitution.

We are not in this decrying the courts. That was reserved for the Chicago Convention in its plank respecting impeachment. Impeachment implies the proof of dishonesty. We do not question the general honesty of the courts. But in applying to present-day social conditions the general prohibitions that were intended originally as safeguards to the citizen against the arbitrary power of government in the hands of caste and privilege, these prohibitions have been turned by the courts from safeguards against political and social privilege into barriers against political and social justice and advancement.

Our purpose is not to impugn the courts, but to emancipate them from a position where they stand in the way of social justice; and to emancipate the people, in an orderly way, from the iniquity of enforced submission to a doctrine which would turn constitutional provisions which were intended to favor social justice and advancement into prohibitions against such justice and advancement.

We in America have peculiar need thus to make the acts of the courts subject to the people, because, owing to causes which I need not now discuss, the courts have here grown to occupy a position unknown in any other country, a position of superiority over both the legislature and the Executive. Just at this time, when we have begun in this country to move toward social and industrial betterment and true industrial democracy, this attitude on the part of the courts is of grave portent, because privilege has intrenched itself in many courts just as it formerly intrenched itself in many legislative bodies and in many executive offices. Even in

England, where the constitution is based upon the theory of the supremacy of the legislative body over the courts, the cause of democracy has at times been hampered by court action. In a recent book by a notable English Liberal leader, Mr. L. T. Hobhouse, there occur the following sentences dealing with this subject:

"Labor itself had experienced the full brunt of the attack. It had come, not from the politicians, but from the judges; but in this country we have to realize that within wide limits the judges are in effect legislators, and legislators with a certain persistent bent which can be held in check only by the constant vigilance and repeated efforts of the recognized organ for the making and repeal of law."

It thus appears that even in England it is necessary to exercise vigilance in order to prevent reactionary thwarting of the popular will by courts that are subject to the power of the legislature. In the United States, where the courts are supreme over the legislature, it is vital that the people should keep in their own hands the right of interpreting their own Constitution when their public servants differ as to the interpretation.

I am well aware that every upholder of privilege, every hired agent or beneficiary of the special interests, including many well-meaning parlor reformers, will denounce all this as "Socialism" or "anarchy"—the same terms they used in the past in denouncing the movements to control the railways and to control public utilities. As a matter of fact, the propositions I make constitute neither anarchy nor Socialism, but, on the contrary, a corrective to Socialism and an antidote to anarchy.

I especially challenge the attention of the people to the need of dealing in far-reaching fashion with our human resources, and therefore our labor power. In a century and a quarter as a nation the American people have subdued and settled the vast reaches of a continent; ahead lies the greater task of building up on this foundation, by themselves, for themselves, and with themselves, an American commonwealth which in its social and economic structure shall be four square with democracy. With England striving to make good the human wreckage to which a scrap-heap scheme of industrialism has relegated her, with Germany putting the painstaking resources of an empire at the work of developing her crafts and industrial sciences, with the Far East placing in the hands of its millions the tools invented and fashioned by Western civilization, it behooves Americans to keep abreast of the great industrial changes and to show that the people themselves, through popular self-government, can meet an age of crisis with wisdom and strength.

In the last twenty years an increasing percentage of our people have come to depend on industry for their livelihood, so that to-day the wage-workers in industry rank in importance side by side with the tillers of the soil. As a people we cannot afford to let any group of citizens or any individual citizen live or labor under conditions which are injurious to the common welfare. Industry, therefore, must submit to such public regulation as will make it a means of life and health, not of death or inefficiency. We must protect the crushable elements at the base of our present industrial structure.

The first charge on the industrial statesmanship of the day is to prevent human waste. The dead weight of orphanage and depleted craftsmanship, of crippled workers and workers suffering from trade diseases, of casual labor, of insecure old age, and of household depletion due to industrial conditions are, like our depleted soils, our gashed mountainsides and flooded river-bottoms, so many strains upon the national structure, draining the reserve strength of all industries and showing beyond all peradventure the public element and public concern in industrial health.

Ultimately we desire to use the government to aid, as far as can safely be done, in helping the industrial tool-users to become in part tool-owners, just as our farmers now are. Ultimately the government may have to join more efficiently than at present in strengthening the hands of the working men who already stand at a high level, industrially and socially, and who are able by joint action to serve themselves. But the most pressing and immediate need is to deal with the cases of those who are on the level, and who are not only in need themselves, but because of their need tend to jeopardize the welfare of those who are better off.

We hold that under no industrial order, in no commonwealth, in no trade, and in no establishment should industry be carried on under conditions inimical to the social welfare. The abnormal, ruthless, spendthrift industry of establishment tends to drag down all to the level of the least considerate.

Here the sovereign responsibility of the people as a whole should be placed beyond all quibble and dispute.

The public needs have been well summarized as follows:

1. We hold that the public has a right to complete knowledge of the facts of work.

2. On the basis of these facts and with the recent discoveries of physicians and neurologists, engineers and economists, the public can formulate minimum occupational standards below which, demonstrably, work can be prosecuted only at a human deficit.

3. In the third place, we hold that all industrial conditions which fall below such standards should come within the scope of governmental action and control in the same way that subnormal sanitary conditions are subject to public regulation and for the same reason—because they threaten the general welfare.

To the first end, we hold that the constituted authorities should be empowered to require all employers to file with them for public purposes such wage scales and other data as the public element in industry demands. The movement for honest weights and measures has its counterpart in industry. All tallies, scales, and check systems should be open to public inspection and inspection of committees of the workers concerned. All deaths, injuries, and diseases due to industrial operation should be reported to public authorities.

To the second end, we hold that minimum wage commissions should be established in the nation and in each State to inquire into wages paid in various industries and to determine the standard which the public ought to sanction as a minimum; and we believe that, as a present instalment of what we hope for in the future, there should be at once established in the nation and its several States minimum standards for the wages of women, taking the present Massachusetts law as a basis from which to start and on which to improve.

We pledge the Federal Government to an investigation of industries along the lines pursued by the Bureau of Mines with the view to establishing standards of sanitation and safety; we call for the standardization of mine and factory inspection by interstate agreement or the establishment of a Federal standard. We stand for the passage of legislation in the nation and in all States providing standards of compensation for industrial accidents and death, and for diseases clearly due to the nature of conditions of industry, and we stand for the adoption by law of a fair standard of compensation for casualties resulting fatally which shall clearly fix the minimum compensation in all cases.

In the third place, certain industrial conditions fall clearly below the levels which the public to-day sanction.

We stand for a living wage. Wages are subnormal if they fail to provide a living for those who devote their time and energy to industrial occupations. The monetary equivalent of a living wage varies according to local conditions, but must include enough to secure the elements of a normal standard of living—a standard high enough to make morality possible, to provide for education and recreation, to care for immature members of the family, to maintain the family during periods of sickness, and to permit of reasonable saving for old age.

Hours are excessive if they fail to afford the worker sufficient time to recuperate and return to his work thoroughly refreshed. We hold that the night labor of women and children is abnormal and should be prohibited; we hold that the employment of women over forty-eight hours per week is abnormal and should be prohibited. We hold that the seven-day working week is abnormal, and we hold that one day of rest in seven should be provided by law. We hold that the continuous industries, operating twenty-four hours out of twenty-four, are abnormal, and where, because of public necessity or of technical reasons (such as molten metal), the twenty-four hours must be divided into two shifts of twelve hours or three shifts of eight, they should by law be divided into three of eight.

Safety conditions are abnormal when, through unguarded machinery, poisons, electrical voltage, or otherwise, the workers are subjected to unnecessary hazards of life and limb; and all such occupations should come under governmental regulation and control.

Home life is abnormal when tenement manufacture is carried on in the household. It is a serious menace to health, education, and child-hood, and should therefore be entirely prohibited. Temporary construc-tion camps are abnormal homes and should be subjected to governmental sanitary regulation.

The premature employment of children is abnormal and should be prohibited; so also the employment of women in manufacturing, com-merce, or other trades where work compels standing constantly; and also any employment of women in such trades for a period of at least eight weeks at time of childbirth.

Our aim should be to secure conditions which will tend everywhere toward regular industry, and will do away with the necessity for rush periods, followed by out-of-work seasons, which put so severe a strain on wage-workers.

It is abnormal for any industry to throw back upon the community the human wreckage due to its wear and tear, and the hazards of sickness, accident, invalidism, involuntary unemployment, and old age should be provided for through insurance. This should be made a charge in whole or in part upon the industries, the employer, the employee, and perhaps the people at large to contribute severally in some degree. Wherever such standards are not met by given establishments, by given industries, are unprovided for by a legislature, or are balked by unenlightened courts, the workers are in jeopardy, the progressive employer is penalized, and the community pays a heavy cost in lessened efficiency and in misery. What Germany has done in the way of old-age pensions or insurance should be studied by us, and the system adapted to our uses, with whatever modifications are rendered necessary by our different ways of life and habits of thought.

Working women have the same need to combine for protection that working men have; the ballot is as necessary for one class as for the other; we do not believe that with the two sexes there is identity of function; but we do believe that there should be equality of right; and therefore we favor woman suffrage. Surely, if women could vote, they would strengthen the hands of those who are endeavoring to deal in efficient fashion with evils such as the white-slave traffic; evils which can in part be dealt with nationally, but which in large part can be reached only by determined local action, such as insisting on the wide-spread publication of the names of the owners, the landlords, of houses used for immoral purposes.

No people are more vitally interested than working men and working women in questions affecting the public health. The pure-food law must be strengthened and efficiently enforced. In the National Government one department should be intrusted with all the agencies relating to the public health, from the enforcement of the pure-food law to the administration of quarantine. This department, through its special health service, would co-operate intelligently with the various State and municipal bodies established for the same end. There would be no discrimination against or for any one set of therapeutic methods, against or for any one school of medicine or system of healing; the aim would be merely to secure under one administrative body efficient sanitary regulation in the interest of the people as a whole.

There is no body of our people whose interests are more inextricably interwoven with the interests of all the people than is the case with the farmers. The Country Life Commission should be revived with greatly increased powers; its abandonment was a severe blow to the interests of our people.

The welfare of the farmer is a basic need of this nation. It is the men from the farm who in the past have taken the lead in every great movement within this nation, whether in time of war or in time of peace. It is well to have our cities prosper, but it is not well if they prosper at the expense of the country. I am glad to say that in many sections of our country there has been an extraordinary revival of recent years in intelligent interest in and work for those who live in the open country. In this movement the lead must be taken by the farmers themselves; but our people as a whole, through their governmental agencies, should back the farmers. Everything possible should be done to better the economic condition of the farmer, and also to increase the social value of the life of the farmer, the farmer's wife, and their children. The burdens of labor and loneliness bear heavily on the women in the country; their welfare should be the especial concern of all of us. Everything possible should be done to make life in the country profitable so as to be attractive from the economic standpoint and also to give an outlet among farming people for those forms of activity which now tend to make life in the cities especially desirable for ambitious men and women. There should be just the same chance to live as full, as well-rounded, and as highly useful lives in the country as in the city.

The government must co-operate with the farmer to make the farm more productive. There must be no skinning of the soil. The farm should be left to the farmer's son in better, and not worse, condition because of its cultivation. Moreover, every invention and improvement, every discovery and economy, should be at the service of the farmer in the work of production; and, in addition, he should be helped to co-operate in business fashion with his fellows, so that the money paid by the consumer for the product of the soil shall, to as large a degree as possible, go into the pockets of the man who raised that product from the soil. So long as the farmer leaves co-operative activities with their profit-sharing to the city man of business, so long will the foundations of wealth be undermined and the comforts of enlightenment be impossible in the country communities.

In every respect this nation has to learn the lessons of efficiency in production and distribution, and of avoidance of waste and destruction; we must develop and improve instead of exhausting our resources. It is entirely possible by improvements in production, in the avoidance of waste, and in business methods on the part of the farmer to give him an increased income from his farm while at the same time reducing to the consumer the price of the articles raised on the farm. Important although education is, everywhere, it has a special importance in the country. The country school must fit the country life; in the country as elsewhere, education must be hitched up with life. The country church and the country Young Men's and Young Women's Christian Associations have great parts to play. The farmers must own and work their own land; steps must be taken at once to put a stop to the tendency toward absentee landlordism and tenant-farming; this is one of the most imperative duties confronting the nation. The question of rural banking and rural credits is also of immediate importance.

The present conditions of business cannot be acepted as satisfactory. There are too many who do not prosper enough, and of the few who prosper greatly there are certainly some whose prosperity does not mean well for the country. Rational Progressives, no matter how radical, are well aware that nothing the government can do will make some men prosper, and we heartily approve the prosperity, no matter how great, of any man, if it comes as an incident to rendering service to the community; but we wish to shape conditions so that a greater number of the small men who are decent, industrious, and energetic shall be able to succeed, and so that the big man who is dishonest shall not be allowed to succeed at all.

Our aim is to control business, not to strangle it—and, above all, not to continue a policy of make-believe strangle toward big concerns that do evil, and constant menace toward both big and little concerns that do well.

Our aim is to promote prosperity, and then see to its proper division. We do not believe that any good comes to any one by a policy which means destruction of prosperity; for in such cases it is not possible to divide it because of the very obvious fact that there is nothing to divide. We wish to control big business so as to secure among other things good wages for the wage-workers and reasonable prices for the consumers. Wherever in any business the prosperity of the business man is obtained by lowering the wages of his workmen and charging an excessive price to the consumers, we wish to interfere and stop such practices. We will not submit to that kind of prosperity any more than we will submit to prosperity obtained by swindling investors or getting unfair advantages over business rivals. But it is obvious that unless the business is prosperous the wage-workers employed therein will be badly paid and the consumers badly served. Therefore not merely as a matter of justice to the business man, but from the standpoint of the self-interest of the wage-worker and the consumer, we desire that business shall prosper; but it should be so supervised as to make prosperity also take the shape of good wages to the wage-worker and reasonable prices to the consumer, while investors and business rivals are insured just treatment, and the farmer, the man who tills the soil, is protected as sedulously as the wage-worker himself.

Unfortunately, those dealing with the subject have tended to divide into two camps, each as unwise as the other. One camp has fixed its eyes only on the need of prosperity, loudly announcing that our attention must be confined to securing it in bulk, and that the division must be left to take care of itself. This is merely the plan, already tested and found wanting, of giving prosperity to the big men on top, and trusting to their mercy to let something leak through to the mass of their countrymen below—which, in effect, means that there shall be no attempt to regulate the ferocious scramble in which greed and cunning reap the largest rewards. The other set has fixed its eyes purely on the injustices of distribution, omitting all consideration of the need of having something to distribute, and advocates action which, it is true, would abolish most of the inequalities of the distribution of prosperity, but only by the unfortunately simple process of abolishing the prosperity itself. This means merely that conditions are to be evened, not up, but down, so that all shall stand on a common level, where nobody has any prosperity at all. The task of the wise radical must be to refuse to be misled by either set of false advisers; he must both favor and promote the agencies that make for prosperity, and at the same time see to it that these agencies are so used as to be primarily of service to the average man.

Again and again while I was President, from 1902 to 1908, I pointed out that under the antitrust law alone it was neither possible to put a stop to business abuses nor possible to secure the highest efficiency in the service rendered by business to the general public. The antitrust law must be kept on our statute-books, and, as hereafter shown, must be rendered more effective in the cases where it is applied. But to treat the antitrust law as an adequate, or as by itself a wise, measure of relief and betterment is a sign not of progress, but of Toryism and reaction. It has been of benefit so far as it has implied the recognition of a real and great evil, and the at least sporadic application of the principle that all men alike must obey the law. But as a sole remedy, universally applicable, it has in actual practice completely broken down; as now applied it works more mischief than benefit. It represents the waste of effort— always damaging to a community—which arises from the attempt to meet new conditions by the application of outworn remedies instead of fearlessly and in common-sense fashion facing the new conditions and devising the new remedies which alone can work effectively for good. The antitrust law, if interpreted as the Baltimore platform demands it shall be interpreted, would apply to every agency by which not merely industrial but agricultural business is carried on in this country; under such an interpretation it ought in theory to be applied universally, in which case practically all industries would stop; as a matter of fact, it is utterly out of the question to enforce it universally; and, when enforced sporadically, it causes continual unrest, puts the country at a disadvantage with its trade competitors in international commerce, hopelessly puzzles honest business men and honest farmers as to what their rights are, and yet, as has just been shown in the cases of the Standard Oil and the Tobacco Trusts, it is no real check on the great trusts at which it was in theory aimed, and indeed operates to their benefit. Moreover, if we are to compete with other nations in the markets of the world as well as to develop our own material civilization at home, we must utilize those forms of industrial organization that are indispensable to the highest industrial productivity and efficiency.

An important volume entitled "Concentration and Control" has just been issued by President Charles R. Van Hise, of the University of Wisconsin. The University of Wisconsin has been more influential than any other agency in making Wisconsin what it has become, a laboratory for wise social and industrial experiment in the betterment of conditions. President Van Hise is one of those thoroughgoing but sane and intelligent radicals from whom much of leadership is to be expected in such a matter. The subtitle of his book shows that his endeavor is to turn the attention of his countrymen toward practically solving the trust problem of the United States. In his preface he states that his aim is to suggest a way to gain the economic advantages of the concentration of industry and at the same time to guard the interests of the public, and to assist in the rule of enlightenment, reason, fair play, mutual consideration, and toleration. In sum, he shows that unrestrained competition as an economic principle has become too destructive to be permitted to exist and that the small men must be allowed to co-operate under penalty of succumbing before their big competitors; and yet such co-operation, vitally necessary to the small man, is criminal under the present law. He says:

With the alternative before the business men of cooperation or failure, we may be sure that they will cooperate. Since the law is violated by practically every group of men engaged in trade from one end of the country to the other, they do not feel that in combining they are doing a moral wrong. The selection of the individual or corporation for prosecution depends upon the arbitrary choice of the attorney-general, perhaps somewhat influenced by the odium which attaches to some of the violators of the law. They all take their chance, hoping that the blow will fall elsewhere. With general violation and sporadic enforcement of an impracticable law, we cannot hope that our people will gain respect for it.

In conclusion, there is presented as the solution of the difficulties of the present industrial situation, concentration, co-operation, and control. Through concentration we may have the economic advantages coming from magnitude of operations. Through co-operation we may limit the wastes of the competitive system. Through control by commission we may secure freedom for fair competition, elimination of unfair practices, conservation of our natural resources, fair wages, good social conditions, and reasonable prices.

Concentration and co-operation in industry in order to secure efficiency are a world-wide movement. The United States cannot resist it. If we isolate ourselves and insist upon the subdivision of industry below the highest economic efficiency and do not allow co-operation, we shall be defeated in the world's markets. We cannot adopt an economic system less efficient than our great competitors, Germany, England, France, and Austria. Either we must modify our present obsolete laws regarding concentration and co-operation so as to conform with the world movement, or else fall behind in the race for the world's markets. Concentration and co-operation are conditions imperatively essential for industrial advance; but if we allow concentration and co-operation there must be control in order to protect the people, and adequate control is only possible through the administrative commission. Hence concentration, co-operation, and control are the key-words for a scientific solution of the mighty industrial problem which now confronts this nation.

In his main thesis President Van Hise is unquestionably right. The Democratic platform offers nothing in the way of remedy for present industrial conditions except, first, the enforcement of the antitrust law in a fashion which, if words mean anything, means bringing business to a standstill; and, second, the insistence upon an archaic construction of the States'-rights doctrine in thus dealing with interstate commerce— an insistence which, in the first place, is the most flagrant possible violation of the Constitution to which the members of the Baltimore Convention assert their devotion, and which, in the next place, nullifies and makes an empty pretense of their first statement. The proposals of the platform are so conflicting and so absurd that it is hard to imagine how any attempt could be made in good faith to carry them out; but, if such attempt were sincerely made, it could only produce industrial chaos. Were such an attempt made, every man who acts honestly would have something to fear, and yet no great adroit criminal able to command the advice of the best corporation lawyers would have much to fear.

What is needed is action directly the reverse of that thus confusedly indicated. We Progressives stand for the rights of the people. When these rights can best be secured by insistence upon States' rights, then we are for States' rights; when they can best be secured by insistence upon national rights, then we are for national rights. Interstate commerce can be effectively controlled only by the nation. The States cannot control it under the Constitution, and to amend the Constitution by giving them control of it would amount to a dissolution of the government. The worst of the big trusts have always endeavored to keep alive the feeling in favor of having the States themselves, and not the nation, attempt to do this work, because they know that in the long run such effort would be ineffective. There is no surer way to prevent all successful effort to deal with the trusts than to insist that they be dealt with by the States rather than by the nation, or to create a conflict between the States and the nation on the subject. The well-meaning ignorant man who advances such a proposition does as much damage as if he were hired by the trusts themselves, for he is playing the game of every big crooked corporation in the country. The only effective way in which to regulate the trusts is through the exercise of the collective power of our people as a whole through the governmental agencies established by the Constitution for this very purpose. Grave injustice is done by the Congress when it fails to give the National Government complete power in this matter; and still graver injustice by the Federal courts when they endeavor in any way to pare down the right of the people collectively to act in this matter as they deem wise; such conduct does itself tend to cause the creation of a twilight zone in which neither the nation nor the States have power. Fortunately, the Federal courts have more and more of recent years tended to adopt the true doctrine, which is that all these matters are to be settled by the people themselves, and that the conscience of the people, and not the preferences of any servants of the people, is to be the standard in deciding what action shall be taken by the people. As Lincoln phrased it: "The [question] of national power and State rights as a principle is no other than the principle of generality and locality. Whatever concerns the whole should be confided to the whole—to the general government; while whatever concerns only the State should be left exclusively to the State."

It is utterly hopeless to attempt to control the trusts merely by the antitrust law, or by any law the same in principle, no matter what the modifications may be in detail. In the first place, these great corporations cannot possibly be controlled merely by a succession of lawsuits. The administrative branch of the government must exercise such control. The preposterous failure of the Commerce Court has shown that only damage comes from the effort to substitute judicial for administrative control of great corporations. In the next place, a loosely drawn law which promises to do everything would reduce business to complete ruin if it were not also so drawn as to accomplish almost nothing.

As construed by the Democratic platform, the antitrust law would, if it could be enforced, abolish all business of any size or any efficiency. The promise thus to apply and construe the law would undoubtedly be broken, but the mere fitful effort thus to apply it would do no good whatever, would accomplish wide-spread harm, and would bring all trust legislation into contempt. Contrast what has actually been accomplished under the interstate commerce law with what has actually been accomplished under the antitrust law. The first has, on the whole, worked in a highly efficient manner and achieved real and great results; and it promises to achieve even greater results (although I firmly believe that if the power of the commissioners grows greater, it will be necessary to make them and their superior, the President, even more completely responsible to the people for their acts). The second has occasionally done good, has usually accomplished nothing, but generally left the worst conditions wholly unchanged, and has been responsible for a considerable amount of downright and positive evil.

What is needed is the application to all industrial concerns and all co-operating interests engaged in interstate commerce in which there is either monopoly or control of the market of the principles on which we have gone in regulating transportation concerns engaged in such commerce. The antitrust law should be kept on the statute-books and strengthened so as to make it genuinely and thoroughly effective against every big concern tending to monopoly or guilty of antisocial practices. At the same time, a national industrial commission should be created which should have complete power to regulate and control all the great industrial concerns engaged in interstate business—which practically means all of them in this country. This commission should exercise over these industrial concerns like powers to those exercised over the railways by the Interstate Commerce Commission, and over the national banks by the comptroller of the currency, and additional powers if found necessary.

The establishment of such a commission would enable us to punish the individual rather than merely the corporation, just as we now do with banks, where the aim of the government is, not to close the bank, but to bring to justice personally any bank official who has gone wrong.

This commission should deal with all the abuses of the trusts—all the abuses such as those developed by the government suit against the Standard Oil and Tobacco Trusts—as the Interstate Commerce Commission now deals with rebates. It should have complete power to make the capitalization absolutely honest and put a stop to all stock watering.

Such supervision over the issuance of corporate securities would put a stop to exploitation of the people by dishonest capitalists desiring to declare dividends on watered securities, and would open this kind of industrial property to ownership by the people at large. It should have free access to the books of each corporation and power to find out exactly how it treats its employees, its rivals, and the general public. It should have power to compel the unsparing publicity of all the acts of any corporation which goes wrong. The regulation should be primarily under the administrative branch of the government, and not by lawsuit. It should prohibit and effectually punish monopoly achieved through wrong, and also actual wrongs done by industrial corporations which are not monopolies, such as the artificial raising of prices, the artificial restriction on productivity, the elimination of competition by unfair or predatory practices, and the like; leaving industrial organizations free within the limits of fair and honest dealing to promote through the inherent efficiency of organization the power of the United States as a competitive nation among nations, and the greater abundance at home that will come to our people from that power wisely exercised.

Any corporation voluntarily coming under the commission should not be prosecuted under the antitrust law as long as it obeys in good faith the orders of the commission. The commission would be able to interpret in advance, to any honest man asking the interpretation, what he may do and what he may not do in carrying on a legitimate business. Any corporation not coming under the commission should be exposed to prosecution under the antitrust law, and any corporation violating the orders of the commission should also at once become exposed to such prosecution; and when such a prosecution is successful, it should be the duty of the commission to see that the decree of the court is put into effect completely and in good faith, so that the combination is absolutely broken up, and is not allowed to come together again, nor the constituent parts thereof permitted to do business save under the conditions laid down by the commission. This last provision would prevent the repetition of such gross scandals as those attendant upon the present Administration's prosecution of the Standard Oil and the Tobacco Trusts. The Supreme Court of the United States in condemning these two trusts to dissolution used language of unsparing severity concerning their actions. But the decree was carried out in such a manner as to turn into a farce this bitter condemnation of the criminals by the highest court in the country. Not one particle of benefit to the community at large was gained; on the contrary, the prices went up to consumers, independent competitors were placed in greater jeopardy than ever before, and the possessions of the wrong-doers greatly appreciated in value. There never was a more flagrant travesty of justice, never an instance in which wealthy wrong-doers benefited more conspicuously by a law which was supposed to be aimed at them, and which undoubtedly would have brought about severe punishment of less wealthy wrong-doers.

The Progressive proposal is definite. It is practicable. We promise nothing that we cannot carry out. We promise nothing which will jeopardize honest business. We promise adequate control of all big business and the stern suppression of the evils connected with big business, and this promise we can absolutely keep.

Our proposal is to help honest business activity, however extensive, and to see that it is rewarded with fair returns so that there may be no oppression either of business men or of the common people. We propose to make it worth while for our business men to develop the most efficient business agencies for use in international trade; for it is to the interest of our whole people that we should do well in international business. But we propose to make those business agencies do complete justice to our own people.

Every dishonest business man will unquestionably prefer either the programme of the Republican convention or the programme of the Democratic convention to our proposal, because neither of these programmes means nor can mean what it purports to mean. But every honest business man, big or little, should support the Progressive programme, and it is the one and only programme which offers real hope to all our people; for it is the one programme under which the government can be used with real efficiency to see justice done by the big corporation alike to the wage-earners it employs, to the small rivals with whom it competes, to the investors who purchase its securities, and to the consumers who purchase its products, or to the general public which it ought to serve, as well as to the business man himself.

We favor co-operation in business, and ask only that it be carried on in a spirit of honesty and fairness. We are against crooked business, big or little. We are in favor of honest business, big or little. We propose to penalize conduct and not size. But all very big business, even though honestly conducted is fraught with such potentiality of menace that there should be thoroughgoing governmental control over it, so that its efficiency in promoting prosperity at home and increasing the power of the nation in international commerce may be maintained, and at the same time fair play insured to the wage-workers, the small business competitors, the investors, and the general public. Wherever it is practicable we propose to preserve competition; but where under modern conditions competition has been eliminated and cannot be successfully restored, then the government must step in and itself supply the needed control on behalf of the people as a whole.

It is imperative to the welfare of our people that we enlarge and extend our foreign commerce. We are pre-eminently fitted to do this because as a people we have developed high skill in the art of manufacturing; our business men are strong executives, strong organizers. In every way possible our Federal Government should co-operate in this important matter. Any one who has had opportunity to study and observe first-hand Germany's course in this respect must realize that their policy of co-operation between government and business has in comparatively few years made them a leading competitor for the commerce of the world. It should be remembered that they are doing this on a national scale and with large units of business, while the Democrats would have us believe that we should do it with small units of business, which would be controlled not by the National Government but by forty-nine conflicting State sovereignties. Such a policy is utterly out of keeping with the progress of the times and gives our great commercial rivals in Europe—hungry for international markets—golden opportunities of which they are rapidly taking advantage.

I very much wish that legitimate business would no longer permit itself to be frightened by the outcries of illegitimate business into believing that they have any community of interest. Legitimate business ought to understand that its interests are jeopardized when they are confounded with those of illegitimate business; and the latter, whenever threatened with just control, always tries to persuade the former that it also is endangered. As a matter of fact, if legitimate business can only be persuaded to look cool-headedly into our proposition, it is bound to support us.

There are a number of lesser, but still important, ways of improving our business situation. It is not necessary to enumerate all of them; but I desire to allude to two, which can be adopted forthwith. Our patent laws should be remodelled; patents can secure ample royalties to inventors without our permitting them to be tools of monopoly or shut out from general use; and a parcel-post, on the zone principle, should be established.

I believe in a protective tariff, but I believe in it as a principle, approached from the standpoint of the interests of the whole people, and not as a bundle of preferences to be given to favored individuals. In my opinion, the American people favor the principle of a protective tariff, but they desire such a tariff to be established primarily in the interests of the wage-worker and the consumer. The chief opposition to our tariff at the present moment comes from the general conviction that certain interests have been improperly favored by over-protection. I agree with this view. The commercial and industrial experience of this country has demonstrated the wisdom of the protective policy, but it has also demonstrated that in the application of that policy certain clearly recognized abuses have developed. It is not merely the tariff that should be revised, but the method of tariff-making and of tariff administration. Wherever nowadays an industry is to be protected it should be on the theory that such protection will serve to keep up the wages and the standard of living of the wage-worker in that industry with full regard for the interest of the consumer. To accomplish this the tariff to be levied should as nearly as is scientifically possible approximate the differential between the cost of production at home and abroad. This differential is chiefly, if not wholly, in labor cost. No duty should be permitted to stand as regards any industry unless the workers receive their full share of the benefits of that duty. In other words, there is no warrant for protection unless a legitimate share of the benefits gets into the pay-envelope of the wage-worker.

The practice of undertaking a general revision of all the schedules at one time and of securing information as to conditions in the different industries and as to rates of duty desired chiefly from those engaged in the industries, who themselves benefit directly from the rates they propose, has been demonstrated to be not only iniquitous but futile. It has afforded opportunity for practically all of the abuses which have crept into our tariff-making and our tariff administration. The day of the log-rolling tariff must end. The progressive thought of the country has recognized this fact for several years, and the time has come when all genuine Progressives should insist upon a thorough and radical change in the method of tariff-making.

The first step should be the creation of a permanent commission of nonpartisan experts whose business shall be to study scientifically all phases of tariff-making and of tariff effects. This commission should be large enough to cover all the different and widely varying branches of American industry. It should have ample powers to enable it to secure exact and reliable information. It should have authority to examine closely all correlated subjects, such as the effect of any given duty on the consumers of the article on which the duty is levied; that is, it should directly consider the question as to what any duty costs the people in the price of living. It should examine into the wages and conditions of labor and life of the workmen in any industry, so as to insure our refusing protection to any industry unless the showing as regards the share labor receives therefrom is satisfactory. This commission would be wholly different from the present unsatisfactory Tariff Board, which was created under a provision of law which failed to give it the powers indispensable if it was to do the work it should do.

It will be well for us to study the experience of Germany in considering this question. The German tariff commission has proved conclusively the efficiency and wisdom of this method of handling tariff questions. The reports of a permanent, expert, and non-partisan tariff commission would at once strike a most powerful blow against the chief iniquity of the old log-rolling method of tariff-making. . . .

The Democratic platform declares for a tariff for revenue only, asserting that a protective tariff is unconstitutional. To say that a protective tariff is unconstitutional, as the Democratic platform insists, is only excusable on a theory of the Constitution which would make it unconstitutional to legislate in any shape or way for the betterment of social and industrial conditions. The abolition of the protective tariff or the substitution for it of a tariff for revenue only, as proposed by the Democratic platform, would plunge this country into the most wide-spread industrial depression we have yet seen, and this depression would continue for an indefinite period. There is no hope from the standpoint of our people from action such as the Democrats propose. The one and only chance to secure stable and favorable business conditions in this country, while at the same time guaranteeing fair play to farmer, consumer, business man, and wage-worker, lies in the creation of such a commission as I herein advocate. Only by such a commission and only by such activities of the commission will it be possible for us to get a reasonably quick revision of the tariff schedule by schedule—revision which shall be downward and not upward, and at the same time secure a square deal not merely to the manufacturer, but to the wage-worker and to the general consumer.

There can be no more important question than the high cost of living necessities. The main purpose of the Progressive movement is to place the American people in possession of their birthright, to secure for all the American people unobstructed access to the fountains of measureless prosperity which their Creator offers them. We in this country are blessed with great natural resources, and our men and women have a very high standard of intelligence and of industrial capacity. Surely, such being the case, we cannot permanently support conditions under which each family finds it increasingly difficult to secure the necessaries of life and a fair share of its comforts through the earnings of its members. The cost of living in this country has risen during the last few years out of all proportion to the increase in the rate of most salaries and wages; the same situation confronts alike the majority of wage-workers, small business men, small professional men, the clerks, the doctors, clergymen.

Now, grave though the problem is there is one way to make it graver, and that is to deal with it insincerely, to advance false remedies, to promise the impossible. Our opponents, Republicans and Democrats alike, propose to deal with it in this way. The Republicans in their platform promise an inquiry into the facts. Most certainly there should be such inquiry. But the way the present Administration has failed to keep its promises in the past, and the rank dishonesty of action on the part of the Penrose-Barnes-Guggenheim national convention, makes their every promise worthless. The Democratic platform affects to find the entire cause of the high cost of living in the tariff, and promises to remedy it by free trade, especially free trade in the necessaries of life. In the first place, this attitude ignores the patent fact that the problem is world-wide, that everywhere, in England and France, as in Germany and Japan, it appears with greater or less severity; that in England, for instance, it has become a very severe problem, although neither the tariff nor, save to a small degree, the trusts, can there have any possible effect upon the situation. In the second place, the Democratic platform, if it is sincere, must mean that all duties will be taken off the products of the farmer. Yet most certainly we cannot afford to have the farmer struck down. The welfare of the tiller of the soil is as important as the welfare of the wage-worker himself, and we must sedulously guard both. The farmer, the producer of the necessities of life, can himself live only if he raises these necessities for a profit. On the other hand, the consumer who must have that farmer's product in order to live, must be allowed to purchase it at the lowest cost that can give the farmer his profit, and everything possible must be done to eliminate any middleman whose function does not tend to increase the cheapness of distribution of the product; and, moreover, everything must be done to stop all speculating, all gambling with the bread-basket which has even the slightest deleterious effect upon the producer and consumer. There must be legislation which will bring about a closer business relationship between the farmer and the consumer. Recently experts in the agricultural department have figured that nearly fifty per cent of the price for agricultural products paid by the consumer goes into the pockets, not of the farmer, but of various middlemen; and it is probable that over half of what is thus paid to middlemen is needless, can be saved by wise business methods (introduced through both law and custom), and can therefore be returned to the farmer and the consumer.

Through the proposed interstate industrial commission we can effectively do away with any arbitrary control by combinations of the necessities of life. Furthermore, the governments of the nation and of the several States must combine in doing everything they can to make the farmer's business profitable, so that he shall get more out of the soil, and enjoy better business facilities for marketing what he thus gets. In this manner his return will be increased while the price to the consumer is diminished. The elimination of the middleman by agricultural exchanges and by the use of improved business methods generally, the development of good roads, the reclamation of arid lands and swamplands, the improvement in the productivity of farms, the encouragement of all agencies which tend to bring people back to the soil and to make country life more interesting as well as more profitable—all these movements will help not only the farmer but the man who consumes the farmer's products.

There is urgent need of non-partisan expert examination into any tariff schedule which seems to increase the cost of living, and, unless the increase thus caused is more than countervailed by the benefit to the class of the community which actually receives the protection, it must of course mean that that particular duty must be reduced. The system of levying a tariff for the protection and encouragement of American industry so as to secure higher wages and better conditions of life for American laborers must never be perverted so as to operate for the impoverishment of those whom it was intended to benefit. But, in any event, the effect of the tariff on the cost of living is slight; any householder can satisfy himself of this fact by considering the increase in price of articles, like milk and eggs, where the influence of both the tariff and the trusts is negligible. No conditions have been shown which warrant us in believing that the abolition of the protective tariff as a whole would bring any substantial benefit to the consumer, while it would certainly cause unheard-of immediate disaster to all wage-workers, all business men, and all farmers, and in all probability would permanently lower the standard of living here. In order to show the utter futility of the belief that the abolition of the tariff and the establishment of free trade would remedy the condition complained of, all that is necessary is to look at the course of industrial events in England and in Germany during the last thirty years, the former under free trade, the latter under a protective system. During these thirty years it is a matter of common knowledge that Germany has forged ahead relatively to England, and this not only as regards the employers, but as regards the wage-earners—in short, as regards all members of the industrial classes. Doubtless, many causes have combined to produce this result; it is not to be ascribed to the tariff alone, but, on the other hand, it is evident that it could not have come about if a protective tariff were even a chief cause among many other causes of the high cost of living.

It is also asserted that the trusts are responsible for the high cost of living. I have no question that, as regards certain trusts, this is true. I also have no question that it will continue to be true just as long as the country confines itself to acting as the Baltimore platform demands that we act. This demand is, in effect, for the States and National Government to make the futile attempt to exercise forty-nine sovereign and conflicting authorities in the effort jointly to suppress the trusts, while at the same time the National Government refuses to exercise proper control over them. There will be no diminution in the cost of trust-made articles so long as our government attempts the impossible task of restoring the flintlock conditions of business sixty years ago by trusting only to a succession of law-suits under the antitrust law—a method which it has been definitely shown usually results to the benefit of any big business concern which really ought to be dissolved, but which causes disturbance and distress to multitudes of smaller concerns. Trusts which increase production—unless they do it wastefully, as in certain forms of mining and lumbering—cannot permanently increase the cost of living; it is the trusts which limit production, or which, without limiting production, take advantage of the lack of governmental control, and eliminate competition by combining to control the market, that cause an increase in the cost of living. There should be established at once, as I have elsewhere said, under the National Government an interstate industrial commission, which should exercise full supervision over the big industrial concerns doing an interstate business into which an element of monopoly enters. Where these concerns deal with the necessaries of life the commission should not shrink, if the necessity is proved, of going to the extent of exercising regulatory control over the conditions that create or determine monopoly prices.

By such action we shall certainly be able to remove the element of contributory causation on the part of the trusts and the tariff toward the high cost of living. There will remain many other elements. Wrong taxation, including failure to tax swollen inheritances and unused land and other natural resources held for speculative purposes, is one of these elements. The modern tendency to leave the country for the town is another element; and exhaustion of the soil and poor methods of raising and marketing the products of the soil make up another element, as I have already shown. Another element is that of waste and extravagance, individual and national. No laws which the wit of man can devise will avail to make the community prosperous if the average individual lives in such fasion that his expenditure always exceeds his income.

National extravagance—that is, the expenditure of money which is not warranted—we can ourselves control, and to some degree we can help in doing away with the extravagance caused by international rivalries.

These are all definite methods by which something can be accomplished in the direction of decreasing the cost of living. All taken together, will not fully meet the situation. There are in it elements which as yet we do not understand. We can be certain that the remedy proposed by the Democratic party is a quack remedy. It is just as emphatically a quack remedy as was the quack remedy, the panacea, the universal cure-all which they proposed sixteen years ago. It is instructive to compare what they now say with what they said in 1896. Only sixteen years ago they were telling us that the decrease in prices was fatal to our people, that the fall in the production of gold, and, as a consequence, the fall in the prices of commodities, was responsible for our ills. Now they ascribe these ills to diametrically opposite causes, such as the rise in the price of commodities. It may well be that the immense output of gold during the last few years is partly responsible for certain phases of the present trouble—which is an instructive commentary on the wisdom of those men who sixteen years ago insisted that the remedy for everything was to be found in the mere additional output of coin, silver and gold alike. There is no more curious delusion than that the Democratic platform is a progressive platform. The Democratic platform, representing the best thought of the acknowledged Democratic leaders at Baltimore, is purely retrogressive and reactionary. There is no progress in it. It represents an effort to go back; to put this nation of a hundred millions, existing under modern conditions, back to where it was as a nation of twenty-five millions in the days of the stage-coach and canal-boat. Such an attitude is Toryism, not Progressivism.

In addition, then, to the remedies that we can begin forthwith, there should be a fearless, intelligent, and searching inquiry into the whole subject made by an absolutely non-partisan body of experts, with no prejudices to warp their minds, no object to serve, who shall recommend any necessary remedy, heedless of what interest may be helped or hurt thereby, and caring only for the interests of the people as a whole.

We believe that there exists an imperative need for prompt legislation for the improvement of our national currency system. The experience of repeated financial crises in the last forty years has proved that the present method of issuing, through private agencies, notes secured by government bonds is both harmful and unscientific. This method was adopted as a means of financing the government during the Civil War through furnishing a domestic market for government bonds. It was largely successful in fulfilling that purpose; but that need is long past, and the system has outlived this feature of its usefulness. The issue of currency is fundamentally a governmental function. The system to be adopted should have as its basic principles soundness and elasticity. The currency should flow forth readily at the demand of commercial activity, and retire as promptly when the demand diminishes. It should be automatically sufficient for all of the legitimate needs of business in any section of the country. Only by such means can the country be freed from the danger of recurring panics. The control should be lodged with the government, and should be safeguarded against manipulation by Wall Street or the large interests. It should be made impossible to use the machinery or perquisites of the currency system for any speculative purposes. The country must be safeguarded against the overexpansion or unjust contraction of either credit or circulating medium.

There can be no greater issue than that of conservation in this country. Just as we must conserve our men, women, and children, so we must conserve the resources of the land on which they live. We must conserve the soil so that our children shall have a land that is more and not less fertile than that our fathers dwelt in. We must conserve the forests, not by disuse but by use, making them more valuable at the same time that we use them. We must conserve the mines. Moreover, we must insure so far as possible the use of certain types of great natural resources for the benefit of the people as a whole. The public should not alienate its fee in the water-power which will be of incalculable consequence as a source of power in the immediate future. The nation and the States within their several spheres should by immediate legislation keep the fee of the water-power, leasing its use only for a reasonable length of time on terms that will secure the interests of the public. Just as the nation has gone into the work of irrigation in the West, so it should go into the work of helping reclaim the swamp-lands of the South. We should undertake the complete development and control of the Mississippi as a national work, just as we have undertaken the work of building the Panama Canal. We can use the plant, and we can use the human experience, left free by the completion of the Panama Canal in so developing the Mississippi as to make it a mighty highroad of commerce, and a source of fructification and not of death to the rich and fertile lands lying along its lower length.

In the West, the forests, the grazing-lands, the reserves of every kind, should be so handled as to be in the interests of the actual settler, the actual homemaker. He should be encouraged to use them at once, but in such a way as to preserve and not exhaust them. We do not intend that our natural resources shall be exploited by the few against the interests of the many, nor do we intend to turn them over to any man who will wastefully use them by destruction, and leave to those who come after us a heritage damaged by just so much. The man in whose interests we are working is the small farmer and settler, the man who works with his own hands, who is working not only for himself but for his children, and who wishes to leave to them the fruits of his labor. His permanent welfare is the prime factor for consideration in developing the policy of conservation: for our aim is to preserve our natural resources for the public as a whole, for the average man and the average woman who make up the body of the American people.

Alaska should be developed at once, but in the interest of the actual settler. In Alaska the government has an opportunity of starting in what is almost a fresh field to work out various problems by actual experiment. The government should at once construct, own, and operate the railways in Alaska. The government should keep the fee of all the coal-fields and allow them to be operated by lessees with the condition in the lease that non-use shall operate as a forfeit. Telegraph-lines should be operated as the railways are. Moreover, it would be well in Alaska to try a system of land taxation which will, so far as possible, remove all the burdens from those who actually use the land, whether for building or for agricultural purposes, and will operate against any man who holds the land for speculation, or derives an income from it based, not on his own exertions, but on the increase in value due to activities not his own. There is very real need that this nation shall seriously prepare itself for the task of remedying social injustice and meeting social problems by well-considered governmental effort; and the best preparation for such wise action is to test by actual experiment under favorable conditions the devices which we have reason to believe will work well, but which it is difficult to apply in old settled communities without preliminary experiment.

In international affairs this country should behave toward other nations exactly as an honorable private citizen behaves toward other private citizens. We should do no wrong to any nation, weak or strong, and we should submit to no wrong. Above all, we should never in any treaty make any promise which we do not intend in good faith to fulfil. I believe it essential that our small army should be kept at a high pitch of perfection, and in no way can it be so damaged as by permitting it to become the plaything of men in Congress who wish to gratify either spite or favoritism, or to secure to localities advantages to which those localities are not entitled. The navy should be steadily built up; and the process of upbuilding must not be stopped until—and not before—it proves possible to secure by internationl agreement a general reduction of armaments. The Panama Canal must be fortified. It would have been criminal to build it if we were not prepared to fortify it and to keep our navy at such a pitch of strength as to render it unsafe for any foreign power to attack us and get control of it. . . .

Now, friends, this is my confession of faith. I have made it rather long because I wish you to know what my deepest convictions are on the great questions of to-day, so that if you choose to make me your standard-bearer in the fight you shall make your choice understanding exactly how I feel—and if, after hearing me, you think you ought to choose some one else, I shall loyally abide by your choice. The convictions to which I have come have not been arrived at as the result of study in the closet or the library, but from the knowledge I have gained through hard experience during the many years in which, under many and varied conditions, I have striven and toiled with men. I believe in a larger use of the governmental power to help remedy industrial wrongs, because it has been borne in on me by actual experience that without the exercise of such power many of the wrongs will go unremedied. I believe in a larger opportunity for the people themselves directly to participate in government and to control their governmental agents, because long experience has taught me that without such control many of their agents will represent them badly. By actual experience in office

I have found that, as a rule, I could secure the triumph of the causes in which I most believed, not from the politicians and the men who claim an exceptional right to speak in business and government, but by going over their heads and appealing directly to the people themselves. I am not under the slightest delusion as to any power that during my political career I have at any time possessed. Whatever of power I at any time had, I obtained from the people. I could exercise it only so long as, and to the extent that, the people not merely believed in me, but heartily backed me up. Whatever I did as President I was able to do only because I had the backing of the people. When on any point I did not have that backing, when on any point I differed from the people, it mattered not whether I was right or whether I was wrong, my power vanished. I tried my best to lead the people, to advise them, to tell them what I thought was right; if necessary, I never hesitated to tell them what I thought they ought to hear, even though I thought it would be unpleasant for them to hear it; but I recognized that my task was to try to lead them and not to drive them, to take them into my confidence, to try to show them that I was right, and then loyally and in good faith to accept their decision. I will do anything for the people except what my conscience tells me is wrong, and that I can do for no man and no set of men; I hold that a man cannot serve the people well unless he serves his conscience; but I hold also that where his conscience bids him refuse to do what the people desire, he should not try to continue in office against their will. Our government system should be so shaped that the public servant, when he cannot conscientiously carry out the wishes of the people, shall at their desire leave his office and not misrepresent them in office; and I hold that the public servant can by so doing, better than in any other way, serve both them and his conscience.

Surely there never was a fight better worth making than the one in which we are engaged. It little matters what befalls any one of us who for the time being stands in the forefront of the battle. I hope we shall win, and I believe that if we can wake the people to what the fight really means we shall win. But, win or lose, we shall not falter. Whatever fate may at the moment overtake any of us, the movement itself will not stop. Our cause is based on the eternal principles of righteousness; and even though we who now lead may for the time fail, in the end the cause itself shall triumph. Six weeks ago, here in Chicago, I spoke to the honest representatives of a convention which was not dominated by honest men; a convention wherein sat, alas! a majority of men who, with sneering indifference to every principle of right, so acted as to bring to a shameful end a party which had been founded over a half-century ago by men in whose souls burned the fire of lofty endeavor. Now to you men, who, in your turn, have come together to spend and be spent in the endless crusade against wrong, to you who face the future resolute and confident, to you who strive in a spirit of brotherhood for the betterment of our nation, to you who gird yourselves for this great new fight in the never-ending warfare for the good of humankind, I say in closing what in that speech I said in closing: We stand at Armageddon, and we battle for the Lord.

# The New Freedom

## *Woodrow Wilson*

*While Theodore Roosevelt battled for the Lord, the Democrats battled for the White House. The distinction was not merely rhetorical. The conventions which nominated Roosevelt and Taft must have sensed that the split between them had ruined the chances of either to win, and as if to underscore the emptiness of the honor they both completed their jobs on the first ballot. In unseemly but logical contrast the Democrats, assembled in Baltimore during a late July heat wave, snarled and clawed at each other for forty-four ballots before a nominee emerged. Why not? The prize was clearly worth a battle: a Democratic victory in November was certain, no matter who the candidate; the party was starved for blood, for they had controlled the presidency only eight years in the previous forty-four and not at all in the previous sixteen; and the prize was conspicuously up for grabs. Bryan, thrice beaten, his silver appeal irreparably tarnished, had lost most of the political magic which had so often commended him to the party leaders. Tammany Hall and the stalwarts, backed by William Randolph Hearst, pushed Champ Clark, Missourian and conservative Speaker of the House. Eastern liberals, fearful of both Bryan and Tammany, supported Woodrow Wilson, reform Governor of New Jersey. A stalemate threatened, but when Wilson gained successively the support of the southern liberals, the Chicago political machine, and Bryan's personal endorsement, the convention at last closed ranks to acclaim a certain winner in the contest to follow. On August 7, the day following Roosevelt's stand at Armageddon, Wilson opened his campaign with a ringing endorsement of national progressivism and thereby assured its triumph in November.*

*By conventional measures of personality and career few men appeared less promising for the part of politician, yet Wilson was soon to establish himself as one of the half-dozen most effective political leaders in American history. To account for his success we need to probe for some complex factors of character and historical circumstance. Born in Virginia five years before the fall of Fort Sumter, raised in the chaotic culture of post-*

*war Georgia, he attended Princeton and spent most of his life north and east of the Potomac. As he was also moderate on those issues which for seventy years had split the Democratic Party north and south, he was thus able to contribute substantially, as a symbol and as a party leader, to its renewed sense of unity in the afterglow of the 1912 election; he was and still is the only southerner since Andrew Jackson to have occupied the White House. Though he had held no public office until his fifty-fourth year, his long career as a scholar of government and the political process and his eight years as president of Princeton were scarcely years of waste for a politician, as no one familiar with university life would be surprised to hear; and his short term as Governor of New Jersey revealed him as one of the most effective executive tacticians in the history of state government.*

*When all this is said, we have still not fully explained the nature and significance of Wilson's rise to the presidency in a generation studded with men as skillful in politics as he. Of the two leading candidates in 1912 Roosevelt seemed the more exciting, and while they expounded almost precisely similar doctrines, Roosevelt appeared to have the more to say. They both agreed that the power of government should be returned to the people, that the laws must be enforced alike on the powerful and the weak, that monopoly agreements must be curtailed, and that the national government must help expand the economic base of natural wealth and guarantee the equal access of all citizens to that wealth. Wilson repeatedly asserted that a victorious Roosevelt would lack the essential support of a party in Congress and that the Bull Moose proposals to regulate monopoly would merely permit the powerful to grow at the expense of the small. But though Wilson scored consistently with these major points, for the most part he reduced himself to the negative strategy of attacking the details of his opponent's position while offering in its place only a generalized promise to support the substance of that position. It has sometimes been suggested that he gained ground on the obvious force of his intellect. Yet he was not a profound or unusually learned scholar; he confessed to Ida Tarbell in 1916 that he had not read a book in fourteen years, and it could be convincingly argued that in the truly favorable sense of the word Roosevelt was at least as much of an "intellectual."*

*What finally stamped Wilson for greatness was a power of verbal eloquence scarcely matched in his or any previous generation. It was coupled with a mastery of extemporaneous phrase, delivered (when spoken) from the briefest of notes; but it was the power of mood even more than the manner of his words that caught and held fast the mind of America in 1912 and in the years to follow. Words, he once said, were swords to cut with, and for most of his life he had trained himself in the use of this weapon as assiduously as any medieval warrior with sword or pike. He possessed the brilliant rhetorical capacity to reawaken in his hearers the moral vision of a land of glowing promise, of abundant opportunity and equal justice for all, a vision of the kind of righteous social order which had been imprinted in their consciences, deep and half-forgotten, bestowed from a generation of childhood sermons, schoolhouse lessons, and parental injunctions at the rural hearthsides of the nineteenth century. By common testimony the effect of this reawakening was as if a coiled spring had been suddenly tripped, releasing in campaign audiences everywhere forces of moral resolve that had been accruing for generations. If Roosevelt was the greatest politician of the progressive era, Wilson was its greatest spokesman. Roosevelt had prepared the way. By the overwhelming mandate of their combined vote, Wilson would be permitted the chance to finish a job substantially begun.*

*The selections which follow have been taken from John W. Davidson's excellent edition of Wilson's campaign speeches, the first to publish the original texts of each address precisely as it was delivered. The selections have been chosen to present Wilson at his best as well as to demonstrate the range of his position. The Columbus Day address is placed at the end, slightly out of chronological order, because in many ways its conclusion best expresses the core of Wilson's progressivism—the image of a classless social order of free men.*

ADDRESS AT MEMORIAL HALL, COLUMBUS, OHIO, SEPTEMBER 20, 1912

Governor Harmon, Chairman Finley, ladies and gentlemen:

I consider it a real privilege to take part in the opening of this great campaign in the noble state of Ohio; and I want to thank Governor Harmon for the very generous and gracious words with which he has introduced me. I feel just the responsibility which he has indicated. The people of this country are tired of assertion. They are now waiting to consider their own affairs and decide them upon the evidence, upon the proof of intention, upon the offering of a program which they can see from the outset will work them the permanent advantage they now wait for.

Before I started west and was considering what would be worth presenting to this great audience, it occurred to me that this singular thing had happened: that the Republican party and the third party had already handed over to the Democratic speakers the two chief issues of the campaign. They are not even professing to know how, or upon

Selections from Woodrow Wilson's campaign speeches as reproduced in John W. Davidson's edition, *A Crossroads of Freedom* (New Haven: Yale University Press, 1956), pp. 218-228, 234-238, 244-271, 425-428, 459-467.

what principle, the tariff ought to be revised, and neither of them is proposing to meet the question of monopoly by way of remedy. The only thing proposed is to mollify it, to make it as mild, as governable, as bearable, as possible. So that the very heart of our difficulties is avoided and declined by the orators of both the regular Republican party and of the very irregular Republican party.

I do not know how it would be possible to characterize the third party, because it is made up of so many elements that no characterization would fit all of its elements. In the first place, it is made up of a great many Republicans who feel simply this: that their consciences couldn't any longer stand what the regular Republican party was doing. And in the second place, it is made up of a great many public-spirited people who have been looking for somebody who would profess their program but have not stopped to consider sufficiently whether they have found somebody that can carry out that program. And in the third place, it consists of a certain number of persons about whom the less said the better. It would be very interesting if I could mention some of their names, but I have laid upon myself certain restrictions of etiquette in this campaign which I do not care to overstep.

For I am not interested in individuals. I am not interested in candidates. I am interested in the feasibility of reform, and the validity and reality of it; and I know that reform cannot begin with such a government as either Mr. Taft or Mr. Roosevelt will supply us with, for the simple reason that neither of these gentlemen proposes to supply us with a government which is free to act in the interests of the people. The first thing we must get is a free government—we haven't a free government now. And we know why we haven't a free government. The government of the United States is not free, because it takes its counsel with regard to the economic policy of the people of the United States from a very limited group of persons; and so long as it takes its counsel from that limited group of persons it cannot serve the interests of the nation as a whole.

My chief indictment against the program of both the other parties is that they do not propose to cure the causes. They merely propose to treat and try to remedy the results. For the causes are plain enough. Take the tariff: I am not going to discuss the tariff here tonight in any analytical fashion, but I want to point out to you that they haven't even realized that the tariff question is an absolutely new question. The most that either of the other platforms says is that some of the schedules are too high, and the most that one of the candidates says is that they are too high, chiefly because there isn't enough of the "prize money" that goes into the pay envelope of the employee. He doesn't object to the high prices when he speaks of the tariff. He doesn't admit that the high prices are due to the tariff. He simply says that there isn't an equitable division of the spoils. And he doesn't realize that there wouldn't be any spoils under the tariff system if it weren't an absolutely new question.

I say that it is an absolutely new question for this reason: When Mr. McKinley used to argue for high protective duties, when Mr. Blaine used so brilliantly to defend them, when the older apostles who built up the system, like Henry Clay, laid the foundations of their argument, what was it? It was that, while it was true that we had excluded foreign competition, it was also true that we had established in the United States such a splendid arrangement of domestic free trade and free competition that prices would be kept at their normal level by reason of the clashing genius of men inside America who would compete with one another for the markets of the great continent. And for a long time prices were kept at a reasonable and normal level by that very competition; and if that competition had continued, I dare say it would have been very difficult to make the people of the United States as uneasy as they now are about the tariff.

For why are they uneasy about it? They used to be told that it was for the benefit of the American workingman; and now they know that the American workingman hasn't got the benefit that was intended for him. They used to be told that it was for the stimulation of American industry, and now they see some power closing in on American industry which has deprived it of its elasticity and of its power to expand. And they see what has laid its hand on us.

Under what spell are we? There is fear in the air. Of what are we afraid? There is paralysis. What withholds our hands? Why, chiefly that this domestic competition has largely disappeared, and that in all the greater fields of industry men have banded themselves together to see that no fresh competitors come into the field of contest.

There isn't a businessman in the United States who doesn't realize that this is true not only, but that there is more than the machinery of combination; there is the machinery of the Clearing House Association, for example, where the leading bankers of whole regions of the country exchange information as to how much particular firms and business concerns are borrowing and suggest upon occasion that so and so, and so and so, and so and so, ought not to be extended any further credit. So that there is getting to be a "black list" with respect of credit, and a preferred list, by the cooperation of a force that is drawing more and more together and that is interlocked with the very men who do not desire competitors. Because, when you take the directors of any one of the great monopolistic organizations like the Standard Oil Company, or the United States Steel Corporation, and then find that those same gentlemen are in the boards of directors of railways and banks and mining companies and manufacturing institutions of every sort and degree, until one man will be found upon the lists of as many as sixty boards of directors, and that these gentlemen who control transportation also control credit, you will know how likely it is that if you start an enterprise that will interfere with theirs you will get money enough to get very far beyond your first beginning.

And so held in the hand of monopoly, we look about us and see what gave these men a chance to grapple us thus. And just as soon as you ask the question, you will see that the laws of this country have failed to do what laws were originally and only intended to do. Laws are not intended for the assistance of the strong. They are intended for the protection of the weak. And the thing that has done this is the thing which before the era of combinations was the very thing that stimulated us. Just as it may turn out that while protection once stimulated us, it is now choking us and enthralling us. The thing that once stimulated us was individual competition. But when you set against the individual, or a little group of individuals, a vast combination of capital (against which it is impossible for him to do anything, but which will break his strength), then you know that what you are suffering from is unrestricted and unregulated competition; and that just so soon as we learn how, as we can easily learn how, to regulate competition, then we will defend the newcomers into the lists. Then we will see to it that the man with only a local market is allowed to live long enough until he gets a market as wide as his state, as wide as his region, as wide as his genius will carry him with wings of commerce from one end of the globe to the other. We will see to it that we establish this rule that the entries to the race are absolutely open and free, and nobody shall be excluded.

We are not going to regulate the strength of the competitors. We are going to say to the newcomers: "It depends upon your genius, upon your initiative, upon your power to originate and use inventions, upon your knowledge of how to organize business and economize processes, upon your art of getting customers and widening your market; but what we are going to see to is that no man uses any means except brains and a better business capacity than yours to beat you." That is what we have got to see to. . . .

The tariff has created the opportunity of monopoly. And monopoly is going to be adopted by this irregular Republican host as the only means of directing the economic development of this country and the life of the working people of this country. They throw their hands up in impotence and say: "We have created a thing which has become our master, and the most that we can do is to see that it does not absolutely crush us. We must see that these proud men who ride this car of juggernaut are not disturbed as they go crashing through the opportunities of men in every community, mastering credit and controlling production." What a monstrous program! What an inconceivable program for men who call themselves statesmen and friends of liberty! And so it is amazing to me; it is nothing less than the confession of failure that neither of these parties even attempts to face the two central issues of the campaign, this monopoly-breeding tariff and this absolute control of American industry and American development by the monopolies which the tariff has created.

Ah, gentlemen, I wish that every man here had been for a little while on the inside of the administration of government. I wish that you knew some of the heart-rending details of how men are made to do the bidding of these great powers. I wish you knew how many business-men in this great country of ours, businessmen of high standing, have come to me and told me that they were utterly in agreement with me and then begged me never to mention their names or to say that they had told me. They were afraid, and they were justly afraid, for there are powers in this country that could crush them. You criticize your legisla-ture. You say that they do not represent you, that is to say, the great body of the people. You say that they do the bidding of special interests. Well, do you know what sometimes happens? You don't pay these legislators enough to make them independent upon their legislative salary. Most of them are lawyers, businessmen, men whose support of them-selves and of those whom they love depends upon somebody else's em-ployment, and never upon opportunities made in the great field of business itself. And when you remember that there are places—I could name them—where if they didn't obey orders, their notes would be un-timely called and they would be sent into bankruptcy; when you know, as I know, instances where within the region that they are known there isn't a bank that would give them further credit if their notes were once called by one member of the confederacy. Then put yourself in their position and remember that they are ordered to vote for this, that, or the other or take the consequences. You would feel gladder than ever that you had at least given yourselves the opportunity in Ohio to pass laws for yourselves. Because they can't call everybody's note. They can't call the notes of a whole community. They can't put everybody out of busi-ness. They can't penetrate the secrets of the voting booth and find out how their employees and dependents voted. They will merely know that this is a free people, which by hook or by crook is going to have the laws which will maintain its liberty. For the detail of tyranny which is possible under the existing circumstances is beyond belief. I never would have ventured to become a governor of a state if I had had a note in the bank. Because, although I dare say they couldn't overawe me, they might have made an end of me.

I tell you frankly, it is hard to withhold one's mind from passion when these things are dissected in the raw, as they are. And yet we are just, and with our knowledge of how these things have come about, we will withhold ourselves from passion. These things have grown up within twenty years, gentlemen. The men concerned have not realized what they were doing. They really believe that they know more how to conduct the business of this nation than anybody else does. They really think that it is for our benefit that they should be our trustees and masters. They are honest men, many of them, and very few of them are malevolent men. Some of them don't care how much blood trickles through their fingers, but most of them don't dream that there is any blood in the business. Most of them repeat that old heartless pagan maxim that "busines is business," which means that business has no touch of humanity in it, that business need have no justice in it, that business is power, and the man that gets crushed by power merely gets crushed by the natural processes of nature herself. I say that that is pagan, not Christian, heartless, inconceivable. If men will but realize how many have their backs to the wall, how many find that life is a hopeless struggle, how many carry the burden of the day and see no outlet whatever!

Here at the turning of the ways, when we are at last asking ourselves, "Can we get a free government that will serve us, and when we get it, will it set us free?" they say: "No, you can't have a free government, and you ought not to desire to be set free. We know your interests, we will obtain everything that you need by beneficent regulation; it isn't necessary to set you free, it is only necessary to take care of you." Ah, that way lies the path of tyranny; that way lies the destruction of independent, free institutions; because all through the highways of history stand those permanent indestructible fingers which say, "This is the way to the destruction of human liberty and of human life." And no man who has any imagination, or in thought traveled those desolate ways, can do anything but tremble to see America standing and questioning as to whether she shall start out upon that path or not. And then these gentlemen, who say that they are going to take care of you, promise to be beneficent, offer in their largess of generosity to be a Providence to you, declare that they know what your interest is and that you need not fear if they take charge of your interest. Whereas, all the processes of liberty are turned about.

The processes of liberty are that if I am your leader, you should talk to me, not that if I am your leader I should talk to you. I must listen, if I be true to the pledges of leadership, to the voices out of every hamlet, from every sort and condition of men. I must listen to the cry of those who are just coming into the lists. I must even be very still and hear the cry of the next approaching generation saying: "Is America to be free for us? Are we to have a heritage? Are we to be children taken care of and directed, or are we to be men and give America another lusty generation of achievement?" I must listen to the voices that the politician does not hear. I must listen to the voices which the self-appointed savior cannot hear, the voices that seem to pulse with the movement of the blood, the voices that are accompanied by those shining eyes of hope and of confidence which are the distinguishing characteristics of America.

Did you ever take a trip to the other side of the Atlantic, and note the difference between the people in the steerage on the outward-bound voyage and the people in the steerage on the incoming voyage? Did you never notice the difference between the eyes of men who have been in America and the eyes and countenances of men who have never been in America? If you have noticed it, would you ever thereafter wish us to close the doors of America against these people who will have the fires of hope lighted in their countenances if they can but touch our altars? Would you wish America to be less than she is, the fertilizing ground of the world, where men coming add richness to richness, energy to energy, hope to hope, knowing that they are building up a great composite people, whose unity shall be their love of freedom, whose energy shall come from those indestructible instincts, those universal powers of mankind, which are excited to action only when men lift their heads in proud independence, where there is no man to make them afraid?

The only thing to be afraid of is the thing that isn't true. The only thing to quail before is iniquity. If you are right why should you quail? Men have to die anyhow. Isn't it better to die with your face to the light than to fall like a craven with the light shining on your back? Shall the torch of liberty fall from our hands? Shall we not take it up, man after man of us, and run that race of freedom which shall end only when the torch is lifted high upon those uplands where no light is needed, but where shines the brilliancy of the justice of God?

ADDRESS AT SCRANTON, PENNSYLVANIA, SEPTEMBER 23, 1912
[Wilson was in part retorting to Roosevelt's accusation that he had adopted the political theories of Thomas Jefferson.]
. . . I know that the government of the United States is not a free instrument, and that it is our duty to set it free. Very well, set it free from whom? And how set it free? . . . I have always been impatient of the talk of abstract propositions. That may seem a strange statement to be made by a man whose opponents whenever they can't answer his arguments call him "academic," but I have always been opposed to the mere presentation to audiences of the abstract conceptions of government.

Of course, this was intended to be a government of free citizens and of equal opportunity, but how are we going to make it such? That is the question. Because I realize that while we are followers of Jefferson, there is one principle of Jefferson's which no longer can obtain in the practical politics of America. You know that it was Jefferson who said that the best government is that which does as little governing as possible, which exercises its power as little as possible. That was said in a day when the opportunities of America were so obvious to every man, when every individual was so free to use his powers without let or hindrance, that all that was necessary was that the government should withhold its hand and see to it that every man got an opportunity to act if he would. But that time is past. America is not now, and cannot in the future be, a place for unrestricted individual enterprise. It is true that we have come upon an age of great cooperative industry. It is true that we must act absolutely upon that principle.

Let me illustrate what I mean. You know that it used to be true in our cities that every family occupied a separate house of its own, that every family had its own little premises, that every family was separated in its life from every other family. But you know that that is no longer the case, and that it cannot be the case, in our great cities. Families live in layers, they live in tenements, they live in flats, they live on floors; they are piled layer upon layer in the great tenement houses of our crowded districts, and not only are they piled layer upon layer, but they are associated room by room, so that there is in each room, sometimes, in our congested districts, a separate family.

Now, what has happened in foreign countries, in some of which they have made much more progress than we in handling these things, is this: In the city of Glasgow, for example, which is one of the model cities of the world, they have made up their minds that the entries and the hallways of great tenements are public streets. Therefore, the policeman goes up the stairway, and patrols the corridors; the lighting department of the city sees to it that the corridors are abundantly lighted and the staircases. The city does not deceive itself into supposing that that great building is a unit from which the police are to keep out and the city authority to be excluded, but it says: "These are the highways of human movement; and wherever light is needed, wherever order is needed, there we will carry the authority of the city."

I have likened that to our modern industrial enterprises. You know that a great many corporations, like the Steel Corporation, for example, are very like a great tenement house; it isn't the premises of a single commercial family; it is just as much a public business as a great tenement house is a public highway.

When you offer the securities of a great corporation to anybody who wishes to purchase them, you must open that corporation to the inspection of everybody who wants to purchase. There must, to follow out the figure of the tenement house, be lights along the corridor, there must be police patrolling the openings, there must be inspection wherever it is known that men may be deceived with regard to the contents of the premises. If we believe that fraud lies in wait for us, we must have the means of determining whether fraud lies there or not. Similarly, treatment of labor by the great corporations is not now what it was in Jefferson's time. Who in this great audience knows his employer? I mean among those who go down into the mines or go into the mills and factories. You never see, you practically never deal with, the president of the corporation. You probably don't know the directors of the corporation by sight. The only thing you know is that by the score, by the hundred, by the thousand, you are employed with your fellow workmen by some agent of an invisible employer. Therefore, whenever bodies of men employ bodies of men, it ceases to be a private relationship. So that when a court, when a court in my own state, held that workingmen could not peaceably dissuade other workingmen from taking employment and based the decision upon the analogy of domestic servants, they simply showed that their minds and understandings were lingering in an age which had passed away two or three generations ago. This dealing of great bodies of men with other bodies of men is a matter of public scrutiny, and should be a matter of public regulation.

Similarly, it was no business of the law in the time of Jefferson to come into my house and see how I kept house. But when my house, when my property, when my so-called private property, became a great mine, and men went along dark corridors amidst every kind of danger to dig out of the bowels of the earth things necessary for the industries of a whole nation, and when it was known that no individual owned these mines, that they were owned by great stock companies, that their partnership was as wide as great communities, then all the old analogies absolutely collapsed and it became the right of the government to go down into those mines and see whether human beings were properly treated in them or not; to see whether accidents were properly safeguarded against; to see whether the modern methods of using these inestimable riches of the world were followed or were not followed. And so you know that by the action of a Democratic House only two years ago the Bureau of Mines and Mining was first equipped to act as foster father of the miners of the United States, and to go into these so-called private properties and see that the life of human beings was just as much safeguarded there as it could be in the circumstances, just as much safeguarded as it would be upon the streets of Scranton, because there are dangers on the streets of Scranton. If somebody puts a derrick improperly erected and secured on top of a building or overtopping the street upon any kind of structure, then the government of the city has the right to see that that derrick is so secured that you and I can walk under it and not be afraid that the heavens are going to fall on us. Similarly, in these great beehives where in every corridor swarm men of flesh and blood it is similarly the privilege of the government, whether of the state or of the United States, as the case may be, to see that human life is properly cared for and that the human lungs have something to breathe.

What I am illustrating for you is this: it is something that our Republican opponents don't seem to credit us with intelligence enough to comprehend. Because we won't take the dictum of a leader who thinks he knows exactly what should be done for everybody, we are accused of wishing to minimize the powers of the government of the United States. I am not afraid of the utmost exercise of the powers of the government of Pennsylvania, or of the Union, provided they are exercised with patriotism and intelligence and really in the interest of the people who are living under them. But when it is proposed to set up guardians over those people to take care of them by a process of tutelage and supervision in which they play no active part, I utter my absolute objection. Because the proposal of the third party, for example, is not to take you out of the hands of the men who have corrupted the government of the United States but to see to it that you remain in their hands and that that government guarantees to you that it will be humane to you.

The most corrupting thing in this country has been this self-same tariff. . . . The workingmen of America are not going to allow themselves to be deceived by a colossal bluff any longer. One of the corporations in the United States which has succeeded in mastering the laborer and saying to him, "You shall not organize; you shall not exercise your liberty of cooperating though we who employ you are using the power of organization to the outmost point of absolute control"—namely, the United States Steel Corporation—paid enormous dividends and still more enormous bonuses to those who promoted its organization at the same time that it was making men work twelve hours, seven days in a week, at wages which in the three hundred and sixty-five days of the year did not allow enough to support a family. If they have millions to divide among themselves and get those millions as they profess to get them from the opportunities created by the tariff, where does the workingman come in?

Mr. Roosevelt himself has spoken of the profits which they get as "prize money." And his objection is just the objection that I am raising. He says that not enough of the prize money gets into the pay envelope. And I am quite agree with him. But I want to know how he proposes to get it there. I search his program from top to bottom, and the only proposal I can find is this: that there shall be an industrial commission charged with the supervision of the great monopolistic combinations which have been formed under the protection of the tariff, and that the government of the United States shall see to it that these gentlemen who have conquered labor shall be kind to labor.

I say, then, the proposition is this: that there shall be two masters, the great corporation and over it the government of the United States; and I ask: Who is going to be the master of the government of the United States? It has a master now—those who in combination control these monopolies. And if the government controlled by the monopolies in its turn controls the monopolies, the partnership is finally consummated.

I don't care how benevolent the master is going to be. I will not live under a master. That is not what America was created for. America was created in order that every man should have the same chance with every other man to exercise mastery over his own fortunes. . . .

ADDRESS AT HARTFORD, CONNECTICUT, SEPTEMBER 25, 1912

Mr. Chairman, ladies and gentlemen:

It is a great pleasure to me to stand on this platform. I like to recall the two very happy years that I spent as your not very distant neighbor, at Middletown, in this state, and I want to tell you that as a consequence of that two years of residence I am not unacquainted with the character of the audience which I face.

I know that there are a great many misguided persons present—persons who, with the best intentions and the clearest conscience, have voted the wrong ticket. I also know that for the very best of reasons a Connecticut audience is a conservative audience, because Connecticut has had a great deal to conserve that was worth conserving, and she has arranged her constitution so that she has got to conserve it. So that, all things taken together, my first thought was almost apologetic, because I know that, in some quarters at any rate, I have acquired the reputation of being a radical, and I might have been expected to apologize to you for coming before you, a conservative community, to present radical points of view. But I don't think that anybody is any longer very much frightened by the word "radical"—and there are all sorts of radicals. It depends upon the kind I am whether I shall have to be apologetic or not.

But to speak seriously, the theme that I want to discuss with you this afternoon is simply this: Are those thoughtful men amongst us who fear that we are now about to disturb the ancient foundations of our institutions justified in their fear? For if they are, we ought to go very slowly about the process of change. If it is indeed true that we have grown tired of the institutions which we have so carefully and sedulously built up, then we ought to go just as slowly and just as carefully about the very dangerous task of altering them. We ought, therefore, to ask ourselves, first of all: Are we justified in the impression that at any rate the sober men among the leaders of progressive thought in this country are intending to do anything by which we shall retrace our steps, or by which we shall change the whole direction of our development?

I believe for one that you cannot tear up ancient rootages and safely plant the tree of liberty in soil which is not native to it. I believe that the ancient traditions of a people are its ballast; that you cannot make a *tabula rasa* upon which to write political programs. You cannot take a new sheet of paper and determine what your life shall be tomorrow. You must knit the new into the old. You cannot put new patches in ancient garments without destroying or endangering the construction of the ancient garment; unless you know that it mustn't be a patch, but must be something woven into the fiber, of practically the same pattern, of the same texture and intention. If I did not believe that to be progressive was to preserve the essentials of our institutions, I for one could not be progressive.

I have several times used an illustration which to my mind expresses the situation just about as well as a whimsical illustration could express it. I believe most of you have had the great pleasure of reading that very delightful book of nonsense, *Alice through the Looking Glass,* the companion of *Alice in Wonderland.* Alice in the book, you remember, is seized by the hand by the red chess queen, who races her off at a breathless pace until both of them can run no further for lack of breath; then they stop and Alice looks around and says: "But we are just where we were when we started." "O, yes," says the Red Queen, "you have to run twice as fast as that to get anywhere else."

Now, that is to my mind the image of progressivism. The laws of this country have not kept up with the change of economic circumstances in this country; they have not kept up with the change of political circumstances in this country; and therefore we are not where we were when we started. We are back of the place that we were when we started. And we will have to run, not until we are out of breath, but until we have caught up with our own conditions, before we shall be where we were when we started; when we started this great experiment which has been the hope and the beacon of the world. And we would have to run twice as fast as any rational progressive program I have seen in order to get anywhere else.

I am, therefore, a progressive because we have not kept up with our own changes of conditions, either in the economic field or in the political field. We have not kept up as well as other nations have. We have not adjusted our practices to the facts of the case. And until we do, and unless we do, the facts of the case will always have the better of the argument, because if you do not adjust your laws to the facts, so much the worse for the laws, not for the facts, because law trails along after the facts. Only that law is unsafe which runs ahead of the facts and beckons to them and makes it follow imaginative programs and will-o'-the-wisps.

Let us ask ourselves, therefore, what it is that disturbs us. In some commonwealths I find a great many conservative men who do not believe, for example, in the direct primary; and they are very diligent in collecting all sorts of evidence that the people do not take very much interest in the direct primaries, and that it simply creates confusion. I must say, parenthetically, that after yesterday's result of the direct primary in New Jersey I am reassured as to its operation.

The primary is a means of determining on the part of the people whom they wish to see put into office and whom they wish to exclude from office. And I maintain that the critical part of every political process is the selection of the men who are going to occupy the office, and not the election of them. And that when as in the past the two cooperative party machines have seen to it that both tickets had men of the same kind on them, it was Tweedledum or Tweedledee, so far as the voter was concerned; that those who managed politics had hem coming and had them going, and it didn't make any difference so far as the interests governing politics were concerned which of the tickets was elected at the election by the voters.

So that what we have established the direct primary for is this: to break up inside determination of who shall be selected to conduct the government and make the laws of our commonwealth and of our nation. And everywhere the impression is growing stronger that there will be no means of dominating those who have dominated us except by taking this process of selection into our own hands. Does that upset any ancient foundation? Ah! gentlemen, are we in danger of being hypocrites, some of us?

What do you talk about on the Fourth of July, if you are talking in public? You talk about the Declaration of Independence, and then you back up the Declaration of Independence with its splendid utterances in our earliest state constitutions, which have been copied in all later ones, taken from the Petition of Rights, or the Declaration of Rights, in the history of the struggle for liberty in England. And there we read these uncompromising sentences: that, when at any time the people of a commonwealth find that their governments are not suitable to the circumstances of their lives or the promotion of their liberties, it is their privilege to alter them at their pleasure. That is the foundation, that is the central doctrine, that is the ancient vision of America with regard to affairs, and this arrangement of the direct primary simply squares with that.

If they cannot find men whom they can trust, to select their tickets, they will select them for themselves. That is what the direct primary means. They do not always do it; they are sometimes too busy. The electorate of the United States is like the god Baal: it is sometimes on a journey, it is sometimes asleep; but when it does wake up, it does not represent the god Baal in the slightest degree. It resembles a great self-possessed power which takes possession, takes control of its own affairs. I am willing to wait. I am among those who believe so in the essential doctrines of democracy that I am willing to wait on the convenience of this great sovereign, provided that I know he has got the instrument to dominate whenever he chooses to grasp it.

Then there is another thing that conservative people are disturbed about: the direct election of United States senators. I have seen some thoughtful men discuss that with a sort of shiver, as if to disturb the ancient constitution of the United States Senate was to do something touched with impiety, touched with irreverence for the Constitution. But the first thing necessary to reverence the United States Senate is to respect the United States senators. I am not one of those who condemns the United States senators as a body; for no matter what has happened there, no matter how questionable the practices, how corrupt the influences which have filled some of the seats in the United States Senate, it must in fairness be said that the majority of that body has all the years through been untouched by that stain, and that there has always been there a sufficient number of men to safeguard the self-respect and the hopefulness of America with regard to her institutions.

But you need not be told, and it would be painful to repeat to you, some of the processes by which seats have been bought in the United States Senate; and you know, as the whole people of the United States knows, that a little group of senators holding the balance of power, has again and again been able to defeat programs of reform upon which the whole country had set its heart; and that whenever you analyzed the power that was behind those little groups you found that it was not the power of public opinion, but some private influence, hardly to be disclosed by superficial scrutiny, which had put those men there to do that thing.

Now, returning to the original principles upon which we profess to stand, have the people of the United States not a right to see to it that every seat in the United States Senate represents the unbought influences of America? Does direct election of senators touch anything except the private control of seats in the Senate? For you must remember another thing, gentlemen: you must remember that we have not been without our suspicions about some of the legislatures which elect senators. Some of the suspicions which we entertained in New Jersey about that turned out to be founded upon very solid facts indeed. And until two years ago New Jersey had not in half a generation been represented in the United States Senate by the men who would have been chosen if the process had been free.

So that we are not now to deceive ourselves by putting our heads in

the sand and saying, "Everything is all right." Didn't Mr. Gladstone say
that the American Constitution was the most perfect constitution ever
devised by the brain of man? Haven't we been praised all over the world
for our genius in setting up successful states? Yes, we have, but a very
thoughtful Englishman, and a very witty one, said an instructive thing
about it. He said that to show that the American Constitution has worked
well is not to prove that it is an excellent constitution, because the Americans could run any constitution—a compliment which is also a comment, a compliment which we lay like a sweet unction to our souls, but a
criticism which ought to set us thinking.

And while it is true that while American forces are awake they can
conduct American processes without serious departures from the ideals
of the Constitution, it is nevertheless true that we have had many shameful instances of practices which we can absolutely remove by the direct
election of senators by the people themselves. And, therefore, I, for one,
will not allow any man who knows his history to say to me that I am
acting inconsistently with either the spirit or the form of the American
government in advocating the direct election of United States senators.

Take another matter, for let's get another step deeper. I hope you
won't any of you think that I am going too far in even mentioning in your
presence those extreme doctrines of the initiative and the referendum and
the recall. It is the last word that makes most men shrink. There are communities, there are states in the Union, in which I am quite ready to admit
that it is perhaps premature, that perhaps it will never be necessary to
discuss these measures. But I want to call your attention to the fact that
these measures have been discussed and have been adopted in those states
where the electorate had become convinced that they did not have representative government.

Let no man deceive himself by the fallacy that anybody proposes to
substitute direct legislation by the people, or the direct reference of laws
voted in the legislature, to the vote of the people for representative
government. The most eager advocates of these reforms have always said
that they were intended to recover representative government; that they
had no place where those who were elected to legislative chambers were
really representative of the communities which they professed to serve.
The initiative is a means of recapturing the seat of legislative authority
on behalf of the people themselves, and the referendum is a means of
seeing to it that unrepresentative measures are not put upon the statute
books but are checked by being submitted to the vote of the people.

When you come to the recall, the principle is that if an administrative
officer—for we will begin with administrative officers—is corrupt or so
unwise as to be doing things that are likely to lead to all sorts of mischief,
in the future it will be possible by a steady and slow process prescribed

by the law to get rid of that officer before the end of his term. Because you must admit that it is a little inconvenient sometimes to have what someone called an astronomical system of government, a system of government in which you can't change anything until there has been a certain number of revolutions of the seasons. And nobody in New England ought to find any very grave objection to the recall of administrative officers, because in most parts of New England the ordinary administrative term is a single twelvemonth. You haven't been willing in New England to trust any man out of your sight more than twelve months, so that your elections are a sort of continuous performance, based on the very fundamental idea that we are discussing, that you will not take your own hands off your own affairs. That is the principle of the recall. I don't see how any man who is grounded in the traditions of American affairs, particularly as they derive their origins from New England, can find any valid objection to the recall of administrative officers.

It is another matter when it comes to the judiciary. I myself have never been in favor of the recall of judges. [*Applause.*] But now that that has received your approval, let me tell you why. Not because some judges haven't deserved to be recalled—that isn't the point—but because that is treating the symptom instead of the disease. The disease lies deeper, and sometimes it is very virulent and very dangerous. Gentlemen, there have been courts in the United States that were controlled by private interests. There have been supreme courts in our states at which men without privilege could not get justice. There have been corrupt judges; there have been controlled judges; there have been judges who acted as other men's servants and not as the servants of the public. And there can be no moral objection to removing such men from public service. Ah, there are some shameful chapters in that story! Think of it! The reason you applauded just now was that you feel, as I feel, that the judicial process is the last and ultimate safeguard of the things that we want to hold stable in this country. But suppose that that safeguard is corrupted; suppose that it doesn't guard my interests and yours, but guards merely the interests of a very small group of individuals; and that whenever your interest clashes with theirs, yours will have to give way, though you represent ninety per cent of your fellow citizens, and they only ten per cent. Then where is your safeguard? And what is it safeguarding, I would like to know?

The great processes of equitable thought must control the judiciary as they control every other instrument of government. But there are ways and ways of controlling it. If—mark you I say "if"—at one time the Union Pacific Railroad—or rather the Southern Pacific Railroad—owned the Supreme Court of the state of California, what was the trouble? Would you remedy it by recalling the judges of the Supreme Court of California? Not so long as the Southern Pacific Railroad could substitute others for them. You would not be cutting deep enough. Where you want to go is to the seat of the trouble; where you want to go is to the place and the process by which those judges were picked out. And when you get there, you lead to the moral of the whole of this discussion, because the moral of it all is that the people of the United States have suspected, until their suspicions have been justified by all sorts of substantial and un-answerable evidence, that, in place after place, at turning point after turning point in the history of this country, we have been controlled by private understandings and not by the public interest; and that influences which were improper, if not corrupt, have determined everything from the making of laws to the administration of justice. They have suspected that the Southern Pacific Railroad owned the Supreme Court of that great and beautiful state that stretches her fair acres up and down the coast of the Pacific, and because of that they have said: "We are going to go to the heart of this matter and dislodge these men who have been controlling our affairs; and no man who understands anything about liberty, or anything about economic prosperity, ought to find it in his con-science or in his heart to withhold his hands."

This thing that grows like a canker in our vitals must be cut out, though I grant you it must be cut out with the skill and the knowledge and the tenderness of the surgeon who will not disturb the vital tissues to which this ugly thing is attached. Let us keep the integrity and the purity of our whole structure, but let us get rid of these things that are corrupting it; for the people of the United States have made up their minds that they are going to unearth the beast in the jungle. They know that their forests have constituted a sort of jungle in which when they hunted they were caught by the beast instead of catching him. They have determined, therefore, to take an axe and to level the jungle, and then see where the beast will find cover, to be ready when the jungle is cut out to bag their game. I, for my part, bid them Godspeed. The jungle breeds nothing but infection.

That, if you choose to call it radicalism, is the kind of radicalism I be-lieve in. If that be radicalism, then the preservation of our life and beauty as a nation is a radical proposition, and it is in the literal meaning of the word. Because, if I am correctly informed, "radical" means "rootical"— it goes to the root of the matter. But where does it all come from? There is no use, as I have just now said, dealing with the symptoms. Where is the seat of the disease? Where is the foundation of corruption?

For I tell you, my fellow citizens, that the choice of this campaign is not a choice among these things that I have been talking about. I have been using these illustrations to draw your thought to the central point where lie the sources of all that we are discussing. The radical circum-stance—the circumstance that is the taproot of the whole matter—is that we have not now a free government; that some secret influences are controlling it; and it is absolutely impossible to pursue any program of reform, no matter how handsome and hopeful it may be, until we get an instrument of our own with which to pursue it. You know where the seat of the corruption lies. If you can, or think that you can, conduct your business only by getting special favors from the government, if you know that you can carry on some of the enterprises that you are now carrying on only if you can see to it that some of the laws of the United States are not changed, then you are going to do—some of you are going to do thoughtlessly, it may be, but nevertheless rather systematically—what has been done for so many years: you are going to contribute your money to the party that will guarantee to you that these privileges are not taken away. . . .

And there comes in your political morals. For these gentlemen do not act directly upon the government of the United States; they act through an interesting class of persons known as political bosses. Political bosses are not politicians at all. They are the business agents on the political side of certain kinds of business. They are the experts who instruct these gentlemen how they can manage not to be embarrassed either by those who occupy executive or by those who occupy legislative offices. And they are well paid for their services, not necessarily in cash, but by being on the inside of many large transactions.

The trouble with bosses is that they are not politicians. By a boss I would like to tell you what I mean. I don't mean the leader of a political organization; I mean the manipulation of a machine. Now, a machine is that part of a political organization which has been taken out of the hands of the rank and file of the organization and has gone to seed in the hands of a few chosen men. It is the part that has ceased to be political and become a business agency for the determination of the public policy of states and of the nation.

You have your complete series, therefore, of suspicions about nominations for office, about the election of United States senators, about the rejection of laws, traced down to the tap root—this great colossal system of special privilege, on account of which men feel obliged to keep their hands upon the sources of power.

You know in the great state of Oregon on the Pacific coast they have the initiative and the referendum. There is a certain gentleman named Mr. U'Ren, who is at the center of a group of men who busy themselves in suggesting certain legislative reforms to be carried out upon the initiative of the people themselves, and these gentlemen by commending these measures to the general public have transformed the government of the state of Oregon. But the point I was about to make is this. When I last visited the state of Oregon I reached the city of Portland in that great state on a morning when there happened to be in the leading newspaper of the city an editorial to this effect, that there were two legislatures in Oregon—I think it was set with a scare headline—one was at Salem, the capital of the state, and the other one under Mr. U'Ren's hat. I digested this statement, and when I came to speak in the evening I ventured upon this remark. I quoted the editorial and said: "Now, I don't wish anybody to understand me as advocating the concentration of power in any man or in any group of men, but I simply wish to say that if I had my choice between a legislature that went around under the hat of someone in particular whom I could identify and find, and a legislature that went around under God knows whose hat, I would choose the legislature that goes around under the hat of the recognizable individual." For I knew, and could tell those people until very recent months, nobody knew who wore the hat of the legislature of New Jersey. And that because the wearer of the hat was not disclosed, was not recognizable, could not be mentioned by name, the people of New Jersey had gone half a generation cheated after every election out of every reform upon which they had insisted.

Who had controlled the legislature at Salem? Perhaps it would be impolite for me to say—I will leave that for some citizen of the state of Oregon. Because I do not venture to mention any names that do not belong within my bailiwick. If I should be transferred to a higher sphere, I will have a larger list of names. I would take great pleasure in publishing them at stated intervals. But more to the point, we must realize that we are choosing.

The thought I want to leave with you is this; here is the choice you have to take: The Democrats are proposing to interevene, and, by lowering those duties which have protected special privilege, expose special privilege to a very wholesome, chastening kind of competition; and then to adopt a process of legislation by which competition will be so regulated that big business can't crush out little business; and that little business can grow—instead of being built by private understanding—into big business and put every man who is manufacturing or engaged in commerce in this country on his mettle to beat, not the capital, but the brains of his competitors. Whereas, on the other hand, the leaders of the third party are proposing to you—I would say parenthetically that the leaders of the regular Republican party are not proposing anything—the leaders of the third party are proposing that you accept the established monopolies as inevitable, their control as permanent, and undertake to regulate them through a commission which will not itself be too carefully restricted by law but will have the right to make rules by which they will accomplish what the platform calls "constructive regulation." In short, it proposes to leave the government in the hands and under the influences which now control it, and shall so long as they can control it make it absolutely impossible that we should have a free instrument by which to restore the rule and the government of the people themselves.

ADDRESS AT NEW HAVEN, CONNECTICUT, SEPTEMBER 25, 1912

Your Excellency, Mr. Chairman, and fellow citizens:

. . . I am interested to learn from Governor Baldwin that this is the opening of the present campaign in New Haven. That gives me leave to do what I should like very much to do, to introduce to some gentlemen in this audience who are not well acquainted with it the great Democratic party; for I know that there are many men sitting before me who are here on the anxious bench. I know that they are now thinking of changing their course of life. I know that they are now "sicklied o'er with the pale cast of thought," and I would if I could commend to their consideration in the choice of their future course in politics the great party which I represent. That party, ladies and gentlemen, is great by recent proof. For the Democratic party has been a minority party for sixteen years in this nation. And during those sixteen years it has grown in power, in clearness of thought, in determinateness of action. It did not wait for the year 1912 to discover the program which was necessary for the rectification of conditions in the United States. It has foreseen the greater part of that program for half a generation. It has been calling through all these years of discouragement upon the American people to bear witness to the fact that they did not have access to their own government and were not being governed in their own general interest. This steadfastness in principle in the face of adversity is, to my mind, a proof of greatness, particularly when in the midst of adversity the party has grown stronger and stronger, and its vision clearer and clearer. For there have been many vacillations in politics. And after a while there came a day when the ranks of the Republican party began in part to waver and to break.

We saw the day in New Jersey when there arose a little group of Republicans who called themselves the "New Idea" Republicans; when the idea of serving the whole people was a new idea with the Republican party. Then there arose in the far state of Iowa another group of men who began to see that the crux of the whole business was the protective tariff, and they began to shake the faith of the West in the time-honored traditions of the Republican party with regard to that policy.

Then there arose that sturdy little giant in Wisconsin who is now such an indomitable, unconquerable champion of progressive ideas all along the line. I mean Senator La Follette. Men who seek expediency rather than pursue principle took him up for a little while and pretended to follow him, and then rejected him, not because he was not the genuine champion of their principles, but because they apparently saw their interest lie in another direction. I do not believe there are many chapters of personal history in the records of parties in this country more difficult to reconcile with principles of honor than that. I feel myself close kin to these men who have been fighting the battle of progressive democracy, for no matter what label they bear we are of one principle.

I remember hearing a story not long ago. I have told it a number of times but perhaps you will bear with me if I tell it again because it interprets my feeling. A very deaf old lady was approached by her son, who wanted to introduce a stranger to her, and he said: "Mama, this is Mr. Stickpin." "I beg your pardon," she said; "what did you say the name was?" "Mr. Stickpin." "I don't catch it," she said. "Mr. Stickpin." "Oh," she said, "it's no use; it sounds exactly like Stickpin." Now, when I talk of men of La Follette's way of thinking in politics I feel like saying: "I beg your pardon, what did say you were?" "A Republican." "A what?" "A Republican." "No use; it sounds to me just like Democrat." . . .

We turn, then, to the introduction to which I invited your attention. I want to introduce you to the present Democratic party; a party that has come through fire, has been purified, has been shown such errors as it has committed in past years and is now absolutely and enthusiastically united upon the progressive program, a platform which the whole country is seeking. That is the new Democratic party; new because it never grows old; new, because the principles in which it is rooted and grounded never can grow old; new, because they are the identical principles upon which . . . the great Declaration of Independence itself was founded, and that other document with which Jefferson had so much to do, the incomparable Virginia Bill of Rights. And so this is the party which is now being questioned with respect to its purposes by the leaders of parties which are either breaking up or have not yet attained to the bone and sinew of manhood.

These gentlemen are saying: "If you give power to the Democrats, you will do all sorts of things. In the first place, you will have free trade." Ah, that ancient bogy! How long will they continue to dress this thing of their imagination in the old clothes of an ancient stump orator. There cannot be free trade in the United States so long as the established fiscal policy of the federal government is maintained.

The federal government has chosen throughout all the generations that have preceded us to maintain itself chiefly on indirect instead of direct taxation. I dare say we shall never see a time when it can alter that policy in any substantial degree; and there is no Democrat of thoughtfulness that I have met who contemplates a program of free trade.

But what we have been doing and what we intend to do, what the House of Representatives has been attempting to do and will attempt to do again, and succeed, is to weed this garden that we have been cultivating. Because, if we have been laying at the roots of our industrial enterprises this fertilization of protection, if we have been stimulating it by this policy, originated at any rate in its present form by Henry Clay, we have found that the stimulation was not equal in respect of all the growths in the garden, and that there are some growths, which every man can distinguish with the naked eye, which have so overtopped the rest, which have so thrown the rest into destroying shadows, that it is impossible for the industries of the United States as a whole to prosper under their destroying shade. In other words, we have found out that this that professes to be a process of protection has become a process of favoritism, and that the favorites of this policy have flourished at the expense of all the rest. And now we are going into this garden and weed it. We are going into this garden and give the little plants air and light in which to grow. We are going into this garden and pull up every root that has so spread itself as to draw all the nutriment of the soil from the other roots. We are going in there to see to it that the fertilization of intelligence, of invention, of origination is once more applied to a set of industries now threatening to be stagnant, because we think it to be too much concentrated. That is the policy of the Democratic party in regard to the protective tariff.

The President said the other day that if the Democratic party was put in power there would come a series of rainy days for those engaged in the industries of the country. I recall the time when he condemned that preposterous Schedule K under which the wool monopoly flourishes, and I want to ask him if he doesn't think that rainy days came long ago to the poor mill hands in Lawrence, Massachusetts. What kind of days are those that are enjoyed by some of the employees of the overshadowing steel monopoly who have to work seven days in the week, twelve hours every one of the seven, and can't, when the three hundred and sixty-five weary days have passed and a year is tolled, find their bills paid or their little families properly sustained? Are they waiting for rainy days? I want to call your attention to the fact that men all over this country in industries not protected see more sun during the day than those who are in most of the protected industries. They get higher wages, they have shorter hours, they are enabled to maintain themselves with a degree of respectability which is denied to the rest.

I say that the policy of the Democratic party will so variegate and multiply the new undertakings in this country that there will be a wider market and a greater competition for labor, that the sun will come through the clouds, and there will no longer be lead in the skies and a burden intolerable to carry for the servants and creatures of some of the protected industries. I tell you, ladies and gentlemen, the time has gone by for statements which cannot be sustained by the facts. And I very earnestly and respectfully protest against arguments which do not square with the facts. For the fact is that the Democratic party has not proposed to change the established fiscal policy of this country, except where it furnishes root for special privilege; and that wherever special privilege grows there American labor languishes.

Then there is another thing it is said will happen if the Democratic party comes in. You know that one of the interesting things that Mr. Jefferson said in those early days of simplicity which marked the beginnings of our government was that the best government consisted in as little government as possible. And there is still a sense in which that is true. It is still intolerable for the government to interfere with our individual activities except where it is necessary to interfere with them in order to free them. I have long had an image in my mind of what constitutes liberty. Suppose that I were building a great piece of powerful machinery, and suppose that I should so awkwardly and unskillfully assemble the parts of it that every time one part tried to move it would be interfered with by the others; the whole thing would buckle up and be checked. And liberty for the several parts would consist in the best possible assembling and adjustment of the various parts, would it not? If you want the great piston of the engine to run with absolute freedom, you give it absolutely perfect alignment and adjustment with the other parts of the machine, so that it is free, not when you let it alone, but when you associate it most skillfully and carefully with the other parts of the great structure. And so I feel confident that if Jefferson had lived in our day he would see what we see: that the individual is caught in a great confused mix-up of all sorts of complicated circumstances, and that to let him alone is to leave him helpless as against the obstacles with which he has to contend; and that, therefore, law in our day must come to the assistance of the individual.

The Democratic party does not stand for the limitation of powers of government, either in the field of the state or in the field of the federal government. There is not a Democrat that I know who is afraid to have the powers of the government exercised to the utmost. But there are a great many of us who are afraid to see them exercised at the discretion of individuals. There are a great many of us who still adhere to that ancient principle that we prefer to be governed by the power of laws, and not by the power of men.

Therefore, we favor as much power as you choose, but power guided by knowledge, power extended in detail, not power given out in the lump to a commission set up as is proposed by the third party and unencumbered by the restrictions of law, to set up a "constructive regulation," as their platform calls it, of the trusts and monopoly. But we wish a law which takes its searchlight and casts its illuminating rays down the secret corridors of all the processes by which monopoly has been established and polices those corridors so that highway robbery is no longer committed on them, so that men are no longer waylaid upon them, so that the liberty of individuals to compete is no longer checked by the power of combinations stronger than any possible individual can be. We want to see the law administered. We are not afraid of commissions.

It is said, with a good deal of force, I want frankly to admit, that merely to make laws and leave their application to the present courts with their present procedure is not a very likely way of reform, because the present procedure of our courts means that individuals must challenge the power that is being exerted against them, that an individual must wait until he is injured and then go to the court for redress, and that he must have money enough and courage enough to go to the court and ask for redress. For the worst of our present situation, ladies and gentlemen, is that it requires courage to challenge the power of the men now in control of our industries by resorting to any tribunal whatever. Therefore, I am ready to admit that we may have to have special tribunals, special processes, and I am not afraid, for my part, of the creation of special processes and special tribunals; but I am absolutely opposed to leaving it to the choice of those tribunals what the processes of law shall be and the means of remedy.

Therefore, the difference between the Democratic and the Republican parties, or rather between the Democratic party and those various other groups that are masquerading under all sorts of names, is that they are willing to accept the discretionary power of individuals, and we are not willing to accept anything except the certainty of law. That is the only thing that has ever afforded salvation or safety.

I want to draw a few illustrations. There is the great policy of conservation, for example; and I do not conceive of conservation in any narrow term. There are forests to conserve, there are great water powers to conserve, there are mines whose wealth should be deemed exhaustible, not inexhaustible, and whose resources should be safeguarded and preserved for future generations. But there is much more than that in the policy of conservation.

There are the lives and fortunes of the citizens of the United States to be conserved. It covers not only forest reservations and forest cultivation and the safeguarding of water powers and mines, but it includes pure food and the public health and the conditions of labor and all those things which government must see to minutely and courageously, if we are not to be sapped of our vitality and disappointed of our hopes. Now, the thing that stands in the way of the proper policy of conservation and makes it impossible to form that policy is that the government of the United States is now under the influence of men who want to control the forests, control the water courses, control the mines; who will not admit that these are public properties which we hold in trust for future generations as well as for ourselves, and are resisting the efforts of those of us who would extend the threads of law all through these industrial processes which threaten our resources and threaten our lives and vitality.

Then there is the matter of the regulation of hours of labor, of the conditions of labor, of the sanitation of factories, of the limitation of the hours of work for women and children, of the limitation of hours for men, questions which are in part state questions but also in part federal questions. All of these matters have to be treated by knowledge and pursued by a constancy of purpose which no special interests should be allowed to stand in the way of. And the government of the United States under the Democratic party will attempt to put all through this nation the structural steel of law, so that no man can doubt what his rights are, or doubt the stability of the thing that he is walking on.

Sometimes, when I think of the growth of our economic system, it seems to me as if, leaving our law just about where it was before any of the modern inventions or developments took place, we had simply at haphazard extended the old family residence, added an office here and a workroom there, and a new set of sleeping rooms there, built up higher on the foundation, put out new foundations and new wings, little lean-tos and ancient jalousies, until we have a structure that has no character whatever. Now the problem is to continue to live in the house and yet change it.

Well, we are architects in our time, and architects are also engineers in our time. We don't have to stop using a terminal because a new railway station is being built. We don't have to stop any of the processes of our lives because we are rearranging the structures in which we conduct those processes. I say that what we have to undertake is to systematize the foundations of the house, then to thread all the old parts of the structure with the steel which will be laced together in modern fashion, accommodated to all the modern knowledge of structural strength and elasticity, and then slowly change the partitions, relay the walls, let in the light through new aperatures, improve the ventilation; until finally a generation or two from now, the scaffolding will be taken away, and there will be the family in a great building whose noble architecture will at last be disclosed, where men can live as a single family, cooperative as in a perfectly coordinated beehive, not afraid of any storm of nature, not afraid of any artificial storm of imitation thunder and lightning, knowing that the foundations go down to the bedrock of principle, knowing that the structure will stand as long as the solid globe, and knowing that whenever they please they can change that plan again and accommodate it as they please to the altering necessity of their lives. That is the figure I have

carried in my mind as I have thought of the future. This minute inter-
lacing of ancient life with modern law, such is the program of the
Democratic party.

But there are a great many men who don't like the idea. You know that
some wit recently said, in view of the fact that most of our American
architects are trained in the École des Beaux Arts at Paris, that all American architecture in recent years was either bizarre or *"Beaux Arts."* I
think that our economic architecture is decidedly bizarre; and I am afraid
that there is a great deal to learn about the architecture from the same
source from which our architects have learned a great many things. I
don't mean the School of Fine Arts at Paris, but the experience of France;
from the other side of the water men can now hold up against us the
reproach that we have not adjusted our lives to modern conditions to the
same extent that they have adjusted theirs. . . .

What I want to suggest to you is that the only basis, the only standard
of readjustment proposed or suggested by our opponents, is the standard
of expediency, and that only the Democratic party offers a standard of
principle. The expediency of the situation is merely to see to it that those
who receive the privileges behave themselves, whereas our principle is
that nobody ought to receive privileges and that every special privilege
shall be destroyed, not with a ruthless hand, not in such a fashion as suddenly to upset the conditions of business, but nevertheless with the firmness and kindness of the judicious parent.

The government of the United States at present is a mere foster child
of the special interests. It is not allowed to have a will of its own. It is told
at every move, "Don't do that. You will interfere with our prosperity!" And
we ask "Where is our prosperity lodged?" and a certain group of gentlemen say, "With us."

Now, I, for my part, don't want to belong to a nation, and prettily believe that I do not belong to a nation, that needs to be taken care of by
guardians. I want to belong to a nation, and I am proud that I do belong
to a nation, that knows how to take care of itself. If I thought that the
American people were reckless, were ignorant, were vindictive, do you
suppose I would want to put the government in their hands? But the
beauty of democracy is that when you are reckless you destroy your own
established conditions of life; when you are vindictive you wreak your
vengeance upon yourself; and that the whole stability of democratic polity
rests upon the fact that every interest is every man's interest. If it were
not so, there could be no community; if it were not so, there could be no
cooperation; if it were not so, there could be no renewal, and that to my
mind is the most important part of the whole matter. For what I am
anxious about, ladies and gentlemen, is the conditions which the next
generation will find.

The present generation finds this: that if, for example, you add to the reputation of America for ingenuity by originating a great invention, a great industrial invention, a singular thing happens to you. If you want, let us say, a million dollars to build a plant and advertise your product and employ your agents and make a market for it, where are you going to get the million dollars? Because the minute you apply for the million dollars this proposition is put to you: This invention will interfere with the established processes and market control of certain great industries. We are already financing those industries, their securities are in our hands; we will lend you the money if you will make an arrangement with those industries and go in with them. If you will not, then you can't have the money.

I am generalizing the statement, but I could particularize it. I could tell you instances where exactly that thing happened. And by the combination of great industries, processes are not only being standardized, but they are being kept at a single point of development and efficiency of operation. The increase of the power to produce in proportion to the cost of production is not studied in America as it used to be studied, because, if you don't have to improve your processes in order to excel a competitor— if you are human—you aren't going to improve your processes. And if you can prevent the competitor from coming into the field, then you can sit at your leisure, and behind this wall of protection which prevents the brains of any foreigner competing with you, you can rest at your ease for a whole generation.

And so I say that I want to see those conditions created which will permit this: Let a man begin his business on ever so small a scale and let him be safe in beginning it on a small scale. He is not safe now, because if he enters a field where a great combination has established a market, that great combination will undersell him in his local market, which is his only market, making its necessary profits in other parts of the country until he is killed off and enterprise after enterprise is nipped in its infancy by the monopolistic control of our industrial markets.

So that America is about to see another generation which must be a generation of employees, unless it makes up its mind to be a generation of masters. The great militant, fighting, triumphant America is a nation of officers, a nation of men who are their own masters, a nation of men who will originate their own processes of industry and of life. And we shall never see the day, I confidently predict, where America will allow itself to be employed and patronized and taken care of.

I hope I have succeeded, therefore, in introducing to you the present-day Democratic party. It has been here all along but you weren't paying any attention. You are just now beginning to take notice, because there was a solid phalanx, a solid organized rush line, between you and the prospects. The whole horizon was shut out from you by the towering figures of the men who held so closely together in order to dominate the situation. Now these ranks are broken, a little bit of the horizon can be glimpsed and beyond these towering figures you see the great resurgent mass of the American people, and you see certain gentlemen, I hope modest gentlemen, trying to speak for them, saying: "We have been waiting for your attention for a long time. Now will you be kind enough to listen? Will you be kind enough to realize what our ideals are? Will you be kind enough to open your eyes to the vision which has led us on through dark days for a whole generation?"

For we would not have carried this burden of exile if we had not seen a vision. We could have traded; we could have got into the game; we could have surrendered and made terms; we could have played the role of patrons to the men who wanted to dominate the interests of the country—and here and there gentlemen who pretended to be Democrats did make those arrangements. I could mention some of them. I have known them. They couldn't stand the pace. They couldn't stand the privation. There was too little in it. And you never can stand it unless you have some imperishable food within you upon which to sustain life and courage, the food of those visions of the spirit where a table is set before you loaded with palatable fruits, the fruits of hope, the fruits of imagination, those invisible things of the spirit which are the only things upon which we can carry ourselves through this weary world without fainting. We have carried in our minds—after you have thought you had obscured them—we have carried in our minds what those men saw who first set their foot upon America, those little bands who came to make a little foothold in the wilderness, because the great teeming nations that they had left behind them had forgotten what human liberty was, liberty of thought, liberty of religion, liberty of residence, liberty of action; and so we set up an asylum. For whom? For the world.

Is it not a beautiful thought that there are nations of Europe that have dreamed dreams that they never could realize on their native soil and have sent their vanguard to America to discover? Why, in that ancient kingdom of Hungary, for example, contemporary with the great Magna Charta, to which we look back as the source of our constitutional liberties, there was proclaimed upon a notable day the terms of the great Golden Bull, which ran almost in the identical terms of the Magna Charta, but Hungary never could get a foothold for the execution of those principles until she began to send eager multitudes across the ocean to find in America what they had vainly hoped for in Hungary. Then when you take the great Italian race, going back to the stern Roman days and coming down to the days of Garibaldi and the visionary but practical Cavour, who built a nation out of separated kingdoms, and accommodated the temporal with the spiritual power as they had never been accommodated before, and find them coming in multitudes over to America, pleased that they could find even more than Garibaldi and Cavour could give them. Then those pathetic heroic struggles that mark the dark days in Cologne and the struggling multitudes that came from Poland to find their home in America. Why, you could go through the lists of the European nations and find in every instance that we had either realized their hopes for them or grossly deceived them. For we are trustees of all the confidence of mankind in liberty. If we do not redeem the trust, if we do not fulfill the pledge, then we are of all nations the most to be pitied; for the more high your aim, the more disastrous your failure to reach it; and the more glorious your program, the more contemptible your failure. Why did we lift this vision of peace before mankind if we did not know the terms in which peace could be realized? And so, like an army indomitable, irresistible, we have enlisted in such wise that no prolonged night of darkness and extinguished campfires can make us the less confident that the morning will dawn, and when the morning dawns and the mists rise, then men shall discover their manhood again and put on that armor of the righteousness of God which makes any nation unconquerable.

ADDRESS AT DUQUESNE GARDEN, PITTSBURGH, PENNSYLVANIA, OCTOBER 18, 1912

Mr. Chairman and fellow citizens:

As I stand here, facing this extraordinary body of people, and realize that I am the Democratic candidate for the Presidency, it is difficult for me to believe that I am in Pittsburgh. Some change has come over the spirit of your dreams that you should turn out with such cordiality to greet the candidate of the party whom you have hitherto suspected of trying to undermine the very life of your community. There was a time when nobody even ventured to discuss the tariff in Pittsburgh. The very air of Pittsburgh was murky with the fumes of the tariff. Every man in it seemed devoted first of all to his business; and that I should just now have come from a great body of twelve or thirteen hundred diners, seventy-five or eighty per cent of whom I was told had hitherto been Republicans, shows me that something has happened in Pittsburgh.

Here is the stronghold, as the country supposed, of those who stand pat, of those who insist that all the static conditions of the country shall be maintained, and that nobody shall move in any direction for fear of upsetting the nice equipoise of affairs; because the most timid people I have ever known are the high protectionists. They are so afraid that something will happen. They are so afraid that some favor of the government will be withdrawn from the communities in which they live, and that the American people will actually have to live on their brains.

That would be a sad calamity, wouldn't it? Because our brains are so inferior to the brains of any other people in the world that we especially need to be taken care of by our government.

This getting under cover of the genius of the American people is the most extraordinary thing that the history of mankind has ever witnessed. A people able to match its brains against all the world, unwilling to undertake the high enterprise for which it is specially qualified! And, after all, we can now in Pittsburgh discuss the tariff.

You know that the Republican ranks have for some ten or fifteen years been slowly crumbling, largely on that very question. Because there is something that is superior to the arguments of the average protectionist, and that is the course of American history. The most difficult thing that the protectionist has to do is to square his arguments with the actual facts. For example, I dare say that the great body of working-men in the city of Pittsburgh have always seen the level of their wages rise with the increase of the tariff schedules. Have you not? I suppose that whenever there was a revision of the tariff upward every working-man in Pittsburgh found it easier to pay his bills. Did he not? At last it has dawned upon the American people that they have been imposed upon by an argument which does not square with the facts. And now nobody pays any attention to those posters on innumerable billboards which put up the old familiar bluff that the industries of this country will stop if the Democratic party is successful. Before Grover Cleveland was elected, they deliberately closed factories all over this country; and the only way they can be closed again will be as grand a bluff.

Because the whole purpose of the United States now is to think its problems out and decide according to the verdict. They want leadership in thinking—leadership in the settlement of the great questions by the reason that runs through the questions, by the facts that sustain and justify the question. America has discovered the character of its life and it is now going to take charge of that life. We have been trusting to the thinking, or at any rate to what passed for the thinking, of a very small number of persons. And we have discovered two things: either that they can't think at all or that they can't think for us. There has been a grand trust in this country which has overshadowed all the other trusts, and that is the trust in the thinking out and settlement of public questions. Very few persons have been consulted and those that have been consulted knew what they were going to say before the conference took place. A government surrounded by men who knew exactly what they wanted and exactly the arguments and the threats by which to get it is not a government that squares with American principles.

Now, the government of the United States is a possible government to maintain only so long as the people of the United States do their own thinking, and only that government can succeed in the United States which is conducted by men who undertake to be the spokesmen of the common thought of the country at large.

As I was saying in another place tonight, I am for government by discussion, not government by control. But you all agree to these general principles, and the only question that has ever bothered you is: Can we trust the Democratic party to do the job?

I want to point out to you several qualifications that the Democratic party possesses. In the first place, it understood this thing about half a generation before the Republican leaders understood it. They have known for quite two decades and a half what it was that needed to be done in the United States, and they have been waiting for you to see it too. That is their first qualification, and it is a pretty handsome qualification. Do you think that it is no small matter for a great party to have stayed out in the chilly minority of a great nation, simply fighting for principle and getting nothing substantial in return? Do you think that a great body of men mustering millions strong will stand steadfast in season and out of season merely because they are stubborn, merely because they are fanatical, merely because it is pleasant to them to differ with the majority of their fellow citizens?

Don't you see that the steadfastness of a minority looks very like the steadfastness of absolute faith? The Democratic party has stood steadfast in a deep-rooted faith which they could not deny, and it is a faith as old as human liberty. It is a faith—the only faith that has ever buoyed up the human race—the only faith that has ever made the intolerable burden of life possible to bear, namely, the faith that every man ought to have the interest of every other man at his heart. The faith that we would at last set up a government in the world where the average man, the plain man, the common man, the unlearned man, the unaccomplished man, the poor man, had a voice equal to the voice of anybody else in the settlement of the common affairs—an ideal never before realized in the history of the world but which we have all along steadfastly determined should some day be realized in America.

And in these later years what has made some of us fear for the future of the United States has been this: that groups of men have built together a power which seemed so great that the individual merely destroyed himself by throwing himself against it; a power so great that everybody took it for granted that the government of the United States would submit and succumb to it; a power so great that men shrugged their shoulders and said: "Well, monopoly has come to stay, and all that we can do is to make the burden as easy to bear as possible." If that is true then the mission of America has been disappointing; the expectation of the world has been disappointing; America has given over her title deeds; she has admitted her failure to realize the ideals which have underlain every undertaking that she has made.

Ah, gentlemen, we have not quite reached the point of despair, but I do not need to tell you how many neighbors of yours have reached the point of cynicism; I need not tell you how many men were flocking over to the standard of the Socialists, saying neither party any longer bears aloft the ancient torch of liberty, and we must find it elsewhere, so that America began to display a broken field, disordered hosts, men divided in opinion, groups contending for new ways to settle new questions; whereas there is but one way to settle questions, new or old, and that is by the old way of righteousness, of righteousness and justice.

It is not righteous that there should be monopoly. I absolutely subscribe to that sentence which has been repeated again and again in Democratic platforms that private monopoly is indefensible and intolerable.

There can be no righteousness—there can be no just opportunity in the field of business—so long as there is private monopoly in the United States. I do not mean so long as there is big business, for there are two kinds of bigness. There is the kind that comes by growth, and there is the kind that comes by inflation. There is the kind that comes by the increase of natural and wholesome and legitimate strength and ascendancy; and there is the kind that comes by private understanding, by those combinations intended to establish monopoly and not intended to establish efficiency. Justice is never interfered with by efficiency. If big business controls the field of affairs in the United States by serving the country better than it could be served in any other way, then there could be no question to be settled now. But big business does not serve as well as the country could be served under a free competitive system.

Are you businessmen satisfied with the present economic organization of the United States? Do you like these interlocked directorates which unite all the big businesses together? Do you like this limitation of credit to those who can get the approval of these interlocked interests? Do you like superintended increase of industry in the United States? Do you like the control of the markets in which goods are sold and the markets in which labor is sold? Do you believe that that is a free air with which to fill your lungs? Do you believe that that is a free field upon which to spend your energies?

Do you believe that your sons will have the same chance to build up big business independently of these interests that you had when you were youngsters? Don't you see that the whole field has changed in the United States? It used to be a field of domestic competition. Now it is a field organized against competition. And just so soon as the field was organized against competition, then all beginners were served notice, all those who first undertook to get a foothold were notified, that they must stand in with the powers that be or else be destroyed.

The future of America, the economic future of America, depends upon the choice made by the voters of America on the fifth of November. There are two things proposed to you. On the one hand, it is proposed to perpetuate the existing order of things with such modulations, such removal of the worst features, as the law can bring about. And on the other hand, there is proposed to you a series of laws which will see to it that competition is not interfered with, shall see to it that the unfair methods of competition which have built up monopoly in this country are made criminal, and the men who undertook them. You cannot put a corporation in jail, but you can put men who use the power of a corporation wrongly in jail.

You can see to it that the raw materials of this country are accessible to every man in it on the same terms. Not terms fixed by the government, but merely a condition of law, a regulation of law which will see to it that men are not discriminated against, and that everybody gets it upon the same terms. Then there will be a law, if we are to have justice in this country, that no great concern can refuse to sell to retail dealers because they are also buying of competitors. And we can see to it that goods are sold at a uniform price so that the man who is trying to get a local foothold is not killed in his own community. Why, the wrongs that have been committed in the name of free competition are what have destroyed free competition in the United States. It is the wrong use of power that law was always intended to prevent and that law, God willing, will prevent in the United States.

And when we turn to that sensitive matter of the tariff, I look upon the tariff as an unweeded garden. There are some rank growths there that are killing out all the other growths, and they are sustained by an artificial method of cultivation which some men can discover with great ease in particular schedules of the tariff. We are not going in with a pruning knife wielded by men who don't know which are the weeds and which are the flowers; but there is going to be a pruning knife, and the weeds are going to be cut out.

Some of them are very handsome-looking weeds. Some of them are weeds that counterfeit the appearance of flowers. Some of them are weeds which have been there so long that we mistake them for the legitimate growths of the forest. But the minute you put the tariff under this question, where are the special favors and where is the general stimulation, then you will find that the general stimulation is increased by the weeding out of the special favors. And we have got rid of the chief gardeners already.

The most cunning custodian of that old garden that is so extraordinarily running to weeds was the one-time senior Senator from the state of Rhode Island. It is astonishing how big a grip that little state got on the development of the industries of the United States. And it is astonishing how many things Senator Aldrich knew that he never told anybody else. I object to a government which is conducted upon the basis of private information.

If every manufacturer will lay his cards on the table and let us see the real truth about the relation of his profits to the protective tariff, we can come to a satisfactory understanding in twenty-four hours, and the only thing the Democratic party is going to insist on is that we know what the facts are and act accordingly. There isn't going to be any earthquake. There isn't going to be any pulling up by the roots of any wholesome or legitimate business in the United States.

You aren't going to see any storms in the air immediately following the fourth of March, 1913. On the contrary, you are going to see a clearing of the air, and you are going to hear an invitation issued to every man who knows anything and has anything to say to stand up and say it. We are going to break up immediately only one monopoly, and that is the monopoly of the conduct of the government of the country. We are going to consult a great many people instead of a very few people. And I know just how sober, just how conservative, just how good-natured the great American people are. I know it by one infallible proof. No other nation in the world would have stood so long for such a government.

It is your government, and yet you have sat on the side lines and watched other people run it, and sat with infinite patience applauding the few good plays and keeping dumbly silent over the bad ones. Aren't you a little tired being outside? Wouldn't you like to have a look-in? Wouldn't you like to feel that your opinion told for something at the ballot box? Wouldn't you like to feel that you were voting a ticket that really meant what you wanted to do? You haven't done that in a long time.

You have sometimes done it in the city of Pittsburgh, but you haven't often done it at a national election. You have generally done what you were told to do and were thankful to get off with that. I have had the greatest pleasure in recent months in defending the people of Pennsylvania, and trying to convince people in distant parts of the country that they really didn't manage their government. I have drawn an analogy from your neighbors on the other side of the Delaware.

New Jersey seemed at one time to be just as content with privately owned and personally conducted government as you are. But they were really not content. They were looking for a way out, and to their great surprise, I suspect, they found a way out in 1910 through the instrumentality of an inexperienced and perfectly innocent person, who did not have any better sense or understanding of politics than to think that it consisted of finding out everything he could and then talking about it. I must admit to you before you vote for me that I have the fatal habit of talking about what I know.

I know a great deal more about the government of New Jersey than I did before I got on the inside, and I dare say that it may fall to my lot to know a great deal more than I do now about the inside of the government of the United States. If I should find things out, I promise you now and here that I will come back and tell you about them. Because you constitute the only jury that I am interested in.

I am perfectly willing that these gentlemen who have been running the government of the United States should be part of the people of the United States, but I am not willing that they should be all of them. And if they will come in on the principle of share and share alike, they are most welcome. The door will never be closed in their faces. Because, ladies and gentlemen, while we talk of restoring government to the people, it is a very great and a very solemn undertaking. It is not a thing that can be accomplished by words. It is a thing that can be accomplished only by the voters of the United States determining to see the facts as they are, allowing no man to gloss them over or change them in the exposition. And that then they will choose men and measures irrespective of parties.

We have come to the time now when we cannot afford to vote the way our fathers voted, simply because our fathers voted in another age and in the presence of other questions. And they would be ashamed of us if we didn't exercise the same individual choice that they exercised when they built up parties and created governments.

The United States has lost her prestige if she depends upon groups of politicians to tell her which way she should turn. Politicians are to serve the people, not to direct them. And my highest ambition is to be, so far as it is possible to be with the gifts that God has given me, the spokesman, the interpreter, the servant of the people of the United States.

ADDRESS AT THE ASTOR HOTEL, NEW YORK CITY, COLUMBUS DAY, OCTOBER 12, 1912

. . . I suppose that the discovery of America by Columbus must always appeal afresh to the imagination, no matter how often we think of it. There are a great many interpretations that may be put upon it and upon the character of Columbus in undertaking it, but there can be only one judgment as to what the event was significant of. For whether you look at it in one light or in another, this is what happened: The Atlantic had been at the back of Europe. All the face of Europe was turned eastward, not westward. All the routes of trade, all the impulses of energy ran from the west to the east; and that little kingdom of

England, that little green jewel of Ireland, was out at the back of the nation on the edge of an unknown sea into which men hardly dared to venture. And then suddenly, with the closing of the route to the East by the conquest of Constantinople by the Turks, Europe had either to face about or else to lack any direction in which she could release her energies—and so she swung about and faced the Atlantic. It was necessary that somebody should undertake to be a pioneer upon that trackless sea, and so soon as that happened the whole aspect of the world changed because the world had not known itself.

Columbus did not expect to find a continent occupied by only a few tribes of savage Indians; he expected to find Cathay, which Marco Polo had visited going eastward out of Europe, and find the kingdoms of far Asia. And instead of that he found not civilization but a continent, so far as civilization was concerned, thoroughly unoccupied, unused, unknown; so that the world turned out to be twice as big as he had supposed it to be, twice as big as anybody ever dreamed that it was. And it was necessary to put into that vacant half of the world, so far, at any rate, as North America was concerned, a new continent; and the significance in the history of the world is, if it has any significance, that the contents, the purposes, the impulses, the civilization established on that vacant continent was new, shot through with new impulses.

Under the impulse of new ideals, conceived with a new set of purposes, it became, instead of a mere seaman's ambition, a moral adventure to create a new world—creating a new world from out of this beautiful continent which no man approached without, as you remember the old voyagers all narrate, receiving a sweet air with the breath that came off the continent, out of woods aflame with flowers. And as they approached, the quiet sound of flowing water, nature in all her beauty, waiting to be touched by the touch of life, not waiting to be touched by the life which men had known in the old world, but waiting to be touched by new conceptions; not only waiting to be touched by the things that had wearied, and in some cases debauched and debased the old world, but defiled if touched in her virgin beauty by these old things that had made older peoples groan under the burden of things intolerable to bear.

And so the whole thing springs into the imagination like the creation of a vision, as well as the discovery of a continent—a vision such as those who found it did not expect to see. I suppose that the receptive soul seldom receives the vision that it is looking for. I suppose that the vision comes in between. The vision is given, not created, by the eye that sees. And so there sprang up in this western country a new age for the life of men, an age that could have dignity only if it were lifted to a new spiritual level.

The year 1492, therefore, is not so remote as we might conceive from the year 1912, because unless we can continue to consecrate this great continent upon which we live to a higher level of spiritual life for mankind, we may some day learn to regret that it was ever discovered; we may some day feel that it was a disgrace to have had a free field in which to do new things and yet not have done them, or to have failed in the doing of them at the very point of trial and of crisis.

The serious thing about America is that we are now about to try this question out: Can we realize our ideals? Now that our youth is past, now that it is no longer easy to live in America, now that we know her resources are no longer inexhaustible, now that we know that we are in hot contact class with class, in hot competition, selfishness with idealism, can we again lift it into the air in which it was lifted at the beginning? For no man can look at that ship of Columbus without knowing, now standing where we do, what it signified. For one thing, we have talked of America as if it were an Anglo-Saxon possession, which is contrary to every indication of its birth and to every fact of its history. It was the eye of an Italian captain that first beheld America and again and again I, for my part, have been reminded of the ideals of America by learning of what were the hopes of those who came out of the old countries to join us on this side of the sea.

I have sometimes thought that the American vision was fresher in the eyes of many an immigrant than it was in the eyes of men born and bred in America. And as many an immigrant bears America with him in his hope, in his imagination, in his confident expectation, so we may say that this first immigrant, this gallant Italian, brought the suggestion of America across the sea, out of that old land—not the land from which he was nourished but the land from which he had originally come— that ran all the threads of its history back through the annals of Rome and touched the beginnings of civilization in Europe.

This is the image of America, the hope of the world, the aspiration of those not in it, as well as the care of those that are in it, the fulfillment of what the human race has hoped for, the guarantee that the fund of hope is not expended and exhausted, but that it lies here in bank in our hand from generation to generation as if we were trustees to see that it was handed on unimpaired to those who seek to realize an opportunity. And, therefore, it seems to me very stimulating for men in the midst of affairs, whether they be their own affairs or public affairs, for men in the midst of business and in the midst of politics to dream a little while about that ship coming in, and ask if the freight that she brought has been debased in any way by our treatment of it—ask if the eyes that now look from the other side of the water towards America are dulled and robbed of that bright gleam of anticipation which must have shone in the faces of those sailors. Because it is the interesting task of every generation in a free country not to receive the ideals of that country by way of inheritance, but to reconceive them and realize them all over again. For there must be a renaissance of fresh birth and renewal in our own conception of the ideals of America or else they will decline and disappear.

Politics in America is a more serious business than it is anywhere else in the world, because there are so many precedents that you dare not reverse, and there are so many plans that you dare not cut off; there are so many boasts, let us say, that you dare not fail to redeem; there is so much behind us, the pace is so tremendous, and the impulse so irresistible that every generation in America must be better than the generation before it or else it will be discredited.

And so my interest in politics in this present year of grace—for it promises to be a year of grace—is that there is some prospect that we shall end the misunderstandings in America; that we shall bring classes to comprehend one another; that we shall bring about common counsel again; that we shall cease the fruitless contests of interest with interest and unite all interests upon a basis, not of generosity but of mutual understanding and of mutual comprehension, and put all through the life of America again that sense of brotherhood, that sense of a common enterprise in behalf of mankind which will not only make us happy, but make us prosperous; which will not only make us properous, but keep us great.

# PART IV

# THE OUTWARD REACH
## OF POWER

# The Caribbean, the Canal, and Righteous Peace

## *Theodore Roosevelt*

*Progressives often questioned the depth and solidity of Theodore Roosevelt's commitment to domestic reform, but no one seriously challenged his reputation as the preeminent spokesman for America's expanding power in foreign affairs at the beginning of the new century. The vigor and elan of the Pacific squadron in its destruction of the Spanish fleet off Manila in 1898 owed much to the vigor with which the Assistant Naval Secretary had prepared it to strike. The public image of Spain's retreat from Cuba overlooked the crucial role of naval fire power and centered instead on the symbol of an intrepid colonel charging uphill with his regiment of volunteers against an entrenched foe. The sharp sting of American intervention in the economic affairs of Caribbean governments was somewhat softened (for Americans, if for no one else) by the disingenuous but plausible explanation of the President of the United States that the ancient Monroe Doctrine needed strengthening if it would continue to serve us. Sometimes the President explained too much. When the American government aggressively extended its naval lifeline across the Caribbean to the Pacific it did so primarily to be assured greater security in a shrinking world, but this purpose was made unnecessarily obscure by the moral arguments which Roosevelt habitually invoked to justify his strategies. Whatever the result, Roosevelt's central part in the drama of foreign affairs stimulated the sort of sharp debate that is likely to occur, whenever a strong policy is uniquely embodied in a controversial public figure.*

*Roosevelt's personal views inspired in his critics a persistent stereotype. Liberals deplored what they imagined was his commitment to doctrines of race supremacy. Champions of peace saw him as a saber-rattling imperialist. Others suspected him of glorying in the stimulation of military adventures. Roosevelt, said William James with more curiosity than* condemnation, "gushes over war and treats peace as a condition of blubberlike and swollen ignobility." If James exaggerated the case, the fault could be traced to Roosevelt himself, who often attempted to fulfill the roles assigned him even when in fact he did not. Brand Whitlock, a reformer and writer on good terms with the President, entered the White House study one evening for a chat. "I will tell you where you and I disagree," said Roosevelt, pointing a vigorous finger at Whitlock before either had exchanged a word. "You think that nobody ought to be killed and I think that the world would be a great deal better off if some undesirable people were put out of it." Whitlock knew Roosevelt well enough to take the remark in partial jest, but for a large number of Americans Roosevelt appeared to consider himself sufficiently equipped with moral insight to decide on his own which were the undesirable people and which were not. Some of the public uneasiness over American foreign policy stemmed from its view of the President as a man of overly righteous conviction and irresponsible impulse.

The public view of Roosevelt was often more than half wrong. He plainly admired the British, German, and Japanese nations, while his disdain for Chinese, Indian, and Latin peoples was ill-concealed. Though he did not always take pains to clarify his meaning, it is now fairly clear that he was not subscribing to racism, the double view that specific traits of character were to be found concentrated in biologically distinct peoples and that character was genetically foreordained. Rather, he was passing judgment on traits of political custom which he tended to ascribe to specific national states, such as the effectiveness of nations to act vigorously in their own interests. If he believed that the United States possessed moral standards superior to those of its neighbors, he also expressed the characteristic hope of progressives that, given our example and a proper change of environment, our neighbors could in time become like us. His was an environmental, not a biological, interpretation of peoples, and he shared this view with most of the liberals of his day.

On questions of power Roosevelt also risked being misunderstood. Anti-imperialists construed his spectacular decision to send the American navy around the world as warmongering. Roosevelt, who had just received the Nobel Prize for peace, viewed the voyage as a bold step to head off war. The mood of the Japanese nation in 1907 seemed ominous; British and German sources warned Roosevelt of a possible move against the Philippines. "The only thing which will prevent war," said Roosevelt to Elihu Root, his Secretary of War, "is the Japanese feeling that we shall not be beaten." Roosevelt proposed to reveal to the Japanese fifth-ranked navy what the world's second-ranked navy looked like; the fleet sailed plainly armed but painted white; and peace in the Pacific was preserved. Roosevelt applauded physical courage and efficiency in military *maneuvers; he insisted that any honorable citizenry must be prepared and eager to defend its national interests. For him a dazzling cruise across four oceans embodied the twofold virtue of preserving peace in the best interests of a modern commercial state and of exercising the moral muscles of its people. If Roosevelt glorified soldiers and sailors, he did so not because they went forth to kill but because to defend the honor of their nation they were willing to risk being killed.*

*It was partly to end these misunderstandings that Roosevelt published his autobiography, first in the* Outlook *(serially in 1913) and then as a book in time to enhance his hopes for a political comeback in 1916. Two chapters recounted American foreign affairs during the progressive era and his own role in fashioning them. These we have chosen to reprint. For the most part his narrative succeeded in setting straight a controversial record and may be regarded as fundamentally reliable, but in a few notable instances it unfortunately twisted the truth still further. Roosevelt, for example, writes about the Caribbean and the Far East as though considerations of naval power and security had had nothing to do with American decisions in Cuba, Puerto Rico, and the Philippines. Nor would anyone who took seriously his account of the Panama Canal be likely to realize that the sovereign Colombian legislature had in fact a perfect legal right to refuse to ratify a treaty which its ambassador had signed, or that the weight of history was entirely on its side when it sought to extract the greatest possible price for a choice piece of its own real estate. The reader is not told that the Panamanian "revolution" against Colombia was engineered in New York by former agents of the French company who had hoped that the United States would see fit to purchase its rights to the property. Despite Roosevelt's explicit denial, these agents kept the White House and the State Department informed of their plottings and in return were given to understand that the United States would (as in fact it did) prevent Colombian troops from interfering in a revolt against the authority of the Colombian government on soil that was unquestionably Colombian.*

*But if parts of Roosevelt's account are misleading, the spirit of his account is revealing. The canal was a prodigious plume in Roosevelt's cap. Within the year (January, 1914) it would open to the traffic of the world. The ex-President was anxious that no confusion remain as to who had done more than any other man to guarantee that the United States would build it and own it. He was also anxious to identify the canal as a national achievement. As a general rule Roosevelt avoided the mystical flag-waving of Senator Beveridge and the earlier jingoists. What emerged instead was a half-conscious formulation of a view congenial to his progressive generation: for international affairs as for one's personal career, conduct must be judged by the codes and principles of moral, high-minded Christian men, seeking to preserve peace and to build a triumphant prosperity. Any great nation must first be certain that its interests were consistent with justice and honor and then be ready to use power to protect its interests. That was Roosevelt's creed, the creed of a man who generally could make the issues of his day appear simpler than they really were.*

No nation can claim rights without acknowledging the duties that go with the rights. It is a contemptible thing for a great nation to render itself impotent in international action, whether because of cowardice or sloth, or sheer inability or unwillingness to look into the future. It is a very wicked thing for a nation to do wrong to others. But the most contemptible and most wicked course of conduct is for a nation to use offensive language or be guilty of offensive actions toward other people and yet fail to hold its own if the other nation retaliates; and it is almost as bad to undertake responsibilities and then not fulfil them. During the seven and a half years that I was President, this Nation behaved in international matters toward all other nations precisely as an honorable man behaves to his fellow-men. We made no promise which we could not and did not keep. We made no threat which we did not carry out. We never failed to assert our rights in the face of the strong, and we never failed to treat both strong and weak with courtesy and justice; and against the weak when they misbehaved we were slower to assert our rights than we were against the strong.

As a legacy of the Spanish War we were left with peculiar relations to the Philippines, Cuba, and Porto Rico, and with an immensely added interest in Central America and the Caribbean Sea. As regards the Philippines my belief was that we should train them for self-government as rapidly as possible, and then leave them free to decide their own fate. I did not believe in setting the time-limit within which we would give them independence, because I did not believe it wise to try to forecast how soon they would be fit for self-government; and once having made the promise I would have felt that it was imperative to keep it. Within a few months of my assuming office we had stamped out the last armed resistance in the Philippines that was not of merely sporadic character; and as soon as peace was secured we turned our energies to developing the islands in the interests of the natives. We established schools everywhere; we built roads; we administered an even-handed justice; we did everything possible to encourage agriculture and industry; and in constantly increasing measure we employed natives to do their own governing, and finally provided a legislative chamber. No higher grade of

*Theodore Roosevelt: an Autobiography* (New York: Scribner's, 1913), pp. 543-605.

public officials ever handled the affairs of any colony than the public officials who in succession governed the Philippines. With the possible exception of the Sudan, and not even excepting Algiers, I know of no country ruled and administered by men of the white race where that rule and that administration have been exercised so emphatically with an eye single to the welfare of the natives themselves. The English and Dutch administrators of Malaysia have done admirable work; but the profit to the Europeans in those States has always been one of the chief elements considered; whereas in the Philippines our whole attention was concentrated upon the welfare of the Filipinos themselves, if anything to the neglect of our own interests.

I do not believe that America has any special beneficial interest in retaining the Philippines. Our work there has benefited us only as any efficiently done work performed for the benefit of others does incidentally help the character of those who do it. The people of the islands have never developed so rapidly, from every standpoint, as during the years of the American occupation. The time will come when it will be wise to take their own judgment as to whether they wish to continue their association with America or not. There is, however, one consideration upon which we should insist. Either we should retain complete control of the islands, or absolve ourselves from all responsibility for them. Any half and half course would be both foolish and disastrous. We are governing and have been governing the islands in the interests of the Filipinos themselves. If after due time the Filipinos themselves decide that they do not wish to be thus governed, then I trust that we will leave; but when we do leave it must be distinctly understood that we retain no protectorate—and above all that we take part in no joint protectorate—over the islands, and give them no guarantee, of neutrality or otherwise; that, in short, we are absolutely quit of responsibility for them, of every kind and description.

The Filipinos were quite incapable of standing by themselves when we took possession of the islands, and we had made no promise concerning them. But we had explicitly promised to leave the island of Cuba, had explicitly promised that Cuba should be independent. Early in my administration that promise was redeemed. When the promise was made, I doubt if there was a single ruler or diplomat in Europe who believed that it would be kept. As far as I know, the United States was the first power which, having made such a promise, kept it in letter and spirit. England was unwise enough to make such a promise when she took Egypt. It would have been a capital misfortune to have kept the promise, and England has remained in Egypt for over thirty years, and will unquestionably remain indefinitely; but though it is necessary for her to do so, the fact of her doing so has meant the breaking of a positive promise and has been a real evil. Japan made the same guarantee about Korea, but as far as can be seen there was never even any thought of keeping the promise in this case; and Korea, which had shown herself utterly impotent either for self-government or self-defense, was in actual fact almost immediately annexed to Japan.

We made the promise to give Cuba independence; and we kept the promise. Leonard Wood was left in as Governor for two or three years, and evolved order out of chaos, raising the administration of the island to a level, moral and material, which it had never before achieved. We also by treaty gave the Cubans substantial advantages in our markets. Then we left the island, turning the government over to its own people. After four or five years a revolution broke out, during my administration, and we again had to intervene to restore order. We promptly sent thither a small army of pacification. Under General Barry, order was restored and kept, and absolute justice done. The American troops were then withdrawn and the Cubans reëstablished in complete possession of their own beautiful island, and they are in possesison of it now. There are plenty of occasions in our history when we have shown weakness or inefficiency, and some occasions when we have not been as scrupulous as we should have been as regards the rights of others. But I know of no action by any other government in relation to a weaker power which showed such disinterested efficiency in rendering service as was true in connection with our intervention in Cuba.

In Cuba, as in the Philippines and as in Porto Rico, Santo Domingo, and later in Panama, no small part of our success was due to the fact that we put in the highest grade of men as public officials. This practice was inaugurated under President McKinley. I found admirable men in office, and I continued them and appointed men like them as their successors. The way that the custom-houses in Santo Domingo were administered by Colton definitely established the success of our experiment in securing peace for that island republic; and in Porto Rico, under the administration of affairs under such officials as Hunt, Winthrop, Post, Ward and Grahame, more substantial progress was achieved in a decade than in any previous century.

The Philippines, Cuba, and Porto Rico came within our own sphere of governmental action. In addition to this we asserted certain rights in the Western Hemisphere under the Monroe Doctrine. My endeavor was not only to assert these rights, but frankly and fully to acknowledge the duties that went with the rights.

The Monroe Doctrine lays down the rule that the Western Hemisphere is not hereafter to be treated as subject to settlement and occupation by Old World powers. It is not international law; but it is a cardinal principle of our foreign policy. There is no difficulty at the present day in maintaining this doctrine, save where the American power whose interest is threatened has shown itself in international matters both weak and delinquent. The great and prosperous civilized commonwealths, such as the Argentine, Brazil, and Chile, in the Southern half of South America, have advanced so far that they no longer stand in any position of tutelage toward the United States. They occupy toward us precisely the position that Canada occupies. Their friendship is the friendship of equals for equals. My view was that as regards these nations there was no more necessity for asserting the Monroe Doctrine than there was to assert it in regard to Canada. They were competent to assert it for themselves. Of course if one of these nations, or if Canada, should be overcome by some Old World power, which then proceeded to occupy its territory, we would undoubtedly, if the American Nation needed our help, give it in order to prevent such occupation from taking place. But the initiative would come from the Nation itself, and the United States would merely act as a friend whose help was invoked.

The case was (and is) widely different as regards certain—not all—of the tropical states in the neighborhood of the Caribbean Sea. Where these states are stable and prosperous, they stand on a footing of absolute equality with all other communities. But some of them have been a prey to such continuous revolutionary misrule as to have grown impotent either to do their duties to outsiders or to enforce their rights against outsiders. The United States has not the slightest desire to make aggressions on any one of these states. On the contrary, it will submit to much from them without showing resentment. If any great civilized power, Russia or Germany, for instance, had behaved toward us as Venezuela under Castro behaved, this country would have gone to war at once. We did not go to war with Venezuela merely because our people declined to be irritated by the actions of a weak opponent, and showed a forbearance which probably went beyond the limits of wisdom in refusing to take umbrage at what was done by the weak; although we would certainly have resented it had it been done by the strong. In the case of two states, however, affairs reached such a crisis that we had to act. These two states were Santo Domingo and the then owner of the Isthmus of Panama, Colombia.

The Santo Domingan case was the less important; and yet it possessed a real importance, and moreover is instructive because the action there taken should serve as a precedent for American action in all similar cases. During the early years of my administration Santo Domingo was in its usual condition of chronic revolution. There was always fighting, always plundering; and the successful graspers for governmental power were always pawning ports and custom-houses, or trying to put them up as guarantees for loans. Of course the foreigners who made loans under such conditions demanded exorbitant interest, and if they were Europeans expected their governments to stand by them. So utter was the disorder that on one occasion when Admiral Dewey landed to pay a call of ceremony on the President, he and his party were shot at by revolutionists in crossing the square, and had to return to the ships, leaving the call unpaid. There was default on the interest due to the creditors; and finally the latter insisted upon their governments intervening. Two or three of the European powers were endeavoring to arrange for concerted action, and I was finally notified that these powers intended to take and hold several of the seaports which held custom-houses.

This meant that unless I acted at once I would find foreign powers in partial possession of Santo Domingo; in which event the very individuals who, in the actual event deprecated the precaution taken to prevent such action, would have advocated extreme and violent measures to undo the effect of their own supineness. Nine-tenths of wisdom is to be wise in time, and at the right time; and my whole foreign policy was based on the exercise of intelligent forethought and of decisive action sufficiently far in advance of any likely crisis to make it improbable that we would run into serious trouble.

Santo Domingo had fallen into such chaos that once for some weeks there were two rival governments in it, and a revolution was being carried on against each. At one period one government was at sea in a small gunboat, but still stoutly maintained that it was in possession of the island and entitled to make loans and declare peace or war. The situation had become intolerable by the time that I interfered. There was a naval commander in the waters whom I directed to prevent any fighting which might menace the custom-houses. He carried out his orders, both to his and my satisfaction, in thoroughgoing fashion. On one occasion, when an insurgent force threatened to attack a town in which Americans had interests, he notified the commanders on both sides that he would not permit any fighting in the town, but that he would appoint a certain place where they could meet and fight it out, and that the victors should have the town. They agreed to meet his wishes, the fight came off at the appointed place, and the victors, who if I remember rightly were the insurgents, were given the town.

It was the custom-houses that caused the trouble, for they offered the only means of raising money, and the revolutions were carried on to get possession of them. Accordingly I secured an agreement with the governmental authorities, who for the moment seemed best able to speak for the country, by which these custom-houses were placed under American control. The arrangement was that we should keep order and prevent any interference with the custom houses or the places where they stood, and should collect the revenues. Forty-five percent of the revenue was then turned over to the Santo Domingan Government, and fifty-five per cent put in a sinking fund in New York for the benefit of the creditors. The arrangement worked in capital style. On the forty-five per cent basis the Santo Domingan Government received from us a larger sum than it had ever received before when nominally all the revenue went to it. The creditors were entirely satisfied with the arrangement, and no excuse for interference by European powers remained. Occasional disturbances occurred in the island, of course, but on the whole there ensued a degree of peace and prosperity which the island had not known before for at least a century.

All this was done without the loss of a life, with the assent of all the parties in interest, and without subjecting the United States to any charge, while practically all of the interference, after the naval commander whom I have mentioned had taken the initial steps in preserving order, consisted in putting a first-class man trained in our insular service at the head of the Santo Domingan customs service. We secured peace, we protected the people of the islands against foreign foes, and we minimized the chance of domestic trouble. We satisfied the creditors and the foreign nations to which the creditors belonged; and our own part of the work was done with the utmost efficiency and with rigid honesty, so that not a particle of scandal was ever so much as hinted at.

Under these circumstances those who do not know the nature of the professional international philanthropists would suppose that these apostles of international peace would have been overjoyed with what we had done. As a matter of fact, when they took any notice of it at all it was to denounce it; and those American newspapers which are fondest of proclaiming themselves the foes of war and the friends of peace violently attacked me for averting war from, and bringing peace to, the island. They insisted I had no power to make the agreement, and demanded the rejection of the treaty which was to perpetuate the agreement. They were, of course, wholly unable to advance a single sound reason of any kind for their attitude. I suppose the real explanation was partly their dislike of me personally, and unwillingness to see peace come through or national honor upheld by me; and in the next place their sheer, simple devotion to prattle and dislike of efficiency. They liked to have people come together and talk about peace, or even sign bits of paper with something about peace or arbitration on them, but they took no interest whatever in the practical achievement of a peace that told for good government and decency and honesty. They were joined by the many moderately well-meaning men who always demand that a thing be done, but also always demand that it be not done in the only way in which it is, as a matter of fact, possible to do it. The men of this kind insisted that of course Santo Domingo must be protected and made to behave itself, and that of course the Panama Canal must be dug; but they insisted even more strongly that neither feat should be accomplished in the only way in which it was possible to accomplish it at all. . . .

By far the most important action I took in foreign affairs during the time I was President related to the Panama Canal. Here again there was much accusation about my having acted in an "unconstitutional" manner —a position which can be upheld only if Jefferson's action in acquiring Louisiana be also treated as unconstitutional; and at different stages of the affair believers in a do-nothing policy denounced me as having "usurped authority"—which meant, that when nobody else could or would exercise efficient authority, I exercised it.

During the nearly four hundred years that had elapsed since Balboa crossed the Isthmus, there had been a good deal of talk about building an Isthmus canal, and there had been various discussions of the subject and negotiations about it in Washington for the previous half century. So far it had all resulted merely in conversation; and the time had come when unless somebody was prepared to act with decision we would have to resign ourselves to at least half a century of further conversation. Under the Hay-Pauncefote Treaty signed shortly after I became President, and thanks to our negotiations with the French Panama Company, the United States at last acquired a possession, so far as Europe was concerned, which warranted her in immediately undertaking the task. It remained to decide where the canal should be, whether along the line already pioneered by the French company in Panama, or in Nicaragua. Panama belonged to the Republic of Colombia. Nicaragua bid eagerly for the privilege of having the United States build the canal through her territory. As long as it was doubtful which route we would decide upon, Colombia extended every promise of friendly coöperation: at the Pan-American Congress in Mexico her delegate joined in the unanimous vote which requested the United States forthwith to build the canal; and at her eager request we negotiated the Hay-Herran Treaty with her, which gave us the right to build the canal across Panama. A board of experts sent to the Isthmus had reported that this route was better than the Nicaragua route, and that it would be well to build the canal over it provided we could purchase the rights of the French company for forty million dollars; but that otherwise they would advise taking the Nicaragua route. Ever since 1846 we had had a treaty with the power then in control of the Isthmus, the Republic of New Granada, the predecessor of the Republic of Colombia and of the present Republic of Panama, by which treaty the United States was guaranteed free and open right of way across the Isthmus of Panama by any mode of communication that might be constructed, while in return our Government guaranteed the perfect neutrality of the Isthmus with a view to the preservation of free transit.

For nearly fifty years we had asserted the right to prevent the closing of this highway of commerce. Secretary of State Cass in 1858 officially stated the American position as follows:

"Sovereignty has its duties as well as its rights, and none of these local governments, even if administered with more regard to the just demands of other nations than they have been, would be permitted, in a spirit of Eastern isolation, to close the gates of intercourse of the great highways of the world, and justify the act by the pretension that these avenues of trade and travel belong to them and that they choose to shut them, or, what is almost equivalent, to encumber them with such unjust relations as would prevent their general use."

We had again and again been forced to intervene to protect the transit across the Isthmus, and the intervention was frequently at the request of Colombia herself. The effort to build a canal by private capital had been made under De Lesseps and had resulted in lamentable failure. Every serious proposal to build the canal in such manner had been abandoned. The United States had repeatedly announced that we would not permit it to be built or controlled by any old-world government. Colombia was utterly impotent to build it herself. Under these circumstances it had become a matter of imperative obligation that we should build it ourselves without further delay.

I took final action in 1903. During the preceding fifty-three years the Governments of New Granada and of its successor, Colombia, had been in a constant state of flux; and the State of Panama had sometimes been treated as almost independent, in a loose Federal league, and sometimes as the mere property of the Government at Bogota; and there had been innumerable appeals to arms, sometimes for adequate, sometimes for inadequate, reasons [averaging one a year for fifty-three years]. . . . One of them lasted for nearly three years before it was quelled; another for nearly a year. In short, the experience of over half a century had shown Colombia to be utterly incapable of keeping order on the Isthmus. Only the active interference of the United States had enabled her to preserve so much as a semblance of sovereignty. Had it not been for the exercise by the United States of the police power in her interest, her connection with the Isthmus would have been sundered long before it was. In 1856, in 1860, in 1873, in 1885, in 1901, and again in 1902, sailors and marines from United States warships were forced to land in order to patrol the Isthmus, to protect life and property, and to see that the transit across the Isthmus was kept open. In 1861, in 1862, in 1885, and in 1900, the Colombian Government asked that the United States Government would land troops to protect Colombian interests and maintain order on the Isthmus. The people of Panama during the preceding twenty years had three times sought to establish their independence by revolution or secession—in 1885, in 1895, and in 1899. . . .

Meanwhile Colombia was under a dictatorship. In 1898 M. A. Sanclamente was elected President, and J. M. Maroquin Vice-President, of the Republic of Colombia. On July 31, 1900, the Vice-President, Maroquin, executed a "coup d'état" by seizing the person of the President, Sanclamente, and imprisoning him at a place a few miles out of Bogota. Maroquin thereupon declared himself possessed of the executive power because of "the absence of the President"—a delightful touch of unconscious humor. He then issued a decree that public order was disturbed, and, upon that ground, assumed to himself legislative power under another provision of the constitution; that is, having himself disturbed the public order, he alleged the disturbance as a justification for seizing absolute power. Thenceforth Maroquin, without the aid of any legislative body, ruled as a dictator, combining the supreme executive, legislative, civil, and military authorities, in the so-called Republic of Colombia. The "absence" of Sanclamente from the capital became permanent by his death in prison in the year 1902. When the people of Panama declared their independence in November, 1903, no Congress had sat in Colombia since the year 1898, except the special Congress called by Maroquin to reject the canal treaty, and which did reject it by a unanimous vote, and adjourned without legislating on any other subject. The constitution of 1886 had taken away from Panama the power of self-government and vested it in Colombia. The *coup d'état* of Maroquin took away from Colombia herself the power of government and vested it in an irresponsible dictator.

Consideration of the above facts ought to be enough to show any human being that we were not dealing with normal conditions on the Isthmus and in Colombia. We were dealing with the government of an irresponsible alien dictator, and with a condition of affairs on the Isthmus itself which was marked by one uninterrupted series of outbreaks and revolutions. As for the "consent of the governed" theory, that absolutely justified our action; the people on the Isthmus were the "governed"; they were governed by Colombia, without their consent, and they unanimously repudiated the Colombian government, and demanded that the United States build the canal.

I had done everything possible, personally and through Secretary Hay, to persuade the Colombian Government to keep faith. Under the Hay-Pauncefote Treaty, it was explicitly provided that the United States should build the canal, should control, police and protect it, and keep it open to the vessels of all nations on equal terms. We had assumed the position of guarantor of the canal, including, of course, the building of the canal, and of its peaceful use by all the world. The enterprise was recognized everywhere as responding to an international need. It was a mere travesty on justice to treat the government in possession of the Isthmus as having the right—which Secretary Cass forty-five years before had so emphatically repudiated—to close the gates of intercourse on one of the great highways of the world. When we submitted to Colombia the Hay-Herran Treaty, it had been settled that the time for delay, the time for permitting any government of anti-social character, or of imperfect development, to bar the work, had passed. The United States had assumed in connection with the canal certain responsibilities not only to its own people but to the civilized world which imperatively demanded that there should be no further delay in beginning the work. The Hay-Herran Treaty, if it erred at all, erred in being overgenerous toward Colombia. The people of Panama were delighted with the treaty, and the President of Colombia, who embodied in his own person the entire government of Colombia, had authorized the treaty to be made. But after the treaty had been made the Colombia Government thought it had the matter in its own hands; and the further thought, equally wicked and foolish, came into the heads of the people in control at Bogota that they would seize the French Company at the end of another year and take for themselves the forty million dollars which the United States had agreed to pay the Panama Canal Company.

President Maroquin, through his Minister, had agreed to the Hay-Herran Treaty in January, 1903. He had the absolute power of an unconstitutional dictator to keep his promise or break it. He determined to break it. To furnish himself an excuse for breaking it he advised the plan of summoning a Congress especially called to reject the canal treaty. This the Congress—a Congress of mere puppets—did, without a dissenting vote; and the puppets adjourned forthwith without legislating on any other subject. The fact that this was a mere sham, and that the President had entire power to confirm his own treaty and act on it if he desired, was shown as soon as the revolution took place, for on November 6 General Reyes of Colombia addressed the American Minister at Bogota, on behalf of President Maroquin, saying that "if the Government of the United States would land troops and restore the Colombian sovereignty" the Colombian President would "declare martial law; and, by virtue of vested constitutional authority, when public order is disturbed, would approve by decree the ratification of the canal treaty as signed; or, if the Government of the United States prefers, would call an extra session of the Congress—with new and friendly members—next May to approve the treaty." This, of course, is proof positive that the Colombian dictator had used his Congress as a mere shield, and a sham shield at that, and it shows how utterly useless it would have been further to trust his good faith in the matter.

When, in August, 1903, I became convinced that Colombia intended to repudiate the treaty made the preceding January, under cover of securing its rejection by the Colombian Legislature, I began carefully to consider what should be done. By my direction Secretary Hay, personally and through the Minister at Bogota, repeatedly warned Colombia that grave consequences might follow her rejection of the treaty. The possibility of ratification did not wholly pass away until the close of the session of the Colombian Congress on the last day of October. There would then be two possibilities. One was that Panama would remain quiet. In that case I was prepared to recommend to Congress that we should at once occupy the Isthmus anyhow, and proceed to dig the canal; and I had drawn out a draft of my message to this effect. But from the information I received, I deemed it likely that there would be a revolution in Panama as soon as the Colombian Congress adjourned without ratifying the treaty, for the entire population of Panama felt that the immediate building of the canal was of vital concern to their well-being. Correspondents of the different newspapers on the Isthmus had sent to their respective papers widely published forecasts indicating that there would be a revolution in such event.

Moreover, on October 16, at the request of Lieutenant-General Young, Captain Humphrey and Lieutenant Murphy, two army officers who had returned from the Isthmus, saw me and told me that there would unquestionably be a revolution on the Isthmus, that the people were unanimous in their criticism of the Bogota Government and their disgust over the failure of that Government to ratify the treaty; and that the revolution would probably take place immediately after the adjournment of the Colombian Congress. They did not believe that it would be before October 20, but they were confident that it would certainly come at the end of October or immediately afterwards, when the Colombian Congress had adjourned. Accordingly I directed the Navy Department to station various ships within easy reach of the Isthmus, to be ready to act in the event of need arising.

These ships were barely in time. On November 3 the revolution occurred. Practically everybody on the Isthmus, including all the Colombian troops that were already stationed there, joined in the revolution, and there was no bloodshed. But on that same day four hundred new Colombian troops were landed at Colon. Fortunately, the gunboat *Nashville,* under Commander Hubbard, reached Colon almost immediately afterwards, and when the commander of the Colombian forces threatened the lives and property of the American citizens, including women and children, in Colon, Commander Hubbard landed a few score sailors and marines to protect them. By a mixture of firmness and tact he not only prevented any assault on our citizens, but persuaded the Colombian commander to reëmbark his troops for Cartagena. On the Pacific side a Colombian gunboat shelled the City of Panama, with the result of killing one Chinaman—the only life lost in the whole affair.

No one connected with the American Government had any part in preparing, inciting, or encouraging the revolution, and except for the reports of our military and naval officers, which I forwarded to Congress, no one connected with the Government had any previous knowledge concerning the proposed revolution, except such as was accessible to any person who read the newspapers and kept abreast of current questions and current affairs. By the unanimous action of its people, and without the firing of a shot, the state of Panama declared themselves an independent republic. The time for hesitation on our part had passed.

My belief then was, and the events that have occurred since have more than justified it, that from the standpoint of the United States it was imperative, not only for civil but for military reasons, that there should be the immediate establishment of easy and speedy communication by sea between the Atlantic and the Pacific. These reasons were not of convenience only, but of vital necessity, and did not admit of indefinite delay. The action of Colombia had shown not only that the delay would be indefinite, but that she intended to confiscate the property and rights of the French Panama Canal Company. The report of the Panama Canal Committee of the Colombian Senate on October 14, 1903, on the proposed treaty with the United States, proposed that all consideration of the matter should be postponed until October 31, 1904, when the next Colombian Congress would have convened, because by that time the new Congress would be in condition to determine whether through lapse of time the French company had not forfeited its property and rights. "When that time arrives," the report significantly declared, "the Republic, without any impediment, will be able to contract and will be in more clear, more definite and more advantageous possession, both legally and materially." The naked meaning of this was that Colombia proposed to wait a year, and then enforce a forfeiture of the rights and property of the French Panama Company, so as to secure the forty million dollars our Government had authorized as payment to this company. If we had sat supine, this would doubtless have meant that France would have interfered to protect the company, and we should then have had on the Isthmus, not the company, but France; and the gravest international complications might have ensued. Every consideration of international morality and expediency, of duty to the Panama people, and of satisfaction of our own national interests and honor, bade us take immediate action. I recognized Panama forthwith on behalf of the United States, and practically all the countries of the world immediately followed suit. The State Department immediately negotiated a canal treaty with the new Republic. One of the foremost men in securing the independence of Panama, and the treaty which authorized the United States forthwith to build the canal, was M. Philippe Bunau-Varilla, an eminent French

engineer formerly associated with De Lesseps and then living on the
Isthmus; his services to civilization were notable, and deserve the fullest
recognition.

From the beginning to the end our course was straightforward and in
absolute accord with the highest of standards of international morality.
Criticism of it can come only from misinformation, or else from a sentimentality which represents both mental weakness and a moral twist. To
have acted otherwise than I did would have been on my part betrayal
of the interests of the United States, indifference to the interests of
Panama, and recreancy to the interests of the world at large. Colombia
had forfeited every claim to consideration; indeed, this is not stating the
case strongly enough: she had so acted that yielding to her would have
meant on our part that culpable form of weakness which stands on a
level with wickedness. As for me personally, if I had hesitated to act,
and had not in advance discounted the clamor of those Americans who
have made a fetish of disloyalty to their country, I should have esteemed
myself as deserving a place in Dante's inferno beside the faint-hearted
cleric who was guilty of "il gran rifiuto." The facts I have given above
are mere bald statements from the record. They show that from the
beginning there had been acceptance of our right to insist on free transit,
in whatever form was best, across the Isthmus; and that towards the
end there had been a no less universal feeling that it was our duty to the
world to provide this transit in the shape of a canal—the resolution of
the Pan-American Congress was practically a mandate to this effect.
Colombia was then under a one-man government, a dictatorship, founded
on usurpation of absolute and irresponsible power. She eagerly pressed
us to enter into an agreement with her, as long as there was any chance
of our going to the alternative route through Nicaragua. When she thought
we were committed, she refused to fulfil the agreement, with the avowed
hope of seizing the French company's property for nothing and thereby
holding us up. This was a bit of pure bandit morality. It would have
achieved its purpose had I possessed as weak moral fiber as those of my
critics who announced that I ought to have confined my action to feeble
scolding and temporizing until the opportunity for action passed. I did
not lift my finger to incite the revolutionists. The right simile to use is
totally different. I simply ceased to stamp out the different revolutionary
fuses that were already burning. When Colombia committed flagrant
wrong against us, I considered it no part of my duty to aid and abet
her in her wrongdoing at our expense, and also at the expense of Panama,
of the French company, and of the world generally. There had been
fifty years of continuous bloodshed and civil strife in Panama; because
of my action Panama has now known ten years of such peace and prosperity as she never before saw during the four centuries of her existence

—for in Panama, as in Cuba and Santo Domingo, it was the action of the American people, against the outcries of the professed apostles of peace, which alone brought peace. We gave to the people of Panama self-government, and freed them from subjection to alien oppressors. We did our best to get Colombia to let us treat her with a more than generous justice; we exercised patience to beyond the verge of proper forbearance. When we did act and recognize Panama, Colombia at once acknowledged her own guilt by promptly offering to do what we had demanded, and what she had protested it was not in her power to do. But the offer came too late. What we would gladly have done before, it had by that time become impossible for us honorably to do; for it would have necessitated our abandoning the people of Panama, our friends, and turning them over to their and our foes, who would have wreaked vengeance on them precisely because they had shown friendship to us. Colombia was solely responsible for her own humiliation; and she had not then, and has not now, one shadow of claim upon us, moral or legal; all the wrong that was done was done by her. If, as representing the American people, I had not acted precisely as I did, I would have been an unfaithful or incompetent representative; and inaction at that crisis would have meant not only indefinite delay in building the canal, but also practical admission on our part that we were not fit to play the part on the Isthmus which we had arrogated to ourselves. I acted on my own responsibility in the Panama matter. John Hay spoke of this action as follows: "The action of the President in the Panama matter is not only in the strictest accordance with the principles of justice and equity, and in line with all the best precedents of our public policy, but it was the only course he could have taken in compliance with our treaty rights and obligations."

I deeply regretted, and now deeply regret, the fact that the Colombian Government rendered it imperative for me to take the action I took; but I had no alternative, consistent with the full performance of my duty to my own people, and to the nations of mankind. . . . The canal would not have been built at all save for the action I took. If men choose to say that it would have been better not to build it, than to build it as the result of such action, their position, although foolish, is compatible with belief in their wrongheaded sincerity. But it is hypocrisy, alike odious and contemptible, for any man to say both that we ought to have built the canal and that we ought not to have acted in the way we did act.

After a sufficient period of wrangling, the Senate ratified the treaty with Panama, and work on the canal was begun. The first thing that was necessary was to decide the type of canal. I summoned a board of engineering experts, foreign and native. They divided on their report. The majority of the members, including all the foreign members, approved a sea-level canal. The minority, including most of the American members, approved a lock canal. Studying these conclusions, I came to the belief that the minority was right. The two great traffic canals of the world were the Suez and the Soo. The Suez Canal is a sea-level canal, and it was the one best known to European engineers. The Soo Canal, through which an even greater volume of traffic passes every year, is a lock canal, and the American engineers were thoroughly familiar with it; whereas, in my judgment, the European engineers had failed to pay proper heed to the lessons taught by its operation and management. Moreover, the engineers who were to do the work at Panama all favored a lock canal. I came to the conclusion that a sea-level canal would be slightly less exposed to damage in the event of war; that the running expenses, apart from the heavy cost of interest on the amount necessary to build it, would be less; and that for small ships the time of transit would be less. But I also came to the conclusion that the lock canal at the proposed level would cost only about half as much to build and would be built in half the time, with much less risk; that for large ships the transit would be quicker, and that, taking into account the interest saved, the cost of maintenance would be less. Accordingly I recommended to Congress, on February 19, 1906, that a lock canal should be built, and my recommendation was adopted. Congress insisted upon having it built by a commission of several men. I tried faithfully to get good work out of the commission, and found it quite impossible; for a many-headed commission is an extremely poor executive instrument. At last I put Colonel Goethals in as head of the commission. Then, when Congress still refused to make the commission single-headed, I solved the difficulty by an executive order of January 6, 1908, which practically accomplished the object by enlarging the powers of the chairman, making all the other members of the commission dependent upon him, and thereby placing the work under one-man control. Dr. Gorgas had already performed an inestimable service by caring for the sanitary conditions so thoroughly as to make the Isthmus as safe as a health resort. Colonel Goethals proved to be the man of all others to do the job. It would be impossible to overstate what he has done. It is the greatest task of any kind that any man in the world has accomplished during the years that Colonel Goethals has been at work. It is the greatest task of its own kind that has ever been performed in the world at all. Colonel Goethals has succeeded in instilling into the men under him a spirit which elsewhere has been found only in a few victorious armies. It is proper and appropriate that, like the soldiers of such armies, they should receive medals which are allotted each man who has served for a sufficient length of time. A finer body of men has never been gathered by any nation than the men who have done the work of building the Panama Canal; the conditions under which they have lived and have done their work have been better than in any similar work ever undertaken in the tropics; they have all felt an eager pride in their work; and they have made not only America but the whole world their debtors by what they have accomplished. . . .

There can be no nobler cause for which to work than the peace of righteousness; and high honor is due those serene and lofty souls who with wisdom and courage, with high idealism tempered by sane facing of the actual facts of life, have striven to bring nearer the day when armed strife between nation and nation, between class and class, between man and man shall end throughout the world. Because all this is true, it is also true that there are no men more ignoble or more foolish, no men whose actions are fraught with greater possibility of mischief to their country and to mankind, than those who exalt unrighteous peace as better than righteous war. The men who have stood highest in our history, as in the history of all countries, are those who scorned injustice, who were incapable of oppressing the weak, or of permitting their country, with their consent, to oppress the weak, but who did not hesitate to draw the sword when to leave it undrawn meant inability to arrest triumphant wrong.

All this is so obvious that it ought not to be necessary to repeat it. Yet every man in active affairs, who also reads about the past, grows by bitter experience to realize that there are plenty of men, not only among those who mean ill, but among those who mean well, who are ready enough to praise what was done in the past, and yet are incapable of profiting by it when faced by the needs of the present. During our generation this seems to have been peculiarly the case among the men who have become obsessed with the idea of obtaining universal peace by some cheap patent panacea.

There has been a real and substantial growth in the feeling for international responsibility and justice among the great civilized nations during the past threescore of fourscore years. There has been a real growth of recognition of the fact that moral turpitude is involved in the wronging of one nation by another, and that in most cases war is an evil method of settling international difficulties. But as yet there has been only a rudimentary beginning of the development of international tribunals of justice, and there has been no development at all of any international police power. Now, as I have already said, the whole fabric of municipal law, of law within each nation, rests ultimately upon the judge and the policeman; and the complete absence of the policeman, and the almost complete absence of the judge, in international affairs, prevents there being as yet any real homology between municipal and international law.

Moreover, the questions which sometimes involve nations in war are far more difficult and complex than any questions that affect merely individuals. Almost every great nation has inherited certain questions, either with other nations or with sections of its own people, which it is quite impossible, in the present state of civilization, to decide as matters between private individuals can be decided. During the last century at least half of the wars that have been fought have been civil and not foreign wars. There are big and powerful nations which habitually commit, either upon other nations or upon sections of their own people, wrongs so outrageous as to justify even the most peaceful persons in going to war. There are also weak nations so utterly incompetent either to protect the rights of foreigners against their own citizens, or to protect their own citizens against foreigners, that it becomes a matter of sheer duty for some outside power to interfere in connection with them. As yet in neither case is there any efficient method of getting international action; and if joint action by several powers is secured, the result is usually considerably worse than if only one Power interfered. The worst infamies of modern times— such affairs as the massacres of the Armenians by the Turks, for instance —have been perpetrated in a time of nominally profound international peace, when there has been a concert of big Powers to prevent the breaking of this peace, although only by breaking it could the outrages be stopped. Be it remembered that the peoples who suffered by these hideous massacres, who saw their women violated and their children tortured, were actually enjoying all the benefits of "disarmament." Otherwise they would not have been massacred; for if the Jews in Russia and the Armenians in Turkey had been armed, and had been efficient in the use of their arms, no mob would have meddled with them.

Yet amiable but fatuous persons, with all these facts before their eyes, pass resolutions demanding universal arbitration for everything, and the disarmament of the free civilized powers and their abandonment of their armed forces; or else they write well-meaning, solemn little books, or pamphlets or editorials, and articles in magazines or newspapers, to show that it is "an illusion" to believe that war ever pays, because it is expensive. This is precisely like arguing that we should disband the police and devote our sole attention to persuading criminals that it is "an illusion" to suppose that burglary, highway robbery and white slavery are profitable. It is almost useless to attempt to argue with these well-intentioned persons, because they are suffering under an obsession and are not open to reason. They go wrong at the outset, for they lay all the emphasis on peace and none at all on righteousness. They are not all of them physically timid men; but they are usually men of soft life; and they rarely possess a high sense of honor or a keen patriotism. They rarely try to prevent their fellow countrymen from insulting or wronging the people of other nations; but they always ardently advocate that we, in our turn, shall tamely submit to wrong and insult from other nations. As Americans their folly is peculiarly scandalous, because if the principles they now uphold are right, it means that it would have been better that Americans should never have achieved their independence, and better that, in 1861, they should have peacefully submitted to seeing their country split into half a dozen jangling confederacies and slavery made perpetual. If unwilling to learn from their own history, let those who think that it is an "illusion" to believe that a war ever benefits a nation look at the difference between China and Japan. China has neither a fleet nor an efficient army. It is a huge civilized empire, one of the most populous on the globe; and it has been the helpless prey of outsiders because it does not possess the power to fight. Japan stands on a footing of equality with European and American nations because it does possess this power. China now sees Japan, Russia, Germany, England and France in possession of fragments of her empire, and has twice within the lifetime of the present generation seen her capital in the hands of allied invaders, because she in very fact realizes the ideals of the persons who wish the United States to disarm, and then trust that our helplessness will secure us a contemptuous immunity from attack by outside nations.

The chief trouble comes from the entire inability of these worthy people to understand that they are demanding things that are mutually incompatible when they demand peace at any price, and also justice and righteousness. I remember one representative of their number, who used to write little sonnets on behalf of the Mahdi and the Sudanese, these sonnets setting forth the need that the Sudan should be both independent and peaceful. As a matter of fact, the Sudan valued independence only because it desired to war against all Christians and to carry on an unlimited slave trade. It was "independent" under the Mahdi for a dozen years, and during those dozen years the bigotry, tyranny, and cruel religious intolerance were such as flourished in the seventh century, and in spite of systematic slave raids the population decreased by nearly two-thirds, and practically all the children died. Peace came, well-being came, freedom from rape and murder and torture and highway robbery, and every brutal gratification of lust and greed came, only when the Sudan lost its independence and passed under English rule. Yet this well-meaning little sonneteer sincerely felt that his verses were issued in the cause of humanity. Looking back from the vantage point of a score of years, probably every one will agree that he was an absurd person. But he was not one whit more absurd than most of the more prominent persons who advocate disarmament by the United States, the cessation of up-building the navy, and the promise to agree to arbitrate all matters, including those affecting our national interests and honor, with all foreign nations.

These persons would do no harm if they affected only themselves. Many of them are, in the ordinary relations of life, good citizens. They are exactly like the other good citizens who believe that enforced universal vegetarianism or anti-vaccination is the panacea for all ills. But in their particular case they are able to do harm because they affect our relations with foreign powers, so that other men pay the debt which they themselves have really incurred. It is the foolish, peace-at-any-price persons who try to persuade our people to make unwise and improper treaties, or to stop building up the navy. But if trouble comes and the treaties are repudiated, or there is a demand for armed intervention, it is not these people who will pay anything; they will stay at home in safety, and leave brave men to pay in blood, and honest men to pay in shame, for their folly.

The trouble is that our policy is apt to go in zigzags, because different sections of our people exercise at different times unequal pressure on our government. One class of our citizens clamor for treaties impossible of fulfillment, and improper to fulfill; another class have no objection to the passage of these treaties so long as there is no concrete case to which they apply, but instantly oppose a veto on their application when any concrete case does actually arise. One of our cardinal doctrines is freedom of speech, which means freedom of speech about foreigners as well as about ourselves; and inasmuch as we exercise this right with complete absence of restraint, we cannot expect other nations to hold us harmless unless in the last resort we are able to make our own words good by our deeds. One class of our citizens indulges in gushing promises to do everything for foreigners, another class offensively and improperly reviles them; and it is hard to say which class more thoroughly misrepresents the sober, self-respecting judgment of the American people as a whole. The only safe rule is to promise little, and faithfully to keep every promise; to "speak softly and carry a big stick."

A prime need for our nation, as of course for every other nation, is to make up its mind definitely what it wishes, and not to try to pursue paths of conduct incompatible one with the other. If this nation is content to be the China of the New World, then and then only can it afford to do away with the navy and the army. If it is content to abandon Hawaii and the Panama Canal, to cease to talk of the Monroe Doctrine, and to admit the right of any European or Asiatic power to dictate what immigrants shall be sent to and received in America, and whether or not they shall be allowed to become citizens and hold land—why, of course, if America is content to have nothing to say on any of these matters and to keep silent in the presence of armed outsiders, then it can abandon its navy and agree to arbitrate all questions of all kinds with every foreign power. In such event it can afford to pass its spare time in one continuous round of universal peace celebrations, and of smug self-satisfaction in having earned the derision of all the virile peoples of mankind. Those who advocate such a policy do not occupy a lofty position. But at least their position is understandable.

It is entirely inexcusable, however, to try to combine the unready hand with the unbridled tongue. It is folly to permit freedom of speech about foreigners as well as ourselves—and the peace-at-any-price persons are much too feeble a folk to try to interfere with freedom of speech—and yet to try to shirk the consequences of freedom of speech. It is folly to try to abolish our navy, and at the same time to insist that we have a right to enforce the Monroe Doctrine, that we have a right to control the Panama Canal which we ourselves dug, that we have a right to retain Hawaii and prevent foreign nations from taking Cuba, and a right to determine what immigrants, Asiatic or European, shall come to our shores, and the terms on which they shall be naturalized and shall hold land and exercise other privileges. We are a rich people, and an unmilitary people. In international affairs we are a short-sighted people. But I know my countrymen. Down at bottom their temper is such that they will not permanently tolerate injustice done to them. In the long run they will no more permit affronts to their National honor than injuries to their national interest. Such being the case, they will do well to remember that the surest of all ways to invite disaster is to be opulent, aggressive and unarmed.

Throughout the seven and a half years that I was President, I pursued without faltering one consistent foreign policy, a policy of genuine international good will and of consideration for the rights of others, and at the same time of steady preparedness. The weakest nations knew that they, no less than the strongest, were safe from insult and injury at our hands; and the strong and the weak alike also knew that we possessed both the will and the ability to guard ourselves from wrong or insult at the hands of any one.

It was under my administration that the Hague Court was saved from becoming an empty farce. It had been established by joint international agreement, but no Power had been willing to resort to it. Those establishing it had grown to realize that it was in danger of becoming a mere paper court, so that it would never really come into being at all. M. d'Estournelles de Constant had been especially alive to this danger. By correspondence and in personal interviews he impressed upon me the need not only of making advances by actually applying arbitration—not merely promising by treaty to apply it—to questions that were up for settlement, but of using the Hague tribunal for this purpose. I cordially sympathized with these views. On the recommendation of John Hay, I succeeded in getting an agreement with Mexico to lay a matter in dispute between the two republics before the Hague Court. This was the first case ever brought before the Hague Court. It was followed by numerous others; and it definitely established that court as the great international peace tribunal. By mutual agreement with Great Britain, through the decision of a joint commission, of which the American members were Senators Lodge and Turner, and Secretary Root, we were able peacefully to settle the Alaska Boundary question, the only question remaining between ourselves and the British Empire which it was not possible to settle by friendly arbitration; this therefore represented the removal of the last obstacle to absolute agreement between the two peoples. We were of substantial service in bringing to a satisfactory conclusion the negotiations at Algeciras concerning Morocco. We concluded with Great Britain, and with most of the other great nations, arbitration treaties specifically agreeing to arbitrate all matters, and especially the interpretation of treaties, save only as regards questions affecting territorial integrity, national honor and vital national interest. We made with Great Britain a treaty guaranteeing the free use of the Panama Canal on equal terms to the ships of all nations, while reserving to ourselves the right to police and fortify the canal, and therefore to control it in time of war. Under this treaty we are in honor bound to arbitrate the question of canal tolls for coastwise traffic between the Western and Eastern coasts of the United States. I believe that the American position as regards this matter is right; but I also believe that under the arbitration treaty we are in honor bound to submit the matter to arbitration in view of Great Britain's contention—although I hold it to be an unwise contention—that our position is unsound. I emphatically disbelieve in making universal arbitration treaties which neither the makers nor any one else would for a moment dream of keeping. I no less emphatically insist that it is our duty to keep the limited and sensible arbitration treaties which we have already made. The importance of a promise lies not in making it, but in keeping it; and the poorest of all positions for a nation to occupy in such a matter is readiness to make impossible promises at the same time that there is failure to keep promises which have been made, which can be kept, and which it is discreditable to break.

During the early part of the year 1905, the strain on the civilized world caused by the Russo-Japanese War became serious. The losses of life and of treasure were frightful. From all the sources of information at hand, I grew most strongly to believe that a further continuation of the struggle would be a very bad thing for Japan, and an even worse thing for Russia. Japan was already suffering terribly from the drain upon her men, and especially upon her resources, and had nothing further to gain from continuance of the struggle; its continuance meant to her more loss than gain, even if she were victorious. Russia, in spite of her gigantic strength, was, in my judgment, apt to lose even more than she had already lost if the struggle continued. I deemed it probable that she would no more be able successfully to defend Eastern Siberia and Northern Manchuria than she had been able to defend Southern Manchuria and Korea. If the war went on, I thought it, on the whole, likely that Russia would be driven west of Lake Baikal. But it was very far from certain. There is no certainty in such a war. Japan might have met defeat, and defeat to her would have spelt overwhelming disaster; and even if she had continued to win, what she thus won would have been of no value to her, and the cost in blood and money would have left her drained white. I believed, therefore, that the time had come when it was greatly to the interest of both combatants to have peace, and when therefore it was possible to get both to agree to peace.

I first satisfied myself that each side wished me to act, but that, naturally and properly, each side was exceedingly anxious that the other should not believe that the action was taken on its initiative. I then sent an identical note to the two powers proposing that they should meet, through their representatives, to see if peace could not be made directly between them, and offered to act as an intermediary in bringing about such a meeting, but not for any other purpose. Each assented to my proposal in principle. There was difficulty in getting them to agree on a common meeting place; but each finally abandoned its original contention in the matter, and the representatives of the two nations finally met at Portsmouth, in New Hampshire. I previously received the two delegations at Oyster Bay on the U. S. S. Mayflower, which, together with another naval vessel, I put at their disposal, on behalf of the United States Government, to take them from Oyster Bay to Portsmouth.

As is customary—but both unwise and undesirable—in such cases, each side advanced claims which the other could not grant. The chief difficulty came because of Japan's demand for a money indemnity. I felt that it would be better for Russia to pay some indemnity than to go on with the war, for there was little chance, in my judgment, of the war turning out favorably for Russia, and the revolutionary movement already under way bade fair to overthrow the negotiations entirely. I advised the Russian Government to this effect, at the same time urging them to abandon their pretensions on certain other points, notably concerning the southern half of Saghelien, which the Japanese had taken. I also, however, and equally strongly, advised the Japanese that in my judgment it would be the gravest mistake on their part to insist on continuing the war for the sake of a money indemnity; for Russia was absolutely firm in refusing to give them an indemnity, and the longer the war continued the less able she would be to pay. I pointed out that there was no possible analogy between their case and that of Germany in the war with France, which they were fond of quoting. The Germans held Paris and half of France, and gave up much territory in lieu of the indemnity, whereas the Japanese were still many thousand miles from Moscow, and had no territory whatever which they wished to give up. I also pointed out that in my judgment whereas the Japanese had enjoyed the sympathy of most of the civilized powers at the outset of and during the continuance of the war, they would forfeit it if they turned the war into one merely for getting money—and, moreover, they would almost certainly fail to get the money, and would simply find themselves at the end of a year, even if things prospered with them, in possession of territory they did not want, having spent enormous additional sums of money, and lost enormous additional numbers of men, and yet without a penny of remuneration. The treaty of peace was finally signed.

As is inevitable under such circumstances, each side felt that it ought to have got better terms; and when the danger was well past each side felt that it had been over-reached by the other, and that if the war had gone on it would have gotten more than it actually did get. The Japanese Government had been wise throughout, except in the matter of announcing that it would insist on a money indemnity. Neither in national nor in private affairs is it ordinarily advisable to make a bluff which cannot be put through—personally, I never believe in doing it under any circumstances. The Japanese people had been misled by this bluff of their Government; and the unwisdom of the Government's action in the matter was shown by the great resentment the treaty aroused in Japan, although it was so beneficial to Japan. There were various mob outbreaks, especially in the Japanese cities; the police were roughly handled, and several Christian churches were burned, as reported to me by the American Minister. In both Russia and Japan I believe that the net result as regards myself was a feeling of injury, and of dislike of me, among the people at large. I had expected this; I regarded it as entirely natural; and I did not resent it in the least. The Governments of both nations behaved toward me not only with correct and entire propriety, but with much courtesy and the fullest acknowledgment of the good effect of what I had done; and in Japan, at least, I believe that the leading men sincerely felt that I had been their friend. I had certainly tried my best to be the friend not only of the Japanese people but of the Russian people, and I believe that what I did was for the best interests of both and of the world at large.

During the course of the negotiations I tried to enlist the aid of the Governments of one nation which was friendly to Russia, and of another nation which was friendly to Japan, in helping bring about peace. I got no aid from either. I did, however, receive aid from the Emperor of Germany. His Ambassador at St. Petersburg was the one Ambassador who helped the American Ambassador, Mr. Meyer, at delicate and doubtful points of the negotiations. Mr. Meyer, who was, with the exception of Mr. White, the most useful diplomat in the American service, rendered literally invaluable aid by insisting upon himself seeing the Czar at critical periods of the transaction, when it was no longer possible for me to act successfully through the representatives of the Czar, who were often at cross purposes with one another.

As a result of the Portsmouth peace, I was given the Nobel Peace Prize. This consisted of a medal, which I kept, and a sum of $40,000, which I turned over as a foundation of industrial peace to a board of trustees which included Oscar Straus, Seth Low and John Mitchell. In the present state of the world's development industrial peace is even more essential than international peace; and it was fitting and appropriate to devote the peace prize to such a purpose. In 1910, while in Europe, one of my most pleasant experiences was my visit to Norway, where I addressed the Nobel Committee, and set forth in full the principles upon which I had acted, not only in this particular case but throughout my administration. . . .

Of course what I had done in connection with the Portsmouth peace was misunderstood by some good and sincere people. Just as after the settlement of the coal strike, there were persons who thereupon thought that it was in my power, and was my duty, to settle all other strikes, so after the peace of Portsmouth there were other persons—not only Americans, by the way—who thought it my duty forthwith to make myself a kind of international Meddlesome Mattie and interfere for peace and justice promiscuously over the world. Others, with a delightful non-sequitur, jumped to the conclusion that inasmuch as I had helped to bring about a beneficent and necessary peace I must of necessity have changed my mind about war being ever necessary. A couple of days after peace was concluded I wrote to a friend: "Don't you be misled by the fact that just at the moment men are speaking well of me. They will speak ill soon enough. As Loeb remarked to me to-day, some time soon I shall have to spank some little international brigand, and then all the well-meaning idiots will turn and shriek that this is inconsistent with what I did at the Peace Conference, whereas in reality it will be exactly in line with it."

To one of my political opponents, Mr. Schurz, who wrote me congratulating me upon the outcome at Portsmouth, and suggesting that the time was opportune for a move towards disarmament, I answered in a letter setting forth views which I thought sound then, and think sound now. The letter ran as follows:

Oyster Bay, N. Y.,
September 8, 1905.

*My dear Mr. Schurz:*    I thank you for your congratulations. As to what you say about disarmament—which I suppose is the rough equivalent of "the gradual diminution of the oppressive burdens imposed upon the world by armed peace"—I am not clear either as to what can be done or what ought to be done. If I had been known as one of the conventional type of peace advocates I could have done nothing whatever in bringing about peace now, I would be powerless in the future to accomplish anything, and I would not have been able to help confer the boons upon Cuba, the Philippines, Porto Rico and Panama, brought about by our action therein. If the Japanese had not armed during the last twenty years, this would indeed be a sorrowful century for Japan. If this country had not fought the Spanish War; if we had failed to take the action we did about Panama; all mankind would have been the loser. While the Turks were butchering the Armenians the European powers kept the peace and thereby added a burden of infamy to the Nineteenth Century, for in keeping that peace a greater number of lives were lost than in any European war since the days of Napoleon, and these lives were those of women and children as well as of men; while the moral degradation, the brutality inflicted and endured, the aggregate of hideous wrong done, surpassed that of any war of which we have record in modern times. Until people get it firmly fixed in their minds that peace is valuable chiefly as a means to righteousness, and that it can only be considered as an end when it also coincides with righteousness, we can do only a limited amount to advance its coming on this earth. There is of course no analogy at present between international law and private or municipal law, because there is no sanction of force for the former, while there is for the latter. Inside our own nation the law-abiding man does not have to arm himself against the lawless simply because there is some armed force—the police, the sheriff's posse, the national guard, the regulars—which can be called out to enforce the laws. At present there is no similar international force to call on, and I do not as yet see how it could at present be created. Hitherto peace has often come only because some strong and on the whole just power has by armed force, or the threat of armed force, put a stop to disorder. In a very interesting French book the other day I was reading how the Mediterranean was freed from pirates only by the "pax Britannica," established by England's naval force. The hopeless and hideous bloodshed and wickedness of Algiers and Turkestan was stopped, and could only be stopped, when civilized nations in the shape of Russia and France took possession of them. The same was true of Burma and the Malay States, as well as Egypt, with regard to England. Peace has come only as the sequel to the armed interference of a civilized power which, relatively to its opponent, was a just and beneficent power. If England had disarmed to the point of being unable to conquer the Soudan and protect Egypt, so that the Mahdists had established their supremacy in northeastern Africa, the result would have been a horrible and bloody calamity to mankind. It was only the growth of the European powers in military efficiency that freed eastern Europe from the dreadful scourge of the Tartar and partially freed it from the dreadful scourge of the Turk. Unjust war is dreadful; a just war may be the highest duty. To have the best nations, the free and civilized nations, disarm and leave the despotisms and barbarisms with great military force, would be a calamity compared to which the calamities caused by all the years of the nineteenth century would be trivial. Yet it is not easy to see how we can by international agreement state exactly which power ceases to be free and civilized and which comes near the line of barbarism or despotism. For example, I suppose it would be very difficult to get Russia and Japan to come to a common agreement on this point; and there are at least some citizens of other nations, not to speak of their governments, whom it would also be hard to get together.

This does not in the least mean that it is hopeless to make the effort. It may be that some scheme will be developed. America, fortunately, can cordially assist in such an effort, for no one in his senses would suggest our disarmament; and though we should continue to perfect our small navy and our minute army, I do not think it necessary to increase the number of our ships—at any rate as things look now—nor the number of our soldiers. Of course our navy must be kept up to the highest point of efficiency, and the replacing of old and worthless vessels by first-class new ones may involve an increase in the personnel; but not enough to interfere with our action along the lines you have suggested. But before I would know how to advocate such action, save in some such way as commending it to the attention of The Hague Tribunal, I would have to have a feasible and rational plan of action presented.

It seems to me that a general stop in the increase of the war navies of the world *might* be a good thing; but I would not like to speak too positively offhand. Of course it is only in continental Europe that the armies are too large; and before advocating action as regards them I should have to weigh matters carefully—including by the way such a matter as the Turkish army. At any rate nothing useful can be done unless with the clear recognition that we object to putting peace second to righteousness.

Sincerely yours,

THEODORE ROOSEVELT.

In my own judgment the most important service that I rendered to peace was the voyage of the battle fleet round the world. I had become convinced that for many reasons it was essential that we should have it clearly understood, by our own people especially, but also by other peoples, that the Pacific was as much our home waters as the Atlantic, and that our fleet could and would at will pass from one to the other of the two great oceans. It seemed to me evident that such a voyage would greatly benefit the navy itself; would arouse popular interest in and enthusiasm for the navy; and would make foreign nations accept as a matter of course that our fleet should from time to time be gathered in the Pacific, just as from time to time it was gathered in the Atlantic, and that its presence in one ocean was no more to be accepted as a mark of hostility to any Asiatic power than its presence in the Atlantic was to be accepted as a mark of hostility to any European power. I determined on the move without consulting the Cabinet, precisely as I took Panama without consulting the Cabinet. A council of war never fights, and in a crisis the duty of a leader is to lead and not to take refuge behind the generally timid wisdom of a multitude of councillors. At that time, as I happen to know, neither the English nor the German authorities believed it possible to take a fleet of great battleships round the world. They did not believe that their own fleets could perform the feat, and still less did they believe that the American fleet could. I made up my mind that it was time to have a show down in the matter; because if it was really true that our fleet could not get from the Atlantic to the Pacific, it was much better to know it and be able to shape our policy in view of the knowledge. Many persons publicly and privately protested against the move on the ground that Japan would accept it as a threat. To this I answered nothing in public. In private I said that I did not believe Japan would so regard it because Japan knew my sincere friendship and admiration for her and realized that we could not as a Nation have any intention of attacking her; and that if there were any such feeling on the part of Japan as was alleged that very fact rendered it imperative that that fleet should go. When in the spring of 1910 I was in Europe I was interested to find that high naval authorities in both Germany and Italy had expected that war would come at the time of the voyage. They asked me if I had not been afraid of it, and if I had not expected that hostilities would begin at least by the time that the fleet reached the Straits of Magellan? I answered that I did not expect it; that I believed that Japan would feel as friendly in the matter as we did; but that if my expectations had proved mistaken, it would have been proof positive that we were going to be attacked anyhow, and that in such event it would have been an enormous gain to have had the three months' preliminary preparation which enabled the fleet to start perfectly equipped. In a personal interview before they left I had explained to the officers in command that I believed the trip would be one of absolute peace, but that they were to take exactly the same precautions against sudden attack of any kind as if we were at war with all the nations of the earth; and that no excuse of any kind would be accepted if there were a sudden attack of any kind and we were taken unawares.

My prime purpose was to impress the American people; and this purpose was fully achieved. The cruise did make a very deep impression abroad; boasting about what we have done does not impress foreign nations at all, except unfavorably, but positive achievement does; and the two American achievements that really impressed foreign peoples during the first dozen years of this century were the digging of the Panama Canal and the cruise of the battle fleet round the world. But the impression made on our own people was of far greater consequence. No single thing in the history of the new United States Navy has done as much to stimulate popular interest and belief in it as the world cruise. This effect was forecast in a well-informed and friendly English periodical, the London *Spectator*. Writing in October, 1907, a month before the fleet sailed from Hampton Roads, the *Spectator* said:

All over America the people will follow the movements of the fleet; they will learn something of the intricate details of the coaling and commissariat work under warlike conditions; and in a word their attention will be aroused. Next

time Mr. Roosevelt or his representatives appeal to the country for new battleships they will do so to people whose minds have been influenced one way or
the other. The naval programme will not have stood still. We are sure that,
apart from increasing the efficiency of the existing fleet, this is the aim which
Mr. Roosevelt has in mind. He has a policy which projects itself far into the
future, but it is an entire misreading of it to suppose that it is aimed narrowly
and definitely at any single Power.

I first directed the fleet, of sixteen battleships, to go round through the
Straits of Magellan to San Francisco. From thence I ordered them to
New Zealand and Australia, then to the Philippines, China and Japan,
and home through Suez—they stopped in the Mediterranean to help the
sufferers from the earthquake at Messina, by the way, and did this work
as effectively as they had done all their other work. Admiral Evans commanded the fleet to San Francisco; there Admiral Sperry took it; Admirals
Thomas, Wainwright and Schroeder rendered distinguished service under
Evans and Sperry. The coaling and other preparations were made in such
excellent shape by the Department that there was never a hitch, not so
much as the delay of an hour, in keeping every appointment made. All
the repairs were made without difficulty, the ship concerned merely falling
out of column for a few hours, and when the job was done steaming at
speed until she regained her position. Not a ship was left in any port; and
there was hardly a desertion. As soon as it was known that the voyage was
to be undertaken men crowded to enlist, just as freely from the Mississippi
Valley as from the seaboard, and for the first time since the Spanish War
the ships put to sea overmanned—and by as stalwart a set of men-of-war's
men as ever looked through a porthole, game for a fight or a frolic, but
withal so self-respecting and with such a sense of responsibility that in
all the ports in which they landed their conduct was exemplary. The
fleet practiced incessantly during the voyage, both with the guns and in
battle tactics, and came home a much more efficient fighting instrument
than when it started sixteen months before.

The best men of command rank in our own service were confident that
the fleet would go round in safety, in spite of the incredulity of foreign
critics. Even they, however, did not believe that it was wise to send the
torpedo craft around. I accordingly acquiesced in their views, as it did not
occur to me to consult the lieutenants. But shortly before the fleet started,
I went in the Government yacht Mayflower to inspect the target practice
off Provincetown. I was accompanied by two torpedo boat destroyers, in
charge of a couple of naval lieutenants, thorough gamecocks; and I had
the two lieutenants aboard to dine one evening. Towards the end of the
dinner they could not refrain from asking if the torpedo flotilla was to go
round with the big ships. I told them no, that the admirals and captains
did not believe that the torpedo boats could stand it, and believed that

the officers and crews aboard the cockle shells would be worn out by the constant pitching and bouncing and the everlasting need to make repairs. My two guests chorused an eager assurance that the boats could stand it. They assured me that the enlisted men were even more anxious to go than were the officers, mentioning that on one of their boats the terms of enlistment of most of the crew were out, and the men were waiting to see whether or not to reënlist, as they did not care to do so unless the boats were to go on the cruise. I answered that I was only too glad to accept the word of the men who were to do the job, and that they should certainly go; and within half an hour I sent out the order for the flotilla to be got ready. It went round in fine shape, not a boat being laid up. I felt that the feat reflected even more credit upon the navy than did the circumnavigation of the big ships, and I wrote the flotilla commander the following letter:

May 18, 1908.

*My dear Captain Cone:*
A great deal of attention has been paid to the feat of our battleship fleet in encircling South America and getting to San Francisco; and it would be hard too highly to compliment the officers and enlisted men of that fleet for what they have done. Yet if I should draw any distinction at all it would be in favor of you and your associates who have taken out the torpedo flotilla. Yours was an even more notable feat, and every officer and every enlisted man in the torpedo boat flotilla has the right to feel that he has rendered distinguished service to the United States navy and therefore to the people of the United States; and I wish I could thank each of them personally. Will you have this letter read by the commanding officer of each torpedo boat to his officers and crew?

Sincerely yours,

THEODORE ROOSEVELT.

There were various amusing features connected with the trip. Most of the wealthy people and "leaders of opinion" in the Eastern cities were panic-struck at the proposal to take the fleet away from Atlantic waters. The great New York dailies issued frantic appeals to Congress to stop the fleet from going. The head of the Senate Committee on Naval Affairs announced that the fleet should not and could not go because Congress would refuse to appropriate the money—he being from an Eastern seaboard State. However, I announced in response that I had enough money to take the fleet around to the Pacific anyhow, that the fleet would certainly go, and that if Congress did not choose to appropriate enough money to get the fleet back, why, it would stay in the Pacific. There was no further difficulty about the money.

It was not originally my intention that the fleet should visit Australia, but the Australian Government sent a most cordial invitation, which I gladly accepted; for I have, as every American ought to have, a hearty admiration for, and fellow feeling with, Australia, and I believe that America should be ready to stand back of Australia in any serious emergency. The reception accorded the fleet in Australia was wonderful, and it showed the fundamental community of feeling between ourselves and the great commonwealth of the South Seas. The considerate, generous, and open-handed hospitality with which the entire Australian people treated our officers and men could not have been surpassed had they been our own countrymen. The fleet first visited Sidney, whch has a singularly beautiful harbor. The day after the arrival one of our captains noticed a member of his crew trying to go to sleep on a bench in the park. He had fixed above his head a large paper with some lines evidently designed to forestall any questions from friendly would-be hosts: "I am delighted with the Australian people. I think your harbor the finest in the world. I am very tired and would like to go to sleep."

The most noteworthy incident of the cruise was the reception given to our fleet in Japan. In courtesy and good breeding, the Japanese can certainly teach much to the nations of the Western world. I had been very sure that the people of Japan would understand aright what the cruise meant, and would accept the visit of our fleet as the signal honor which it was meant to be, a proof of the high regard and friendship I felt, and which I was certain the American people felt, for the great Island Empire. The event even surpassed my expectations. I cannot too strongly express my appreciation of the generous courtesy the Japanese showed the officers and crews of our fleet; and I may add that every man of them came back a friend and admirer of the Japanese. Admiral Sperry wrote me a letter of much interest, dealing not only with the reception in Tokio but with the work of our men at sea; I herewith give it almost in full:

28 October, 1908.

*Dear Mr. Roosevelt:*

My official report of the visit to Japan goes forward in this mail, but there are certain aspects of the affair so successfully concluded which cannot well be included in the report.

You are perhaps aware that Mr. Denison of the Japanese Foreign Office was one of my colleagues at The Hague, for whom I have a very high regard. Desiring to avoid every possibility of trouble or misunderstanding, I wrote to him last June explaining fully the character of our men, which they have so well lived up to, the desirability of ample landing places, guides, rest houses and places for changing money in order that there might be no delay in getting the men away from the docks on the excursions in which they delight. Very few of them go into a drinking place, except to get a resting place not to be found elsewhere, paying for it by taking a drink.

I also explained our system of landing with liberty men an unarmed patrol, properly officered, to quietly take in charge and send off to their ships any men who showed the slightest trace of disorderly conduct. This letter he showed to the Minister of the Navy, who highly approved of all our arrangements, including the patrol, of which I feared they might be jealous. Mr. Denison's reply reached me in Manila, with a memorandum from the Minister of the Navy which removed all doubts. Three temporary piers were built for our boat landings, each 300 feet long, brilliantly lighted and decorated. The sleeping accommodations did not permit two or three thousand sailors to remain on shore, but the ample landings permitted them to be handled night and day with perfect order and safety.

At the landings and railroad station in Yokohama there were rest houses or booths, reputable money changers and as many as a thousand English-speaking Japanese college students acted as volunteer guides, besides Japanese sailors and petty officers detailed for the purpose. In Tokyo there were a great many excellent refreshment places, where the men got excellent meals and could rest, smoke and write letters, and in none of these places would they allow the men to pay anything, though they were more than ready to do so. The arrangements were marvelously perfect.

As soon as your telegram of October 18, giving the address to be made to the Emperor, was received, I gave copies of it to our Ambassador to be sent to the Foreign Office. It seems that the Emperor had already prepared a very cordial address to be forwarded through me to you, after delivery at the audience, but your telegram reversed the situation and his reply was prepared. I am convinced that your kind and courteous initiative on this occasion helped cause the pleasant feeling which was so obvious in the Emperor's bearing at the luncheon which followed the audience. X., who is reticent and conservative, told me that not only the Emperor but all the Ministers were profoundly gratified by the course of events. I am confident that not even the most trifling incident has taken place which could in any way mar the general satisfaction, and our Ambassador has expressed to me his great satisfaction with all that has taken place.

Owing to heavy weather encountered on the passage up from Manila the fleet was obliged to take about 3500 tons of coal.

The Yankton remained behind to keep up communication for a few days, and yesterday she transmitted the Emperor's telegram to you, which was sent in reply to your message through our Ambassador after the sailing of the fleet. It must be profoundly gratifying to you to have the mission on which you sent the fleet terminate so happily, and I am profoundly thankful that, owing to the confidence which you displayed in giving me this command, my active career draws to a close with such honorable distinction.

As for the effect of the cruise upon the training, discipline and effectiveness of the fleet, the good cannot be exaggerated. It was a war game in every detail. The wireless communication has been maintained with an efficiency hitherto unheard of. Between Honolulu and Auckland, 3850 miles, we were out of communication with a cable station for only one night, whereas three [non-American] men-of-war trying recently to maintain a chain of only 1250 miles, between Auckland and Sydney, were only able to do so for a few hours.

The officers and men as soon as we put to sea turn to their gunnery and tactical work far more eagerly than they go to functions. Every morning certain ships leave the column and move off seven or eight thousand yards as targets for range measuring fire control and battery practice for the others, and at night certain ships do the same thing for night battery practice. I am sorry to say that this practice is unsatisfactory, and in some points misleading, owing to the fact that the ships are painted white. At Portland, in 1903, I saw Admiral Barker's white battleships under the searchlights of the army at a distance of 14,000 yards, seven sea miles, without glasses, while the Hartford, a black ship, was never discovered at all, though she passed within a mile and a half. I have for years, while a member of the General Board, advocated painting the ships war color at all times, and by this mail I am asking the Department to make the necessary change in the Regulations and paint the ships properly. I do not know that any one now dissents from my view. Admiral Wainwright strongly concurs, and the War College Conference recommended it year after year without a dissenting voice.

In the afternoons the fleet has two or three hours' practice at battle maneuvers, which excite as keen interest as gunnery exercises.

The competition in coal economy goes on automatically and reacts in a hundred ways. It has reduced the waste in the use of electric light and water, and certain chief engineers are said to keep men ranging over the ships all night turning out every light not in actual and immediate use. Perhaps the most important effect is the keen hunt for defects in the machinery causing waste of power. The Yankton by resetting valves increased her speed from 10 to 11½ knots on the same expenditure.

All this has been done, but the field is widening, the work has only begun. . . .

C. S. Sperry.

When I left the Presidency I finished seven and a half years of administration, during which not one shot had been fired against a foreign foe. We were at absolute peace, and there was no nation in the world with whom a war cloud threatened, no nation in the world whom we had wronged, or from whom we had anything to fear. The cruise of the battle fleet was not the least of the causes which ensured so peaceful an outlook.

When the fleet returned after its sixteen months' voyage around the world I went down to Hampton Roads to greet it. The day was Washington's Birthday, February 22, 1907. Literally on the minute the homing battlecraft came into view. On the flagship of the Admiral I spoke to the officers and enlisted men, as follows:

Admiral Sperry, Officers and Men of the Battle Fleet: Over a year has passed since you steamed out of this harbor, and over the world's rim, and this morning the hearts of all who saw you thrilled with pride as the hulls of the mighty warships lifted above the horizon. You have been in the Northern and the Southern Hemispheres; four times you have crossed the line; you have steamed through all the great oceans; you have touched the coast of every continent. Ever your general course has been westward; and now you come back to the port from which you set sail. This is the first battle fleet that has ever circumnavigated the globe. Those who perform the feat again can but follow in your footsteps.

The little torpedo flotilla went with you around South America, through the Straits of Magellan, to our own Pacific Coast. The armored cruiser squadron met you, and left you again, when you were half way round the world. You have falsified every prediction of the prophets of failure. In all your long cruise not an accident worthy of mention has happened to a single battleship, nor yet to the cruisers or torpedo boats. You left this coast in a high state of battle efficiency, and you return with your efficiency increased; better prepared than when you left, not only in personnel but even in material. During your world cruise you have taken your regular gunnery practice, and skilled though you were before with the guns, you have grown more skilful still; and through practice you have improved in battle tactics, though here there is more room for improvement than in your gunnery. Incidentally, I suppose I need hardly say that one measure of your fitness must be your clear recognition of the need always steadily to strive to render yourselves more fit; if you ever grow to think that you are fit enough, you can make up your minds that from that moment you will begin to go backward.

As a war machine, the fleet comes back in better shape than it went out. In addition, you, the officers and men of this formidable fighting force, have shown yourselves the best of all possible ambassadors and heralds of peace. Wherever you have landed you have borne yourselves so as to make us at home proud of being your countrymen. You have shown that the best type of fighting man of the sea knows how to appear to the utmost possible advantage when his business is to behave himself on shore, and to make a good impression in a foreign land. We are proud of all the ships and all the men in this whole fleet, and we welcome you home to the country whose good repute among nations has been raised by what you have done.

# Mr. Dooley on the Philippine Peace and the Hague Conference

## Finley Peter Dunne

*Theodore Roosevelt's foreign policy and his vigorous defense of it continued to draw fire throughout the progressive era. In conservative realists like William Graham Sumner, Yale's formidable sociologist and economist, the whole adventure with Spain and the subsequent flirtation with imperialism and naval power aroused a deep revulsion. They doubted whether a democracy had any moral business undertaking to rule subject peoples, and they feared a subsequent rise of militarism, a centralization of authority, and a constriction of the nation's free-wheeling economic structure. Liberals who sympathized with the aspirations of native peoples for independence suspected the influence of Wall Street on the government's aggressive diplomacy and erratic colonialism. Advocates of world peace could not be persuaded that a major war was ever made less likely by the maneuvers of a navy, regardless of the white paint on its guns.*

*No more apt commentary on the ambiguities and difficulties in American foreign policy can be found than in the continuous fire of Finley Peter Dunne's observations during the early years of America's colonial and naval adventures. Two of Mr. Dooley's "conversations," reprinted here, may serve to represent the open skepticism of many citizens which greeted our new world-wide stance.*

THE PHILIPPINE PEACE

" 'Tis sthrange we don't hear much talk about th' Ph'lippeens," said Mr. Hennessy.

"Ye ought to go to Boston," said Mr. Dooley. "They talk about it there in their sleep. Th' raison it's not discussed annywhere else is that ivrything

Finley Peter Dunne, *Observations by Mr. Dooley* (New York: Scribner's, 1902), pp. 115-120; *Mr. Dooley Says* (New York: Scribner's, 1910), pp. 204-213.

is perfectly quiet there. We don't talk about Ohio or Ioway or anny iv
our other possissions because they'se nawthin' doin' in thim parts. Th'
people ar-re goin' ahead, garnerin' th' products iv th' sile, sindin' their
childher to school, worshipin' on Sundah in th' churches an' thankin'
Hiven f'r th' blessin's iv free govermint an' th' pro-tiction iv th' flag above
thim.

"So it is in th' Ph'lippeens. I know, f'r me frind Gov'nor Taft says so,
an' they'se a man that undherstands con-tintmint whin he sees it. Ye
can't thrust th' fellows that comes back fr'm th' jools iv th' Passyfic an' tells
ye that things ar-re no betther thin they shud be undher th' shade iv th'
cocoanut palm be th' blue wathers iv th' still lagoon. They mus' be
satisfied with our rule. A man that isn't satisfied whin he's had enough
is a glutton. They're satisfied an' happy an' slowly but surely they're
acquirin' that love f'r th' govermint that floats over thim that will make
thim good citizens without a vote or a right to thrile be jury. I know it.
Guv'nor Taft says so.

"Says he: 'Th' Ph'lippeens as ye have been tol' be me young but speech-
ful frind, Sinitor Bivridge, who was down there f'r tin minyits wanst an'
spoke very highly an' at some lenth on th' beauties iv th' scenery, th'
Ph'lippeens is wan or more iv th' beautiful jools in th' diadem iv our fair
nation. Formerly our fair nation didn't care f'r jools, but done up her hair
with side combs, but she's been abroad some since an' she come back with
beautiful reddish goolden hair that a tiara looks well in an' that is betther
f'r havin' a tiara. She is not as young as she was. Th' simple home-lovin'
maiden that our fathers knew has disappeared an' in her place we find a
Columbya, gintlemen, with machurer charms, a knowledge iv Euro-peen
customs an' not averse to a cigareet. So we have pinned in her fair hair
a diadem that sets off her beauty to advantage an' holds on th' front iv
th' hair, an' th' mos' lovely pearl in this ornymint is thim sunny little
isles iv th' Passyfic. They are almost too sunny f'r me. I had to come away.

" 'To shift me language suddintly fr'm th' joolry counther an' th'
boodore, I will say that nawthin' that has been said even be th' gifted an'
scholarly sinitor, who so worthily fills part iv th' place wanst crowded be
Hendricks an' McDonald, does justice to th' richness iv thim islands. They
raise unknown quantities iv produce, none iv which forchnitly can come
into this counthry. All th' riches iv Cathay, all th' wealth iv Ind, as
Hogan says, wud look like a second morgedge on an Apache wickeyup
compared with th' untold an' almost unmintionable products iv that
gloryous domain. Me business kept me in Manila or I wud tell ye what
they are. Besides some iv our lile subjects is gettin' to be good shots an'
I didn't go down there f'r that purpose.

" 'I turn to th' climate. It is simply hivenly. No other wurrud describes
it. A white man who goes there seldom rayturns unless th' bereaved
fam'ly insists. It is jus' right. In winter enough rain, in summer plinty iv

heat. Gin'rally speakin' whin that throupical sky starts rainin' it doesn't stop till it's impty, so th' counthry is not subjected to th' sudden changes that afflict more northerly climes. Whin it rains it rains; whin it shines it shines. Th' wather frequently remains in th' air afther th' sun has been shinin' a month or more, th' earth bein' a little overcrowded with juice an' this gives th' atmosphere a certain cosiness that is indescribable. A light green mould grows on th' clothes an' is very becomin'. I met a man on th' boat comin' back who said 'twas th' finest winter climate in th' wurruld. He was be profission a rubber in a Turkish bath. As f'r th' summers they are delicious. Th' sun doesn't sit aloft above th' jools iv th' Passyfic. It comes down an' mingles with th' people. Ye have heard it said th' isles was kissed be th' sun. Perhaps bitten wud be a betther wurrud. But th' timprachoor is frequently modified be an eruption iv th' neighborin' volcanoes an' th' inthraduction iv American stoves. At night a coolin' breeze fr'm th' crather iv a volcano makes sleep possible in a hammock swung in th' ice-box. It is also very pleasant to be able to cuk wan's dinner within wan.

"'Passin' to th' pollytical situation, I will say it is good. Not perhaps as good as ye'ers or mine, but good. Ivry wanst in a while whin I think iv it, an iliction is held. Unforchnitly it usually happens that those ilicted have not yet surrindhered. In th' Ph'lippeens th' office seeks th' man, but as he is also pursooed be th' sojery, it is not always aisy to catch him an' fit it on him. Th' counthry may be divided into two parts, pollytically,—where th' insurrection continues an' where it will soon be. Th' brave but I fear not altogether cheery army conthrols th' insurrected parts be martiyal law, but th' civil authorities are supreme in their own house. Th' diff'rence between civil law an' martiyal law in th' Ph'lippeens is what kind iv coat th' judge wears. Th' raysult is much th' same. Th' two branches wurruks in perfect harmony. We bag thim in th' city an' they round thim up in th' counthry.

"'It is not always nicessry to kill a Filipino American right away. Me desire is to idjacate thim slowly in th' ways an' customs iv th' counthry. We ar-re givin' hundherds iv these pore benighted haythen th' well-known, ol'-fashioned American wather cure. Iv coorse, ye know how 'tis done. A Filipino, we'll say, niver heerd iv th' histhry iv this counthry. He is met be wan iv our sturdy boys in black an' blue iv th' Macabebee scouts who asts him to cheer f'r Abraham Lincoln. He rayfuses. He is thin placed upon th' grass an' given a dhrink, a baynit bein' fixed in his mouth so he cannot reject th' hospitality. Undher th' inflooence iv th' hose that cheers but does not inebriate, he soon warrums or perhaps I might say swells up to a ralization iv th' granjoor iv his adoptive counthry. One gallon makes him give three groans f'r th' constitchoochion. At four gallons, he will ask to be wrapped in th' flag. At th' dew pint he sings Yankee Doodle. Occasionally we run acrost a stubborn an' rebellyous man who wud sthrain at me idee iv human rights an' swallow th' Passyfic Ocean, but I mus' say mos' iv these little fellows is less hollow in their pretintions. Nachrally we have had to take a good manny customs fr'm th' Spanyard, but we have improved on thim. I was talkin' with a Spanish gintleman th' other day who had been away f'r a long time an' he said he wudden't know th' counthry. Even th' faces iv th' people on th' sthreets had changed. They seemed glad to see him. Among th' mos' useful Spanish customs is reconcenthration. Our reconcenthration camps is among th' mos' thickly populated in th' wurruld. But still we have to rely mainly on American methods. They are always used fin'lly in th' makin' iv a good citizen, th' garotte sildom.

"'I have not considhered it advisable to inthrajooce anny fads like thrile be jury iv ye'er peers into me administhration. Plain sthraight-forward dealin's is me motto. A Filipino at his best has on'y larned half th' jooty iv mankind. He can be thried but he can't thry his fellow man. It takes him too long. But in time I hope to have thim thrained to a pint where they can be good men an' thrue at th' inquest.

"'I hope I have tol' ye enough to show ye that th' stories iv disordher is greatly exaggerated. Th' counthry is pro-gressin' splindidly, th' ocean still laps th' shore, th' mountains are there as they were in Bivridge's day, quite happy apparently; th' flag floats free an' well guarded over th' governmint offices, an' th' cherry people go an' come on their errands— go out alone an' come back with th' throops. Ivrywhere happiness, contint, love iv th' shtep-mother counthry, excipt in places where there ar-re people. Gintlemen, I thank ye.'

"An' there ye ar-re, Hinnissy. I hope this here lucid story will quite th' waggin' tongues iv scandal an' that people will let th' Ph'lippeens stew in their own happiness."

"But sure they might do something f'r thim," said Mr. Hennessy.

"They will," said Mr. Dooley. "They'll give thim a measure iv freedom."

"But whin?"

"Whin they'll sthand still long enough to be measured," said Mr. Dooley.

## THE HAGUE CONFERENCE

"I see," said Mr. Hennessy, "we're goin' to sind th' navy to th' Passyfic."

"I can't tell," said Mr. Dooley, "whether th' navy is goin' to spend th' rest iv its days protectin' our possessions in th' Oryent or whether it is to remain in th' neighborhood iv Barnstable makin' th' glaziers iv New England rich beyond th' dhreams iv New England avarice, which ar-re hopeful dhreams. Th' cabinet is divided, th' Sicrety iv th' Navy is divided, th' Prisidint is divided an' th' press is divided. Wan great iditor, fr'm his post iv danger in Paris, has ordhered th' navy to report at San Francisco at four eight next Thursday. Another great iditor livin' in Germany has warned it that it will do so at its peril. Nawthin' is so fine as to see a great modhern journalist unbend fr'm his mighty task iv selectin' fr'm a bunch iv phottygrafts th' prettiest cook iv Flatbush or engineerin' with his great furrowed brain th' Topsy Fizzle compytition to trifle with some light warm-weather subjick like internaytional law or war. But men such as these can do annything.

"But, annyhow, what diff'rence does it make whether th' navy goes to th' Passyfic or not? If it goes at all, it won't be to make war. They've dumped all th' fourteen inch shells into th' sea. Th' ammunition hoists ar-re filled with American beauty roses an' orchids. Th' guns are loaded with confetty. Th' officers dhrink nawthin' sthronger thin vanilla an' sthrawberry mixed. Whin th' tars go ashore they hurry at wanst to th' home iv th' Christyan Indeavor Society or throng th' free libries readin' religious pothry. Me frind Bob Evans is goin' to conthribute a series iv articles to th' *Ladies' Home Journal* on croshaying.* F'r th' Hague Peace Conference has abolished war, Hinnissy. Ye've seen th' last war ye'll iver see, me boy.

"Th' Hague conference, Hinnissy, was got up be th' Czar iv Rooshya just befure he moved his army agin th' Japs. It was a quiet day at Saint Pethersburg. Th' Prime Minister had just been blown up with dinnymite, th' Czar's uncle had been shot, an' wan iv his cousins was expirin' fr'm a dose iv proosic acid. All was comparitive peace. In th' warrum summer's afthernoon th' Czar felt almost dhrousy as he set in his rile palace an' listened to th' low, monotonous drone iv bombs bein' hurled at th' Probo-jensky guards, an' picked th' broken glass out iv th' dhrink that'd just been brought to him be an aged servitor who was prisidint iv th' Saint Pethers-burg lodge iv Pathriotic Assassins. Th' monarch's mind turned to th' subjick iv war an' he says to himsilf: 'What a dhreadful thing it is that such a beautiful wurruld shud be marred be thousands iv innocint men bein' sint out to shoot each other f'r no cause whin they might betther stay at home an' wurruk f'r their rile masthers,' he says. 'I will disguise mesilf as a moojik an' go over to th' tillygraf office an' summon a meetin' iv th' Powers,' he says.

"That's how it come about. All th' powers sint dillygates an' a g-reat manny iv th' weaknesses did so too. They met in Holland an' they have been devotin' all their time since to makin' war impossible in th' future. Th' meetin' was opened with an acrimonyous debate over a resolution offered be a dillygate fr'm Paryguay callin' f'r immeejit disarmamint,

---

* Rear Admiral Robley D. Evans commanded the Atlantic Fleet on the first leg of the voyage to San Francisco in 1907. A lifelong sailor, he had fought for the Union in the Civil War. [ED.]

which is th' same, Hinnissy, as notifyin' th' Powers to turn in their guns to th' man at th' dure. This was carrid be a very heavy majority. Among those that voted in favor iv it were: Paryguay, Uryguay, Switzerland, Chiny, Bilgium, an' San Marino. Opposed were England, France, Rooshya, Germany, Italy, Austhree, Japan, an' the United States.

"This was regarded be all present as a happy auggry. Th' convintion thin discussed a risolution offered be th' Turkish dillygate abolishin' war altogether. This also was carried, on'y England, France, Rooshya, Germany, Italy, Austhree, Japan, an' th' United States votin' no.

"This made th' way clear f'r th' discussion iv th' larger question iv how future wars shud be conducted in th' best inthrests iv peace. Th' conference considhered th' possibility iv abolishin' th' mushroom bullet which, entherin' th' inteeryor iv th' inimy not much larger thin a marble, soon opens its dainty petals an' goes whirlin' through th' allyminthry canal like a pin-wheel. Th' Chinese dillygate said that he regarded this here insthrumint iv peace as highly painful. He had an aunt in Pekin, an estimable lady, unmarried, two hundred an' fifty years iv age, who received wan without warnin' durin' th' gallant riscue iv Pekin fr'm th' foreign legations a few years ago. He cud speak with feelin' on th' subjick as th' Chinese army did not use these pro-jictyles but were armed with bean-shooters.

"Th' English dillygate opposed th' resolution. 'It is,' says he, 'quite thrue that these here pellets are in many cases harmful to th' digestion, but I think it wud be goin' too far to suggest that they be abolished ontil their mannyfacther is betther undherstud be th' subjick races,' he says. 'I suppose wan iv these bullets might throw a white man off his feed, but we have abundant proof that whin injicted into a black man they gr-reatly improve his moral tone. An' afther all, th' improvemint iv th' moral tone is, gintlemen, a far graver matther thin anny mere physical question. We know fr'm expeeryence in South Africa that th' charmin' bullet now undher discussion did much to change conditions in that enlightened an' juicy part iv his Majesty's domains. Th' darky that happened to stop wan was all th' betther f'r it. He retired fr'm labor an' give up his squalid an' bigamious life,' he says. 'I am in favor, howiver, iv restrictin' their use to encounters with races that we properly considher infeeryor,' he says. Th' dillygate fr'm Sinagambya rose to a question iv privilege. 'State ye'er question iv privilege,' says th' chairman. 'I wud like to have th' windows open,' says th' dillygate fr'm Sinagambya. 'I feel faint,' he says.

"Th' Hon'rable Joe Choate, dillygate fr'm th' United States, moved that in future wars enlisted men shud not wear ear-rings. Carried, on'y Italy votin' no.

"Th' conference thin discussed blowin' up th' inimy with dinnymite, poisinin' him, shootin' th' wounded, settin' fire to infants, bilin' prisoners-iv-war in hot lard, an' robbin' graves. Some excitemint was created durin' th' talk be th' dillygate fr'm th' cannybal islands who proposed that prisoners-iv-war be eaten. Th' German dillygate thought that this was carryin' a specyal gift iv man power too far. It wud give th' cannybal islands a distinct advantage in case iv war, as Europeen sojers were accustomed to horses. Th' English dillygate said that while much cud be said against a practice which personally seemed to him rather unsportsmanlike, still he felt he must reserve th' right iv anny cannybal allies iv Brittanya to go as far as they liked.

"Th' Hon'rable Joe Choate moved that in future wars no military band shud be considered complete without a base-dhrum. Carrid.

"Th' entire South American dillygation said that no nation ought to go to war because another nation wanted to put a bill on th' slate. Th' English dillygate was much incensed. 'Why, gintlemen', says he, 'if ye deprived us iv th' right to collect debts be killin' th' debtor ye wud take away fr'm war its entire moral purpose. I must ask ye again to cease thinkin' on this subjick in a gross mateeryal way an' considher th' moral side alone,' he says. Th' conference was much moved be this pathetic speech, th' dillygate fr'm France wept softly into his hankerchef, an' th' dillygate fr'm Germany wint over an' forcibly took an openface goold watch fr'm th' dillygate fr'm Vinzwala.

"Th' Hon'rable Joe Choate moved that in all future wars horses shud be fed with hay wheriver possible. Carrid.

"A long informal talk on th' reinthroduction iv scalpin' followed. At last th' dillygate fr'm Chiny arose an' says he: 'I'd like to know what war is. What is war annyhow?' 'Th' Lord knows, we don't,' says th' chairman. 'We're all profissors iv colledges or lawyers whin we're home,' he says. 'Is it war to shoot my aunt?' says th' dillygate fr'm Chiny. Cries iv 'No, no.' 'Is it war to hook me father's best hat that he left behind whin he bashfully hurrid away to escape th' attintions iv Europeen sojery?' he says. 'Is robbery war?' says he. 'Robbery is a nicissry part iv war,' says th' English dillygate. 'F'r th' purpose iv enfoorcin' a moral example,' he says.

"'Well,' says old Wow Chow, 'I'd like to be able to go back home an' tell thim what war really is. A few years back ye sint a lot iv young men over to our part iv th' wurruld an' without sayin' with ye'er leave or by ye'er leave they shot us an' they hung us up be our psyche knots an' they burned down our little bamboo houses. Thin they wint up to Pekin, set fire to th' town, an' stole ivry thing in sight. I just got out iv th' back dure in time to escape a jab in th' spine fr'm a German that I niver see befure. If it hadn't been that whin I was a boy I won th' hundred yards at th' University iv Slambang in two hours an' forty minyits, an' if it hadn't happened that I was lightly dhressed in a summer overskirt an' a thin blouse, an' if th' German hadn't stopped to steal me garters, I wudden't

be here at this moment,' says he. 'Was that war or wasn't it?' he says. 'It
was an expedition,' says th' dillygate fr'm England, 'to serve th' high moral
jooties iv Christyan civvylization.' 'Thin,' says th' dillygate fr'm Chiny,
puttin' on his hat, 'I'm fr war,' he says. 'It ain't so rough,' he says. An' he
wint home."

# PART V

# AMERICAN SOCIETY: POSSIBILITIES

# Drift and Mastery

## *Walter Lippmann*

*Woodrow Wilson's second presidential inaugural in March, 1917, closed the first act in the drama of American liberalism. On a comprehensive record of legislative reforms and on his fervent efforts to keep America from entering a war which threatened to shatter a progressive world, he had appealed to the electorate for a second term and had won by a hairbreadth margin. "We have sought," he said, summarizing the achievements of his generation on that early March day, "to set our house in order, correct the grosser errors and abuses of our industrial life, and lift our politics to a broader view of the people's essential interests." Then, admitting that much was left to do at home, he warned his people that the problems of war and peace were henceforth paramount, that American fortunes were now hopelessly involved in the outcome whether Americans would have it so or not. Within precisely four weeks of his inaugural, having sought to the very end to keep America neutral, Wilson asked Congress to declare war on Germany.*

*Twenty months later the decimated and exhausted peoples of the western world were permitted to begin the task of rebuilding a peace.*

*Reform did not die with the war, but its spirit and mood were changed. The aging leaders and spokesmen of its first era faltered and fell. Scarred by the frustrations of his war years, Roosevelt died in rage against Wilson, his League, and his leadership. Bryan lived into the 1920's serenely impervious to the currents of the urban world which had once feared his flailing words and now merely laughed at his antique foolishness. Wilson, ravaged by presidential cares, his mind clear but brittle, his body half-paralyzed, stumbled through his last two years in office; for a harsh, corrosive period he was to become the symbol of everything about reform, in war and in peace, that Americans preferred to forget. For some years now the voices of younger men, seeking to reshape the liberal dream, had been speaking a bolder language with fresher words.*

*The most brilliant of the younger men was Walter Lippmann. An urban*

431

*New Yorker, raised in comfort amid the stimulation of books and talk, he took Harvard by storm and won a degree in three years. He wrote articles which struck the attention of the faculty, formed a Socialist club to study Marxism and to investigate the urban political order, and so impressed Graham Wallas, a visiting British Socialist, that Wallas paid this under-graduate the unprecedented compliment of dedicating a book to him. Lippmann returned to New York in 1910 to work for Lincoln Steffens, on the editorial staff of Everybody's. Under the older reporter's eye he trained himself to write with a clarity and precocity few in his generation could match. Though he soon grew restless for active politics, a term of service in the Socialist municipal government of Schenectady in 1912 con-vinced him that he could more effectively influence men as a thinker and political essayist. Within two more years he had renounced Socialism and had set forth in a pair of remarkable books—A Preface to Politics and Drift and Mastery—an incisive commentary on the politics and social ideals of his generation. He was not yet twenty-five.*

*Of the two books, Drift and Mastery was the more thoughtful and persuasive; it was indeed the clearest and most confident of a number of works to call at the height of progressivism for a national emancipation from the political and intellectual formulas of the past and present, in-cluding some of the dogmas of progressivism itself. Lippmann ingeniously bestowed on the reform generation both a young disciple's measured tribute and a young rebel's devastating critique. In A Preface to Politics Lippmann had prophesied the contemporary liberation of men's psychic energies from outworn Victorian assumptions about man's nature and the social order; in so doing he had been proclaiming what historian Henry May has penetratingly described as "the end of American innocence." Now, in his second book, he was to call on the reformers to infuse their achievements with the spirit of scientific planning and conscious, un-dogmatic experiment. Lippmann in passing censured Woodrow Wilson and the New Freedom Democrats for their supposedly outworn and futile attack on the organizational trends in business and industry; it was this feature of Drift and Mastery which must have prompted Roosevelt to praise the author for unusual perception. But Lippmann was not writing a tract for the New Nationalism, nor did he seek merely to revisit the battleground of 1912. He was after bigger game. Drift and Mastery set forth the faith of all those young men who had been liberated by the teachings of William James and were now to discover Sigmund Freud. It was the faith of the pragmatist and the social scientist in the ordering of human affairs through the systematic understanding of man's irrational nature. The progressive vision, thought Walter Lippmann on the eve of world war, had taken America only so far. The future lay in the hands of those who could probe deeper than Wilson, Roosevelt, or Debs into the mystery and potentiality of the social animal in an organized industrial world.*

## THE THEMES OF MUCKRAKING

There is in America today a distinct prejudice in favor of those who make the accusations. Thus if you announced that John D. Rockefeller was going to vote the Republican ticket it would be regarded at once as a triumph for the Democrats. Something has happened to our notions of success: no political party these days enjoys publishing the names of its campaign contributors, if those names belong to the pillars of society. The mere statement that George W. Perkins is an active Progressive has put the whole party somewhat on the defensive. And there is more than sarcasm in the statement of the New York Times Annalist that:

"If it be true that the less bankers have to do with a scheme of banking and currency reform the more acceptable it will be to the people, it follows that the Administration's Currency Bill . . . must command popular admiration."

You have only to write an article about some piece of corruption in order to find yourself the target of innumerable correspondents, urging you to publish their wrongs. The sense of conspiracy and secret scheming which transpire is almost uncanny. "Big Business," and its ruthless tentacles, have become the material for the feverish fantasy of illiterate thousands thrown out of kilter by the rack and strain of modern life. It is possible to work yourself into a state where the world seems a conspiracy and your daily going is beset with an alert and tingling sense of labyrinthine evil. Everything askew—all the frictions of life are readily ascribed to a deliberate evil intelligence, and men like Morgan and Rockefeller take on attributes of omnipotence, that ten minutes of cold sanity would reduce to a barbarous myth. I know a socialist who seriously believes that the study of eugenics is a Wall Street scheme for sterilizing working-class leaders. And the cartoons which pictured Morgan sitting arrogantly in a chariot drawn by the American people in a harness of ticker tape—these are not so much caricatures as pictures of what no end of fairly sane people believe. Not once but twenty times have I been told confidentially of a nation-wide scheme by financiers to suppress every radical and progressive periodical. But even though the most intelligent muckrakers have always insisted that the picture was absurd, it remains to this day a very widespread belief. I remember how often

Walter Lippmann, *Drift and Mastery* (New York: Kennerly, 1914), pp. 1-49, 240-334.

Lincoln Steffens used to deplore the frightened literalness with which some of his articles were taken. One day in the country he and I were walking the railroad track. The ties, of course, are not well spaced for an ordinary stride, and I complained about it. "You see," said Mr. Steffens with mock obviousness, "Morgan controls the New Haven and he prefers to make the people ride."

Now it is not very illuminating to say that this smear of suspicion has been worked up by the muckrakers. If business and politics really served American need, you could never induce people to believe so many accusations against them. It is said, also, that the muckrakers played for circulation, as if that proved their insincerity. But the mere fact that muckraking was what people wanted to hear is in many ways the most important revelation of the whole campaign.

There is no other way of explaining the quick approval which the muckrakers won. They weren't voices crying in a wilderness, or lonely prophets who were stoned. They demanded a hearing; it was granted. They asked for belief; they were believed. They cried that something should be done and there was every appearance of action. There must have been real causes for dissatisfaction, or the land notorious for its worship of success would not have turned so savagely upon those who had achieved it. A happy husband will endure almost anything, but an unhappy one is capable of flying into a rage if his carpet-slippers are not in the right place. For America, the willingness to believe the worst was a strange development in the face of its traditional optimism, a sign perhaps that the honeymoon was over. For muckraking flared up at about the time when land was no longer freely available and large scale industry had begun to throw vast questions across the horizon. It came when success had ceased to be easily possible for everyone.

The muckrakers spoke to a public willing to recognize as corrupt an incredibly varied assortment of conventional acts. That is why there is nothing mysterious or romantic about the business of exposure—no putting on of false hair, breaking into letter-flies at midnight, hypnotizing financiers, or listening at keyholes. The stories of graft, written and unwritten, are literally innumerable. Often muckraking consists merely in dressing up a public document with rhetoric and pictures, translating a court record into journalese, or writing the complaints of a minority stockholder, a dislodged politician, or a boss gone "soft." No journalist need suffer from a want of material.

Now in writing this chapter I started out to visualize this material in systematic and scholarly fashion by making a list of the graft revelations in the last ten years. I wished for some quantitative sense of the number and kinds of act that are called corrupt. But I found myself trying to classify the industrial, financial, political, foreign and social relations of the United States, with hundreds of sub-heads, and a thousand gradations of credibility and exaggeration. It was an impossible task. The popular press of America is enormous, and for years it has been filled with "probes" and "amazing revelations." And how is a person to classify, say, the impeachment of a Tammany governor by a Tammany legislature? A mere list of investigations would fill this book, and I abandoned the attempt with the mental reservation that if anyone really desired that kind of proof, a few German scholars, young and in perfect health, should be imported to furnish it.

They could draw up a picture to stagger even a jaded American. Suppose they began their encyclopedia with the adulteration of foods. There would follow a neat little volume on the aliases of coffee. The story of meat would help the vegetarians till the volume on canned foods appeared. Milk would curdle the blood, bread and butter would raise a scandal, candy—the volume would have to be suppressed. If photographs could convey odors the study of restaurants might be done without words. The account of patent medicines, quack doctors, beauty parlors, mining schemes, loan sharks, shyster lawyers, all this riff-raff and fraud in the cesspool of commercialism would make unendurable reading. You would rush to the window, cursing the German pedants, grateful for a breath of that air which filters through in spite of the unenforced smoke ordinance of your city.

But the story would proceed. Think of your state of mind after you had read all about the methods of drummers, advertising agents, lobbyists, publicity men, after you knew adulteration of every description, and had learned the actual motives and history of political conferences, of caucuses, and consultations with the boss; suppose you understood the underground history of legislatures, the miscarriages of justice, the relations of the police to vice and crime, of newspapers to advertisers and wealthy citizens, of trade union leaders to their unions, the whole fetid story of the war between manufacturers and labor organizations. A study of the public domain in America would employ a staff of investigators. What railroads have done to the public, to their employees, what directors do to the stockholders and the property, the quantitative record of broken trust, the relation of bankers to the prosperity of business enterprise, of stock gamblers to capitalization—taking merely all that is known and could be illustrated, summed up and seen at once, what a picture it would make.

And yet such a picture would be false and inept. For certainly there must be some ground for this sudden outburst of candor, some ground beside a national desire for abstract truth and righteousness. These charges and counter-charges arose because the world has been altered radically, not because Americans fell in love with honesty. If we condemn what we once honored, if we brand as criminal the conventional acts of twenty years ago, it's because we have developed new necessities and new expectations.

They are the clue to the clouds of accusation which hang over American life. You cannot go very far by reiterating that public officials are corrupt, that business men break the law. The unbribed official and the law-abiding business man are not ideals that will hold the imagination very long. And that is why the earlier kind of muckraking exhausted itself. There came a time when the search for not-dishonest men ceased to be interesting. We all know now what tepid failures were those first opponents of corruption, the men whose only claim to distinction was that they had done no legal wrong. For without a vivid sense of what politics and business might be, you cannot wage a very fruitful campaign.

Now if you study the chief themes of muckraking I think it is possible to see the outlines of what America has come to expect.

The first wave of exposure insisted upon the dishonesty of politicians. Close upon it came widespread attack upon big business men, who were charged with bribing officials and ruining their competitors. Soon another theme appeared: big business men were accused of grafting upon the big corporations which they controlled. We are entering upon another period now: not alone big business, but all business and farming too, are being criticized for inefficiency, for poor product, and for exploitation of employees.

This classification is, of course, a very rough one. It would be easy enough to dispute it, for the details are endlessly complicated and the exceptions may appear very large to some people. But I think, nevertheless, that this classification does no essential violence to the facts. It doesn't matter for my purposes that some communities are still in what I call the first period, while others are in the third. For a nation like ours doesn't advance at the same rate everywhere. All I mean to suggest is that popular muckraking in the last decade has shifted its interest in something like this order: First, to the corruption of aldermen and mayors and public servants by the boss acting for a commercial interest, and to the business methods of those who built up the trusts. Then, muckraking turned, and began to talk about the milking of railroads by banks, and of one corporation by another. This period laid great emphasis on the "interlocking directorate." Now, muckraking is fastening upon the waste in management, upon working conditions as in the Steel Mills or at Lawrence, or upon the quality of service rendered by the larger corporations. These have been the big themes.

Why should they have been? Why, to begin with, should politicians have been attacked so fiercely? Some people would say flatly: because politicians were dishonest. Yet that is an utterly unfounded generalization. The morals of politicians cannot by any stretch of the imagination be described as exceptionally bad. Politicians were on the make. To be sure. But who in this sunny land isn't? They gave their relatives and friends pleasant positions. What father doesn't do that for his son if he can, and with every feeling of righteousness? They helped their friends, they were loyal to those who had helped them: who will say that in private life these are not admirable virtues? And what were the typical grafts in politics—the grafts for which we tried to send politicians to jail? The city contracts for work, and the public official is in league with the contractor; but railroads also contract for work, and corporation officials are at least as frequently as politicians, financially interested in the wrong side of the deal. The city buys real estate, and the city official manages to buy it from himself or his friends. But railroad directors have been known to sell their property to the road they govern.

We can see, I think, what people meant by the word graft. They did not mean robbery. It is rather confused rhetoric to call a grafter a thief. His crime is not that he filches money from the safe but that he betrays a trust. The grafter is a man whose loyalty is divided and whose motives are mixed. A lawyer who takes a fee from both sides in some case; a public official who serves a private interest; a railroad director who is also a director in the supply company; a policeman in league with outlawed vice: those are the relationships which the American people denounce as "corrupt." The attempt to serve at the same time two antagonistic interests is what constitutes "corruption."

The crime is serious in proportion to the degree of loyalty that we expect. A President of the United States who showed himself too friendly to some private interest would be denounced, though he may not have made one cent out of the friendship. But where we have not yet come to expect much loyalty we do very little muckraking. So if you inquired into the ethics of the buyer in almost any manufacturing house, you would find him doing things daily that would land the purchasing agent of a city in jail. Who regards it as especially corrupt if the selling firm "treats" the buyer, gives him or her a "present," perhaps a commission, or at least a "good time"? American life is saturated with the very relationship which in politics we call corrupt. The demand for a rake-off penetrates to the kitchen where a sophisticated cook expects a commission from the butcher, and tampers with the meat if it is refused; you can find it in the garage where the chauffeur has an understanding about the purchase of supplies; it extends to the golf caddie who regards a "lost" ball as his property and proceeds to sell it to the next man for half the original cost—it extends to the man who buys that ball; and it ramifies into the professions when doctors receive commissions from specialists for sending patients to them; it saturates the work-a-day world with tips and fees and "putting you on to a good thing" and "letting you in on the ground floor." But in the politician it is mercilessly condemned.

That is because we expect more of the politician. We say in effect that no public servant must allow himself to follow the economic habits of his countrymen. The corrupt politician is he who brings into public service the traditions of a private career. Perhaps that is a cynical reflection. I do not know how to alter it. When I hear politicians talk "reform," I know they are advocating something which most drummers on the road would regard as the scruples of a prig, and I know that when business men in a smoking-room are frank, they are taking for granted acts which in a politician we should call criminal.

For the average American will condemn in an alderman what in his partner he would consider reason for opening a bottle of champagne. In literal truth the politician is attacked for displaying the morality of his constituents. You might if you didn't understand the current revolution, consider that hypocrisy. It isn't: it is one of the hopeful signs of the age. For it means that unconsciously men regard some of the interests of life as too important for the intrusion of commercial ethics.

Run a government to-day, with the same motives and vision that you run a dry goods store, and watch for the activity of the muckrakers. Pursue in the post office the methods which made you a founder of colleges, you will be grateful for a kind word from Mr. Lorimer. Poor as they are, the standards of public life are so much more social than those of business that financiers who enter politics regard themselves as philanthropists. The amount of work and worry without reward is almost beyond the comprehension of the man whose every act is measured in profit and loss. The money to be accumulated in politics even by the cynically corrupt is so small by comparison that able men on the make go into politics only when their motives are mixed with ambition, a touch of idealism, vanity, or an imaginative notion of success.

But the fact that a public official took no bribe soon ceased to shield him from popular attack. Between the honest adherent of machine politics and the corruptionist himself the muckrakers made no sharp distinction. And that was because they had in a vague way come to expect positive action from men in office. They looked for better school systems, or health campaigns, or a conservation policy, that is for fairly concrete social measures, and officials who weren't for them were lumped together and denounced. The official might have read too much Adam Smith, or been too much of a lawyer, or taken orders from the boss, or a bribe from a lobbyist—the rough result was the same: he wasn't for what public opinion had come to expect, and the muckrakers laid their traps for him.

I suppose that from the beginning of the republic people had always expected their officials to work at a level less self-seeking than that of ordinary life. So that corruption in politics could never be carried on with an entirely good conscience. But at the opening of this century, democratic people had begun to see much greater possibilities in the government than ever before. They looked to it as a protector from economic tyranny and as the dispenser of the prime institutions of democratic life.

But when they went to the government, what they found was a petty and partisan, slavish and blind, clumsy and rusty instrument for their expectations. That added to the violence of their attacks. When they had no vision of what a democratic state might do, it didn't make so very much difference if officials took a rake-off. The cost of corruption was only a little money, and perhaps the official's immortal soul. But when men's vision of government enlarged, then the cost of corruption and inefficiency rose: for they meant a blighting of the whole possibility of the state. There has always been corruption in American politics, but it didn't worry people very much, so long as the sphere of government was narrowly limited. Corruption became a real problem when reform through state action began to take hold of men's thought.

As muckraking developed, it began to apply the standards of public life to certain parts of the business world. Naturally the so-called public service corporation was the first to feel the pressure. There is obviously a great difference in outlook between the Vanderbilt policy of "the public be damned" and the McAdoo policy of "the public be pleased." The old sense of private property is very much modified: few railroad men to-day would deny that they are conducting a quasi-public enterprise, and that something more is demanded of them than private exploitation. Thus President Mellen of the New Haven railroad could not have been handled more roughly by the people of New England if they had elected him to office. And his successor, President Howard Elliott, finds it necessary to remind the people that "the railroad is a public servant in fact as well as in name and that the service which it renders depends largely upon the treatment which it receives from its master." Mr. Elliott's grandfather would, I think, have said that his descendant lacked a sense of private property. That is true: Mr. Elliott's remark is a recognition that the cultural basis of property is radically altered, however much the law may lag behind in recognizing the change. So if the stockholders think they are the ultimate owners of the Pennsylvania railroad, they are colossally mistaken. Whatever the law may be, the people have no such notion. And the men who are connected with these essential properties cannot escape the fact that they are expected to act increasingly as public officials.

That expectation has filtered into the larger industrial corporations. I have here, for example, a statement by Roger Babson, a recognized financial expert:

Suppose the mayor of a town should appoint his brother police commissioner; his daughter's husband, fire commissioner; his uncle, superintendent of the water works; and put his son in charge of the street cleaning department. How long would it be before the good citizens would hold an indignation meeting? It would not be long. No city in America would stand that kind of graft. Yet pick up the letterhead of a private corporation and what are you likely to find? It usually reads something like this: Quincy Persimmon, president; Quincy Persimmon, Jr., vice-president; Persimmon Quincy, treasurer; Howard Lemon, secretary. The presence of Howard Lemon in this select family circle is somewhat puzzling until one learns that Prunella Quincy Persimmon is the wife of Howard Lemon. Then all is clear. To be sure, the general manager of the concern, who is the man to see on any matter of special importance, is a man named Hobbs or Smith or Hogan, but it soon appears that the salary of the general manager is just about what it costs young Lemon to run his motor for one year. . . . Has there ever been an American mayor who dared to run his city as this private corporation is run? In their leisure moments the Persimmons, Quincys and the Lemons are constantly advising their fellow citizens of the danger of permitting an American city to advance one step toward the sort of municipal work which is done by a great many foreign cities with success. The reason against this is given as the graft in public life.

Now when the Persimmons are muckraked, what puzzles them beyond words is that anyone should presume to meddle with *their* business. What they will learn is that it is no longer altogether *their* business. The law may not have realized this, but the fact is being accomplished, and it's a fact grounded deeper than statutes. Big business men who are at all intelligent recognize this. They are talking more and more about their "responsibilities," their "stewardship." It is the swan-song of the old commercial profiteering and a dim recognition that the motives in business are undergoing a revolution.

But muckraking has grown in scope, which is another way of saying that it has come to expect still more. We hear now about the inefficiency of business. Men like Brandeis, Redfield, Taylor have taken the lead in this criticism. Try if you can to imagine a merchant in the '70's subject to criticism on a national scale because he didn't know how to run his business. He would have sputtered and exploded at the impudence of such a suggestion. As a matter of fact some remnants of that age have sputtered and exploded at the impudence of Mr. Brandeis. But in the main the younger business men have been willing to listen. They do not think it a preposterous notion when the Secretary of Commerce suggests that if they are to conduct business they must do it efficiently.

Then too, the farmers are being criticized. They are no longer deluged with adulation: they are being told quite frankly that they have a very great deal to learn from the government and the universities. And now there is a tremendous agitation about the quality of the goods and the conditions of labor under which they are produced.

Why all this has happened: why there are new standards for business men, why the nature of property is altered, why the workers and the purchasers are making new demands—all this muckraking never made very clear. It was itself considerably more of an effect than a sign of leadership. It expressed a change, and consequently it is impossible to say that muckraking was either progressive or reactionary in its tendency. The attack upon business men was listened to by their defeated competitors as well as by those who looked forward to some better order of industrial life. Muckraking is full of the voices of the beaten, of the bewildered, and then again it is shot through with some fine anticipation. It has pointed to a revolution in business motives; it has hinted at the emerging power of labor and the consumer—we can take those suggestions, perhaps, and by analyzing them, and following them through, gather for ourselves some sense of what moves beneath the troubled surface of events.

NEW INCENTIVES

We say in conversation: "Oh, no, he's not a business man—he has a profession." That sounds like an invidious distinction, and no doubt there is a good deal of caste and snobbery in the sentiment. But that isn't all there is. We imagine that men enter the professions by undergoing a special discipline to develop a personal talent. So their lives seem more interesting, and their incentives more genuine. The business man may feel that the scientist content with a modest salary is an improvident ass. But he also feels some sense of inferiority in the scientist's presence. For at the bottom there is a difference of quality in their lives—in the scientist's a dignity which the scramble for profit can never assume. The professions may be shot through with rigidity, intrigue, and hypocrisy: they have, nevertheless, a community of interest, a sense of craftsmanship, and a more permanent place in the larger reaches of the imagination. It is a very pervasive and subtle difference, but sensitive business men are aware of it. They are not entirely proud of their profit-motive: bankers cover it with a sense of importance, others mitigate it with charity and public work, a few dream of railroad empires and wildernesses tamed, and some reveal their sense of unworthiness by shouting with extra emphasis that they are not in business for their health.

It is a sharp commentary on the psychological insight of the orthodox economist who maintains that the only dependable motive is profit. Most people repeat that—parrot-fashion, but in the rub they don't act upon it. When we began to hear recently that radium might subdue cancer, there was a fairly unanimous demand that the small supply available should be taken over by the government and removed from the sphere of private exploitation. The fact is that men don't trust the profiteer in a crisis, or whenever the interest at stake is of essential importance. So the public regards a professor on the make as a charlatan, a doctor on the make as a quack, a woman on the make as an adventuress, a politician on the make as a grafter, a writer on the make as a hack, a preacher on the make as a hypocrite. For in science, art, politics, religion, the home, love, education—the pure economic motive, profiteering, the incentive of business enterprise is treated as a public peril. Wherever civilization is seen to be in question, the Economic Man of commercial theorists is in disrepute.

I am not speaking in chorus with those sentimentalists who regard industry as sordid. They merely inherit an ancient and parasitic contempt for labor. I do not say for one instant that money is the root of evil, that rich men are less honest than poor, or any equivalent nonsense. I am simply trying to point out that there is in every-day life a widespread rebellion against the profit motive. That rebellion is not an attack on the creation of wealth. It is, on the contrary, a discovery that private commercialism is an antiquated, feeble, mean, and unimaginative way of dealing with the possibilities of modern industry.

The change is, I believe, working itself out under our very eyes. Each day brings innumerable plans for removing activities from the sphere of profit. Endowment, subsidy, state aid, endless varieties of consumers' and producers' coöperatives; public enterprise—they have been devised to save the theater, to save science and invention, education and journalism, the market basket and public utilities from the life-sapping direction of the commercialist. What is the meaning of these protean efforts to supersede the profiteer if not that his motive produces results hostile to use, and that he is a usurper where the craftsman, the inventor and the industrial statesman should govern? There is no sudden substitution of sacrifice for selfishness. These experiments are being tried because commercialism failed to serve civilization: the coöperator intrenched behind his wiser organization would smile if you regarded him as a patient lamb on the altar of altruism. He knows that the old economists were bad psychologists and superficial observers when they described man as a slot machine set in motion by inserting a coin.

It is often asserted that modern industry could never have been created had it not been given over to untrammeled exploitation by commercial adventurers. That may be true. There is no great point in discussing the question as to what might have happened if something else had happened in the past. Modern industry was created by the profiteer, and here it is, the great fact in our lives, blackening our cities, fed with the lives of children, a tyrant over men and women, turning out enormous stocks of produce, good, bad, and horrible. We need waste no time arguing whether any other motive could have done the work. What we are finding is that however effective profit may have been for inaugurating modern industry, it is failing as a method of realizing its promise. That is why men turn to coöperatives and labor unions; that is why the state is interfering more and more. These blundering efforts are the assertion of all the men and all those elements of their natures which commercialism has thwarted. No amount of argument can wipe out the fact that the profit-system has never commanded the whole-hearted assent of the people who lived under it. There has been a continuous effort to overthrow it. From Robert Owen to John Stuart Mill, from Ruskin through Morris to the varied radicalism of our day, from the millionaire with his peace palaces to Henry Ford with his generous profit-sharing, through the consumer organizing a coöperative market, to the working-men defying their masters and the economists by pooling their labor, you find a deep stream of uneasiness, of human restlessness against those impositions which are supposed to rest on the eternal principles of man's being.

There is scarcely any need to press the point, for no one questions the statement that endowment, coöperation, or public enterprise are attempts to employ motives different from those of the profiteer. The only dispute is whether these new motives can be extended and made effective. It is, I think, a crucial question. It lies at the root of most theoretical objection to socialism in the famous "human nature" argument. Far from being a trivial question, as socialist debaters like to pretend—it is the hardest nut they have to crack. They are proposing a reconstruction of human society, and in all honesty, they cannot dodge the question as to whether man as we know him is capable of what they ask. Persian, Mexican, Turkish and Chinese experience with constitutional democracies ought to show how easy it is, as Macaulay said, for a tailor to measure the clothes of all his customers by the Apollo Belvedere. In a matter like this there is little to choose between the socialist who is sure his plan will work and the "anti" who is sure it will not. The profit-motive is attacked, that is certain; that more or less successful attempts are made to supplant it, is obvious, but how far we can go, that remains an open question. We cannot answer it by analogy: it does not follow from the success of a coöperative grocery that the Steel Trust can be governed on the same plan. If our expectations are to have any solidity we must find evidence for them in those great private industries which seem to be completely in the hands of profit. That is where the issues join. The theater has always been a stamping ground for "queer" people; scholars are notoriously incompetent in "business"; scientific research pays so well, is so undeniably valuable, that few dare grudge it a subsidy; public utilities, like the highways, are by tradition not business propositions; and coöperatives have had a stormy history. There are, of course, the army and navy, which no man wishes to see organized by private individuals on the make. The most conservative have doubted recently whether armaments should be manufactured for profit. Yet such analogies, impressive as they are, offer nothing conclusive. But if we find that in the staple industries like steel and oil a silent revolution is in progress, then we have a basis for action. If there the profit-motive is decadent and new incentives ready, then perhaps what look like irresponsible outcries and wanton agitation will assume the dignity of a new morality.

In the last thirty years or so American business has been passing through a reorganization so radical that we are just beginning to grasp its meaning. At any rate for those of us who are young to-day the business world of our grandfathers is a piece of history that we can reconstruct only with the greatest difficulty. We know that the huge corporation, the integrated industry, production for a world market, the network of combinations, pools and agreements have played havoc with the older political economy. The scope of human endeavor is enormously larger, and with it has come, as Graham Wallas says, a general change of social scale. Human thought has had to enlarge its scale in order to meet the situation. That is why it is not very illuminating to say, for example, that the principles of righteousness are eternal and that the solution of every problem is in the Golden Rule. The Golden Rule in a village, and the Golden Rule for a nation of a hundred million people are two very different things. I might possibly treat my neighbor as myself, but in this vast modern world the greatest problem that confronts me is to find my neighbor and treat him at all. The size and intricacy which we have to deal with have done more than anything else, I imagine, to wreck the simple generalizations of our ancestors. After all, they were not prophets, and the conservative to-day makes an inhuman demand when he expects them to have laid out a business policy for a world they never even imagined. If anyone thinks that the Fathers might have done this let him sit down and write a political economy for the year 1950.

"Since the Sherman Act was passed (1890)," says President Van Hise of Wisconsin University, "a child born has attained its majority." Indeed he has, much to the surprise of the unwilling parents. Now a new business world has produced a new kind of business man. For it requires a different order of ability to conduct the Steel Trust, than it did to manage a primitive blast-furnace by means of a partnership. The giant corporation calls for an equipment unlike any that business has ever known: the minds of the managers are occupied with problems beyond the circle of ideas that interested the old-fashioned chop-whiskered merchants. They have to preserve intimate contact with physicists and chemists, there is probably a research laboratory attached to the plant. They have to deal with huge masses of workingmen becoming every day more articulate. They have to think about the kind of training our public schools give. They have to consider very concretely the psychology of races, they come into contact with the structure of credit, and a money squeeze due to the Balkan war makes a difference in their rate of output. They have to keep thousands of ignorant stockholders somewhere in the back of their mind, people who don't know the difference between puddling and pudding. They may find themselves an issue in a political campaign, and if they are to be successful they must estimate correctly the social temper of the community. Diplomacy is closely related to the selling department, and perhaps at times they may have to dabble in Latin-American revolutions.

Mr. Louis D. Brandeis commented on this change of scale in his testimony before the Committee on Interstate Commerce.

Anyone who critically analyzes a business learns this: that success or failure of an enterprise depends usually upon one man. . . . Now while organization has made it possible for the individual man to accomplish infinitely more than he could before, aided as he is by new methods of communication, by the stenographer, the telephone, and system, still there is a limit for what one man can do well. . . . When, therefore, you increase your business to a very great extent, and the multitude of problems increases with its growth, you will find, in the first place, that the man at the head has a diminishing knowledge of the facts, and, in the second place, a diminishing opportunity of exercising careful judgment upon them.

In this statement, you will find, I believe, one of the essential reasons why a man of Mr. Brandeis's imaginative power has turned against the modern trust. He does not believe that men can deal efficiently with the scale upon which the modern business world is organized. He has said quite frankly, that economic size is in itself a danger to democracy. This means, I take it, that American voters are not intelligent enough or powerful enough to dominate great industrial organizations. So Mr. Brandeis, in company with many important thinkers the world over, has turned de-centralizer. The experience of history justifies his position in many respects: there is no doubt that an organization like the Holy Roman Empire was too large for the political capacity of human beings. It is probably true that the Morgan empire had become unwieldly. It may be that the Steel Trust is too large for efficiency. The splendid civilizations of the past have appeared in small cities. To-day if you go about the world you find that the small countries like Belgium, Holland, Denmark, are the ones that have come nearest to a high level of social prosperity. I once heard George Russell (Æ), the Irish poet and reformer, say that an ideal state would be about the size of County Cork.

Yet it is not very helpful to insist that size is a danger, unless you can specify what size.

The senators asked Mr. Brandeis that question. They pressed him to state approximately what percentage of an industry he considered an effective unit. He hesitated between ten per cent. and forty per cent., and could not commit himself. Obviously—for how could Mr. Brandeis be expected to know? Adam Smith thought the corporations of his day doomed to failure on the very same grounds that Mr. Brandeis urges against the modern corporation. Now the million dollar organization is not too large for efficiency and the billion dollar one may be. The ideal unit may fall somewhere between? Where? That is a problem which experiments alone can decide, experiments conducted by experts in the new science of administration.

The development of that science is the only answer to the point Mr. Brandeis raises. Remarkable results have already been produced. Every one of us, for example, must wonder at times how the President of the United States ever does all the things the papers say he does. When, for example, does the man sleep? And is he omniscient? The fact is that administration is becoming an applied science, capable of devising executive methods for dealing with tremendous units. No doubt the President with his increasing responsibilities is an overworked man. No doubt there are trusts badly administered. No doubt there are inflated monopolies created for purely financial reasons. But just what the limits of administrative science are, a legislature is no more capable of determining than was Mr. Brandeis. Only experience, only trial and ingenuity, can demonstrate, and in a research so young and so swift in its progress, any effort to assign by law an arbitrary limit is surely the most obvious meddling. Say to-day that one unit of business is impossible, to-morrow you may be confronted with an undreamt success. Here if anywhere is a place where negative prophecy is futile. It is well to remember the classic case of that great scientist Simon Newcomb, who said that man would never fly. Two years before that statement was made, the Wright brothers had made secret flights.

It may well be that the best unit is smaller than some of the modern trusts. It does not follow that we must break up industry into units of administration whose ideal efficiency is spent in competing with one another. I can understand, for example, the desire of many people to see Europe composed of a larger number of small nations. But I take it that everyone wishes these small nations to coöperate in the creation of a common European civilization. So it is with business. The unit of administration may be whatever efficiency demands. It may be that the steel industry would gain if it were conducted by forty corporations. But at the same time there are advantages in common action which we cannot afford to abandon. Technical improvement must be for the whole industry, the labor market must be organized and made stable, output must be adjusted to a common plan. The appearance of federal organization seems to suggest a possible compromise in which the administrative need for decentralization is combined with the social demand for a unified industrial policy.

No one, surely, proposes to revive the little business monarch who brooded watchfully over every operation in factory and office, called his workingmen by their pet names, and was impelled at almost every turn by Adam Smith's "natural propensity to truck and barter." For just as in political government "the President" does a hundred things every day he may never even hear of, just as the English Crown acts constantly through some unknown civil servant at $1,500 a year—so in big business —the real government is passing into a hierarchy of managers and deputies, who, by what would look like a miracle to Adam Smith, are able to coöperate pretty well toward a common end. They are doing that, remember, in the first generation of administrative science. They come to it unprepared, from a nation that is suspicious and grudging. They have no tradition to work with, the old commercial morality of the exploiter and profiteer still surrounds these new rulers of industry. Perhaps they are unaware that they are revolutionizing the discipline, the incentives, and the vision of the business world. They do brutal and stupid things, and their essential work is obscured. But they are conducting business on a scale without precedent in history.

The real news about business, it seems to me, is that it is being administered by men who are not profiteers. The managers are on salary, divorced from ownership and from bargaining. They represent the revolution in business incentives at its very heart. For they conduct gigantic enterprises and they stand outside the higgling of the market, outside the shrewdness and strategy of competition. The motive of profit is not their personal motive. That is an astounding change. The administration of the great industries is passing into the hands of men who cannot halt before each transaction and ask themselves: what is my duty as the Economic Man looking for immediate gain? They have to live on their salaries, and hope for promotion, but their day's work is not measured in profit. There are thousands of these men, each with responsibilities vaster than the patriarchs of industry they have supplanted. It is for the commercial theorists to prove that the "ability" is inferior, and talent less available.

It is no accident that the universities have begun to create graduate schools of business-administration. Fifty years ago industry was an adventure or perhaps a family tradition. But to-day it is becoming a profession with university standing equal to that of law, medicine, or engineering. The universities are supplying a demand. It is big business, I believe, which has created that demand. For it is no longer possible to deal with the present scale of industry if your only equipment is what men used to call "experience," that is, a haphazard absorption of knowledge through the pores. Just as it is no longer possible to become a physician by living with doctors, just as law cannot be grasped by starting as a clerk in some attorney's office, so business requires a greater preparation than a man can get by being a bright, observant, studious, ambitious office boy, who saves his money and is good to his mother.

What it will mean to have business administered by men with a professional training is a rather difficult speculation. That it is a very far-reaching psychological change, I have no doubt. The professions bring with them a fellowship in interest, a standard of ethics, an esprit de corps, and a decided discipline. They break up that sense of sullen privacy which made the old-fashioned business man so impervious to new facts and so shockingly ignorant of the larger demands of civilized life. I know that the professions develop their pedantry, but who was ever more finicky, more rigid in his thinking than the self-satisfied merchant? It would be idle to suppose that we are going suddenly to develop a nation of reasonable men. But at least we are going to have an increasing number of "practical" men who have come in contact with the scientific method. That is an enormous gain over the older manufacturers and merchants. They were shrewd, hard-working, no doubt, but they were fundamentally uneducated. They had no discipline for making wisdom out of their experience. They had almost no imaginative training to soften their primitive ambitions. But doctors and engineers and professional men, generally, have something more than a desire to accumulate and outshine their neighbors. They have found an interest in the actual work they are doing. The work itself is in a measure its own reward. The instincts of workmanship, of control over brute things, the desire for order, the satisfaction of services rendered and uses created, the civilizing passions are given a chance to temper the primal desire to have and to hold and to conquer. . . .

BOGEYS

There are people who are always waiting for the heavens to fall. In 1879, when Massachusetts granted school suffrage to women, a legislator arose and said: "If we make this experiment we shall destroy the race, which will be blasted by Almighty God." That silly man was not a prehistoric specimen. He is always with us. And he is in the soul of most of us. He is the panic that seized Chicago over the Haymarket anarchists; he is what makes preachers cry out that the tango is wrecking the nation; he is the white slave legend; he is Mr. Taft contemplating the recall of judges.

I know how bogeys are made. I was a child of four during the panic of '93, and Cleveland has always been a sinister figure to me. His name was uttered with monstrous dread in the household. Then came Bryan, an ogre from the West, and a waiting for the election returns of 1896 with beating heart. And to this day I find myself with a subtle prejudice against Democrats that goes deeper than what we call political conviction.

I can remember a birthday "party" for two or three chums which developed into a "rough-house." In the excitement we used cakes as ammunition, leaving the carpet in a shocking state. This angered the maid who was responsible for the tidiness of my room to such a pitch that only religion seemed adequate for the occasion. In the late afternoon she began to talk to me in a solemn voice. I would have preferred a thousand beatings to that voice in the wretched gaslight which used to darken homes before electricity reached the middle-class. The flickering shadows on the cake-strewn carpet were unbearable and accusing shapes full of foreboding to boys lost in sin. I burst into tears at the impending wrath of God. And for years God was the terror of the twilight.

With that somehow or other was associated a belief that the world was about to come to an end. I think the nurse had read the predictions of some astronomer in a newspaper, and the news was communicated to me. It became part of the twilight, and was mixed up with thunderstorms, and going into a dark room. Then too, there were ghosts, but I laid them one night after everyone had gone to bed in what is undoubtedly the most heroic exploit of my life. I still glow with pride in the telling. I got out of bed and turned on the light, identified the ghost with the lace curtain, went back to bed, turned on the light once more, made sure that the ghost *was* the curtain, and felt immeasurably happier.

Generally, however, we create the bogey by pulling the bed-clothes over our heads. A friend of mine couldn't be cured of his socialist phobia until he happened one day to see the most terrible agitator of them all buying a pair of suspenders. For in the seclusion and half-light of class tradition and private superstition, in a whispered and hesitant atmosphere, phantoms thrive. But in direct contact by an unromantic light evil is no longer a bogey but a problem. That is the way to approach evil: by stating it and manhandling it: the fevered gloom subsides, for that gloom does not belong to evil; it is merely the feeling of a person who is afraid of evil. "Death," said a wise man, "is not feared because it is evil, but it is evil because it is feared."

To overcome the subjective terrors: that is an important aspect of the age-long struggle out of barbarism. Romantic persons like to paint savages as care-free poets living in thoughtless happiness from day to day. Nothing could be further from the facts. The life of a savage is beset by glowering terrors: from birth to death he lives in an animated world; where the sun and the stars, sticks, stones, and rivers are obsessed with his fate. He is busy all the time in a ritual designed to propitiate the abounding jealousies of nature. For his world is magical and capricious, the simplest thing is occult. In that atmosphere there is no possibility of men being able to face their life without heroics and without terror, simply and gladly. They need authority: they need to be taken in charge; they cannot trust themselves.

That is why the exorcising of bogeys is so intimate a part of the effort at self-government. Think of the ordinary business man's notion of an anarchist, or the anarchist's notion of a business man; many men's feeling about Theodore Roosevelt, or Bill Haywood, or the Capitalist Class, or the Money Power, or Sex Reform—I use capital letters because these fantasies have become terrific monsters of the imagination. Our life is overwrought with timidities and panics, distorting superstitions and fantastic lures: our souls are misshapen by the plucking of invisible hands.

The regiment of bogeys is waiting for people at birth, where the cruellest unreason clusters about illegitimacy. It attacks the young child who asks how he was born. For answer he is given lies and a sense of shame; for ever afterwards he too lies and is ashamed. And so we begin to build up the sense of sin and the furtiveness of sex. The body becomes the object of a sneaking curiosity, of a tingling and embarrassing interest. We surround the obvious with great wastes of silence, and over the simplest facts we teach the soul to stutter.

What we call purity is not honest and temperate desire, but a divided life in which our "Better Nature" occasionally wins a bankrupt victory. Children are immured in what their parents fondly picture to be a citadel of innocence. In reality, they are plunged into fantastic brooding or into a haphazard education. Behind innocence there gathers a clotted mass of superstition, of twisted and misdirected impulse; clandestine flirtation, fads, and ragtime fill the unventilated mind.

Then too the whole edifice of class-feeling—what "is done" and what "isn't done," and who are "the best people" and who are the "impossible," and sleepless nights over whether you were correctly dressed, or whether you will be invited to be seen with Mrs. So-and-So. It makes sheep out of those who conform and freaks out of those who rebel. Every fairly intelligent person is aware that the price of respectability is a muffled soul bent on the trivial and the mediocre. The mere fact that the weight of custom is on the accidents of class is a tremendous item in the lives of those who try to live in a human sphere. No one escapes the deformity altogether. Certainly not the modern rebel. His impulse is to break away from the worship of idols to central human values. But the obstruction of class feeling is so great that he becomes a kind of specialist in rebellion. He is so busy asserting that he isn't conventional that the easy, natural humanity he professes to admire is almost the last thing he achieves. Hence the eccentricity and the paradox, the malice and the wantonness of the iconoclast.

The fear of losing one's job, the necessity of being somebody in a crowded and clamorous world, the terror that old age will not be secured, that your children will lack opportunity—there are a thousand terrors which arise out of the unorganized and unstable economic system under which we live. These are not terrors which can be blown away by criticism; they will go only when society is intelligent enough to have made destitution impossible, when it secures opportunity to every child, when it establishes for every human being a minimum of comfort below which he cannot sink. Then a great amount of social hesitancy will disappear. Every issue will not be fought as if life depended upon it, and mankind will have emerged from a fear economy. There are those who cannot conceive of a nation not driven by fear. They seem to feel that enterprise would diminish in a sort of placid contentment. That, it seems to me, is a serious error. The regime of fear produces dreaming and servile races, as in India and China and parts of Ireland. The enterprise that will be fruitful to modern civilization is not the undernourished child of hard necessity, but the high spirits and exuberant well-being of a happy people.

It is a common observation that no man can live well who fears death. The over-careful person is really dying all his life. He is a miser, and he pays the miser's penalty: he never enjoys his own treasure because he will not spend it. And so when we hear that he who would find his own soul must lose it first, we are not listening to an idle paradox or to some counsel of perfection. Those who hold life lightly are the real masters of it: the lavish givers have the most to give.

But anyone who picks his way through the world as if he were walking on eggs will find it a difficult and unsatisfactory place. Writers and scientists and statesmen who are forever preoccupied with their immediate reputation, always counting the costs, are buying rubbish for a fortune. The thinker who has a mortal fear of being wrong will give all that is valuable in himself to that little ambition. A mistake matters far less than most of us imagine: the world is not brittle, but elastic.

If we could know the inner history of weakness, of what disappoints us in leaders, the timidity of thought, the hesitancy and the drift, we should find in endless cases that the imagination had been blinded and the will scattered by the haunting horror of constructed evils. We falter from childhood amidst shames and fears, we move in closed spaces where stale tradition enervates, we grow hysterical over success and failure, and so by surrounding instinct with terror, we prepare the soul for weakness.

There is a brilliant statement of Freud's that in the Middle Ages people withdrew to a monastery, whereas in modern times they become nervous. He means that formerly men could find refuge from their sense of sin, their bogeys, and their conflicts, in a special environment and a fulfilling religion. But to-day they are the victims of their weakness. So if confidence is to become adequate for us we must set about expunging that weakness and disciplining a new strength.

A great deal can be done by exorcising bogeys—by refusing to add the terrors of the imagination to the terrors of fact. But there is in addition more positive work to do. We have to build up a disciplined love of the real world. It is no easy task. As yet, we see only in the vaguest way the affirmative direction of democratic culture. For the breakdown of absolutism is more evident than the way to mastery.

### POVERTY, CHASTITY, OBEDIENCE

Poverty, chastity, and obedience are not the ideals of a self-governing people. Occasionally, however, some well-fed old gentleman announces that it would be wrong to abolish want because poverty is such an excellent training ground for character. The sentiment does not attract the poor, of course, and even the friends of the old gentleman wish that he had not made an ass of himself. And of course, there are not many modern people who could agree with the mediæval theory that celibacy is more blessed than marriage. They prefer a father and a mother to a monk and a nun, and St. Paul's dictum that it is better to marry than burn will not seem to them a very noble tribute to the family. As to obedience, they continue to like it pretty well in other people, no doubt, and yet their greatest admiration goes out to those who stand on their own feet.

These mediæval vows are the true discipline of authority. In their absolute form they were meant only for those who sought absolute perfection. But to ordinary mortals, who could accept them only in moderation, they were still the best atmosphere for a world in which democracy was impossible. I do not mean to imply that the Church deliberately created an ideal which sapped the possibility of self-government. That would be to endow the Church with an inconceivably deliberate intelligence. All I mean is that in the undemocratic world which the Church dominated, ideals grew up which expressed the truth about that world.

The desire for self-government has become vivid with the accumulation of a great surplus of wealth. Man to-day has at last seen the possibility of freeing himself from his supreme difficulty. It wasn't easy to think much of the possibilities of this world while he lived on the edge of starvation. Resignation to hardship was a much more natural outlook. But in the midst of plenty, the imagination becomes ambitious, rebellion against misery is at last justified, and dreams have a basis in fact.

Of course, there are immense sections of the globe where the hard conditions of the older life still prevail, and there the ideal of democracy is still a very ineffective phrase. But the United States has for the most part lifted itself out of primitive hardship, and that fact, more than our supposedly democratic constitution, is what has justified in some measure the hope which inspires our history. We have been far from wise with the great treasure we possessed, and no nation has such cause for shame at the existence of poverty. We have only our shortsighted selves to blame. But the blunders are not fatal: American wealth has hardly been tapped. And that is why America still offers the greatest promise to democracy.

The first item in the program of self-government is to drag the whole population well above the misery line. To create a minimum standard of life below which no human being can fall is the most elementary duty of the democratic state. For those who go below the line of civilized decency not only suffer wretchedly: they breed the poisons of self-government. They form the famous slum proletariat about whom even the socialists despair. Occasionally some dramatic figure rises out of them, occasionally they mutter and rebel and send the newspapers into a panic. But for the purposes of constructive revolution this submerged mass is of little use, for it is harassed, beaten, helpless. These last will not be first. They may scare the rest of us into a little reform. But out of sheer wretchedness will come little of the material or the power of democracy, for as Walter Weyl has said, "A man or a class, crushed to earth—is crushed to earth."

Unfit for self-government, they are the most easily led, the most easily fooled, and the most easily corrupted. You can't build a modern nation out of Georgia crackers, poverty-stricken negroes, the homeless and helpless of the great cities. They make a governing class essential. They are used by the forces of reaction. Once in a while they are used by revolutionists for agitation, but always they are used. Before you can begin to have democracy you need a country in which everyone has some stake and some taste of its promise.

Now to link chastity with poverty as one of the props of absolutism is to prepare for yourself a peck of trouble. "Do you advocate unchastity?" shrieks the frightened person. As unchastity means to most people promiscuity, I say emphatically, "No, it isn't unchastity that we wish." We don't wish poverty, but that doesn't mean that we are for parvenus and millionaires. And so for sex, we don't seek Don Juans or ascetics, we seek fathers and mothers, and a life that isn't swamped by sex.

Life can be swamped by sex very easily if sex is not normally satisfied.

Those who can't have a piece of flesh, said Nietzsche, often grasp at a piece of spirit. I must confess I never saw anything very noble or pure in the dreams of St. Theresa. And as for St. Anthony in the Wilderness— surely that was no solution of the sex problem. But it was a wonderful way of cementing loyalty, to deny men and women a human life, and suggest that they marry the Church. The mediæval vow of chastity did not mean a sudden disappearance of the sexual life: it meant a concentration of that life upon the spiritual authority.

With poverty and chastity effectively enforced, there would have been very little need to preach obedience. That was necessary only because human nature didn't permit of any thoroughgoing application of the first two vows. Had the Church achieved its full ambition, to be glorious and rich amidst poverty, to offer the only spiritual compensation to thwarted lives, then the Church would have had few disloyal sons. But as it didn't succeed completely, it had to demand the third vow—obedience—as a kind of extra prop if the other two failed.

It is no wonder then, that the upholders of authority recognize in the labor movement and the women's awakening their mortal foes, or that Ibsen in that classic prophecy of his, should have seen in these same movements the two greatest forces for human emancipation. They are the power through which there will be accomplished that transvaluation of values which democracy means. They are pointed toward a frank worldliness, a coöperation among free people, they are pointed away from submissive want, balked impulse, and unquestioned obedience.

We can begin to see, then, a little of what democratic culture implies. There was a time, not so long ago, when scholars, and "cultured people" generally, regarded Ruskin's interest in political economy as the unfortunate perversion of a man who was born to better things. We do no longer regard it as "sordid" to take an interest in economic problems. I have met artists who deplore Mr. George Russell's interest in agricultural coöperation as unworthy of the poet who is known to the world by the mystic letters Æ. The interest of the working-class in its bread and butter problem is still occasionally the chance for a scolding about its "materialism." But in the main, modern democrats recognize that the abolition of poverty is the most immediate question before the world to-day, and they have imagination enough to know that the success of the war against poverty will be the conquest of new territory for civilized life.

So too, the day is passing when the child is taught to regard the body as a filthy thing. We train quite frankly for parenthood, not for the ecstasies of the celibate. Our interest in sex is no longer to annihilate it, but to educate it, to find civilized opportunities for its expression. We hope to organize industry and housekeeping so that normal mating shall not be a monstrously difficult problem. And there is an increasing number of people who judge sexual conduct by its results in the quality of human life. They don't think that marriage justifies licentiousness, nor will they say that every unconventional union is necessarily evil. They know the tyrannies that indissoluble marriage produces, and they are beginniing to know the equal oppressions of what is called "Free love." They are becoming concrete and realistic about sex. They are saying that where love exists with self-respect and joy, where a fine environment is provided for the child, where the parents live under conditions that neither stunt the imagination nor let it run to uncontrolled fantasy, there you have the family that modern men are seeking to create. They desire such a family not because they are afraid not to advocate it, but because they have reason to believe that this is the most fruitful way of ordering human life.

When we speak of the modern intellect we mean this habit of judging rules by their results instead of by their sources. The fact that an idea is old or that it is "advanced," that the Pope said it or Bernard Shaw, all that is of no decisive importance. The real question always turns on what an idea is worth in the satisfaction of human desire.

Objections will arise at once. It will be said that you can't judge rules or life or beliefs by their results, because many an idea of the greatest value may at first be very disagreeable. In other words, it is often necessary to sacrifice immediate advantages to distant results. That is perfectly true, of course, and the balancing of present wants against the future is really the central problem of ethics. Will you weigh action by its results on this particular venture, or on your whole life, or by its results on your generation, or on the generations to come? There is no simple answer to those questions. Every human being makes his own particular compromise. There are few people so concentrated on the immediate that they don't look ahead a little, if it's only to the extent of taking out a life insurance policy. There have been a few fanatics who lived so absolutely for the millennium that they made a little hell for their companions. But the wiser a man is, it seems to me, the more vividly he can see the future as part of the evolving present. He doesn't break the flow of life, he directs it, hastens it, but preserves its continuity. The people who really matter in social affairs are neither those who wish to stop short like a mule, or leap from crag to crag like a mountain goat.

But of course, to act for results instead of in response to authority requires a readiness of thought that no one can achieve at all times. You cannot question everything radically at every moment. You have to do an infinite number of acts without thinking about their results. I have to follow the orders of my physician. We all of us have to follow the lead of specialists.

And so, it is easy to score points against anyone who suggests that modern thought is substituting the pragmatic test by results for the old obedience to authority. It can't do that altogether. We cannot be absolute pragmatists. But we judge by results as much as we can, as much as our human limitations allow. Where we have to accept dogmas without question we do so not because we have any special awe of them, but because we know that we are too ignorant, or too busy, to analyze them through. I know how unphilosophical this will sound to those who worship neatness in thought.

Well, if they can find some surer key to the complexity of life, all power to them. But let them be careful that they are not building a theory which is symmetrical only on the printed page. Nothing is easier than to simplify life and then make a philosophy about it. The trouble is that the resulting philosophy is true only of that simplified life. If somebody can create an absolute system of beliefs and rules of conduct that will guide a business man at eleven o'clock in the morning, a boy trying to select a career, a woman in an unhappy love affair—well then, surely no pragmatist will object. He insists only that philosophy shall come down to earth and be tried out there.

In some such spirit as I have tried to suggest, the modern world is reversing the old virtues of authority. They aimed deliberately to make men unworldly. They did not aim to found society on a full use of the earth's resources; they did not aim to use the whole nature of man; they did not intend him to think out the full expression of his desires. Democracy is a turning upon those ideals in a pursuit, at first unconsciously, of the richest life that men can devise for themselves.

## MASTERY

The Dyaks of Borneo, it is said, were not accustomed to chopping down a tree, as white men do, by notching out V-shaped cuts. "Hence," says Mr. Marett in telling the story, "any Dyak caught imitating the European fashion was punished by a fine. And yet so well aware were they that this method was an improvement on their own that, when they could trust each other not to tell, they would surreptitiously use it."

If you went to an elder of the Dyak race and asked him why the newer method was forbidden, he would probably have told you that it was wrong. The answer would not have satisfied you, but the Dyak would have inquired no further. What was wrong was filled with impending calamity. Now, of course, there is no end of conservatism to-day which is just as instinctive, just as fearful of unimagined evil, and just as dumbly irrational as the Dyaks'. I have heard a middle-aged woman say "It isn't done" as if the voice of the universe spoke through her. But there is a rationalized conservatism. If you go to an elder of the Boston race and ask why new projects are so unexceptionally bad, he will tell you that without reverence for tradition life becomes unsettled, and a nation loses itself for lack of cohesion.

These essays are based upon that observation, but added to it is the observation, just as important, that tradition will not work in the complexity of modern life. For if you ask Americans to remain true to the traditions of all their Fathers, there would be a pretty confusion if they followed your advice. There is great confusion, as it is, due in large measure to the persistency which men follow tradition in a world unsuited to it. They modify a bit, however, they apply "the rule of reason" to their old loyalties, and so a little adjustment is possible. But there can be no real cohesion for America in following scrupulously the inherited ideals of our people. Between the Sons of the Revolution, the Ancient Order of Hibernians, the Orangemen, the plantation life of the South, the refugees from Russia, the Balkan Slavs, there is in their traditions a conflict of prejudice and custom that would make all America as clamorous as the Stock Exchange on a busy day. Nor is there going to be lasting inspiration for Bulgarian immigrants in the legend of the Mayflower.

The only possible cohesion now is a loyalty that looks forward. America is preëminently the country where there is practical substance in Nietzsche's advice that we should live not for our fatherland but for our children's land.

To do this men have to substitute purpose for tradition: and that is, I believe, the profoundest change that has ever taken place in human history. We can no longer treat life as something that has trickled down to us. We have to deal with it deliberately, devise its social organization, alter its tools, formulate its method, educate and control it. In endless ways we put intention where custom has reigned. We break up routines, make decisions, choose our ends, select means.

The massive part of man's life has always been, and still is, subconscious. The influence of his intelligence seems insignificant in comparison with attachments and desires, brute forces, and natural catastrophes. Our life is managed from behind the scenes: we are actors in dramas that we cannot interpret. Of almost no decisive event can we say: this was our own choosing. We happen upon careers, necessity pushing, blind inclination pulling. If we stop to think we are amazed that we should be what we are. And so we have come to call mysterious everything that counts, and the more mysterious the better some of us pretend to think it is. We drift into our work, we fall in love, and our lives seem like the intermittent flicker of an obstinate lamp. War panics, and financial panics, revivals, fads sweep us before them. Men go to war not knowing why, hurl themselves at cannon as if they were bags of flour, seek impossible goals, submit to senseless wrongs, for mankind lives to-day only in the intervals of a fitful sleep.

There is indeed a dreaming quality in life: moved as it is from within by unconscious desires and habits, and from without by the brute forces of climate and soil and wind and tide. There are stretches in every day when we have no sense of ourselves at all, and men often wake up with a start: "Have I lived as long as I'm supposed to have lived? . . . Here I am, this kind of person who has passed through these experiences—well, I didn't quite know it."

That, I think, is the beginning of what we call reflection: a desire to realize the drama in which we are acting, to be awake during our own lifetime. When we cultivate reflection by watching ourselves and the world outside, the thing we call science begins. We draw the hidden into the light of consciousness, record it, compare phases of it, note its history, experiment, reflect on error, and we find that our conscious life is no longer a trivial iridescence, but a progressively powerful way of domesticating the brute.

This is what mastery means: the substitution of conscious intention for unconscious striving. Civilization, it seems to me, is just this constant effort to introduce plan where there has been clash, and purpose into the jungles of disordered growth. But to shape the world nearer to the heart's desire requires a knowledge of the heart's desire and of the world. You cannot throw yourself blindly against unknown facts and trust to luck that the result will be satisfactory.

Yet from the way many business men, minor artists, and modern philosophers talk you would think that the best world can be created by the mere conflict of economic egotisms, the mere eruption of fantasy, and the mere surge of blind instinct. There is to-day a widespread attempt to show the futility of ideas. Now in so far as this movement represents a critical insight into the emotional basis of ideas, it is a fundamental contribution to human power. But when it seeks to fall back upon the unconscious, when the return to nature is the ideal of a deliberate vegetable, this movement is like the effort of the animal that tried to eat itself: the tail could be managed and the hind legs, but the head was an insurmountable difficulty. You can have misleading ideas, but you cannot escape ideas. To give up theory, to cease formulating your desire is not to reach back, as some people imagine, to profounder sources of inspiration. It is to put yourself at the mercy of stray ideas, of ancient impositions or trumped-up fads. Accident becomes the master, the accident largely of your own training, and you become the plaything of whatever happens to have accumulated at the bottom of your mind, or to find itself sanctified in the newspaper you read and the suburb that suited your income.

There have been fine things produced in the world without intention. Most of our happiness has come to us, I imagine, by the fortunate meeting of events. But happiness has always been a precarious incident, elusive and shifting in an unaccountable world. In love, especially, men rejoice and suffer through what are to them mysterious ways. Yet when it is suggested that the intelligence must invade our unconscious life, men shrink from it as from dangerous and clumsy meddling. It is dangerous and clumsy now, but it is the path we shall have to follow. We have to penetrate the dreaming brute in ourselves, and make him answerable to our waking life.

It is a long and difficult process, one for which we are just beginning to find a method. But there is no other way that offers any hope. To shove our impulses underground by the taboo is to force them to virulent and uncontrolled expression. To follow impulse wherever it leads means the satisfaction of one impulse at the expense of all the others. The glutton and the rake can satisfy only their gluttonous and rakist impulses, and that isn't enough for happiness. What civilized men aim at is neither whim nor taboo, but a frank recognition of desire, disciplined by a knowledge of what is possible, and ordered by the conscious purpose of their lives.

There is a story that experimental psychology grew from the discovery that two astronomers trying to time the movement of the same heavenly body reached different results. It became necessary then to time the astronomers themselves in order to discount the differences in the speed of their reactions. Now whether the story is literally true or not, it is very significant. For it symbolizes the essential quality of modern science —its growing self-consciousness. There have been scientific discoveries all through the ages. Heron of Alexandria invented a steam-turbine about 200 B.C. They had gunpowder in Ancient China. But these discoveries lay dormant, and they appear to us now as interesting accidents. What we have learned is to organize invention deliberately, to create a record for it and preserve its continuity, to subsidize it, and surround it with criticism. We have not only scientific work, but a philosophy of science, and that philosophy is the source of fruitful scientific work. We have become conscious about scientific method; we have set about studying the minds of scientists. This gives us an infinitely greater control of human invention, for we are learning to control the inventor. We were able already to discount some of the limitations of those engaged in research; we should not, for example, send a man who was color blind to report on the protective coloring of animals; we begin to see how much it matters in many investigations whether the student is an auditory or a visualizing type. Well, psychology opens up greater possibilities than this for the conscious control of scintific progress. It has begun to penetrate emotional prejudice, to show why some men are so deeply attached to authority, why philosophers have such unphilosophical likes and dislikes. We ask now of an economist, who his friends are, what his ambitions, his class bias. When one thinker exalts absolute freedom, another violent repression, we have ceased to take such ideas at their face value, and modern psychology, especially the school of Freud, has begun to work out a technique for cutting under the surface of our thoughts.

The power of criticizing the scientific mind is, I believe, our best guarantee for the progress of scientific discovery. This is the inner sanctuary of civilized power. For when science becomes its own critic it assures its own future. It is able, then, to attack the source of error itself; to forestall its own timidities, and control its own bias.

If the scientific temper were as much a part of us as the faltering ethics we now absorb in our childhood, then we might hope to face our problems with something like assurance. A mere emotion of futurity, that sense of "vital urge" which is so common to-day, will fritter itself away unless it comes under the scientific discipline, where men use language accurately, know fact from fancy, search out their own prejudice, are willing to learn from failures, and do not shrink from the long process of close observation. Then only shall we have a substitute for authority. Rightly understood science is the culture under which people can live forward in the midst of complexity, and treat life not as something given but as something to be shaped. Custom and authority will work in a simple and unchanging civilization, but in our world only those will conquer who can understand.

There is nothing accidental then in the fact that democracy in politics is the twin-brother of scientific thinking. They had to come together. As absolution falls, science arises. It *is* self-government. For when the impulse which overthrows kings and priests and unquestioned creeds becomes self-conscious we call it science.

Inventions and laboratories, Greek words, mathematical formulæ, fat books, are only the outward sign of an attitude toward life, an attitude which is self-governing, and most adequately named humanistic. Science is the irreconcilable foe of bogeys, and therefore, a method of laying the conflicts of the soul. It is the unfrightened, masterful and humble approach to reality—the needs of our natures and the possibilities of the world. The scientific spirit is the discipline of democracy, the escape from drift, the outlook of a free man. Its direction is to distinguish fact from fancy; its "enthusiasm is for the possible"; its promise is the shaping of fact to a chastened and honest dream.

MODERN COMMUNION

But, you will say, granted that the breakdown of authority in a complicated world has left men spiritually homeless, and made their souls uneasy; granted that it may be possible to exorcise many of the bogeys which haunt them, and to cultivate a natural worldliness in which economic and sexual terror will have been reduced; granted that women are tending to create a new environment for the child in which the property sense will not be stimulated morbidly, and where coöperation will become as obvious as obedience and isolation were in the past; suppose too, that an expanding civilization gives such varied resources that man will live more fully, and rely less on the compensations of thwarted desire; suppose that the spirit of science pervades his daily work, not as a mutilated specialty, but as a rich interest in the world with a vivid desire to shape it— suppose all that, would there not be lacking the one supreme virtue of the older creeds, their capacity for binding the world together?

There would be justice in such a criticism. There is a terrible loneliness that comes to men when they realize their feebleness before a brutally uninterested universe. In his own life-work, say as a teacher, a person may be making some one class-room more serviceable to a few children. But he will feel, as the more imaginative teachers do, that his work is like that of Sisyphus, he no sooner achieves a thing than it is undone. How can he educate a child for a few hours a day, when the home, the streets, the newspapers, the movies, the shop, are all busy miseducating? Wherever there is a constructive man at work you are likely to find this same complaint, that he is working alone. He may be heartwhole and eager, without bogeys or unnecessary fears. He may be free of the weaknesses that have reared so many faiths, and yet he seeks assurance in a communion with something outside himself, at the most perhaps, in a common purpose, at least, in a fellowship of effort.

Religions have placed human action in a large and friendly setting. They have enabled men to play their little rôle by making it essential to the drama of eternity. "God needs me, Christ died for me, after all I may be a poor creature, but I'm indispensable." And, as if by feeling themselves part of greatness, men have added to their stature. So even the meekest freshman in a grandstand is a more exalted person because his college team has captured the front page of the newspapers. He may be merely one in thousands who cheered for the eleven heroes, yet somehow he has partaken of their heroism. He is like the cockney who talks of "our Empire," like the Irish immigrants who tell how we licked the British at Yorktown, like the crank whose society of eight people is entitled "Association for Advancing the Human Race." It is well known that in a strike it matters enormously whether the men are fighting for a "fair day's wage" or for "the emancipation of labor."

The history of martyrs is the history of people who expanded to their faith. Indeed, men have shaken destiny because they felt they embodied it. Patriotism, the Cause, Humanity, Perfection, Righteousness, Liberty— all of them large and windy abstractions to outsiders, are more powerful than dynamite to those who feel them. "My country is the world," said Garrison, while Boston hated him. "I fight for women," says Mrs. Pankhurst. "I am a fate," said Nietzsche. "This is the true joy in life," says Bernard Shaw, "the being used for a purpose recognized by yourself as a mighty one."

It is no idle question then to ask what there is in the outlook of a modern man to bind his world together. Well, if he is looking for absolute assurance, an infallible refuge in weakness and terror, we have to answer that there is no such certainty. He may learn that while there is no promise of ultimate salvation, there is at least no fear of ultimate damnation; that in the modern world things are not so irremediable, and he may meet a large charity in its endless variety. He can find some understanding, an assurance perhaps of life's resiliency, he may come to know that nothing is so final as he thought it was, that the future is not staked on one enterprise, that life rises out of its own ashes, and renews its own opportunities. But if he demands personal guarantees, he may have to lie in order to get them.

Almost all men do require something to focus their interest in order to sustain it. A great idea like Socialism has done that for millions. But Socialism simply as a great passion can easily produce its superstitions and its barbarisms. What men need in their specialties in order to enable them to coöperate is not alone a binding passion, but a common discipline. Science, I believe, implies such a discipline. It is the fact that scientists approach the world with an understood method that enables them to give and take from each other whether they live in Calcutta or in San Francisco. The scientific world is the best example we have to-day of how specialists can coöperate. Of course there are profound disagreements, intrigues, racial and national prejudices, even among scientific men, for a common method will not wipe out the older cleavages, and it is not a perfectly cohesive force. But for the kind of civilization we are entering it is as yet the best we know.

There are undoubtedly beginnings of such a common method in public affairs. We read English books for help in dealing with American conditions. Social legislation is to-day a world-wide interest, so that reformers in Oregon may draw upon Australasian experiment. The labor movement has international organization with the result that its experience becomes available for use. There is no need to multiply examples. Instruments of a coöperative mind are being forged, be it the world-wide moving picture or some immense generalization of natural science.

This work has aroused in many men the old sense of cosmic wonder, and called forth devotion to impersonal ends. Nor can it be denied that in the study of institutions, in laboratories of research, there have appeared the same loyalty and courage to which the old religions could point as to their finest flower. Moreover, these devotions which science can show, come in the main redeemed from barbarism and pointed to civilized use. There is, to be sure, a certain raw novelty in modern forms of devotion, as there is in uninhabited houses, in new clothes and in new wine—they have hardly felt the mellowing of human contact, that saturation of brute things with the qualities of their users, which makes men love the old, the inadequate, the foolish, as against what is sane and clean, but unfamiliar. Science, too, is a concrete and essentially humble enterprise; spiritually sufficient it may be, to-day, only for the more robust. But the release from economic want, the emancipation from manufactured bogeys, the franker acceptance of normal desire, should tend to make men surer of themselves. And so most of them may not find it necessary to believe the impossible, but will reach their satisfaction in contemplating reality, in decorating it, shaping it, and conquering it.

They may find, as Santayana suggests, that "to see better what we now see, to see by anticipation what we should actually see under other conditions, is wonderfully to satisfy curiosity and to enlighten conduct. At the same time, scientific thinking involves no less inward excitement than dramatic fiction does. It summons before us an even larger number of objects in their fatal direction upon our interests. Were science adequate it would indeed absorb those passions which now, since they must be satisfied somehow, have to be satisfied by dramatic myths. . . . All pertinent dramatic emotion, joyous or tragic, would then inhere in practical knowledge. As it is, however, science abstracts from the more musical overtones of things in order to trace the gross and basal processes within them; so that the pursuit of science seems comparatively dry and laborious, except where at moments the vista opens through to the ultimate or leads back to the immediate. Then, perhaps, we recognize that in science we are surveying all it concerns us to know, and in so doing are becoming all that it profits us to be."

For the discipline of science is the only one which gives any assurance that from the same set of facts men will come approximately to the same conclusion. And as the modern world can be civilized only by the effort of innumerable people we have a right to call science the discipline of democracy. No omnipotent ruler can deal with our world, nor the scattered anarchy of individual temperaments. Mastery is inevitably a matter of coöperation, which means that a great variety of people working in different ways must find some order in their specialties. They will find it, I think, in a common discipline which distinguishes between fact and fancy, and works always with the implied resolution to make the best out of what is possible.

For behind this development of common method there are profound desires at work. As yet they are vaguely humanitarian. But they can be enriched by withdrawing them from vague fantasy in order to center them on a conception of what human life might be. This is what morality meant to the Greeks in their best period, an estimate of what was valuable, not a code of what should be forbidden. It is this task that morality must resume, for with the reappearance of a deliberate worldliness, it means again a searching for the sources of earthly happiness.

In some men this quest may lead to luminous passion. "The state-making dream," Wells calls it, and he speaks of those who "have imagined cities grow more powerful and peoples made rich and multitudinous by their efforts, they thought in terms of harbors and shining navies, great roads engineered marvellously, jungles cleared and deserts conquered, the ending of muddle and dirt and misery; the ending of confusions that waste human possibilities; they thought of these things with passion and desire as other men think of the soft lines and tender beauty of women. Thousands of men there are to-day almost mastered by this white passion of statecraft, and in nearly everyone who reads and thinks you could find, I suspect, some sort of answering response." And then with careful truth he adds, "But in every one it presents itself extraordinarily entangled and mixed up with other, more intimate things."

We begin to recognize a vague spirit which may suggest a common purpose. We live in a fellowship with scientists whose books we cannot read, with educators whose work we do not understand. Conservative critics laugh at what they call the futurist habit of mind. It is very easy to point out how blind and unintelligent is the enthusiasm of liberal people, how eager they are to accept Bergson, Montessori, Freud and the Cubists. But there is something fundamentally dull in these sneers. For granted the faddishness of modern people, there is yet more than faddishness in being friendly to novelty in a novel environment. It is the glimmer of intention, the absurd, human contradictory sign of faith. Men call it by different names—progress, the welfare of the race—it is perhaps not ready for precise formulation in a neat and inspiring slogan. But nevertheless, it is the business of critics to understand these beginnings, for they are already a great practical force. They enable men to share their hopes with strangers, to travel about and talk to people of widely different professions and origin, yet to find the assurance that they are part of a great undertaking.

### FACT AND FANCY

Most people still feel that there is something inhuman about the scientific attitude. They think at once of a world grown over-precise, of love regulated by galvanometers and sphygmographs, of table talk abolished because nutrition is confined to capsules prepared in a laboratory, of babies brought up in incubators. Instead of desire, statistical abstracts; a chilly, measured, weighed, and labelled existence. There is a famous cartoon of Max Beerbohm's in which H. G. Wells is depicted "conjuring up the darling future." A spectacled mother holds in her arm a spectacled infant, mostly head like a pollywog, while she dangles before it a pair of geometrical dividers. Mr. Chesterton's nightmare of a future in which jolly beer and jolly dirt and jolly superstition shall have disappeared is

merely a somewhat violently literary expression of what the average man
feels. Science as it comes through the newspapers announces that kissing
is unhygienic and that love is a form of lunacy. Science is the occupation
of absent-minded professors, of difficult and unsociable persons, wise
enough, no doubt, but not altogether in their right minds. And then, of
course, when wireless telegraphy is perfected, science becomes an omnipotent magic, wonderful or fearful, infinite in its power, but always something above and beyond the ordinary thoughts of men. So the suggestion
that Twentieth Century democracy is bound up with the progress of the
scientific spirit will make many people think of

> Organized charity, all cold and iced,
> In the name of a cautious, statistical Christ.

There is a basis for these fears. Scientists have often been very arrogant, unnecessarily sure of themselves, and only too glad to pooh-pooh
what they couldn't fit into some theory. This was especially true of those
who grew up in the controversies of the nineteenth century. There was a
kind of malicious fun in telling a devout man that thought depended on
phosphor and that his magnificent visions were merely an excitation of
the cortex. Of course, far-seeing men like Huxley protested that the sensation of red had not been destroyed because light-waves had been
measured.

Yet there were plenty of scientific bigots who would have liked to
annihilate what they could not weigh. Certainly it is true that the general
effect of science at first was to create impatience with the emotional life.
Many proud possessors of the Spencerian mind devoted their glowing
youth to a study of those bleak books which used to pass for scientific
manuals. They regarded religion with scorn and art with condescension,
and sometimes they nerved themselves up to admire beauty as one of
the necessary weaknesses of an otherwise reasonable man. Truth for them
was as neat as a checkerboard, and they made you feel like the man from
Corinth who asked a Spartan "whether the trees grew square in his
country."

It always surprises one of these hardheaded people to be told that he
lives in a world, which has a fantastic resemblance to a cubist painting.
For the rationalist's vision expresses his own love of form, while it dis-
torts the object. Now in a thinker who pretends to be dealing with actual
events this is a dangerous delusion. He will come to believe that square
things, sharply defined things, very tangible things, are somehow more
genuine than elusive and changing ones. It's a short step from this to
denying the existence of anything which is not easily defined. But note
what he has done: seduced by a method of thought, the rigorous, classify-
ing method where each color is all one tone, he has come to regard his

method as more important than the blendings and interweavings of reality. Like any dreamer he gives up the search for truth in order to coddle himself in his simple, private universe. The hardness of such a rationalist is on the surface only: at bottom there is a weakness which clings to stiff and solid frames of thought because the subtlety of life is distressing.

It is a great deal easier, for example, to talk of Labor and Capital than to keep in mind all the different kinds of workers or how they shade off into capitalists. It is immensely difficult to think about the actual complexity in the relations of men, and that is why eager and active people substitute for the facts those large abstractions with their rigid simplicity. But the workingman who is something of a capitalist himself, the employer who works as hard as anyone under him, can't see how the straight conflict between Exploited and Exploiter, Labor and Capital, applies in the particular situation.

What puzzles them is one of the oldest difficulties of thought: that any large classification fits each single fact very badly. They are like "the bewildered porter in Punch" quoted by Graham Wallas, "who had to arrange the subtleties of nature according to the unsubtle tariff-schedule of his company. 'Cats . . . is dogs, and guinea-pigs is dogs, but this 'ere tortoise is a hinsect.'"

Now we all have to do the same injustice to the tortoise, or in the language of philosophy, we have to use concepts. How much we shall use them depends upon what we are trying to do. For the purposes of the soap-box a few very rough distinctions are about all anyone can handle. In a group of friends, you can be a bit subtler. The moment you act in some real situation, say in some labor dispute, your large generalizations have to undergo enormous modification. For you will find yourself dealing there with a particular employer who is not exactly like any other employer and with workers for whom race and education, the fact that it's a cold winter, and a hundred other little complications turn the balance.

The only rule to follow, it seems to me, is that of James: "Use concepts when they help, and drop them when they hinder understanding." For "the world we practically live in is one in which it is impossible, except by theoretic retrospection, to disentangle the contributions of intellect from those of sense. They are wrapped and rolled together as a gunshot in the mountains is wrapt and rolled in fold on fold of echo and reverberative clamor. . . . The two mental functions thus play into each other's hands. Perception prompts our thought, and thought in turn enriches our perception. The more we see, the more we think; while the more we think, the more we see in our immediate experiences, and the greater grows the detail and the more significant the inarticulateness of our perception."

There is nothing in the scientific temper which need make it inevitably hostile to the variety of life. But many scientists have been hostile. And the reason for that is not so difficult to see. The first triumphs of the scientific mind were in mathematics, astronomy, and physics, out of which grows engineering. The habit of mind which produced such great results was naturally exalted, so that men began to feel that science which wasn't mechanical, wasn't science. They dreamt of a time when living bodies, consciousness and human relations, would be adjusted with the accuracy of a machine. But they were merely following an analogy, which a real scientist would abandon the moment it appeared that living organisms differ from the inert. I do not know whether any such distinction must be made, but there is nothing in the scientific temper which would preclude it.

In the long controversy with religious belief the true temper of the scientific mind was revealed. There have been hasty people who announced boldly that any interest in the immortality of the soul was "unscientific." William James, in fact, was accused of treason because he listened to mystics and indulged in psychical research. Wasn't he opening the gates to superstition and obscurantism? It was an ignorant attack. For the attitude of William James toward "ghosts" was the very opposite of blind belief. He listened to evidence. No apostle of authority can find the least comfort in that. For the moment you test belief by experience you have destroyed the whole structure of authority. It may well happen that the growth of knowledge will prove the wisdom in many a popular saying, or confirm the truth of a "superstition." It would be surprising if it didn't, for the long adjustments of the race must have accumulated much unconscious truth. But when these truths are held because there is evidence for them, their whole character is changed. They are no longer blind beliefs; they are subject to amendment when new evidence appears, and their danger is gone.

The last few years have produced a striking illustration of this within the Catholic Church. The Modernist movement is nothing but an outburst of the scientific spirit in the very citadel of authority. For the Modernists propose to accept Catholicism on the basis of experience. It is no wonder, then, that the Pope issued his Encyclical letter denouncing the Modernists root and branch, for once you substitute evidence for authoritative revelation the ruin of absolutism is prepared. There is no compromise possible between authority and the scientific spirit. They may happen to agree on some particular point to-day, but there is no guarantee that they will not disagree to-morrow. The Modernist may subscribe to the whole creed, but from the point of view of the absolutist his heresy is of the deepest and subtlest kind. All the fixity of eternal principles comes crashing about your head if you derive them simply from human experience. There is a sentence of Santayana's which destroys with a terrible brevity the ambitions of those who accept the scientific spirit and cling to traditional authority. "The gods are demonstrable only as hypotheses but as hypotheses they are not gods."

There is no question that science has won its way, in part, by insult and blindness, often by a harsh ignorance of the value of older creeds. It is associated with a certain hardness of mind and narrowness of feeling, as if it were a vandal in a sanctuary. But that also is not essential to the scientific mind; it is rather an accompaniment of the bitter controversy in which science grew up.

We can begin now to define the attitude of science toward the past. It may be summed up, I think, by saying that only when we have destroyed the authority of tradition can we appreciate its treasure. So long as tradition is a blind command it is for our world an evil and dangerous thing. But once you see the past merely as a theater of human effort, it overflows with suggestion.

Men can reverence the dead if they are buried. But they will no longer sit at table with corpses, ghosts, and skeletons. They can respect both life and death; they must resent a confusion of life and death. The conservative has made such a confusion, and out of it arises our contempt for the traditionalist mind. Scorn of the antiquarian has been transferred to antiquity. Modern men have said in a way that rather than deal with the past through a conservative, they would leave it to him as his exclusive domain.

There is hardly need to rehearse the grounds of this contempt. Whenever evil is defended or tyranny devised, it is done in the name of tradition. So the loss of a sense of the past has come to mean a definite emancipation. Then, too, it looks at times as if men felt they could not move forward if they stared backward—that Greece and Rome are a fatal lure which enervate and render dry-as-dust. They think of pedants in closed university ground, walled in from all enthusiasm, tangled in the creepers that shackle with their beauty.

Modern men are afraid of the past. It is a record of human achievement, but its other face is human defeat. Too often it speaks through the words of Koheleth the Preacher—that which is crooked cannot be made straight. History is full of unbearable analogies which make enthusiasm cold and stale. It tells of the complications that are not foreseen, of the successes that caricature the vision. Conservatives may dwell upon the perspective which history gives. It is just this perspective which men fear, the looking at life through the wrong end of the opera glass. It is a good instinct which refuses to see the present as a bubble on the stream of time. For the bubble in which we live is more of our concern than all the rivers which have flowed into the sea.

And yet, the past can be a way to freedom. The present order is held very lightly and without undue reverence in a mind which knows how varied is human experience. An imagination fed on the past will come to see the present as a very temporary thing. Wherever routine and convention become unbearable weights, the abundance of the past is a source of liberty. Merely to realize that your way of living is not the only way, is to free yourself from its authority. It brings a kind of lucidity in which society is rocked by a devastating Why? Why should men who have one life to live submit to the drudgeries and vexations that we call civilization? The whole shell is strained by a wild rationality.

The past has been used to throttle the present. Why should we not turn around and use it for a different purpose? We have sunk under the weight of its gloomy sanctity. Can we not free ourselves in the light of its great variety?

That is just what the best scholarship of our time has tried to do. The Nineteenth Century undoubtedly meant a shattering of the traditional faiths. And yet no century has ever been so eager to understand the very idols it was breaking. The same period in which the secular spirit won its greatest triumphs saw the first real effort at an understanding of superstition and magic, ritual and taboo, religious need and doctrinal sources. Indeed, the interest of the scientific spirit in the past has been so masterful that all previous history looks like village gossip. It is utterly untrue, therefore, to say that the modern outlook means an abrupt break with the accumulated wisdom of the past. It has meant a break with blind obedience to an ignorant fabrication about the past. But that break is what has opened to us the lessons of history as they have never been opened to any other people. It has been said that we know more about Homer than Plato did; no one would dream of comparing the modern knowledge of classical antiquity with Dante's or with Shakespeare's. The Biblical scholars of the last hundred years, in spite of all their so-called atheism, have, I believe, seen deeper into the basis of Christianity than the Church which has represented it. And while they have undoubtedly shaken authority, they have built up a sympathetic understanding of the human values it contained. All this is the sheerest commonplace, yet conservatives continue to accuse the scientific spirit of blindness to the great past. They deceive themselves in their outcry. They don't really fear a neglect of the past. They don't really mean that modern men ignore it. What they miss in modern science is submission. They feel vaguely that scientific interest in the past makes of history a double-edged weapon. The absolutist has suddenly discovered that a study of the very thing he adores destroys obedience to it. The men who talk most about reverence for the American Constitution are the last people in the world to welcome a study of its origin. For the conservative is not devoted to a real past. He is devoted to his own comfortable image of it.

We have come to look at history with ease and without too much reverence. To be sure that puts a bridle on a great deal of haphazard optimism. There is a strain of doubt in the speculations of an historian. But there is a full compensation for the loss of barren hopes in the bodily warmth that comes from knowing how millions of men have acted, have hoped, have built better than they knew, or failed. If the dream of perfection and endless progress fades, is that necessarily so great a loss? It does not seem possible that life will lose its flavor because we have robbed it of a few abstract and careless dreams. For the modern sense of what the past contains can give a new realization of the fertility in existence. That is a rock upon which to build. Instead of a "featureless future," instead of an aspiring vacuum, which ends in disappointment, we may see a more modest future, but one inhabited by living people. This is the great boon of the past, that it saturates thought with concrete images. And it leaves scope for invention, for the control of nature and buoyant living. For by taking with a certain levity our schemes for improvement we shatter the sects and liberate thought.

There is, however, a persistent feeling that science means the abandonment of the imagination for a grubby absorption in facts. It is far truer to say that with the scientific spirit the imagination comes into its own. Fantasy has been a solace in defeat, a refuge from reality, a compensation to the thwarted, a dreaming desire for better things. But under the discipline of science, desire becomes concrete: it not only imagines, but it creates as well. So we can say with real justice that vision is for the first time able to direct the shaping of a world.

One of the myths that modern critics are overthrowing is the notion that science is a passionless pursuit of dead facts. For even in the most "disinterested" inquiry, there is, as Bertrand Russell says, some interest that determines the direction of our curiosity. Men will endow medical schools and institutes of technology, but only very idle and superfluously rich persons would think of devoting much time to the use of adverbs in the Bible or to the comparative history of Icelandic particles. Science is a very human thing. It springs from a need, is directed by curiosity to choose an interesting field of study, and in that field seeks results that concern men. The ideal of science, it seems to me, is to seek interesting truth critical of one's interest. If the student is merely disinterested, he is a pedant; if he seeks only what catches his passing fancy, he is romantic. The true scientist is inspired by a vision without being the victim of it.

Before the scientific spirit can reach its full bloom, it will have to acquire an honest sense of the rôle that fantasy plays in all its work. This is true especially of the social sciences. We are just beginning to realize the importance in economics of the economist's utopia. We are learning the determining influence of a thinker's dream. Thus Adam Smith's utopia was a place where enterprise was unshackled: he longed for a freedom which the corporate guilds and feudal restrictions of his time denied. He had seen Watts persecuted for his steam engine; had seen him take refuge in the university grounds at Glasgow from a crusted society that had no use for disturbing inventions. So Adam Smith endowed nature and men with the virtues that Eighteenth Century England lacked—he dreamed his utopia of laissez-faire. Guided by that utopia, he sought facts and built arguments into a science of economics. He justified his dream. It was timely, for it uttered the hopes of England. His facts were plausible almost immediately, his arguments swam with the flood-tide of opinion. The "Wealth of Nations" became the Bible of English trade—like all Bibles it was true to hope and practical for those who used it.

One man, at least, in the Nineteenth Century, achieved a result similar to Adam Smith's. Ricardo didn't. As Prof. Marshall points out, Ricardo, who was a stockbroker, erected the "pure science" of economics on the very limited motives he knew. Even a fine spirit like John Stuart Mill was doomed to a large measure of sterility because he did not grasp the revolutionary dream that was rising in his time. What Ricardo had no idea of doing, what Mill failed to do, Karl Marx did. In his own time, the '50's and '60's, Marx saw through a bewildering maze of facts and put his hand upon the revolutionary trend. And so he stood in as commanding a position to the middle age of capitalism as Adam Smith did to its infancy. Marx won out, not because his books are easy reading: they are not, except for occasional bursts of irony and wrath. He did not win out because the respectable of the world founded universities in his honor; they didn't. He won out because his vision was a rising one in the facts of his time.

The facts have changed in sixty years, and with them our vision: Marx was not omniscient, and the revolutionary movement is no longer adequately expressed by him. You do not have to go to the hostile critics of Marx. The inadequacy of Marx for the present age is freely admitted by a rising group within the socialist movement. In many essential ways, events have not justified his prophecies. The middle class has not disappeared: in this country it is the dominant power expressing itself through the Progressives, and through the Wilson Administration. The middle class has put the "Money Power" on the defensive. Big business is losing its control of the government. The farmers are a class with enormous power, misunderstood and neglected by the city-bred theories of socialism. The great line-up of two hostile classes hasn't happened. There have been fierce conflicts between employers and employees, but a united working class facing united capitalists is an unreal picture of American conditions. Labor has within itself innumerable deep conflicts of interest. Business men are divided by trades and by sections. And there is an unexpected burst of sheerly democratic impulse which blurs class lines. Internationalism is still a very distant dream, and while men are less provincial, it is doubtful whether the national idea is any weaker. Patriotism itself has gained a new dignity by its increasing alliance with democratic reform, and there is actually ground for supposing that love of country is coming to mean love of country and not hatred of other countries. There is a growth of that abused thing, public spirit, and the growth is so powerful that it may be able to ride the mere clashing of self-interest.

I repeat these commonplaces with no intention of casting any doubts upon the historic service of Karl Marx. If they go to show anything it is this: that the probabilities have changed, and that only by expressing that fact can *our* social science be built up. Adam Smith and Karl Marx, each in his own way, took a revolutionary purpose and expressed it. One can say without fear of contradiction that they are the two most fertile minds that have dealt with the modern problem. But the orthodox economists and the orthodox Marxians are out of touch with the latent forces of this age: both have proved themselves largely sterile. They have built a dialectic, one might almost say, a dialect, upon the texts of their masters; they have lost their command over change, and so they have become apologetic, and eager to save their faces in the wreck of their creed. The effect on socialism has been very disastrous. In America, to borrow no unnecessary trouble, socialist thinking has almost come to a standstill. The leaders of the movement write one weary book after another in which the old formulæ are restated. But not a single study of any depth has been made by an American Marxian of the American trust, trade union, political system or foreign policy. And as for the underlying spiritual habits of the American people, there is hardly any recognition that such habits exist. There has been on the other hand a very noticeable hostility to original effort. Yet even if Karl Marx captured the secret of social evolution (which is doubtful), and even if Karl Kautsky is his vicar, the necessity still remains of showing concretely how that key unlocks the American difficulty. A principle is at best a guide: it is certainly not an open sesame to the future to be applied without hesitation by any pamphleteer. It is no longer very illuminating to meet the American problem with the stale vision of continental Europe in 1850.

The first way to estimate a social philosophy is to test the vision which it embodies. For this is what determines the direction of the thinker's interest, and from it his arguments take their lead. But you cannot always trust his own statement as to his purpose. Every thinker is abstractedly devoted to truth, and almost everybody presents himself as a lover of justice and righteousness. But he may see justice in almost anything—in the unfettered action of business men, or the "dictatorship of the proletariat." Real criticism would find out what he sees and admires instinctively—what are, in short, the governing assumptions of his thought. Thus Woodrow Wilson's "New Freedom" is laid in the main upon sympathy with "those on the make," with the man looking for a career; upon horror at the crimes of monopoly, and little recognition of the crimes of competition. It is, I believe, a vigorous restatement of the traditional American utopia in which justice is to be attained by the balance of self-interest. There is a kind of hope that an equality in push will neutralize all dangers, and produce an automatic coöperation. So Wilson seems to see the working man merely as a possible shop-keeper. The assumptions are those of a generous commercialism. It is a vision of chivalrous enterprise. Or take the message of Haywood: he sees the unskilled laborer, the genuine proletarian without property in things or in craft; he sees the outcast, the convict, the casual, the bum, the peon, with such wonderful warmth and great understanding that they have come to embody for him the whole social problem. What are the troubles of a business man harassed by a bad credit system to these ultimate miseries in which are concentrated the failures of our civilization? Do you think there will be any "reason" for Haywood in a social philosophy which seems to forget the very things which fill his sky? He has only to take a walk through Union Square to feel what fools his critics are.

It may seem curious to approach a pretentiously scientific volume with the question: What is this man's dearest wish? The usual method is to regard that as of no importance, and to turn immediately to testing of logic or criticism of fact. It is no wonder that writers are not convinced by hostile reviews, or that editorials make so little impression on propagandists. Unless you go to the passionate source of ideas, you are a cat looking at a king. What does it matter to the suffragettes that they are called hysterical and lectured about their mistaken tactics? That is so much scrubby, withered stupidity fit only to set off vividly the grandeur of ideas it attacks. Or does anyone suppose that feminism is dependent on the logic of its supporters or opponents? Certainly not. Until you begin to see in feminism the opposition of attitudes toward life, drawn by hope and pushed by events, you are still the six-weeks convert who can rattle off her argument and repartee in a fusilade across the dinner-table.

Criticism will have to slough off the prejudices of the older rationalism if it is to have any radical influence on ideas. It is sophomoric to suppose that the emotional life can be treated as a decadent survival. Men's desires are not something barbaric which the intellect must shun. Their desires are what make their lives, they are what move and govern. You are not talking of human beings when you talk of "pure reason." And, therefore, anyone who deepens the conflict between thought and feeling is merely adding confusion to difficulty. The practical line of construction is to saturate feeling with ideas. That is the only way in which men can tap their own power—by passionate ideas. There is, of course, no greater difficulty in thought than to attain a delicate adjustment of our own desires to what is possible. All important thinking achieves such an adjustment, and we recognize its success by the fact that it gives us control over brute things. That sense of control is the yielding of fact to intelligent desire. But if we try to ignore the desire that moves our thought, if we try in short to be "absolutely objective," we succeed only in accumulating useless facts, or we become the unconscious victims of our wishes. If thinking didn't serve desire, it would be the most useless occupation in the world.

The only reason, of course, for casting suspicion upon the emotional life is that it does so often falsify the world and build a fool's paradise in a human hell. But when you have faced this fully, there is still no reason for attempting the vain effort of jumping out of our human skins. The danger means simply that desire has to be subjected to criticism. It is a difficult task. But it is one that we are capable of beginning, for the great triumph of modern psychology is its growing capacity for penetrating to the desires that govern our thought.

There have been a large number of very frank attempts to express the vision of an ideal commonwealth. Plato, More, Bacon, Campanella, Fourier, William Morris, Bellamy, H. G. Wells, are only a few among many. From them come the obvious utopias, pictures of a better world by gifted and dissatisfied men. They are strangely alike. Generally the utopia is located in Peru, or a mythical island, or in the year two thousand, or centuries back, or Nowhere. Life is fixed: the notion of change is rare, for men do not easily associate perfection with movement. Moreover, the citizens of these utopias are the disciplined servants of the community. They are rigorously planned types with sharply defined careers laid out for them from birth to death. A real man would regard this ideal life as an unmitigated tyranny. But why are the utopias tyrannical? I imagine it is because the dreamer's notion of perfection is a place where everything and everybody is the puppet of his will. In a happy dream the dreamer is omnipotent: that is why it is a happy dream. So utopias tend toward a scrupulous order, eating in common mess halls, mating by order of the state, working as the servant of the community. There is no democracy in a utopia—no willingness to allow intractable human beings the pleasure of going to the devil in their own way. Even in the utopias which pretend to be democratic, that is, where the citizens vote, the assumption always exists that the citizens vote as the dreamer would have them vote. He simply calls his will the will of the people.

Now these qualities, so obvious in the utopias, can be detected in all sorts of thinking which would be horrified at the word utopian. Most economics is about life either on Robinson Crusoe's island, or at least in some imaginary and ideally simplified nation. Few economists can remember that their reasoning is built upon on unreal picture of man and industry. By the time the details are worked out, economists have the greatest difficulty in recalling the fact that they have been talking about an imaginary world, a world which pleases their fancy because it yields to their logic.

Classical economics is related to the utopias in that it deals with some place, not England and not the United States, where motives are utterly simple, and rigorously automatic. The imaginary world of the economist is not, however, a generous fantasy of a fine life. It is a crass abstraction, industrialism idealized until it is no longer industrialism.

The bureaucratic dreams of reformers often bear a striking resemblance to the honest fantasies of the utopians. What we are coming to call "State Socialism" is in fact an attempt to impose a benevolent governing class on humanity. Oh, for wise and powerful officials to bring order out of chaos, end the "muddle," and make men clean, sober and civic-minded. There is no real understanding of democracy in the State Socialist, for he doesn't attempt to build with the assent and voluntary coöperation of men and women. But he avoids the laborious and disheartening method of popular education, and takes satisfaction in devising a ruling class, inspired by him, as a short-cut to perfection.

But let no one suppose that the "revolutionist" who denounces State Socialism is thereby free from the utopian habit of mind. He may scorn the brutal fictions of the economist or the depressing benevolence of the bureaucrat, only to imagine a world more unreal than either. I have before me a syndicalist utopia written by two of the most prominent leaders in France. It is a picture of the Revolution which is going to happen. The working men of France do just what the syndicalist dream says they should do. Suddenly, when the crash comes, there is an exhibition of skill in organizing; there rises to the surface a coöperative power epoch-making in the history of the race. Millions of men who fight and curse each other every day, their interests divided by trade and locality, suddenly become unanimous and efficient. Why? Because the authors of the book would like it so, because they have imagined that their will had become the will of the people. They have treated French working men as the puppets of their fancy.

And yet, as Oscar Wilde said, no map of the world is worth a glance that hasn't Utopia on it. Our business is not to lay aside the dream, but to make it plausible. We have to aim at visions of the possible by subjecting fancy to criticism. The usual thing to do is to follow fiction unreservedly: that produces the castle in Spain and news from nowhere. Or to deny fancy, and suppress it: that means that the thinker becomes the victim of his prejudice, the unconscious slave of his desires. The third course is to drag dreams out into the light of day, show their sources, compare them with fact, transform them to possibilities. They should not run wild. They cannot be discarded. So they must be disciplined. For modern civilization demands something greater than the fantasies of a child or the close observation of patient investigators, something greater than is born of their union: it calls for a dream that suffuses the actual with a sense of the possible.

This is the creative imagination, and to it we owe all attempts to bridge the gap between what we wish and what we have. Romanticism can falter: "it would be lovely, if——"; Philistia can answer: "what is, is"; but the disciplined imagination alone can say, "I will." Mere fantasy gives up the struggle with actual affairs in order to find a temporary home in the warmth of memory and the fervor of impossible hopes. So in the intimacies of his own life each man confesses by his dreams that he and his world are at odds: that his desires overflow experience and ask for more than they can ever have. If he remains there, he may build splendid utopias, and shirk the effort to realize them; he is the eternal Peer Gynt, hero of his own epic, dawdler and coward in the world. He is uncompromising in his dreams, and acquiescent in his deeds. At the other pole is the philistine with his smug sense of the comfort of life, pledged to his routine, convinced that change is over, satisfied that he and his are the pinnacles of creation. Nothing is possible for him, because nothing more is desirable: the long travail of creation is done, and there he is. To all wild dreams he presents a shrewd and well-seasoned knowledge of genuine affairs. Vision beats in vain against his solid world.

In the creative imagination no relevant fact is shirked; yet over all the things that are there hovers a feeling for what they might be. A sharp and clear sense of existence is shot through with the light of its possibilities. Each fact is a place where the roads fork. Each event is a vista. Each moment is a choice. To the man who lives without question from day to day, life is just one thing after another; to the mere dreamer it is harsh and unyielding. But to the creative imagination fact is plastic, and ready to be moulded by him who understands it.

That, I believe, is the spirit of invention: around each observation there gathers an aura of conjectures. The scientific discoverer can penetrate the crevices of fact with moving guesses; each experiment is suspended in pregnant hypotheses. It is the spirit of the working artist, embodied in the fine myth that the block of marble imprisoned a statue which the sculptor released. To the artist his material is not dead clay or a silent palette, but a living substance clamoring for its form. It is the dilettante who could do a fine work if it weren't for the hardness of the stone. It is the esthete who can do everything but write his poems. It is the amateur who complains about the conflict between matter and spirit. Not the producing artist: his medium is a friendly thing, the very substance of his dream. It is the spirit of education: not to produce a row of respectable automata, but to draw out of each child the promise that is in it.

It is the spirit of valuable statecraft: the genius among politicians is he who can deal in his own time with the social forces that lead to a better one. He does not ask for a world of angels before he can begin. He does not think his duty in life is merely to keep old institutions in good repair. He grasps the facts of his age, sees in the confusion of events currents like the union, the trust, the coöperative—suffuses them with their promise, and directs them into the structure of the future.

It is the spirit of all fine living: to live ready, to lighten experience by a knowledge of its alternatives, to let no fact be opaque, but to make what happens transparent with the choices it offers.

To escape from barren routine and vain fantasy in order to leaven reality with its possibilities: this must be the endless effort of a democratic people. To stand-pat on whatever happens to exist is to put yourself at the mercy of all the blind mutterings and brute forces that move beneath the surface of events. The labor movement, the women's awakening, industry on a national scale, will work themselves out to distorted and wasted ends, if they come merely as blind pushes against invincible ignorance. But if they are left to themselves, if the labor movement becomes the plaything of its own visions, if it is not welded and disciplined to the other interests of civilization, then its wonderful possibilities will be frittered away. And likewise, so long as the large organization of business is in the hands of economic adventurers or attacked by its defeated competitors, there is no chance to make of it what it could be.

The method of a self-governing people is to meet every issue with an affirmative proposal which draws its strength from some latent promise. Thus the real remedy for violence in industrial disputes is to give labor power that brings responsibility. The remedy for commercialism is collective organization in which the profiteer has given way to the industrial statesman. The incentive to efficiency is not alone love of competent work but a desire to get greater social values out of human life. The way out of corrupt and inept politics is to use the political state for interesting and important purposes. The unrest of women cannot be met by a few negative freedoms: only the finding of careers and the creation of positive functions can make liberty valuable. In the drift of our emotional life, the genuine hope is to substitute for terror and weakness, a frank and open worldliness, a love of mortal things in the discipline of science.

These are not idle dreams: they are, it seems to me, concrete possibilities of the actual world in which we live. I have tried in this book to suggest a few of them, to make clearer to myself by illustrations, the attitude of mind with which we can begin to approach our strangely complex world. It lacks precision, it lacks the definiteness of a panacea, and all of us rebel against that. But mastery in our world cannot mean any single, neat, and absolute line of procedure. There is something multitudinous about the very notion of democracy, something that offends our inherited intellectual prejudices. This book would have a more dramatic climax if I could say that mastery consisted in some one thing: say in a big union of the working class, or the nationalization of all business. But it isn't possible to say that because there are too many factors which compete for a place, too many forces that disturb a simple formula. Mastery, whether we like it or not, is an immense collaboration, in which all the promises of to-day will have their vote.

Our business as critics is to make those promises evident, to give to the men who embody them a consciousness of them, to show how they clash with facts, to bathe them in suggestion. In that atmosphere we can go about organizing the new structure of society, building up producers' and consumers' controls, laying down plans for wise uses of our natural resources, working wherever we happen to be, or wherever our abilities call us, on the substitution of design for accident, human purposes for brute destiny. It is not easy, nor as yet a normal attitude toward life. The sustained effort it requires is so great that few can maintain it for any length of time. Anyone who has tried will report that no intellectual discipline is comparable in the severity of its demands: from the weariness it engenders men fall either into sheer speculation or mechanical repetition. How often does a book begin truly, and turn off exhausted into a conventional ending. You can almost see the point where the author gave up his struggle, and called in the claptrap of a happy accident. How often does a reformer begin with penetration, entangle himself in officialdom, and end in excuses for uninspired deeds. Who has not wept over the critical paper which started off so bravely, handling each event with freshness and skill, only to become cluttered in its own successes and redundant with stale virtues. Everyone has met the man who approached life eagerly and tapered off to a middle age where the effort is over, his opinions formed, his habits immutable, with nothing to do but live in the house he has built, and sip what he has brewed.

Effort wells up, beats bravely against reality, and in weariness simmers down into routine or fantasy. No doubt much of this is due to physiological causes, some of which lie beyond our present control. And yet in large measure the explanation lies elsewhere. There are fine maturities to give our pessimism the lie. This abandonment of effort is due, I imagine, to the fact that the conscious mastery of experience is, comparatively speaking, a new turn in human culture. The old absolutisms of caste and church and state made more modest demands than democracy does: life was settled and fantasy was organized into ritual and riveted by authority. But the modern world swings wide and loose, it has thrown men upon their own responsibility. And for that gigantic task they lack experience, they are fettered and bound and finally broken by ancient terrors that huddle about them. Think of the enormous effort that goes into mere rebellion, think of the struggle that young men and women go through in what they call a fight for independence, independence which is nothing but an opportunity to begin. They have to break with habits rooted in the animal loyalties of their childhood, and the rupture has consequences greater than most people realize. The scars are very deep, even the most successful rebel is somewhat crippled. No wonder then that those who win freedom are often unable to use it; no wonder that liberty brings its despair.

There are people who think that rebellion is an inevitable accompaniment of progress. I don't see why it should be. If it is possible to destroy, as I think we are doing, the very basis of authority, then change becomes a matter of invention and deliberate experiment. No doubt there is a long road to travel before we attain such a civilization. But it seems to me that we have every right to look forward to it—to a time when childhood will cease to be assaulted by bogeys, when eagerness for life will cease to be a sin. There is no more reason why everyone should go through the rebellions of our time than that everyone should have to start a suffrage movement to secure his vote.

To idealize rebellion is simply to make a virtue out of necessity. It shows more clearly than anything else that the sheer struggle for freedom is an exhausting thing, so exhausting that the people who lead it are often unable to appreciate its uses. But just as the men who founded democracy were more concerned with the evils of the kingly system than they were with the possibilities of self-government, so it is with working men and women, and with all those who are in revolt against the subtle tyrannies of the school and the home and the creed. Only with difficulty does the affirmative vision emerge.

Each of us contributes to it what he can in the intervals of his battle with surviving absolutisms. The vision is clearer to-day than it was to the rebels of the nineteenth century. We are more used to freedom than they were. But in comparison with what we need our vision is murky, fragmentary, and distorted. We have dared to look upon life naturally, we have exorcised many bogeys and laid many superstitions, we have felt reality bend to our purposes. We gather assurance from these hints.

# The Moral Equivalent of War

## *William James*

*The central question of our time has proven not to be the collective capacity of men to extract and distribute nature's abundance or even to manage their own societies. The central question is whether men can understand their own nature well enough to learn how to live in peace with each other. Nineteenth-century America had won world acclaim for the surpassing excellence of at least two products: its small firearms and its small organizations to achieve universal peace. Americans in the progressive era were not so naive about the nature of men as to overlook the irony of this dualism or to believe that economic and political engineering would alone assure peace. They were chiefly absorbed in finding solutions to other questions which pressed more insistently on their daily lives: for half a century until 1916 they simply had not needed to think hard and soberly about peace and war. By 1914 many of the notions of the earlier pacifists seemed shallow and tired, but it is a striking comment on the intellectual vigor of the progressive generation that even before the war burst on their world a few perceptive thinkers like Jane Addams and William James managed to infuse a shopworn debate with fresh insights derived from new advances in the scientific study of man's behavior. With the appearance in 1910 of James's immensely popular essay on "The Moral Equivalent of War" it could be said that the central issue was at last posed in terms which a subsequent generation would find compelling and significant.*

*William James, lifelong psychologist and expounder of an open-ended pragmatism in the search for the good society, acknowledged to being a pacifist of sorts but questioned the popular notion that a Christian commitment to a love of one's fellow man, however desirable, was sufficient to solve any of the disturbing riddles of war. Nor would a state of peace furnish a satisfactory substitute for some of war's attractions. Peace in fact did not always reveal man at his best. What is required, said James, is to reproduce the constructive passions of war in time of peace. The essay which set forth this view sold 30,000 copies and was twice reprinted in contemporary magazines. It furnished an intellectual and emotional bridge from the outlook and assumptions of the followers of Theodore Roosevelt to the assumptions of a later generation who would find in a Peace Corps and in scores of similar enterprises over the world a crucial and valid fulfillment of the progressive dream.*

The war against war is going to be no holiday excursion or camping party. The military feelings are too deeply grounded to abdicate their place among our ideals until better substitutes are offered than the glory and shame that come to nations as well as to individuals from the ups and downs of politics and the vicissitudes of trade. There is something highly paradoxical in the modern man's relation to war. Ask all our millions, north and south, whether they would vote now (were such a thing possible) to have our war for the Union expunged from history, and the record of a peaceful transition to the present time substituted for that of its marches and battles, and probably hardly a handful of eccentrics would say yes. Those ancestors, those efforts, those memories and legends, are the most ideal part of what we now own together, a sacred spiritual possession worth more than all the blood poured out. Yet ask those same people whether they would be willing in cold blood to start another civil war now to gain another similar possession, and not one man or woman would vote for the proposition. In modern eyes, precious though wars may be, they must not be waged solely for the sake of the ideal harvest. Only when forced upon one, only when an enemy's injustice leaves us no alternative, is a war now thought permissible.

It was not thus in ancient times. The earlier men were hunting men, and to hunt a neighboring tribe, kill the males, loot the village and possess the females, was the most profitable, as well as the most exciting, way of living. Thus were the more martial tribes selected, and in chiefs and peoples a pure pugnacity and love of glory came to mingle with the more fundamental appetite for plunder.

Modern war is so expensive that we feel trade to be a better avenue to plunder; but modern man inherits all the innate pugnacity and all the love of glory of his ancestors. Showing war's irrationality and horror is of no effect upon him. The horrors make the fascination. War is the *strong* life; it is life *in extremis*; war-taxes are the only ones men never hesitate to pay, as the budgets of all nations show us.

History is a bath of blood. The Iliad is one long recital of how Diomedes

William James, "The Moral Equivalent of War," *International Conciliation*, No. 27 (February, 1910).

and Ajax, Sarpedon and Hector *killed*. No detail of the wounds they made is spared us, and the Greek mind fed upon the story. Greek history is a panorama of jingoism and imperialism—war for war's sake, all the citizens being warriors. It is horrible reading, because of the irrationality of it all —save for the purpose of making "history"—and the history is that of the utter ruin of a civilization in intellectual respects perhaps the highest the earth has ever seen.

Those wars were purely piratical. Pride, gold, women, slaves, excitement, were their only motives. In the Peloponnesian war, for example, the Athenians ask the inhabitants of Melos (the island where the "Venus of Milo" was found), hitherto neutral, to own their lordship. The envoys meet, and hold a debate which Thucydides gives in full, and which, for sweet reasonableness of form, would have satisfied Matthew Arnold. "The powerful exact what they can," said the Athenians, "and the weak grant what they must." When the Meleans say that sooner than be slaves they will appeal to the gods, the Athenians reply: "Of the gods we believe and of men we know that, by a law of their nature, wherever they can rule they will. This law was not made by us, and we are not the first to have acted upon it; we did but inherit it and we know that you and all mankind, if you were as strong as we are, would do as we do. So much for the gods; we have told you why we expect to stand as high in their good opinion as you." Well, the Meleans still refused, and their town was taken. "The Athenians," Thucydides quietly says, "thereupon put to death all who were of military age and made slaves of the women and children. They then colonized the island, sending thither five hundred settlers of their own."

Alexander's career was piracy pure and simple, nothing but an orgy of power and plunder, made romantic by the character of the hero. There was no rational principle in it, and the moment he died his generals and governors attacked one another. The cruelty of those times is incredible. When Rome finally conquered Greece, Paulus Aemilius, was told by the Roman Senate to reward his soldiers for their toil by "giving" them the old kingdom of Epirus. They sacked seventy cities and carried off a hundred and fifty thousand inhabitants as slaves. How many they killed I know not; but in Etolia they killed all the senators, five hundred and fifty in number. Brutus was "the noblest Roman of them all," but to reanimate his soldiers on the eve of Philippi he similarly promises to give them the cities of Sparta and Thessalonica to ravage, if they win the fight.

Such was the glory nurse that trained societies to cohesiveness. We inherit the warlike type; and for most of the capacities of heroism that the human race is full of we have to thank this cruel history. Dead men tell no tales, and if there were any tribes of other type than this they have left no survivors. Our ancestors have bred pugnacity into our bone and marrow, and thousands of years of peace won't breed it out of us. The popular imagination fairly fattens on the thought of wars. Let public opinion once reach a certain fighting pitch, and no ruler can withstand it. In the Boer war both governments began with bluff, but couldn't stay there, the military tension was too much for them. In 1898 our people had read the word WAR in letters three inches high for three months in every newspaper. The pliant politician McKinley was swept away by their eagerness, and our squalid war with Spain became a necessity.

At the present day, civilized opinion is a curious mental mixture. The military instincts and ideals are as strong as ever, but are confronted by reflective criticisms which sorely curb their ancient freedom. Innumerable writers are showing up the bestial side of military service. Pure loot and mastery seem no longer morally avowable motives, and pretexts must be found for attributing them solely to the enemy. England and we, our army and navy authorities repeat without ceasing, arm solely for "peace," Germany and Japan it is who are bent on loot and glory. "Peace" in military mouths to-day is a synonym for "war expected." The word has become a pure provocative, and no government wishing peace sincerely should allow it ever to be printed in a newspaper. Every up-to-date Dictionary should say that "peace" and "war" mean the same thing, now *in posse,* now *in actu.* It may even reasonably be said that the intensely sharp competitive *preparation* for war by the nations *is the real war,* permanent, unceasing; and that the battles are only a sort of public verification of the mastery gained during the "peace"-interval.

It is plain that on this subject civilized man has developed a sort of double personality. If we take European nations, no legitimate interest of any one of them would seem to justify the tremendous destructions which a war to compass it would necessarily entail. It would seem as though common sense and reason ought to find a way to reach agreement in every conflict of honest interests. I myself think it our bounden duty to believe in such international rationality as possible. But, as things stand, I see how desperately hard it is to bring the peace-party and the war-party together, and I believe that the difficulty is due to certain deficiencies in the program of pacificism which set the militarist imagination strongly, and to a certain extent justifiably, against it. In the whole discussion both sides are on imaginative and sentimental ground. It is but one utopia against another, and everything one says must be abstract and hypothetical. Subject to this criticism and caution, I will try to characterize in abstract strokes the opposite imaginative forces, and point out what to my own very fallible mind seems the best utopian hypothesis, the most promising line of conciliation.

In my remarks, pacificist tho' I am, I will refuse to speak of the bestial side of the war-régime (already done justice to by many writers) and consider only the higher aspects of militaristic sentiment. Patriotism no one thinks discreditable; nor does any one deny that war is the romance of history. But inordinate ambitions are the soul of every patriotism, and the possibility of violent death the soul of all romance. The militarily patriotic and romantic-minded everywhere, and especially the professional military class, refuse to admit for a moment that war may be a transitory phenomenon in social evolution. The notion of a sheep's paradise like that revolts, they say, our higher imagination. Where then would be the steeps of life? If war had ever stopped, we should have to re-invent it, on this view, to redeem life from flat degeneration.

Reflective apologists for war at the present day all take it religiously. It is a sort of sacrament. Its profits are to the vanquished as well as to the victor; and quite apart from any question of profit, it is an absolute good, we are told, for it is human nature at its highest dynamic. Its "horrors" are a cheap price to pay for rescue from the only alternative supposed, of a world of clerks and teachers, of co-education and zoophily, of "consumer's leagues" and "associated charities," of industrialism unlimited, and feminism unabashed. No scorn, no hardness, no valor any more! Fie upon such a cattleyard of a planet!

So far as the central essence of this feeling goes, no healthy minded person, it seems to me, can help to some degree partaking of it. Militarism is the great preserver of our ideals of hardihood, and human life with no use for hardihood would be contemptible. Without risks or prizes for the darer, history would be insipid indeed; and there is a type of military character which every one feels that the race should never cease to breed, for every one is sensitive to its superiority. The duty is incumbent on mankind, of keeping military characters in stock—of keeping them, if not for use, then as ends in themselves and as pure pieces of perfection—so that Roosevelt's weaklings and mollycoddles may not end by making everything else disappear from the face of nature.

This natural sort of feeling forms, I think, the innermost soul of army-writings. Without any exception known to me, militarist authors take a highly mystical view of their subject, and regard war as a biological or sociological necessity, uncontrolled by ordinary psychological checks and motives. When the time of development is ripe the war must come, reason or no reason, for the justifications pleaded are invariably fictitious. War is, in short, a permanent human *obligation*. General Homer Lea, in his recent book "the Valor of Ignorance," plants himself squarely on this ground. Readiness for war is for him the essence of nationality, and ability in it the supreme measure of the health of nations.

Nations, General Lea says, are never stationary—they must necessarily expand or shrink, according to their vitality or decrepitude. Japan now is culminating; and by the fatal law in question it is impossible that her statesmen should not long since have entered, with extraordinary foresight, upon a vast policy of conquest—the game in which the first moves were her wars with China and Russia and her treaty with England, and of which the final objective is the capture of the Philippines, the Hawaiian Islands, Alaska, and the whole of our Coast west of the Sierra Passes. This will give Japan what her ineluctable vocation as a state absolutely forces her to claim, the possession of the entire Pacific Ocean; and to oppose these deep designs we Americans have, according to our author, nothing but our conceit, our ignorance, our commercialism, our corruption, and our feminism. General Lea makes a minute technical comparison of the military strength which we at present could oppose to the strength of Japan, and concludes that the islands, Alaska, Oregon, and Southern California, would fall almost without resistance, that San Francisco must surrender in a fortnight to a Japanese investment, that in three or four months the war would be over, and our republic, unable to regain what it had heedlessly neglected to protect sufficiently, would then "disintegrate," until perhaps some Caesar should arise to weld us again into a nation.

A dismal forecast indeed! Yet not unplausible, if the mentality of Japan's statesmen be of the Caesarian type of which history shows so many examples, and which is all that General Lea seems able to imagine. But there is no reason to think that women can no longer be the mothers of Napoleonic or Alexandrian characters; and if these come in Japan and find their opportunity, just such surprises as "the Valor of Ignorance" paints may lurk in ambush for us. Ignorant as we still are of the innermost recesses of Japanese mentality, we may be foolhardy to disregard such possibilities.

Other militarists are more complex and more moral in their considerations. The "Philosophie des Krieges," by S. R. Steinmetz is a good example. War, according to this author, is an ordeal instituted by God, who weighs the nations in its balance. It is the essential form of the State, and the only function in which peoples can employ all their powers at once and convergently. No victory is possible save as the resultant of a totality of virtues, no defeat for which some vice or weakness is not responsible. Fidelity, cohesiveness, tenacity, heroism, conscience, education, inventiveness, economy, wealth, physical health and vigor—there isn't a moral or intellectual point of superiority that doesn't tell, when God holds his assizes and hurls the peoples upon one another. *Die Weltgeschichte ist das Weltgericht;* and Dr. Steinmetz does not believe that in the long run chance and luck play any part in apportioning the issues.

The virtues that prevail, it must be noted, are virtues anyhow, superiorities that count in peaceful as well as in military competition; but the strain on them, being infinitely intenser in the latter case, makes war infinitely more searching as a trial. No ordeal is comparable to its winnow-ings. Its dread hammer is the welder of men into cohesive states, and no-where but in such states can human nature adequately develop its capacity. The only alternative is "degeneration."

Dr. Steinmetz is a conscientious thinker, and his book, short as it is, takes much into account. Its upshot can, it seems to me, be summed up in Simon Patten's word, that mankind was nursed in pain and fear, and that the transition to a "pleasure-economy" may be fatal to a being wielding no powers of defense against its distintegrative influences. If we speak of the *fear of emancipation from the fear-regime,* we put the whole situation into a single phrase; fear regarding ourselves now taking the place of the ancient fear of the enemy.

Turn the fear over as I will in my mind, it all seems to lead back to two unwillingnesses of the imagination, one aesthetic, and the other moral: unwillingness, first to envisage a future in which army-life, with its many elements of charm, shall be forever impossible, and in which the destinies of peoples shall nevermore be decided quickly, thrillingly, and tragically, by force, but only gradually and insipidly by "evolution"; and, secondly, unwillingness to see the supreme theatre of human strenuousness closed, and the splendid military aptitudes of men doomed to keep always in a state of latency and never show themselves in action. These insistent unwillingnesses, no less than other esthetic and ethical insistencies have, it seems to me, to be listened to and respected. One cannot meet them effectively by mere counter-insistency on war's expensiveness and horror. The horror makes the thrill; and when the question is of getting the extremest and supremest out of human nature, talk of expense sounds ignominious. The weakness of so much merely negative criticism is evident—pacificism makes no converts from the military party. The military party denies neither the bestiality nor the horror, nor the expense; it only says that these things tell but half the story. It only says that war is *worth* them; that, taking human nature as a whole, its wars are its best protection against its weaker and more cowardly self, and that mankind cannot *afford* to adopt a peace-economy.

Pacificists ought to enter more deeply into the esthetical and ethical point of view of their opponents. Do that first in any controversy, says J. J. Chapman, *then move the point,* and your opponent will follow. So long as anti-militarists propose no substitute for war's disciplinary function, no *moral equivalent* of war, analogous, as one might say, to the mechanical equivalent of heat, so long they fail to realize the full inwardness of the situation. And as a rule they do fail. The duties, penalties, and sanctions pictured in the utopias they paint are all too weak and tame to touch the military-minded. Tolstoy's pacificism is the only exception to this rule, for it is profoundly pessimistic as regards all this world's values, and makes the fear of the Lord furnish the moral spur provided elsewhere by the fear of the enemy. But our socialistic peace-advocates all believe absolutely in this world's values; and instead of the fear of the Lord and the fear of the enemy, the only fear they reckon with is the fear of poverty if one be lazy. This weakness pervades all the socialistic literature with which I am acquainted. Even in Lowes Dickinson's exquisite dialogue, high wages and short hours are the only forces invoked for overcoming man's distaste for repulsive kinds of labor. Meanwhile men at large still live as they always have lived, under a pain-and-fear economy—for those of us who live in an ease-economy are but an island in the stormy ocean—and the whole atmosphere of present-day utopian literature tastes mawkish and dishwatery to people who still keep a sense for life's more bitter flavors. It suggests, in truth, ubiquitous inferiority.

Inferiority is always with us, and merciless scorn of it is the keynote of the military temper. "Dogs, would you live forever?" shouted Frederick the Great. "Yes," say our utopians, "let us live forever, and raise our level gradually." The best thing about our "inferiors" to-day is that they are as tough as nails, and physically and morally almost as insensitive. Utopianism would see them soft and squeamish, while militarism would keep their callousness, but transfigure it into a meritorious characteristic, needed by "the service," and redeemed by that from the suspicion of inferiority. All the qualities of a man acquire dignity when he knows that the service of the collectivity that owns him needs them. If proud of the collectivity, his own pride rises in proportion. No collectivity is like an army for nourishing such pride; but it has to be confessed that the only sentiment which the image of pacific cosmopolitan industrialism is capable of arousing in countless worthy breasts is shame at the idea of belonging to *such* a collectivity. It is obvious that the United States of America as they exist to-day impress a mind like General Lea's as so much human blubber. Where is the sharpness and precipitousness, the contempt for life, whether one's own, or another's? Where is the savage "yes" and "no," the unconditional duty? Where is the conscription? Where is the blood-tax? Where is anything that one feels honored by belonging to?

Having said thus much in preparation, I will now confess my own utopia. I devoutly believe in the reign of peace and in the gradual advent of some sort of a socialistic equilibrium. The fatalistic view of the war-function is to me nonsense, for I know that war-making is due to definite motives and subject to prudential checks and reasonable criticisms, just like any other form of enterprise. And when whole nations are the armies, and the science of destruction vies in intellectual refinement with the sciences of production, I see that war becomes absurd and impossible from its own monstrosity. Extravagant ambitions will have to be replaced by reasonable claims, and nations must make common cause against them. I see no reason why all this should not apply to yellow as well as to white countries, and I look forward to a future when acts of war shall be formally outlawed as between civilized peoples.

All these beliefs of mine put me squarely into the anti-militarist party. But I do not believe that peace either ought to be or will be permanent on this globe, unless the states pacifically organized preserve some of the old elements of army-discipline. A permanently successful peace-economy cannot be a simple pleasure-economy. In the more or less socialistic future towards which mankind seems drifting we must still subject ourselves collectively to those severities which answer to our real position upon this only partly hospitable globe. We must make new energies and hardihoods continue the manliness to which the military mind so faithfully clings. Martial virtues must be the enduring cement; intrepidity, contempt of softness, surrender of private interest, obedience to command, must still remain the rock upon which states are built—unless, indeed, we wish for dangerous reactions against commonwealths fit only for contempt, and liable to invite attack whenever a centre of crystallization for military-minded enterprise gets formed anywhere in their neighborhood.

The war-party is assuredly right in affirming and reaffirming that the martial virtues, although originally gained by the race through war, are absolute and permanent human goods. Patriotic pride and ambition in their military form are, after all, only specifications of a more general competitive passion. They are its first form, but that is no reason for supposing them to be its last form. Men now are proud of belonging to a conquering nation, and without a murmur they lay down their persons and their wealth, if by so doing they may fend off subjection. But who can be sure that *other aspects of one's country* may not, with time and education and suggestion enough, come to be regarded with similarly effective feelings of pride and shame? Why should men not some day feel that it is worth a blood-tax to belong to a collectivity superior in *any* ideal respect? Why should they not blush with indignant shame if the community that owns them is vile in any way whatsoever? Individuals, daily more numerous, now feel this civic passion. It is only a question of blowing on the spark till the whole population gets incandescent, and on the ruins of the old morals of military honour, a stable system of morals of civic honour builds itself up. What the whole community comes to believe in grasps the individual as in a vise. The war-function has graspt us so far; but constructive interests may some day seem no less imperative, and impose on the individual a hardly lighter burden.

Let me illustrate my idea more concretely. There is nothing to make one indignant in the mere fact that life is hard, that men should toil and suffer pain. The planetary conditions once for all are such, and we can stand it. But that so many men, by mere accidents of birth and opportunity, should have a life of *nothing else* but toil and pain and hardness and inferiority imposed upon them, should have *no* vacation, while others natively no more deserving never get any taste of this campaigning life at all—*this* is capable of arousing indignation in reflective minds. It may end by seeming shameful to all of us that some of us have nothing but campaigning, and others nothing but unmanly ease. If now—and this is my idea—there were, instead of military conscription a conscription of the whole youthful population to form for a certain number of years a part of the army enlisted against *Nature,* the injustice would tend to be evened out, and numerous other goods to the commonwealth would follow. The military ideals of hardihood and discipline would be wrought into the growing fibre of the people; no one would remain blind as the luxurious classes now are blind, to man's real relations to the globe he lives on, and to the permanently sour and hard foundations of his higher life. To coal and iron mines, to freight trains, to fishing fleets in December, to dish-washing, clothes-washing, and window-washing, to road-building and tunnel-making, to foundries and stoke-holes, and to the frames of skyscrapers, would our gilded youths be drafted off, according to their choice, to get the childishness knocked out of them, and to come back into society with healthier sympathies and soberer ideas. They would have paid their blood-tax, done their own part in the immemorial human warfare against nature, they would tread the earth more proudly, the women would value them more highly, they would be better fathers and teachers of the following generation.

Such a conscription, with the state of public opinion that would have required it, and the many moral fruits it would bear, would preserve in the midst of a pacific civilization the manly virtues which the military party is so afraid of seeing disappear in peace. We should get toughness without callousness, authority with as little criminal cruelty as possible, and painful work done cheerily because the duty is temporary, and threatens not, as now, to degrade the whole remainder of one's life. I spoke of the "moral equivalent" of war. So far, war has been the only force that can discipline a whole community, and until an equivalent discipline is organized, I believe that war must have its way. But I have no serious doubt that the ordinary prides and shames of social man, once developed to a certain intensity, are capable of organizing such a moral equivalent as I have sketched, or some other just as effective for preserving manliness of type. It is but a question of time, of skillful propagandism, and of opinion-making men seizing historic opportunities.

The martial type of character can be bred without war. Strenuous honour and disinterestedness abound elsewhere. Priests and medical men

are in a fashion educated to it, and we should all feel some degree of it
imperative if we were conscious of our work as an obligatory service to
the state. We should be *owned,* as soldiers are by the army, and our pride
would rise accordingly. We could be poor, then, without humiliation, as
army officers now are. The only thing needed henceforward is to inflame
the civic temper as past history has inflamed the military temper. H. G.
Wells, as usual, sees the centre of the situation. "In many ways," he says,
"military organization is the most peaceful of activities. When the contemporary man steps from the street, of clamorous insincere advertise-
ment, push, adulteration, underselling and intermittent employment, into
the barrack-yard, he steps on to a higher social plane, into an atmosphere
of service and co-operation and of infinitely more honourable emulations.
Here at least men are not flung out of employment to degenerate because there is no immediate work for them to do. They are fed and drilled
and trained for better services. Here at least a man is supposed to win
promotion by self-forgetfulness and not by self-seeking. And beside
the feeble and irregular endowment of research by commercialism, its
little short-sighted snatches at profit by innovation and scientific economy,
see how remarkable is the steady and rapid development of method and
appliances in naval and military affairs! Nothing is more striking than to
compare the progress of civil conveniences which has been left almost
entirely to the trader, to the progress in military apparatus during the
last few decades. The house-appliances of to-day for example, are little
better than they were fifty years ago. A house of to-day is still almost as
ill-ventilated, badly heated by wasteful fires, clumsily arranged and
furnished as the house of 1858. Houses a couple of hundred years old are
still satisfactory places of residence, so little have our standards risen. But
the rifle or battleship of fifty years ago was beyond all comparison inferior
to those we possess; in power, in speed, in convenience alike. No one has
a use now for such superannuated things."

Wells adds that he thinks that the conception of order and discipline,
the tradition of service and devotion, of physical fitness, unstinted
exertion, and universal responsibility, which universal military duty is
now teaching European nations, will remain a permanent acquisition,
when the last ammunition has been used in the fireworks that celebrate
the final peace. I believe as he does. It would be simply preposterous if
the only force that could work ideals of honour and standards of efficiency
into English or American natures should be the fear of being killed by the
Germans or the Japanese. Great indeed is Fear; but it is not, as our
military enthusiasts believe and try to make us believe, the only stimulus
known for awakening the higher ranges of men's spiritual energy. The
amount of alteration in public opinion which my utopia postulates is

vastly less than the difference between the mentality of those black warriors who pursued Stanley's party on the Congo with their cannibal war-cry of "Meat! Meat" and that of the "general-staff" of any civilized nation. History has seen the latter interval bridged over: the former one can be bridged over much more easily.

# Suggestions for Further Reading

(Books starred are available in recent paperback editions.)

### GENERAL INTERPRETATION

Within the past twelve years a number of interpretive essays of book length have gained wide circulation and deserved popularity for the light they have shed on the Progressive years and on our own subsequent era. Richard Hofstadter, *The Age of Reform* (1955),* is indispensable, provocative, and gracefully composed. One of the most original and thoughtful essays on recent aspects of American history is David Potter's *People of Plenty* (1954).* Samuel P. Hays, *Response to Industrialism, 1885-1914* (1957),* provides a fresh, challenging, and persuasive summary of the reform impulse. Eric Goldman, *Rendezvous with Destiny* (1953),* views modern reform from a mid-century perspective which is both informative and entertaining. Henry S. Commager, *The American Mind* (1950),* surveys social thought since 1890 in a book crammed with thumbnail interpretations and opinions.

### LABOR, SOCIAL PROBLEMS, AND URBAN REFORM

Influential in exposing the plight of the slum dwellers and the urban working classes was Jacob Riis, *The Battle with the Slum* (1902), a journalistic account which helped pave the way for the De Forest and Veiller report. Jane Addams' memoir of the Chicago social settlement was followed by Lillian Wald, *The House on Henry Street* (1915), an account of a New York settlement. One of the most eloquent contemporary discussions of the principal social problem of the city was Robert Hunter's *Poverty* (1904). Lincoln Steffens first won national attention with *The Shame of the Cities* (1903),* and he later put his experiences as a reporter and student of public affairs into the perspective of one of the few great memoirs in American history, his *Autobiography* (1931). Steffens' friend Brand Whitlock described his own career as urban reformer in *Forty Years of It* (1914), while Whitlock's Ohio colleague in politics, Frederic C. Howe, later wrote *Confessions of a Reformer* (1925), both books outstanding for their literary craft and their introspection on the strengths and weaknesses of reform. Less graceful, but a classic of its kind, is Samuel Gompers, *Seventy Years of Life and Labor* (2 vols., 1925). Eugene V. Debs' *Writings and Speeches* have been collected by Arthur M. Schlesinger, Jr. (1948), and Louis Filler presents a discriminating collection of Finley Peter Dunne's essays in *Mr. Dooley Now and*

493

*Forever* (1954).\* Among the innumerable works of fiction to reveal the conditions of urban America in the Progressive years, the following are classics: Frank Norris, *The Octopus* (1899); Theodore Dreiser, *Sister Carrie* (1901), *The Financier* (1912), and *The Titan* (1914); and Upton Sinclair, *The Jungle* (1906).

Modern historians have written incisively about this period. Ray Ginger has ably recaptured the mood and the significance of Chicago in the ferment of the 1890's and 1900's in *Altgeld's America* (1957). Roy Lubove is the first scholar to do justice to "Lawrence Veiller and the New York State Tenement House Commission of 1900," in the *Mississippi Valley Historical Review*, March, 1961. Walton Bean provides a wealth of detail and perspective on Boss Reuf's San Francisco (1952), and George Mowry, in *The California Progressives* (1951), has written the best account of state reform politics to have appeared in modern scholarship. Vann Woodward, *Origins of the New South, 1877-1913* (1953), offers original insights and a brilliant synthesis for a major region. Louis Filler, *Crusaders for American Liberalism* (1939),\* tells of the reform journalists and their influence. The most powerful banker in America is discussed with objective sympathy in Frederick Lewis Allen's short study, *The Great Pierpont Morgan* (1949),\* while the most revolutionary "modern" industrialist of the progressive period is accorded definitive treatment in Allan Nevins' splendid biography of *Ford* (Vol. I, 1954). American labor and union history for this period has been done scant justice. The most comprehensive account is Selig Perlman and Philip Taft, *Labor Movements* (1930), but its style is turgid. Ray Ginger has written warmly and with insight about Debs in *The Bending Cross* (1948). The simplest and most objective account of American Socialism is to be found in David Shannon's able study, *The Socialist Party of America* (1955). Oscar Handlin's *The Uprooted* (1952) is by now a modern classic in its rendering of the meaning and impact of American urban life on the immigrant.

## THE FORCES OF NATIONAL POLITICS AND EXPANSION

The central figure in the progressive era was also one of its most prolific writers: Theodore Roosevelt's *Works*, collected in 1925, run to twenty-four volumes, including his autobiography; in the 1950's Elting Morison and a staff of associates published a useful collection of Roosevelt's *Letters* in eight volumes with superior editorial apparatus and penetrating comments; even so, the larger part of Roosevelt's correspondence remains unpublished. A similar project for Woodrow Wilson's letters is under way at Princeton; meanwhile Wilson's *New Freedom* (1913),\* has been reissued, and in 1927 Ray Stannard Baker edited six volumes of Wilson's *Public Papers*.

Most national figures in the progressive period have been fortunate in their recent biographers. Henry F. Pringle, *Theodore Roosevelt* (1931),* is still the most penetrating for Roosevelt's career through 1907, and for the later period George Mowry, *Theodore Roosevelt and the Progressive Era* (1946),* is imaginative, fast-paced, and scholarly. John Blum, *The Republican Roosevelt* (1954), is a model of compression and trenchant prose. The best general account of American politics and society in the period 1900-1912 is to be found in George Mowry's new book, *The Era of Theodore Roosevelt* (1958). Important phases of expanding American interests and policy abroad are examined with clarity and authority in Julius Pratt, *America's Colonial Experiment* (1951); Howard K. Beale, *Theodore Roosevelt and the Rise of America to World Power* (1956); and Gerstle Mack, *The Land Divided* (1944), the most satisfying and literate account of the Panama Canal and the tangled history which preceded it. Of the major figures of the Roosevelt period, Gifford Pinchot has done himself justice in his autobiography, *Breaking New Ground* (1947), while Claude Bowers has done a midwesterner more than justice in *Beveridge and the Progressive Era* (1932). William Allen White's *Autobiography* (1951) is charming, a little slick, and drops so many names as to be required reading for the politics of progressivism. A. T. Mason has written a superb but overly sympathetic biography of *Brandeis* (1946), and John Garraty's *Right-Hand Man* (1960) ably places George W. Perkins in a perspective which reveals the strengths and weaknesses of American financial politics in the reform period as few recent books have done. Woodrow Wilson is the subject of a scholarly and almost epic biography by Arthur S. Link, of which the first two volumes, *Wilson: The Road to the White House* (1947) and *Wilson: The New Freedom* (1958), reveal with masterful control the forces of domestic politics in the years through 1915. The ablest short interpretation of Wilson's total career is Herbert Bell's *Woodrow Wilson and the People* (1945).

## THE PROGRESSIVE MIND: CHANGE AND POSSIBILITIES

The social currents of the old century met those of the new in a virtual riptide of intellectual activity beginning about 1910. In that year came William James' *Pragmatism*,* and within the next four years there appeared James Harvey Robinson, *The New History* (1912); Walter Weyl, *The New Democracy* (1912); George Santayana, *Winds of Doctrine* (1913); Walter Lippmann, *A Preface to Politics* (1913) and *Drift and Mastery* (1914); Herbert Croly, *Progressive Democracy* (1914); and Charles Beard, *Contemporary American History* (1914). Fully as significant were the writings of three disturbing commentators on the philosophy of the age. They are found best represented in *The Mind and*

*Faith of Justice Holmes* (1943) and *The Portable Veblen* (1950),* both compiled by Max Lerner; and in John Dewey's *Reconstruction in Philosophy* (1920). The watershed character of this period of thought has nowhere been more clearly delineated than in Henry F. May, *The End of American Innocence* (1959), while Morton White, *Social Thought in America* (1947),* analyzes the views of five leading rebels against "formalism," including Dewey, Veblen, and Holmes. Lawrence Cremin, *The Transformation of the School* (1961), is a superior study of progressivism as embodied in a major institution. Ralph Barton Perry's classic biography, *The Thought and Character of William James* (1954), attempts to define the qualities which enabled America's leading philosopher to underwrite the response which Americans were to make to the turmoil and challenge of a new century.